A Guide to Reviewing
Nosotros, los jóvenes

Focusing on communication in everyday situations, *Nosotros, los jóvenes* helps students develop proficiency in listening, speaking, reading, and writing in Spanish. It also increases students' knowledge and appreciation of diverse cultures in Spanish-speaking countries.

Use the list below as a convenient guide to reviewing *Nosotros, los jóvenes.* Page references provide examples of key features.

▶ Clearly delineated sections with specific communicative functions provide a "purpose" for language learning (page 287).

▶ Each section opens with an appealing situation rich in ideas for lively communication (page 201).

▶ Each section includes a cultural note—**Sabes que . . .**—that provides interesting facts about Spanish-speaking people to increase students' cultural awareness (page 152).

▶ Each section includes one or more **Se dice así** entries that summarize the key phrases and sentences needed to express the communicative functions (page 205).

▶ Throughout the textbook, photographic essays depict the lifestyles of Spanish-speaking people and enhance students' understanding of Spanish attitudes and customs (pages 278–284).

▶ **Try Your Skills** activities provide "real-life" opportunities for students to use new language skills (pages 320–322).

▶ Cross-referenced to the communicative functions in each unit, **¿Lo sabes?** helps students monitor their progress (page 266).

▶ Word-study activities included with most unit vocabulary lists help students review vocabulary effectively (page 185).

▶ In each unit, **Vamos a leer** helps students develop reading skills in Spanish (page 186). Activities following each selection check comprehension and relate reading to students' personal experiences (page 189).

▶ A wealth of supplements, including the *Teacher's Edition* and the *Teacher's ResourceBank*™, provides a rich variety of teaching resources for *Nosotros, los jóvenes*.

HBJ Harcourt Brace Jovanovich, Inc.
School Department

Nosotros, los jóvenes

The Spanish program that has everybody talking!

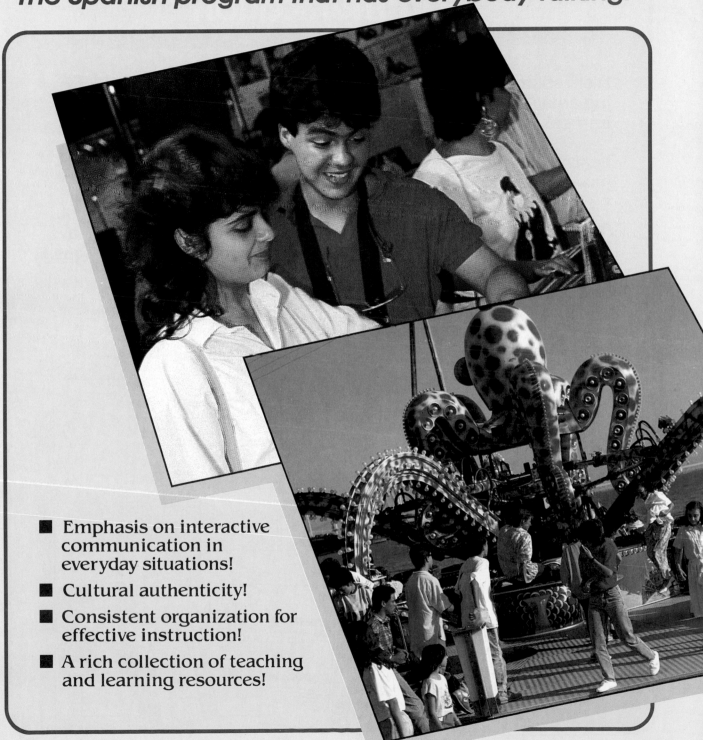

- ■ Emphasis on interactive communication in everyday situations!
- ■ Cultural authenticity!
- ■ Consistent organization for effective instruction!
- ■ A rich collection of teaching and learning resources!

Functional language for proficient communication

From asking about a friend's health to offering advice, from expressing amazement to asking for permission, ***Nosotros, los jóvenes*** immerses students in the world of *real* language in *real* situations!

Learning activities that develop basic concepts

Through a variety of activities, ***Nosotros, los jóvenes*** provides specific practice for basic vocabulary and grammar concepts.

Each section opens with an appealing situation rich in ideas for lively communication.

Application activities for proficient communication

Motivating activities invite students to apply what they have learned to real-life situations.

A balance of activities for learning and application helps students become proficient in listening, speaking, reading, and writing in Spanish.

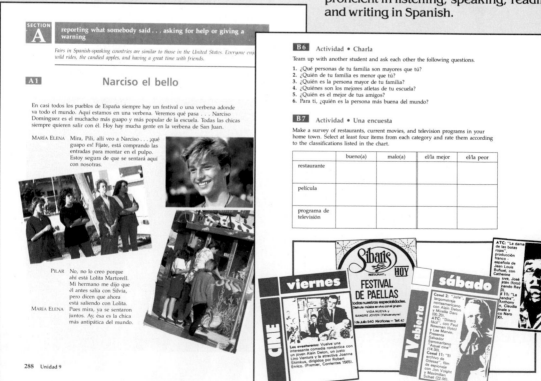

1   Los clasificados

Use what you have learned in this unit and the advertisements below as models to write a classified ad in Spanish for one of the following professions or trades.

secretaria   vendedor   arquitecto
mesero   programadora   ingeniero
recepcionista   cajero   plomero

320   Unidad 9

Application activities in **Try Your Skills** provide "real-life" opportunities for students to use their new language skills.

Reading selections in a variety of formats—including letters, job interviews, folktales, and articles, as well as narratives—help students develop reading skills in Spanish. Activities, following each selection, check comprehension and relate reading to students' personal experiences.

VAMOS A LEER

Antes de leer

In Spanish, many narratives, folk tales, or legends begin with one of the following phrases: Había una vez . . . ; Cuentan que . . . ; Dicen que . . . .
These phrases give the story a sense of oral tradition. In many instances, stories that begin in this manner have been told for several generations.

Preparación para la lectura

Before you read the following folk tale, answer these questions.
1. ¿Leíste cuentos y leyendas cuando eras niño? ¿Cuáles leíste?
2. ¿De qué habla el cuento? ¿Qué te dice el título?
3. Organiza las siguientes expresiones de más lejos a más cerca: un poco lejos, bastante lejos, nada lejos, muy lejos, lejísimo.
4. Conoces el verbo **extrañar** (to miss), pero aquí **extraño** es un cognado, es decir, una palabra similar a su traducción al inglés. ¿Puedes adivinar qué significa?
5. Mira el último párrafo del cuento. Parecen dos proverbios, ¿verdad? ¿Qué relación hay entre la narración y ese párrafo?

Cuestión de opinión

Había una vez una familia que vivía en el campo. Faltaban pocos días para las grandes fiestas del pueblo y el padre decidió que era buen momento para vender uno de los burros° que tenía. Necesitaba dinero para comprar abrigos para el invierno y algunos regalos de Reyes.

Todavía hacía muy buen tiempo y el hombre le preguntó a su hijo menor si quería ir con él al mercado. Al muchacho le gustaba mucho ir con su padre al mercado y hablar con la gente. Al día siguiente, salieron el hombre y su hijo con el burro, que se llamaba Cristóbal y nunca tenía prisa. Tenían bastante tiempo. El pueblo° estaba un poco lejos, pero era muy temprano.

Cuando tenían hambre, paraban para comer unas uvas que llevaban. Caminando y caminando, encontraron° entonces a unas mujeres a quienes ellos no conocían. Oyeron que la tercera mujer dijo:

burros *donkeys*   pueblo *village*   encontraron *they met*

186   Unidad 5

Cultural awareness to broaden understanding

Positive cultural attitudes

To help students understand and appreciate Spanish-speaking people and countries, **Nosotros, los jóvenes** interweaves cultural insights and information. Teaching more than just the language, the program depicts everyday life, such as family and peer relations and social customs, in the Spanish world.

Cultural authenticity

To immerse students in Spanish culture, the textbook includes facsimiles of authentic documents, photos shot on location, numerous cultural notes, and such special features as colorful photographic essays. To ensure authenticity, the textbook was written and illustrated by native speakers of Spanish and is based on many interviews with Spanish students. In addition, the annotated *Teacher's Edition* and *Teacher's ResourceBank* ™ provide abundant cultural information and realia to enhance learning experiences.

Each selection includes a cultural note—**Sabes que...**—that provides interesting facts about Spanish-speaking people to increase students' cultural awareness.

Depicting the lifestyles of Spanish-speaking people, colorful photo essays enhance students' understanding of Spanish attitudes and customs.

Viñeta cultural 1

Los españoles y los hispanoamericanos

La América hispana, al igual que España, es una de las regiones de más variedad étnica de nuestro planeta.

Estos jóvenes del Instituto Municipal del Turismo de Barcelona son de gran ayuda para los miles de turistas que visitan la bella capital catalana.

Cada región de España tiene sus trajes típicos que los jóvenes y los mayores por igual llevan con orgullo (pride) en las celebraciones y fiestas de la región.

En España se encuentra una gran variedad de tipos, como podemos ver en esta foto.

Los españoles y los hispanoamericanos 1

El equipo de béisbol cubano está considerado como uno de los mejores del mundo a nivel amateur.

En Venezuela el béisbol es tan popular como en los Estados Unidos.

El deporte nacional de las islas del Caribe, sobre todo de Cuba, la República Dominicana y Puerto Rico es el béisbol. Este deporte también se juega *(is played)* en Venezuela, Panamá, Nicaragua y México. Varias estrellas del béisbol, como el mexicano Fernando Valenzuela y el cubano José Canseco, juegan en los Estados Unidos para equipos *(teams)* de las grandes ligas *(Major Leagues)*. Entre *(Among)* los miembros del Salón de la Fama *(Hall of Fame)* figuran el dominicano Juan Marichal y el puertorriqueño Roberto Clemente.

Fernando Valenzuela, el lanzador (pitcher) mexicano, juega en Los Ángeles.

El cubano José Canseco fue nombrado (was named) el jugador más valioso de la Liga Americana por ser un gran bateador (batter).

Sólo hay admiración cuando se recuerda al gran pelotero puertorriqueño (Puerto Rican), Roberto Clemente.

Los deportes 141

Sample pages are reduced. Actual sizes are 8"x10". All pages are from *Level 2*.

Consistent organization for effective teaching and learning

Manageable content

Designed as a one-year course, **Nosotros, los jóvenes** promotes active learning at a comfortable pace. Instruction progresses logically without overwhelming students, introducing a manageable amount of new grammar and vocabulary to support the communicative functions.

Clear learning objectives

Consistent unit organization with clearly defined objectives ensures success in learning. As students move through each new lesson, they build self-confidence and self-motivation.

Clearly delineated sections with specific communicative functions provide a "purpose" for language learning.

UNIDAD 7

La tecnología y el progreso

In Spanish America, very much like in the United States, young people are interested in the future and in progress. However, since there are fewer opportunities for employment after graduation, students have to be more careful in deciding what they are going to study. This important decision is usually made with the help of their parents.

In this unit you will:

SECTION A	express displeasure and ask for help . . . direct others to do something
SECTION B	advise others . . . describe your plans for the future . . . express time factors
SECTION C	inquire whether something is considered possible or impossible . . . request favors or help
TRY YOUR SKILLS	use what you've learned
VAMOS A LEER	read for practice and pleasure

231

Frequent review

Periodic review helps students apply what they have learned to new and different situations. Self-checks in each unit allow students to monitor their grasp of important concepts and skills. Review units provide numerous activities that teachers may select to reinforce learning and satisfy special needs.

Cross-referenced to the communicative functions, **¿Lo sabes?** helps students monitor their progress.

¿LO SABES?

Let's review some of the points you've learned in this unit.

SECTION A

Are you able to express yourself in Spanish when you are disappointed?
Form five sentences showing your dissatisfaction or annoyance with someone or with something. Then ask for help. Here are some ideas:
You bought a new television set and you can't make it work.
You are having problems with your motorcycle.
Your portable radio is old, and it is not working well.

Can you give commands in Spanish to others?
Make a list of the six most common commands you receive from your parents.

SECTION B

Can you say what you will do tomorrow?
Write five sentences in Spanish indicating what you will do tomorrow.

Do you know how to express your predictions for the future in Spanish?
Using your imagination, write a paragraph predicting at least five different things that will happen in the future.

Are you able to discuss how often or how quickly you can do something?
Explain how often you do the following activities.
1. pasear por el parque
2. andar en bicicleta
3. cortar el césped
Now explain how quickly you do each of the following things.
1. hacer la tarea
2. arreglarse para salir
3. salir de la escuela por la tarde

SECTION C

Are you able to express logical conclusions in Spanish?
Pair up with a partner and discuss your Spanish course, following the model.
A la corta o a la larga tendremos que estudiar más.

Do you know how to express what you would do in each of the following situations?
1. You were accepted to a well-known college in Spain.
2. You needed to raise your grade point average to graduate.
3. You made the basketball and swim teams, but you could only participate in one sport.
4. You visited friends in Madrid and got lost.

When you receive an invitation, how would you politely decline that invitation by expressing other obligations?
Pair up with a classmate who will invite you to do five different things.
Tell him/her that you would like to do those things, but you have other plans.

Can you ask somebody to help you in Spanish?
Ask a classmate to help you with your computer. Then ask two other classmates to do you a favor.

266   Unidad 7

Throughout the textbook, a simple color-code system helps students recognize new material, activities, and cultural information (not shown).

Sample pages are reduced. Actual sizes are 8"x10". All pages are from *Level 2*.

P7

A wealth of teaching resources for a range of needs

Flexible resources

Nosotros, los jóvenes provides a range of resources to satisfy a variety of teaching preferences and individual learning rates and styles.

Teacher's Edition

The easy-to-use annotated *Teacher's Edition* contains numerous convenient features:

- A scope and sequence chart for each unit
- Detailed teaching suggestions— including ideas for cooperative learning—conveniently located before each unit
- Cultural background notes for each section of every unit
- Provisions for students of different abilities
- Scripts and answers for listening comprehension exercises
- Annotated pupil's pages with answers to exercises

Sample pages are reduced.
Actual sizes are 8"x10" (Teacher's Edition, Level 2).

Sample page

with a partner. You may wish to discuss one or more items with the class to help them get started. Add other questions not included in the activity in order to check the students' comprehension.

¿Compro la blusa?
¿Mando la carta?
¿Abrimos las ventanas?
¿Vendemos los libros?

A 16   Actividad • El gerente

Present the activity as explained in A15, but this time the students should answer the questions negatively. Review with the class. For writing practice, you may wish to have the students write the sentences and review by correcting them on the board or a transparency.

A 17   Actividad • Instrucciones

Assign this activity for homework or have the students work in pairs to complete the activity in the form of a dialog.

SLOWER-PACED LEARNING   Brainstorm with the class the types of instructions a store manager might give the employees. Write the list on the board or a transparency. Then have the students use the list as a guide to write the instructions in command forms.

CHALLENGE   After the students have completed the activity, ask them to look at the realia at the bottom of page 99. Have them write as many commands as possible based on the information found in the advertisement. The commands may be singular or plural, or affirmative or negative. For example, the first sentence in the realia, **Porque garantizamos mayor surtido**, can be converted into the command form: **Garanticen mayor surtido.**

A 18   Actividad • ¡A escribir!

Ask the students to prepare a commercial for each of the items listed. Suggest that they include at least four different commands, two reasons for using the product, and information on where it may be obtained. Students may also write about a local restaurant or store. Explain that they may not translate other commercials.

SLOWER-PACED LEARNING   You may wish to define the new vocabulary found in the realia that may be difficult for students to comprehend.

gente que sabe   *people that know*
mariscos   *shellfish*
Descubra Ud.   *discover*
saboreando   *tasting*
calzado   *footwear*

SITUACIÓN • Pidiendo y dando información

Before presenting the dialog, call on volunteers to summarize the events in A1, pp. 92–93. You may also wish to re-enter the expressions used for giving and following directions, such as **a la derecha, a la izquierda, delante de**, and **atrás de.** Draw a simple map on the board and use a paper doll or cardboard figure to demonstrate. Then present the new vocabulary: **cuadras, esquina, doblen a la derecha, sigan derecho.**

Unidad 3   Teacher's Notes   **T77**

UNIDAD **3**   A16–19

Teacher's Notes provide specific strategies for each part of the unit—including basic material, activities, and reading selections. Notes include special projects, variations of textbook exercises, and suggestions for accommodating different learning styles. Tabbed pages allow quick location of **Teacher's Notes.**

Challenge and **Slower-Paced Learning** activities satisfy individual learning needs.

Teacher's ResourceBank™

The *Teacher's ResourceBank™* includes useful *Teacher's Resource Materials* —learning and teaching strategies, proficiency practice cards, games, songs, vocabulary lists with exercises, realia, components correlation charts, a glossary of grammatical terms, and a pronunciation guide. The *Teacher's ResourceBank™* also contains a Unit Theme Posters Sampler; an Overhead Transparencies Sampler and Planning Guide; the *Student's Test Booklet*; the *Teacher's Test Guide;* and the *Unit Cassette Guide.* A three-ring binder with convenient tabbed dividers provides organized storage for these teaching resources.

Additional components for students and teachers

Exercise Workbook with Teacher's Edition

The *Exercise Workbook (Manual de ejercicios)* provides practice in grammar and vocabulary. The accompanying *Teacher's Edition* contains answers for all exercises.

Activity Workbook with Teacher's Edition

Rich in illustrations and realia, the *Activity Workbook (Manual de actividades)* provides entertaining and challenging activities to develop communication skills. The accompanying *Teacher's Edition* contains answers for all activities.

Testing Program

The comprehensive Testing Program—consisting of the *Student's Test Booklet, Teacher's Test Guide,* and *Test Cassettes*—assesses both achievement and proficiency in Spanish. The perforated *Student's Test Booklet* includes section quizzes, unit tests, review tests, mid-year and final examinations, and proficiency-based tests. The *Teacher's Test Guide* includes recording scripts for the listening portions of all quizzes and tests, speaking tests for each unit, suggestions for administering and scoring tests, and

an answer key. *Test Cassettes* contain the listening portions of all quizzes and tests as well as a model for administering the speaking portion of a proficiency-based test.

Teacher's Resource Materials

Teacher's Resource Materials provide a variety of copying masters, including:

- Proficiency practice cards with situations and activities for use with each review unit to help students improve communication skills
- Games to enrich and enliven learning
- Spanish songs for group singing activities
- Vocabulary lists with exercises for reinforcement and enrichment
- Realia—including authentic menus, transportation schedules, invoices, and forms—with teaching suggestions and cross-references to textbook units
- Components correlation charts
- A glossary of grammatical terms with examples
- A pronunciation guide with suggestions for pronunciation practice
- Answer forms for listening comprehension exercises

Unit Cassettes

Cassettes for instructional and review units include basic material, selected activities, listening comprehension and pronunciation exercises, reading selections, and photo essays—all recorded by native speakers with pauses for student repetition and response, where appropriate. They also provide Spanish songs.

Unit Cassette Guide

The *Unit Cassette Guide* includes an index to the *Unit Cassettes*, recording scripts for all *Unit Cassettes*, and answer forms for the listening comprehension exercises in the textbook.

Overhead Transparencies

Overhead Transparencies, with copying masters, accompany each instructional unit. Full-color map transparencies include overlays with geographical names. In addition, a Planning Guide contains suggestions for classroom use.

Unit Theme Posters

Colorful posters feature captivating photographs to enhance each unit in the textbook.

Nosotros, los jóvenes

Teacher's Edition

Teacher's Edition Writers

Roberto Fernández
Florida State University
Tallahassee, FL

Nancy Ann Humbach
Finneytown High School
Cincinnati, OH

Dora Kennedy
Prince George's County Public Schools
Landover, MD

Nosotros, los jóvenes

Teacher's Edition

HBJ HARCOURT BRACE JOVANOVICH, PUBLISHERS
Orlando   San Diego   Chicago   Dallas

Printed in the United States of America
ISBN 0-15-388351-0

We do not include a Teacher's Edition automatically with each shipment of a classroom set of textbooks. We prefer to send a Teacher's Edition only when it is part of a purchase order or when it is requested by the teacher or administrator concerned or by one of our representatives. A Teacher's Edition can be easily mislaid when it arrives as part of a shipment delivered to a school stockroom, and, since it contains answer materials, we would like to be sure it is sent directly to the person who will use it, or to someone concerned with the use or selection of textbooks.

If your class assignment changes and you no longer are using or examining this Teacher's Edition, you may wish to pass it on to a teacher who may have use for it.

CONTENTS

TO THE TEACHER

SCOPE AND SEQUENCE CHARTS AND TEACHER'S NOTES

TO THE TEACHER

In creating the new Harcourt Brace Jovanovich Spanish Program, we have incorporated suggestions from foreign language teachers in all parts of the country. We are grateful to you for talking and writing to us. We feel that, based on your suggestions and on what we have observed about general trends in foreign language teaching, we have produced a program that you and your students will profit from and enjoy.

Philosophy and Goals

The primary goal of the Harcourt Brace Jovanovich Spanish Program is to help students develop proficiency in the four basic skills: listening, speaking, reading, and writing. At the same time, it aims to increase the students' knowledge and appreciation of the diverse cultures of the countries whose language they are learning.

In order to become proficient in a foreign language, students must not only learn the vocabulary and structures of the language, but also apply what they have learned. Thus, students learn and practice the material in each unit, and they also have many opportunities to apply their skills. Given ample opportunity for creative expression, students are on their way to developing proficiency.

The emphasis is on communication. The approach is based on the communicative purposes of young people at this level—to invite, inform, inquire, exclaim, agree, disagree, compliment, express emotions and opinions, and so on. These communicative purposes, or functions, in turn determine the selection and the amount of vocabulary and grammar that students need to learn. The communicative functions, grammar, and vocabulary are presented in culturally authentic situations that appeal to young people. They are followed by a variety of activities that promote both learning and application of the language, ultimately leading students to function with increasing proficiency in many new situations. The question to be asked constantly in measuring students' success is, "What can they do with the language they are learning, and how well?"

Description of the HBJ Spanish Program

We have designed the materials of this program to be highly adaptable. You will be able to offer a variety of experiences in learning and using the foreign language, choosing materials that correspond to the learning needs of each student. The various parts of the program are:

Components of the program

- Pupil's Edition
- Teacher's Edition
- Activity Workbook
- Activity Workbook, Teacher's Edition
- Exercise Workbook
- Exercise Workbook, Teacher's Edition
- Overhead Transparencies
- Unit Theme Posters

- Testing Program
  Student's Test Booklet
  Teacher's Test Guide
  Test Cassettes
- Audio Program
  Unit Cassettes
  Unit Cassette Guide
- Teacher's Resource Materials
- Videocassettes

Pupil's Edition

Organization
of the
textbook

The student textbook is the core of the HBJ Spanish program. The book contains twelve units grouped into three Parts, each Part consisting of one photo essay *(Viñeta cultural)*, three instructional units *(Unidades)*, and one review unit *(Repaso)*. A reference section at the back of the textbook provides summaries of the communicative functions, grammar, and vocabularies for all the lessons. Culturally authentic photographs, art, and realia, which appear throughout the book, enhance student comprehension of the cultural diversity of the Spanish-speaking world.

Organization of Instructional Units

Each instructional unit starts with two pages of photographs that illustrate the theme of the unit. These pages also contain a brief introduction and an outline of the unit that lists, section by section, the performance objectives, or communicative functions, that the students should expect to achieve.

Communica-
tive functions

The instructional portion of each unit is divided into three sections, each equivalent to a regular lesson—Section A, Section B, and Section C. The communicative functions are repeated at the beginning of the section, followed by a brief introduction to the theme of the section. Each section includes basic material, presented in the form of a dialog, narrative, letter, an ad, captions to illustrations, or a memo; a grouping of the words and phrases necessary to the communicative function *(Se dice así)*; grammar *(Estructuras esenciales)*; a cultural note *(Sabes que . . .)*; a listening comprehension exercise *(Comprensión)*; and numerous activities *(Actividades)*, both oral and written. The activities range from those that help students acquire new skills and knowledge through practice to those that provide opportunities for them to apply their newly acquired skills in simulated real-life situations. Personalized questions encourage students to relate the material to their own experiences, while open-ended activities provide them with the opportunity to use what they have learned to express their own points of view. Many of the activities recommend that students work in pairs or groups.

Color coding

All headings are color-coded. Blue signifies new material, communicative functions, and grammar. Orange signals activities. Green calls attention to the cultural notes.

Application

Following Section C is the Try Your Skills section. Some of the activities in this section are open-ended. They create situations in which students can apply what they have learned, bringing together the communicative functions, grammar, and vocabulary presented in the preceding sections. The Try Your Skills section is essential to the development of proficiency. At the end of the Try Your Skills section there are dictation exercises that help students practice listening comprehension and writing in context.

Self-check

A complete pronunciation section *(Pronunciación)* follows the Try Your Skills section. These exercises point out letter-sound correspondences, intonation, and linking. A one-page self-check *(¿Lo sabes?)* contains a few key questions and check-up exercises to help students assess their achievement of the objectives listed on the opening pages of the unit. You may use the self-check after completing Sections A, B, and C and

Try Your Skills, or you may choose to use the appropriate part of the self-check after completing the corresponding section of the unit.

Vocabulary

On the page opposite the self-check is a list of active vocabulary items *(Vocabulario)* and their English equivalents, grouped by section. Below the list, a word-study exercise *(Práctica del vocabulario)* focuses attention on the vocabulary list; it gives students practice in developing word-attack skills while expanding their Spanish vocabulary.

Reading

The unit closes with a reading selection *(Vamos a leer)* linked to the theme of the unit. The selection is preceded by *Antes de leer,* which contains guided reading questions and statements, and by *Preparación para la lectura,* which includes pre-reading questions that help build a background for reading comprehension. The activities that follow the reading selection seek to further develop reading skills in Spanish and to encourage critical thinking through open-ended questions.

The basic material, some of the activities, the listening comprehension and pronunciation exercises, and the reading selection of each unit are recorded on the Unit Cassettes.

Organization of Review Units

The three review units *(Repasos)*—Units 4, 8, and 12— are considerably shorter than the nine instructional units. A review unit presents familiar material in a different context. No new vocabulary, grammar, or communicative functions are presented. Like the Try Your Skills section within an instructional unit, a review unit contains activities that encourage students to combine and apply the skills they acquired in the preceding instructional units. The situations presented in the review unit may differ from those the students encountered previously; using skills in new situations is crucial to developing proficiency. Selected material from the review units is also recorded on the Unit Cassettes.

Teacher's Edition

Annotations

The Teacher's Edition is designed to be of maximum assistance to you. It includes the pages of the Pupil's Edition, fully annotated with background notes, answers to activities, teaching suggestions, and variations.

Teacher's Notes

In addition, special Teacher's Notes—pages tabbed in blue—accompany each unit. For your convenience the Teacher's Notes for each unit are placed immediately before the annotated pupil pages of that unit. The Teacher's Notes address not only each section of the unit but every item within the section. The teaching suggestions are cross-referenced to the corresponding material (A1, A2, etc.) in the pupil pages.

Scope and Sequence chart

The Teacher's Notes begin with a detailed Scope and Sequence chart for the unit that also contains suggestions for the consistent re-entry of previously learned material. Below the chart is a list of the relevant ancillary components of the program and suggested materials that you may wish to prepare or gather. The Teacher's Notes state objectives, provide cultural background, suggest motivating activities, and offer teaching suggestions for all basic material, for the functions, grammar, cultural notes, and for each activity. To help you adapt instruction to meet different learning styles, suggestions are given on how to accommodate slower-paced learning and how to provide a challenge. Also included are suggestions for using cooperative learning and TPR (Total Physical Response) techniques (see page T7) and for combining the different language skills. The scripts of the listening comprehension exercises and the pronunciation exercises also appear in the Teacher's Notes.

Activity Workbook

The Activity Workbook *(Manual de actividades)* offers additional activities, puzzles, and games that give students practice with communicative functions, vocabulary, and structure in a variety of entertaining and challenging ways. Culturally authentic art and realia add an appealing visual dimension. All the exercises and activities are cross-referenced to those in the textbook.

The Teacher's Edition of the Activity Workbook provides you with the answers to the activities, printed in place.

Exercise Workbook

The Exercise Workbook *(Manual de ejercicios)* contains exercises of a more structured nature, all of which are cross-referenced to the textbook. The grammar points taught in the textbook are restated in the Exercise Workbook, where they are followed by extensive practice.

The Teacher's Edition of the Exercise Workbook, like that of the Activity Workbook, contains the answers to the exercises, printed in place.

Testing Program

Student's Test Booklet

Section quizzes

Unit tests

Proficiency-based tests

The Student's Test Booklet has three parts. The first part contains quizzes based on every section of the nine instructional units in the textbook. The second part includes a unit test for each instructional unit, three review tests covering the three Parts of the textbook, a midterm test, and a final exam. Listening comprehension is an integral part of each quiz and test. The third part of the Student's Test Booklet contains three optional proficiency-based tests that are designed to assess students' levels of proficiency in all four language skills. You may wish to use the first two tests for practice during the second half of the school year and the third proficiency-based test at the end of the year. Although related to the content of the textbook, the proficiency-based tests do not measure students' mastery of specific material. Rather, they present a variety of situations in which students are expected to demonstrate their ability to function in Spanish.

Teacher's Test Guide

The Teacher's Test Guide consists of several parts. The introduction describes the testing program and offers suggestions on how you may administer and score the quizzes and tests.

Following the introduction are the scripts of the listening parts of the quizzes, tests, and proficiency-based tests.

Speaking tests

The next section of the Teacher's Test Guide presents speaking tests for each unit in the textbook. Although these tests are optional, you are urged to administer them at the appropriate times. Suggestions for administering and scoring the speaking tests are given in the introduction to the Teacher's Test Guide.

The answer key to the entire testing program forms the final part of the Teacher's Test Guide.

Test Cassettes

The listening parts of the quizzes, tests, and proficiency-based tests are recorded on cassettes. Included is a recording of an examiner administering the speaking portion of a proficiency-based test to a student; it is intended to serve as a model if you are not familiar with proficiency testing.

Audio Program

Unit Cassettes

For each unit the recordings include the new or basic material, some of the activities, the listening and pronunciation exercises, and the reading selections. The texts of the three photo essays are also recorded. Where appropriate, pauses are provided for student repetition or response. In the textbook, items that are recorded are designated by means of a cassette symbol ▭ . The scripts of the recordings are provided in the Unit Cassette Guide. One of the Unit Cassettes contains several songs; the lyrics are provided in the Teacher's Resource Materials.

Unit Cassette Guide

The Unit Cassette Guide includes the reference index to the Unit Cassettes, the scripts of the Unit Cassettes, and student answer forms for the listening comprehension exercises in each unit.

Overhead Transparencies

Copying masters

A set of overhead transparencies with copying-master duplicates supplements the textbook. The set includes one transparency for each section of the nine instructional units, one for each of the three review units, and three maps. Each transparency depicts a situation that is closely related to the one in the corresponding section of the unit. The transparencies are accompanied by a Planning Guide booklet that offers suggestions on how to use them effectively.

Teaching suggestions

The transparencies are a valuable teaching aid. Students may be asked to describe what they see and then to imagine themselves in the situation and converse appropriately. Used in this manner, the transparencies serve to involve students in interactive communication. You may wish to use the transparencies in your presentation of basic material. As students learn new vocabulary and communicative functions, transparencies from previous units may be reintroduced to provide additional situations for the practice of the new material. When students view a new transparency, they may be encouraged to re-enter previously learned communicative functions and vocabulary. The copying masters enable you to reproduce and distribute copies of the transparencies for use in cooperative learning groups, for individual or group writing assignments, and for homework.

Unit Theme Posters

Twelve full-color posters are available. Each poster displays photographs relevant to the theme of the corresponding unit in the textbook. An accompanying guide suggests ways in which you might use the posters. Aside from creating a cultural ambiance in the classroom, they can be an effective teaching aid when you present and review a unit.

Teacher's Resource Materials

**Proficiency
practice**

The Teacher's Resource Materials booklet contains numerous teaching aids. One section discusses learning and teaching strategies, such as Total Physical Response (TPR), group learning, study hints, and suggestions for planning total immersion experiences. Another provides copying masters for role-playing situations to be used with each review unit. You may reproduce and distribute them to the students to stimulate extemporaneous communication, oral or written.

**Vocabulary
exercises**

Also included in the Teacher's Resource Materials are the vocabulary lists of the nine instructional units with the words regrouped according to parts of speech. Supplementary vocabulary exercises complement each list. Enrichment vocabulary and useful classroom expressions complete the vocabulary section.

Realia

Games/songs

The booklet contains several pages of realia, authentic documents that you may reproduce for classroom use. In addition, there are suggestions for classroom games and the lyrics of favorite songs. The music has been recorded on one of the Unit Cassettes. Also included are a glossary of grammar terms and a listing of additional sources of instructional materials (magazines, films, software, etc.).

Videocassettes

The videocassettes show a series of dramatic episodes that closely parallel the themes of the units in the textbook. Filmed on location, the programs are authentic representations of the foreign culture. Students see and hear Spanish-speaking young people doing and saying things that they themselves have simulated in the classroom. Special interactive segments involve the students. A guide suggests ways to use the videocassettes in the classroom.

Using the HBJ Spanish Program

The following procedures and techniques are suggested to meet diverse learning styles and classroom circumstances and to help students achieve communicative competence.

Developing Proficiency in the Four Skills

Listening

From the beginning, students are eager to say things in the foreign language, but they should also hear authentic language, even if they do not grasp the meaning of every word. You will wish to provide an abundance of listening activities.

Authentic input

For this purpose, the textbook is a primary source. The basic material and selected activities in each unit are recorded so that students may hear authentic language spoken by a variety of native speakers. In addition, each section of every unit contains a listening exercise. When playing the recordings in class, consider that students need time to listen to the new material before you ask them to repeat it or apply it.

Listening strategies

Listening requires active mental participation. You may want to share these listening strategies with your students: (1) they should listen for key words that tell what the situation is about; (2) they should not feel that they must understand every word; (3) they should make guesses and verify their hunches by repeated listening.

TPR (Total Physical Response)

The TPR (Total Physical Response) technique is an effective means of developing proficiency in listening. TPR is a physical response to an oral stimulus. Students listen to instructions or commands and give nonverbal responses according to their comprehension of the message. These responses may include moving about the classroom, interacting silently with classmates, drawing, or arranging pictures in sequence. Some activities in the student textbook call for TPR techniques. Suggestions for applying the TPR technique to other activities are also given in the Teacher's Edition.

By minimizing the use of English in the classroom from the beginning, you provide more opportunity for students to hear the foreign language. You may want to make a practice of relating personal experiences and local or world happenings to the students in the foreign language. Students will pick up a great deal of this "incidental" language.

Speaking

Students want most to be able to speak the foreign language they are studying. Keep in mind that the speaking skill is the most fragile; it takes careful nurturing and encouraging, uninhibited by rigid standards. It is very important to encourage fluency from the start of the course.

Interactive communication

Each of the units in the textbook focuses on the speaking skill. The majority of the activities are designed to lead to interaction and communication among students. Managed properly, these activities will provide the optimum speaking experiences for the students. The use of various grouping techniques will facilitate this procedure (see page T13).

Developing speaking proficiency

The development of the speaking skill follows this pattern: (1) repeating after adequate listening; (2) responding, using words and expressions of the lesson (up to this point no degree of proficiency should be expected); (3) manipulating learned material and recombining parts; (4) using what was previously learned in a new context.

When students use a previously learned expression spontaneously in a simulated situation as a natural thing to say at that time, they are truly beginning to speak the language. Students must be engaged in the application phase in order to develop proficiency beyond the novice level. Application activities are found particularly in the Try Your Skills section of each unit and in each review unit.

Reading

It is appropriate for students to read material they have been practicing, but they should also develop their reading skills using unfamiliar material. Require students to skim, scan, draw inferences, determine the main idea, and so forth. They should begin their reading by extracting the general ideas before they approach the details of a reading selection. The aim should be global comprehension in reading just as in listening.

Developing reading skills

You may help students approach reading selections through prereading strategies. Key words or expressions that might cause difficulty may be clarified, preferably in the foreign language. Students may be encouraged to examine the title and illustrations of a reading selection in search of clues to its meaning. You may elicit students' background knowledge of the subject of the reading through preliminary discussion; comprehension is definitely influenced by the prior information that students bring to a reading selection. All reading selections in the *Vamos a leer* sections are preceded by reading strategies grouped under *Antes de leer* and *Preparación para la lectura*.

Critical thinking

Also consider conducting directed reading lessons, requiring students to read selected passages silently with a purpose: to find answers to questions; to find reasons for actions and events; to find descriptions of characters. Students may be asked to write down all they recall of the content of a passage they have just read silently. In the follow-up lesson, you may wish to inquire not only about the who, what, and where of the content, but also to encourage critical thinking by asking why.

The TPR technique may be used to develop reading proficiency as well as listening proficiency. In the case of reading, students are expected to respond nonverbally to directions they have read.

Writing

The development of the writing skill is analogous to that of the speaking skill. Although the first stage may consist of copying, learning to spell, filling in the blanks, and writing from dictation, this training does not constitute writing. Writing is transferring thoughts to paper. Hence, students should progress from directed writing to more creative expression. To this end, a variety of controlled and open-ended writing activities appear in the textbook. The Teacher's Notes identify other activities suitable for writing practice and suggest additional writing activities.

Writing activities

Communicative Functions

When people communicate with each other—either orally or in writing—they use language for a specific purpose: to describe, persuade, argue, express emotions and opinions, praise, complain, agree, and so on. The term "communicative functions," or simply "functions," is used to refer to these purposes for which people communicate.

In the HBJ Spanish Program, the objectives of each instructional unit are phrased as communicative functions. They are clearly stated in the unit opener and are repeated in the section openers so that students can readily see the purpose for learning the language. Within the sections, the communicative functions are presented in new, or basic, material in a culturally authentic situation of interest to young people.

New (Basic) Material

Each section of an instructional unit opens with the presentation of basic material. In some sections there may be more than one presentation of new material. The basic material may take different forms; it may be a dialog, an interview, a monolog, or a narrative. Its purpose is to introduce the expressions, grammar, and vocabulary necessary to the communicative function(s) to be learned in the section. Previously learned functions may reappear in the basic material where appropriate. Also, in any basic material there will necessarily appear the new functions to be practiced in the section. Another purpose of the basic material is to provide cultural information, either directly or indirectly.

Before introducing any basic material, consult the list of communicative functions in the Scope and Sequence chart in the Teacher's Notes for that unit. The new material should be presented in ways that emphasize these communicative functions.

Students should approach basic material with these questions in mind, "What is the communicative purpose of the native speakers in this particular situation, and how are they using their language to accomplish it?" Students should not be required to memorize the basic material. The dialogs and narratives in the textbook are only samples of what a particular speaker of Spanish might say in a given situation; they should not be taught as fixed and rigid sentences. The aim should be to transfer the communicative functions from the basic material to other situations. Students should use the language functions to communicate naturally and spontaneously in real situations.

To help students, the communicative function is restated and the expressions necessary to achieve it are grouped together under the heading *Se dice así*. As the title suggests, this is how you say it, how you accomplish the communicative purpose or function. The expressions listed are primarily those introduced in the basic material. There may also be expressions from previous units that are appropriate to the communicative function; expressions that are learned to carry out one function may also be applied to carry out others. *Se dice así*, then, is a statement of a communicative function and the expressions to accomplish it.

After students have read the basic material and done the related activities, direct their attention to the expressions in *Se dice así*. You might make some statements in Spanish and have students choose appropriate responses from the expressions listed. Or, you might have students suggest ways to use Spanish to elicit the expressions from classmates. The activities that follow *Se dice así* give students opportunities to carry out the intended communicative function.

You will find detailed suggestions on how to present basic material and *Se dice así* in the Teacher's Notes preceding each unit. All basic material is recorded on the Unit Cassettes.

Activities

Practice/
application

The heading *Actividad* identifies the exercises in the textbook. There are two basic types of activities: (1) those that reinforce learning of the new material through practice and (2) those that require students to apply what they have learned.

The activities that follow the basic material are arranged in a planned progression from practice to application of the communicative functions, grammar, and vocabulary. Try Your Skills and review units mostly contain activities of the application type. Many application activities are designed to have the students converse in pairs or groups in order to foster communication and encourage creative expression.

The activities in the textbook may take many different forms. Those that relate to the basic material include questionnaires, sentence completions, true and false statements, identifications, and the sequencing of events. Personalized questions encourage students to relate the basic material to their own experiences. (Be careful to respect the privacy of individuals.) Grammar explanations are followed by practice exercises. Then, since the grammar is meant to support the communicative function(s), additional activities lead students to use the grammar in communicative situations.

Writing

Writing activities of various kinds appear throughout the textbook. Controlled exercises provide practice in writing the forms and structures of the language. Others provide opportunities for creative written expression. Dictation exercises *(Dictados)* in the Try Your Skills sections provide practice in both listening comprehension and writing skills. For further writing practice, many of the oral activities may be assigned to be written.

Listening

One or more listening comprehension activities, identified by the heading *Comprensión,* appear in each instructional section of a unit. These listening exercises are recorded on the Unit Cassettes, and student answer forms for them are located in both the Unit Cassette Guide and the Teacher's Resource Materials booklet. The scripts of the listening comprehension exercises are reproduced in the Teacher's Notes preceding each unit in the Teacher's Edition, as well as in the Unit Cassette Guide.

Optional activities

A few activities have been identified in the Teacher's Notes as optional Usually found at the end of a section, these activities are intended to enrich vocabulary. You may choose to use them or not, as time permits.

Pronunciation

In each instructional unit, following the Try Your Skills section, you will find a pronunciation section. This section, called *Pronunciación,* is designed to teach the sounds of Spanish. The sounds are presented first in a listening-speaking exercise that gives the students practice in saying them. This exercise is followed by one that presents the sounds in context in sentences. An exercise that recombines all of the sounds taught in the section concludes the *Pronunciación* section. These exercises are recorded on the Unit Cassettes; the scripts are located in the Unit Cassette Guide.

Recordings

This cassette symbol signals the activities that are recorded on the Unit Cassettes. Frequently, activities have been modified to adapt them for recording. You will find that a communicative activity in the textbook may be more structured when recorded. For this reason, you will want to consult the scripts in the Unit Cassette Guide before you play the cassettes. In certain circumstances, you may wish to play the recorded version of an activity first and then have the students perform the activity as directed in the textbook.

Answers to all activities are indicated (in blue) in the annotated pupil pages of the Teacher's Edition.

Grammar

In each section of every unit except the review units, the main grammar points relating to the functional objectives of the unit are summarized.

Grammar may be approached inductively or deductively, depending on the nature of the item and on student learning styles. Younger students, in general, respond favorably to an inductive approach that leads them to draw conclusions about the forms they have been practicing and applying.

On the other hand, because of the relative complexity of some structures, there may be a need to explain them before the students practice and apply them. In this case, the deductive approach may be more effective. You will want to determine which approach is more suitable.

Grammar and proficiency

Regardless of the approach, it is important to remember that in the development of proficiency, grammar is a means and not an end. Only the grammar that is relevant to the communicative function is necessary at this point.

Vocabulary

Vocabulary and proficiency

As in the case of grammar, consider the extent to which the amount and type of vocabulary presented serves the communicative purpose at hand. The introduction of excessive or irrelevant vocabulary, however interesting, may only complicate the task. The goal is to use vocabulary to communicate. Like grammar, vocabulary is a means, not an end.

Vocabulary is presented in context and listed at the end of each unit. A word-study activity following the list helps students understand and remember the vocabulary by pointing out word families, relationships, derivations, and so on.

You may use word games, puzzles, and mnemonic aids to teach vocabulary. An effective motivational practice is to have students devise their own games, puzzles, illustrative posters, and picture dictionaries.

Culture

Cultural expression

We hope to instill cultural awareness by exposing students to different kinds of cultural expression—authentic written and spoken language, a rich collection of photographs showing a cross-section of people and places, an abundance of realia, and special culture notes in Spanish. We want students to get to know what Spanish-speaking young people are like and to develop a feel for the everyday life in the foreign culture.

Throughout this Teacher's Edition we have noted additional cultural points that may interest you and your students or that clarify situations depicted in the units. The Teacher's Notes preceding each unit provide additional background information on the unit themes. You may want to consult these pages as you prepare to introduce each unit.

Photo essays

Sources for cultural awareness are present on almost every page of the textbook. They are especially concentrated, however, in the photo essays that precede Units 1, 5, and 9. To help you in presenting the photo essays, we have included background information on the various topics and some details about specific photographs in the Teacher's Notes preceding the review units.

Projects

Encourage your students to personalize the Spanish-speaking cultures as they study and practice the themes and vocabulary of the units. Suggestions for projects are given in the units and in the Teacher's Notes; assign as many projects as possible. In doing projects, students not only practice their skills, but they also share in an experience that helps them learn about the particular country's culture in a direct and personal way.

You can enhance students' cultural awareness and appreciation by utilizing community resources and, if possible, by taking school trips to regions or countries where the foreign language is spoken.

Review

Quizzes

Frequent feedback is essential to assess your students' progress toward proficiency and their need for review. The quizzes based on each section of a unit are one means of assessment. They are short and are best checked immediately during the same class period.

The textbook itself is structured to ensure adequate review. The self-check (*¿Lo sabes?*) and the Try Your Skills section at the end of each unit, as well as the three review units, provide opportunities for students to review and recombine previously presented material.

Re-entry

In addition, you will want to make a practice of systematically re-entering material from previous units, especially during warm-up activities at the beginning of a class period. You will find suggestions for the re-entry of previously learned material in the Scope and Sequence chart in the Teacher's Notes preceding each instructional unit.

Testing and Evaluation

Evaluation is an ongoing process. Informal assessment should take place in the classroom on an almost daily basis, whether by observing students during their group work or by engaging individuals or groups briefly in conversation. The section quizzes and the unit tests in the Student's Test Booklet provide a formal check on progress in the areas of listening, reading, and writing. You may wish to administer a short speaking test after each unit. To save you preparation time, speaking tests are supplied in the Teacher's Test Guide.

Proficiency
tests

Unlike achievement testing, which is the assessment of the immediate objectives of a lesson, proficiency testing measures how well students use the language in contexts that approximate real-life situations. Since proficiency develops slowly, assessments of proficiency should be made less frequently. Proficiency-based tests are a vital part of this program. There are two practice tests and a final test. Meant to be given during the second half of the year, they require students to demonstrate their abilities in all four language skills in situations beyond—but not unrelated to—the textbook.

Suggestions for Classroom Management

Classroom Climate

As you know, students are more enthusiastic and responsive in a friendly, nonthreatening atmosphere of mutual respect that fosters self-confidence.

A tense atmosphere may inhibit the spontaneous use of the foreign language which is so necessary to the development of proficiency.

You may wish to consider the importance of organization and keeping students on task. Ground rules for classroom procedures will help you create an effective environment for learning. These procedures should include an explanation of how English is to be used and the distribution of a list of classroom expressions in Spanish that students will gradually begin to use with confidence.

Another—but not the least—consideration is the positive effect of a classroom decorated with posters, maps, pictures, realia, and students' papers and projects.

English in the Classroom

The use of the foreign language in the classroom is basic to helping students develop listening proficiency. Students should become accustomed to hearing classroom directions in the foreign language. You will find lists of classroom expressions in Spanish in the vocabulary section of the Teacher's Resource Materials.

It is natural for students to ask for explanations and want to make comments in English. You may wish to set aside a short segment of time at the end of a class period for clarifications in English.

Classroom Strategies

Two fundamental approaches to classroom instruction can be described as teacher-centered and student-centered. Both have a place in the foreign language classroom. In either approach the student is the primary focus.

A teacher-centered approach is most effective in the learning phase. You may wish to use this approach for directed teaching activities, such as presenting new material and conducting drills and question/answer sessions. Consider using various student-centered activities, such as simulated social situations and conversations, in the application phase to develop the independence that eventually leads to proficiency beyond the novice stage.

Grouping

Grouping maximizes opportunities for interaction among students in lifelike situations. It is an especially useful strategy in classes that have combined levels of students with varied learning styles and abilities.

Cooperative learning

Cooperative learning is one way in which students and teachers can achieve learning goals. In cooperative learning, small groups of students collaborate to achieve a common goal. There are four basic benefits of a cooperative learning group: (1) positive interdependence; (2) face-to-face interaction; (3) individual accountability; (4) appropriate use of interpersonal skills. Following are some suggestions for structuring cooperative learning activities.

Forming cooperative learning groups

1. Be sure the task is clear to everyone.
2. Set a time limit. Completion of the task and reporting to the class should take place during the class period.
3. Circulate among the students and assist them as needed.
4. Assign specific tasks to each group member.

5. Clarify any limitations of movement during the activity.
6. Select the group size most suited to the activity. Pairs are appropriate for many activities.
7. Assign students to groups. Heterogeneous groups are more desirable. Groups should not be permanent.
8. Evaluate the group's task when completed and discuss with the group the interaction of the members.

Many activities in the textbook lend themselves to cooperative learning.

Providing for Different Learning Styles

Different students learn best in different ways. Some learn new material most easily when they are allowed to listen to it and repeat it. Others do best when they see it in writing. Still others respond best to visual experiences—photographs, drawings, overhead transparencies. And some students need to be involved physically or emotionally with the material they are learning and to respond concretely and personally. Moreover, all students need variety in the learning experience; the same student may respond differently on different days.

Slower-paced learning

Slower-paced learning requires that you present and adapt materials differently than you do when a greater challenge is called for. The Teacher's Notes that precede each unit contain numerous suggestions for teaching strategies to be used in a slower-paced learning environment and in a challenge situation.

Challenge

In general, you may wish to consider strategies for slower-paced learning that involve breaking down an activity into smaller tasks and then rebuilding it gradually. Accept short answers and elicit passive, non-linguistic responses more often. On the other hand, when you deal with students who need a greater challenge, consider expanding activities and adding new twists that require critical thinking and creativity.

Forming heterogeneous cooperative learning groups and pairing students of different learning abilities can be effective means of assisting all students, both academically and socially.

Homework

Differentiated assignments

Homework that reinforces and enriches class work should be an integral part of instruction. You may want to consider giving differentiated homework assignments to suit the varied needs of students instead of issuing identical assignments to all. For this purpose, the Activity Workbook and the Exercise Workbook provide numerous exercises of various types that are designed to meet different learning styles.

Homework should be collected and checked; otherwise students will not respect the practice. You may devise a system for students to check their own homework, but you must take care to avoid spending an entire class period checking homework. Long-term homework projects as well as short-term assignments are effective.

Use of Audio-Visual Materials

Audio-visual components

Students need to hear a variety of voices speaking Spanish. The Unit Cassettes provide an auditory program to develop listening proficiency.

Students also need to see authentic representations of the foreign culture. The photographs in the textbook—in each unit and in the photo essays—can be used to motivate students before they launch into new material and also to increase cultural awareness. In addition, the unit theme posters and the transparencies related to each section of a unit depict culturally authentic situations.

Additional materials

You may want to use an overhead projector with a transparency instead of writing on the board to focus students' attention more directly. Where the facilities exist, students may create their own skits based on the units and record them on a videocassette for classroom viewing. Showing rented films, displaying posters, and sharing realia are other means you may consider to add a visual dimension to classroom instruction.

Planning

Pacing

Controlling the pace

It is helpful to devise a schedule of instruction for the year. Planning ahead is essential to setting the pace most appropriate for your classroom. The textbook is designed to be completed in one school year. Where needed, you can control the time spent on each unit by including or omitting optional exercises, by doing some or all of the activities in the review unit, by insisting on total mastery of material before progressing or relying on the cumulative acquisition of the language.

Unit planning

Your schedule will vary according to the grade and ability level of your students and the number of interruptions in your school program. In general, an instructional unit can be taught in three weeks; in some cases an additional day may be needed for the unit test. A review unit will take one week, including the review test. Sufficient time should remain for discussing the cultural notes and photo essays, administering midterm, final tests, and proficiency-based tests, and conducting optional enrichment activities.

Lesson Plans

You will probably want to prepare a daily lesson plan that incorporates various language skills. Plans may vary, but the basic lesson should include the following to some degree, at least over a span of two days.

Planning sequence

- A warm-up activity, usually involving review
- A quiz or test when appropriate
- The presentation of new material preceded by a motivating activity and a statement of objectives
- Developmental activities and guided practice
- Application by the students of what they have learned
- Summarizing statements, preferably elicited from the students
- Closure (a review with the students of what they have learned)
- Assignment, planning ahead, or previewing the next lesson
- Periodic long-range planning with the students

Unit Planning Guide

The following plan suggests how the material in Unit 2 may be distributed over fifteen days. You may wish to prepare similar lesson plans, adjusting them to suit the needs and interests of your students. For a faster pace, the exercises in parentheses might be assigned as homework or omitted.

	Daily Plans	Unit Resources
Day 1	Objective: To talk about family relationships Unit opener: discussion Section A: motivating activity Basic material A1 Actividades A2, (A3), A4 Sabes que . . . A5 Se dice así A6 Actividades A7, (A8)	Unit 2 Poster Overhead Transparency 4 Unit 2 Cassette Activity Workbook Exercise Workbook
Day 2	Objective: To talk about family relationships Estructuras esenciales A9 Actividades A10, (A11), A12 Estructuras esenciales A13 Actividades A14, A15	Unit 2 Cassette Activity Workbook Exercise Workbook
Day 3	Objective: To make comparisons Sabes que . . . A16 Estructuras esenciales A17 Actividades A18, A19 Estructuras esenciales A20 Actividad A21 Comprensión A22 Actividad A23 Assign review of Section A	Unit 2 Cassette Activity Workbook Exercise Workbook Overhead Transparency 4
Day 4	Objective: To make excuses Quiz on Section A Section B: motivating activity Basic material B1 Actividades B2, (B3)	Quiz 4 Overhead Transparency 5 Unit 2 Cassette Activity Workbook Exercise Workbook
Day 5	Objective: To make excuses Sabes que . . . B4 Actividad B5 Se dice así B6 Actividad B7 Basic material B8 Actividades (B9), B10	Unit 2 Cassette Activity Workbook Exercise Workbook
Day 6	Objective: To express your point of view Estructuras esenciales B11 Actividades B12, B13, (B14) Sabes que . . . B15 Actividades B16, B17	Unit 2 Cassette Activity Workbook Exercise Workbook

	Daily Plans	**Unit Resources**

Day 7	Objective: To make suggestions
	  Basic material B18
	  Actividades B19, (B20)
	  Comprensión B21
	  Estructuras esenciales B22
	  Actividad B23
	  Assign review of Section B
		Unit 2 Cassette
		Activity Workbook
		Exercise Workbook
		Overhead Transparency 5

Day 8	Objective: To persuade somebody to lend
	you something, to confirm expected
	courses of action
	  Quiz on Section B
	  Section C. motivating activity
	  Basic material C1
	  Actividades C2, (C3)
	  Sabes que . . . C4
	  Se dice así C5
		Quiz 5
		Unit 2 Cassette
		Overhead Transparency 6
		Activity Workbook
		Exercise Workbook

Day 9	Objective: To persuade somebody to lend
	you something, to confirm expected
	courses of action
	  Estructuras esenciales C6
	  Actividades C7, C8, (C9)
	  Comprensión C10
	  Actividad (C11)
		Unit 2 Cassette
		Activity Workbook
		Exercise Workbook

Day 10	Objective: To persuade someone
	to lend you something
	  Se escribe así C12
	  Estructuras esenciales C13
	  Actividades C14, C15, (C16), C17
	  Assign review of Section C
		Unit 2 Cassette
		Activity Workbook
		Exercise Workbook
		Overhead Transparency 6

Day 11	Objective: To use what you've learned
	  Quiz on Section C
	  Basic material Try Your Skills 1
	  Actividades 2, (3), 4, 5, 6
		Quiz 6
		Unit 2 Cassette
		Activity Workbook

Day 12	Objective: To use what you've learned
	  Actividades (7), 8, 9, (10), 11
	  Pronunciación
		Unit 2 Cassette
		Activity Workbook

Day 13	Objective: To prepare for Unit 2 Test
	  ¿Lo sabes?
	  Vocabulario
	  Práctica del vocabulario
		Activity Workbook
		Exercise Workbook
		Overhead Transparencies
		  4, 5, 6
		Unit 2 Poster

Day 14	Objective: To assess progress Unit 2 Test	Unit 2 Test

TO THE TEACHER

	Daily Plans	Unit Resources
Day 15	Objective: To read for practice and pleasure Vamos a leer: El coquí de Puerto Rico Actividades (Choice of other reading selections)	Unit 2 Cassette

Beyond the Classroom

In School

A vibrant foreign language program extends outside the classroom to other disciplines, the entire school, the community, and beyond.

Relating to other disciplines

By its very nature, the study of foreign languages is interdisciplinary. You may wish to consider cooperating with social studies teachers to promote global education. Since you deal with the art, music, and literature of the foreign culture, you complement the work of the art, music, and English teachers. Foreign language study raises students' level of general linguistic awareness, thereby reinforcing their work in English language arts. Learning about sports in other countries may increase the enthusiasm for sports among your students.

Foreign language classes should have an impact on the total school environment. You may have the students label areas of the building and prepare public address announcements in the foreign language. Staging assemblies, participating in school fairs, and celebrating foreign festivals schoolwide are other ways to provide students with opportunities to use their knowledge and skills outside the classroom, particularly during National Foreign Language Week in March.

Outside School

Your efforts to heighten enthusiasm for foreign language study might reach out into the community through field trips to ethnic restaurants, museums, embassies, and local areas where the foreign language is spoken. Encourage your students to present special foreign language programs in nursing homes and hospitals. If you receive radio and television programs in Spanish, or if foreign movies are shown in your region, you will want your students to take advantage of them to improve their language skills as well as their cultural awareness.

The ultimate extension of foreign language study is a trip to or a stay in a country where the language is spoken. Working with school authorities, you may be able to arrange trips abroad for your students.

Total immersion

However, a total foreign language experience need not require travel outside the area. For a day, a weekend, or a longer period during a school vacation, the foreign culture can be recreated at the school, at a camp, or at a university to provide a total immersion experience. This activity requires detailed planning and preparation. Suggestions for planning total immersion experiences are presented in the Teacher's Resource Materials.

Whatever the nature of the endeavor to extend foreign language study beyond the classroom, you will need to develop guidelines with the students in addition to any school rules governing such activities. Adherence to an organized plan results in a more productive experience.

Career Awareness

For many students, foreign language study will form the basis of their life's work or enhance it.

Career awareness activities can be a strong motivating force to learn a foreign language. Students should be made aware of the types of professions and occupations prevailing in the foreign culture and those in their own culture that either depend on foreign language skills or are enhanced by such skills.

You may want to collaborate with guidance counselors in your school to provide up-to-date information concerning career opportunities related to foreign languages. Many schools have career fairs in which you might consider participating.

Conclusion

Many teachers have found the following guidelines practical in planning their foreign language courses. You, too, may find them useful.

- Establish a positive climate.
- Have a classroom decor that reflects the foreign culture.
- Establish a fair-but-firm policy for classroom management.
- Take student interests into consideration when planning.
- Have a written plan.
- Discuss objectives with the students.
- Provide for varied learning styles and rates.
- Avoid lecturing.
- Maximize student involvement.
- Provide positive verbal and nonverbal feedback.
- Evaluate class procedures and outcomes with the students.

The aim of proficiency-oriented instruction is not that students learn language lessons. Rather, the goal is to encourage and guide students to use what they have learned in new situations. Without this application phase in the instructional procedure, proficiency will not be achieved. Therein lies the challenge to the foreign language teacher. We wish you much success in this exciting undertaking.

Specific suggestions for teaching each unit appear in the blue-tabbed pages preceding the unit. Additional suggestions and answers to activities are provided in the annotated pupil pages.

Nosotros, los jóvenes

Foreign Language Programs

SPANISH

- **Nuevos amigos**
  Level 1

- **Nosotros, los jóvenes**
  Level 2

- **Nuestro mundo**
  Level 3

Nosotros, los jóvenes

HBJ HARCOURT BRACE JOVANOVICH, PUBLISHERS
Orlando   San Diego   Chicago   Dallas

Printed in the United States of America
ISBN 0–15–388350–2

PHOTO CREDITS Key: (t) top, (b) bottom, (l) left, (r) right, (c) center, (fl) far left, (fr) far right
COVER: HBJ Photo/Peter Menzel
TABLE OF CONTENTS: page vii(all), HBJ Photo except (bc), HBJ Photo/Peter Menzel; viii, HBJ Photo/Peter Menzel; x. HBJ Photo; xii, HBJ Photo/Peter Menzel; xiv, HBJ Photo; xvi, HBJ Photo xviii, NASA; xx, HBJ Photo/Mark Antman; xxii, HBJ Photo/Peter Menzel; xxiv, HBJ Photo/Mark Antman; 1(tl, bl), Craig Aurness/West Light; 1(tr, br), HBJ Photo; 2(tl, bl), HBJ Photo/Peter Menzel; 2(tr, br), HBJ Photo; 3(all), HBJ Photo/Peter Menzel; 4(tl), HBJ Photo; 4(c,br), HBJ Photo/Saúl o. Iglesias; 4(tr), HBJ Photo/Peter Menzel; 5(tl, br), HBJ Photo; 5(tr), HBJ Photo/Saúl O. Iglesias; 5(bl), HBJ Photo/Peter Menzel; 6(tl, tr), HBJ Photo/Mimi Fernández; 6(bl), Victor Englebert/Black Star; 6(br), HBJ Photo; 7(tl, bl), HBJ Photo/Peter Menzel; 7(tr, br), HBJ Photo/Gerhard Gscheidle; 8(tl, bl, tr), HBJ Photo/Peter Menzel; 8(br), HBJ Photo

Continued on page 459

iv

ACKNOWLEDGMENTS

We wish to express our thanks to the students pictured in this textbook and to the parents who allowed us to photograph these young people in their homes and in other places. We also thank the teachers and the families who helped us find these young people; the school administrators who allowed us to photograph the students in their schools; and the merchants who permitted us to photograph the students in their stores and other places of business.

YOUNG PEOPLE
Pilar Abad, Monserrat de Udaeta, José Granada Domenich, Pepita Llaurado, José Ponson, Severo Hiller, Andrea Hiller

TEACHERS AND FAMILIES
María Clara Grau, Carmen Cortéz, Arturo Llaureado, José Ponson, Carlos Hiller

CONTENTS

COMMUNICATIVE FUNCTIONS	GRAMMAR	CULTURE
Exchanging information • Describing what one did	Review of the preterit tense, regular **-ar, -er,** and **-ir** verbs The preterit tense of **scr, ir, ver,** and **dar**	Ancient Indian civilizations in Mexico
Exchanging information • Reporting past events • Asking and explaining how something was **Expressing feelings and emotions** • Expressing satisfaction and dissatisfaction	Verbs ending in **-car, -gar,** and **-zar** The preterit tense of **tener, estar,** and **poder**	Early Spanish missions in the United States
Socializing • Meeting and greeting people • Sending greetings and saying that someone sends regards • Writing salutations and complimentary closings	The preterit tense of **saber** and **conocer** Adverbs ending in **-mente** Using **por** and **para** *(Review)*	Spanish names, surnames, and nicknames
Recombining communicative functions, grammar, and vocabulary		Dinner with a Spanish-speaking family
Reading for practice and pleasure		Your name and its origin

	BASIC MATERIAL

COMMUNICATIVE FUNCTIONS	GRAMMAR	CULTURE
Socializing • Extending an invitation • Congratulating someone **Exchanging information** • Expressing time (morning, afternoon, or evening) • Inquiring about age	The infinitive after a preposition *(Review)* Ordinal numbers The imperfect tense of regular verbs	Honoring Christopher Columbus in the New World Saint's day in the Spanish-speaking world
Exchanging information • Describing events in the past **Expressing feelings and emotions** • Expressing intention	The imperfect tense forms of **ver, ir,** and **ser** Some uses of the imperfect tense	Festivities and holidays in Spain and Spanish America
Expressing feelings and emotions • Expressing regret • Expressing how you feel about others and about yourself	The imperfect and the preterit tenses contrasted Verbs ending in **-cer** and **-cir**	Teenage parties in the Spanish-speaking world
Recombining communicative functions, grammar, and vocabulary		Celebrating Valentine's Day
Reading for practice and pleasure		A Spanish folk tale

	BASIC MATERIAL

COMMUNICATIVE FUNCTIONS	GRAMMAR	CULTURE
Exchanging information • Talking about what one does every day • Describing emotions	Reflexive pronouns The definite article with the parts of the body and with personal possessions	A look at Lima, Peru
Expressing feelings and emotions • Asking and stating how one feels • Expressing sympathy	Affirmative and negative expressions The preterit tense of **querer** and **poner** The verb **gustar** (*Review*)	Native American foods discovered by the early Europeans Tropical fruits of America
Exchanging information • Discussing unplanned events **Socializing** • Paying compliments	Verbs used with reflexive pronouns The present indicative tense of **traer** and **oír**	Grooming and fashion in Spanish America
Recombining communicative functions, grammar, and vocabulary		Keeping fit in Spanish America
Reading for practice and pleasure		The ancient origin of the potato

TERCERA PARTE

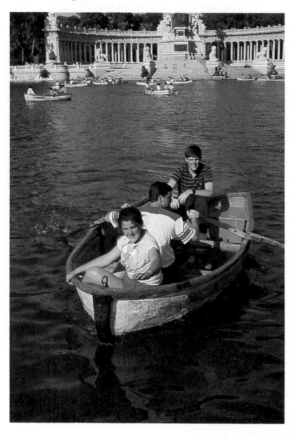

COMMUNICATIVE FUNCTIONS	GRAMMAR	CULTURE
Exchanging information • Reporting what others say **Persuading** • Asking for help or giving a warning	Review of the Spanish indicative mood The superlative construction	Fairs and festivals celebrated in Spain
Expressing feelings and emotions • Expressing amazement and pity • Expressing desire **Socializing** • Writing salutations and complimentary closings for business letters	Irregular forms of comparatives and superlatives The Spanish subjunctive mood The subjunctive to express demands, wishes, and requests Present subjunctive of some irregular verbs	Household chores in Spanish-speaking countries
Socializing • Congratulating someone • Writing common introductions for business letters **Persuading** • Directing others to tell someone else to do something	Irregular verbs and verbs ending in **-car**, **-gar**, and **-zar** in the present subjunctive Indirect commands	Summer vacation and the youth of Hispanic America
Recombining communicative functions, grammar, and vocabulary		Classified ads in Spanish
Reading for practice and pleasure		Strategies for a better job interview

COMMUNICATIVE FUNCTIONS	GRAMMAR	CULTURE
Exchanging information • Reporting, describing, and narrating • Describing things you have done in the past	The present perfect tense Stem-changing verbs in the preterit tense	The diversity of Argentina's population
Expressing feelings and emotions • Expressing your likes and dislikes **Persuading** • Warning others to refrain from doing something	Negative familiar commands Some irregular past participles	The Spanish origin of some American words from the West
Expressing attitudes and opinions • Expressing obligation or necessity **Expressing feelings and emotions** • Expressing doubt, disbelief, or denial	The subjunctive to express doubt, disbelief, or denial The use of **se** for indefinite subjects	Protecting the environment in Spanish America
Recombining communicative functions, grammar, and vocabulary		Cultural highlights from the three preceding units
Reading for practice and pleasure		The music, dance, and crafts of Spanish America

COMMUNICATIVE FUNCTIONS	GRAMMAR	CULTURE
Expressing feelings and emotions • Expressing emotions **Expressing and finding out moral attitudes** • Expressing agreement or lack of preference • Expressing approval or satisfaction with emphasis	The use of the subjunctive to express feelings and emotions The use of the subjunctive to express the indefinite	Learning about Cataluña, Spain
Expressing attitudes and opinions • Expressing what is needed or expected • Expressing probability or denial **Persuading** • Making suggestions	The use of the subjunctive in impersonal expressions Softened commands	Vacationing in Spain A visit to Montjuich, Barcelona, Spain
Socializing • Attracting attention **Expressing feelings and emotions** • Expressing uncertainty	The expression **¡ojalá!** The subjunctive with **tal vez** and **quizás**	Exploring Barcelona **La sardana:** A folk dance from Cataluña
Recombining communicative functions, grammar, and vocabulary		Traveling in Spain
Reading for practice and pleasure		The varied regions of Spain
Reviewing communicative functions, grammar, and vocabulary		The end-of-the-school-year celebrations in Spanish-speaking countries

FOR REFERENCE

Los españoles y los hispanoamericanos

OBJECTIVE To read in Spanish for cultural awareness

MOTIVATING ACTIVITY Ask the students what they know about Spanish-speaking people, about Spain, and about Spanish America. List their impressions on the board or a transparency. Compare these to the impressions they develop after reading the photo essay.

CULTURAL BACKGROUND You may wish to discuss the great ethnic variety within the Spanish-speaking world. Point out its size, indicating that it includes Spain, parts of North America, Central America, the Caribbean, and South America. Show Transparencies 31–35 and point out that Spanish is spoken by approximately 308 million people in those countries. You may wish to add that about 20 million Americans also speak Spanish. Stress the value of learning Spanish because of its growing importance, both for international trade and international relations. It is important to point out to the students that in spite of this diversity of types and ethnic backgrounds, the common language of people throughout the Hispanic world is Spanish. Government affairs, street signs, private business issues, newspapers, and all kinds of publications are in Spanish. Thus, Spanish-speaking people traveling in the Hispanic world have no difficulty understanding each other, just as Americans traveling through Australia, South Africa, or England have no problem communicating.

Explain to the students that it will become obvious from this photo essay that there is an infinite ethnic variety in the Spanish-speaking world, but that people can communicate because they have a common language. Go back to Transparency 34 and Overlay 34A or a map of Spain. Locate **Cataluña** on the map and point out the photograph of the two young guides on page 1. Explain that they are from the **Instituto Municipal del Turismo** in Barcelona. You may wish to ask the class to identify the meaning of **Instituto Municipal del Turismo.** If they need help, point out that there are three cognates in the name: **Instituto, Municipal,** and **Turismo.** Add that in addition to Spanish, the Catalonians speak a language called **catalán;** thus, they are bilingual.

Point out the different types of people found in Spain. Draw the students' attention to the photographs of the two young people in regional costumes and the group on the lower-right side of page 1. This variety can also be seen in the photographs on page 2 (excluding the photo on the lower left). Using the transparency or a map of Spain, point out the geographical location of Madrid. Explain that the **Plaza Mayor** was once the center of the city. It is very famous because of its beautiful baroque architecture.

As you continue to present the information on page 3, you may wish to explain to the students that there is also ethnic diversity in South America. Point out the strong Indian influence that is present in its culture and people. Use Transparency 32 and Overlay 32A, or a map of South America to show the students that the Inca Empire encompassed Peru,

Ecuador, southern portions of Colombia, and parts of Bolivia. Point out the city of Cuzco on the map and explain that Cuzco was the ancient capital of the Incas. Now, have the students compare the photo of the hand-woven cloth with the photo of the Peruvian shawl. Point out that they are similar because during pre-Columbian times there was commerce among ancient Peru, Colombia, and parts of Central America and Mexico, and that merchants used to travel in caravans carrying products back and forth.

On page 4 there are several photos showing the countries of the Caribbean basin: Venezuela, Santo Domingo, and Puerto Rico. Use Transparency 31 and Overlay 31A, or a map of Central America and the West Indies, to point out the location of these countries. Also show the location of Cuba and Central America on the map. Explain that Santo Domingo shares the island of Hispaniola with Haiti, and add that there is a great deal of African influence in the music and culture of these islands.

Explain to the students that on his first voyage, **Cristóbal Colón** departed from the port of Palos de Moguer, Spain, with three vessels **(carabelas)** called the Pinta, the Niña, and the Santa María. Ask them to open their books to page 370 and point out the photograph of the replica of a **carabela.** Tell the students that these vessels were not very large in comparison to the ships of today. Now, ask the students to turn to page 152 and explain that **Cristóbal Colón** first reached the Caribbean in 1492. The red lines at the upper left side of the illustration mark his arrival and how he traveled by Cuba and Santo Domingo before returning to Spain.

CULTURAL BACKGROUND   In Chile there are a great many people of Indian descent. When the Spaniards arrived in Chile, they had to fight a group of Indians called the **araucanos.** The **araucanos** defended their territory fiercely and won many battles before being conquered. Alonso de Ercilla, a Spanish soldier in the war against the **araucanos,** was also a poet and writer. He wrote a famous epic poem called **"La araucana"** that was based on his experiences during the war.

Peru, Ecuador, and Bolivia all were part of the Inca Empire and had a highly advanced civilization. The empire had large cities, such as Cuzco, and was well populated. The legacy of the Inca Empire remains strong throughout these countries because the descendents of the Incas constitute much of the population today in Peru, Ecuador, and Bolivia. When the Spaniards invaded Peru, they occupied the principal cities of the Inca Empire, including Cuzco, its capital. After the conquest, the Spaniards founded many cities. One of theses cities is Lima, used by the Spaniards as the seat of government during colonial times. It greatly resembled Spanish cities of the period in its layout and architectural styles. Many stories and legends of this colonial period have been popularized by the work of Ricardo Palma (1833–1919), author of *Tradiciones peruanas.*

As you present the information and photographs on pages 5–8, have the students take note of the great diversity of cultures and ethnic characteristics of Spanish-speaking people. Stress that in most Spanish-American countries, the Spaniards were the largest immigrant group. The one exception is Argentina, which received a great many immigrants from Italy and other European countries during the nineteenth and twentieth centuries. Today in Argentina the largest population group is of Italian descent, with people of Spanish descent the second largest. There are very few people of Indian descent in Argentina. This explains why the European tradition rather than the Indian one is the strongest influence on the arts and literature. In this aspect Argentina is unique, since Indian conflicts, customs, and traditions are pervasive in South American literature.

UNIDAD 1 El regreso de las vacaciones
Scope and Sequence

	BASIC MATERIAL	COMMUNICATIVE FUNCTIONS
SECTION A	En la puerta de la escuela (A1)	**Exchanging information** • Describing what one did
SECTION B	Páginas de mi diario (B1)	**Exchanging information** • Reporting past events • Asking and explaining how something was **Expressing feelings and emotions** • Expressing satisfaction and dissatisfaction
SECTION C	Saludos y presentaciones (C1) Una carta (C9)	**Socializing** • Meeting and greeting people • Sending greetings • Saying that someone sends his or her regards • Writing salutations and complimentary closings
TRY YOUR · SKILLS	Una comida en casa de Tere Dictado	

■ **Pronunciación** (letters **g** and **j**)
■ **¿Lo sabes?** ■ **Vocabulario**

VAMOS A LEER	**¿Te gusta tu nombre?** (Would you like to change your name?)

WRITING   A variety of controlled and open-ended writing activities appear in the Pupil's Edition. The Teacher's Notes identify other activities suitable for writing practice.

COOPERATIVE LEARNING   Many of the activities in the Pupil's Edition lend themselves to cooperative learning. The Teacher's Notes explain some of the many instances where this teaching strategy can be particularly effective. For guidelines on how to use cooperative learning, see page T13.

GRAMMAR	CULTURE	RE-ENTRY
The preterit tense of **ser** and **ir** (A9) The preterit tense of **ver** and **dar** (A17)	Guadalajara and the Mariachis The pre-Columbian culture of Mexico	Review of the preterit tense, regular **-ar**, **-er**, and **-ir** verbs
Verbs ending in **-car, -gar,** and **-zar** (B6) The preterit tense of **tener, estar,** and **poder** (B12)	The Spanish missions Hispanic influence in the United States	Keeping the same sound in the preterit tense
The preterit tense of **saber** and **conocer** (C11) Adverbs ending in **-mente** (C17)	A look at San Antonio Spanish names	The verbs **saber** and **conocer** Using **por** and **para** Nicknames The use of **usted**

Recombining communicative functions, grammar, and vocabulary

Reading for practice and pleasure

Section A Map of Mexico, photographs of summer activities
Section B Pictures of sports activities, pictures of Spanish missions, map of the United States
Section C Map of the United States, pictures of San Antonio, postcards, toy telephones, pictures of a city

Manual de actividades, Unit 1
Manual de ejercicios, Unit 1
Unit 1 Cassettes
Transparencies 1–3
Quizzes 1–3
Unit 1 Test

OBJECTIVES **To exchange information:** describe what one did

CULTURAL BACKGROUND Point out Guadalajara on a map of Mexico. Then explain that Guadalajara, Mexico's second largest city, is known for its lovely parks. The tradition of the **mariachis** is very strong in Guadalajara. The **mariachis** are groups of strolling musicians who play a variety of stringed and brass instruments. They dress in the traditional suits of the **charro,** the cowboy of Mexico. The trousers are tight and tapered with silver trim on the side seams. Boots and spurs are often worn as well. A short jacket, white shirt, and bow tie complete the outfit. Their songs are traditional and can often be heard throughout the streets of the neighborhoods in the early hours of the morning. At these hours, on special occasions, young men may have hired the group to serenade their girlfriends.

MOTIVATING ACTIVITY Bring photographs depicting summer activities, such as camping, fishing, swimming, cycling, and water skiing. Review the Spanish names of these activities. Then have the students discuss three activities they like and three they dislike.

A1 En la puerta de la escuela

To create a cultural setting for **El regreso de las vacaciones,** after you have discussed the cultural notes, point out on a map of Mexico, the cities of Guadalajara, Mérida, Chichén Itzá, and Mazatlán.

When you begin the presentation of the dialog, concentrate on the specific objectives of the activity in progress. You should not interrupt to explain grammar or to define new vocabulary. Explanation of these items may be done before, or may follow later.

Three of the main objectives of the presentation materials are: to provide a natural and coherent semantic context that includes the functions, the vocabulary, and the grammar presented in the section; to help the students develop oral production, including pronunciation, rhythm, and intonation; and to aid in the students' development of an auditory memory in the foreign language by familiarizing them with the sounds of spoken Spanish.

While presenting and practicing the dialog in class, try to keep a fast tempo in order to maintain as much of the students' attention as possible. Insist on a normal delivery—as close as possible to that of a native speaker. Particular attention should be given to the linking of words, syllable length, and intonation.

You may prefer to play the cassette or to read aloud small portions of the dialog first. Then call for choral and individual repetition. Choral and individual repetition should be alternated in order to avoid boredom. When you have completed the dialog, you may wish to call on students to role-play parts of the dialog. You should not expect total memorization of the exchanges, but the students should become familiar with the situation and should learn the new vocabulary in context. Try not to spend too much time presenting the dialog the first day. Ten to twelve minutes of class time should be sufficient. You can extend the presentation over several days.

A2 Actividad • Preguntas y respuestas

You may wish to do this activity orally with books closed, or you may ask the students to work with a partner to answer the questions. For writing practice, you may wish to ask them to write the answers in complete sentences for homework. Discuss their answers in class.

SLOWER-PACED LEARNING Ask the students to write the answers in complete sentences for homework. Discuss their answers in class.

A3   Actividad • ¿Es cierto o no?

Activities A2 and A3 will help you determine student comprehension of the basic material in A1. If student comprehension is low, you should review A1, and go over the vocabulary again.

A4   Sabes que...

Discuss the various groups of Indians found in Mexico, such as the **olmecas** from La Venta, Chiapas, and Tabasco, the **totonacas** from Veracruz, the **zapotecas** from Oaxaca, the **toltecas** from north of Mexico City, the **aztecas** from Mexico City, the **mayas** from Yucatán, and the **tarahumaras** from northwest Mexico. Each of these major groups had its own identity, tradition, and language. Even today, many of these languages can be heard. The Spanish spoken in Mexico is rich with vocabulary taken from these groups, particularly words from **náhuatl,** the language of the Aztecs. Much of the architecture bears the influence of the Indian cultures, for though the Spaniards designed the early buildings, the craftsmen were the Indians. An example of this architecture is visible in the interior of the church of Santa María Tonantzintla near Puebla. It is covered with figures of angels, each of which has Indian features.

A5   ¿RECUERDAS?

Using pictures to cue responses, ask the students if they participated in a number of activities this summer. For example: **¿Nadaste mucho? Sí, nadé mucho.** To begin your review, use only **-ar** verbs. Remind the students that the preterit is used to refer to completed past actions, much in the same way as the English simple past tense.

Ask other students if they did the same activities. Move to the third person, asking if student 2 did the activity. Move through the paradigm until the class appears to have a good grasp of the **-ar** verb endings. Have the students work with a partner and name two activities they or a family member did last summer and two things they did not do. When finished, repeat the process with **-er** and **-ir** verb endings.

A6   Actividad • ¿Qué lugares visitaron?

List several archaeological sites on the board and locate them on the map of Mexico on page 14. Present the activity, asking the students to select a site they would like to visit.

Explain to the students that the realia is a ticket for the Light and Sound **(luz y sonido)** show at Uxmal. Point out Uxmal on the map on page 14. Add that many countries in Spanish America offer shows for tourists in English and Spanish.

CHALLENGE   Have the students research a town or a city in Mexico that interests them. Then have them report their findings to the class.

Actividad • Y tú, ¿qué dices?

Have the students answer in complete sentences, either orally or on paper for writing practice.

Have the students compare the ticket for the English light and sound show on page 15 to the ticket for the same show in Spanish on the top right of page 16. Ask the students to identify as many Spanish words as possible on the ticket on page 16. Write the new vocabulary on the board.

Point out the realia at the top left of page 16. Explain that this is a ticket to enter the **casa de las artesanías,** an arts and crafts store. Also ask the students to identify the familiar words and to try to guess the meanings of words that are new to them. The following list includes the vocabulary from the realia that students might not know.

bejuco	*rattan*	ropa típica	*traditional clothing*
henequén	*henequen (a fiber)*	filigrana	*filigree*
caracol	*shell*	fomento	*promotion; development*
piedra	*stone*	artesanía	*popular art; folk art*

Finally, draw the students' attention to the realia on the top center of page 16. Explain that **camión** is the Mexican word for *bus.* In other countries where Spanish is spoken **bus** or **autobús** is used. In the Caribbean, **guagua** is the word used for *bus.*

Comprensión

> You will hear a series of sentences. If the activity took place in the past, check **ya pasó** on your answer sheet. If it is happening now, check **ocurre ahora.** For example, you will hear: **Hace una semana que llegó Elisa.** You place your mark in the row labeled **ya pasó,** since the event already happened.
>
> 1. El junio pasado viajamos a Acapulco.   *Ya pasó.*
> 2. Trabajamos mucho en esta clase todos los días.   *Ocurre ahora.*
> 3. El año pasado cantamos en el coro.   *Ya pasó.*
> 4. Tomás viajó a España este año.   *Ya pasó.*
> 5. Mi hermano estudió en la universidad.   *Ya pasó.*
> 6. Toco el violín en la orquesta.   *Ocurre ahora.*
> 7. ¿Fuiste al cine el sábado?   *Ya pasó.*
> 8. Pedro comió en la cafetería el lunes.   *Ya pasó.*
> 9. Les escribí tres cartas a mis primas.   *Ya pasó.*
> 10. Corremos todos los martes.   *Ocurre ahora.*
> 11. Bebimos mucho jugo de naranja.   *Ya pasó.*
> 12. Marta viajó a San Francisco.   *Ya pasó.*
>
> Now check your answers. *Read each sentence again and give the correct answer.*

ESTRUCTURAS ESENCIALES

Write a number of place names on the board or a transparency. Using the same procedure you used for the presentation of **-ar, -er,** and **-ir** verbs in A5 (p. T27), discuss where you did or did not go during the summer. Then rapidly review the forms of the verb. Switch to a situation in which you "accuse" the students of having borrowed something of yours. Make it clear that you are not angry. You will want to distribute several items from your desk such as a pencil, a book, a cassette, and a dictionary. Ask the following: **¿Quién tomó mi lápiz? ¿Fuiste tú, (Marta)?** Then prompt the student to respond: **No, no fui yo. Fue (David).**

A 10   Actividad • ¿Y Gilberto?

Have the students work with a partner. When they have finished, review the activity with the class. You could ask about people the students have known from previous classes.

A 11   Actividad • ¿Adónde fueron?

Ask the students to complete this activity with a partner, or you may wish to complete it together with the entire class.

SLOWER-PACED LEARNING   Do the activity orally in class. Then assign it for written homework to be corrected in class the following day.

A 12   Actividad • ¿Qué hiciste?

Have the students choose a partner and take turns asking and answering the questions. They should take notes on their partner's responses. Then call on volunteers to report what their partners said.

A 13   Actividad • Todos quieren saber

Review the answers with the class or have the students exchange papers with a partner for correction. You may wish to point out the various Mexican cities on the map and discuss their location relative to that of your city.

A 14   Actividad • Mi viaje a México

Before completing this activity orally, discuss several places of interest the students would like to visit in Mexico. Locate them on the map and point out the types of activities they would like to do there.

A 15   Actividad • ¡A escribir!

Assign the first composition of the year to be written in class so that you will have the opportunity to help the students as they write. Suggest that the students use the questions and answers in A14 as a guide.

A 16   SE DICE ASÍ

Stress the communicative aspect of this entry. Indicate the importance of these expressions with the verb **dar.** After reviewing the examples in the book, you may wish to cover other functions of the verb **dar.** For example, **dar** may be used to ask someone to come along for a walk: **¿Qué te parece si damos una vuelta?, ¿Quieres dar una vuelta por (el parque)?,** or **¿Damos una vuelta por (la plaza)?**

CHALLENGE   Write the following paragraph on the board or a transparency, omitting the underlined words. Ask the students to fill in the blanks with expressions from A16 and the information found in the realia at the bottom of page 19.

Dimos un viaje a Mérida, Yucatán, México. Tomamos un avión de Aeroméxico. Fue el vuelo número 502. Necesitamos un pase de abordar para entrar en el avión. En Mérida nos quedamos *(we stayed)* en el hotel El Conquistador. El hotel está en la calle 56-A. El número de teléfono es el 26-21-10.

A 17 **ESTRUCTURAS ESENCIALES**

With books closed, present the forms of **ver** by discussing things you saw this summer. You may wish to use magazine pictures to stimulate the presentation. For example: **Vi las pirámides de Teotihuacán. Visité la Estatua de la Libertad.** Continue until the students can function fairly well with the forms. Then switch to the verb **dar.** Demonstrate by giving a book to a student and then saying: **Le di el libro a Juan.** Then have the student give the book to another student and say: **Él le dio el libro a Carolina.**

Once all forms have been completed, ask the students to list the preterit forms of **dar** and **ver.** Write them on the board or a transparency. Then ask the students to open their books and continue with the material.

A 18 **Actividad • Conversación**

Allow the students to work in cooperative learning groups of two or three to complete the questions in survey form. Ask them to keep notes and report their findings to another group or to the class.

SLOWER-PACED LEARNING After the students have completed the activity orally, have them begin writing the answers in class so that they are able to relate the oral and written work.

A 19 **Actividad • ¿Qué hicieron ayer?**

Complete the activity orally with the class. Write the students' responses on the board or a transparency for correction. Personalize the activities by having a brief discussion with the students.

A 20 **Actividad • ¿Quién vio a quién?**

Ask the students to write the missing forms of the verb **ver.** Review the activity orally.

OBJECTIVES **To exchange information:** report past events, ask and explain how something was; **to express feelings and emotions:** express satisfaction and dissatisfaction

CULTURAL BACKGROUND Fray Junípero Serra, a Spanish missionary known as the Apostle of California, went from Spain to Mexico in 1749 and lived there until 1769. Then he went north and founded **Misión San Diego** in California. Between 1770 and 1782 he founded eight additional missions where he established schools, provided medical care, and built centers where Spanish culture could be disseminated. He also introduced cattle, sheep, grains, and fruits from Mexico and Spain. Fray Junípero Serra died in 1784 and is remembered as a defender of the Indians and a colonizer of California.

MOTIVATING ACTIVITY Allow the students a few moments to take notes and think of things they did during each of the following time periods.

ayer	la semana pasada
el mes pasado	el año pasado
hace dos semanas	anteayer
el fin de semana pasado	

Then ask the students to form groups of two or three. The object is to guess what each person did during the time periods mentioned above by asking questions that require a yes or no answer.

—¿Fuiste al cine ayer?
—No, no fui al cine.
—¿Fuiste a la biblioteca?
—Sí, fui a la biblioteca.

B1   Páginas de mi diario

To present the narratives, you may wish to follow a similar procedure as described in A1, on p. T26. Then use pictures to introduce the activities that are included in the diary entries, such as camping, fishing, horseback riding, cycling, and hiking. Present each entry individually, asking the students to follow along in their books while you read aloud or play the cassette. Allow the students time to fully comprehend the material before you begin to discuss it. You may also ask questions to check comprehension. You may call for choral and individual repetition, alternating them to avoid boredom.

    Before you complete the second entry, you may wish to show the students pictures of several California missions, such as Santa Barbara and San Juan Capistrano. Show them a map that has the Camino Real marked. The local AAA (American Automobile Association) or other organization will be able to provide you with maps and information concerning the missions.

SLOWER-PACED LEARNING   Write several of the new words used in the diary entries on the board or a transparency, and illustrate their meanings through the use of pictures. Then continue with the reading. Once the students have been exposed to the material, they will feel more comfortable with it.

B2   Actividad • Preguntas y respuestas

You may wish to complete the activity with books closed and to divide the questions into four groups to be answered after each of the diary entries in B1. Questions 1–3 accompany the first entry. Question 4 accompanies the second entry. Questions 5 through 7 accompany the third, and the last three questions accompany the fourth entry.

ANSWERS:

1. Luis acampó cerca de un lago.
2. Luis pescó muchas truchas.
3. Luis cocinó las truchas en una sartén.
4. Miguel y su hermano dieron un viaje en bicicleta por California.
5. Rosalía fue a un parque nacional de Maine.
6. Rosalía y sus padres vieron muchas montañas.
7. Dieron muchos paseos por el parque.
8. Las vacaciones de Pedro no fueron muy divertidas.
9. Pedro tuvo que ir a la escuela de verano para tomar un curso de programación.

B3   Actividad • Combinación

Ask the students to write complete sentences by combining the elements in the box. Then call on volunteers to read aloud their sentences for correction.

    Activities B2 and B3 will help you determine student comprehension of the basic material in B1. If student comprehension is low, you should review B1, and go over the vocabulary again.

B4 **Actividad • ¡A escribir!**

Set a limit of at least ten sentences you will require for each entry of the diary. The students should use six different verbs in the preterit tense. They may also wish to illustrate their entries.

CHALLENGE Ask the students to use the realia on page 25 to answer the following questions. Pointing to the boarding pass, ask:

> ¿Cómo fuiste?
> ¿A qué hora salió el vuelo?
> ¿Cuál fue el número del asiento?
> ¿En qué vuelo saliste?

Now using the information contained in the advertisement for Mérida as a guide, ask the students to give several reasons for visiting Mérida, Yucatán.

B5 **Sabes que . . .**

You may wish to use transparency number 30 with the accompanying overlay 30A, **España en los Estados Unidos,** to show the students the route of the missions in California, **El Camino Real.** Point out the various missions founded by Fray Junípero Serra and his followers in the eighteenth century. Also draw attention to other missions founded by the Spaniards in Arizona, New Mexico, and Florida. Explain that the oldest North American city, St. Augustine, was established in Florida by Pedro Menéndez de Avilés in 1565.

B6 **ESTRUCTURAS ESENCIALES**

You may wish to have the students write out the **yo** forms of several verbs ending in **-car, -zar,** and **-gar.** Some examples are **marcar, pescar, buscar, llegar, pagar, empezar, almorzar,** and **comenzar.** Stress that the changes in verbs ending in **-car** and **-gar** are made in order to maintain the sound of the final consonant of the stem. You may illustrate this with the example: **buscar-busqué.** Mention that without the change, the verb would be pronounced as **buscé.** With respect to the verbs ending in **-zar,** the change is simply a spelling change, since **z** in Spanish is not used before **e** or **i.**

B7 **Actividad • ¡Yo también!**

You may wish to complete this activity first in the affirmative and then in the negative. Introduce the word **tampoco,** for example: **Eduardo no practicó la guitarra. Yo no practiqué la guitarra tampoco.**

ANSWERS:

1. Yo jugué al básquetbol también.
2. Yo expliqué el problema también.
3. Yo busqué la solución también.
4. Yo pagué la cuenta también.
5. Yo comencé a estudiar también.
6. Yo choqué la moto también.
7. Yo toqué el piano también.
8. Yo marqué el número de teléfono también.
9. Yo indiqué dónde está Uxmal también.

B 8   **Actividad • Entrevista**

After the students complete the interview, ask them to share the details with a third person. Then call on a few volunteers to present their findings to the class. Remind the students to change all the entries to the third person.

B 9   **Actividad • ¡A escribir!**

Have the students write a short article about their partners' vacation. Have them give specific details. Ten sentences and six different verbs would provide an adequate length for practice.

B 10   **SE DICE ASÍ**

With books closed, ask the students about certain events in school or in the community. For example: **¿Cómo fue el baile?** Then elicit a response, such as: **La pasamos de maravilla.** You may have to prompt the students to get the appropriate responses. After several students have responded correctly, allow them to open their books and read the material.

B 11   **Comprensión**

You will hear several conversations about vacations. For each of them, decide whether the person had a good time (**la pasó bien**) or whether the vacation was not good (**la pasó mal**). For example, you will hear: **Cuéntame cómo fueron tus vacaciones.** The response is: **No te puedes imaginar lo fantásticas que fueron.** You place your mark in the row labeled **la pasó bien,** since the person had a good time.

1. —Fuiste a las montañas, ¿no? Me imagino que fue fantástico.
   —Sí, pero llovió todos los días y no pude salir del hotel. *La pasó mal.*
2. —Di un viaje a la playa. Todo fue fantástico.
   —¡Qué envidia! Tus vacaciones fueron estupendas. *La pasó bien.*
3. —¿Adónde fuiste el verano pasado?
   —Pues, chico, hicimos un viaje interesantísimo a México. ¡Fue increíble! *La pasó bien.*
4. —¿Qué tal tus vacaciones, Paco?
   —No lo vas a creer. Tuve un accidente el primer día. Acampé en California, pero alguien me llevó todo el dinero. *La pasó mal.*
5. —Oye, Eduardo, ¿cuándo regresaste de California?
   —Pues anoche, Roberto. Visitamos varias misiones cerca de Los Ángeles. Fue el mejor viaje de todos. *La pasó bien.*
6. —Buenas tardes, Sra. Gómez. Veo que ya regresaron de su viaje a España.
   —Fuimos a Madrid a visitar a nuestros hijos. Fue un viaje que nos gustó mucho. *La pasó bien.*
7. —Hola, Elena. Te llamo para saber cómo pasaste las vacaciones.
   —¿Qué vacaciones, Pilar? Tuve que trabajar todo el verano y no pude hacer mi viaje a Miami. ¡Qué aburrido! *La pasó mal.*
8. —¿Quieres ver las fotos de mis vacaciones?
   —Sí, claro. ¿Adónde fuiste?
   —Pues, fuimos a una playa hermosísima. Nadamos todo el día y practiqué el esquí acuático. ¡Y la comida! ¡Ay, qué buena! *La pasó bien.*

Now check your answers. *Read each exchange again and give the correct answer.*

B 12 ESTRUCTURAS ESENCIALES

Introduce the preterit tense of the verbs **tener, estar,** and **poder** separately, incorporating them into conversations. You might start with a discussion about the homework the students had last night.

> ¿Tuviste mucha tarea anoche?
> ¿Estuviste muy cansado(a)?
> ¿Pudiste estudiar mucho?

Use these themes to develop conversations in the class until the students seem comfortable with the forms. You may wish to point out the stem change of the irregular preterit endings. You may also note that these have no accents.

CHALLENGE   You may wish to have the students write a short paragraph using the verbs **tener, estar,** and **poder.** Allow them to choose the topic of the paragraph and then read it aloud to the class.

B 13 Actividad • ¡Qué suerte!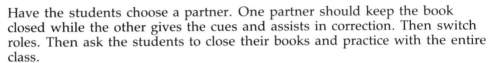

Have the students choose a partner. One partner should keep the book closed while the other gives the cues and assists in correction. Then switch roles. Then ask the students to close their books and practice with the entire class.

CHALLENGE   Ask the students to form original sentences with **tener, poder,** and **estar.** They should use the cues for each subject of their sentences. Call on volunteers to read their sentences aloud.

ANSWERS:

1. Yo tuve un trabajo bueno.
   Pude ahorrar mucho dinero.
   Estuve en México de vacaciones.
2. Mis amigos tuvieron un trabajo bueno.
   Pudieron ahorrar mucho dinero.
   Estuvieron en México de vacaciones.
3. Luis y yo tuvimos un trabajo bueno.
   Pudimos ahorrar mucho dinero.
   Estuvimos en México de vacaciones.
4. Los chicos tuvieron un trabajo bueno.
   Pudieron ahorrar mucho dinero.
   Estuvieron en México de vacaciones.
5. Tú tuviste un trabajo bueno.
   Pudiste ahorrar mucho dinero.
   Estuviste en México de vacaciones.
6. Raúl y Eva tuvieron un trabajo bueno.
   Pudieron ahorrar mucho dinero.
   Estuvieron en México de vacaciones.
7. María Laura tuvo un trabajo bueno.
   Pudo ahorrar mucho dinero.
   Estuvo en México de vacaciones.
8. Tomás tuvo un trabajo bueno.
   Pudo ahorrar mucho dinero.
   Estuvo en México de vacaciones.

B 14 Actividad • ¿Cómo te fue?

Allow the students several minutes to read through the selections and choose the proper responses. Discuss the answers with the class.

B 15 **Actividad • ¿Pudiste ir a la conferencia?**

Have the students choose a partner. They should alternate responses to this activity. When finished, you may wish to have them repeat the activity with a sentence-combining practice. Have them use the conjunction **porque** in their responses.

▮ Silvia no pudo ir porque tuvo que ir al hospital.

CHALLENGE Ask the students to create six new sentences similar to the ones in B15 in which they state that they or a friend could not do something because of a conflict.

ANSWERS:

1. Eduardo no pudo ir. Tuvo que terminar la tarea.
2. Luisa no pudo ir. Tuvo que cocinar las truchas en la sartén.
3. Ana y Cecilia no pudieron ir. Tuvieron que acompañar a su tía Julia.
4. Sonia y Andrés no pudieron ir. Tuvieron que ahorrar dinero para un viaje.
5. Yo no pude ir. Tuve que tomar fotos.
6. Tu primo no pudo ir. Tuvo que escalar una montaña.
7. Roberto no pudo ir. Tuvo que estudiar para un examen.
8. Cristina no pudo ir. Tuvo que montar a caballo.

B 16 **SE DICE ASÍ**

Introduce the expressions by discussing and asking questions about a school event. Allow the students to respond to your questions. After they respond appropriately, review the statements in the book. To practice the new expressions, allow the students to work with a partner to ask about two different events. Partners should respond accordingly.

As part of the warm-up for the next several days, ask questions about an event that happened the day before. Allow the students to give free responses.

B 17 **Actividad • ¿Cómo fue?**

Complete this activity orally. With books opened, ask several questions and allow the students to choose the appropriate answers. Then allow them to personalize the questions and answers. Discuss last Saturday's events or those of a recent weekend. You may list a number of activities on the board or a transparency. Allow the students to comment on the activities.

SLOWER-PACED LEARNING For writing practice, have the students write the completed sentences as a homework assignment. Then, the following day, have them exchange papers with a partner to check their answers.

B 18 **Actividad • El partido de béisbol**

Have the students complete this activity on paper. Monitor their answers as they write. Review the completed work with the class.

B 19 **Actividad • Cuéntanos**

After the students have had time to work with their classmates, ask several individuals to share comments and experiences of others with the class.

SECTION **C**

OBJECTIVES **To socialize:** meet and greet people, send greetings, say that someone sends his or her regards, write salutations and complimentary closings

CULTURAL BACKGROUND Locate San Antonio on the map. You may wish to discuss a few facts in Spanish, such as the large Mexican-American population. Remind the students that San Antonio was the site of the Battle of the Alamo, in which Mexican forces defeated Texan revolutionaries during the Texas Revolution in 1836. You may also wish to show pictures or slides of San Antonio.

MOTIVATING ACTIVITY Allow the students to form groups of three. Ask them to think of all the places they might visit in Mexico and what they might see there. They should mention a city and name as many places of interest in the city as possible.

> Mexico City: las ruinas de Teotihuacán, Museo Nacional de Antropología
> Acapulco: la playa, los clavadistas *(high divers)*, el ballet folklórico

C1   Saludos y presentaciones

For additional information on how to present the basic material, you may wish to refer to A1, on p. T26. Then ask two students to role-play the dialog through the second speech by Rafael, ending with . . . **Nuevo México.** Then have the students use the phrases with a partner, and ask them to personalize the material. After two or three minutes, ask several pairs to model their conversations for the class.

Continue role-playing the conversation until reaching Tomás's comment: **"Encantado".** Act out several introductions with the students. Be sure to include the handshake and explain its importance. Then complete the dialog. Allow the students to follow along as you play the cassette or read the dialog aloud.

Using stick figures, present several words before you begin reading the letters. Teach **vecina** by drawing two houses next to each other. Ask the students to give the name of an imaginary person for each house. Explain that they are **vecinos.** Ask the students to write the new words in the vocabulary section of their notebooks. Then play the cassette or read the letters, one at a time, aiding comprehension by acting out some of the phrases or by using synonyms. For example, a synonym of **mil gracias** is **muchas gracias.** Show the students several postcards as you teach the word **postales.** To present **noticias,** mention the name of a well-known newscaster and say: **Tom Brokaw anuncia las noticias.** To introduce **extrañar,** draw two stick figures on the board. Explain that they love each other but that one lives in New York and the other lives in California. Then say: **se extrañan,** and ask the students: **¿Cómo se dice?**

C2   Actividad • Preguntas y respuestas

Have the students complete the activity with a partner, taking notes of the answers. When they have finished, call on volunteers to share their answers with the class. If necessary, they may refer to C1 as a guide.

C3   Sabes que . . .

Review Hispanic names with the students by reading the cultural note. Then ask the students the following questions:

If Rafael López Hernández marries María Teresa Hidalgo Fortín, what is her name? (*María Teresa Hidalgo de López*)
Their children's names are Luis Manuel and Patricia. What are their complete names? (*Luis Manuel López Hidalgo* and *Patricia López Hidalgo*)

You might also point out that when a woman is widowed her name changes. For example, Patricia López de Cuevas becomes Patricia López Vda. (**viuda**—*widow*) de Cuevas. When a woman is divorced, she always drops her husband's name and reverts to her maiden name, even if she has children. Often people with common last names hyphenate their last names in order to force the use of both surnames. A famous example is the Music Director of the National Symphony Orchestra of Spain and also of the Cincinnati Symphony Orchestra, Jesús López-Cobos.

SLOWER-PACED LEARNING   You may wish to have the students identify all the compound names in the realia.

Marcos Roberto	Sara Alexandra	Rafael Ángel
Carmen Martha	Rolando Atilio	Elena del Carmen
Félix Rolando	Ana Daysi	Ana Isabel

C4   SE DICE ASÍ

You may wish to review nicknames with the students. Also re-enter the uses of **usted.** Elicit comments from the students about when their parents use their entire name and when they use their nicknames. They may note that parents often use their child's full name during a reprimand.

C5   Actividad • Charla

Ask the students to work in groups of three to complete the dialog. Have them present the dialog to the class, including appropriate gestures, such as a handshake.

CHALLENGE   Call on volunteers to present a formal dialog using **usted** and the appropriate gestures. Then have them present an informal dialog using **tú,** nicknames, and the appropriate gestures, such as a kiss on the cheek.

C6   Comprensión

Listen to each of the ten conversational exchanges. If the second speaker gives a logical response to the first speaker's question, check **lógico** on your answer sheet. If not, check **absurdo.** For example, you will hear: **¿Cómo viajaste?** and the response: **No pudimos viajar hasta el sábado.** You should place your mark in the row labeled **absurdo,** since the response does not make sense.

1. —Hola, Pilar. ¿Qué tal te fue en las vacaciones?
   —No sé. Voy a visitar a mi tía mañana.   *absurdo*
2. —¿Fuiste a acampar en Colorado?
   —Sí, y me fue de maravilla.   *lógico*
3. —¿Te acompañó tu amiga?
   —No pudo ir conmigo porque su mamá estuvo enferma.   *lógico*
4. —¿Qué hicieron?
   —Pues, chica, acampamos, escalamos montañas y visitamos un parque nacional.   *lógico*

5. —¿Sacaste muchas fotos?
   —¿Puedes creer? Olvidé mi cámara antes de salir de
   casa. *lógico*
6. —¿Cómo estuvo el tiempo?
   —Dos semanas, más o menos. *absurdo*
7. —¿Lo pasaste bien?
   —De lo más bien. Te digo que fueron las mejores vacaciones de
   todas. *lógico*
8. —¿Quieren volver?
   —Sí, pero quiero visitar otros lugares. *lógico*
9. —¿Sabes adónde fue Adela?
   —No pudo venir porque está trabajando. *absurdo*
10. —¿Hablaste con Mariana?
    —No, todavía está de vacaciones. *lógico*

Now check your answers. *Read each exchange again and give the correct answer.*

C7   SE DICE ASÍ

Present the expressions with a conversation. Call on two volunteers to assist
as you continue the conversation that began in C5. Add expressions, such
as: **Saludos a tus padres.** Remind the students to respond with **gracias.**
Practice the exchanges with other members of the class.

C8   Actividad • ¡Saludos!

Ask the students to complete the activity orally. Then you might wish to
have them pretend they are calling their partner long distance. Have them
send regards from classmates and friends. If possible, use toy telephones to
complete the activity. In many areas, the Bell System has teletrainers that
are available on loan. These are working phones with speakers that allow
the entire class to hear a conversation with a student outside the class.

C9   SITUACIÓN • Una carta

You may wish to have the students complete a matching activity using the
words **frecuentemente, distinta,** and **lleno.** You may write the synonyms or
antonyms on the board and ask the students to match them with the correct
words. Ask them to read Julian's letter. Then discuss several facts about
Chicago and ask the students questions to check their comprehension.

C10   Actividad • ¿Es cierto o no?

Allow the students to work on this activity in one of three ways:

1. They may work with a partner to identify and correct the false
   statements.
2. They may work alone to complete the activity on paper.
3. You may work with the entire class to complete the activity,
   discussing the answers as you work through the exercise.

C11 ESTRUCTURAS ESENCIALES

Re-enter the present tense forms of the verbs **saber** and **conocer.** You may wish to do a personalized question/answer drill such as: **¿Sabes que Los Ángeles está en California? ¿Conoces a Bruce Springsteen personalmente?** Then elicit from the students the differences between the two verbs.

Begin to present the preterit forms of **saber** by making a few outrageous statements to catch the students' attention. **¿Supiste que hoy van a servir filete mignon en la cafetería?** Continue with several statements before allowing the students to respond. Work through the entire paradigm in this manner. When finished, ask them to identify the forms as you write them on the board or a transparency. Indicate that the preterit forms of the verb **saber** are irregular. Compare them with the preterit forms of **conocer,** which are regular.

Continue in the same manner with the verb **conocer.** Once again, indicate that the preterit forms of **conocer** are regular. Ask the students to add the verbs to the vocabulary section of their notebooks, and point out that the forms of **saber** and **conocer** must be memorized. Compare them to the other three irregular verbs in Section B.

C12 Actividad • ¡A completar!

For writing practice, have the students write the completed sentences. When they have finished, call on volunteers to write their sentences on the board or a transparency for correction.

C13 Actividad • El estudiante nuevo

Ask the students to work in pairs as you monitor their responses. Halfway through the activity, have them choose another partner and repeat the questions.

C14 Actividad • La visita a Chicago

Allow the students several minutes to complete the activity by filling in the blanks with the appropriate verb form. Have the students check their work by writing the paragraph on the board or a transparency.

C15 SE ESCRIBE ASÍ

Present the material in the box. Then write a list of names on the board, mixing formal and informal titles, and ask the students to choose the appropriate **saludo** and **despedida** for each name. Here are some examples:

Pati **(Querida Pati; Afectuosamente)**
señor González **(Estimado señor González; Atentamente)**
tía Anita **(Querida tía Anita; Un abrazo de)**
señorita Márquez **(Estimada señorita Márquez; Cordialmente)**
abuelita **(Querida abuelita; Cariñosamente)**

Review the students' choices and discuss any misunderstandings.

SLOWER-PACED LEARNING Have the students choose a partner. They must write two short thank-you notes: one to a friend and one to a friend of their parents whom they do not know. They must use the appropriate salutation and complimentary closing. They may wish to read the notes aloud to the class.

C16 Actividad • ¡A escribir tarjetas postales!

Ask the students to bring postcards to class or have them use clippings from magazines glued to 3×5 cards. Allow them to write messages, prompting them to use the appropriate **saludo** and **despedida.** Collect the postcards and display them in the classroom if you wish. The students may also address the cards to students in another Spanish class. You or a volunteer may act as **"cartero"** between the classes.

C17 ESTRUCTURAS ESENCIALES

Ask the students to recall the word **frecuentemente** from C9. Write several other words on the board or a transparency, such as **rápidamente, inteligentemente,** and **lentamente.** Demonstrate **rápidamente** and **lentamente** by walking quickly or slowly until the students understand their meanings. Ask them to compare **-mente** with an ending in English. If no one makes the comparison, write a few examples from the book on the board. Then encourage the students to form other adverbs after you have presented the material in C17.

C18 Actividad • Mis amigos y yo corremos

Ask the students to complete this activity on paper while you monitor their progress. Review the answers with the class by writing them on the board or a transparency.

C19 Actividad • A completar lógicamente

The students may complete this activity in pairs, or you may wish to complete it with the entire class. For writing practice, have the students write each sentence at home or in class.

C20 ¿RECUERDAS?

Review with the students the explanation and examples in the box. Then ask them to think of other examples for each of the uses of **por** and **para.** Write their suggestions on the board or a transparency.

SLOWER-PACED LEARNING Have the students form cooperative learning groups of three to think of examples using **por** and **para.** Choose several groups to write their responses on the board. Then discuss and correct the examples with the class.

C21 Actividad • ¿Por o para?

Ask the students to complete the activity on paper. Monitor their progress and discuss their answers, using a transparency. You may wish to review the material orally.

C22 **Actividad • ¿Qué pasó ayer?**

This activity is an ideal homework assignment or it may be completed in class. In either case, ask the students to write their sentences on the board or a transparency for a review by the entire class.

POSSIBLE ANSWERS:
Graciela trabajó para su papá.
Los turistas salieron para Guadalajara.
Yo pesqué por tres horas.
Juan Carlos fue para Uxmal.
Gustavo llegó por avión.
Roberto y Pepe corrieron por el parque.
Yo pasé por tu casa.

TRY
YOUR
SKILLS

OBJECTIVE To recombine communicative functions, grammar, and vocabulary

CULTURAL BACKGROUND You may wish to review the cultural information in this unit with the students. For cooperative learning, form small groups to identify the following items. Give extra points to the winning group or groups.

olmecas	mariachi
náhuatl	Oaxaca
Fray Junípero Serra	zócalo
Monte Albán	zapoteca
Teotihuacán	maya
totonaca	

1 # Una comida en casa de Tere

Introduce the selection by asking the students what they might expect if they invited their music teacher to dinner. Ask what they might serve and what type of entertainment they might plan. Then play the cassette or read the selection aloud. Ask the students to tell what happened at Tere's dinner in their own words.

2 **Actividad • Preguntas y respuestas**

Allow the students to answer the questions with a partner. You may also wish to ask them to complete the answers on paper. A third alternative is to answer the questions orally with the class.

ANSWERS:

1. Tere y su familia invitaron al nuevo profesor de música y a su esposa a cenar.
2. Los invitados fueron el profesor José Fernández López y su esposa Elena.
3. La cena fue a las siete y media.
4. Tuvieron dos invitados.
5. Comieron pescado, verduras y arroz.
6. Comieron en casa de Tere.
7. Después de la cena, el profesor Fernández López tocó el piano y todos cantaron.
8. La comida fue muy divertida.

3   Actividad • La semana pasada

Set a time limit of approximately five minutes for this activity. Instruct the students to write a sentence describing what they did on each of the last seven days. They should use the verbs listed in the book. Then write the verbs in separate columns on the board. Call on volunteers to write one of their sentences in the column below the verb that they used in that sentence.

4   Actividad • Entrevista

Instruct the students to use the activities in Skills 3 to form questions. Allow them to walk throughout the room to question classmates in order to find someone who did the same activities. Set a time limit of five to eight minutes, after which you may wish to ask the students about their findings.

5   Actividad • Proyecto

Allow the students several minutes to write a summary of their findings. For cooperative learning, form groups of two or three to complete the activity. Each member must participate, but call on one member to report the group's findings to the class.

6   Actividad • Lo que pasó

Have the students prepare for the class presentation at home. They should bring drawings, photographs, or news clippings of the events they are narrating to the class. Give specific instructions, such as the following:

1. Use only preterit verb forms.
2. Use a minimum of ten verbs.
3. Seven verbs must be different; three can be repeated.
4. Begin the presentation with one of the following: **La semana pasada . . . , Cuando fui a la fiesta . . . ,** or **El otro día tuve que . . .**

Collect and correct the narratives. Then call on volunteers to present their narratives to the class.

7   Actividad • Saber o conocer

Review the preterit forms of **saber** and **conocer** with the students. Allow them to write sentences according to the instructions in the book. Prepare a transparency on which you can write their sentences as they dictate them. Discuss the meanings of each of the sentences.

8   **Actividad • Una tarjeta postal**

Assign the activity for homework. Have the students write the postcard, and encourage them to write it from one of the places they have discussed in this unit. You may wish to review the correct **saludo** and **despedida** with them before they write the card.

9   **Actividad • Para o por**

Review the uses of **por** and **para** with the students. Allow them ten minutes or more to write the note. Collect and correct the notes.

SLOWER-PACED LEARNING   You may wish to have the class write a collective note. Call on students and write their sentences on the board or a transparency as they dictate.

10   **Dictado**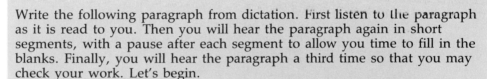

Write the following paragraph from dictation. First listen to the paragraph as it is read to you. Then you will hear the paragraph again in short segments, with a pause after each segment to allow you time to fill in the blanks. Finally, you will hear the paragraph a third time so that you may check your work. Let's begin.

El verano pasado mis amigos *(pause)* Gustavo y Gisela fueron de vacaciones *(pause)* a lugares diferentes. *(pause)* Gustavo fue a un parque nacional *(pause)* con su hermano Gilberto. *(pause)* Gisela hizo un viaje a México *(pause)* con su hermana. *(pause)* Todos la pasaron de lo mejor.

PRONUNCIACIÓN

Model the different **g** sounds for the students. After reading the explanations and words aloud or playing the cassette, ask the students to practice the columns of words chorally. After several minutes, you may wish to ask several students to read selections from the columns. Then prepare a transparency with a mixture of words containing **g** and **j** sounds. Ask the students to distinguish between the sounds. You may also wish to prepare flashcards with the words. As you show a card to the class, instruct them to pronounce correctly. Do not spend a great deal of time on this section. The drills are strictly for practicing sounds, and not for communicating a message, thus, students' attention span is short.

Actividad • Práctica de pronunciación

Have the students listen and repeat as you read the sentences aloud or play the cassette. Stress the importance of linking, rhythm, and intonation, paying particular attention to syllable length.

¿LO SABES?

Allow the students several minutes to collect their thoughts about their summer vacation. Review the expressions with them. Then ask the students to describe their vacations orally or in writing.

Instruct the students to prepare five sentences to describe the school event. Allow them to tell their story to a partner. You may wish to ask several students to retell their experience to the class. To review asking questions, have the students work in pairs. Instruct them to imagine they were on a trip if they have not just returned from a trip.

To review introductions, divide the class into groups of three or four and allow the students to role-play introductions. You may also wish to have each student introduce another student to you. After they complete the postcards, have them make a collage on the bulletin board with the postcards. They may use magazine pictures to illustrate.

VOCABULARIO

To practice new vocabulary, you may wish to play a word game. Have the students form a circle. Then call on a student to name a word from the unit vocabulary that begins with the letter **a.** Then, the person to the right must identify a word that begins with **b.** The game continues until all the letters of the alphabet have been used. If there is not a word from the unit vocabulary that corresponds to a letter of the alphabet, the student must say, **"No hay"** and continue with the next letter of the alphabet.

PRÁCTICA DEL VOCABULARIO

Ask the students to find the names of places where people go on vacation. Allow them to work in groups of three to make up sentences with each of the expressions. The first group to complete each section with the most correct sentences receives extra points.

VAMOS A LEER

OBJECTIVE   To read for practice and pleasure

Preparación para la lectura

Review the techniques suggested in part A with the students. Then, continue with the questions in part B.

¿TE GUSTA TU NOMBRE?

Ask the students to turn to the first paragraph of the reading selection. Ask them to find the following words in Spanish.

> name   image
> to create   exotic

Review with the students the words they have found. Have them read the paragraph silently. Ask them to find three facts about names and to locate the following:

> . . . es muy importante . . .
> . . . crear tu imagen . . .

Cuatro de cada cinco personas no están contentas con su nombre. Ask the students, **¿Qué nombre te gustaría tener?** Help them understand the question if necessary. Ask them what their new name would be and why. Encourage simple responses, such as **es bonito, es elegante, me gusta,** or **es el nombre de mi cantante favorito.**

Continue through the selection in the same manner. For cooperative learning, you may wish to have small groups read each paragraph and decipher the meanings of new words. Then ask the groups to summarize the content of the reading selection for the class.

Actividad • Preguntas y respuestas

Allow the students to work with a partner to complete the activity orally. As an alternative, you may wish to call on students at random to answer the questions.

Actividad • ¿Cuál es el diminutivo?

As the students dictate the diminutives, write them on the board or a transparency.

Actividad • Los nombres españoles

This is an optional activity that can be assigned for homework. Offer extra points to the person who completes the assignment first.

Actividad • Charla

Allow the students to work in groups of three to complete the sentences in the form of a conversation. Review the activity by asking them about their classmates' preferences.

Viñeta cultural 1

Los españoles y los hispanoamericanos

La América hispana, al igual que España, contiene muchas regiones de gran variedad étnica.

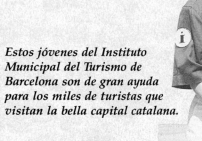

Estos jóvenes del Instituto Municipal del Turismo de Barcelona son de gran ayuda para los miles de turistas que visitan la bella capital catalana.

Cada región de España tiene sus trajes típicos que los jóvenes y los mayores por igual llevan con orgullo (pride) en las celebraciones y fiestas de la región.

En España se encuentra una gran variedad de tipos, como podemos ver en esta foto.

Si España es una mezcla (*combination*) de los distintos pueblos que habitaron (*inhabited*) la península ibérica a través de (*throughout*) los siglos—íberos, celtas, fenicios, griegos, cartagineses, romanos, germanos, árabes y judíos—en Hispanoamérica convergen gentes de varios continentes, que se mezclan con las poblaciones (*people*) ya existentes en el Nuevo Mundo (*New World*).

Los cafés al aire libre (outdoor) *de la Plaza Mayor de Madrid son un lugar de reunión favorito para los madrileños.*

Dos amigos miran el menú en una cafetería madrileña.

Jóvenes estudiantes de secundaria en Caracas, Venezuela

Escena callejera (Street scene) *en un pueblo de la Costa Brava, Cataluña, España*

Así, encontramos que en Guatemala, Ecuador, Bolivia, Perú y Paraguay, el indio es el elemento predominante. Tal es *(Such is)* la influencia india en estos países *(countries)* que en Perú y Paraguay, además *(in addition to)* del español, el quechua y el guaraní respectivamente son lenguas *(languages)* oficiales. La unidad monetaria del Perú se llama el inti, que quiere decir **sol** en quechua, y la unidad monetaria del Paraguay se llama el guaraní.

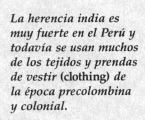

La herencia india es muy fuerte en el Perú y todavía se usan muchos de los tejidos y prendas de vestir (clothing) *de la época precolombina y colonial.*

Jóvenes estudiantes de secundaria en el famoso balneario de Miraflores, en el Perú

En Guatemala todavía se sigue fabricando tejidos (hand-woven products are being produced), *como el que vemos en la foto, siguiendo* (following) *la tradición maya.*

El Día de las Madres también se celebra (is celebrated) *en el mundo hispánico, aunque la fecha no siempre coincide con la de los Estados Unidos. Estos niños participan en la celebración en Cuzco, Perú.*

La influencia africana es considerable en el área del Caribe, sobre todo *(especially)* en Cuba, Puerto Rico, Panamá, y en las costas de Venezuela, Colombia, Honduras y Costa Rica.

Un grupo de estudiantes de secundaria en Santo Domingo

Calle típica en el Viejo San Juan, Puerto Rico

Tres jóvenes venezolanos sentados (seated) a la puerta del liceo "25 de Julio" en Caracas, Venezuela

Estudiantes de secundaria, en la biblioteca de una escuela en Caracas, Venezuela

Venezuela tiene algunas de las playas más bellas de Suramérica. En la foto podemos ver un grupo de jóvenes divirtiéndose (having fun) en la playa de Todasana.

Los españoles fueron el elemento colonizador predominante y en casi todos los países hispanoamericanos fueron el grupo de inmigrantes europeos más numeroso.

Joven argentina de origen alemán **(German)**

Grupo de compradores conversan en El Rastro, el famoso mercado de objetos y antigüedades **(antiques)** *en Madrid, España.*

Las siempre populares tunas estudiantiles **(student musicians)** *en un concierto para los inválidos en Barcelona, España*

Niños juegan en la playa de Horcón, un pueblo de pescadores **(fishing village)** *en la accidentada costa* **(rough coast)** *chilena.*

Biblioteca escolar en Buenos
Aires, Argentina

Sin embargo *(However)*, en tres países hispánicos, Argentina, Uruguay y Costa Rica, llegaron
una gran cantidad de inmigrantes italianos, ale-
manes *(German)* y eslavos *(Slavic)* a finales del
siglo XIX y a principios del siglo XX. Tan es así
(So much so), que hoy día hay más argentinos de
origen italiano que de origen español.

Tres jóvenes uruguayas sonríen (smile) *a la cámara en
Montevideo, Uruguay.*

Los mercados de objetos usados y antigüedades (antiques)
*son muy populares en España, como podemos ver aquí,
en una bella ciudad de la Costa Brava, con sus edificios
medievales al fondo* (background).

Aprendiz (Beginner) *de gaucho,
se apoya pensativamente* (leans
thoughtfully) *en una cerca
(fence) de la Pampa, Argentina.*

En otros países hispánicos una gran parte de la población es india o mestiza. La palabra (word) **mestizo** quiere decir descendiente de padres de distinta raza, en este caso india con europea.

Escuela comercial en Mérida, Yucatán, México

En México, los descendientes de los aztecas mantienen su cultura.

La Plaza de Armas en Santiago de Chile es el lugar favorito de los santiagueros para pasear o conversar.

Festival en Guadalajara, México

Todos estos grupos étnicos han contribuido (*have contributed*) al mejoramiento del mundo hispánico, y cada uno de ellos ha dejado su huella (*has left its mark*) en la formación e historia de estos países. Su herencia (*heritage*) cultural se manifiesta en los diversos aspectos de la sociedad hispánica, ya sea en (*be it in*) las artes, como la música, el baile, la pintura (*painting*) o la literatura, o en las ciencias, como en el campo de la medicina, la física o la química.

Pareja sentada (**Couple seated**) *en frente a su casa, en Horcón, Chile*

Jóvenes exploradores (**Boy Scouts**) *en la puerta de una casa típica de origen colonial en Muna, Yucatán, México*

Dos niñas de origen indio en Pisac, Perú

Esta foto de varios estudiantes de secundaria de la escuela San Juan Bautista muestra (**shows**) *la diversidad de tipos en el mundo hispánico.*

It's back to school after a summer of fun spent with families at the beach or visiting relatives in other places. On the first day of school, students greet each other and talk about their summer vacation. They renew old friendships, make new ones, and think of the friends that are no longer there. In this unit you'll meet many of these students and will learn how to greet them.

You'll learn about Spanish-speaking teenagers and their family relationships. You'll also meet the relatives of these students and will learn the differences, and the similarities, between the Spanish-American culture and yours.

Do you like to go shopping? Most Spanish-American teen-agers enjoy it as much as you do. You'll learn what an experience shopping can be in different countries and what the currency is in each of these. You'll learn how to ask for what you want and how to bargain in order to get it. Meet two Spanish-speaking teenagers as they set out to go shopping and join them as they ask for directions on how to get where they want to go.

Is reality stranger than fiction? Find out as you join Marcos and Cristina, two classmates from Los Angeles who meet by chance in the pyramids of Teotihuacán, near Mexico City.

UNIDAD 1

El regreso de las vacaciones

Most Spanish teenagers spend their summer vacations with their families. Some usually go to the beach, to the country, or to visit relatives. Deciding where to go represents a major issue that is discussed by the whole family. It is not easy for young people to find summer jobs. A few of them work with their parents in the family business or in the business of a relative.

In this unit, you will:

SECTION A	describe what one did . . . exchange information
SECTION B	report past events . . . express satisfaction and dissatisfaction
SECTION C	meet and greet people . . . send regards
TRY YOUR SKILLS	use what you've learned
VAMOS A LEER	read for practice and pleasure

SECTION A

describing what one did . . . exchanging information

The starting of the new school year gives you the opportunity to meet old friends, to comment about your summer vacation, and to inquire about theirs.

A1

En la puerta de la escuela 🔲

Adela y Agustín, dos chicos de Guadalajara que son compañeros de clase, cambian impresiones sobre sus vacaciones de verano.

AGUSTÍN ¿Adónde fueron?
ADELA Fuimos a muchos lugares. En una excursión visitamos las ruinas de Monte Albán en Oaxaca. En otra, salimos de Mérida y vimos las pirámides mayas de Chichén Itzá y Uxmal. En fin, viajamos por casi todo Yucatán.
AGUSTÍN ¿Ganaste mucho dinero?
ADELA Bueno, según papá, fui la mejor guía de la agencia. No gané mucho dinero . . . pero sí gasté mucho.
AGUSTÍN Bueno, ¡también paseaste mucho!

ADELA Hola, Agustín. ¿Cómo pasaste las vacaciones?
AGUSTÍN ¡De lo mejor! Fui a acampar a las montañas y luego fui a Mazatlán a tomar el sol. Y ¿qué tal tus vacaciones?
ADELA Así, así . . . Trabajé con mi hermano Jorge en la agencia de viajes de mi papá.
AGUSTÍN Y ¿qué hiciste en la agencia?
ADELA Fui guía de turistas. Acompañé a muchos de ellos en varias excursiones que dio la agencia. Fue muy interesante.

A2   Actividad • Preguntas y respuestas

Answer the following questions based on the dialog in A1.

1. ¿Quiénes son Adela y Agustín?
2. ¿Qué hacen ellos?
3. ¿Qué hizo Agustín en sus vacaciones?
4. ¿Con quién trabajó Adela?
5. ¿Dónde trabajó ella?
6. ¿A quiénes acompañó Adela?
7. ¿Qué visitaron en Monte Albán?
8. ¿Qué otros lugares visitaron?
9. ¿De dónde salió la excursión por Yucatán?
10. ¿Ganó mucho dinero Adela?

1. Adela y Agustín son dos chicos de Guadalajara. Son compañeros de clase. 2. Cambian impresiones sobre sus vacaciones de verano. 3. Agustín fue a acampar a las montañas y luego fue a Mazatlán. 4. Adela trabajó con su hermano Jorge. 5. Trabajó en la agencia de viajes de su papá. 6. Adela acompañó a muchos turistas en varias excursiones que dio la agencia. 7. En Monte Albán visitaron las ruinas. 8. Visitaron las pirámides mayas de Chichén Itzá y Uxmal en Yucatán. 9. La excursión salió de Mérida. 10. No, Adela no ganó mucho dinero.

A3   Actividad • ¿Es cierto o no?

Decide whether each statement is true or false according to A1. Correct the false statements.

1. Agustín es un chico de Mérida.   Agustín es un chico de Guadalajara.
2. Jorge y Agustín fueron a acampar a las montañas.   Jorge no fue a acampar a las montañas.
3. Adela acompañó a muchos turistas.   Es cierto.
4. Los turistas visitaron Mazatlán.   Los turistas visitaron Monte Albán, Chichén Itzá y Uxmal.
5. Agustín fue a Monte Albán a tomar el sol.   Agustín fue a Mazatlán a tomar el sol.
6. Adela visitó las pirámides mayas de Uxmal y Chichén Itzá.   Es cierto.
7. Jorge gastó mucho dinero.   Adela gastó mucho dinero.
8. Adela pasó las vacaciones de lo mejor.   Adela pasó las vacaciones así, así.

Las culturas prehispánicas de México

Sabes que . . .

Las antiguas civilizaciones indias poblaron *(inhabited)* México mucho antes de la llegada de los españoles. Estas civilizaciones dejaron una muestra increíble *(incredible example)* de su cultura en las ruinas de sus ciudades y centros religiosos.

En Teotihuacán están las pirámides del Sol y de la Luna, maravillosas ruinas toltecas. En Tula, la antigua capital de los toltecas, hay unas famosas esculturas de piedra *(stone sculptures)*. Estas esculturas colosales están agrupadas en patios o plazas gigantescas.

En el estado de Oaxaca está Monte Albán, centro de la cultura zapoteca. Esta ciudad fue abandonada *(was abandoned)* misteriosamente en el año 1.000 d.C. (después de Cristo).

En la península de Yucatán están las grandes ruinas de la civilización maya: Chichén Itzá, Uxmal y Tulum. Estas ruinas sorprenden al viajero por su extensión y belleza, y por su buen estado de conservación.

14   Unidad 1

¿RECUERDAS?
Review of the preterit tense, regular **-ar, -er,** *and* **-ir** *verbs*

The following chart reviews the preterit forms of regular **-ar, -er,** and **-ir** verbs.

trabajar	*to work*	aprender	*to learn*	salir	*to leave*
	é				í
	aste				iste
trabaj-	ó	aprend-			ió
	amos	sal-			imos
	asteis				isteis
	aron				ieron

Review the preterit forms chorally. After going over the explanation, you may wish to mention that stem-changing verbs that end in *-ar* and *-er* are regular in the preterit tense. For example: "pensar (pensé, pensaste, etc.), volver (volví, volviste, etc.)."

Ellos **trabajaron** en la agencia de viajes de papá el verano pasado.
They worked at Dad's travel agency last summer.

Los turistas **aprendieron** mucho en el viaje.
The tourists learned a lot during the trip.

Tú **saliste** de Cuernavaca en julio.
You left Cuernavaca in July.

Adela **visitó** las ruinas de Monte Albán.
Adela visited the ruins at Monte Albán.

1. Remember that regular **-er** and **-ir** verbs have the same endings in the preterit.

2. The Spanish preterit is used to express completed past actions. In many instances, its use is similar to the simple past tense in English.

    Trabajé por tres horas.   *I worked for three hours.*
    ¿Trabajó Ud. ayer?   *Did you work yesterday?*

A 6   Actividad • ¿Qué lugares visitaron?   Answers will vary.

Suppose that you have just returned from a tour of ancient Mexican archeological sites.
A classmate will ask you the following questions. Answer them, then switch roles.

1. ¿Qué lugares visitaron?
2. ¿Quién los acompañó?
3. ¿De dónde salieron?
4. ¿Cuántos turistas fueron?
5. ¿Visitaron otros lugares? ¿Cuáles?
6. ¿Aprendiste mucho sobre los mayas?
7. ¿Gastaste mucho dinero? ¿Cuánto?
8. ¿Con quiénes cambiaste impresiones durante el viaje?

A 7   Actividad • Y tú, ¿qué dices?
Answers will vary.
Answer the following personal questions.

1. ¿A quién visitaste la semana pasada?
2. ¿Con quién saliste el sábado pasado?
3. ¿Qué lección estudiaste anoche?
4. ¿A quién llamaste por teléfono ayer?
5. ¿Comiste mucho en el desayuno? ¿Qué comiste?
6. ¿Quiénes hablaron en clase esta mañana?

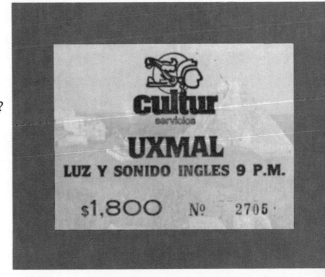

cultur
servicios
UXMAL
LUZ Y SONIDO INGLES 9 P.M.
$1,800   Nº   2705

For information on how to present the realia, see p. T28.

Ruta 61
CAMION 17
$ 1.50

Conserve su Boleto
NO LO DEVUELVA

Nº   3957

PATRONATO DE LUZ Y SONIDO
DE UXMAL
ADMISION $ 300.oo

Nº 199203

E S P A Ñ O L

FECHA _____
HORA _____

NOTA: Es válido para la fecha y hora
arriba indicadas.

A8 Comprensión   For script, see p. T28.

Decide whether each activity took place in the past, **ya pasó** *(it already happened)*, or **ocurre ahora** *(it is happening now).* Check the appropriate space on your answer sheet.

MODELO   Hace una semana que llegó Elisa. *(Ya pasó.)*

	Ocurre ahora	Ya pasó		Ocurre ahora	Ya pasó
1.		✓	7.		✓
2.	✓		8.		✓
3.		✓	9.		✓
4.		✓	10.	✓	
5.		✓	11.		✓
6.	✓		12.		✓

A9 ESTRUCTURAS ESENCIALES
The preterit tense of ser *and* ir

Remind the students that they already know the preterit forms of the verb "ir." Stress that both "ir" and "ser" have identical preterit forms. You may wish to review the explanation of the verb "ir."

The preterit forms of the verbs **ser** and **ir** are identical. You already learned these forms when you studied the preterit of the verb **ir.**

ser *to be* / **ir** *to go*	
fui	fuimos
fuiste	fuisteis
fue	fueron

Él **fue** mi profesor de español.   *He was my Spanish professor.*
Él **fue a** California el verano pasado.   *He went to California last summer.*

1. The context of the sentence makes clear which verb you are using.

2. Remember that the verb **ir** is often followed by the preposition **a.**

3. Notice that none of these forms take a written accent.

Actividad • ¿Y Gilberto? Answers will vary.

What did all these people do for a living? Choose a profession from the box, and then answer following the model. Remember to use feminine or plural forms when necessary.

guía de turistas		profesor de español	ingeniero	fotógrafo
	doctor		agente de viajes	
camarero		vendedor		reportero

MODELO ¿Y Gilberto?
Fue agente de viajes.

1. ¿Y Carlos?
2. ¿Y Roberto y Juan?
3. ¿Y Pedro y Ana?
4. ¿Y Georgina?

5. ¿Y Gisela?
6. ¿Y tú?
7. ¿Y Ana María?
8. ¿Y tú y tu amigo?

A 11 **Actividad • ¿Adónde fueron?**

Look at the illustrations and tell where the people went for their vacation. Follow the model.

MODELO Elena / el verano pasado

Elena fue a las montañas el verano pasado.

1. Carlos y Alberto / el año pasado   Carlos y Alberto fueron a la playa el año pasado.

2. Martín y yo / el mes pasado   Martín y yo fuimos a acampar el mes pasado.

El regreso de las vacaciones   **17**

3. María Elena / el verano pasado   **4.** Yo / el invierno pasado

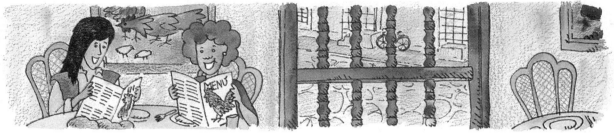

5. María y Ana / el viernes pasado   María y Ana fueron a un restaurante el viernes pasado.

A 12   Actividad • ¿Qué hiciste? Answers will vary.

Your best friend was away all summer, and now you have a lot of catching up to do. Ask each other the following questions.

1. ¿Qué hiciste en el verano? ¿Adónde fuiste?
2. ¿Tomaste el sol muchas veces? ¿Dónde?
3. ¿Visitaste a tus amigos? ¿A quiénes?
4. ¿Tomaste muchas fotos? ¿De qué?
5. ¿Trabajaste en el verano? ¿Por qué?
6. ¿Ganaste o gastaste mucho dinero? ¿Cómo?

A 13   Actividad • Todos quieren saber

Some friends are talking. Who talks to whom? Match the answers on the right with the corresponding questions on the left. Then write down each exchange.

1. ¿Saliste de Cuernavaca?   No, viajó a Mazatlán.
2. ¿Acompañaron a los turistas?   No, sólo visité Cuernavaca.
3. ¿Ellos hablaron en español?   No, acompañamos a Carmen.
4. ¿Viajó tu padre a Mérida?   No, salí de Guadalajara.
5. ¿Visitaste muchas ciudades?   No, hablaron en inglés.

A 14 Actividad • Mi viaje a México *Answers will vary.*

Pair up with a classmate and imagine that you both took a tour to Mexico. Ask each other the following questions.

1. ¿Adónde fuiste?
2. ¿Con quién fuiste?
3. ¿Cuándo fuiste de viaje?
4. ¿Qué lugares visitaste?
5. ¿Quién fue tu guía?
6. ¿Quién fue el fotógrafo?
7. ¿Hablaste inglés o español?
8. ¿Conociste a muchos mexicanos?
9. ¿Qué comida mexicana comiste?
10. ¿Qué compraste?
11. ¿Cuándo regresaste?
12. ¿Te gustó el viaje? ¿Por qué?

A 15 Actividad • ¡A escribir! *Answers will vary.*

Now put together all your answers to A14. Add the necessary linking words, such as **y, luego, también, en fin, después, por, para, con,** and so on. When you finish, you will have a brief composition about your trip.

A 16 SE DICE ASÍ
Describing what one did For information on how to present the realia, see p. T29.

Tomás **dio dinero** para la fiesta.	Tomás gave money for the party.
Dimos una vuelta por el mercado.	We went for a walk around the marketplace.
Dimos un viaje a las pirámides.	We took a trip to the pyramids.
Dieron un paseo por el parque.	They went for a walk in the park.
La profesora **dio la clase** a las ocho.	The teacher gave the class at eight o'clock.

The verb **dar** is used in many different idiomatic expressions in Spanish, such as: **dar un viaje** *(to take a trip)*, **dar un paseo** *(to take a walk)*, **dar un concierto** *(to give a concert)*, **dar una película** *(to show a movie)*.

The following chart shows the forms of **ver** and **dar** in the preterit.

ver	*to see*	dar	*to give*
vi	vimos	di	dimos
viste	visteis	diste	disteis
vio	vieron	dio	dieron

Ellos **vieron** las fotos del viaje a México.
Los chicos **dieron** un concierto el viernes pasado.
El guía les **dio** el mapa a los turistas.

They saw the photos of the trip to Mexico.
The kids gave a concert last Friday.
The tour guide gave the map to the tourists.

1. Note that the verb **ver** has the regular **-er** verbs endings in the preterit.
2. The verb **dar** uses the regular **-er** verb endings in the preterit just like **ver.**
3. None of the preterit forms of these two verbs take a written accent.
4. When **dar** is used with an indirect object, remember to use the indirect/object pronoun, even when the indirect object is stated.

Juan | le dio | los libros | a la profesora.

Juan gave the books to the teacher.

A 18 **Actividad • Conversación** Answers will vary. Possible answers are given.

Team up with a classmate and ask each other the following questions.

1. ¿Diste un viaje a México? ¿Cuándo? Sí, di un viaje a México. No, no di...
2. ¿Cuándo diste una vuelta por la ciudad? Di una vuelta por la ciudad....
3. ¿Quién dio la clase por la mañana? ... dio la clase por la mañana.
4. ¿Diste un paseo con tus amigos ayer? ¿Adónde?
5. ¿Qué grupo dio un concierto el sábado?
6. ¿Cuándo dio el examen la profesora?

4. Sí, ayer di.... No, ayer no di...
5. El grupo... dio un concierto el sábado.
6. La profesora dio el examen...

Tell a classmate what the people in the illustrations did yesterday. Follow the model.

MODELO   La mamá / ayer
           La mamá le dio la comida al niño ayer.

1. Pablo / el día de su cumpleaños   **2.** María y Ana / ayer

3. Los estudiantes / la semana pasada   **4.** La profesora / el jueves

5. José y Elisa / el mes pasado   **6.** Papá / anoche

1. Pablo le dio un regalo a su mamá el día de su cumpleaños.
2. María y Ana dieron un paseo por la playa ayer.
3. Los estudiantes le dieron los libros al profesor la semana pasada.
4. La profesora dio un examen el jueves.
5. José y Elisa dieron un viaje el mes pasado.
6. Papá le dio dinero anoche.

El regreso de las vacaciones   **21**

Supply the missing forms of the verb **ver.**

Anoche Julio y yo fuimos al concierto del grupo *Miami Sound Machine*.
Nosotros __vimos__ a Luisa, pero ella no nos __vio__. Gerardo y Roberto también fueron
al concierto, pero yo no los __vi__ porque ellos llegaron tarde. Mucha gente __vio__ el
concierto por televisión. ¿Lo __viste__ tú también?

Do you keep a diary? Many young people in the United States and in the Hispanic world enjoy jotting down their opinions or writing about the most important events of their lives.

B1 Páginas de mi diario

Luis, Miguel, Rosalía y Pedro escribieron un diario sobre sus vacaciones de verano.

Luis

Hice un viaje a Colorado y acampé cerca de un lago. Llegué por la tarde y fui a pescar varias veces. Pesqué muchas truchas, las cociné en una sartén . . . ¡qué sabrosas! También monté mucho a caballo.

Miguel

Mi hermano y yo dimos un viaje en bicicleta por California. Estuvimos en algunas de las misiones españolas del Camino Real. Tomamos muchas fotos y la pasamos muy bien.

Rosalía

Yo estuve con mis padres en un parque nacional de Maine. Visitamos muchos lugares en el parque y vimos muchas montañas. Nosotros no escalamos las montañas, pero dimos muchos paseos por el bosque. Fue interesantísimo.

Pedro

Mis vacaciones no fueron muy divertidas. Tuve que ir a la escuela de verano para tomar un curso de programación. Fue un curso difícil, pero pude aprender mucho y saqué buenas notas. Me fue muy bien en el curso, pero no tuve mucho tiempo libre. También tuve un trabajo durante parte del verano.

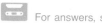
Answer the following questions according to B1.

1. ¿Dónde acampó Luis?
2. ¿Qué pescó Luis?
3. ¿Qué hizo Luis con las truchas?
4. ¿Qué hicieron Miguel y su hermano?
5. ¿Adónde fue Rosalía?

6. ¿Qué vieron Rosalía y sus padres?
7. ¿Qué hicieron en el parque nacional?
8. ¿Cómo fueron las vacaciones de Pedro?
9. ¿Qué hizo Pedro en las vacaciones?

B3   Actividad • Combinación

Based on what you have read in B1, join elements from each column to form five
logical sentences.

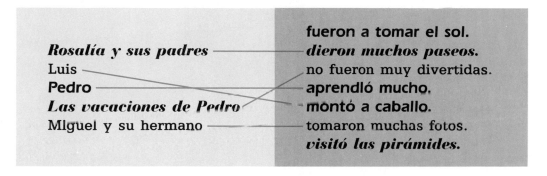

Rosalía y sus padres	fueron a tomar el sol.
Luis	*dieron muchos paseos.*
Pedro	no fueron muy divertidas.
Las vacaciones de Pedro	**aprendió mucho.**
Miguel y su hermano	**montó a caballo.**
	tomaron muchas fotos.
	visitó las pirámides.

B4   Actividad • ¡A escribir!   Answers will vary. For information on
how to present the realia, see p. T32.

Prepare an entry for your diary about a real or imaginary trip you have recently taken.
Base your entry on B1.

Some hints: ¿Adónde fuiste? ¿Con quién? ¿Por cuánto tiempo? ¿Te gustó? ¿Por qué? . . .

25

Muchos territorios que hoy forman parte *(that are now part)* de los Estados Unidos antes fueron territorios españoles. Allí vivieron algunas tribus indias y España trató de entrar en contacto con estos indios. Los nativos muchas veces combatieron contra *(fought against)* los españoles. Uno de los métodos que usó España para colonizar estos territorios fue el sistema de misiones. En las misiones los indios trabajaron y aprendieron muchas cosas, entre ellas: diversos oficios *(several trades)*, la religión católica y la lengua española. Ya en 1570 encontramos *(Already in 1570 we find)* la primera misión en la Florida. De la Florida el sistema de misiones pasó a Nuevo México, Texas, Arizona y California. Miles *(Thousands)* de indios vivieron en estas misiones. En California está el famoso Camino Real *(The King's Highway)*. A lo largo de *(along)* este camino, Fray Junípero Serra y otros misioneros establecieron más de veinte misiones. Hoy día podemos visitar, admirar la arquitectura y apreciar la historia de las misiones españolas en los Estados Unidos.

UNA MISIÓN ESPAÑOLA

B6 ESTRUCTURAS ESENCIALES
Verbs ending in -car, -gar, *and* -zar

Voy a **pescar** al lago.	*I'm going to the lake to fish.*
Ayer **pesqué** muchas truchas.	*Yesterday I caught many trout.*
Juan va a **llegar** a las tres.	*Juan will arrive at three o'clock.*
Yo **llegué** a las dos.	*I arrived at two o'clock.*
Comencé a trabajar el domingo.	*I started to work on Sunday.*

1. Note that the **yo** form of **pescar** in the preterit tense is **pesqué.** It is spelled with **qu** instead of **c.** This is to preserve the **k** sound of the stem, since **c** is pronounced with a soft **s** sound (as in **cine** and **cero**) when followed by **e** or **i.** All other forms follow the regular pattern. Other verbs that end in **-car** and follow the **pescar/pesqué** pattern in the preterit tense are: **buscar** *(to look for, to search)*, **indicar** *(to indicate)*, **practicar** *(to practice)*, **tocar** *(to touch)*, **chocar** *(to hit, to collide)*, and **marcar** *(to mark, to dial)*.

2. The **yo** form of **llegar** in the preterit tense is **llegué.** It is spelled with **gu** instead of **g.** This is to preserve the **g** sound of the stem. All other forms follow the regular pattern. Other verbs that end in **-gar** and that follow the **llegar/llegué** pattern are **pagar** *(to pay)* and **jugar** *(to play)*.

3. The **yo** form of **comenzar** in the preterit tense is **comencé.** It is spelled with **c** instead of **z.** All other forms follow the regular pattern. Another verb that ends in **-zar** and that follows the **comenzar/comencé** pattern is **empezar** *(to begin)*.

B7 Actividad • ¡Yo también! 📼 For answers, see p. T32.

Imagine that you did everything that your friends did. Rewrite each sentence as if you also did what was described. Follow the model.

MODELO   Eduardo practicó la guitarra.
         Yo practiqué la guitarra también.

1. Marisol jugó al básquetbol.
2. Luis y Antonio explicaron el problema.
3. La señora Ramírez buscó la solución.
4. Silvia pagó la cuenta.
5. Carolina comenzó a estudiar.

6. Andrés chocó la moto.
7. Roberto tocó el piano.
8. Celia marcó el número de teléfono.
9. Ella indicó dónde está Uxmal.

B8 Actividad • Entrevista   Answers will vary.

Working with a partner, find out about her or his summer vacation. Make up the details, if you like. You could try questions like these:

1. ¿Adónde fuiste? ¿Fuiste solo(a) o con tus padres?
2. ¿Llegaste temprano? ¿A qué hora?
3. ¿Saliste muchas veces? ¿Adónde fuiste?
4. ¿Cómo la pasaste?
5. ¿Fuiste de pesca? ¿Pescaste mucho?
6. ¿Tuviste tiempo para ir de compras? ¿Qué compraste?
7. ¿Tuviste mucho tiempo libre? ¿Qué hiciste?
8. ¿Cuándo regresaste de vacaciones?
9. ¿Te gustaron tus vacaciones? ¿Por qué?

B9 Actividad • ¡A escribir!   Answers will vary.

Your school newspaper would like you to write an article about your partner's vacation. Prepare the article, basing it on the information you gathered in the interview in B8. Remember to use the necessary connecting words, such as **y, luego, también, después, para, por,** and **con.**

Expressing satisfaction and dissatisfaction

Me fue bien en el examen.	I did well on the test.
La pasamos muy bien en la playa.	We had a very good time at the beach.
Nos fue de lo mejor en el paseo.	Things went very well for us during the outing.
La pasamos de maravilla en el picnic.	We had a marvelous time at the picnic.
No nos fue bien.	It did not go well for us.
Nos fue muy mal.	It went very badly for us.
La pasamos muy mal.	We had a terrible time.

B 11 Comprensión  For script, see p. T33.

Listen to each conversation and decide whether the person had a good time on vacation, **la pasó bien,** or not, **la pasó mal.** Check the appropriate space on your answer sheet.

MODELO — Cuéntame cómo fueron tus vacaciones.
— No te puedes imaginar lo fantásticas que fueron.

	La pasó bien	La pasó mal		La pasó bien	La pasó mal
0.	✔		**5.**	✔	
1.		✔	**6.**	✔	
2.	✔		**7.**		✔
3.	✔		**8.**	✔	
4.		✔			

ESTRUCTURAS ESENCIALES
The preterit tense of tener, estar, *and* poder

The verbs **tener, estar,** and **poder** are irregular in the preterit, but they have the **u** stem in common.

After B13, you may wish to do an individualized question/ answer drill using the students' real names. For example: "_____, ¿estuviste en el centro comercial la semana pasada? ¿Pudiste ir de compras? ¿Tuviste también tiempo de ir al cine?" (Try to use different subjects.)

tener *to have*	estar *to be*	poder *to be able to*
tuve	estuve	pude
tuviste	estuviste	pudiste
tuvo	estuvo	pudo
tuvimos	estuvimos	pudimos
tuvisteis	estuvisteis	pudistcis
tuvieron	estuvieron	pudieron

1. **Poder** means *to be able to*. It is usually followed by an infinitive.

El curso de programación fue difícil, pero **pude aprender** mucho.
The programming course was difficult, but I was able to learn a lot.

No **pudieron trabajar** en la agencia de mi padre durante el verano.
They couldn't work at my father's agency during the summer.

2. Remember that **tener** means *to have* or *to possess*.

Sólo **tuve** dos semanas de vacaciones.
I only had two weeks of vacation.

José **tuvo** una bicicleta roja.
José had a red bicycle.

3. You already know that **tener que** means *to have to*. It is followed by an infinitive.

Gabriela **tuvo que sacar** buenas notas para poder entrar a la universidad.
Gabriela had to get good grades to be able to get into the university.

4. Use **estar** when you want to express location or current condition.

Estuve en Guadalajara el verano pasado.
I was in Guadalajara last summer.

Genaro **estuvo** enfermo la semana pasada, pero ya **está** bien.
Genaro was sick last week, but he is fine now.

B 13 Actividad • ¡Qué suerte! For answers, see p. T34.

Use the verbs **tener, poder,** and **estar** to describe what each of the following persons did last year. Follow the model.

MODELO Julia   Julia tuvo un trabajo bueno.
Pudo ahorrar mucho dinero.
Estuvo en México de vacaciones.

1. yo
2. mis amigos
3. Luis y yo
4. los chicos
5. tú
6. Raúl y Eva
7. María Laura
8. Tomás

Actividad • ¿Cómo te fue?

Who talks to whom? Complete each exchange by finding the reply in the box on the right.

ANA	¿Tuviste mucho trabajo?	ROSA	**Sí, y también tuve mucho calor.**
INÉS	¿Estuviste en el hospital?	ELSA	**Sí, estuve muy ocupada.**
LUIS	¿Tuviste mucha sed?	JORGE	**No, sólo tuve dolor de cabeza.**
ELENA	¿Estuviste muy cansado?	TERE	**No, tuve visitas.**
RAÚL	¿Estuviste sola?	RAFA	**Sí, no tuve ganas de ir.**

B15 Actividad • ¿Pudiste ir a la conferencia? For answers, see p. T35.

Héctor wondered who went to the lecture on Saturday. Everyone had something else to do. Follow the model.

MODELO   Silvia / ir al hospital
         Silvia no pudo ir. Tuvo que ir al hospital.

1. Eduardo / terminar la tarea
2. Luisa / cocinar las truchas en la sartén
3. Ana y Cecilia / acompañar a su tía Julia
4. Sonia y Andrés / ahorrar dinero para un viaje
5. Yo / tomar fotos
6. Tu primo / escalar una montaña
7. Roberto / estudiar para un examen
8. Cristina / montar a caballo

B16   SE DICE ASÍ
         Asking and explaining how something was

¿Qué tal estuvo el partido de béisbol? ¿Cómo fue el partido de béisbol?	How was the baseball game?
No sé. Yo no fui, pero Antonio fue.	I don't know. I didn't go, but Antonio went.
Fue un partido muy bueno.	It was a very good game.
Estuvo muy bueno. Fue un partido muy malo. No fue muy bueno.	It was very good. It was a very bad game. It was not very good.

Remember that even though **ir** and **ser** have identical forms in the preterit, they have different meanings. The context of the sentence clarifies their meaning.

Actividad • ¿Cómo fue?

Elisa and Nora are discussing last Saturday's events. Match the questions with the appropriate answers.

1. ¿Quiénes fueron al baile?
2. ¿Cuándo salieron?
3. ¿Llegó Marisela de Texas?
4. ¿Cómo fue el partido de fútbol?
5. ¿Qué contestó Juan Antonio?
6. ¿Fuiste al concierto? ¿Cómo estuvo?

Sí, fue una gran sorpresa.

Que él fue a pescar.

Marta, Tomás y Julieta

No sé. Yo no fui.

No fue muy bueno.

Fue antes de las doce.

1. Marta, Tomás y Julieta   2. Fue antes de las doce.   3. Sí, fue una gran sorpresa.   4. No fue muy bueno.
5. Que él fue a pescar.   6. No sé. Yo no fui.

B18 **Actividad • El partido de béisbol**

Francisco and Javier got tickets to a baseball game last night. They tell their friends about the game, using the preterit tense.

Anoche nosotros (poder) _____ ver un partido   pudimos
de béisbol. El partido (ser) _____ entre los   fue
Serafines de California y los Atléticos de Oakland
y (estar) _____ muy interesante. Los Atléticos   estuvo
(ganar) _____ el partido y los jugadores José   ganaron
jugaron   Canseco y Mark McGwire (jugar) _____ bien. Nosotros
(tener) _____ la oportunidad de hablar con ellos y   tuvimos
después del partido, (ir) _____ a casa a comer.   fuimos

B19 **Actividad • Cuéntanos** *Tell us*   Answers will vary.

You already know about Luis, Miguel, Rosalía, and Pedro and their vacations. Now tell us about yours. Prepare notes on three or four activities that you enjoyed while you were on vacation, and also about some of the things that you did not like. Discuss them with a classmate. Some hints:

¿Cuándo fuiste?   ¿Practicaste algún deporte?
¿Fue cerca o lejos?   ¿Qué otra cosa hiciste?
¿Cómo fuiste?   ¿Vas a volver allí?

It's sad to think about the old friends who are no longer in school with you, but it's always nice to meet new friends.

C1 # Saludos y presentaciones

En San Antonio, Texas, poco después de las vacaciones de verano, varios estudiantes mexicanoamericanos conversan cerca de la entrada de la escuela.

RAFAEL	¡Hola, Tere! ¡Qué gusto verte de nuevo!
TERE	¡Rafa! ¿Qué tal de vacaciones? ¿Cómo te fue?
RAFAEL	Pues, muy bien. Di un viaje a Nuevo México . . . pero mira, Tere, te presento a Tomás Hinojosa, un estudiante nuevo.
TERE	Mucho gusto, Tomás.
TOMÁS	Encantado.

RAFAEL	Sabes, Tere, Tomás vivió en Los Ángeles por mucho tiempo. Es el primo de Guadalupe.
TERE	Ah, Lupe, y ¿dónde está Lupe? No la vi llegar.
TOMÁS	Mi prima llegó temprano y entró en la clase para escribir unas cartas.

Mientras los muchachos conversan . . . Lupe, sola en la clase, le escribe unas cartas a doña Rosario, su vecina, y a Leticia, su mejor amiga.

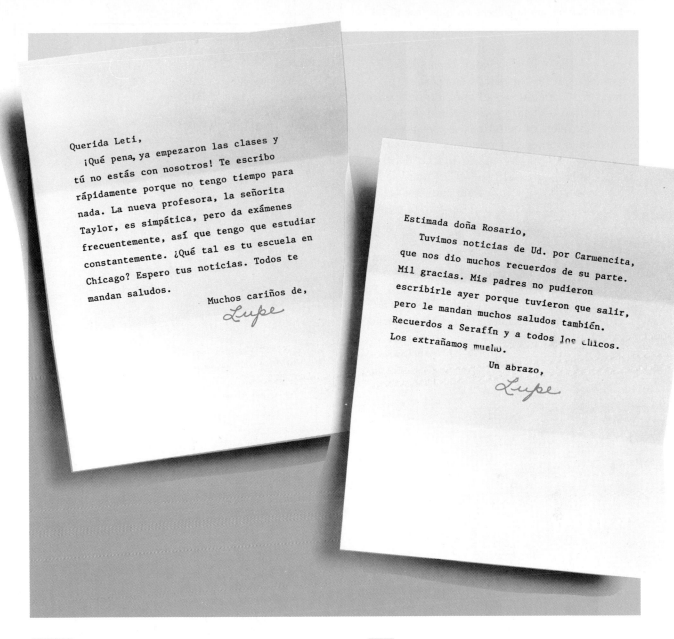

Querida Leti,
    ¡Qué pena, ya empezaron las clases y tú no estás con nosotros! Te escribo rápidamente porque no tengo tiempo para nada. La nueva profesora, la señorita Taylor, es simpática, pero da exámenes frecuentemente, así que tengo que estudiar constantemente. ¿Qué tal es tu escuela en Chicago? Espero tus noticias. Todos te mandan saludos.

Muchos cariños de,
Lupe

Estimada doña Rosario,
    Tuvimos noticias de Ud. por Carmencita, que nos dio muchos recuerdos de su parte. Mil gracias. Mis padres no pudieron escribirle ayer porque tuvieron que salir, pero le mandan muchos saludos también. Recuerdos a Serafín y a todos los chicos. Los extrañamos mucho.

Un abrazo,
Lupe

C2   Actividad • Preguntas y respuestas

Answer the following questions according to C1.

1. ¿Qué hizo Rafa durante sus vacaciones?   Durante las vacaciones Rafa dio un viaje a Nuevo México.
2. ¿Quién le presentó a Tomás a Tere?   Rafael le presentó a Tomás a Tere.
3. ¿Dónde vivió Tomás?   Tomás vivió en Los Ángeles.
4. ¿Cómo se llama la prima de Tomás?   La prima de Tomás se llama Guadalupe.
5. ¿Por qué llegó Lupe temprano a clase?   Lupe llegó temprano para escribir unas cartas.
6. ¿Quién es Leti?   Leti es la mejor amiga de Lupe.
7. ¿Quién le dio noticias de doña Rosario a Lupe?   Carmencita le dio noticias de doña Rosario a Lupe.
8. ¿A quién le mandó recuerdos Lupe?   Lupe les mandó muchos recuerdos a Serafín y a todos los chicos.
9. ¿Cómo es la señorita Taylor?   La señorita Taylor es simpática, pero da exámenes frecuentemente.
10. ¿Qué le mandan a Leti los chicos de la escuela?   Los chicos de la escuela le mandan saludos a Leti.

El regreso de las vacaciones   33

C3 Sabes que . . .

Como ya sabes (*as you already know*), los hispanos usan dos apellidos (*surnames*). El primer (*first*) apellido es el apellido del padre, y el segundo (*second*) es el apellido de la madre. También es común (*it is common*), entre los hispanos, tener dos nombres, como por ejemplo: María Luisa o José Antonio. Uno de los nombres es, por lo general, el nombre de uno de los santos de la iglesia católica. (Los calendarios hispánicos incluyen [*include*] el nombre de uno o más santos para cada día del año.) El otro nombre es generalmente el nombre del padre, de la madre o de un familiar (*relative*) querido. Los nombres españoles, como los americanos, tienen apodos (*nicknames*). Así los amigos llaman Rafa a Rafael, Manolo a Manuel o Lola a Dolores. Frecuentemente, por cariño, llamamos a una persona por el diminutivo de su nombre, así de Clara, Clarita; de José, Joseíto; y de Diego, Dieguito.

MARCOS ROBERTO MATA

DR. MANUEL CONTRERAS LOPEZ

Elena del Carmen Muñoz

Infantil
Sara Alexandra, hija del ingeniero Rafael Angel Zaldaña y doña Carmen Martha Lozano de Zaldaña, celebró recientemente la grata fecha de su cumpleaños.

Marta Pacheco de Gutiérrez

Cumpleañero
Celebrando su cumpleaños estuvo el niño Rolando Atilio, hijo del arquitecto Félix Rolando Bran y doña Ana Daysi Lozano de Bran, quienes por tal motivo lo agasajaron con una fiesta infantil, durante la que recibió múltiples felicitaciones.

Ana Isabel Gutiérrez

C4 SE DICE ASÍ
Meeting and greeting people

Remind students that "encantado, -a" should agree in number and gender with the subject.

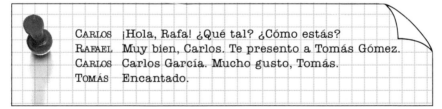

CARLOS   ¡Hola, Rafa! ¿Qué tal? ¿Cómo estás?
RAFAEL   Muy bien, Carlos. Te presento a Tomás Gómez.
CARLOS   Carlos García. Mucho gusto, Tomás.
TOMÁS   Encantado.

You may use a nickname with a person you address as **tú.** Use a full name for formal occasions, such as introducing someone.

C5 Actividad • Charla

Laura, Ignacio, and Cecilia are talking. Get together with two classmates to complete the following conversation.

—Buenos días, Ignacio, _____ .
—¡Laura! ¿ _____ ?
—Muy bien, ¿y tú?
—Así, así. Laura, _____ a Cecilia Sandoval.
—Mucho gusto, Cecilia.
— _____ .

¿qué tal?
¿Cómo estás?
te presento
Encantada

Decide if the second speaker gives a logical response to the first speaker's questions. If the response is logical, check **lógico** on your answer sheet. If it is not, check **absurdo.**

MODELO   —¿Cómo viajaste?
            —No pudimos viajar hasta el sábado. *(absurdo)*

	Lógico	Absurdo		Lógico	Absurdo
1.		✓	6.		✓
2.	✓		7.	✓	
3.	✓		8.	✓	
4.	✓		9.		✓
5.	✓		10.	✓	

C7   SE DICE ASÍ
Sending greetings and saying that someone sends regards

Sending greetings to . . .	Giving regards from . . .
Recuerdos a Serafín y a los chicos.	Maribel te **manda recuerdos.**
Say hello to Serafín and the children.	Maribel sends regards.
Saludos de mi parte.	Carmencita me **dio saludos** para ti.
Best regards.	Carmencita told me to say hello to you.
	Mis padres le **mandan muchos saludos.**
	My parents send greetings.
	Todos te **mandan recuerdos.**
	Everyone says hello.

The English equivalent for **mandar saludos** can be either *to say hello* or *to send greetings.*

C8   Actividad • ¡Saludos!   Answers will vary.
                                  Possible answers are given.

You are calling your grandparents long distance. Ask them how they are, and tell them you are having a good time. Also tell them that your family and friends send their regards. Finish by sending your own.

Hola, abuelos. Habla . . . ¿Cómo están? Yo la paso de lo mejor. Mamá, papá y mis amigos les mandan saludos. Yo también les mando recuerdos.

Julián, un compañero de clase que vive ahora en Chicago, le escribe una carta a su amigo Daniel.

Querido amigo,
Chicago es una ciudad grande, pero muy distinta a Los Ángeles. Voy al centro frecuentemente. Está lleno de rascacielos pero hace mucho viento. Estuve allí el otro día y vi muchas cosas interesantes.
Tengo algunos amigos nuevos y conocí a varias chicas mexicanas en una fiesta. ¿Tienes que venir a pasar unos días con nosotros. Hasta pronto.
Muchos saludos de

C10 Actividad • ¿Es cierto o no?

Correct these statements, if necessary, to make them agree with the information in C9.

1. Julián vive en Los Ángeles.   Julián vive en Chicago.
2. Daniel le escribió la carta a Julián.   Julián le escribió la carta a Daniel.
3. Chicago es una ciudad pequeña.   Chicago es una ciudad grande.
4. Daniel conoció a varias chicas peruanas.   Julián conoció a varias chicas mexicanas.
5. Julián invitó a Daniel a pasar unos días con él.   Es cierto.

C11 ESTRUCTURAS ESENCIALES
The preterit tense of saber *and* conocer

saber	*to know, to find out*	conocer	*to meet*
supe	supimos	conocí	conocimos
supiste	supisteis	conociste	conocisteis
supo	supieron	conoció	conocieron

Supimos que Tomás es el primo de Lupe.
Estrella **conoció** a Rafa en el concierto.

We found out that Tomás is Lupe's cousin.
Estrella met Rafa at the concert.

1. The verb **saber** is irregular in the preterit.

2. Notice that **saber** has two meanings in the preterit tense. Besides *to know,* it also means *to find out* or *to hear about.*

Supe que Genaro está enfermo.
Supimos la noticia por la radio.
Carolina no **supo** qué decir.

I found out that Genaro is sick.
We heard the news on the radio.
Carolina didn't know what to say.

3. The preterit tense forms of **conocer** are regular.

4. Notice that the verb **conocer** in the preterit tense usually means *to meet.*

Laura, ¿**conociste** al estudiante nuevo?
Pues sí, lo **conocí** en la fiesta de Roberto.

Laura, did you meet the new student?
Well yes, I met him at Roberto's party.

C12 Actividad • ¡A completar!

Complete the following sentences with the preterit tense of **saber** or **conocer.**

1. ¡Qué pena! Yo no _____ qué decir. supe
2. Dieguito _____ que Rafa no habla inglés. supo
3. Lupe y yo _____ que Leti visitó un rascacielos en Chicago. supimos
4. ¿_____ ellos al estudiante nuevo? Conocieron
5. ¿_____ tú si él tiene hermanos? Supiste
6. El ingeniero _____ a la señorita Taylor en la feria. conoció

C13 Actividad • El estudiante nuevo Answers will vary. Possible answers are given.

Your friend was absent from class yesterday and asks you about a new student.
Answer in complete sentences, using the preterit of **saber** or **conocer.**

1. ¿Conociste al estudiante nuevo? Sí, conocí al estudiante nuevo.
2. ¿Supiste cómo se llama? Sí, supe que se llama Alfredo Peña.
3. ¿Supieron ustedes si habla español? No, no supimos si habla español.
4. ¿Conoció él a tu hermana? Sí, conoció a mi hermana.
5. ¿Supieron las chicas dónde vive el estudiante nuevo? Sí, las chicas supieron dónde vive el estudiante nuevo.

Actividad • La visita a Chicago

Complete the following paragraph with the correct preterit form of **saber** or
conocer, as needed.

Yo ____ que Leti fue a Chicago la semana pasada y que   supe
____ a un muchacho muy guapo que se llama Rafa. Leti   conoció
y Rafa ____ que los amigos de Leti, Ana Gloria y Rolando,   supieron
quieren ir a Chicago también. Ellos visitaron la ciudad hace
años y ____ mucha gente interesante.   conocieron

C15   SE ESCRIBE ASÍ
Salutations and complimentary closings

Saludos	Salutations
Informal	*Formal*
Querida Rita,	Estimada doña Rosario,
Querido amigo,	Estimado señor Gómez,
Queridos papá y mamá,	Estimada señora Ruiz,
Queridas primas,	Estimadas señoras,
Despedidas	**Complimentary Closings**
Informal	*Formal*
Cariñosamente,	Afectuosamente,
Un abrazo de,	Cordialmente,
Muchos recuerdos/saludos de,	Saludos,
Todos te mandan saludos,	Atentamente,

C16   Actividad • ¡A escribir tarjetas postales!   Answers will vary.

You are writing postcards in Spanish to some of your relatives or friends. Tell
them what you did during your summer vacation and what you are doing in
school. Read C15 carefully and make sure that you use the correct **saludo** and
despedida. Write postcards to at least four relatives or friends.

ESTRUCTURAS ESENCIALES
Adverbs ending in -mente

Te escribo **rápidamente** porque no tengo tiempo para nada.	*I'm writing to you quickly because I don't have time for anything.*
La profesora nueva da exámenes **frecuentemente**.	*The new teacher gives tests frequently.*
Evita escribe **lentamente**.	*Evita writes slowly.*
Tengo que estudiar **constantemente**.	*I have to study constantly.*

1. In Spanish, many adverbs are formed by adding **-mente** to the feminine form of the adjective: **rápido→rápida→rápidamente**. Notice that if the adjective has an accent, the accent remains in the adverb form.

2. Adjectives that have only one form for both masculine and feminine add **-mente** to that form: **frecuente→frecuentemente; fácil→fácilmente.**

3. The ending **-mente** in Spanish is equivalent to the ending *-ly* in English: **rápidamente**, *rapidly.*

C18 Actividad • Mis amigos y yo corremos

You want to tell the class how you and your friends jog in the park. Change the adjectives in parentheses to adverbs.

Yo voy al parque (frecuente) _____ y siempre veo que mis amigos Gustavo y Guido corren (rápido) _____ . Mi otro amigo, Andrés, corre (lento) _____ porque no practica (diario) _____ . Yo puedo correr (fácil) _____ porque practico (constante) _____ .

frecuentemente
rápidamente
lentamente
diariamente   fácilmente
constantemente

C19 Actividad • A completar lógicamente

Complete the sentences by changing adjectives to adverbs ending in **-mente**.

1. Manuel no estudia mucho y contesta las preguntas (tonto) _____ .
2. Pedro cocina las truchas (delicioso) _____ .
3. Me gusta mucho la comida, (especial) _____ la mexicana.

4. El profesor mexicanoamericano explica la lección (estupendo) _____ .
5. La señorita Taylor me saludó (cariñoso) _____ .
6. (Final) _____ ,Pedro pudo salir con Cecilia.

1. tontamente
2. deliciosamente
3. especialmente

4. estupendamente
5. cariñosamente
6. Finalmente

¿RECUERDAS?
Using por *and* para

You have been using **por** and **para** for a while. Do you recall the following uses?

Por is used to indicate:	**Para** is used to indicate:

1. Motion
    Los muchachos pasaron **por** la tienda.
	1. Destination: to a place
	    Nos vamos **para** Mazatlán.

2. Means, manner
    Siempre viajamos **por** avión.
    Le mandé una carta **por** correo.
	2. Destination: to a recipient
	    Compré este libro **para** ti.

3. Period of time
    Voy a clase **por** la mañana.
	3. Time limit
	    Necesito la tarea **para** mañana.

4. Frequency; in exchange for
    dos discos **por** $10
    tres veces **por** semana
	4. Purpose
	    Como **para** vivir.
	    Necesitas billete **para** entrar.

C21   Actividad • ¿Por o para?

Complete the following sentences with **por** or **para.**

1. El tren salió _para_ Madrid.
2. La composición es _para_ la semana próxima.
3. Dos veces _por_ semana vamos al cine.
4. ¿Pasaste _por_ las misiones españolas?
5. No, porque viajé _por_ avión.

6. La entrevista es _para_ el periódico.
7. Tuve noticias de Juan _por_ correo.
8. ¿Es ese regalo _para_ mí? ¡Mil gracias!
9. Si paso _por_ Houston, te voy a visitar.
10. A ella le gusta mucho hablar _por_ teléfono.

C22   Actividad • ¿Qué pasó ayer?   Answers will vary. For possible answers, see p. T41.

Combine the words in each of the columns and you will know what happened
yesterday. Use the correct preterit form of the verb in the second column, and choose
por or **para** as needed.

Graciela	trabajar		su papá.
Los turistas	salir		Guadalajara.
Yo	pescar	por	tres horas.
Juan Carlos	pasar	para	Uxmal.
Gustavo	llegar		avión.
Roberto y Pepe	correr		el parque.
Yo	ir		tu casa.

1   Una comida en casa de Tere

El viernes pasado los padres de Tere invitaron al nuevo profesor de música, José Fernández López, y a su esposa, Elena, a cenar con ellos. Después de la cena, el profesor Fernández López tocó el piano y todos cantaron. ¡Fue muy divertido!

2   Actividad • Preguntas y respuestas   For answers, see p. T41–42.

Answer in complete sentences. Base your answers on the information and illustration in Skills 1.

1. ¿Qué hicieron Tere y su familia el viernes?
2. ¿Quiénes fueron los invitados?
3. ¿A qué hora fue la cena?
4. ¿Cuántos invitados tuvieron ellos?
5. ¿Qué comieron?
6. ¿Dónde comieron?
7. ¿Qué hicieron después de la cena?
8. ¿Cómo fue la comida?

3 Actividad • La semana pasada

You want to write down the things that you did every day last week, beginning with **lunes.** Write seven different things that you did, one thing for each day, using the verbs below.

MODELO estudiar
El lunes estudié la lección.

caminar   ir   ver   dar
comer   salir   escribir

4 Actividad • Entrevista

Now let's see if other people in the class did the same things you did last week. Ask your classmates seven different questions to find out what they did each day.

5 Actividad • Proyecto

Write the answers to Skills 4, and report your findings to the class.

6 Actividad • Lo que pasó

Do you recall a recent event you've seen? Narrate the event to the class. Some hints:

La semana pasada . . .
Cuando fui a la fiesta . . .
El otro día tuve que . . .

7 Actividad • Saber o conocer

Write four sentences about someone you've just met or someone you know by using the preterit of **saber** or **conocer.**

8 Actividad • Una tarjeta postal

You are away on vacation. Write a postcard in Spanish to your teacher, using the correct **saludo** and **despedida.** Don't forget to send greetings to your classmates.

9 Actividad • Para o por

Write a short note (eight sentences) to your best friend, using **por** and **para.** You can write about your vacation, your weekend, or your school.

10 Dictado For script, see p. T43.

Get ready to complete the following paragraph from dictation.

El _____ pasado mis _____ Gustavo y Gisela fueron de _____ a
_____ diferentes. Gustavo _____ a un _____ nacional con su hermano
_____ . Gisela _____ un _____ a _____ con su hermana. Todos la pasaron
de lo _____ .

The letter *g*

1. The Spanish consonant **g**, followed by **a**, **o**, or **u**, has a sound similar to the English *g* in the word *guy*.

ganar	gracias	goma
gastar	tengo	guapo
gusto	guante	Guadalupe
amigo	agosto	pregunta

No gané mucho, pero gasté mucho.
Mucho gusto, Guadalupe.
Muchas gracias, amigo.
Tengo una pregunta.

2. The Spanish consonants **g** (before **e** and **i**) and **j** (in all positions) have a sound similar to a strongly pronounced English *h*.

juego	agencia	trabajé
Gerardo	tarjeta	gente
Jorge	trabajaron	Georgina

Juego con Jorge y Gerardo.
Voy a la agencia.
Trabajé con la gente.
Georgina y Gerardo van de viaje.

3. In the combinations **gue** and **gui**, the **u** is not pronounced.

Miguel	guía	Dieguito	pagué
jugué	llegué	guitarra	Guido

Actividad • Práctica de pronunciación

Listen carefully to the following sentences, then repeat.

La gente vio a Gisela y a Gilberto.
Gerardo Jiménez es ingeniero.
Juan Gualberto habla una lengua antigua.
Gabriel y Graciela dieron las gracias por el regalo.
Guido Guedes tocó la guitarra cuando llegó.

¿LO SABES?

Let's review some important points you've learned in this unit.

SECTION A

Answers will vary.

Can you remember the things that you did during your summer vacation?
Write five complete sentences, telling five different things you did during your summer vacation. Here are some hints: **Fui a . . . y llegué. Vimos muchas . . . Pesqué todos los días . . .**

Use the following expressions to tell others about your vacation.
Dimos un viaje . . .
Dimos muchos paseos por . . .
Dieron un concierto/una película . . .
Visité muchos . . .
Trabajé por _____ semanas . . .
Pasé las vacaciones . . .

SECTION B

Answers will vary.

Can you tell about a recent event at school?
Briefly report it to the class.
Some ideas: la última fiesta en la escuela
el último juego de básquetbol
una excursión de la escuela
un proyecto de la clase de español

What would you ask somebody who has just returned from a summer trip?
Think of five questions and ask a classmate.

SECTION C

Answers will vary.

Do you know how to introduce someone in Spanish? What do you say when you are being introduced to someone?
Get together with two classmates. Introduce each other. One student should play the role of an adult.

Are you able to write a postcard in Spanish?
Write a postcard to a friend. Include each of the following:
send greetings
give your regards to someone else
include the complimentary closing

VOCABULARIO

You may wish to have the students read the vocabulary at home before each section is introduced.

SECTION A

acampar *to camp out*
la **agencia de viajes** *travel agency*
aprender *to learn*
así, así *so-so*
cambiar impresiones *to exchange views*
el **compañero de clase** *classmate*
dar *to give*
  dar una clase *to teach a class*
  dar un concierto *to give a concert*
  dar dinero *to give money*
  dar un paseo *to take a walk*
  dar un viaje *to take a trip*
¡de lo mejor! *wonderfully!*
en fin *really; actually; after all*
ganar *to earn (money)*
gastar *to spend*
el **guía de turistas** *tour guide*
interesantísimo, -a *very interesting*
luego *then; later*
maya *Mayan*
la **montaña** *mountain*
la **pirámide** *pyramid*
el **regreso** *return*
las **ruinas** *ruins (archeological)*
según *according to*
tomar el sol *to sunbathe*

SECTION B

el **bosque** *forest*
el **caballo** *horse*

el **curso** *course*
de maravilla *marvelous; great*
durante *during*
enfermo, -a *sick*
escalar *to climb (a mountain)*
el **lago** *lake*
me fue bien *things went well for me*
me fue mal *things went badly for me*
montar (a caballo) *to ride (on horseback)*
pasarla bien *to have a good time*
pasarla mal *to have a bad time*
pescar *to fish*
la **programación** *programming*
sacar buenas notas *to get good grades*
el **trabajo** *job*
la **trucha** *trout*
varias veces *several times*

SECTION C

el **abrazo** *hug; embrace*
afectuosamente *affectionately*
atentamente *sincerely; very truly yours*
el **cariño** *affection*
cariñosamente *affectionately*
el **centro** *downtown*
constantemente *constantly*
cordialmente *cordially*
de nuevo *again*
la **despedida** *complimentary closing*
distinto, -a *different*

doña *title of respect for mature women*
encantado, -a *pleased to meet you*
estimado, -a *dear; esteemed*
extrañar *to miss (someone or something)*
fácilmente *easily*
frecuentemente *frequently*
lentamente *slowly*
lleno, -a *full*
mexicanoamericano, -a *Mexican American*
mientras *while*
mil gracias *thank you very much*
muchos recuerdos *many regards*
no tengo tiempo para nada *I don't have time for anything*
presentar *to introduce; to present*
pues *well*
¡qué gusto (verte)! *what a pleasure (to see you)!*
rápidamente *rapidly*
el **rascacielos** *skyscraper*
los **recuerdos** *regards*
  dar recuerdos (a, para) *to give regards (to)*
  dar recuerdos de *to give regards from*
  mandar recuerdos *to send regards*
solo, -a *alone*
tener noticias de *to hear from (about)*
un abrazo de . . . *a hug from . . .*

PRÁCTICA DEL VOCABULARIO

1. Go through the unit vocabulary list and find the names of places where people go on vacation. la montaña, las ruinas, el bosque, el lago, las pirámides

2. Now make up at least five sentences in the preterit tense with the words you selected. Then classify them in your preferred order of importance. Answers will vary.

VAMOS A LEER

Antes de leer

Let's get ready for the reading! Here are some strategies that will help you to read the selection. The activities that follow the selection will help you develop your reading skills.

Preparación para la lectura

A. Try to guess the meaning of unfamiliar words by identifying the familiar words in a sentence. Also, pick out the cognates; that is, words that are spelled similarly and have the same meaning in English and Spanish. For instance, many Spanish words that end in a vowel have an English equivalent without the vowel, such as: **excepto,** *except.* How many cognates can you find in the selection?

Cognates:
contenta
exótico
diferente
diminutivo
norte
novela
histórico
famosa

B. Answer the following questions before reading.

1. ¿Te llama todo el mundo por tu nombre o tienes un apodo?   Answers will vary.

2. ¿Te gusta tu nombre? ¿Por qué?   Answers will vary.

3. Después de buscar rápidamente en la lectura, ¿sabes cuál es la idea general?

    a. apodos   b. diminutivos   c. cambios de nombre

4. Si miras rápidamente la lectura, también vas a poder encontrar otros nombres que puede usar una persona que se llama Dolores. ¿Cuáles son?   Son Lola, Lolita, Loló y Lolina.

5. ¿Cómo traduces al inglés los nombres José, Pepe y Pepito?   Joseph, Joe, Joey

¿Te gusta tu nombre?

Tu nombre es para toda la vida. ¿Te gusta? ¿O quieres cambiarlo? ¿Te aburre el tuyo°? Tu nombre es muy importante: te ayuda a crear tu imagen, eres tú. Cuatro de cada cinco personas no están contentas con su nombre. ¿Eres tú una de ellas? ¿Quieres un nombre exótico o solamente diferente?

Los primeros días de clase son una buena ocasión para cambiar de nombre, especialmente si vas a otra escuela donde nadie te conoce. En muchas clases de español los estudiantes usan su nombre en español o escogen uno nuevo en ese idioma. Hay muchas posibilidades.

Quizás una tía o alguien de tu familia te llama por un apodo que nadie más sabe. O quizás tu nombre ya tiene un apodo. ¿Te llamas José? Pues tienes muchos apodos de donde escoger: Pepe, Pepito, Pepín, Joseíto, Cheo, Cheíto. ¿Te llamas Dolores? Puedes cambiar a Lola, Lolita, Loló o Lolina. La verdad es que Dolores es un nombre muy bonito . . . y muy español. Si tu nombre tiene un apodo y nunca lo usaste, ése es el cambio más fácil que puedes hacer.

Quizás nunca, excepto en familia, usas el diminutivo de tu nombre. Éste es también un cambio muy fácil, pero no muy diferente. Sólo tienes que añadir **-ito/-ita** a tu nombre. Así, de Rosa tienes Rosita; de Miguel, Miguelito. Si tu nombre termina en **n** o **r**, entonces añades **-cita/-cito,** como Carmencita, Leonorcita, Ramoncito. A veces el diminutivo necesita escribirse de manera diferente, como Francisquita, de Francisca. Y el diminutivo no es igual° en todas partes. En el norte de España prefieren la terminación° **-ín,** como Tomasín, de Tomás; o Dominguín de Domingo. En el Caribe a veces favorecen la terminación **-ico,** como Robertico y Humbertico.

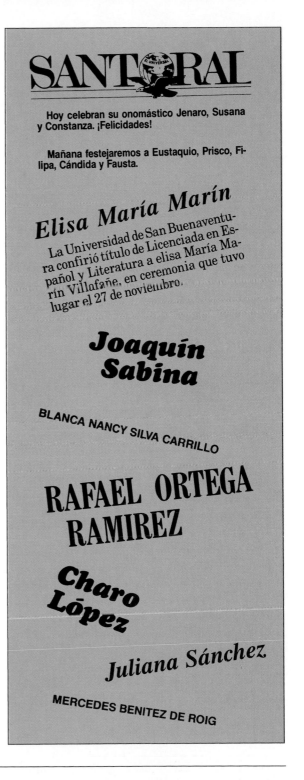

SANTORAL

Hoy celebran su onomástico Jenaro, Susana y Constanza. ¡Felicidades!

Mañana festejaremos a Eustaquio, Prisco, Filipa, Cándida y Fausta.

Elisa María Marín
La Universidad de San Buenaventura confirió título de Licenciada en Español y Literatura a elisa María Marín Villafañe, en ceremonia que tuvo lugar el 27 de noviembro.

Joaquín Sabina

BLANCA NANCY SILVA CARRILLO

RAFAEL ORTEGA RAMIREZ

Charo López

Juliana Sánchez

MERCEDES BENITEZ DE ROIG

---

el tuyo *yours*   **igual** *the same*   **terminación** *ending*

Otro cambio fácil es hacer tu nombre más corto. Si te llamas Teresa, puedes usar Tere. Si te llamas Gabriela, Gaby, o si Guillermo, Guille. Puedes también usar la última parte de tu nombre: de Georgina, Gina; de Guadalupe, Lupe.

Si tienes dos nombres, como María Luisa, puedes hacer un solo nombre de los dos: Marilú. Así, de María Soledad tienes Marisol; de María Isabel, Maribel. También puedes usar uno solo, por ejemplo, de María Luisa puedes usar o María o Luisa. Si quieres, puedes usar un apodo como Maruca o Lulú.

Por supuesto, si no encuentras manera de hacer tu nombre diferente, puedes cambiarlo por otro legalmente, pero ése es un problema muy grande. Necesitas tiempo y dinero. Además, es muy difícil para tu familia y tus amigos llamarte de una manera totalmente diferente. ¿Qué hacer entonces?

Estudia primero tu nombre. ¿Por qué te lo dieron tus padres? ¿Es el nombre de alguna persona muy querida para ellos? ¿O quizás de alguien famoso a quien le tuvieron mucha admiración? ¿Es un nombre de novela° o histórico? ¿Es el nombre de una diosa°, como Diana? ¿O de un héroe o un rey? ¿O de una flor, como Margarita o Jacinto? ¿O tiene significado°, como Alba, que quiere decir *amanecer* y también *blanca*? Estudia qué personas famosas se llaman como tú. ¿Quiénes son? ¿Qué hacen?

Recuerda que tus padres te dieron con cariño° el nombre que llevas°. Y que cuando alguien te llama por tu nombre con cariño, tu nombre suena° mejor, más dulce°. En realidad, tu personalidad es más importante. Tu nombre eres tú.

DON GREGORIO RODRIGUEZ ACOSTA

Roberto González

DON LUIS MARTIN GARCIA

MANUEL CLAVERO PEREZ

DOÑA BLANCA DE ONIS LOPEZ

Pedro Juan Caballero

DOÑA MARIA PIEDAD YRISARRY

---

de novela *from a novel*   **diosa** *goddess*   **significado** *meaning*   **con cariño** *with affection*   **llevas** *(you) have*
suena *sounds*   **más dulce** *sweeter*

Actividad • Preguntas y respuestas

Answer these questions according to **¿Te gusta tu nombre?**

1. ¿Hay muchas personas contentas con su nombre, según la lectura?
2. ¿Por qué cambia la gente de nombre?
3. ¿Cuándo es un buen momento para cambiar de nombre?
4. ¿De qué nombre es Lolina el apodo?
5. ¿Sabes que Carmen quiere decir *canción*? ¿Cuál es el diminutivo?
6. Maribel puede ser la combinación de dos nombres. ¿Cuáles?
7. ¿Sabes el significado de tu nombre? ¿Cuál es?
8. ¿Sabes cómo se dice tu nombre en español?

1. Según la lectura, hay muchas personas que no están contentas con su nombre. 2. La gente cambia de nombre porque no le gusta el suyo. 3. Un buen momento para cambiar de nombre es durante los primeros días de clase, especialmente si vas a otra escuela donde nadie te conoce. 4. Lolina es el apodo de Dolores. 5. El diminutivo de Carmen es Carmencita. 6. Maribel puede ser la combinación de María e Isabel. 7. *Answers will vary.* 8. *Answers will vary.*

Actividad • ¿Cuál es el diminutivo?

Write the diminutives of the following names.

Raquelita	Marianita	Tomasito	Albertico	Juliancito	Estrellita
Raquel	Mariana	Tomás	Alberto	Julián	Estrella
Diego	Paco	Olga	Andrés	Manolo	Susana
Dieguito/Dioguín	Paquito/Paquín	Olguita	Andresito/Andresín	Manolito/Manolín	Susanita

Actividad • Los nombres españoles

Find names you like of two kings and two queens of Spain. Also find the Spanish names of two flowers that are used as first names, and of four Spanish people you may know.

Kings and queens: Felipe, Juan Carlos, Alfonso, Carlos, Fernando, Pedro, Sofía, Isabel, María, Mercedes
Flowers: Margarita, Jazmín

Actividad • Charla   Answers will vary.

Get together with a classmate and discuss names and nicknames you like and dislike. Talk about the names you would choose if you had to change your names. You can start your discussion with one of the following:

No me gusta mi nombre. Prefiero _____ .
Yo prefiero el apodo _____ .
Me gusta el nombre _____ .

UNIDAD 2 Con la familia
Scope and Sequence

	BASIC MATERIAL	COMMUNICATIVE FUNCTIONS
SECTION A	Unos días con los abuelos (A1)	**Expressing attitudes and opinions** • Comparing and expressing preferences **Exchanging information** • Comparing age and quality
SECTION B	Obligaciones familiares (B1) Algunos animales (B8) ¿Me dan permiso? (B18)	**Expressing attitudes and opinions** • Making excuses • Expressing points of view **Persuading** • Making suggestions
SECTION C	Problemas y más problemas (C1)	**Persuading** • Persuading somebody to lend you something **Expressing attitudes and opinions** • Confirming expected courses of action
TRY YOUR SKILLS	Vacaciones en México Dictado	

■ **Pronunciación** (diphthongs and stressed syllables)
■ **¿Lo sabes?**　■ **Vocabulario**

VAMOS A LEER	**El coquí de Puerto Rico** (The serenade of a tiny frog from Puerto Rico)

WRITING　A variety of controlled and open-ended writing activities appear in the Pupil's Edition. The Teacher's Notes identify other activities suitable for writing practice.

COOPERATIVE LEARNING　Many of the activities in the Pupil's Edition lend themselves to cooperative learning. The Teacher's Notes explain some of the many instances where this teaching strategy can be particularly effective. For guidelines on how to use cooperative learning, see page T13.

GRAMMAR	CULTURE	RE-ENTRY
Stressed possessive adjectives (A9) Possessive pronouns: fewer words to say the same thing (A13) Comparisons of equality: **tan . . . como . . .** (A17) Comparisons of equality: **tanto . . . como . . .** (A20)	Puerto Rico (The Island of Enchantment) Old San Juan	Names of family relationships Short form of possessive adjectives Meeting and greeting people Adverbs ending in **-mente**
Stem changing verbs like **pedir (e→i)** (B11) The preterit tense of the irregular verb **decir** (B22)	The Spanish-American family Two words for *fish*	Indirect-object pronouns
Two-pronoun groups (I.O./D.O.) (C6) The pronoun **se** in two-pronoun groups (C13)	Spanish-American teenagers	Direct- and indirect-object pronouns The verbs **prestar** and **dar**

Recombining communicative functions, grammar, and vocabulary

Reading for practice and pleasure

TEACHER-PREPARED MATERIALS
Section A Magazine picture of twins, Puerto Rican music, world map
Section B Pictures of animals, construction paper or poster board
Section C Bingo tokens

UNIT RESOURCES
Manual de actividades, Unit 2
Manual de ejercicios, Unit 2
Unit 2 Cassettes
Transparencies 4–6
Quizzes 4–6
Unit 2 Test

SECTION A

OBJECTIVES **To express attitudes and opinions**: compare and express preferences; **to exchange information:** compare age and quality

CULTURAL BACKGROUND Puerto Rico is the easternmost of the islands that are known as the Greater Antilles. It is part of the West Indies. A coastal plain surrounds the central mountain range called **La Cordillera Central.** Puerto Ricans living in the United States may vote, and many have served in the United States Armed Forces.

Puerto Rico earns much of its income from tourism. The beautiful beaches and colorful towns provide a wealth of activities. In addition, there is a beautiful rain forest, **El Yunque,** that attracts many visitors each year. Education in Puerto Rico is very similar to that in the United States. English is the preferred foreign language in Puerto Rico.

MOTIVATING ACTIVITY Write the following puzzle on the board. Then ask the students to help find the missing word.

```
        primo
  abuela
   madre
       tío
  padre
      nuera
      tía
    (hermano)   (Leave this space blank and elicit the word from the
     suegro      students.)
```

The word is **parientes.**

A1   **Unos días con los abuelos**

You may wish to follow the procedures described in Unit 1, A1, p. T26, to present the basic material. Then read the introduction to the letter with the students and ask several questions to test comprehension. Play the cassette or read the letter aloud as the students follow along in their books. You may wish to call for choral and individual repetition, alternating them to avoid boredom. Then ask the students to review the letter silently. You may also wish to have the students find specific information as they read. For example, write the following list on the board or a transparency.

los nombres de los tíos   la bicicleta de Miguel
el nombre del amigo   el estéreo de Miguel
la tía del amigo

Ask the students to find the information that describes each item or person. Then review the letter with the class for detailed information. You may also wish to have the students repeat sections of the letter for pronunciation practice.

A2   **Actividad • Preguntas y respuestas**

You may wish to have the students complete the activity with books closed, and call on individuals to answer the questions. As a variation, have the students work with a partner to ask and answer each question.

For writing practice, you may wish to ask the students to write their answers at home or in class.

A3   Actividad • ¡A escoger!

Ask the students to complete this activity individually to check comprehension. Upon completion, you may wish to review parts of the letter with which they had difficulty.

You may also ask several students to talk about the contents of the letter by having each student add something of importance contained in it. You may wish to start the discussion by adding an introductory sentence, such as: **Juan Pablo está de vacaciones con sus abuelos.**

Activities A2 and A3 will help you determine student comprehension of the basic material in A1. If student comprehension is low, you should review A1, and review the vocabulary again.

A4   Actividad • Tu familia

Ask the students to work in pairs. They will interview each other, take notes concerning the answers, and report their findings to the class. You may wish to call the students' attention to the word **gemelos** by showing a magazine picture of twins. Also remind the students that the masculine plural noun can include both males and females. If necessary, re-enter names of family relationships by having the students complete the following or similar sentences.

1. El padre de mi padre es mi *abuelo.*
2. El hijo de mi tía es mi *primo.*
3. El esposo de mi madre es mi *padre.*
4. El hijo de mi mamá es mi *hermano.*
5. La madre de mi padre es mi *abuela.*

SLOWER-PACED LEARNING   Before completing the activity in small groups, ask individuals: **¿Eres el mayor o el menor de tu familia?** Then ask the ages of their brothers and sisters and write their names and ages on the board or a transparency. Establish who is **el mayor** and **el menor.** Be prepared to teach the students to say: **No soy ni el mayor ni el menor.** When teaching **tíos,** you may wish to ask: **¿Cuántos hermanos tiene tu padre?** Point out that these people are the **tíos.**

For cooperative learning, form groups of three or four to respond to the questions and discuss their real or imaginary families. Then review the answers with the class by having several students report their findings.

A5   Sabes que . . .

Locate Puerto Rico on a map and introduce the cardinal points **norte, sur, este,** and **oeste** by drawing a compass star on the board. Talk about the major cities located on the island and the position of the mountains. You may wish to point out that the island was under Spanish rule until the end of the Spanish-American War, and that Puerto Ricans speak Spanish. There are many famous Puerto Rican baseball players, baseball being the most popular sport in Puerto Rico. You may wish to ask the students to name several of them, beginning with perhaps the most famous of all, Roberto Clemente. He was killed in a plane crash in the early 1970s as he was taking emergency supplies to the Nicaraguans following an earthquake that destroyed the city of Managua.

A 6   SE DICE ASÍ

Write several names of students and their ages on the board or a transparency as follows:

Marta:	16 años
José:	18 años
Rafael:	15 años

Review **mayor que** and **menor que** by making statements about the students indicated. Then ask the ages of several other class members. Write the information on the board or a transparency and call on volunteers to make comparisons using **mayor que** and **menor que.**

    To present **mejor que** and **peor que,** bring in pairs of items to compare quality. You may also ask the students to bring in items, such as an old tennis shoe and a new tennis shoe, ragged clothes and new clothes, or broken records and new records. As you point to the objects, say: **El zapato de tenis azul es mejor que el rojo. El vestido negro es mejor que el blanco. El disco viejo es peor que el nuevo.** Then call on volunteers to compare other objects using **mejor que** and **peor que.**

A 7   Actividad • ¡A completar!

Ask the students to complete this activity orally. You may wish to ask them to first write their answers to use as a guide.

A 8   Actividad • ¿Mejor o peor?

This activity may be used as a quick review or you may wish to have the students complete the activity in writing as a practice quiz. Review the material with the entire class.

A 9   ESTRUCTURAS ESENCIALES

Re-enter the short form of possessive adjectives by collecting items from the students' desks and questioning them about the owners. Write the short form of possessive adjectives on the board or a transparency. Then introduce the stressed possessive adjectives by repeating the questioning with the classroom objects. Indicate how differences in word order reflect differences in emphasis. With the short forms, the emphasis is on the thing possessed: **mi** *lápiz.* With the stressed possessive adjective, the emphasis is on the possessor: **el lápiz** *mío.* Compare with English where the emphasis is done with vocal stress and intonation. Ask the students to generalize about the use of the stressed forms. Have them open their books to review the chart and the explanation. Once again, orally review the several forms in context.

CHALLENGE   Have the students write ten sentences with possessive adjectives. Five sentences should include the short forms and five should include the stressed forms. Then collect and correct their papers.

A 10   Actividad • Y ésta es . . .

Begin the activity with the class by presenting a model and one or two items. Then have the students complete the activity with a partner.

    For further practice, ask the students to review how to introduce friends by acting out an introduction in class. Model the conversation with three students. Then ask the class to practice in groups of four. Finally, call several volunteers to present their dialog.

A 11   Actividad • De regreso

For writing practice, have the students write the completed sentences. Remind them again that the possessive form agrees with the item possessed, not the possessor.

A 12   Actividad • ¿Quién es?

Review the various meanings of **suyo.** Then complete the model and one or two items. Ask the students to complete the activity with a partner.

SLOWER-PACED LEARNING   For writing practice, you may wish to have the students write their answers and then transfer them to the board or a transparency for correction.

A 13   ESTRUCTURAS ESENCIALES

Choose several objects from your desk and describe their color, size, newness, and so on.

> El libro mío es más grande que el libro de Anita.
> La regla tuya es nueva.

Repeat the sentences, deleting the nouns.

> El mío es más grande que el de Anita.
> La tuya es nueva.

Then read aloud the sample sentences and explanation in the book.

A 14   Actividad • ¡Demasiadas palabras!

Complete the activity with the entire class. You may also wish to have the students write the paragraph for homework or in class. Write the corrected paragraph on the board or a transparency. Then ask the students to exchange papers to correct their work.

> ANSWERS:
> Tú tienes ya los discos míos y los tuyos. Necesitamos todos los tuyos y todos los míos. Mañana necesitamos también los de Cheo, el radio grande y el nuevo. La música es para la fiesta de cumpleaños, el mío y el de Marilú, mi hermana gemela.

A 15   Actividad • Charla

Have the students work together to discuss their real or imaginary family members. Partners should take notes so that they will be able to share information with the class. You may wish to have the students limit their comments to only one member of their family.

CHALLENGE   Ask the students to talk about their favorite or most interesting family member.

A 16   Sabes que . . .

Play the cassette or read the cultural note aloud as the students follow along in their books. After discussing the pictures and the cultural note, elicit comments about attitudes that may have changed. You may also wish to play tapes of Puerto Rican music, such as the classic piece, "Borinquén." Mention that the word **Borinquén** was the name the natives used for Puerto Rico before the Spaniards arrived.

A 17 ESTRUCTURAS ESENCIALES

Collect several identical items from the classroom in order to demonstrate **tan . . . como** to the class. Use common adjectives and adverbs as you show pictures or objects to the class. Ask the students to join in the conversation. You may also wish to call on volunteers to write your comments on the board or a transparency. When you have practiced enough to give the class an idea of the new structure, ask the students to refer to the chart in their books. Review the material with them. Remind them that **tan . . . como** can be used with adjectives and adverbs.

To practice comparisons of equality with **tan . . . como,** ask the students to form several sentences as you write cues on the board or a transparency. For example, you may write **rápido** and the students may respond: **El metro es tan rápido como el autobús.**

A 18 Actividad • En Puerto Rico

Have the students complete this activity with a partner or have them write the sentences for homework. Review all the material on the board or a transparency.

ANSWERS:
1. ¿Cuál es más caliente, el Atlántico o el Caribe?
   El Atlántico es tan caliente como el Caribe.
2. ¿Cuál es más interesante, la capital o el campo?
   La capital es tan interesante como el campo.
3. ¿Cuál es más famoso, El Morro o El Yunque?
   El Morro es tan famoso como El Yunque.
4. ¿Cuál es más divertido, el Viejo San Juan o el San Juan moderno?
   El Viejo San Juan es tan divertido como el San Juan moderno.
5. ¿Cuál es más azul, el mar o el cielo?
   El mar es tan azul como el cielo.
6. ¿Cuál es más viejo, el disco mío o el de ella?
   El disco mío es tan viejo como el de ella.

A 19 Actividad • Mis amigos

Ask the students to complete the activity in groups of two or three. They may wish to use a friend's name or any Spanish name to complete the activity. You may wish to remind them that **-mente** is the equivalent of *-ly* in English.

A 20 ESTRUCTURAS ESENCIALES

To present **tanto . . . como,** you may wish to follow the procedure as suggested in A17 above. Then on the board or a transparency, write several examples, such as the following:

María: tres libros
yo: tres libros

Ask the students to form a sentence with the examples given, making sure the students use the correct gender.

María tiene tantos libros como yo.

A 21 Actividad • El fanfarrón

Have the students complete this activity orally. Then assign it for writing practice, either in class or for homework. Call on volunteers to write the answers on the board or a transparency for correction.

ANSWERS:
1. Tú tienes tantos primos como Cheo.
   ¡Oh, no! Yo tengo más primos que Cheo.
2. Paco tiene tantos amigos como tú.
   ¡Oh, no! Yo tengo más amigos que Paco.
3. Yo tengo tantos videos como tú.
   ¡Oh, no! Yo tengo más videos que tú.
4. Carlos tiene tanto tiempo como tú.
   ¡Oh, no! Yo tengo más tiempo que Carlos.
5. Tú tienes tantos libros como yo.
   ¡Oh, no! Yo tengo más libros que tú.
6. Tú tienes tantas fotos como Enrique.
   ¡Oh, no! Yo tengo más fotos que Enrique.

A 22 Comprensión

You will hear a statement comparing two people or objects. Each statement will be followed by a conclusion. If the conclusion is true, check **sí** on your answer sheet. If not, check **no.** For example, you will hear: **Alicia tiene quince años y Teresa tiene dieciséis.** The conclusion is: **Teresa es menor que Alicia.** You place your mark in the row labeled **no,** since the conclusion is not correct.

1. —Yo vi una película muy interesante que me gustó mucho. José vio una película horrible y aburrida.
   —La película que yo vi fue mejor que la que vio José. *sí*
2. —Marisol tiene muchos discos. Yo sólo tengo diez.
   —Marisol tiene menos discos que yo. *no*
3. —El estéreo de Pablo costó mil dólares. El mío costó seiscientos dólares.
   —El mío es más caro que el de Pablo. *no*
4. —La bicicleta roja es nueva. La azul es vieja y no funciona.
   —La bicicleta roja es mejor que la azul. *sí*
5. —Mamá tiene treinta y cinco años. Papá tiene cuarenta.
   —Papá es mayor que mamá. *sí*
6. —Eduardo recibió una nota de diez. Fernando recibió siete.
   —La nota de Fernando es peor que la de Eduardo. *sí*
7. —Mi hermana tiene veinte años. Yo tengo quince.
   —Yo soy mayor que mi hermana. *no*
8. —El coche de Anita es muy viejo y no funciona bien. El mío funciona bien aunque es viejo también.
   —El coche de Anita es peor que el mío. *sí*
9. —Mi amiga tiene un libro nuevo. El mío es viejo y feo.
   —El libro de mi amiga es mejor que el mío. *sí*
10. —Voy a la universidad dentro de tres años. Mi hermano va dentro de cinco.
    —Yo soy mayor que mi hermano. *sí*

Now check your answers. *Read each statement and conclusion again, and give the correct answer.*

A 23 Actividad • ¡A escribir!

Before assigning the letter for homework, review the salutations and complimentary closings with the students. Then, ask the students to write the letter in the form they learned earlier in Unit 1, Section C.

SECTION
B

OBJECTIVES **To express attitudes and opinions:** make excuses, express points of view; **to persuade:** make suggestions

CULTURAL BACKGROUND You may wish to discuss the concept of the extended family with the class. When talking about the family, be sure to safeguard the privacy of individuals—some students may not wish to discuss their family situation. Offer the choice of discussing one's real family or a fictitious one. Ask them to complete the following sentences about their real or imaginary families.

> Mi familia consiste de . . .
> Los que viven en mi casa son . . .
> Para las fiestas invito a . . .
> Mis abuelos son . . .
> Mis primos son . . .

Discuss their responses as an introduction to a Hispanic family. All members of the family are close to each other. Grandparents often live with their adult children and grandchildren. First cousins are referred to as **primos hermanos.**

MOTIVATING ACTIVITY Ask the students to list as many good points as possible about the families they are discussing. For example:

> Mi hermano es muy divertido.
> Mi papá toca muy bien el piano.
> Los domingos hacemos una excursión.

Ask the students to share their thoughts with a partner. You may wish to conclude by asking them to mention one or two things about their family of which they are proud or happy.

B 1 Obligaciones familiares

Before presenting the dialog, initiate a discussion of responsibilities the students have at home. Make a list of chores, such as **poner la mesa, quitar la mesa, lavar los platos, lavar la ropa,** and so on. Discuss who does the chores and when they must be completed. Then, review the setting of the dialog, the ages of the characters, and the pronunciation of their names with the class. To continue, read the **División de tareas** with the class and if you wish, select new words from the dialog and ask the students to guess their meanings. You may use pictures to illustrate their meanings or use each new word in a sentence. Then have the students listen as you read the first part of the dialog aloud or play the cassette. To check comprehension, ask questions about its content.

Once the first part of the dialog is understood, continue in the same manner with the second part. When finished, review the list of chores. You may wish to play the cassette once again for comprehension practice. You may call for choral and individual repetition, alternating them to avoid boredom. While presenting and practicing the dialog in class, try to keep a fast tempo in order to maintain as much of the students' attention as possible. Insist on a normal delivery—as close as possible to that of a native speaker. Particular attention should be given to linking of words, syllable length, and intonation.

B 2 ## Actividad • Preguntas y respuestas

You may wish to do this activity with the books closed, or you may prefer to call on two volunteers to read the dialog aloud. Then ask the students to work with a partner to complete the answers to the questions. Review the answers with the class. Refer to the dialog, if necessary.

B 3 ## Actividad • No es así. ¿Cómo es?

Have the students complete this activity in writing. When they have finished, ask them to exchange papers to correct the answers. Then discuss the answers with the class.

B 4 ## Sabes que . . .

You may wish to add that until recent times Spanish–speaking youngsters did not usually help with the household chores, because in most families mothers did not have jobs and many people could afford servants. Nowadays, more Spanish women have jobs and servants are increasingly difficult to find. Prepare the following or similar list of questions to help the students read the cultural note.

> ¿Quién es el cabeza de familia?
> ¿Quién trabaja en la familia?
> ¿Qué hace la familia?
> ¿Qué incluye la familia?
> ¿De qué depende la profesión de los hijos?
> ¿Cómo celebran las fiestas importantes?

Read the cultural note aloud, stopping after each sentence or two to ask questions to check for comprehension. When finished, allow the students to return to the questions you have written on the board or a transparency. Give them a few moments to complete the answers.

CHALLENGE   Have the students prepare a report on their real or imaginary family, comparing it to a Spanish-speaking family. Have them report their findings to the class and have a group discussion.

B 5 ## Actividad • ¡A escribir!

Ask the students to make a list of chores and then assign each one to the members of their family. You may wish to have them find magazine pictures or drawings of people doing each chore. Have the students paste the pictures on colored paper to later use for review.

B 6 ## SE DICE ASÍ

Ask the students to review the expressions with you. Practice making excuses with them by extending an invitation and having them respond by giving an excuse. Then allow time for the students to practice with a partner. You or a volunteer may also read aloud a list of exciting and unpleasant activities. Allow the students to respond freely. Some suggestions are:

> ¿Qué te parece si vamos al cine?
> ¿Quieres limpiar tu cuarto?
> ¿Por qué no vamos al partido de fútbol?
> ¿No prometiste estudiar dos horas esta noche?

B7   Actividad • ¡Siempre tienen una buena excusa!

Role-play the situation with several students, asking them to help with various chores. You may wish to give prizes to the students who create the most original excuses. For cooperative learning, have them work in groups of three to create short dialogs based on the material. Select several groups to present their dialogs to the class.

B8   SITUACIÓN • Algunos animales

Using flashcards, introduce the new vocabulary for animals. You can make flashcards by pasting magazine pictures or illustrations on construction paper or poster board. After most students are able to identify the Spanish names of the animals, have them open their books, cover the captions, and identify the animals pictured in each illustration.

B9   Actividad • Animales domésticos

Ask the students to work in pairs. Each student should alternate the role of the questioner. Review the activity with the entire class, keeping books closed. You may wish to ask questions for choral and individual responses.

ANSWERS:
1. ¿Cepillaste mi caballo?
   No, cepillé el mío.
2. ¿Les diste la zanahoria a mis conejos?
   No, les di la zanahoria a los míos.
3. ¿Cuidaste mi serpiente?
   No, cuidé la mía.
4. ¿Limpiaste la jaula de mi pájaro?
   No, limpié la jaula del mío.
5. ¿Lavaste el plato de mi gata?
   No, lavé el plato de la mía.
6. ¿Bañaste mi perro?
   No, bañé el mío.
7. ¿Les cambiaste el agua a mis ranas?
   No, les cambié el agua a las mías.
8. ¿Hablaste con mi loro?
   No, hablé con el mío.
9. ¿Les diste lechuga a mis ratones blancos?
   No, les di lechuga a los míos.
10. ¿Les diste de comer a mis peces?
    No, les di de comer a los míos.

B10   Actividad • Tus animales preferidos

This activity lends itself to be conducted as an interview. The students may interview another student, but allow them to switch partners and take notes. Ask several volunteers to share their information with the class.

For writing practice, ask the students to combine the answers from the interview to form a paragraph. Then call on volunteers to read their paragraphs aloud.

SLOWER-PACED LEARNING   Ask the students to write five or six sentences describing their pet or a pet they would like to have. Have them illustrate their descriptions with drawings or photographs and display them in the classroom.

B 11 ESTRUCTURAS ESENCIALES

Present the verb **pedir** with a guided question-answer activity using the students' real names:

TEACHER	Yo pido un café. ¿Qué pides tú?
STUDENT I	Yo pido un refresco.
TEACHER	Ella pide un refresco. Y tú, ¿qué pides?
STUDENT II	Yo pido una hamburguesa.
TEACHER	¿Pide él/ella un jugo?
STUDENT III	No, él pide una hamburguesa.

Continue with the conversation until all the forms of **pedir** have been introduced. When most of the students understand the forms, ask them to tell you what they have heard and write the forms on the board or a transparency. Then ask them to open their books and read the explanation to confirm their observations.

Review the preterit forms in the same manner. You may start your conversation in the following manner: **Ayer yo fui a la cafetería. Pedí un café, pero la señora Jones pidió un refresco y un bocadillo.** Then ask the students to identify what they ordered at the school cafeteria yesterday. Make sure to include all verb forms in the conversation.

B 12 Actividad • Todos piden algo

For writing practice, you may wish to have the students write complete sentences. Write the answers on the board or a transparency. Then have the students exchange papers to correct their work. Be sure to circulate throughout the room to help any students who are having problems with the verb forms.

CHALLENGE   Call on volunteers to write the sentences on the board or a transparency, inserting the correct preterit form of the verb **pedir.** They may also wish to write original sentences.

B 13 Actividad • ¡A escoger!

Ask the students to form at least ten sentences with these items. This makes an ideal homework assignment. For writing practice, have the students write the sentences on the board or a transparency from dictation.

B 14 Actividad • La reunión familiar

Have the students make a list of the family members at the reunion. Then ask them to make a statement about what each person wanted. Ask them to share the list with a partner who will take notes and report their information to the class or to another class member. For cooperative learning, form groups of two or three. Allow each group three minutes to form as many sentences as possible. The group with the most correct sentences wins.

B 15 **Sabes que . . .**

Review the material on **pez** and **pescado** with the class. Tell the students they must order **pescado** in a restaurant, not **pez.** Point out that **pescado** refers to fish that are cooked or caught, and **pez** refers to fish in water. Remind them that the **z** changes to **c** when the plural ending is added.

B 16 **Actividad • Y tú, ¿qué hiciste?**

Complete the activity orally with the class in the affirmative form. Then, you may wish to have the students work with a partner. Have them answer negatively after you review some of the excuses they learned in B6, p. 66. Write the list of excuses on the board.

CHALLENGE   Choose several students to play the roles of parent and child. Have them act out several of the exchanges for the class.

B 17 **Actividad • ¿Qué hizo el robot?**

Ask the students to talk about their robots to a classmate, who will then share with the class three things the robot did or did not do. Give small prizes or points to those who remember most of what their partner said. Ask the students to prepare an advertisement about a robot they have for sale. Ask them to include a list of chores the robot will do. These can be made into commercials and art can be added to make the project more realistic.

B 18 **SITUACIÓN • ¿Me dan permiso?**

When you begin the presentation of the dialog, concentrate on the specific objectives of the activity in progess. Do not interrupt to explain grammar or to define new vocabulary. Explanation of these items may follow later.

Play the cassette or read the dialog aloud. Before role-playing the dialog, you may call for choral and individual repetition, alternating them to avoid boredom. Then discuss the various reasons for being grounded. You may wish to ask questions, such as **¿Cuándo es que no te permiten salir tus padres?** The responses may be **tienes malas notas** or **no limpias tu cuarto.**

SLOWER-PACED LEARNING   Ask the students to use the information in B18 to make each of the following sentences agree with the dialog.

1. Lucila está feliz.
2. Lucila quiere ir a la escuela.
3. Lucila no puede ir porque tiene buenas notas.
4. Ella quiere ir con sus amigos por tres días.
5. Los hermanos de Lucila no le dan permiso.

B 19 **Actividad • Por favor, ¡denme permiso!**

You may wish to complete this activity with books closed. Call on individual students to answer the questions orally. For writing practice, have the students write each answer in complete sentences at home or in class. Review the answers with the class.

B 20 **Actividad • ¿Le dieron permiso o no?**

For cooperative learning, form groups of two or three classmates to write a short dialog based on B18. Have the students present their dialogs to the class.

B 21   Comprensión   🔊

The Gómez children are arguing about the family chores. You will hear ten short conversational exchanges. If the two speakers agree, check **de acuerdo** on your answer sheet. If they disagree, check **en desacuerdo.** For example, you will hear: **Tú nunca me ayudas a limpiar el baño.** The response is: **¡No es cierto! Te ayudé la semana pasada.** You check **en desacuerdo** because the two speakers disagree.

1. —Oye, Laura, ayúdame a lavar los platos.
   —En dos minutos. Te ayudo también a secarlos.   *de acuerdo*
2. —Nunca cuidas los peces, Rolando. No sé porque los tienes.
   —No es cierto. Limpié el acuario la semana pasada.   *en desacuerdo*
3. —Luisa, ¿quieres ayudarme a poner la mesa?
   —Yo te ayudo si tú me ayudas a quitarla.   *de acuerdo*
4. —Mamá dice que tenemos que bañar y cepillar al perro.
   —Entonces puedes hacerlo tú, porque yo siempre lo saco a pasear.   *en desacuerdo*
5. —Hermanito, ¿me haces el favor de sacar la basura?
   —Sácala tú. Está lloviendo.   *en desacuerdo*
6. —Hija, llevame la ropa a lavar.
   —Ya voy, mamá. Busco la ropa de José Luis también.   *de acuerdo*
7. —O haces la cama o no sales. ¡Palabra final!
   —Pero mamá, ya es tarde y mis amigos me esperan afuera.   *en desacuerdo*
8. —Vienen tus abuelos esta tarde. Necesito ayuda para ordenar la casa.
   —Yo puedo pasar la aspiradora si quieres.   *de acuerdo*
9. —En esta casa todos ayudamos. Yo pongo y quito la mesa.
   —Y yo siempre lavo los platos. Quique los seca.   *de acuerdo*
10. —Roberto, el perro quiere salir. ¿Puedes sacarlo a pasear?
    —Pero mamá, estoy estudiando para mi examen.   *en desacuerdo*

Now check your answers. *Read each exchange again and give the correct answer.*

B 22   ESTRUCTURAS ESENCIALES

To present the preterit tense of the verb **decir,** follow the same procedure as mentioned in B11 on page T57. Point out to the students that the forms are irregular and that they must be memorized.

B 23   Actividad • Chismes

Have the students complete the activity with a partner. Then have them close their books and respond to cues. Ask for individual and full choral responses.

Re-enter indirect-object pronouns by writing several sentences on the board or a transparency, and have the students find the indirect objects. Then rewrite each sentence below the original, replacing the indirect objects with **me, te, le, nos,** and **les.**

SLOWER-PACED LEARNING   Ask the students to write the sentences in B23. Then ask them to complete this activity as a short practice quiz with books closed. You may also wish to write the activity on the board or a transparency. Then review the answers with the class.

SECTION

C

OBJECTIVES **To persuade:** persuade somebody to lend you something; **to express attitudes and opinions:** confirm expected courses of action

CULTURAL BACKGROUND Puerto Rico is a commonwealth of the United States. In Spanish, *commonwealth* is **Estado Libre Asociado.** As a commonwealth, Puerto Rico has representatives in the U.S. Congress, but they are nonvoting members. Puerto Ricans participate in presidential elections only in a straw poll. Candidates often travel to Puerto Rico, because the Puerto Ricans on the east coast of the United States have a great deal of political influence. This influence is often related to the island, as there is much communication and travel between the mainland and the island.

MOTIVATING ACTIVITY You may wish to discuss the ongoing debate about the future of Puerto Rico with the students. Some Puerto Ricans want the island to become independent. Others want it to become a state in the union. Still others want it to remain as it is at present.

C1

Problemas y más problemas

Before introducing the dialog, present the new vocabulary to the class. Remind the students of the meaning of the verb **prestar** by "borrowing" items from them. You may wish to start with the following question: **¿Me prestas tu libro? ¿lápiz?** Coax the students to respond with **Sí, te presto mi lápiz** or **No, no te presto mi lápiz.**

Next, write the words **moto, tele,** and **bici** on the board or a transparency. Explain that these words are shortened words used in informal conversation. You may wish to have them guess the meanings of these words and ask for a few examples in English, such as *TV, bike, phone,* and so on.

You may prefer to play the cassette or to read aloud small portions of the dialog first. Then call for choral and individual repetition. Choral and individual repetition should be alternated in order to avoid boredom. When you have completed the dialog, you may wish to call on students to role-play parts of the dialog. You should not expect total memorization of the exchanges, but students should become familiar with the situation and should learn the new vocabulary in context. Try not to spend too much time presenting the dialog the first day. Ten to twelve minutes of class time should be sufficient. You can extend the dialog presentation over several days.

SLOWER-PACED LEARNING You may wish to have the students read only the first section of the dialog. Once they understand the first section, continue with the second part in the same manner.

CHALLENGE You may wish to challenge the students by asking them to hold an impromptu conversation with a partner. One student should try to convince the other to lend him or her an item, while the second student should give reasons not to do so.

C2

Actividad • No es así

You may wish to do this activity with books closed. Write the statements on the board and call on individual students to correct them.

As a variation, ask the students to work alone or with a partner to correct the statements. You or a volunteer may wish to write the corrected sentences on the board or a transparency. If necessary, return to the dialog to clarify any misunderstandings.

C3 Actividad • Para completar

Ask the students to complete this activity with books closed. Allow only three or four minutes. Review the answers in class, and if any students have had difficulty in answering, refer them to the dialog in C1.

C4 Sabes que . . .

Begin by asking some of the students about their favorite activities. Ask whether they like to go out in groups, with a friend, or alone and where they go. Then use the following or similar group of words from the selection and ask the students to match them with their English equivalents.

diversiones	*impressions*	impresiones	*entertainment*
grupo	*group*	participan	*they meet*
miembros	*they participate*	reuniones	*members*
se reúnen	*meetings*		

Continue by reading the information aloud or playing the cassette. Pause after each sentence or group of two sentences to ask simple comprehension questions. Then have the students read the cultural note again silently. You may ask for a quick summary in English, or if time allows, have them summarize in Spanish. Ask the students to compare the styles of social life presented in the cultural note to that of their own.

C5 SE DICE ASÍ

Review the examples of tag questions with the students and have them repeat after you for intonation practice. Then have volunteers comment about something in class or at school. Other students should respond using tag questions whenever possible. You might reward those who ask tag questions by giving bingo tokens. Collect the tokens at the end of the class period and assign a point value for extra credit.

C6 ESTRUCTURAS ESENCIALES

Before presenting the structure, you may wish to re-enter direct- and indirect-object pronouns. Begin the section with an oral practice. Return to the dialog in C1, page 72, and your initial presentation of ¿Me prestas . . . ? Then continue your conversation, including the direct-object pronoun for the item you wish to borrow. For example: ¿Me prestas tu lápiz? ¿Me lo prestas? Select a variety of items to allow for a change in pronouns. Write some of the students' responses on the board or a transparency. For example, when you ask: ¿Me prestas tu lápiz? the response should be: ¿Me lo prestas? Once you have written several examples on the board, ask the students to identify the function of each word in the sentence. Then ask them to open their books to review the chart and the explanation.

C7 Actividad • Menos palabras

Before completing this activity, write several sentences on the board or a transparency. Ask the students to replace each direct object with a pronoun.

Te mando la carta. Te la mando.
Te presto las revistas. Te las presto.
Me dio unos libros. Me los dio.

You may also wish to re-enter the verbs **prestar** and **dar** by completing a similar activity with the students. Then, with books open, review the instructions and complete one or two items with the class. Ask the students to complete the activity with a partner.

SLOWER-PACED LEARNING   For further practice with indirect-object pronouns, you may wish to have the students write the sentences, underline or circle the direct object, and identify the pronoun they should use. For writing practice, have them rewrite the sentences using the indirect-object pronouns.

C8 Actividad • ¿Puedes decirme?

Before the students complete the activity, remind them about the final position of the pronoun with infinitives. They may also complete this activity orally with a partner.

As an optional activity, you may wish to write question 4 on the board and ask the students to respond using the information in the realia at the top of the page. You may also wish to ask the following questions.

> ¿Cómo se llama la tienda?
> ¿A qué hora está abierta?
> ¿Cuál es la dirección?

ANSWERS:
1. No puedo hablarle ahora.
2. Voy a prometerles muchas cosas.
3. Raúl quiere prestarme los libros de español.
4. ¿A quién puedo comprarle una bicicleta?
5. Vas a decirme tu nombre, ¿verdad?
6. Voy a extrañarte mucho.

C9 Actividad • ¿Puedes decírmelo otra vez?

Have the students complete this activity orally. If you are unsure they have mastered the concept of attaching direct-object pronouns and indirect-object pronouns to infinitives, have them write complete sentences. You may wish to call on volunteers to write the sentences on the board for correction.

C10 Comprensión

You will hear a series of short conversational exchanges. If the second statement is a logical conclusion to the first, check **lógico** on your answer sheet. If it is not, check **ilógico**. For example, you will hear: **Creo que voy a mandarle el dinero a Elena.** The response is: **Debes mandárselo.** You should check **lógico** because it is a logical conclusion.

1. —Le presté la bicicleta a mi primo ayer.
   —Va a devolvértela hoy, ¿no?   *lógico*
2. —¿Me cuidas el coche?
   —¿Cuándo me lo devuelves?   *ilógico*
3. —Rafael le compró un anillo a su novia.
   —Y, ¿ya se lo dio?   *lógico*

4. —Le voy a mandar una carta a Elena la semana que viene.
   —¿Dijiste que vas a mandármelo pronto? *ilógico*
5. —¿Tienes que darle el número de teléfono a Paco?
   —Sí, tengo que dártelo hoy mismo. *ilógico*
6. —Laura acaba de devolverme mis libros.
   —¿Te los devolvió todos? *lógico*
7. —Tengo muchísimo trabajo. Voy a pedirle ayuda a Mario.
   —Siempre puedes pedírsela a él. Es muy amable. *lógico*
8. —Tengo el dinero para la fiesta.
   —Entonces puedes pagárselo a Raimundo. *lógico*
9. —¿Me prestas tu diccionario?
   —Con mucho gusto te lo presto. *lógico*
10. —Diana le mandó el regalo a su novio en España.
    —Se lo mandó por avión, ¿verdad? *lógico*

Now check your answers. *Read each exchange again and give the correct answer.*

C11 Actividad • Y tú, ¿qué me dices?

The students may have difficulty deciding which pronoun to use in their answers. You may wish to prompt them using gestures and prepositional phrases if they hesitate. Assign the activity for written practice after they have finished.

C12 SE ESCRIBE ASÍ

Review the chart and explanation with the students. Stress that many Spanish words ending in **-ión** are cognates and resemble English words ending in *-tion*. Point out that there is an exception in the following list (**oración**). Have the students try to guess its meaning. You may wish to provide them with the following or similar words they have not seen. Let them guess the meanings and predict which forms need accents.

demostración	construcciones
acción	oración
mansiones	panteón
destrucciones	revoluciones

Ask the students to change the plural words to the singular and vice versa. Write their answers on the board or a transparency. You may wish to delete all the accents and have the students identify the words that need accents.

C13 ESTRUCTURAS ESENCIALES

Return to your original presentation of double-object pronouns in C6 on page T61. Ask two students to present a short dialog in which one asks to borrow something from the other. Following the exchange of the item, state: **José le prestó su lápiz a Marco. José se lo prestó.** Then write the two sentences on the board or a transparency. Ask the students to analyze what happened, using the diagram in the text as a model. You may wish to write several other samples on the board. Once the students have given answers, review the charts and explanation in the book. Prepare the following or similar sentences for the students to write as examples:

Le mandé la carta a José.   Se la mandé.
Les dio el dinero a ellos.   Se lo dio.
Le prestó mi lápiz a Tesera.   Se lo prestó.
Les prestaron la moto.   Se la prestaron.

You may wish to have the students practice this type of activity orally, following the model of the students' dialog. Several pairs of students may ask to borrow items, and the class may make statements about the actions.

C 14   Actividad • ¿Qué va a prestar?

SLOWER-PACED LEARNING   Complete the activity with the entire class or have the students work with a partner. For writing practice, have them write the sentences. You may also wish to have the students find pictures to mount on paper. They should look for three pictures of objects and three pictures of people. The students will then question each other about what is being loaned to whom, showing the pictures and stating a name. For example, holding up a picture of a bicycle and of a boy, student 1 should say: **¿Le prestaste a Juan la bicicleta?** Student 2 should respond: **Sí, se la presté.**

C 15   Actividad • Sólo para mí

Have the students complete the activity in pairs. When they are finished, ask them to tell their partners what items they would not consider lending to anyone. They must also give a reason. Partners should take notes and be prepared to discuss what they have learned with the class.

C 16   Actividad • ¿Lo hago hoy?

Each student may complete this activity alone, either orally or in writing. Review the responses with the class.

C 17   Actividad • Charla

Ask the students to prepare notes about five things they do to help friends or family members, and five things others do to help them. Here are some examples you may wish to share:

Mi mamá me lava la ropa.
Yo le preparo el desayuno a mi hermano.
Mi amiga Marta me ayuda con el álgebra.

Ask each student to share notes with a partner. You may also wish to have individuals share their information with the entire class. In this case, prepare to ask others what the student has said to check comprehension. Another technique is to give a spot quiz, either for a grade or as a game. Take notes on what the students say. When finished, ask questions, such as **¿Quién le prepara el desayuno a su hermano? (María se lo prepara.)** Award extra points or tokens to the students who answer correctly and use complete sentences.

TRY
YOUR
SKILLS

OBJECTIVE   To recombine communicative functions, grammar, and vocabulary

CULTURAL BACKGROUND   You may wish to explain that Xochimilco is the site of the floating gardens. When the Aztecs founded Mexico City, there was no room on the island for crops. The farmers filled shallow baskets called **chinampas** with dirt, lashed them together, and floated them on the lake. They planted their crops in the baskets, and would row small boats between the canals. *Xochitl* (so CHI tl) is the Nahuatl word for *flowers*, so Xochimilco (so chee MEEL co) is the Place of Flowers.

1

Vacaciones en México

Play the cassette or read the letter aloud to the students. Once they have understood the material, allow them to write a response. You may wish to review the salutations and complimentary closings with the students.

2

Actividad • Ahora son amigos tuyos

Allow the students to work through the activity in groups. Then have them act out the material, introducing class members to each other and to you. Review the activity with the class.

3

Actividad • La mía es mejor que ésa

Allow the students several minutes to complete the comparisons. Check their work by completing the same sentences on the board or a transparency.

4

Actividad • El tuyo y el mío

Complete the activity with the class, or you may wish to ask the students to work with a partner. Write the answers on a transparency as you review with the class.

5

Actividad • Bailo tan bien como tú

Allow the students a few moments to write the sentences. Review the completed sentences on the board or a transparency. Then ask the students to make comparisons with members of the class, encouraging polite behavior.

6

Actividad • Tengo tantos como él

You may wish to work with the entire class or have the students divide into groups of two or three. Ask them to make original comparisons, using classroom objects.

7

Actividad • A completar

Write the sentences on the board or a transparency. Call on students to fill in the blanks with the appropriate form of the verb.

8   Actividad • A usar la imaginación

Set a time limit. At the end of the limit, ask the students to turn in their suggested sentences. Give extra points to the students with the most correct sentences. You may wish to ask several people to write their sentences on the board to discuss with the class.

9   Actividad • ¿Vas a decírmelo?

Allow the students to rewrite the sentences. Call on volunteers to write their sentences on the board.

10   Actividad • ¿Cuál puede ser la pregunta?

Review the indirect- and direct-object pronouns with the students. Then ask the students to work in groups of three to create the questions. Write the answers on the board, and allow groups to write a question for each of the responses.

11   Dictado

Write the following paragraph from dictation. First listen to the paragraph as it is read to you. Then you will hear the paragraph again in short segments, with a pause after each segment to allow you time to fill in the blanks. Finally, you will hear the paragraph a third time so that you may check your work. Let's begin.

> Querida prima,
> Paso unos días con mis abuelos. *(pause)* Sabes que viven en Puerto Rico, *(pause)* y hace diez días que estoy aquí. *(pause)* Ayer fui a San Juan con mis tíos *(pause)* y compré muchas cosas. *(pause)* Ayudo a abuela con las tareas de la casa. *(pause)* Esta mañana limpié mi cuarto. *(pause)*
> Muchos recuerdos de
> Juan Pablo

PRONUNCIACIÓN

Review the vowel sounds, asking the students to repeat them. Encourage the students to position their lips or the shape of their mouths correctly for each vowel. Play the cassette or read aloud the words in the first section. Be sure to explain the meaning of the word diphthong, differentiating between the combinations of **a, e,** and **o.**

It is suggested to divide the pronunciation activity into several sessions. You may also wish to re-enter the use of accents before you complete the next section. Ask the students to listen to and repeat the pronunciation of the next two sections as you read aloud or play the cassette.

Actividad • ¿Dónde están los acentos?

Ask the students to write the paragraph in their notebooks and find the accents. You may then call on individuals to read it aloud, stressing the appropriate syllables. This activity is an excellent homework assignment and pronunciation quiz.

ANSWERS:
Ayer Ana limpió los zapatos, cepilló al perro y llevó la ropa a lavar. Después tuvo ensayo y cantó en el coro. No pudo poner la mesa porque llegó tarde. Ella tuvo una buena excusa hoy. Sus hermanos no pudieron decir nada. Ella trabajó bastante.

¿LO SABES?

For the first activity, instruct the students to write a short letter in Spanish to a friend. You may wish to remind them of the expressions used for salutations and complimentary closings. For further practice of the next three activitites, review the various forms of possession. Then collect items from the students and allow them to review the various forms by stating who the owners of the items are. For example, **El lápiz rojo es de María. Es suyo.** To complete the last activity, review the construction **tan . . . como** and **tanto . . . como.** Allow the students to write five sentences using these constructions. Have them choose their best ones to copy on the board or a transparency for review.

To complete the first two activities, ask the students to participate in the formation of a list of chores. Write the list on the board or a transparency. Then have each student give an excuse why they cannot help with a particular chore. For the last activity, choose two students to role-play the situation. Then ask the students to create other similar situations that they will use with a partner. Call on volunteers to re-enact their dialog for the class.

To complete the first activity, persuade a student to "lend" you ten dollars. Then call on volunteers to re-enact your presentation with a partner. For the last activity, you may wish to review the object pronouns. Call on four volunteers to write the sentences in shorter form on the board or a transparency. Then review and correct the sentences with the entire class.

VOCABULARIO

You may wish to play the game **Memoria** to practice new vocabulary. Form groups of three or four students. Ask each group to select twelve words from the unit vocabulary list. The students should write each word and its English definition on separate index cards, totaling 24 cards. After shuffling the cards, students should place them face down on the table. Each student will turn over two cards at a time, attempting to locate and match each word with its English definition. If a student completes the match successfully, he or she takes both cards. When all words and their definitions have been matched, the player with the most pairs wins.

PRÁCTICA DEL VOCABULARIO

Have the class point out the expressions containing a verb and write them on the board or a transparency. Then have each student use each one in a sentence.

VAMOS A LEER

OBJECTIVE   To read for practice and pleasure

Antes de leer

Allow three minutes for the students to scan the selection to identify cognates. Write the words on the board as volunteers read their lists aloud. After the students have completed the reading selection, you may wish to have them add any additional words to the list.

Preparación para la lectura

Try to familiarize the students with Puerto Rico and the **Coquí** before they read the selection. You may wish to show slides or pictures of Puerto Rico. Also, if you would like to know more about **el coquí,** see *Fatherhood in Frogdom* by Daniel S. Townsend.

EL COQUÍ DE PUERTO RICO

Give the students a general idea of the content of the story. Tell them that they will be learning about an animal native to Puerto Rico. Ask them to skim over the paragraphs and find one or two items they recognize. For example, they might find in the first paragraph that the frog "sings" when they read the word **música.** Gloss the paragraph for words. Then ask the students to guess the meaning of these words or phrases.

You may prefer to play the cassette or to read aloud small portions of the reading selection and pause to check comprehension. You should not interrupt to define new vocabulary. Encourage the students to use context clues to identify the meanings of new words. To practice pronunciation, you may wish to have the students read the reading selection aloud.

Actividad • Preguntas y respuestas

When finished with the reading, have the students complete the answers. This may be completed as a homework assignment, in class, or with a partner. You may also wish to have them make up ten true or false statements. Have a round-robin game the next day. Student 1 will call on someone to answer, read his or her statement, and student 2 will respond **verdadero** or **falso.** If the answer is **falso,** student 2 must correct the statement. You may wish to collect the sentences and make up a true or false quiz based on the students' work.

Actividad • ¡A escoger!

Ask the students to review the lists of words and choose the unrelated item. Discuss their choices. You may wish to set a time limit of five minutes for the students to complete the activity.

Actividad • Charla

Work with the entire class to retell what they have learned about the **coquí.** Then ask the students to repeat the process with a partner or in groups of three. Each person in the group should retell part of the selection.

UNIDAD 2

Con la familia

Spanish-speaking teenagers who live in the United States often spend time with relatives in other parts of the country. They make new acquaintances and go out in mixed groups. Like most teenagers everywhere, they often borrow things from their friends. Sometimes they have to be very persuasive to get the things they want to borrow.

In this unit you will:

SECTION A	compare and express preferences . . . talk about family relationships
SECTION B	make excuses . . . express your point of view . . . make suggestions
SECTION C	persuade somebody to lend you something . . . confirm expected courses of action
TRY YOUR SKILLS	use what you've learned
VAMOS A LEER	read for practice and pleasure

SECTION A

comparing and expressing preferences . . . talking about family relationships

Spanish youngsters meet new friends among close neighbors and relatives. Grandchildren are usually very close to their grandparents. Grandparents are an integral part of the Spanish family.

For additional background on Puerto Rico, see p. T48.

A1   Unos días con los abuelos

Juan Pablo es un muchacho de Puerto Rico que ahora vive en Nueva York. Está de visita por unos días en casa de sus abuelos, que viven en Fajardo, Puerto Rico. Juan Pablo les escribe una carta a sus padres y les manda unas fotos.

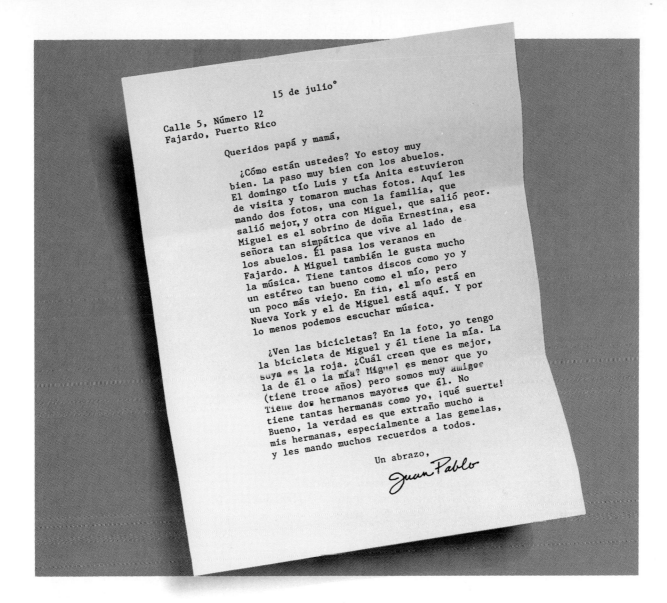

15 de julio°

Calle 5, Número 12
Fajardo, Puerto Rico

Queridos papá y mamá,

¿Cómo están ustedes? Yo estoy muy
bien. La paso muy bien con los abuelos.
El domingo tío Luis y tía Anita estuvieron
de visita y tomaron muchas fotos. Aquí les
mando dos fotos, una con la familia, que
salió mejor, y otra con Miguel, que salió peor.
Miguel es el sobrino de doña Ernestina, esa
señora tan simpática que vive al lado de
los abuelos. Él pasa los veranos en
Fajardo. A Miguel también le gusta mucho
la música. Tiene tantos discos como yo y
un estéreo tan bueno como el mío, pero
un poco más viejo. En fin, el mío está en
Nueva York y el de Miguel está aquí. Y por
lo menos podemos escuchar música.

¿Ven las bicicletas? En la foto, yo tengo
la bicicleta de Miguel y él tiene la mía. La
suya es la roja. ¿Cuál creen que es mejor,
la de él o la mía? Miguel es menor que yo
(tiene trece años) pero somos muy amigos.
Tiene dos hermanos mayores que él. No
tiene tantas hermanas como yo, ¡qué suerte!
Bueno, la verdad es que extraño mucho a
mis hermanas, especialmente a las gemelas,
y les mando muchos recuerdos a todos.

Un abrazo,
Juan Pablo

A2   Actividad • Preguntas y respuestas

Answer the following questions according to Juan Pablo's letter in A1.

1. ¿De dónde es Juan Pablo?   Juan Pablo es de Puerto Rico.
2. ¿Quiénes viven en Fajardo?   Los abuelos de Juan Pablo viven en Fajardo.
3. ¿Dónde viven los padres de Juan Pablo?   Los padres de Juan Pablo viven en Nueva York.
4. ¿Cómo se llama el sobrino de doña Ernestina?   El sobrino de doña Ernestina se llama Miguel.
5. ¿Quién tiene tantos discos como Juan Pablo?   Miguel tiene tantos discos como Juan Pablo.
6. ¿Es el estéreo de Miguel mejor que el de Juan Pablo?   El estéreo de Miguel es tan bueno como el de Juan Pablo, pero un poco más viejo.
7. ¿Es Miguel mayor o menor que Juan Pablo?   Miguel es menor que Juan Pablo.
8. ¿Son los hermanos de Miguel mayores o menores que él?   Los hermanos de Miguel son mayores que él.
9. ¿Cuántos hermanos tiene Miguel?   Miguel tiene dos hermanos.
10. ¿Qué le manda Juan Pablo a su familia?   Juan Pablo le manda muchos recuerdos a su familia. También le manda dos fotos.

°Note that in Spanish you write the day first, then the month, with **de** instead of commas, as in **12 de octubre de 1492.**

Actividad • ¡A escoger!

For each numbered sentence, choose the ending that fits best. Refer to the information in A1.

1. Juan Pablo escribió
   • una tarjeta postal. • <u>una carta.</u> • un telegrama.

2. En Fajardo, Puerto Rico, viven sus
   • <u>abuelos.</u> • tíos. • padres.

3. Doña Ernestina es
   • la abuela de Juan Pablo. • <u>la tía de Miguel.</u> • la mamá de Miguel.

4. Miguel tiene tantos discos como
   • tía Anita. • <u>Juan Pablo.</u> • doña Ernestina.

5. La bicicleta de Miguel es
   • la verde. • la azul. • <u>la roja.</u>

6. En la foto, Miguel tiene
   • <u>la bicicleta de Juan Pablo.</u> • la suya. • la azul.

7. Juan Pablo extraña a
   • su mamá. • su abuela. • <u>las gemelas.</u>

A4 Actividad • Tu familia   Answers will vary.

Answer the following questions about your real or imaginary family.

1. ¿De dónde son tus abuelos? ¿Y tus padres?
2. ¿Tienes hermanos o hermanas? ¿Eres mayor o menor?
3. ¿Qué es mejor, tener hermanos mayores o menores? ¿Por qué?
4. ¿Hay gemelos en tu familia?
5. ¿Cuántos tíos o tías tienes?
6. ¿Cuántos primos tienes?

Al sur *(to the south)* de la península de la Florida hay un grupo de islas *(islands)*, las Antillas *(the West Indies)*. En tres de estas islas se habla español: Cuba, la República Dominicana y Puerto Rico.

   Cristóbal Colón descubrió *(discovered)* la isla de Puerto Rico en 1493 durante su segundo viaje. Ponce de León exploró la isla y fundó *(founded)* la ciudad de San Juan en 1508. La Isla del Encanto *(The Island of Enchantment)*, otro nombre para Puerto Rico, es pequeña en tamaño *(size)*, pero grande en atracciones. San Juan, la capital, es una ciudad moderna, pero tiene una parte antigua, el Viejo San Juan. Allí podemos admirar el aspecto colonial de la isla.

   A la entrada de la bahía de San Juan *(San Juan Bay)* está el famoso castillo de El Morro *(El Morro Fortress)* que defendió la ciudad del ataque de los crueles piratas. La ciudad de Mayagüez da honor al "Descubridor" *(Discoverer)* en la Plaza de Cristóbal Colón. El Yunque es un bosque tropical donde hay cientos de plantas y animales distintos *(different)*. Aquí termina nuestro viaje por Puerto Rico, pero no el deseo *(desire)* de volver a esta encantadora *(charming)* isla.

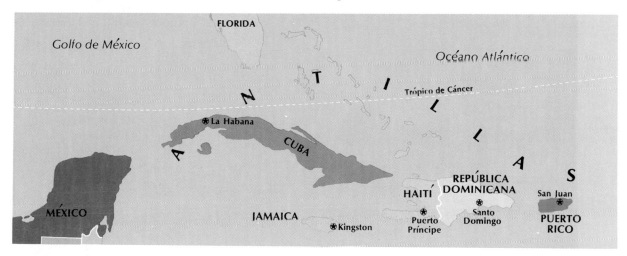

A6   SE DICE ASÍ
Comparing age and quality

You may wish to add that "mayor" and "menor" refer to people and mean *older* and *younger* respectively. The regular forms "(el) más grande," "(el) más pequeño," usually refer to size.

Él es menor que yo.	He is younger than I (am).
Ellas son menores que nosotros.	They are younger than we (are).
Yo soy mayor que ella.	I am older than she (is).
Luis y Elena son mayores que yo.	Luis and Elena are older than I (am).
La roja es mejor que la mía.	The red one is better than mine.
Mis discos son mejores que los de Alberto.	My records are better than Alberto's.
Mi reloj es peor que el de Carlos.	My watch is worse than Carlos's.
Son peores que los de ellos.	They are worse than theirs.

Use **menor/menores** and **mayor/mayores** when comparing age. Use **mejor/mejores** and **peor/peores** to compare quality.

Actividad • ¡A completar! Some answers will vary.

Look at each illustration. Then complete the captions with **mayor, menor, mejor,** or **peor.**

1. Miguel es _____ que Luis. mayor

2. Él me admira porque yo soy _____ que él. mayor

3. Sus hermanos son _____ que él. mayores

4. Yo creo que tener tres hermanas es _____ que no tener hermanas. mejor

5. Mi estéreo es _____ que el suyo. mejor/peor

6. Su bicicleta es _____ que la mía. mejor/peor

Actividad • ¿Mejor o peor?   Answers will vary. Possible answers are given.

Compare the items mentioned in each sentence and decide if one is better or worse than the other. Choose between **mejor que** and **peor que.**

1. Una bicicleta vieja es _____ una nueva.   peor que
2. Las películas divertidas son _____ las películas aburridas.   mejores que
3. Tener muchos discos es _____ tener pocos discos.   mejor que
4. Escribir cartas es _____ leer cartas.   mejor que
5. Ser el menor es _____ ser el mayor.   mejor que
6. Tener una hermana mayor es _____ tener una menor.   peor que
7. Estar de vacaciones es _____ estar en casa.   mejor que

A9   ## ESTRUCTURAS ESENCIALES
Stressed possessive adjectives

There are two sets of possessive adjectives in Spanish. You already know the short forms, **mi, tu, su,** and **nuestro,** which are used before nouns. The following chart shows the stressed possessive adjectives that follow the nouns.

	Masculine	*Feminine*
my	**mío, míos**	**mía, mías**
your (*familiar*)	**tuyo, tuyos**	**tuya, tuyas**
your (*polite*), his, her, its, their	**suyo, suyos**	**suya, suyas**
our	**nuestro, nuestros**	**nuestra, nuestras**

1. Stressed possessive adjectives are used for emphasis and therefore they are stressed in pronunciation. Note that they are generally used with the article.

   la bicicleta **mía**   *my bicycle (the bicycle of mine)*
   el pasaporte **mío**   *my passport (the passport of mine)*

2. Stressed possessive adjectives always follow the noun they modify. They agree in gender and number with the noun.

   mi amigo = **el** amigo **mío**   **mis** amigos = **los** amigos **míos**
   mi amiga = **la** amiga **mía**   **mis** amigas = **las** amigas **mías**

3. Note that the article is usually omitted after the verb **ser** when referring to people.

   Ella es **amiga mía.**   *She is a friend of mine.*
   Ellos son **amigos míos.**   *They are friends of mine.*

4. Following a noun, **suyo (-a, -os, -as)** may have several meanings: *your* (formal), *his, her, its,* or *their.* For clarification, it can be replaced with the following:

$$\text{de} + \begin{cases} \text{Ud., Uds.,} \\ \text{él, ella, ellos, ellas} \end{cases}$$

You may wish to review the short forms "mi," "tu," "su," and "nuestro," before introducing the stressed possessives. Point out how a change in word order affects the emphasis: "mi amigo" vs. "el amigo mío." In the first phrase the emphasis is on "amigo," *friend,* while in the second, it is on the adjective "mío," *mine,* stressing possession.

Actividad • Y ésta es . . . 🔲

You invited your friend Tomás to a family reunion. Now clarify for him who are the members of your family and friends. Follow the model and use stressed possessive adjectives.

> MODELO   David / hermano   Tomás, David es hermano mío.

1. doña Isabel / vecina
2. Roberto / tío
3. Elena / prima

4. Luisa y Ana / hermanas
5. el señor López / amigo
6. Raúl y Rita / primos

1. Tomás, doña Isabel es vecina mía.
2. Tomás, Roberto es tío mío.
3. Tomás, Elena es prima mía.
4. Tomás, Luisa y Ana son hermanas mías.
5. Tomás, el señor López es amigo mío.
6. Tomás, Raúl y Rita son primos míos.

A 11   **Actividad • De regreso**

Getting ready to come home from your vacation, your mother wants to make sure nothing is left behind. Complete each sentence with the correct form of **suyo**.

1. ¿Tiene Elenita la raqueta _suya_ ?
2. ¿Dónde están las maletas _suyas_ , debajo de la cama?
3. ¡Ay, papá no sabe dónde están los cheques de viajero _suyos_ !
4. ¿Tiene Pablo la chaqueta _suya_ ?
5. No encuentro el pasaporte _suyo_ .
6. Éstos son los míos. ¿Dónde están los zapatos de tenis _suyos_ ?
7. Pepe no debe olvidar la cámara _suya_ .
8. Aquí están las fotos _suyas_ .

A 12   **Actividad • ¿Quién es?** 🔲

You are showing a family album to friends. They are confused and need more information about your family members. Change the underlined possessive adjectives to prepositional phrases.

> MODELO   Aquí está Elena con el esposo suyo.
>   Aquí está Elena con el esposo **de ella**.

1. Ésta es mi prima Rosalía, con Cuchi, el perro suyo.   de ella
2. Éste es mi tío Juan con la hija suya.   de él
3. Aquí está doña Elvira al lado de un amigo suyo.   de ella
4. Éstos son mis amigos con unos primos suyos.   de ellos
5. Aquí está la esposa de mi hermano con los padres suyos.   de ella
6. En esta foto estamos con Andrés, María y el esposo suyo.   de ella

Use contrasting examples to further illustrate the explanation: "su bicicleta, la bicicleta suya, la suya (de: él, ella, Ud., Uds.)."
Continue with a personalized question/answer drill addressing the students individually: "—¿Dónde están sus libros? —Los
míos están . . . —¿Dónde están los de él? . . ."

A13 ESTRUCTURAS ESENCIALES
Possessive pronouns: fewer words to say the same thing

El estéreo mío es fantástico.	*My stereo is fantastic.*
El mío es fantástico.	*Mine is fantastic.*
El cuaderno tuyo está aquí.	*Your notebook is here.*
El tuyo está aquí.	*Yours is here.*
Los lápices suyos están en la mesa.	*Your (Her, His, Their) pencils are on the table.*
Los suyos están en la mesa.	*Yours (Hers, His, Theirs) are on the table.*

1. Notice that the stressed possessive adjectives are also used as possessive pronouns by omitting the nouns they accompany.

2. The definite article and the possessive pronoun agree in number and gender with the omitted noun, that is, with the thing possessed.

A14 Actividad • ¡Demasiadas palabras!   For answers, see p. T51.

Everybody knows someone who talks too much. You like to be brief and to say things differently. Eliminate as many unnecessary nouns as you can from the following paragraph. Use possessive pronouns.

Tú tienes ya los discos míos y los discos tuyos. Necesitamos todos los discos tuyos y todos los discos míos. Mañana necesitamos también los discos de Cheo, el radio grande y el radio nuevo. La música es para la fiesta de cumpleaños, el cumpleaños mío y el cumpleaños de Marilú, mi hermana gemela.

A15 Actividad • Charla   Answers will vary.

Tu familia y la mía   Pair up with a classmate. Take turns describing at least five members of your family and maybe a very close friend. Ask each other questions, including all the different ways of indicating possession that you have learned.

MODELO   El tío mío es ingeniero y le gusta tomar fotografías cuando va de viaje.

Con la familia   59

Los colonizadores *(settlers)* españoles fundaron *(founded)* la ciudad de San Juan, hoy el Viejo San Juan, en 1508. Muchas de sus estrechas *(narrow)* calles tienen vista a la bahía *(bay)* y a la ciudad moderna. Allí podemos entrar en sus tiendas de artesanía y galerías de arte. Y podemos descansar en sus frescos parques y plazas. También podemos visitar iglesias y conventos históricos, o almorzar en algunos de los variados *(varied)* restaurantes. La famosa fortaleza *(fortress)* de El Morro queda en esa parte de la ciudad.

FOLLETO TURÍSTICO *(Tourist pamphlet)* — lugares para ver:
1. **El Morro:** defendió *(defended)* la ciudad contra Sir Francis Drake hace más de 350 años.
2. **La Muralla:** sólo queda parte de este famoso muro *(wall)*.
3. **Calles de Escaleras:** Callejón de las Monjas *(Nuns)* y Caleta del Hospital.
4. **La iglesia de San José:** una de las más antiguas y bellas del hemisferio.
5. **La Fortaleza:** palacio del gobernador. Antigua defensa contra los indios.
6. **La Catedral:** saqueada *(looted)* por los ingleses. Restaurada *(restored)* en el siglo XIX.
7. **La Casa Blanca:** casa de la familia de Ponce de León, primer gobernador de Puerto Rico y descubridor *(discoverer)* de la Florida.

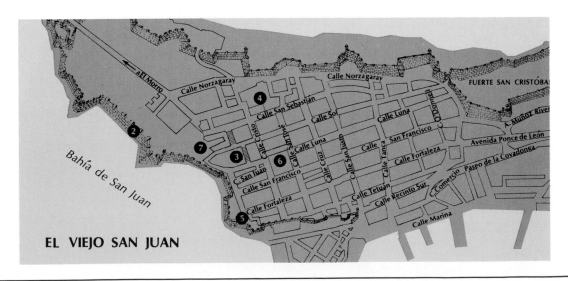

EL VIEJO SAN JUAN

ESTRUCTURAS ESENCIALES
Comparisons of equality: tan . . . como . . .

To express the comparison *as . . . as* in Spanish with adjectives or adverbs, use:

	adjective	
tan +	*or*	+ **como**
	adverb	

Mi estéreo es **tan bueno como** el tuyo.   *My stereo is as good as yours.*
Corro **tan rápidamente como** él.   *I run as fast as he does.*

A 18   Actividad • En Puerto Rico For answers, see p. T52.

Pair up with a classmate. Ask questions following the model.

MODELO lindo playa / sierra — ¿Cuál es más linda, la playa
o la sierra?
— La playa es tan linda como
la sierra.

1. caliente   el Atlántico / el Caribe
2. interesante   la capital / el campo
3. famoso   El Morro / El Yunque
4. divertido   el Viejo San Juan / el San Juan moderno
5. azul   el mar / el cielo
6. viejo   el disco mío / el de ella

A 19   Actividad • Mis amigos Answers will vary.

All your friends have different abilities. Compare seven of them, using complete
sentences. Follow the model. You may use pronouns or your friends' real names to
refer to them.

MODELO bailar bien   Roberto no baila tan bien como Luis.

1. correr rápidamente   5. nadar mal
2. remar fuerte(mente)   6. jugar al tenis frecuentemente
3. escribir claramente   7. patinar bien
4. ganar dinero fácilmente

Con la familia **61**

You may wish to mention that "tanto . . . como" can also be used with verbs: "No escribo tanto como tú. Marta estudia tanto como Paula."

A 20 ESTRUCTURAS ESENCIALES
Comparisons of equality: tanto . . . como . . .

To express the comparisons *as much . . . as* and *as many . . . as* with nouns, in Spanish you use:

tanto (-a, -os, -as)	+	noun	+	**como**

Tengo **tanto tiempo como** tú.   *I have as much time as you do.*
Compré **tantos discos como** él.   *I bought as many records as he did.*

For answers, see p. T53. Notice that this activity, like several others, requires some logical thinking on part of the students. Encourage the students to use the correct subject when working in pairs.

A 21 Actividad • El fanfarrón

No matter what you say, **el fanfarrón** feels the need to upstage you. Get together with a classmate, decide who will be **el fanfarrón** or **la fanfarrona,** and discuss the following items according to the model.

MODELO   Elena / tú   discos   — Elena tiene tantos discos como tú.
                                           — ¡Oh, no! Yo tengo más discos que Elena.

1. tú / Cheo   primos
2. Paco / tú   amigos
3. yo / tú   videos
4. Carlos / tú   tiempo
5. tú / yo   libros
6. tú / Enrique   fotos

A 22 Comprensión   For script, see p. T53.

You will hear ten statements comparing two people or objects. Each statement will be followed by a conclusion. If the conclusion is true, check **sí** on your answer sheet. If it is not, check **no**.

MODELO   Alicia tiene quince años y Teresa tiene dieciséis.
              Teresa es menor que Alicia.

	0	1	2	3	4	5	6	7	8	9	10
Sí		✔			✔	✔	✔		✔	✔	✔
No	✔		✔	✔				✔			

A 23 Actividad • ¡A escribir!   Answers will vary.

Imagine you are visiting relatives. Write a letter to your parents or to a brother or sister. Write the date correctly. Use the salutations and complimentary closings that you learned in Unit 1, Section C. Write about new friends or about members of your family, comparing their preferences.

*In many Hispanic homes, especially those in the United States, household chores are usually
divided among the family members. Each member should do his or her share of the work . . .
Sometimes problems arise.*

B1

Obligaciones familiares 📼

DÍA:	domingo por la noche
LUGAR:	la casa de los Gómez
OCASIÓN:	una agitada reunión familiar
MOTIVO:	dividir las tareas de la casa entre los cuatro hermanos: Luis Andrés, 17 años; Rosalía, 15 años; Mayra, 13 años; y Gerardo, 12 años

DIVISIÓN DE TAREAS

Todos los hermanos deben ayudar y hacer algo en la
casa. Pero, ¿qué es lo que va a hacer cada uno la semana
próxima? No están de acuerdo. Todos quieren hacer
lo menos posible. Nadie está contento. Los chicos,
preocupados, miran la lista de tareas en la puerta
del refrigerador.

ordenar el cuarto
Hacer la cama

poner la mesa
quitar la mesa

Refrío

llevar la ropa
a lavar
sacar la basura

sacar al perro a
pasear. Bañar
y cepillar al
perro.

cuidar los peces
limpiar el acuario

lavar los platos
y secarlos
Pasar la aspiradora

GERARDO	Lo siento, esta semana no puedo ayudarlos. ¡Tengo muchas cosas que hacer!
ROSALÍA	¿Cómo? ¿Otra vez . . . ? Pero, ¿qué dices?
GERARDO	Digo que esta semana no puedo. La semana que viene hago el doble. ¡Les prometo que sí!
LUIS ANDRÉS	¡Qué coraje! La semana pasada dijiste lo mismo. Siempre tienes una excusa. Tú crees que como eres menor . . .
GERARDO	Sí, como soy menor que ustedes, nadie me escucha. Ustedes saben que canté con el coro de la escuela el viernes pasado. Ya les expliqué que esta semana tenemos ensayo todos los días.

Mayra propone una solución

Es tarde y la discusión sigue en la casa de los Gómez.

ROSALÍA	La semana pasada, yo saqué a Cuchi a pasear todos los días. Le di de comer, lo bañé, lo cepillé . . . No le pedí ayuda a nadie.
MAYRA	¡Por favor! Un momento, pido la palabra.
LUIS ANDRÉS	¡Atención! ¡Atención! La señorita Mayra, el genio de la familia Gómez, pidió la palabra. Ahora con ustedes . . .
MAYRA	¡Mayra Gómez!, que les pide silencio, y les da una solución: poner todas las notas del refrigerador en un sombrero y, . . . ¡a escoger!

Actividad • Preguntas y respuestas

Answer the following questions according to B1.

1. ¿Qué deben hacer los cuatro hermanos?
2. ¿Por qué no están contentos?
3. ¿Cuántas tareas hay?
4. ¿Por qué no puede Gerardo participar en las tareas familiares?
5. ¿Qué promete él hacer la semana que viene?
6. ¿Qué dijo Gerardo la semana pasada? ¿Qué hizo?
7. ¿Qué le dice a él su hermano mayor?
8. ¿Quién es el hermano menor?
9. ¿Cuándo tiene ensayo el coro?
10. Gerardo dice que nadie lo escucha. ¿Por qué?
11. ¿Qué hizo Rosalía la semana pasada?
12. ¿Qué solución ofreció Mayra?

1. Los cuatro hermanos deben ayudar y hacer algo en la casa. 2. Porque quieren hacer lo menos posible. 3. Hay doce tareas. 4. Gerardo no puede participar porque tiene muchas cosas que hacer. 5. La semana que viene Gerardo promete hacer el doble. 6. La semana pasada Gerardo dijo lo mismo. No hizo nada. 7. Su hermano mayor le dice a él que siempre tiene una excusa. 8. Gerardo es el hermano menor. 9. El coro tiene ensayo todos los días. 10. Gerardo dice que nadie lo escucha porque es menor que ellos. 11. La semana pasada Rosalía sacó a Cuchi a pasear todos los días, le dio de comer, lo bañó y lo cepilló. 12. Mayra ofreció poner todas las notas del refrigerador en un sombrero y escoger.

B3 Actividad • No es así. ¿Cómo es?

Correct these statements to make them agree with the dialog in B1.

1. La discusión ya terminó en casa de los Gómez.
2. Rosalía propone una solución.
3. La semana pasada, Gerardo sacó a pasear a Cuchi todos los días.
4. Rosalía le dio de comer a su hermano menor.
5. Rosalía les pidió ayuda a todos.
6. Luis Andrés es el genio de la familia.
7. La solución fue poner las notas en la basura.

1. La discusión sigue en casa de los Gómez. 2. Mayra propone una solución. 3. La semana pasada, Rosalía sacó a pasear a Cuchi todos los días. 4. Rosalía le dio de comer a Cuchi. 5. Rosalía no le pidió ayuda a nadie. 6. Mayra es el genio de la familia. 7. La solución fue poner las notas en un sombrero y escoger.

B4 Sabes que . . .

La familia es una institución valiosa (*valuable*) en la sociedad hispana. El padre casi siempre es el cabeza de familia y la madre también es muy importante. Ella dirige (*manages*) la casa y toma parte en las decisiones. [Constantemente aumenta (*increases*) el número de mujeres que trabaja en empleos (*jobs*) y profesiones.] La familia también incluye (*includes*) a otros familiares (*close relatives*): los abuelos, los tíos, los primos. Estos familiares a veces viven todos en una misma casa. Los hijos, si trabajan, ayudan con los gastos (*expenses*). En la familia hispana todos se ayudan (*help each other*). Muchas veces los hijos casados viven en la casa. La profesión de los hijos depende en parte de los padres, pero generalmente los jóvenes pueden escoger. La familia casi siempre va junta de vacaciones, de visita y a otros lugares. Cuando hay alguna fiesta importante, la celebran con una gran reunión familiar donde vienen todos los parientes (*distant relatives*).

B5 Actividad • ¡A escribir!   Answers will vary.

Write a list of at least eight household chores. Then distribute them among the members of your family in any way you would like.

B6 SE DICE ASÍ
Making excuses

Lo siento, no puedo ayudarlos.	I'm sorry, I can't help you.
¡Tengo tantas cosas que hacer!	I have so much to do!
¡Estoy tan ocupado(a)...!	I'm so busy...!
¡Estoy tan cansado(a)...!	I'm so tired...!
La próxima vez...Hoy no, otro día.	Next time...Not today, another day.

B7 Actividad • ¡Siempre tienen una buena excusa!   Answers will vary.
One example is given.

Imagine that you ask some of your friends to help you clean your uncle's garage. Think of six excuses that they might find, and how you might convince them to help.   1. Lo siento, no puedo ayudarte porque es el cumpleaños de mi hermano.
Pero, creo que el cumpleaños de tu hermano es el sábado y hoy es viernes.

B8 SITUACIÓN • Algunos animales

Most people love animals and Spanish Americans are no different. Here are some popular and not so popular animals that they like to keep as pets:

3. el caballo
1. el pájaro
2. el loro
4. los conejos
5. los ratones blancos

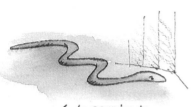

6. la serpiente

7. los peces

8. las ranas

9. la tortuga

B 9 **Actividad • Animales domésticos** For answers, see p. T56.

Carlitos and Mariana love animals. He and his sister have to take care of their pets. Get together with a classmate and play both roles, according to the model.

MODELO   dar de comer / tortuga
— ¿Le diste de comer a mi tortuga?
— No, le di de comer a la mía.

1. cepillar / caballo
2. dar la zanahoria / conejos
3. cuidar / serpiente
4. limpiar la jaula / pájaro
5. lavar el plato / gata

6. bañar / perro
7. cambiar el agua / ranas
8. hablar con / loro
9. dar lechuga / ratones blancos
10. dar de comer / peces

B 10 **Actividad • Tus animales preferidos**   Answers will vary.

Pair up with a classmate and ask the following questions. Then switch roles and repeat the activity.

1. ¿Cuál es tu animal favorito?   Mi animal favorito es . . .
2. ¿Tienes algún animal en tu casa?   Sí, tengo . . .
3. ¿Quién lo cuida?   Yo cuido a mi animal.
4. ¿Cuántas veces al día le das de comer?   Le doy de comer . . .
5. ¿Dónde lo tienes?   Lo tengo en . . .
6. ¿En qué parte de la casa come el animal?   El animal come en . . .
7. ¿Cómo se llama tu animal?   Mi animal se llama . . .
8. ¿Cómo es?   Es muy . . . tiene . . .
9. ¿Hay un animal que no te gusta? ¿Cuál?   No me gusta . . .
10. ¿Cuál o cuáles de los animales en B8 quieres tener?   Quiero tener . . .

ESTRUCTURAS ESENCIALES
Stem-changing verbs like pedir (e→i)

A. Present tense

pedir	*to ask for*
pido	pedimos
pides	pedís
pide	piden

Yo **pido** ayuda.   *I ask for help.*
Nosotros **pedimos** silencio.   *We ask for silence.*

1. You have already learned that in the present indicative some Spanish verbs like **pedir** change the stressed **e** in the stem to **i** in all forms except the **nosotros** and **vosotros** forms.

2. Other verbs like **pedir** are **servir** *(to serve)*, **seguir** *(to follow; to continue)*, **vestir** *(to dress)*, **repetir** *(to repeat)*, and **conseguir** *(to get; to obtain)*.

   Carlitos **repite** la canción.   *Carlitos repeats the song.*
   ¿Quién **consigue** los refrescos?   *Who gets the refreshments?*

B. Preterit tense

pedir	*to ask for*
pedí	pedimos
pediste	pedisteis
pidió	pidieron

Ella no **pidió** excusas.   *She did not ask for excuses.*
Sirvieron el desayuno.   *They served breakfast.*
Conseguí la comida para los peces.   *I got the fish food.*
El profesor **repitió** la pregunta.   *The professor repeated the question.*

Verbs like **pedir** also have the stem change **e** to **i** in the preterit, but *only* in the third person, both singular and plural.

Actividad • **Todos piden algo**

Imagine that it is Sunday morning and everybody is asking for something. Complete the following sentences with the correct form of **pedir.**

1. Papá _____ el desayuno. pide
2. Mamá _____ la leche que está en el refrigerador. pide
3. Nosotros _____ el periódico. pedimos
4. El loro _____ su comida. pide
5. Yo _____ no lavar los platos hoy. pido
6. Mis hermanas mayores _____ silencio. piden
7. Ellas _____ permiso para ir al parque. piden

Actividad • ¡A escoger!

What happened here last weekend? Explain who did what by combining elements from these three columns.   Answers will vary. Possible answers are given.

Mis amigas pidieron ayuda. Un primo suyo sirvió la ensalada. Yo seguí las instrucciones. Mi mejor amigo consiguió unos peces. Nosotros repetimos el número de teléfono.

mis amigas	pedir	ayuda
un primo suyo	servir	las instrucciones
yo	repetir	la ensalada
mi mejor amigo	seguir	unos peces
nosotros	conseguir	el número de teléfono

Actividad • La reunión familiar   Answers will vary.

There was a family reunion at your home last week. There were a lot of people and everyone had fun. You were very busy because everybody was asking for something. Say what each person asked for. Use the verb **pedir**.

Dora y Paco   Los gemelos   Mi primo Luis   Tío Guillermo

Tía Anita   Tú   Nosotros   Mamá y papá   Doña Ana

refresco   chocolate   café con leche   jamón   bocadillo   queso

enchiladas   jugo   vaso de agua   tortilla   gaseosa

Sabes que . . .

Spanish has two words for the English word *fish*. **Los peces** (*sing.*: **pez**) are alive and swimming. **El pescado** is the fish after it has been caught.

Actividad • Y tú, ¿qué hiciste? Answers will vary. Possible answers are given.

It is Friday and your family wants to know if you did all of the
things you were supposed to do before going out. Answer the following
questions. If you didn't do what was asked, explain why not.

> MODELO ¿Pasaste la aspiradora?
> Sí, la pasé. *or* No, no la pasé. No tuve tiempo.

1. ¿Quitaste la mesa? Sí, la quité.
2. ¿Lavaste los platos
   y los secaste? Sí, los lavé y los sequé.
3. ¿Sacaste la basura? No, no la saqué. No tuve tiempo.
4. ¿Le diste de comer al perro? No, no le di de comer. No tuve tiempo.
5. ¿Limpiaste el acuario? Sí, lo limpié.
6. ¿Ordenaste tu cuarto? No, no lo ordené. No tuve tiempo.
7. ¿Llamaste a tu tía? Sí, la llamé.

B17 **Actividad • ¿Qué hizo el robot?** Answers will vary.

Wouldn't it be great to have a robot to do your household chores! Make believe that
you have just bought one. Tell an interested classmate what the robot did during
the first week. Also tell him or her what the robot did not do.

B18 **SITUACIÓN • ¿Me dan permiso?**

Los amigos de Lucila preparan una excursión para el
fin de semana. A Lucila le gusta mucho la idea, pero
no sabe si sus padres le van a dar permiso.

> PAPÁ ¿Qué pasa, Lucila? ¿Por qué tienes esa
> cara tan triste?
> MAMÁ El problema es que tu hija quiere ir de
> excursión el sábado, y no le doy
> permiso. Con las notas que tiene . . .
> PAPÁ Tu madre tiene razón, Lucila. Tú no
> puedes ir.
> LUCILA Pero, por favor . . . es un solo día . . .
> La semana que viene voy a estudiar
> todos los días. Lo prometo.

B19 **Actividad • Por favor, ¡denme permiso!**

Answer the following questions according to the dialog in B18.

1. ¿Por qué está triste Lucila? Lucila está triste porque no sabe si sus padres le van a dar permiso para ir de excursión.
2. ¿Adónde quiere ir? Lucila quiere ir de excursión.
3. ¿Por qué no puede ir? Lucila no puede ir porque no le dan permiso.
4. ¿Quién no le da permiso? Su mamá no le da permiso.
5. ¿Cómo son las notas de Lucila? Las notas de Lucila son malas.
6. ¿Qué promete Lucila? Lucila promete estudiar todos los días la semana que viene.

B 20 Actividad • ¿Le dieron permiso o no? Answers will vary.

Do you think Lucila should go? Act out the conversation with two classmates. Change the kind of activity to: **ir al cine, acampar, bailar,** or **dar un viaje.** Explain why she can't go by using **no limpió su cuarto, no le dio de comer al perro,** and so forth.

B 21 Comprensión For script, see p. T59.

The Gómez children are still arguing about the family chores. You will hear ten short conversational exchanges. If the two speakers agree, check **de acuerdo** *(in agreement)* on your answer sheet. If they disagree, check **en desacuerdo** *(in disagreement).*

MODELO — Tú nunca me ayudas a limpiar el baño.
— ¡No es cierto! Te ayudé la semana pasada.

	0	1	2	3	4	5	6	7	8	9	10
De acuerdo		✔		✔			✔		✔	✔	
En desacuerdo	✔		✔		✔	✔		✔			✔

B 22 ESTRUCTURAS ESENCIALES
The preterit tense of the irregular verb decir

decir *to tell; to say*	
dije	dijimos
dijiste	dijisteis
dijo	dijeron

¿Qué **dijeron?**   *What did they say?*
Dijeron que Luisa no pudo ir.   *They said that Luisa could not go.*

The verb **decir** has a stem change **e→i** in all forms of the preterit. In addition, it changes the **c** to **j** in all forms.

B 23 Actividad • Chismes *Gossip*

You told a secret to your best friend, Orlando, with strict instructions that he not spread it around. But now you hear your own secret from María! Trace the route your secret took by following the model.

MODELO Yo / Orlando   Yo le dije el secreto a Orlando.

1. Orlando / Marilú y Luci
2. Marilú y Luci / ti
3. tú / mis primos
4. mis primos / Margarita
5. Margarita / sus primas
6. sus primas / María

1. Orlando les dijo el secreto a Marilú y a Luci.
2. Marilú y Luci te dijeron el secreto a ti.
3. Tú les dijiste el secreto a mis primos.
4. Mis primos le dijeron el secreto a Margarita.
5. Margarita les dijo el secreto a sus primas.
6. Sus primas le dijeron el secreto a María.

Con la familia   71

persuading somebody to lend you something . . . confirming expected courses of action

Who has not asked somebody for something? Hispanic teenagers are no different from American teenagers, and they also borrow things from their friends. Sometimes one has to be very persuasive.

C1 Problemas y más problemas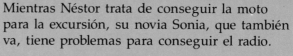

Néstor quiere ir de excursión en la moto¹ de su hermano.

NÉSTOR   Oye, Germán, voy a ir de excursión con mis amigos. ¿Me puedes prestar tu moto?

GERMÁN   ¿Te la piensas llevar todo el fin de semana? ¿Viernes, sábado y domingo?

NÉSTOR   No, me la prestas el sábado solamente. El domingo te la devuelvo sin falta. Yo te dejo mi bicicleta si quieres.

GERMÁN   Bueno, está bien. Te la presto si me la cuidas . . . Pero, si le pasa algo a la moto, tú pagas la reparación, ¿de acuerdo?

Mientras Néstor trata de conseguir la moto para la excursión, su novia Sonia, que también va, tiene problemas para conseguir el radio.

SONIA   ¡Ay, caramba! Si tú no puedes ir a la excursión, no vamos a tener música . . . Marta me dijo que tú nos puedes prestar tu radio. Nos lo prestas, ¿verdad?

HILDA   No sé, el radio no es sólo mío, ¿sabes? Es mío y de mi hermana. Tengo que hablar con ella. Pero creo que te lo podemos prestar.

SONIA   Tú puedes hablar con ella y decírselo, ¿no? Yo te llamo esta tarde. ¿Está bien?

HILDA   De acuerdo. Hasta luego, Sonia.

°**La moto** is the short form for **la motocicleta** and that is why it takes a feminine article. Another word that follows this pattern is **la foto,** a short form of **la fotografía.**

C2 Actividad • No es así

Correct these statements to make them agree with the dialog in C1.

1. Néstor le pide la bicicleta a Germán.   Néstor le pide la moto a Germán.
2. Germán la necesita por todo el fin de semana.   Néstor la necesita solamente para el sábado.
3. Néstor la necesita para ir a la escuela.   Néstor la necesita para ir de excursión con sus amigos.
4. El domingo Néstor le deja su bicicleta a Germán.   El domingo Néstor le devuelve la moto a Germán.
5. Si Néstor no la cuida, Germán paga la reparación.   Si Néstor no la cuida, Néstor paga la reparación.
6. El radio es de Hilda.   El radio es de Hilda y de su hermana.
7. Hilda le puede prestar el radio a la hermana de Sonia.   Hilda cree que le puede prestar el radio a Sonia.
8. Hilda puede decírselo a Sonia.   Hilda puede hablar con su hermana y decírselo.
9. Sonia le dice a Hilda que es tarde.   Sonia le dice a Hilda que la llama esta tarde.

C3 Actividad • Para completar

Use the information in C1 to help you choose the correct ending for each sentence.

1. Néstor no tiene
   • amigos.   • bicicleta.   • moto.

2. Él piensa ir de excursión
   • el sábado.   • el domingo.   • el fin de semana.

3. Si le pasa algo a la moto, Néstor
   • la cuida.   • la devuelve.   • paga la reparación.

4. Hilda no puede
   • ir.   • tener música.   • prestar su moto.

5. El radio es de
   • Hilda.   • su hermana.   • Hilda y su hermana.

6. Sonia tiene que llamar a
   • su hermana.   • Hilda.   • una amiga suya.

7. Hilda cree que puede
   • prestarle el radio.   • llamar esa tarde.   • hablar con Sonia.

A los jóvenes hispanos les gusta hacer las mismas cosas que hacen los jóvenes de todo el mundo. Ahora sí *(However)*, los hispanos prefieren *(prefer)* las diversiones en grupo. Generalmente, los miembros del grupo son compañeros de escuela, familiares o vecinos de una misma clase social. En cada país estos grupos reciben nombres diferentes: la pandilla *(gang)*, la banda, el grupo. Los amigos se reúnen *(meet)* en casa de un miembro del grupo, en un banco del parque *(park bench)*, en una esquina, en el café favorito o en un club social. Las diversiones favoritas son: cambiar impresiones sobre un tópico de interés, escuchar música, mirar televisión o practicar algún deporte. También se reúnen para hacer la tarea, ir al cine o ir a otro lugar. Los miembros del grupo van a fiestas, excursiones y paseos, y en estas reuniones es común *(common)* ver a las personas mayores de la familia. Lo importante es que todos participan.

C5   SE DICE ASÍ
Confirming expected courses of action

Me llamas luego, ¿verdad?	You'll call me later, right?
Puedes hablar con ella, ¿no?	You can talk to her, can't you?
Te llamo esta tarde, ¿está bien?	I'll call you this afternoon, all right?

Tag questions are very common in Spanish. They may have different equivalents in English, such as: *is it?*, *isn't it?*, *are you?*, *aren't you?*, and *all right?*

Actividad • Sólo para mí

There are a few things some people would prefer not to share with anyone. Form sentences with the clues provided. Can you add a few of your own or do you share everything?

MODELO   un secreto / decir   Tengo un secreto, ¡y no quiero **decírselo** a nadie!

1. un estéreo / prestar
2. unos esquís / dar
3. unas tarjetas postales / mandar
4. una bicicleta / vender
5. una amiga / presentar
6. un helado / ofrecer
7. unas cartas / leer

1. Tengo un estéreo, ¡y no quiero prestárselo a nadie!   2. Tengo unos esquís, ¡y no quiero dárselos a nadie! 3. Tengo unas tarjetas postales, ¡y no quiero mandárselas a nadie!   4. Tengo una bicicleta, ¡y no quiero vendérsela a nadie!   5. Tengo una amiga, ¡y no quiero presentársela a nadie!   6. Tengo un helado, ¡y no quiero ofrecérselo a nadie!   7. Tengo unas cartas, ¡y no quiero leérselas a nadie!

C16   Actividad • ¿Lo hago hoy?

You often act without thinking. Today you have decided to stop and think first. Make up nine sentences following the model.

MODELO   le presto los discos   Siempre le presto los discos. ¿Se los presto hoy?

1. le consigo el libro
2. les cuido los perros
3. le preparo el desayuno
4. les compro flores
5. le presto las revistas
6. le doy un beso
7. les digo la verdad
8. le doy permiso
9. le pido la cámara

1. Siempre le consigo el libro. ¿Se lo consigo hoy?   2. Siempre les cuido los perros. ¿Se los cuido hoy?   3. Siempre le preparo el desayuno. ¿Se lo preparo hoy?   4. Siempre les compro flores. ¿Se las compro hoy? 5. Siempre le presto las revistas. ¿Se las presto hoy?   6. Siempre le doy un beso. ¿Se lo doy hoy?   7. Siempre les digo la verdad. ¿Se la digo hoy?   8. Siempre le doy permiso. ¿Se lo doy hoy?   9. Siempre le pido la cámara. ¿Se la pido hoy?

C17   Actividad • Charla   Answers will vary.

Get together with a classmate and ask each other about the favors you do for your friends or members of your family.

For additional background on Xochimilco, see p. T65.

1 Vacaciones en México

Suppose your best friend has gone to Mexico with his or her parents for a vacation. Your friend writes you the following letter.

> Querido amigo:
>
> La paso de maravilla en la Ciudad de México con papá y mamá. El lunes fuimos al Museo de Antropología y mañana vamos a ir a los jardines de Xochimilco. Tomé muchas fotos que te van a gustar mucho. ¿Cómo estás tú? ¿Qué tal los amigos? Les mando muchos recuerdos a todos.
>
> Un abrazo,

Answer the letter, telling your friend how you and your friends are. Also include news about school and the town. Don't forget to wish your friend a happy stay in Mexico before saying goodbye.

2 Actividad • Ahora son amigos tuyos

Introduce Raúl, a friend of yours, to your family and friends. Use stressed possessive adjectives.

MODELO   Carlos / primo   Raúl, Carlos es primo mío.

1. Manolo / amigo
2. Trini y Nora / vecinas
3. Alicia / tía

1. Raúl, Manolo es amigo mío.   2. Raúl, Trini y Nora son vecinas mías.   3. Raúl, Alicia es tía mía.

4. el señor Pérez / profesor
5. Rubén y Andrés / hermanos
6. Virginia / prima

4. Raúl, el señor Pérez es profesor mío.
5. Raúl, Rubén y Andrés son hermanos míos.
6. Raúl, Virginia es prima mía.

3 Actividad • La mía es mejor que ésa

Answers will vary. Possible answers are given.

Compare the following and decide if one is better or worse than the other.

1. Estar triste es _____ estar contento.   peor que
2. Tener muchos amigos es _____ tener pocos.   mejor que
3. Un estéreo viejo es _____ uno nuevo.   peor que
4. Estar con los amigos es _____ estar solo.   mejor que
5. Unas vacaciones largas son _____ que unas cortas.   mejores que
6. Un examen difícil es _____ uno fácil.   peor que
7. Un vestido bonito es _____ uno feo.   mejor que

4 Actividad • El tuyo y el mío

This activity may be done orally or in writing.

Restate each sentence, using fewer words or replacing nouns with pronouns.

1. Aquí está el mío, pero no veo tu disco.   Aquí está el mío, pero no veo el tuyo.
2. Yo no tengo el radio de Elena.   Yo no tengo el suyo.
3. Compramos nuestros regalos ayer.   Compramos los nuestros ayer.
4. Los primos de ellos son simpáticos.   Los suyos son simpáticos.
5. Encontré tu revista allí.   Encontré la tuya allí.

5 Actividad • Bailo tan bien como tú

Your friends are comparing skills. Write complete sentences, using **tan . . . como.**

1. Juanita / Susana   correr / rápido   Juanita corre tan rápido como Susana.
2. yo / tú   ser / simpático   Yo soy tan simpático como tú.
3. Gaby / Rubén   hablar / claramente   Gaby habla tan claramente como Rubén.
4. tú / ella   cantar / mal   Tú cantas tan mal como ella.
5. nosotros / ellos   ahorrar dinero / fácilmente   Nosotros ahorramos dinero tan fácilmente como ellos.

6 Actividad • Tengo tantos como él

No one wants to be number two, but being number one is not always necessary. Make comparisons, using **tanto(s) . . . como.**

MODELO   Tengo tantos videos como tú.

amigos / dinero / primos / discos / revistas / jeans

Tengo tantos amigos como tú.
Tengo tanto dinero como tú.
Tengo tantos primos como tú.
Tengo tantos discos como tú.
Tengo tantas revistas como tú.
Tengo tantos jeans como tú.

7 Actividad • A completar

Complete each sentence with the appropriate form of the verb in parentheses.

1. (pedir) El perro __pide__ su comida.
2. (decir) David siempre __dice__ la verdad.
3. (seguir) El director __siguió__ enfermo.

4. (servir) ¿Quién __sirvió__ la ensalada el lunes pasado?
5. (repetir) Roberto __repitió__ el examen ayer.

8 Actividad • A usar la imaginación   Answers will vary.

See how many sentences in the preterit you can make using one word or phrase from each box.

el primo mío *la gente* **mi tía** la invitada su novio el abuelo	**decir** proponer sacar quitar *secar* **prestar**	la basura los platos *otra fiesta* **la verdad** sus discos la mesa

9 Actividad • ¿Vas a decírmelo?

Rewrite the following sentences using object pronouns.

MODELO   Me vas a cuidar los peces.   Vas a cuidármelos.

1. Me quiero poner el abrigo. Quiero ponérmelo.
2. Luis no te puede escribir la carta. Luis no puede escribírtela.

3. Nos van a prestar el dinero. Van a prestárnoslo.
4. Me tiene que dar el permiso. Tiene que dármelo.
5. Le debo comprar la camisa. Debo comprársela.

10 Actividad • ¿Cuál puede ser la pregunta?   Answers will vary. Possible answers are given.

Write a question that fits each of the following answers.

MODELO   Sí, se lo dije.   ¿Le dijiste el número?

1. Sí, se los pedí. ¿Le pediste los libros?
2. Sí, se la preparó. ¿Le preparó la cena?
3. No, no se las compré. ¿Le compraste las flores?

4. Sí, se la presté. ¿Le prestaste la moto?
5. No, no se lo dijeron. ¿Le dijeron el secreto?
6. Sí, se la hice. ¿Le hiciste la tarea?

11 Dictado   For script, see p. T66.

Copy the following letter to prepare yourself for dictation.

Querida prima,

Paso unos días con _____ . Sabes que _____ Puerto Rico, _____ que estoy _____ .

Ayer _____ a San Juan con _____ y _____ muchas cosas. _____ a abuela con _____ de

la casa. Esta mañana _____ mi cuarto.

Muchos recuerdos de

_____

Diphthongs with *a, e,* and *o*

1. The Spanish vowels **a**, **e**, and **o** combine with **i** and **u** to form diphthongs. Each vowel maintains its individual sound, open and without glides, and **a**, **e**, and **o** are normally stressed. Pronounce each vowel clearly.

jueves	seis	nuestro	piano
baila	siete	Dios	acuario

El jueves seis, Antonio bailó.
Eusebio toca nuestro piano.
Clara tiene seis peces en el acuario.

2. The vowels **a**, **e**, and **o** cannot be combined with each other to form diphthongs. Each one claims a syllable for itself.

mu-se-o	ve-o	es-té-re-o	cum-ple-a-ños
vi-de-o	pe-or	co-rre-o	ca-e

Veo cuadros en el museo.
Mi estéreo es peor que el tuyo.
Mandé la tarjeta de cumpleaños por correo.

Stressed syllables

1. A written accent will tell you that the stress falls on the syllable with the accent mark. Read and compare:

café	cantó	fantástico	Tomás	
llegó	prestármelo	cámara	conseguí	

Atlántico	simpático	matemáticas	bolígrafo	jóvenes
dármelo	vendérmela	mandárnoslo	decírtelo	prestárnoslo

2. Vowels at the end of a word are not normally stressed. When they are stressed, an accent mark will indicate it. Read the following and compare:

llevo→**llevó**	paseo→**paseó**	bajo→**bajó**	cuido→**cuidó**
completo→**completó**	pesco→**pescó**	llego→**llegó**	limpio→**limpió**

Actividad • ¿Dónde están los acentos?   For answers, see p. T67.

Can you find the accents that are missing in the following paragraph? Read the paragraph aloud and try to find where the accents fall.

Ayer Ana limpio los zapatos, cepillo al perro y llevo la ropa a lavar. Después tuvo ensayo y canto en el coro. No pudo poner la mesa porque llego tarde. Ella tuvo una buena excusa hoy. Sus hermanos no pudieron decir nada. Ella trabajo bastante.

¿LO SABES?

Let's review some important points you've learned in this unit.

SECTION A

Answers will vary.

Can you write a letter in Spanish?
Write a letter to a friend or relative. Include the following:
    date   street address   salutation   complimentary closing
Don't forget to send regards.

Can you compare your two cousins, and then your bike and your grades with theirs?
Form as many comparisons as you can, using **mejor, peor, mayor,** and **menor.**
At the same time, emphasize possession with **mío** and **suyo.**

Are you able to clarify which cousin is the "possessor" by changing *suyo* **to some other way of expressing possession?**

Can you refer to the bike without saying the word *bike?*
Give two or three examples.

How do you express the comparison when you dance as well as your friend and you have as many records? Or you run as fast and have as many friends?
Using **tan . . . como** and **tanto . . . como,** write five sentences.

SECTION B

Answers will vary.

Can you mention five chores you do to help around the house?

Do you know how to make excuses?
Give three excuses why you could not help out this week.

Do you know how to make your position clear?
Suppose your brother and you have a conversation. He can't find a record of his, and you answer that you gave it to him. He says that you are not telling the truth and that he will not lend you any more records. You answer that you returned the record last Tuesday.

SECTION C

Can you persuade someone to lend you something?   Answers will vary.
What was the last thing you borrowed from a friend or a relative? Imagine that you need to borrow it again, but this time from a Spanish-speaking friend. How would you ask?

Can you use fewer words to say the same thing?
Change the following sentences by using fewer words.
1. Le voy a prestar el radio a ella.
2. Me tienes que dar las cartas.
3. Te acaban de dar la moto.
4. Raúl nos quiere dar los libros.

1. Se lo voy a prestar.   Voy a prestárselo.
2. Me las tienes que dar.   Tienes que dármelas.
3. Te la acaban de dar.   Acaban de dártela. .
4. Raúl nos los quiere dar.   Raúl quiere dárnoslos.

VOCABULARIO

de visita *visiting*
extrañar *to miss*
gemelo, -a *twin*
la paso muy bien *I'm having a good time*
mayor que *older than*
mejor que *better than*
menor que *younger than*
mío, -a *mine*
la **muchacha** *girl*
el **muchacho** *boy*
peor *worse*
peor que *worse than*
el **reloj** *watch*
salir bien *to turn out well*
suyo, -a *yours*
tan *so*
tan . . . como *as . . . as*
tanto, -a . . . como *as much . . . as*
tantos, -as . . . como *as many . . . as*
tuyo, -a *your*

el **acuario** *aquarium*
el **acuerdo** *agreement*
agitado, -a *excited*
la **aspiradora** *vacuum cleaner*
bañar *to bathe*
la **basura** *trash*

la **canción** *song*
cepillar *to brush*
el **conejo** *rabbit*
conseguir *to get*
contento, -a *happy*
el **coro** *choir*
cosas que hacer *things to do*
cuidar *to take car of*
dividir *to divide*
devolver *to return*
la **división** *division*
el **doble** *double*
el **ensayo** *rehearsal*
estar de acuerdo *to be in agreement*
estar tan cansado, -a . . . *to be so tired . . .*
estar tan ocupado, -a . . . *to be so busy . . .*
la **excusa** *excuse*
gracioso, -a *funny*
la **jaula** *cage*
limpiar *to clean*
lo menos posible *as little as possible*
el **loro** *parrot*
el **motivo** *reason*
la **obligación** *obligation, duty*
la **ocasión** *occasion*
el **pájaro** *bird*
pasar la aspiradora *to vacuum*
pedir la palabra *to ask permission to speak*
el **perro** *dog*
el **pez** (*pl.* **peces**) *fish*

posible *possible*
proponer *to propose*
la **próxima vez . . .** *next time . . .*
¡qué coraje! *what nerve!*
quitar la mesa *to clear the table*
la **rana** *frog*
el **ratón** *mouse*
el **refrigerador** *refrigerator*
la **reparación** *repairs*
repetir (i) *to repeat*
la **reunión** *meeting*
sacar *to take*
secar *to dry*
seguir *to follow; to continue*
la **semana que viene** *next week*
la **serpiente** *snake*
el **silencio** *silence*
tener tantas cosas que hacer *to have so much to do*
la **tortuga** *turtle*

¡ay, caramba! *for heaven's sake!*
ir de excursión *to go on a trip or excursion*
la **novia** *girlfriend*
el **novio** *boyfriend*
prestar *to lend*
sin falta *without fail*

---

1. canción - canciones
   división - divisiones
   obligación - obligaciones
   ocasión - ocasiones
   reparación - reparaciones
   reunión - reuniones
   excursión - excursiones

2. la paso muy bien
   salir bien
   cosas que hacer
   estar de acuerdo
   estar tan cansado
   estar tan ocupado
   pasar la aspiradora
   pedir la palabra
   quitar la mesa
   tener tantas cosas que hacer
   ir de excursión

PRÁCTICA DEL VOCABULARIO

1. Make a list of all words ending in **-ión** you can find in the unit vocabulary list. Write their plurals.
2. Find all the idiomatic expressions containing a verb and write a sentence for each one. *Answers will vary for sentences.*

VAMOS A LEER

Antes de leer

Try to organize your thoughts and recall all you know about Puerto Rico, such as where it is located, its climate, its vegetation, and its wildlife. Before continuing with the **Preparación para la lectura,** scan the reading selection and find as many cognates as possible. For example, on line 2 you will find the words **música** and **favorita.**

Preparación para la lectura

Answer the questions after taking a quick look at the reading selection in order to get a general idea of the subject matter.

1. ¿Conoces Puerto Rico? ¿Dónde está?   Sí. Puerto Rico está en el Caribe.
2. ¿Qué sabes de Puerto Rico?   Puerto Rico es una isla. La capital de Puerto Rico es San Juan. Puerto Rico también se llama la Isla del Encanto.
3. Mira rápidamente la Lectura para tener una idea general. El coquí es
      a. un pájaro.   b. una ranita.   c. una playa.   b. una ranita
4. ¿Conoces algún otro animal como el coquí?   Answers will vary.
5. ¿De qué palabra crees que *chiquitica* es diminutivo? ¿Qué otra forma tiene que tú conoces?   Chiquitica es diminutivo de *chiquita*. Otra forma es *chiquitita*.
6. Y esa palabra, ¿no es diminutivo de otra que tú también conoces?   Sí, de chica.
7. ¿De qué palabra crees es diminutivo *poquitico*?   Poquitico es diminutivo de *poco*.

El coquí de Puerto Rico 📼

"¡Co-quí! ¡Co-quí! ¡Co-co-quí! ¡Co-quí!" Ésta es la música favorita en mi recuerdo de Puerto Rico. Nunca lo pensé. Me gustan los ritmos latinos, la salsa . . . Pero cuando la primera noche en San Juan me quedé un rato en el jardín de la casa de mi amigo Eliseo, tuve que preguntarle qué canto° mágico era ése. Eliseo me dijo que era una rana muy chiquitica que vive en Puerto Rico y que se llama coquí. Para muchas personas, el coquí es el símbolo de la Isla del Encanto. Como campanitas°, este canto mágico me acompañó todas las noches mientras estuve en San Juan. ¡No hay nada igual!

Entonces, decidí aprender° algo sobre la vida° de este animalito fascinante. Descubrí cosas muy interesantes. El mundo de la naturaleza° está lleno de sorpresas.

Las ranas son animales anfibios°. Pero el coquí no necesita ir al agua para poner sus huevos°. La razón es que el coquí, cuando nace° del huevo, ya es una ranita perfectamente formada. Nunca es renacuajo° ni tiene que nadar en el agua hasta convertirse en rana. Todo ese proceso lo hace dentro del huevo. Y, ¿sabes de qué tamaño es el coquí cuando nace? Del tamaño de una hormiga° negra. Después no crece° mucho más. Vive en los árboles y otras plantas y duerme durante el día.

El coquí no pone sus huevos y se va, como otros anfibios. El coquí cuida sus huevos. Pero crees que la madre los cuida, ¿verdad? Pues no. Es el padre quien defiende los huevos de otros coquíes que vienen a comerlos.

El coquí canta para atraer a su compañera y para proteger su territorio. En los trópicos sólo hay dos estaciones, las lluvias y la seca°. De marzo a octubre, que es la estación de las lluvias, miles de coquíes cantan su serenata toda la noche. Pero sólo en Puerto Rico. No hay coquíes en otras partes.

Cuando un coquí encuentra compañera, la lleva a su nido°. La ranita toma toda la noche

---

canto *song*	**campanitas** *little bells*	**aprender** *to learn*	**vida** *life*	**naturaleza** *nature*	**anfibios** *amphibious*			
huevos *eggs*	**nace** *is born*	**renacuajo** *tadpole*	**hormiga** *ant*	**crece** *grows*	**seca** *dry season*	**nido** *nest*		

Con frecuencia tiene que abandonar el nido para buscar un poco de agua en una hoja°. El mayor problema del coquí es defender sus huevos de los otros coquíes que vienen a comerlos. Y, ¿cómo los defiende? Pues canta. Eso casi nunca es suficiente para combatir al agresor. El coquí tiene que sacarlo del nido a la fuerza. Su mejor defensa es morder° al enemigo en una especie de lucha libre°. El enemigo es rápido y a veces el padre pierde algunos huevos. Y la madre, ¿dónde está? Nadie sabe. Pero si vuelve al nido, el padre la saca tan rápidamente como a los otros enemigos.

* * *

Esa noche volví otra vez al jardín para oír el canto del coquí. Todavía me pareció una música mágica. Desde entonces, cuando alguien dice "Puerto Rico", siempre recuerdo el dulce canto del coquí. "Co-quí! ¡Co-quí! ¡Co-co-quí! ¡Co-quí . . . "

para ovular sus huevos. Entonces el macho° los fertiliza. Los huevos son blancos como perlas. Cuando la hembra° termina de poner sus huevos, el padre, que es más pequeño que la madre, la saca del nido a la fuerza°. ¡Él quiere cuidar los huevos!

Mientras el padre cuida los huevos, no sale tanto a cantar como antes. Muchos coquíes no cantan más hasta que sus hijos nacen, en unos veintidós días. El padre toma muy en serio sus labores.

Como otras ranas, los coquíes tienen que mantener su cuerpo° húmedo°. Pero no toman agua. Tienen que buscar lugares donde hay agua y la absorben por su cuerpo. El trabajo más importante del padre, particularmente cuando no llueve, es cubrir los huevos con su cuerpo. Lo hace para mantener los huevos húmedos con el agua que él tiene adentro.

---

macho *male*   **hembra** *female*   **a la fuerza** *by force*   **cuerpo** *body*   **húmedo** *moist*   **hoja** *leaf*
morder *to bite*   **lucha libre** *wrestling match*

Teachers who would like to find out more about the coquí, please refer to "Fatherhood in Frogdom," by Daniel S. Townsend, Natural History, May 1987, pages 28–35.

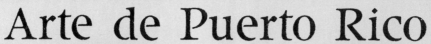

Arte de Puerto Rico

Litografías y Serigrafías
por Artistas de Puerto Rico

Luis Cajigas   Manuel Hernández   Wichi Torres   Tufiño

HENRY J. GARCIA

Director, Arte de Puerto Rico
(212) 562-7601 (Mornings Only)

Actividad • Preguntas y respuestas

Answer the following questions about **El coquí de Puerto Rico.**

1. ¿Qué canto mágico se oye?
2. ¿Qué otro nombre le dan a Puerto Rico?
3. ¿Cuál es el símbolo para muchos?
4. ¿Por qué es diferente el coquí de otros anfibios?
5. ¿Cuántas estaciones hay en Puerto Rico? ¿Cuáles son?
6. ¿Por qué canta el coquí?
7. ¿Quién come los huevos del coquí?
8. ¿Quién es más grande, la madre o el padre?
9. ¿Cuál es el trabajo del padre?
10. ¿Cuál crees que es un título apropiado para esta Lectura?
    a. Un famoso cantante de Puerto Rico
    b. El canto del coquí
    c. Un padre que quiere ser madre

1. Se oye el canto mágico del coquí.
2. Le dan a Puerto Rico el nombre de la Isla del Encanto.   3. Para muchos, el coquí es el símbolo de Puerto Rico.   4. El coquí es diferente porque no necesita ir al agua para poner sus huevos.   5. En Puerto Rico hay dos estaciones: las lluvias y la seca.   6. El coquí canta para atraer a su compañera.   7. Otros coquíes comen los huevos.   8. La madre es más grande.
9. El trabajo del padre es cuidar los huevos.   10. b. El canto del coquí.

Actividad • ¡A escoger!

According to **El coquí de Puerto Rico,** three words from each group are related in one way or another. The fourth word is not. What word is not related?

1. noche	coquí	perla	canto	perla
2. campanita	ranita	huevo	animalito	huevo
3. húmedo	sequía	agua	lluvia	sequía
4. serenata	anfibio	renacuajo	hormiga	serenata
5. campo	árboles	recuerdo	jardín	recuerdo
6. Puerto Rico	San Juan	Eliseo	Isla del Encanto	Eliseo

Actividad • Charla

Explain to a classmate how **el coquí** protects its eggs. Your classmate should tell you how **el coquí** keeps the eggs moist.

El coquí canta y muerde al enemigo en una especie de lucha libre para proteger los huevos.
El coquí cubre los huevos con su cuerpo para mantener los huevos húmedos.

UNIDAD 3 ¡Vamos de compras!
Scope and Sequence

	BASIC MATERIAL	COMMUNICATIVE FUNCTIONS
SECTION A	**Anuncios y más anuncios** (A1) **El departamento de señoras** (A11) **Pidiendo y dando información** (A19)	**Socializing** • Extending, accepting, and refusing invitations **Exchanging information** • Giving directions • Asking for directions and giving information
SECTION B	**En La Barata** (B1) **El departamento de caballeros** (B15)	**Exchanging information** • Identifying what you want • Asking for and giving information in a store
SECTION C	**De regreso** (C1)	**Expressing feelings and emotions** • Expressing satisfaction or displeasure with emphasis **Exchanging information** • Talking about past events
TRY YOUR SKILLS	**¡A dar órdenes!** **Dictado**	

■ **Pronunciación** (diphthongs **a, e,** and **o;** letters **r** and **rr**)
■ **¿Lo sabes?**   ■ **Vocabulario**

VAMOS A LEER	**España y los Estados Unidos** (Spanish influence in the United States)

WRITING   A variety of controlled and open-ended writing activities appear in the Pupil's Edition. The Teacher's Notes identify other activities suitable for writing practice.

COOPERATIVE LEARNING   Many of the activities in the Pupil's Edition lend themselves to cooperative learning. The Teacher's Notes explain some of the many instances where this teaching strategy can be particularly effective. For guidelines on how to use cooperative learning, see page T13.

GRAMMAR	CULTURE	RE-ENTRY
Formal commands (A7) Position of object pronouns with commands (A14) Irregularities in the formal command (A24)	Shopping in Spanish-speaking cities The monetary units of Spanish-speaking countries	Names of colors Directional expressions
The present progressive form (B8) Position of object pronouns with the present progressive (B13)	Venezuelan cities	Uses of the verb **estar** The position of pronouns with infinitives and affirmative commands
The irregular verb **venir** in the preterit tense (C9) Some verbs with spelling changes in the preterit tense (C11)	Three regions of Venezuela	Pronouns used after prepositions Numbers 0–1,000

Recombining communicative functions, grammar, and vocabulary

Reading for practice and pleasure

TEACHER-PREPARED MATERIALS
Section A Items of clothing, activity cards for A23, paper doll, a map of your community
Section B Advertisements from Spanish newspapers, pictures of merchandise, a map of Venezuela, magazine pictures of people in action, items that represent gender, items of clothing
Section C A map of Venezuela, magazine pictures, items of clothing

UNIT RESOURCES
Manual de actividades, Unit 3
Manual de ejercicios, Unit 3
Unit 3 Cassettes
Transparencies 7–9
Quizzes 7–9
Unit 3 Test

SECTION **A**

OBJECTIVES **To socialize:** extend, accept, and refuse invitations; **to exchange information:** give directions, ask for directions and give information

CULTURAL BACKGROUND Shopping in a Spanish-speaking city can be an adventure. They do have great chains of department stores like the ones that are found in the United States and Canada, but one generally looks for smaller specialty stores. Small grocery stores and shops are often located in the neighborhoods, permitting the local residents to walk to the area. The large downtown shopping areas also have many smaller stores. However, there are several chains of stores in Spanish-speaking countries, such as **Ley** in Colombia (much like Woolworth), **El Palacio de Hierro** and **Puerto de Liverpool** in Mexico, and **Galerías Preciados** and **El Corte Inglés** in Spain.

Many large stores, such as the hyper markets in Europe and **Aurrera, Gigante,** and **Comercial Mexicana** in Mexico, are much like K Mart or Walmart in the United States. However, many of the stores also carry groceries and double as supermarkets.

MOTIVATING ACTIVITY Write the following words on flashcards, on the board, or a transparency.

papelería	carnicería
tortillería	panadería
librería	pizzería
frutería	zapatería

Ask the students: **¿Qué puedes comprar en cada una de estas tiendas?** Then, as you write the following words on the board, ask **¿Adónde vas para comprar . . . ?**

café	leche	zapatos
sombreros	relojes	joyas
helado	pasteles	mariscos

Point out to the students that names of stores often contain the name of the items they sell. The suffix **-ería** denotes the store. You may also wish to mention that a similar pattern is true for some types of vendors. Adding **-ero** or **-era** identifies the item and the person who is repairing, preparing, or selling the item. Give a few examples and then ask the students to name a few words.

carnicera	zapatero	lechera	relojero	joyera

A 1

Anuncios y más anuncios

You may wish to follow the procedures outlined in Unit 1, A1, p. T26, to present the basic material. After presenting the selection chorally and individually, review the vocabulary that the students already know. Then write the new vocabulary on the board or a transparency. Allow the students to arrive at the meanings from context and examples. You may also ask them to identify words that relate to those on the board. Mention to them that the word **plata** is slang for *money*. After all new vocabulary has been presented, have the students write the words in the vocabulary section of their notebooks.

Read the introduction with the students, asking questions to check comprehension. Then ask them to follow along in their books as you read aloud or play the cassette. Following the first two commercials, ask additional questions for comprehension. Ask the students their opinion of commercials. Ask them to discuss commercials that are especially good or poor. Continue with the next commercial. When the students understand the commercials, introduce the dialog portion of the material. You may wish to have volunteers role-play the parts of the dialog or you may call for choral and individual repetition, alternating them to avoid boredom. Finally, ask the students to read again silently as you read aloud or play the final portion of the dialog on the cassette.

A2 Actividad • Preguntas y respuestas

You may wish to do this activity with books closed, calling on individual students to answer the questions, or you may ask the students to work alone or with a partner to find the answers to the questions. You may need to review several vocabulary items such as **lema** and **anuncio.** Review the answers with the class.

ANSWERS:
1. El sábado por la mañana los chicos ven un programa de televisión en casa de su prima María Lucía.
2. La Barata es un almacén. En La Barata están al día con la moda.
3. El lema de La Barata es: "La Barata, donde Ud. ahorra plata."
4. En La Casa García hay grandes rebajas en todos los artículos. En La Casa García garantizan mayor surtido.
5. Bernardo dice que los anuncios son odiosos y que hablan muy alto.
6. El lema de La Nación es: "La Nación, donde el cliente siempre tiene la razón."
7. Nati y Marilú van de compras a La Barata.
8. Bernardo no va de compras con Ramiro y Quique porque nunca saben lo que quieren.

SLOWER-PACED LEARNING You may wish to write the answers in scrambled order on the board or a transparency and have the students match the answers to the questions.

A3 Actividad • ¿Es cierto o no?

Review the statements with the students. They may wish to work in pairs to correct the false statements. Call on volunteers to read aloud the corrected statements. These last two activities, A2 and A3, will help you determine student comprehension of the basic material in A1. If student comprehension is low, you must review A1 and go over the vocabulary again.

A4 Sabes que . . .

You may wish to mention that street vendors and door-to-door salespeople often offer goods at lower prices. Knives and scissors may be sharpened at home by a person with a bicycle and a sharpening tool. Vendors of brooms, mops, brushes, and other items sell from door to door. In addition, you may purchase a much smaller amount of any item from a street vendor than from a department store. It is not uncommon to buy a half-kilo or less of coffee, one or two sticks of chewing gum, or a small bag of laundry soap.

A5 SE DICE ASÍ

Introduce the invitations to go shopping. Once everyone feels comfortable with the pronunciation, review the responses. As a variation, you may wish to ask the students to suggest other responses. Have them role-play the contextual exchanges in pairs or groups of three. After a few moments call on a few volunteers to role-play a dialog for the class, using the expressions in the box as a guide. You may also wish to include yourself in the dialogs to make some changes and challenge the students to give different responses.

A6 Actividad • ¡Vamos de compras!

Tell the students to use the expressions from A5, p. 94, as a guide. To encourage conversation, you may wish to have the students move about the room.

A7 ESTRUCTURAS ESENCIALES

Begin the presentation of the command forms by using some of the best-known commands used in the classroom, such as **Abra Ud. la puerta, Abran los libros, Cierren los libros,** and so on. Ask the students to carry out the instructions. Then ask them what kind of statements they have heard. Once they understand that the commands are being used to tell them to do something, continue with the explanation by writing some of the forms on the board. You may wish to have the students repeat what you say. Then ask them to identify the differences in the verb forms. Show examples of verbs until they notice that the endings are different.

Read aloud the material in the chart. After you read item 1, write several different verbs on the board or a transparency, including stem-changes in the **yo** form, and allow the students to form commands. Write their comments on the board, and continue with the rest of the presentation.

Make students aware that stem–changing verbs in the **yo** form of the present indicative keep the change in the formal command. Indicate that verbs ending in **-car, -gar,** and **-zar** also change the **c** to **qu**; the **g** to **gu**; and the **z** to **c** in the formal command.

A8 Actividad • Falta algo

Ask the students to complete this activity silently. Prepare a transparency with the answers or write them on the board or a transparency to review their responses.

A9 Actividad • El suplente

Point out to the students that in most Spanish–American countries and Spain the relationship between the students and their teachers is more formal than in the United States. Thus, students are usually addressed formally, using **usted.**

Ask the students to work in pairs. One will read the sentence, and the other will form the command. Ask them to switch roles. For writing practice, you may wish to have them write the commands either before or after they complete the activity orally.

CHALLENGE Call on several volunteers to play the role of the substitute teacher and to give several commands to the group. The group must do what they are told.

A 10 **Comprensión**

You will hear a statement followed by two responses. Choose the response that best completes the first statement and check the appropriate space on your answer sheet. For example, you will hear: **Yo necesito un suéter nuevo para el invierno.** The responses are: (a) **Pues, búsquelo en el garaje.** (b) **Entonces, búsquelo en el almacén.** You will check **b** because it best completes the first statement.

1. —Mamá, hace mucho calor.
   a. Sí, hijo, debes ponerte el abrigo.
   b. Sí, hijo, ¿por qué no te pones el traje de baño? (√)
2. —Busco unas botas para montar a caballo.
   a. ¿Qué le parecen estos guantes?
   b. Aquí tengo unas botas a buen precio. (√)
3. —Hace mucho frío, ¿verdad?
   a. Sí, debes ponerte el traje.
   b. ¿Por qué no te pones el abrigo? (√)
4. —¿Qué te parece esta falda con un suéter?
   a. Me gusta más esta blusa. (√)
   b. ¿Te parece mejor esta cartera?
5. —Voy a un baile formal. ¿Qué necesito?
   a. Debes tener traje, corbata y camisa blanca. (√)
   b. Debes tener un sombrero, unos pantalones y un suéter.
6. —Paquito, debes ponerte los zapatos.
   a. Vas a perder los calcetines.
   b. Vas a tener los calcetines muy sucios. (√)
7. —Voy a jugar al béisbol.
   a. ¿Viste mis botas?
   b. ¿Viste mi guante? (√)
8. —Mamá va a una cena muy elegante en casa de los Gómez.
   a. Por eso se compró el vestido de seda. (√)
   b. Por eso se compró los jeans.
9. —Me gustaría ver los pañuelos de seda.
   a. ¿Los que están en el sombrero?
   b. ¿Los que están en la mesa? (√)
10. —¿Qué debo llevar a la playa?
    a. Traje de baño y sombrero para el sol. (√)
    b. Bufanda, corbata y zapatos.

Now check your answers. *Read the statements and responses again and give the correct answer.*

A 11 **SITUACIÓN • El departamento de señoras**

Bring in as many items from the vocabulary list as possible. Display them on the desk or on a table, and label them with prices in **bolívares.** To re-enter vocabulary, you may wish to include items taught in **Nuevos amigos.**

Another possibility is to attach pictures of the items with their prices to the board. Introduce the material by asking the students their opinions of the prices, the quality, or the styles. Re-enter the names of colors.

As a variation, you may wish to combine the clothing items for men (from p. 111, B15) and women (from p. 97, A11). To present the new vocabulary, bring a variety of oversized clothes to the classroom. Discuss the clothes as you point to each item.

> Éstos son pantalones.
> Son azules.
> Tienen cuatro bolsillos.

Then have the students put on the clothes (over their own), according to your instructions. The oversized clothing can be taken off using a similar procedure.

A 12 Actividad • Descripción del dibujo

Ask the students to complete the activity in class or for homework. Review the answers in class.

A 13 Sabes que . . .

Read the cultural note aloud as the students follow along in their books. Then ask them to guess what the following monetary units have in common.

> Venezuela: el bolívar   Nicaragua: el córdoba
> Costa Rica: el colón   El Salvador: el colón
> Panamá: el balboa   Ecuador: el sucre

Explain that these monetary units are named after famous people.

> el bolívar: Simón Bolívar, el "Libertador" de las Américas
> el colón: Cristóbal Colón, descubridor de América
> el balboa: Vasco Núñez de Balboa, descubridor del océano Pacífico
> el córdoba: Fernández de Córdoba, conquistador español que fundó las ciudades de León y Granada en Nicaragua.
> el sucre: Antonio José de Sucre, general y político venezolano que liberó al Ecuador.

A 14 ESTRUCTURAS ESENCIALES

Select a number of classroom objects that you might use with commands. Begin with a series of questions and commands, such as the following.

> ¿Los libros? Sí, ábranlos, por favor.
> ¿El papel? Sí, sáquelo, por favor.

Ask the students to repeat the responses as you write them on the board or a transparency. Generalize about the forms and the pronouns. Then have the students open their books and read the first section of the material. Continue with a similar presentation to introduce negative commands, and follow with a reading of the material. You may wish to point out that they may use exclamation marks when commands are meant to be emphasized.

A 15 Actividad • El empleado nuevo

You may wish to have the students complete the activity with books closed, calling on individual students to answer, or you may ask them to work with a partner. You may wish to discuss one or more items with the class to help them get started. Add other questions not included in the activity in order to check the students' comprehension.

> ¿Compro la blusa?
> ¿Mando la carta?
> ¿Abrimos las ventanas?
> ¿Vendemos los libros?

A 16 Actividad • El gerente

Present the activity as explained in A15, but this time the students should answer the questions negatively. Review with the class. For writing practice, you may wish to have the students write the sentences and review by correcting them on the board or a transparency.

A 17 Actividad • Instrucciones

Assign this activity for homework or have the students work in pairs to complete the activity in the form of a dialog.

SLOWER-PACED LEARNING   Brainstorm with the class the types of instructions a store manager might give the employees. Write the list on the board or a transparency. Then have the students use the list as a guide to write the instructions in command forms.

CHALLENGE   After the students have completed the activity, ask them to look at the realia at the bottom of page 99. Have them write as many commands as possible based on the information found in the advertisement. The commands may be singular or plural, or affirmative or negative. For example, the first sentence in the realia, **Porque garantizamos mayor surtido,** can be converted into the command form: **Garanticen mayor surtido.**

A 18 Actividad • ¡A escribir!

Ask the students to prepare a commercial for each of the items listed. Suggest that they include at least four different commands, two reasons for using the product, and information on where it may be obtained. Students may also write about a local restaurant or store. Explain that they may not translate other commercials.

SLOWER-PACED LEARNING   You may wish to define the new vocabulary found in the realia that may be difficult for students to comprehend.

gente que sabe	*people that know*
mariscos	*shellfish*
Descubra Ud.	*Discover*
saboreando	*tasting*
calzado	*footwear*

A 19 SITUACIÓN • Pidiendo y dando información

Before presenting the dialog, call on volunteers to summarize the events in A1, pp. 92–93. You may also wish to re-enter the expressions used for giving and following directions, such as **a la derecha, a la izquierda, delante de,** and **detrás de.** Draw a simple map on the board and use a paper doll or cardboard figure to demonstrate. Then present the new vocabulary: **cuadras, esquina, doblen a la derecha, sigan derecho.**

While presenting and practicing the dialog in class, try to keep a fast tempo in order to maintain as much of the students' attention as possible. Insist on a normal delivery—as close as possible to that of a native speaker. Particular attention should be given to the linking of words, syllable length, and intonation.

You may prefer to play the cassette or to read aloud small portions of the dialog first. Then call for choral and individual repetition. Choral and individual repetition should be alternated in order to avoid boredom. When you have completed the dialog, you may wish to call on students to role-play parts of the dialog. You should not expect total memorization of the exchanges, but the students should become familiar with the situation and should learn the new vocabulary in context. Try not to spend too much time presenting the dialog the first day. Ten to twelve minutes of class time should be sufficient. You can extend the dialog presentation over several days.

A 20 Actividad • **Preguntas y respuestas**

You may wish to do this activity with books closed, calling on individual students to answer the questions.

SLOWER-PACED LEARNING You may wish to write scrambled answers on the board or a transparency. Then ask the students to match the correct answer to each question. As a variation, supply a selection of answers for each question and have the students choose the appropriate answer.

A 21 Actividad • **Cómo llegar a La Nación**

Have the students draw the map and then explain the route in their own words to a partner.

SLOWER-PACED LEARNING Have the students draw a map of the route they would take from their home to school, to a shopping center, or to a supermarket. Ask them to explain the route to a partner.

A 22 SE DICE ASÍ

You may wish to re-enter the following directional expressions.

| al lado de | detrás de | lejos de |
| enfrente de | cerca de | |

Then continue by presenting the directional expressions for asking and giving directions. Using their maps from A21, have the students give instructions on how to get from one point of interest to another.

To further practice giving and following directions, the students should choose a partner. Have each student hide a number of objects around the room. Without mentioning the name of the object, each student should give directions to his or her partner on reaching the object's location. The partner must locate and identify each item. Then switch roles.

A 23 Actividad • **¿Dónde están?**

As a variation, prepare activity cards with the following or similar routes that are familiar to all the students.

de tu casa a la escuela
de la escuela al centro comercial
de tu escuela a otra escuela cercana

Ask the students to present an impromptu dialog in which they ask for directions and give directions to a place indicated on the card.

A 24 ESTRUCTURAS ESENCIALES

Present the verbs in the chart. Ask the students to write them in their notebooks for reference. For writing practice, you may wish to have them write two or three sentences using each verb.

CHALLENGE   You may wish to practice the regular and irregular formal commands, using TPR (Total Physical Response). You may also form teams and have the students compete with one another as they follow your instructions. The following or similar commands may be used.

Vayan a la pizarra.
Pongan el libro en la mesa.
Busquen los cuadernos y pónganlos en el suelo.

A 25 Actividad • El dueño manda

Ask the students to complete this activity in writing, using the correct forms of the formal commands indicated. Call on volunteers to write the sentences on the board or a transparency for correction.

A 26 Actividad • ¡A completar!

You may wish to have this activity written on the board or a transparency. Call on students to provide the correct forms of the verbs. You may also prepare a handout of the advertisement, including the blanks, as an impromptu quiz or activity. Review the completed advertisement with the class.

A 27 SE DICE ASÍ

Present the expressions, using TPR (Total Physical Response). Demonstrate the actions as you give the commands. Then have the students carry out the instructions when you give the command form. For example, ask several students to stand and say: **Doblen a la derecha/izquierda.** Review the material in the book.

A 28 Actividad • Cómo llegamos a nuestra casa

To expand this activity, prepare maps of your community to distribute to the students. Have them take turns giving directions to their classmates, who must trace the routes on their maps.

SECTION

B

OBJECTIVES   **To exchange information:** identify what you want, ask for and give information in a store

CULTURAL BACKGROUND   The shopping center is becoming an important part of the commerce of any major city in Spanish-speaking countries. In Spanish America, the shopping center caters to the middle and upper-middle classes. As in the United States, the shopping center has replaced the old courthouse square in large cities and is a central gathering point for all ages, particularly teens. This is particularly true in suburban areas where most shopping centers are located. Proximity makes it unnecessary for adults and teens to go downtown to courthouse squares or sidewalk cafés. Thus, they are re-enacting the old custom of the **paseo** (girls walking one way around the plaza, boys walking another, and eventually meeting) in shopping malls.

MOTIVATING ACTIVITY   Select various advertisements from Spanish newspapers. Have the students analyze the products and prices. Prepare a list of questions and ask them to use the information in the advertisements to answer them. Also provide the students with the exchange rate for currency in use.

B1   En La Barata

Ask the students to review what was discussed in the opening dialog in A1 on page 92. Remind them of the name of the store and the decisions made by the group about going shopping. Before the students read the dialog, you may wish to present the new vocabulary, using magazine pictures or the actual items. You may wish to call for choral and individual repetition, alternating them to avoid boredom. Mention to the students that the sizes in many Spanish-speaking countries are different from those in the United States. Most guide books to Europe or Spanish America have size-equivalence charts.

Concentrate on the specific objectives of the dialog. You should not interrupt to explain grammar or to define new vocabulary. Play the cassette or read the dialog aloud as the students follow along in their books. For cooperative learning, have them form groups of four to role-play the dialog. Students should not memorize the exchanges. They may use the books or cue cards to role-play.

B2   Actividad • Preguntas y respuestas

Allow the students several minutes to answer the questions. When completed, have them compare their answers with those of a partner. Review with the entire class. Have the students refer to the dialog if necessary. You may also do this activity with books closed calling on individual students to answer the questions.

SLOWER-PACED LEARNING   Prepare a summary of the dialog to distribute to the students. Leave blanks for items they are to complete. You may also wish to have the students complete the following or similar sentences to test comprehension.

1. Roberto Barrera es . . .
2. Bernardo, Marilú y Nati están en . . .
3. Marilú es . . .
4. Marilú y Nati están buscando . . .
5. Bernardo quiere . . .

B3   Actividad • ¿Es cierto o no?

Allow the students to complete the activity as a practice quiz. To check the work, you or a volunteer may write on the board or a transparency as individuals dictate the corrected statements. These last two activities, B2 and B3, will help you determine student comprehension of the basic material in B1. If student comprehension is low, you must review B1 and go over the vocabulary again.

B4 Sabes que . . .

Have the students locate Caracas on a map of Venezuela. Ask them to describe the topography and explain what they might expect the climate to be. Explain to the students that Caracas has nearly three million inhabitants. It is located at the base of Mt. Humboldt, which separates Caracas from La Guaira on the beach. One can reach the top of Mt. Humboldt by cable car and then descend on the other side to La Guaira. At the peak of the mountain there is a lovely hotel and ice rink.

As the students read the cultural note, ask them to name two other major cities in Venezuela and to explain why many Venezuelans prefer shopping in malls. Then read the selection with the class and ask questions to check comprehension.

B5 SE DICE ASÍ

Review the section entitled **dependiente.** When the students are comfortable with the sentences and understand their meanings, continue with those of the **cliente.**

Set up an area of the classroom to resemble a store. Ask the students to take turns enacting the roles of the **dependiente** and the **cliente.** As they master the exchanges, ask them to add lines. You may wish to demonstrate by playing one of the roles.

SLOWER–PACED LEARNING Have the students match a list of statements or questions by the **dependiente** to a scrambled list of responses by the **cliente.** They should then use the exchanges to form a dialog, adding any necessary information.

B6 Actividad • Minidiálogo

Ask the students to complete the activity, using the expressions from B5 as a guide. As a variation, provide them with a list of scrambled words. The students should choose the most appropriate word to complete each sentence.

B7 Comprensión

You will hear a statement by either a clerk or a shopper. Each statement will be followed by three possible responses. Choose the one that best completes the conversation. For example, you will hear: **¿En qué puedo servirle?** and the responses (a) **No, gracias. Es muy caro.** (b) **Estoy buscando unos jeans.** (c) **¿Algo más?** You should select *b* because it best completes the conversation.

1. —Buenos días, señores. ¿Qué desean?
   a. Está barato, ¿no?
   b. Necesitamos un regalo para mamá. (√)
   c. Estoy buscando un vestido muy caro.
2. —¿Dónde está el probador?
   a. Está al fondo y a la derecha. (√)
   b. Está a dos cuadras de aquí.
   c. Lo siento, está en casa de Anita.

3. —¿Algo más?
   a. No, es muy barato.
   b. ¿Puedo probármelo?
   c. No, gracias. Es todo por el momento. (√)

4. —¿Los están atendiendo?
   a. Sí, gracias. Muy amable. (√)
   b. Estoy buscando unos zapatos negros.
   c. Aquí está el vuelto.

5. —¿Cuál es su talla?
   a. Me lo llevo.
   b. No estoy seguro. ¿Puedo probármelo? (√)
   c. No me queda bien.

6. —Me gusta mucho. Me lo llevo.
   a. Muy bien. ¿Algo más? (√)
   b. Aquí está el vuelto.
   c. Está barato.

7. —Me gusta esta camisa. Está barata.
   a. Verdad. Ella es muy amable.
   b. ¿En qué puedo servirle?
   c. Es verdad. No es muy cara. (√)

8. —¿Me quedan bien estos pantalones?
   a. Debes buscar una talla más pequeña. (√)
   b. Necesitas una blusa roja.
   c. ¿Puedo probármelos?

9. —¿Cuál es el precio? ¿Veinticinco bolívares?
   a. Sí, ¿en qué puedo servirle?
   b. Sí, aquí tiene el vuelto.
   c. Sí, señorita. Es un buen precio. (√)

10. —¿Qué le parece esta playera?
   a. No, gracias. Es muy cara.
   b. Prefiero una más grande. (√)
   c. ¿Cuál es su talla, señorita?

Now check your answers. *Read each sentence again and give the correct answer.*

B8   ESTRUCTURAS ESENCIALES

Select magazine pictures of people in action. Choose pictures that depict verbs that the students know very well. Present the present progressive tense by showing the pictures and stating what the people are doing. Ask the students to identify what action is taking place.

Once the students have grasped the idea, ask them to generalize about what they have learned. As they repeat the sentences, write the examples on the board or a transparency. Explain that the present progressive tense is used when describing an action in progress at the moment of speaking. Ask them to compare it to English. Stress that unlike the English progressive tense, the Spanish present progressive tense does not refer to future time or habitual situations. You may add that Spanish uses the present indicative tense to refer to future time or habitual situations. Give some examples contrasting them.

Read the explanation and chart in the book. Give the students a list of ten verbs and ask them to write the **-ndo** forms. You may also wish to re-enter the forms of the verb **estar** at this time.

Ask the students to write the irregular forms listed in number 5 in their notebooks, along with the notes they have just written. Using the pictures, ask them again to describe the actions taking place in each picture.

SLOWER-PACED LEARNING   Ask the students to find five large pictures from magazines to show the class. They must explain what is happening in the pictures. Collect the pictures, paste them on heavy paper, and distribute them to small groups for review practice. The pictures may be collected and placed into a file to be used later for team games and other activities.

B 9   Actividad • ¿Qué está pasando ahora?

Ask the students to complete the activity as a group or with a partner. You may also wish to have them write out the sentences. Watch for the common error of omitting the verb **estar.** For correction, write the sentences on the board or a transparency.

B 10   Actividad • ¿Qué están haciendo?

Ask the students to work with a partner to complete the activity. When finished, write their responses on the board or a transparency. For further practice, make a list of other famous people and ask the students what they think the people may be doing.

CHALLENGE   Have the students think of a famous person. They must tell what they think the person is doing at this time, and other students must identify the person.

B 11   Actividad • Excusas, excusas y más excusas

Ask the students to complete the activity on paper. Then have them role-play the situations with a partner. Choose several pairs to demonstrate their mini-dialogs to the class.

B 12   Actividad • ¿Qué están haciendo los estudiantes?

The students may work in pairs to complete this activity. As a variation, ask them to role-play the situation, using names of their classmates. They must respond by identifying activities that would be typical of the person named.

B 13   ESTRUCTURAS ESENCIALES

To introduce the position of object pronouns with the present progressive tense, bring to the classroom several items that represent both genders, as well as singular and plural forms. Display each item and say, for example: **¿El jugo? Estoy tomándolo.** Ask the students to repeat the sentences as you show the item. Once you have completed your series of items, ask the students to generalize about what they have heard. Write their responses on the board or a transparency. You might also wish to re-enter the position of pronouns with infinitives and with affirmative commands at this time.

Read the explanation aloud to the students to confirm their previous generalizations. You may wish to use your picture collection again to reinforce the structure. Have the students describe the action using an object pronoun with the **-ndo** form. Be sure to have them give the sentence with the pronoun in both positions.

B 14 **Actividad • ¿Qué está pasando allí?**

Ask the students to complete this activity for homework or in class, making sure they include both forms of the sentence. You may also wish to write the elements of the sentences on cardboard. The students must then tell you where to place the pronouns as you place the elements in the correct position on the board or a flannel board. This will also work well with cutouts from a transparency.

> ANSWERS:
> 1. Alberto y Julián están atendiéndolos.
>   Alberto y Julián los están atendiendo.
> 2. El dependiente está aprendiéndolo.
>   El dependiente lo está aprendiendo.
> 3. Los clientes están aprovechándola.
>   Los clientes la están aprovechando.
> 4. Quique está comprándolos.
>   Quique los está comprando.
> 5. Eduardo y yo estamos pagándola.
>   Eduardo y yo la estamos pagando.
> 6. El gerente está rebajándolos.
>   El gerente los está rebajando.
> 7. Clara está vendiéndola.
>   Clara la está vendiendo.
> 8. Nati y su prima están usándola.
>   Nati y su prima la están usando.

B 15 **SITUACIÓN • El departamento de caballeros**

Bring as many of the items pictured as possible to class to present the vocabulary. If you do not have the items, you may wish to demonstrate using clothing the students are wearing. Ask them to stand in front of the class as you present each new item.

B 16 **Actividad • Descripción del dibujo**

Ask the students to answer the questions with complete sentences, orally or in writing. Copy the illustration on a transparency and ask a question as you point to each element in the drawing.

B 17 **Actividad • Las compras**

Ask the students to complete the activity and to take notes on their partner's responses. Have them report their findings to a third person, or select several students to report to the class.

B 18 **Actividad • ¡A escribir!**

Have the students prepare a shopping list for their new winter wardrobe. As a variation, you may wish to tell the students to select items from the realia at the bottom of the page to include in their shopping list. The following items may be suggested.

camisa	suéter
pantalón	corbata
cinturón	saco
medias	zapatos

OBJECTIVES **To express feelings and emotions:** express satisfaction or displeasure with emphasis; **To exchange information:** talk about past events

CULTURAL BACKGROUND Many shopping districts in cities in Spanish America and Spain have restaurants and cafés that cater to people who only want a soft drink or a light snack. They are popular because it is customary to have a cup of coffee or a snack with a friend for a long period of relaxed conversation. Cities that have climates allowing sidewalk and open-air cafés invite shoppers, professionals, and others to take a short break in their day.

MOTIVATING ACTIVITY Ask the students to guess what the following or other famous people might be doing now. Students should respond following this model: **Michael Jackson está cantando.**

Gloria Estefan	Emilio Estévez
Julio Iglesias	David Concepción (or other baseball player)
Diego Maradona	Gabriela Sabatini

C1   De regreso

Introduce the dialog by asking the students to recall the events that occurred in the previous dialogs, from sections A and B. Then, you may wish to follow the procedures outlined in Unit 1, A1, p. T26, to present the basic material. Present the expression **tener la culpa.** Explain that it means *to be at fault.* You may also wish to present other new vocabulary items by having the students identify a previously learned word from the same word family as the new word, such as **almuerzo—almorzar, verdad—verdadero,** and **lluvia—llover.**

Play the cassette or read aloud small portions of the dialog. Then call for choral and individual repetition. This will help the students develop their oral production, which includes pronunciation, rhythm, and intonation. After completing the dialog, you may call on students to role-play. To further aid understanding, ask the following or similar questions.

1. ¿Crees que Quique y Ramiro están contentos? ¿Por qué?
2. ¿Te ocurrió algo similar a ti alguna vez? ¿Qué te pasó?
3. En tu opinión, ¿quién tuvo la culpa? ¿Por qué?

C2   Actividad • Preguntas y respuestas

Allow the students to find the answers to the questions, using the dialog as a guide. They may work in groups or alone. When they are finished, review the material with them. You could also do this activity with the books closed, calling on individual students to answer the questions.

SLOWER-PACED LEARNING You may wish to give the students partial sentences that they must complete. Collect and correct their papers.

ANSWERS:
1. Los chicos están bebiendo unos refrescos en casa de Marilú.
2. Quique y Ramiro tocan el timbre.
3. Ellos dicen que están muertos de tanto caminar.
4. Ellos vieron que la tienda cerró por inventario.
5. La culpa la tuvo el anuncio viejo.
6. Grabaron el anuncio el mes pasado.
7. Ahorraron plata en La Barata porque no compraron nada.

C3 **Actividad • ¡A escoger!**

Allow the students time to review the answers to this activity silently. You may also use the activity as a sample quiz that will not be graded. Activities C2 and C3 will help you determine student comprehension of the basic material in C1. If student comprehension is low, you should review C1 and go over the vocabulary again.

C4 **SE DICE ASÍ**

Review the pronunciation of the items in this section. As a variation, have the students make up situations in which each of the expressions might be used.

> Comimos en Siete Mares cuando estuvimos en Barcelona. Juanita tenía mucha hambre. ¡Huy! ¡Cómo comió Juanita!

SLOWER-PACED LEARNING Provide the students with situations in which they might use the interjections. Allow them to select one interjection for each of the situations you state.

> Son las ocho y las clases empezaron a las siete y media. *(¡Caramba!)*
> No creo que puedo hacer todo. *(¡Bah!)*

C5 **Sabes que . . .**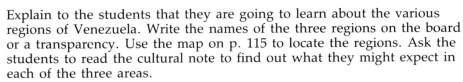

Explain to the students that they are going to learn about the various regions of Venezuela. Write the names of the three regions on the board or a transparency. Use the map on p. 115 to locate the regions. Ask the students to read the cultural note to find out what they might expect in each of the three areas.

CHALLENGE For cooperative learning, form groups of two or three. Have the students research information about **el Salto del Ángel, el río Amazonas, el Pico Bolívar,** or **Maracaibo.** Then call on each group to present the information to the class.

C6 **¿RECUERDAS?**

Select several classroom objects to re-enter the prepositional pronouns. Proceed as follows:

> ¿El libro? Es para Juan. Es para él.
> ¿La carta? Es para mí.

After you have reviewed all of the pronouns, ask the students to recall them as you write them on the board or a transparency. Ask them questions, such as: **¿Quieres ir al cine conmigo?** Then elicit the response: **Sí, quiero ir al cine contigo.**

Explain to the students that **mí** has an accent in order to differentiate it from the possessive adjective **mi.** The same rule applies to **dé** (the command form of **dar**) and **de. Ti** does not have an accent because there is no other word with which it might be confused.

Review the chart and explanation in the book, paying particular attention to the information concerning **conmigo** and **contigo.** Point out that for stress or clarification, the prepositional phrase is often used.

C7 Actividad • Combinación

Allow the students time to complete the activity orally or in writing. Review the activity by calling on individuals to read aloud the sentences as you or a volunteer writes them on the board or a transparency.

C8 Actividad • Yo quiero saber

Have the students work with a partner to complete the activity. When they are finished, review the answers with the entire class.

CHALLENGE Choose two students at a time to present a short dialog for the class about a mystery person. The questions should be based on those in the activity, but the person's name should not be mentioned. The other students must listen to the description and guess the identity of the person.

C9 ESTRUCTURAS ESENCIALES

Present the preterit tense forms of the verb **venir** in conversational form as demonstrated in Unit 2, B11, on page T57. Once all the forms have been presented and used in conversation, ask the students to name the forms as you write them on the board or a transparency. Then have them read the chart and the examples in the book.

C10 Actividad • La visita

Have the students work with a partner to complete the activity. Before they begin, allow them to select imaginary names and identities. They should answer the questions based on their new identities.

C11 ESTRUCTURAS ESENCIALES

Read the explanation and the material in the chart to the students. Note the spelling change of the intervocalic **i,** which, when unaccented, changes to **y.** Practice the forms of **construir, huir,** and **contribuir** in conversation. For writing practice, have them write three sentences with each verb.

The students may ask why **leíste** has an accent mark and **destruiste** does not. Explain that when two weak vowels combine **(iu),** the stress falls on the second one. **Leíste** has the stress on a weak vowel and therefore needs an accent (the same as **María**).

C12 Actividad • La tienda nueva

Provide a transparency with the completed forms for the students to correct their papers. They may also exchange papers with a partner for correction.

C13 Actividad • Las compras

Ask the students to answer the questions silently, making notes that they will use in a presentation to the class. Select a number of students to give their monologs. As they are speaking, take notes and encourage the rest of the class to listen carefully. When the speakers are finished, ask the following or similar questions to test comprehension.

¿Quién compra su ropa en (La Barata)?
¿Quién va de compras solo?

C 14 Actividad • ¿Qué pasó?

Ask the students to first complete the activity orally. Then have them write the sentences. You may wish to call on volunteers to write their answers on the board or a transparency for review by the entire class. The students may also enjoy creating their own illustrations. Then have them write a caption for each illustration using one of the verbs listed in the book.

C 15 Actividad • Aquí está La Barata

Use clothing from home or clothing the students have donated for this activity. Set up several "departments" throughout the classroom to permit the students to work in different areas. Choose clerks and clients, and label all items with prices. The students must then make purchases, using play money in **bolívares.** After a few moments, have them switch roles. Circulate and participate with the students. If actual clothing is not available, use pictures cut from catalogs and paste on colored paper, with the prices attached. Select a number of volunteers to role-play dialogs for the class.

SLOWER-PACED LEARNING Have the students label all the items with prices. Re-enter numbers from 0–1,000 before the students role-play. You may also wish to select a volunteer to demonstrate how to make a purchase in Spanish.

C 16 Comprensión

You will hear a statement or a question followed by a response. If the response is logical, check **lógico** on your answer sheet. If not, check **ilógico.** For example, you will hear: **¿Vas al baile con Juan?** and the response: **Sí, voy con él.** Since the response is logical, you should check the box labeled **lógico.**

1. —Estoy comprando este libro para ti.
   —¿Es para ellos? ¡Qué sorpresa!   *ilógico*
2. —¿De quién es la carta? ¿De Carlos y Gregorio?
   —Sí. Es de ustedes.   *ilógico*
3. —Voy a México con mis amigos Anita y Marcos.
   —¿Por qué vas con ellas?   *ilógico*
4. —¿Quieres ir al cine esta noche?
   —Sí, con mucho gusto voy contigo.   *lógico*
5. —Camila llamó a Roberto anoche para invitarlo a la fiesta.
   —¿A él? ¿No va a invitar a Rafael?   *lógico*
6. —¿Sabes si tu hermana conoce a Pati?
   —Creo que las conoce a ellas.   *ilógico*
7. —¿Compraste este regalo para mí?
   —Sí, es para mí.   *ilógico*
8. —Marilú quiere ir de compras contigo y con Julia.
   —¿Con nosotros?   *lógico*
9. —¿Con quiénes come en la cafetería? ¿Con sus amigos?
   —Sí. Come con ellas.   *ilógico*
10. —¿Juega Arturo al tenis contigo?
    —Sí, juega conmigo todos los sábados.   *lógico*

Now check your answers. *Read each sentence again and give the correct answer.*

C17 Actividad • ¡A escribir y a hablar!

Ask the students to write three paragraphs answering the questions included in the outline.

SLOWER-PACED LEARNING   Provide the first part of the answers to each question contained in the outline and have the students complete the answers with their own personal information. You may also provide connecting words, such as **porque, cuando, y,** and **o**. Collect and correct the compositions. Allow the students to use only notes when they present their compositions orally to the class.

TRY YOUR SKILLS

OBJECTIVE   To recombine communicative functions, grammar, and vocabulary

CULTURAL BACKGROUND   In Venezuela, credit cards are not as popular as they are in the United States. Although bank cards are used, large department stores and other shops do not offer credit. Small boutiques often extend credit to someone the owners know personally, and signatures, paper work, and other formalities are often bypassed for **"amigos."**

1   ¡A dar órdenes!

Review the formation of the commands by working with oral examples. If necessary, write some of the examples on the board or a transparency. Then ask the students to complete the activity in writing. Review orally with the class.

2   Actividad • En la clase

Allow the students to work in pairs to complete the activity orally, and then ask them to write the command forms. Have them exchange papers with a partner for correction.

ANSWERS:
1. Sí, escríbalos. / No, no los escriba.
2. Sí, ábrala. / No, no la abra.
3. Sí, contéstenlas. / No, no las contesten.
4. Sí, pídalos. / No, no los pida.
5. Sí, póngale atención. / No, no le ponga atención.
6. Sí, ahórrenlo. / No, no lo ahorren.
7. Sí, léanla. / No, no la lean.
8. Sí, límpiela y arréglela. / No, no la limpie y no la arregle.
9. Sí, salgan. / No, no salgan.
10. Sí, tráigalos. / No, no los traiga.

3   Actividad • Los dólares en pesos

Have the students complete the activity orally. You may also wish to dictate a series of numbers for comprehension practice.

ANSWERS:
doscientos cuarenta dólares = novecientos sesenta pesos
ciento setenta dólares = seiscientos ochenta pesos
ciento y un dólares = cuatrocientos cuatro pesos
sesenta y seis dólares = doscientos sesenta y cuatro pesos
ciento treinta y seis dólares = quinientos cuarenta y cuatro pesos

4 **Actividad • El cliente**

Ask the students to write the questions. Then call on individuals to read their questions aloud as you or a volunteer writes them on the board or a transparency. Elicit the appropriate responses for each question.

5 **Actividad • En la tienda**

Allow the students to work with a partner to make up a conversation. Choose several pairs to role-play their conversations to the class.

6 **Actividad • ¿Qué pasó ayer?**

Have the students choose a partner and compose a sentence for each verb. Then ask them to write their sentences on the board under columns headed by each of the verbs. Correct the sentences with the whole class.

7 **Actividad • ¿Qué dices?**

Allow the students to work in pairs to match the items. Remind them to use emphasis and gestures when they speak, and to make the situations as realistic as possible.

8 **Actividad • El anuncio**

Allow the students fifteen minutes to write commercials for their favorite stores. While they are writing, circulate to give encouragement and hints. Call on volunteers to present their commercials to the class.

9 **Actividad • ¿Con él o sin él?**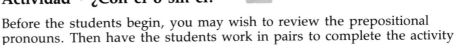

Before the students begin, you may wish to review the prepositional pronouns. Then have the students work in pairs to complete the activity orally.

SLOWER-PACED LEARNING After the students have completed the activity orally, ask them to write the sentences on paper. For correction, call on volunteers to write the responses on the board.

10 **Dictado**

Write the following paragraph from dictation. First listen to the paragraph as it is read to you. Then you will hear the paragraph again in short segments, with a pause after each segment to allow you time to write. Finally, you will hear the paragraph a third time so that you may check your work. Let's begin.

La semana pasada mi prima Rosalía *(pause)* fue de compras conmigo *(pause)*. Cuando llegamos al almacén *(pause)*, vimos muchos artículos en la vitrina *(pause)*. Una dependiente inmediatamente nos preguntó *(pause)*, "¿En qué puedo servirles?" *(pause)* Y nos atendió muy bien *(pause)*. Mi prima compró una playera *(pause)* para mí y un monedero para su sobrina *(pause)*. Yo aproveché la venta liquidación *(pause)* y ahorré mucho dinero.

PRONUNCIACIÓN

Re-enter the formation and pronunciation of the diphthongs with **a, e,** and **o.** Then introduce the formation of the single and the double **r.** Remind the students that the single **r** is like the tt in *butter.* Pay special attention to the sentences, showing the students how to link the words together, and insisting that they keep uniform syllable length. Repeat the exercises with the class before continuing with the tongue twisters. Assign pronunciation practice for homework and review the following day.

Actividad • Dos trabalenguas fáciles

Read each tongue twister aloud or play the cassette. Have the students repeat and practice the pronunciation line by line. Explain to them that before they try to increase the speed in which they say the tongue twisters, they should acquire the correct pronunciation of each word.

¿LO SABES?

SECTION
A

To further practice the command forms, you may do a TPR (Total Physical Response) activity with the class. Have volunteers take turns giving commands. Then ask the students to work with a partner to practice giving directions, and accepting and refusing invitations.

ANSWERS:
Apague la luz.
Déme el libro.
No se lleve el disco.
Quede en su sitio.
Anote todo lo que digo.

SECTION
B

Have the students write the phrases a salesclerk may use, or you may write several of their responses on the board or a transparency. To expand practice with the present progressive forms, use your picture file and encourage the students to state what is happening in each illustration.

SECTION
C

Tell the students to make their lists. Then ask for volunteers to play a game with you. Make up a list of crazy purchases for a girl and for a boy. Include items that would be of no use to the person. Allow the students to correct you.

VOCABULARIO

You may wish to play several word games with the students. Ask them to write the Spanish names of the following groups of items:

1. three directions
2. five verbs having to do with shopping or money
3. a slang word for money
4. as many items of men's clothing as they can think of
5. as many items of women's clothing as they can think of

As a variation, have the students divide into teams. Call out a word from the unit vocabulary list. Each student must then give an expression or a sentence, using the word. For example: **abrir—abrir una cuenta.**

PRÁCTICA DEL VOCABULARIO

Have the students write the lists of clothing at home. Then call on volunteers to read aloud the items on their lists.

VAMOS A LEER

OBJECTIVE To read for practice and pleasure

CULTURAL BACKGROUND More than the dollar sign has come to the United States from Spain. At one time, Spain controlled a large part of the United States territory. St. Augustine, Florida was the first settlement in this country, a city founded by the Spanish. The United States has not only used the dollar sign, it has also adopted the Spanish system of money. It divides the dollar into one hundred cents, just as the Spanish currency had been divided. The United States did not adopt the British system of coinage, but instead opted for the less complicated Spanish system. Many words have also come to English from Spanish, such as:

la reata—*lariat*   **mesa**—*tableland*
cimarrón—*wild calf*   **vigilantes**—*vigilantes*
chaparreras—*chaps*   **corraleja**—*corral*

Antes de leer

Ask the students to work with you as you review the material preceding the selection. Allow them time to find the cognates. Make lists of the cognates on the board or a transparency.

Preparación para la lectura

Have the students answer the questions before completing the reading selection. You may wish to complete the questions orally with the entire class.

ESPAÑA Y LOS ESTADOS UNIDOS

Play the cassette or have the students read the article, paragraph by paragraph, and ask them questions after each. After completing the reading, discuss the contents.

Actividad • Preguntas y respuestas

Divide the questions into groups to correspond with each paragraph. As you complete each paragraph, allow the students to work in groups of two or three to answer the questions. Review the answers with the entire class.

ANSWERS:
1. California, Florida, Nuevo México
2. Porque hay una conexión histórica. España colonizó gran parte del actual territorio de los Estados Unidos.
3. El emperador Carlos V decidió poner en su escudo las dos columnas de Hércules.
4. Hércules es un héroe mitológico y representa un gran poder.
5. La otra parte es la inscripción Plus Ultra.
6. Las colonias inglesas hicieron sus monedas en 1652.
7. Porque Thomas Jefferson propuso el "Spanish pillars" dólar como unidad monetaria de los Estados Unidos.
8. En ese escudo también había las dos columnas de Hércules.
9. El nombre Florida quiere decir en inglés "in full bloom."
10. Son las ciudades más antiguas de los Estados Unidos.
11. Tuvo el nombre de San Francisco de los Tejos.
12. b. La influencia española en los Estados Unidos

Actividad • ¡A ver el mapa!

You may wish to have the students use very detailed maps of their state or of the United States. Ask them to categorize (by states) the lists of the cities and towns with Spanish names. Make a game of the activity by awarding a small prize or bonus points to the person or team that finds the most cities.

Actividad • Charla

Allow the students to work in pairs to tell each other the information requested. Then ask several volunteers to tell their version for the entire class.

¡Vamos de compras!

Where can you shop in a Spanish-speaking country? There are many different types of shops and a variety of currencies. We need to know a little about both in order to pick the right store and pay the correct amount. If you like large department stores, you'll certainly find them. But you will also find small boutiques and specialized stores much favored by Spanish-speaking people. Which do you prefer?

In this unit, you will:

SECTION A	extend, accept, and refuse invitations . . . give and follow directions
SECTION B	identify what you want . . . ask for and give information in a store
SECTION C	express satisfaction or displeasure . . . talk about past events
TRY YOUR SKILLS	use what you've learned
VAMOS A LEER	read for practice and pleasure

extending, accepting, and refusing invitations . . . giving and following directions

In Spanish-speaking countries, television is almost as popular as in the United States. Although everybody complains about the commercials, many people buy the products . . .

Anuncios y más anuncios

En Caracas, un sábado por la mañana, Enrique, Ramiro, Bernardo y Natalia ven un programa de televisión en casa de su prima María Lucía. Como de costumbre, de pronto aparecen los anuncios con sus lemas.

Aproveche la gran venta-liquidación del almacén La Barata . . . Estamos al día con la moda. Visite hoy mismo La Barata y no olvide nuestro lema "La Barata, donde Ud. ahorra plata."

Grandes rebajas en todos los artículos en La Casa García. Garantizamos mayor surtido. No lo deje para mañana. Cómprelos y llévelos a su casa hoy mismo. "Mire que García . . . rebaja la mercancía."

BERNARDO   ¡Qué anuncios tan odiosos y qué alto hablan! Marilú, cambia de canal, por favor.

(Después de cambiar de canal, aparece otro anuncio.)

¡Señoras y señores! Abran una cuenta y usen la tarjeta de crédito de La Nación. Así no tienen que pagar ahora. Ahorren constantemente con nuestras gangas. "La Nación, donde el cliente siempre tiene la razón."

(Marilú apaga el televisor.)

NATI Y MARILÚ	*(A sus otros primos)* ¿Quieren ir de compras a La Barata con nosotros?
QUIQUE Y RAMIRO	No, nosotros vamos a La Nación con Bernardo.
BERNARDO	¡Oh no! . . . ¡Con Uds. yo no voy! Yo voy a La Barata con Nati y Marilú.
QUIQUE Y RAMIRO	Pero, Bernardo . . .
BERNARDO	Ir de compras con Uds. es una locura. Uds. nunca saben lo que quieren.
NATI	Bueno, por favor . . . que no queremos llegar tarde. Vamos, Bernardo. Hasta luego.
QUIQUE Y RAMIRO	Adiós.

For answers, see p. T73.

A2   Actividad • Preguntas y respuestas

Use the information in A1 to answer the following questions.

1. ¿Qué hacen los chicos el sábado por la mañana?
2. ¿Qué es La Barata? ¿Con qué están al día?
3. ¿Cuál es el lema de La Barata?
4. ¿Qué hay en La Casa García? ¿Qué garantizan?
5. ¿Qué dice Bernardo de los anuncios?
6. ¿Cuál es el lema de La Nación?
7. ¿Adónde van de compras Nati y Marilú?
8. ¿Por qué Bernardo no va de compras con Ramiro y Quique?

A3   Actividad • ¿Es cierto o no?

Decide whether each statement is true or false according to A1. Correct the false statements.

1. Natalia y Ramiro son primos de Marilú.
2. Los jóvenes viven en Madrid.
3. La Casa García no tiene lema.
4. Bernardo cambia de canal.
5. En La Barata el cliente siempre tiene la razón.
6. Nati va de compras con Bernardo.

1. Es cierto.
2. Los jóvenes viven en Caracas.
3. La Casa García sí tiene lema.
4. Marilú cambia de canal.
5. En La Barata el cliente ahorra plata.
6. Nati va de compras con Marilú.

¡Vamos de compras!   93

En Venezuela, como en la mayoría de los países de habla hispana *(Spanish-speaking)*, hay diversos tipos de tiendas y lugares en donde comprar. Aquellos compradores que quieren comprar mercancías o artículos a mejores precios que los de los centros comerciales van al centro *(downtown)*. Allí hay muchas tiendas y vendedores ambulantes *(street vendors)* que en general ofrecen un precio mejor y con los cuales *(with whom)* se puede regatear *(bargain)*. Los mercados libres *(open markets)* ofrecen aun *(yet)* mejores precios. Allí uno puede encontrar de todo *(everything)*, desde carne y queso hasta las más bellas flores del mundo. En caso de *(In case of)* necesidad, o porque uno se quedó sin algo *(one ran out of something)*, hay tiendas de barrio *(neighborhood)* llamadas "casas de abastos" o "bodegas," donde se pueden comprar muchas cosas. Lo mejor de las bodegas es que quedan cerca y que el dueño *(owner)* conoce a los clientes *(customers)*. Los conoce tan bien que muchas veces les fía *(gives them credit)* si no tienen dinero.

A5   SE DICE ASÍ
Extending, accepting, and refusing invitations

¿Quieres ir de compras? Do you want to go shopping?	Sí, ¡cómo no! Oh, sure!
¡Vamos de compras! Let's go shopping!	Sí, ¡por supuesto! Yes, of course!
¿Tienes ganas de ir de compras? Do you feel like going shopping?	No, gracias. No puedo. Tengo que… No, thank you. I can't. I have to…
¿Por qué no vamos de compras? Why don't we go shopping?	Lo siento, pero no puedo. Sorry, I can't.
	Hoy no. No tengo ganas. Otro día. Not today. I don't feel like it. Another day.

A6   Actividad • ¡Vamos de compras!
Answers will vary. Possible answers are given.

Using the expressions from A5, invite three classmates to go shopping. Do not use the same expression twice.

¿Quieres ir de compras?
¿Por qué no vamos de compras?
¿Tienes ganas de ir de compras?

Use commands to direct or request one or more persons to do something. In Spanish, commands can be formal or familiar. Formal (or polite) commands are used with people one normally addresses as **Ud.** The following chart shows the formal commands for **usted (Ud.)** and **ustedes (Uds.).**

Verb Endings	Present Indicative		Formal Commands	
	yo form	*stem*	*usted (Ud.)*	*ustedes (Uds.)*
-ar	**entro**	**entr-**	**entre Ud.**	**entren Uds.**
-er	**como**	**com-**	**coma Ud.**	**coman Uds.**
-ir	**abro**	**abr-**	**abra Ud.**	**abran Uds.**

1. To form the **usted (Ud.)** formal command of regular **-ar** verbs, add **-e** to the stem of the **yo** form of the present indicative of the verb.

   ¡Aproveche la gran venta-   *Take advantage of the great*
     liquidación!   *clearance sale!*

2. To form the **usted (Ud.)** formal command of **-er** and **-ir** verbs, add **-a** to the stem of the **yo** form.

   ¡Abra una cuenta hoy mismo!   *Open an account today!*
   ¡Pida su tarjeta de crédito   *Ask for your credit card*
     ahora mismo!   *right now!*

3. To form the plural **ustedes (Uds.)** command, add **-n** to the **usted** command form.

   ¡Visiten hoy La Barata y   *Visit La Barata today and*
     abran una cuenta!   *open an account!*

4. To form negative commands, place **no** in front of the verb.

   No **abra** una cuenta.   *Don't open an account.*
   No **olviden** nuestro lema.   *Don't forget our slogan.*

Actividad • Falta algo

Complete the sentences with the appropriate command form of the following verbs.

llevar   aprovechar   ahorrar   olvidar   visitar   abrir

1. _Aproveche_ (Ud.) nuestra gran venta-liquidación.
2. _Lleve_ (Ud.) los artículos a su casa.
3. _Visiten_ (Uds.) La Nación hoy mismo.
4. _Abra_ (Ud.) una cuenta en La Nación.
5. No _olviden_ (Uds.) nuestro lema.
6. _Ahorre_ (Ud.) dinero con nuestras gangas.

A9   Actividad • El suplente   *The substitute*

Imagine you are a substitute teacher and you are having some problems in class. What instructions would you give in the following situations?

> MODELO   a Marieta, que no quiere entrar en la clase
> Marieta, **entre** en la clase.

1. a dos estudiantes que no quieren hablar español — Hablen español.
2. a un estudiante que come en clase — No coma en clase.
3. a Rolando, que estudia poco — Rolando, estudie más.
4. a Juan Octavio, que no escucha — Juan Octavio, escuche.
5. a los amigos de Andrés que beben refrescos en clase — No beban refrescos en clase.
6. a Rita y a su hermana, que no quieren abrir la puerta — Abran la puerta.
7. a Ramona y a Nati, que no escriben la actividad — Escriban la actividad.
8. a una chica que lee una revista en clase — No lea la revista en clase.
9. a tus amigos que no quieren aprender la lección — Aprendan la lección.
10. a todos los estudiantes que no estudian — Estudien.

For script, see p. T75.

A10   Comprensión

You will hear a statement followed by two responses. Choose the response that better completes the first statement and check the appropriate space on your answer sheet.

> MODELO   Yo necesito un suéter nuevo para el invierno.
>
> **a.** Pues, búsquelo en el garaje.
> **b.** Entonces, búsquelo en un almacén.

	0	1	2	3	4	5	6	7	8	9	10
a.					✓	✓			✓		✓
b.	✓	✓	✓	✓			✓	✓		✓	

1. el mostrador
2. un monedero
3. un par de zarcillos°
4. unas sandalias
5. un anillo
6. la vitrina
7. una bata
8. un vestido de seda
9. una playera
10. un paraguas
11. un par de botas
12. una bufanda

A 12 Actividad • Descripción del dibujo

Describe the illustration by answering the following questions.

1. ¿Cuáles son los artículos que están en la vitrina?
2. ¿De qué color es la bufanda?
3. ¿Cuánto cuesta el paraguas?
4. ¿Cuál es el artículo más caro? ¿Cuánto cuesta?
5. ¿Cuál es el artículo más barato? ¿Cuánto cuesta?
6. ¿Qué compra la señorita?
7. ¿Cómo paga la señorita?
8. ¿Cuánto cuestan las sandalias y las playeras?

1. Los artículos que están en la vitrina son una bata, un vestido de seda, una playera, un paraguas y un par de botas de cuero.   2. La bufanda es roja.   3. El paraguas cuesta 110 bolívares.   4. El artículo más caro es el vestido de seda. Cuesta 1.000 bolívares.   5. El artículo más barato es la playera. Cuesta 85 bolívares.   6. La señorita compra una bufanda.   7. La señorita usa una tarjeta de crédito para pagar.   8. Las sandalias cuestan 570 bolívares y las playeras cuestan 85 bolívares.

°In Venezuela, **zarcillos** (*earrings*) is used. In other Spanish-speaking countries, **aretes** or **pendientes** are also used for *earrings*.

El dinero en el mundo hispánico El nombre de la unidad monetaria en los distintos países hispanoamericanos varía, como también varía su valor *(its worth)* en relación al dólar. La fluctuación del valor de estas monedas es muy grande, y el viajero debe pedir información en un banco antes de salir de viaje.

Nombres de las unidades monetarias		
Argentina: el austral	El Salvador: el colón	Paraguay: el guaraní
Bolivia: el boliviano	España: la peseta	Perú: el sol, el inti
Colombia: el peso	Guatemala: el quetzal	República Dominicana:
Costa Rica: el colón	Honduras: la lempira	el peso
Cuba: el peso	México: el peso	Uruguay: el peso
Chile: el peso	Nicaragua: el córdoba	Venezuela: el bolívar
Ecuador: el sucre	Panamá: el balboa	

Perú: sol

El Salvador: colón

Uruguay: peso

Venezuela: bolívar

A 14 **ESTRUCTURAS ESENCIALES**
Position of object pronouns with commands

You may wish to do a personalized question/answer drill using classroom objects. Nod your head to elicit affirmative responses, and shake it to elicit negative responses.
(holding a book)
—¿Lo pongo allí? *(nod)*
—Sí, póngalo allí.
—¿Lo pongo aquí?
 (shake)
—No, no lo ponga aquí.

1. In all affirmative commands, object pronouns are placed after the verb and attached to it, forming one word. Don't forget to add an accent mark if the verb has more than one syllable.

¿Abro las ventanas?	Sí, ¡ábra**las**!	*Should I open the windows? Yes, open them!*
¿Compro el monedero?	Sí, ¡cómpre**lo**!	*Should I buy the change purse? Yes, buy it!*

2. To form negative commands, place the object pronoun in front of the verb.

> **no** + object pronoun + command

¿Abro la cuenta?	No, no **la** abra.	*Should I open the account?*	*No, don't open it.*
¿Compro las sandalias?	No, no **las** compre.	*Should I buy the sandals?*	*No, don't buy them.*

A 15 Actividad • El empleado nuevo

Pair up with another student. You have just been hired as a salesclerk at La Barata. Since you are not familiar with the procedures, ask your boss (classmate) what to do. Follow the model, using direct and indirect-object pronouns where necessary.

> MODELO ¿Saludo a los clientes?
> Sí, ¡salúdelos!

1. ¿Limpio la vitrina?
2. ¿Les pregunto a los clientes qué desean?
3. ¿Llevo los paraguas al departamento de señoras?
4. ¿Acepto tarjetas de crédito?
5. ¿Rebajo el anillo y los zarcillos que están en el mostrador?
6. ¿Preparo la cuenta?

Sí, ¡límpiela!
Sí, ¡pregúnteles!
Sí, ¡llévelos!
Sí, ¡acéptelas!

Sí, ¡rebájelos!
Sí, ¡prepárela!

A 16 Actividad • El gerente *The manager*

It seems that the new salesclerk isn't catching on very quickly. You have to tell the new salesclerk not to do certain things.

> MODELO ¿Rebajo los artículos?
> No, ¡no los rebaje!

1. ¿Pongo los anillos en el mostrador?
2. ¿Preparo una venta-liquidación de playeras?
3. ¿Llamamos por teléfono a nuestros amigos?
4. ¿Abro las puertas de la tienda a las once?
5. ¿Pido más monederos?
6. ¿Preparo las cuentas?

No, ¡no los ponga!
No, ¡no la prepare!
No, ¡no los llamen!
No, ¡no las abra!
No, ¡no los pida!
No, ¡no las prepare!

A 17 Actividad • Instrucciones
Answers will vary. For information on how to present the realia, see p. T77.

You are the store manager. Since you cannot open the store tomorrow morning, leave a list of instructions for your employees. Use a variety of singular and plural command forms, as well as affirmative and negative commands. Create a list of at least eight instructions.

You have recently been hired as copywriter at El Buen Anuncio, an advertising agency. Write a brief commercial for each of the following companies. (These ads will give you some ideas.)

LA CAVA
DE BARRILITO 🦏🦏🦏

EXQUISITA GASTRONOMIA FRANCESA E INTERNACIONAL

EL RESTAURANT DE LA GENTE QUE SABE

Centro Plaza Los Palos Grandes

Reservaciones: Telfs.:
283.3742 - 283.7424

BravaMar

RESTAURANT BAR

LO MEJOR EN CARNES Y MARISCOS

Avenida Principal La Castellana
Caracas

TELEFONOS: 33.1240
31.5941 - 31.3780

La Galera
Bar Restaurant

Descubra Ud. un nuevo mundo saboreando la exquisita paella en

La Galera

afiliado a su tarjeta de crédito

AVENIDA CASANOVA, CON 2ª
CALLE BELLO MONTE - CARACAS
TELEFONOS: 71.6680 - 71.3935

1. el restaurante Las Delicias

compre hoy
cómoda, fácil y agradablemente

DE: 10 a.m. A: 5 p.m.
Niza · Pasadena · La Esperanza

los 3 elefantes
bueno, bonito y barato!

silos ROPA DEPORTIVA

Porque la vida es un deporte

2. la ropa de deportes El Atleta

Calzados ROCKY, C.A.

Rocky

Ofrece a su distinguida clientela y público en general, el mayor surtido en calzados

Ponga un guante a sus pies con calzados ¡ROCKY!

Oferta Limitada

QUE NOTA

OFERTA 2x1

Tiempo limitado

APROVECHE OFERTA 2 X 1
en nuestra línea de calzado para dama
COMPRE SU PAR Y LLEVE OTRO COMPLETAMENTE GRATIS
Calzado Country Blue
con su gran promoción anual le espera
Dirección: 50 mts. norte del Hotel Balmoral

3. los zapatos Julieta

Quique y Ramiro salen de la casa de Marilú y, como no saben llegar a La Nación, le preguntan a un señor que va por la calle.

QUIQUE Perdone, señor, ¿sabe Ud. dónde queda La Nación?
SEÑOR Bueno . . . conozco esa tienda, pero no sé bien en qué calle está. Miren, vayan a la esquina y pregúntenle al policía de tránsito.
QUIQUE Muchísimas gracias.

(Quique y Ramiro van a la esquina donde está el policía.)

RAMIRO Buenos días, señor. ¿Puede decirnos cómo llegar a La Nación?
POLICÍA Por supuesto, jóvenes. Estén atentos a lo que les digo. Sigan Uds. por esta calle, que es la calle Pino, hasta la esquina de Pino y Paseo de la Fortuna. Doblen a la derecha en Paseo y . . .
QUIQUE Espere un momento, por favor. Déjeme anotarlo.
POLICÍA Sí . . . bueno, sigan por Paseo unas quince cuadras hasta llegar a la calle Flores. Doblen a la izquierda en Flores, caminen dos cuadras más y allí está La Nación.
QUIQUE Y
RAMIRO Muchísimas gracias.

(Quique y Ramiro se van. Después de unos minutos el policía dice algo.)

POLICÍA ¡Ay, caramba! Olvidé decirles que La Nación cerró hoy por inventario . . .

A20   Actividad • Preguntas y respuestas 🔲

Use the information in A19 to answer the following questions.

1. ¿A quién le piden información Quique
   y Ramiro al salir de casa?
2. ¿Qué información les dio el señor?
3. ¿Qué les dice el señor?
4. ¿Dónde está La Nación?
5. ¿Cuáles son las calles que toman
   ellos para ir a La Nación?
6. ¿Qué olvidó decirles el policía?

Quique y Ramiro le piden información a un señor que va por la calle.
El señor no sabe bien dónde está La Nación.
El señor les dice que vayan a la esquina y le pregunten al policía de
La Nación está en la calle Flores.   tránsito.

Ellos toman las calles Pino, Paseo de la Fortuna y Flores.
El policía olvidó decirles que La Nación cerró por inventario.

A21   Actividad • Cómo llegar a La Nación

Following the instructions given to Quique and Ramiro, draw a map showing how
to get to La Nación.

A22   SE DICE ASÍ
Asking for directions and giving information

Perdone, ¿sabe dónde está . . . ?	Excuse me, do you know where . . . is?
Con permiso, ¿sabe dónde queda . . . ?	Excuse me, do you know where . . . is?
¿Podría decirme cómo llegar a . . . ?	Could you please tell me how to get to . . . ?
Sí, con mucho gusto.	Yes, I'd be glad to.
Sí, está a la derecha.	Yes, it's on the right.
Sí, queda a la izquierda.	Yes, it's on the left.
Sí, queda a . . . cuadras de aquí.	Yes, it's . . . blocks away.
Sí, . . . al lado de . . .	Yes, . . . next to . . .
Sí, . . . enfrente de . . .	Yes, . . . in front of . . .
Sí, . . . detrás de . . .	Yes, . . . behind . . .
Sí, . . . cerca de . . .	Yes, . . . near . . .
Sí, . . . lejos de . . .	Yes, . . . far . . .

All of the above expressions can be used with either **está** or **queda.**

A23   Actividad • ¿Dónde están?   Answers will vary. Possible answers are given.

Imagine you are a Hispanic exchange student in your home town. Pair up with
a classmate and ask where three different places are located in relation to your
school. Use the expressions in A22 and exchange roles.   ¿Dónde queda el banco?
                                                     ¿Dónde está el centro comercial?
                                                     ¿Dónde queda el estadio de fútbol?

ESTRUCTURAS ESENCIALES
Irregularities in the formal command

The following verbs have irregular formal commands.

Infinitive	Usted (Ud.) Command	Ustedes (Uds.) Command
dar	**dé**	**den**
estar	**esté**	**estén**
ir	**vaya**	**vayan**
saber	**sepa**	**sepan**
ser	**sea**	**sean**

Déle la tarjeta de crédito al cliente.
Estén en la tienda temprano.
Vayan a clase a tiempo.
Sepan estos verbos para mañana.
Sea bueno con los profesores.

Give the credit card to the customer.
Be in the store early.
Go to class on time.
Know these verbs by tomorrow.
Be good to the teachers.

A 25 **Actividad • El dueño manda** *The owner gives the orders*

You are the new owner of La Nación and you are giving your employees a set of guidelines. Follow the model.

MODELO   Guillermo, (ser) _____ rápido en el trabajo.
Guillermo, **sea** rápido en el trabajo.

1. Carlos y María, (tener) _____ cuidado con los productos.
2. Pedro y Arturo, no (salir) _____ de su departamento.
3. (Venir) (Uds.) _____ temprano al trabajo.
4. Ricardo y Rosalía, (ir) _____ al mostrador.
5. (Darles) (Ud.) _____ buen precio a todos.
6. (Estar) (todos) _____ siempre listos para atender a los clientes.
7. Tú y tu hermana, (poner) _____ atención a los anuncios.
8. Manolo, (pedir) _____ permiso para llamar por teléfono.
9. Pepe y Paco, (saber) _____ el precio de los artículos.
10. Señora Pérez, (conseguir) _____ más clientes.
11. Gonzalo, (cerrar) _____ la tienda.
12. Elena, (hacer) _____ las cuentas del día.

1. tengan	7. pongan
2. salgan	8. pida
3. Vengan	9. sepan
4. vayan	10. consiga
5. Déles	11. cierre
6. Estén	12. haga

Actividad • ¡A completar!

Supply the correct form of each verb in this advertisement.

¡Gran venta para jóvenes! (ahorrar) _____ Ud. como   Ahorre
nunca. (Llevar) _____ a todos sus amigos a La Casa   Lleve
García y (aprovechar) _____ Uds. nuestra   aprovechen
venta-liquidación. (Ver) _____ los magníficos artículos   Vean
que nosotros tenemos en rebaja. Y amigos, no
(olvidar) _____ que "García regala la mercancía."   olviden

A 27 **SE DICE ASÍ**

Giving and following directions

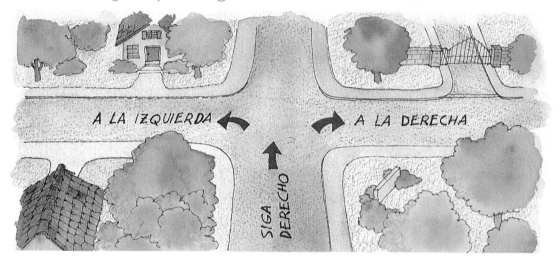

Siga derecho. Go straight ahead.		
	en la esquina. at the corner.
Doble a la derecha Turn right	en la intersección. at the intersection.
Doble a la izquierda Turn left	en la calle . . . at . . . Street.
	en la plaza . . . at . . . square.

The three expressions above will enable you to give or follow directions in Spanish to go almost everywhere.

A 28 **Actividad • Cómo llegamos a nuestra casa**   Answers will vary.

You have learned how to give directions in Spanish. Draw a map showing how to get from your school to your home, and write directions telling how to get there.

*In most large Hispanic cities there are department stores and shopping malls, called **centros
comerciales**. Many people like to shop in these places; others prefer the personal touch of
smaller specialty stores.*

B1   En La Barata 📼

Mientras Quique y Ramiro buscan La Nación, Bernardo, Marilú y Nati están en La
Barata. De pronto oyen que los llaman y allí ven a Roberto Barrera, un vecino de
Marilú que es dependiente del almacén.

ROBERTO	Buenos días, chicos. ¿Ya los están atendiendo?
MARILÚ	Roberto, ¡qué gusto verte!
ROBERTO	Hola, ¿cómo estás, Marilú? ¿En qué puedo servirles?
MARILÚ	Nati y yo estamos buscando unos jeans y unas playeras como las que vimos en la vitrina.

ROBERTO	Ah, los jeans y las playeras están en el departamento de jóvenes, en el último piso.
BERNARDO	Yo quiero una chaqueta de cuero, talla 46.
ROBERTO	Las chaquetas están en el departamento de caballeros. Están a la última moda. Si quieres, te las enseño. Estamos vendiendo miles de ellas.
BERNARDO	Gracias, Roberto. Chicas, las espero a la salida.
NATI Y MARILÚ	Nosotras vamos al último piso. Hasta luego, Roberto, y muchas gracias.

Cuando bajan, las muchachas ven que Bernardo está hablando por teléfono.
Bernardo termina, pero todos tienen que esperar un rato antes de ir a
casa porque ven por la ventana que está cayendo un aguacero muy fuerte.

B2   Actividad • Preguntas y respuestas

Based on the dialog in B1, answer the following questions.

1. ¿Quién es Roberto Barrera?
2. ¿Qué hace él en La Barata?
3. ¿Qué vieron en la vitrina Nati y Marilú?
4. ¿Qué quiere Bernardo?
5. ¿Qué dice Roberto que está a la última moda?
6. ¿Qué ven las muchachas cuando bajan?

Roberto Barrera es un vecino de Marilú.
Él es dependiente del almacén.
Nati y Marilú vieron unos jeans y unas playeras.
Bernardo quiere una chaqueta de cuero.
Roberto dice que las chaquetas están a la última moda.
Las muchachas ven que Bernardo está hablando por teléfono.

B3   Actividad • ¿Es cierto o no?

Decide whether each statement is true or false according to B1. Correct the false statements.

1. Bernardo y Quique están en La Barata.
2. Roberto está atendiendo a los jóvenes.
3. La Barata está vendiendo pocas chaquetas de cuero.
4. Bernardo está buscando unos jeans.
5. Las chaquetas de cuero están en el último piso.

Bernardo, Marilú y Nati están en La Barata.
Es cierto.
La Barata está vendiendo miles de chaquetas de cuero.
Bernardo está buscando una chaqueta de cuero.
Las chaquetas de cuero están en el departamento de caballeros.

B4   Sabes que . . .

Caracas, la capital de Venezuela, fue fundada (*was founded*) por los españoles en 1527. Hoy día es una gran ciudad de casi tres millones de habitantes (*residents*) y muy moderna. Caracas y otras ciudades importantes de Venezuela, como Maracaibo y Valencia, tienen grandes centros comerciales donde los compradores pueden encontrar todo lo que quieren. Estos centros comerciales se parecen mucho a los que hay en los Estados Unidos, con cafeterías, restaurantes, tiendas por departamentos y pequeñas boutiques. Mucha gente prefiere comprar en los centros comerciales, aunque (*even though*) tiene que pagar precios más altos por la mercancía, porque es fácil encontrar estacionamiento (*parking*) y por la comodidad (*convenience*) y elegancia que ofrecen estos lugares.

SE DICE ASÍ
Asking for and giving information in a store

Dependiente	Cliente
¿En qué puedo servirle? How may I help you?	Estoy buscando un . . . I'm looking for a . . .
¿Los están atendiendo? Is someone helping you?	No, es muy caro. No, it is very expensive.
¿Qué desea? What would you like?	¿Puedo probármelo? May I try it on?
¿Cuál es su talla? What's your size?	¿Dónde está el probador? Where is the fitting room?
¿Algo más? Anything else?	¿Me queda bien? Does it fit well?
Aquí está el vuelto. Here is your change.	Me lo llevo. I'll take it.

In some Spanish-speaking countries "el vuelto" or "el cambio" is used for *change.*

B6   Actividad • Minidiálogo

Pair up with a partner to complete the following conversation. Base your answers on the information provided in B1 and B5.

SEÑORITA	Buenos _____ , señor.	días
DEPENDIENTE	Buenos días, señorita. ¿En qué _____ ?	puedo servirle
SEÑORITA	Quiero _____ .	un vestido que vi en la vitrina
DEPENDIENTE	¿Cuál es su talla?	
SEÑORITA	Es la talla 10 americana. ¿Cuál es aquí?	
DEPENDIENTE	Aquí es la talla 36.	
SEÑORITA	Es muy bonito. Me lo _____ .	llevo
DEPENDIENTE	Muy bien. ¿Quiere algo _____ ?	más
SEÑORITA	No, gracias, _____ .	muy amable

B7   Comprensión   For script, see p. T81–82.

You will hear a statement by either a salesclerk or a shopper. Each statement will be followed by three possible responses. Choose the one that best completes the conversation.

MODELO   ¿En qué puedo servirle?

a. No, gracias.
   Es muy caro.
b. Estoy buscando
   unos jeans.
c. ¿Algo más?

	0	1	2	3	4	5	6	7	8	9	10
a.			✓		✓		✓		✓		
b.	✓	✓				✓					✓
c.				✓				✓		✓	

ESTRUCTURAS ESENCIALES
The present progressive form

To describe an action that is in progress at the moment of speaking, that is, right now, Spanish uses the present progressive.

> present tense of **estar** + **-ndo** form = present progressive

Pedro y Luis **están trabajando** en la tienda.	*Pedro and Luis are working in the store.*
Coralia **está vendiendo** las bufandas.	*Coralia is selling the scarfs.*
Yo **estoy escribiendo** la cuenta.	*I am writing the bill.*

1. To form the present progressive, use a present tense form of **estar** as a helping verb plus the **-ndo** form of the main verb called **gerundio**.

   Alicia **está hablando** con Mauricio.   *Alicia is talking to Mauricio.*

2. The **-ndo** form of regular **-ar** verbs consists of the verb stem + **-ando**.

   buscar: **busc** + **ando** = **buscando**

   Las chicas **están buscando** unos jeans.   *The girls are looking for jeans.*

3. The **-ndo** form of regular **-er** and **-ir** verbs consists of the verb stem + **-iendo**.

   atender: **atend** + **iendo** = **atendiendo**
   escribir: **escrib** + **iendo** = **escribiendo**

   ¿Ya los **están atendiendo?**   *Is someone helping you?*
   ¿Qué **estás escribiendo,** Mauricio?   *What are you writing, Mauricio?*

4. Notice that the helping verb **estar** changes to agree with the subject, but the **-ndo** form always remains the same.

   Marilú **está comprando** botas.   *Marilú is buying boots.*
   Marilú y Nati **están comprando** botas.   *Marilú and Nati are buying boots.*

5. Some irregular **-ndo** forms are:

   pedir **pidiendo**
   decir **diciendo**
   venir **viniendo**
   servir **sirviendo**
   caer **cayendo**
   leer **leyendo**
   repetir **repitiendo**
   seguir **siguiendo**

Actividad • ¿Qué está pasando ahora?

Look at the illustrations and describe what these people are doing.

MODELO Rogelio / unas sandalias
Rogelio está comprando unas sandalias.

1. Guillermo / los calcetines

2. Rosendo y Nora / la vitrina

3. El señor Barrera / los precios

4. La dependienta / una chaqueta de cuero

5. María y Adela / el policía

1. Guillermo está comprando los calcetines.
2. Rosendo y Nora están mirando la vitrina.
3. El señor Barrera está rebajando los precios.
4. La dependienta está vendiendo una chaqueta de cuero.

5. María y Adela están hablando con el policía.
6. El gerente está abriendo la puerta.

6. El gerente / la puerta

B 10 Actividad • ¿Qué están haciendo? Cindy Lauper está cantando una canción. Michael Jordan y Magic Johnson están jugando al básquetbol. Tu profesor está explicando la lección. Michael J. Fox está actuando en una película. Judy Bloom está escribiendo un libro.

Use the present progressive form to express what the following people may be doing right now.

Cindy Lauper
Tu profesor
Michael Jordan y Magic Johnson
Judy Bloom
Michael J. Fox

cantar una canción
actuar en una película
explicar la lección
jugar al básquetbol
escribir un libro

B 11 Actividad • Excusas, excusas y más excusas Answers will vary.

Five people are calling you to see if you want to go out right now. Think of five different excuses that you can give in order not to go. Use the present progressive.

MODELO — Hola, (Gregorio), ¿quieres salir?
— No puedo porque estoy trabajando.

B 12 Actividad • ¿Qué están haciendo los estudiantes?

The assistant principal wants to know where your classmates are right now, and you are the only one who knows. Answer by following the model.

MODELO Nacho / jugar al básquetbol
Nacho está jugando al básquetbol.

1. Mario / hacer un examen   Mario está haciendo el examen.
2. Tu hermano / correr en el parque   Tu hermano está corriendo en el parque.
3. Roberto / comer en la cafetería   Roberto está comiendo en la cafetería.
4. Tere y Rafa / estudiar en su casa   Tere y Rafa están estudiando en su casa.
5. Andrés / escuchar la radio   Andrés está escuchando la radio.
6. Carlos y yo / leer una revista   Carlos y yo estamos leyendo una revista.
7. Quique y Ramiro / llamar por teléfono   Quique y Ramiro están llamando por teléfono.
8. Carolina / salir de la escuela   Carolina está saliendo de la escuela.
9. Ellos / cerrar las ventanas   Ellos están cerrando las ventanas.

B 13 ESTRUCTURAS ESENCIALES
Position of object pronouns with the present progressive

There are two positions for object pronouns when used with the present progressive.

Estamos comprándo**lo.** }
Lo estamos comprando. } *We are buying it.*

Están vendiéndo**la.** }
La están vendiendo. } *They are selling it.*

Object pronouns are either attached to the end of the **-ndo** form or placed in front of the verb **estar.** When an object pronoun is attached to the **-ndo** form, add a written accent to maintain the original stress in pronunciation.

B14 **Actividad • ¿Qué está pasando allí?**  For answers, see p. T84.

Change each sentence to the present progressive and replace the direct object with
an object pronoun. Follow the model.

MODELO   Pedro compra la guitarra.
          Pedro está comprándola.
          Pedro la está comprando.

1. Alberto y Julián atienden a los clientes.
2. El dependiente aprende nuestro lema.
3. Los clientes aprovechan la venta-liquidación.
4. Quique compra la chaqueta y el pañuelo.

5. Eduardo y yo pagamos la cuenta.
6. El gerente rebaja los precios.
7. Clara vende una bufanda.
8. Nati y su prima usan la tarjeta de crédito.

B15   **SITUACIÓN • El departamento de caballeros**

1. un llavero
2. un impermeable
3. una camisa de mangas largas
4. una camisa de mangas cortas
5. una camiseta

6. unos pantalones
7. un traje
8. unos pijamas
9. unos calzoncillos
10. un saco

Actividad • Descripción del dibujo

Look at the illustration in B15 and answer the following questions.

1. ¿Qué está haciendo la señora?
2. ¿Qué están mirando los jóvenes?
3. ¿Qué está comprando el señor?
4. ¿Qué está haciendo el niño?
5. ¿Qué le está dando la dependienta al señor?
6. ¿Qué está haciendo la chica?

La señora está llamando a su hijo.
Los jóvenes están mirando un traje.
El señor está comprando una camisa de manga corta.
El niño está corriendo.
La dependienta le está dando el vuelto al señor.
La chica está mirando unos pijamas.

B17 **Actividad • Las compras**   Answers will vary.

Get together with a classmate and discuss the following:

¿Te gusta ir de compras? ¿Por qué?
¿Cuándo fuiste de compras la última vez? ¿Adónde?
¿Qué compraste?
¿Tienes mucha ropa? ¿Qué quieres comprar?

B18 **Actividad • ¡A escribir!**   Answers will vary. For information on how to present the realia, see p. T84.

Prepare a shopping list of seven items you need or would like to buy for a friend at a men's clothing store.

C1

De regreso 📼

Bernardo, Nati y Marilú están bebiendo unos refrescos en casa de Marilú y están comentando sobre los artículos que vieron en La Barata, cuando Quique y Ramiro tocan el timbre.

MARILÚ   ¡Hola! ¡Entren! ¡Huy, qué tarde vinieron!
RAMIRO   ¡Uf! Estamos muertos de tanto caminar.
QUIQUE   ¡Ay! ¡Y qué hambre tengo!
MARILÚ   ¿No almorzaste?
          ¿Qué les pasó?

QUIQUE   Ramiro fue conmigo a La Nación y . . .
          caramba, la tienda cerró hoy por inventario.
NATI   ¡Ay, qué pena!
RAMIRO   Quique, nunca más voy de compras contigo.
QUIQUE   Yo no tuve la culpa. Para mí, la culpa la tuvo
          ese anuncio horrible que están pasando
          por televisión. Es un anuncio viejo
          que grabaron el mes pasado.
RAMIRO   Perdona, la culpa la tuvo el policía
          que no nos dijo que la tienda cerró.
QUIQUE   Bueno, y ustedes, ¿qué compraron?
BERNARDO Pues . . . nada. No compramos nada.
          Y así, de verdad ahorramos plata
          en La Barata.

Use the information in C1 to answer the following questions.

1. ¿Dónde están bebiendo los chicos unos refrescos?
2. ¿Quiénes tocan el timbre?
3. ¿Por qué dicen que están muertos?
4. ¿Qué vieron Quique y Ramiro al llegar a La Nación?
5. Según Quique, ¿quién tuvo la culpa?
6. ¿Cuándo grabaron el anuncio?
7. ¿Por qué dice Bernardo que ahorraron plata en La Barata?

TIENDA CERRADA POR INVENTARIO

C3 Actividad • ¡A escoger!

Choose the correct word or words to complete each statement according to C1.

1. Los muchachos están _____ unos refrescos.
   • comiendo   • <u>bebiendo</u>   • cocinando

2. Quique y Ramiro llegaron _____.
   • temprano   • a tiempo   • <u>tarde</u>

3. Quique no _____.
   • pidió   • <u>descansó</u>   • comió

4. Según Ramiro, la culpa la tuvo _____.
   • <u>el policía</u>   • el anuncio   • la televisión

5. La tienda cerró por _____.
   • artículos   • <u>inventario</u>   • televisión

6. Los muchachos no compraron _____.
   • artículos   • algo   • <u>nada</u>

C4 SE DICE ASÍ

Expressing satisfaction or displeasure with emphasis

¡Uf! Estamos muertos de tanto caminar.	Ugh! We're dead tired from so much walking.
¡Ay! Y yo no tomé el almuerzo.	Boy! And I didn't have lunch.
¡Huy! ¡Cómo comió Juanita!	Wow, did Juanita eat!
¡Bah! Creo que no va a llover.	C'mon! I don't think it is going to rain.
¡Basta! No quiero más.	Enough! I don't want any more.
¡Caramba! Son las siete.	Heavens! It's seven o'clock.

Interjections in Spanish, as well as in English, are used to reaffirm or emphasize what you want to express.

Hablemos un poco del país ahora. Venezuela puede dividirse en tres grandes zonas. **1. La zona montañosa de los Andes:** Inmensas montañas entran al país por Colombia y se extienden por el norte de Venezuela paralelas *(parallel)* a la costa. Su altura máxima *(highest point)* es el Pico Bolívar (5,002 m.). La costa tiene bellísimas playas en el mar Caribe. En esta zona están la moderna capital, Caracas, con más de tres millones de habitantes *(residents)* y la ciudad petrolera *(oil city)* de Maracaibo, al borde del lago Maracaibo. **2. La zona central de los llanos:** Una vasta sabana *(plains)* que es el centro ganadero *(cattle center)* del país. Incluye el delta del río Orinoco, que atraviesa *(crosses)* toda Venezuela. **3. La zona de Guayana:** Allí está el Salto del Ángel, la cascada *(waterfall)* más alta del mundo. También se encuentran en esta zona las selvas *(jungles)* del río Amazonas donde habitan *(live)* indios que no habían español.

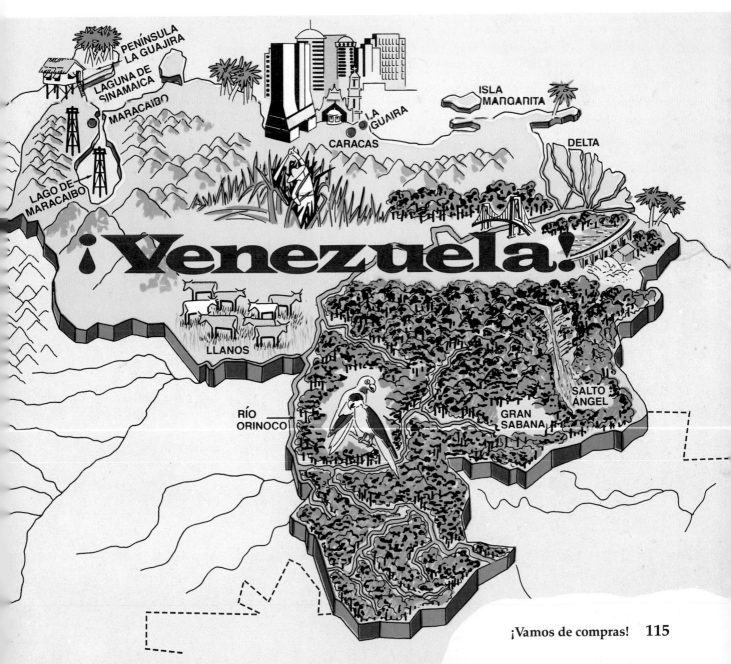

¿RECUERDAS?
Pronouns used after prepositions

You have already learned the prepositional pronouns. The following chart summarizes them:

	Prepositions	Prepositional Pronouns
El regalo es	**para**	**mí.**
Hablaron	**de**	**ti.**
Van de compras	**con**	**ella/él/Ud.**
Piensa	**en**	**nosotros(-as).**
Vamos	**sin**	**ellos/ellas/Uds.**

1. Remember that the prepositional pronouns are the same as the subject pronouns, except that **mí** replaces **yo** and **ti** replaces **tú.**

2. When used with the preposition **con,** the pronouns **mí** and **ti** have special forms.

con + mí = conmigo
con + ti = contigo

Venga **conmigo,** por favor.   *Please come with me.*
Charo, quiero salir **contigo.**   *Charo, I want to go out with you.*

3. With object pronouns, for emphasis or clarification, Spanish uses **a** followed by the prepositional pronoun.

¿Le doy el anillo **a ella?**   *Should I give the ring to her?*
A mí me gusta ahorrar.   *I do like to save.*
A ellos les gusta gastar.   *They like to spend (money).*

C7 Actividad • Combinación

Complete each sentence by selecting the appropriate item from the box.

1. Elena, ¿te importa esto a . . . ?
2. Rolando, voy al cine . . .
3. Leti le habla por teléfono a . . .
4. Nora me ve a . . .
5. Camila, ¿quieres ir de compras . . . ?
6. Andrés los quiere ver a . . .

1. ti
2. contigo.
3. él.
4. mí.
5. conmigo.
6. ustedes.

C8 Actividad • Yo quiero saber   Answers will vary.

You want to know more about the student who sits behind you in class. Pair up with a classmate and ask the following questions.

1. ¿Conoces a la persona que se sienta detrás de mí?
2. ¿Juega al básquetbol contigo?
3. ¿Les habla a tus amigos de mí?
4. ¿Sabes si conoce a mi mejor amigo/a?
5. ¿Estudia contigo?
6. ¿Con quién come en la cafetería?

C9 ESTRUCTURAS ESENCIALES
The irregular verb venir *in the preterit tense*

The verb **venir** is irregular in the preterit tense.

venir	*to come*
vine	vinimos
viniste	vinisteis
vino	vinieron

Ellos **vinieron** en autobús.   *They came by bus.*
Rosita **vino** con Eduardo.   *Rosita came with Eduardo.*

C10 Actividad • La visita   Answers will vary.

Some friends you have not seen in a long time have just arrived in town, and you are talking to one of them on the phone. Work with a partner and ask the following questions.

1. Sí, vine de . . .   4. Answers will vary.
2. Vine . . .   5. Answers will vary.
3. Vine en . . .   6. Vine por . . .

MODELO ¿De dónde viniste?
        Vine de Nueva York.

1. ¿Viniste de vacaciones?
2. ¿Cuándo viniste, hoy o ayer?
3. ¿En qué viniste?

4. ¿Vinieron tus padres contigo?
5. ¿Vino tu primo?
6. ¿Por cuánto tiempo viniste?

ESTRUCTURAS ESENCIALES
Some verbs with spelling changes in the preterit tense

The **-er** and **-ir** verbs that have a stem ending in a vowel change the **i** to **y** in the third person singular and third person plural of the preterit tense.

leer *to read*	caer° *to fall*	oír *to hear*	creer *to believe*	destruir *to destroy*
leí	caí	oí	creí	destruí
leíste	caíste	oíste	creíste	destruiste
leyó	**cayó**	**oyó**	**creyó**	**destruyó**
leímos	caímos	oímos	creímos	destruimos
leísteis	caísteis	oísteis	creísteis	destruisteis
leyeron	**cayeron**	**oyeron**	**creyeron**	**destruyeron**

¿Qué libro **leyó** Ud. ayer? — *What book did you read yesterday?*
La lluvia **cayó** de repente. — *The rain fell suddenly.*
Oyeron la noticia anoche. — *They heard the news last night.*
Gloria **creyó** lo que él dijo. — *Gloria believed what he said.*
La tormenta **destruyó** dos árboles. — *The storm destroyed two trees.*

ATENCIÓN: Another verb conjugated like **destruir** is **construir**.

Ellos **construyeron** la casa. — *They built the house.*
La ciudad **construyó** un centro para las artes. — *The city built an art center.*

C12 Actividad • La tienda nueva

Change all the infinitives in parentheses to the appropriate preterit forms.

Mi hermano (leer) en el periódico que el señor Fernández (construir) una tienda cerca de casa. También (oír) por la radio muchos anuncios sobre una gran venta en esa tienda. Él pensó ir a la tienda, pero un aguacero que (caer) de repente le (destruir) sus planes.

leyó / construyó

oyó

cayó / destruyó

C13 Actividad • Las compras   Answers will vary.

Now you have the chance to talk about yourself by answering the following questions.

1. ¿Te gusta ir de compras? ¿Por qué?
2. Cuando vas de compras, ¿vas solo/a o con alguien?
3. ¿Dónde compras tu ropa?
4. ¿Qué clase de ropa te gusta a ti? ¿Por qué?
5. ¿Cuáles son tus colores favoritos?
6. ¿Qué clase de ropa usas tú para ir a la escuela?
7. ¿Aprovechas las ventas-liquidación? ¿Por qué?

°The verb **caer(se)** is most often used in reflexive constructions. You will learn about reflexives in Unit 6.

Look at the illustrations and tell what happened by using **construir, oír, leer, destruir,** or **caer.**
Follow the model.

MODELO   mi abuelo / anoche
           Mi abuelo leyó el periódico anoche.

1. el avión / al mar ayer

El avión cayó al mar ayer.

2. los ingenieros / el edificio el año pasado

3. yo / el noticiero a las once

4. la tormenta / dos árboles el mes pasado

5. los muchachos / la revista el domingo

2. Los ingenieros construyeron el edificio el año pasado.   3. Yo oí el noticiero a las once.   4. La tormenta destruyó dos
árboles el mes pasado.   5. Los muchachos leyeron la revista el domingo.

Actividad • Aquí está La Barata

Answers will vary.

The classroom will now become La Barata. Some of the students will play the role of customers while others will be the salesclerks. The customers can ask questions about five articles, including prices, sizes, colors, and so on. The salesclerks should provide the correct information.

C16 Comprensión 🔲

For script, see p. T88.

You will hear a statement or a question followed by a response. If the response is logical, check **lógico** on your answer sheet. If it is not, check **ilógico**.

MODELO — ¿Vas al baile con Juan?
— Sí, voy con él.

	0	1	2	3	4	5	6	7	8	9	10
Lógico	✔				✔	✔			✔		✔
Ilógico		✔	✔	✔			✔	✔		✔	

C17 Actividad • ¡A escribir y a hablar!

Answers will vary.

Write a description in Spanish of your favorite store, taking into account the following suggestions.

I. Introducción
   A. Mi tienda favorita es . . .
   B. ¿Cómo conociste la tienda?
   C. ¿Dónde queda?
   D. ¿Cuántas veces al mes compras en la tienda?
II. Desarrollo *(Development)*
   A. ¿Cómo es la tienda?
   B. ¿Tiene muchos empleados?
   C. ¿Son buenos los empleados?
   D. ¿Vende cosas caras o baratas?
   E. ¿Van muchos clientes a la tienda?
   F. ¿Ofrece gangas o ventas-liquidación?
   G. ¿Cómo pagas en la tienda?
III. Conclusión
   A. Me gusta esa tienda porque . . .
   B. Le voy a recomendar esa tienda a . . .

Now present your composition orally in class.

1 ¡A dar órdenes!

Give formal commands to the people in the illustrations.

1. Roberto y Raúl / escribir   ¡Escriban la carta!

2. Luisa / poner   ¡Ponga la mesa!

3. la camarera / servir   ¡Sirva el agua!

4. el dependiente / vender   ¡Venda los zapatos!

5. Mario y Alberto / ir   ¡Vayan a la pizarra!

6. Antonio / leer   ¡Lea el periódico!

7. Ana y Luisa / traer   ¡Traigan los libros!

8. Juan y Andrés / hablar   ¡Hablen más alto!

2 **Actividad • En la clase**   For answers, see p. T89.

Imagine how your teacher will respond if you ask the following questions. Follow the model.

> MODELO   ¿Termino la tarea ahora?
> Sí, termínela.
> *or*
> No, no la termine.

1. ¿Escribo los ejercicios en clase?
2. ¿Abro o cierro la puerta?
3. ¿Contestamos las preguntas?
4. ¿Pido un libro y un lápiz nuevo?
5. ¿Le pongo atención a Tomás?

6. ¿Ahorramos dinero para la excursión?
7. ¿Leemos la composición?
8. ¿Limpio y arreglo la clase?
9. ¿Salimos durante la hora del almuerzo?
10. ¿Traigo la bufanda y el sombrero a la escuela?

3 **Actividad • Los dólares en pesos**   For answers, see p. T89.

Suppose that in the Dominican Republic a dollar is worth four pesos. Read these numbers aloud in Spanish as if they were **dólares;** then change them to **pesos.**

240   170   101   66   136

4 **Actividad • El cliente**   Answers will vary.

Write five questions in Spanish you may ask a salesclerk.

5 **Actividad • En la tienda**   Answers will vary.

Now pair up with another student and role-play a conversation between a salesclerk and a customer. Be sure to ask about four items and their prices.

Mention eight different things that happened recently, using these verbs.

buscar	leer	venir	conocer
gastar	destruir	oír	construir

Choose an appropriate exclamation from the box to precede each of the following statements.

____ ¡Tengo tanta sed!
____ Eso no importa.
____ No puedo comer más.
____ ¡Qué cansado estoy!
____ ¡Qué sorpresa!
____ ¡Cómo bailó Carlos!

¡Basta!   ¡Uf!   ¡Caramba!   ¡Ay!

¡Huy!   ¡Bah!

Write three commercials in Spanish for three of your favorite department stores.

9 Actividad • ¿Con él o sin él? 🔲

Clarisa is asking her brother Pepe about several things, but he always answers negatively. Following the model, use a preposition, such as **con, a, para,** or **sin.** Replace the nouns with the corresponding prepositional pronouns.

MODELO   Pepe, ¿quieres ir al cine? (conmigo)
No, no quiero ir al cine contigo.

1. ¿Compraste el regalo? (papá y mamá)   No, no compré el regalo para ellos.
2. ¿Fuiste al baile? (Luisa)   No, no fui al baile con ella.
3. ¿Viniste a casa? (Felipe y Santiago)   No, no vine a casa con ellos.
4. ¿Le regalaste las flores? (Elena)   No, no le regalé las flores a ella.
5. ¿Vas a almorzar? (nosotros)   No, no voy a almorzar sin ustedes.

10   Dictado 🔲 For script, see p. T90.

Get ready to complete the following paragraph from dictation.

La semana pasada mi prima _____ fue de
compras _____ . Cuando llegamos _____ almacén,
vimos muchos _____ en la _____ . Una
dependienta _____ nos preguntó, "¿_____
_____ ?" Y nos _____ muy bien. Mi prima
compró una _____ para _____ y un _____
para su _____ . Yo _____ la venta
_____ y _____ mucho _____ .

The following questions are based on the realia in #9. Once the activity is finished, you may wish to write these questions on the board and have the students answer them in writing.

1. ¿Cómo se llama la película?
2. ¿Cómo se llama el cine?
3. ¿De quién es la música?
4. ¿Cuál es el ballet?
5. ¿Quiénes fueron los actores?
6. ¿Quién es el director?
7. ¿Qué día hay rebaja?
8. ¿Cuánto rebajan?

Diphthongs with *a, e,* and *o* *(Review)*

In Spanish, the vowels **a, e,** and **o** combine with the weaker vowels **i** and **u** to form diphthongs. Read and repeat the following words and sentences.

aguacero	vuelto	muerto	nuevo
cuenta	paraguas	cierto	tienda

Queremos comprar un nuevo paraguas.
Eugenia quiere abrir una cuenta en la tienda.
Es cierto que hace mucho ruido.
El dependiente no nos dio el vuelto.

Letters *r* (initial) and *rr*

1. The **r** in the initial position and after **l, n,** or **s** is pronounced with a very strong trill. Read and repeat the following words and sentences.

Roberto	rebaja	Enrique	alrededor	Israel
refresco	Raúl	radio	rascacielos	

Roberto rebaja los regalos y Rita regatea.
Raúl bebe refrescos mientras oye la radio.
A Enrique le gusta remar en el río.
Raúl le regala rosas rojas a Ramona.

2. The **rr** is a letter of the Spanish alphabet and is pronounced with a very strong trill. The **rr** can never begin a word. Read and repeat the following words and sentences.

ahorra	perro	arriba	arroz
pelirrojo	corre	horrible	cerró

Rolando el pelirrojo ahorra rápido.
El perro de Rosita corre con la revista.
El ruido es horrible.
El restaurante cerró y no hay arroz.

Actividad • Dos trabalenguas fáciles

Practice the following tongue twisters.

Erre con erre cigarro,
Erre con erre barril.
Rápido corren los carros
por los rieles del ferrocarril.

En tres tristes trastos
comen trigo
tres tristes tigres.

¿LO SABES?

Let's review some important points you've learned in this unit.

SECTION A

For answers, see p. T91.

Can you give formal commands in Spanish?
Use the following verbs to command someone to do something.

apagar   dar   llevar   quedar   anotar

Can you give directions in Spanish?
Ask where a classmate lives. Then explain how to get from his or her home to yours.

Do you know how to accept and refuse invitations?
Pair up with a classmate. Your classmate will ask you three questions inviting you to go shopping. On two occasions answer affirmatively; on one, answer negatively.

SECTION B

Answers will vary.

Can you use your Spanish as a salesclerk?
Write five phrases in Spanish you may use as a salesclerk.

Can you guess what people are doing right now?
Tell what two members of your family are doing right now and what five of your classmates are doing at this very moment.

Are you able to identify items commonly found in the men's or ladies' department of a clothing store?
Name at least five items from each department.

SECTION C

Answers will vary.

Can you express in Spanish some of the things you want to have?
Make a list of five things that you want to buy at a department store. Describe the items in Spanish to your classmates.

Do you know how to use Spanish interjections correctly?
Use each of the following interjections in a sentence to express satisfaction or displeasure.

¡Ay!   ¡Basta!   ¡Huy!   ¡Bah!

Can you talk about the last time you went shopping?
List five items you bought or wanted to buy. Then write a sentence in the preterit tense with each of them.

VOCABULARIO

SECTION A

abrir una cuenta *to open an account*
ahora mismo *right now*
al día *up to date*
el **almacén** *store*
alto *loudly*
el **anillo** *ring*
anotar *to write down*
apagar *to turn off*
aparecer *to appear*
aprovechar *to take advantage of*
los **aretes** *earrings*
el **artículo** *article*
atento, -a *attentive*
la **bata** *robe*
la **bufanda** *scarf*
¡caramba! *heavens!*
la **casa** *business firm*
cerrar (ie) *to close*
como de costumbre *as usual*
¡cómo no! *of course!*
con mucho gusto *I'd be glad to*
la **cuadra** *city block*
doblar *to turn*
doblar a la derecha *to turn right*
doblar a la izquierda *to turn left*
estar al día *to be up to date*
garantizar *to guarantee*
hoy mismo *today*
el **inventario** *inventory*
ir de compras *to go shopping*
el **lema** *slogan*
la **locura** *madness*
llevar *to take (with you)*

más barato *cheaper*
más caro *more expensive*
la **mercancía** *merchandise*
la **moda** *fashion*
el **monedero** *change purse*
el **mostrador** *counter*
muchísimo *very much*
odioso, -a *hateful, odious*
otro día *another day*
el **par** *pair*
el **paraguas** *umbrella*
los **pendientes** *earrings*
perdone *excuse me*
la **plata** *silver; (coll.) money*
la **playera** *tee shirt*
¡por supuesto! *of course!*
quedar *to be (located)*
rebajar *to reduce (price)*
regalar *to give (away)*
las **sandalias** *sandals*
seguir derecho *to go straight ahead*
el **surtido** *stock*
el **tránsito** *traffic*
la **venta-liquidación** *clearance sale*
la **vitrina** *display window*
los **zarcillos** *earrings*

SECTION B

el **aguacero** *downpour*
a la (última) moda *in the latest style*
atender (ie) *to attend; to wait on someone*
el **caballero** *gentleman*
los **calzoncillos** *men's briefs*
la **camiseta** *undershirt*

la **dependienta** *salesclerk (f.)*
el **dependiente** *salesclerk (m.)*
desear *to wish, to want*
enseñar *to show; to teach*
el **impermeable** *raincoat*
el **llavero** *key ring*
el **probador** *fitting room*
probarse (ue) *to try on*
¡qué gusto verte! *what a pleasure to see you!*
el **último piso** *top floor*
la **ventana** *window*
el **vuelto** *change (money)*

SECTION C

almorzar (ue) *to eat lunch*
¡bah! *c'mon!*
caer *to fall; to strike (lightning)*
comentar *to comment*
construir *to build, to construct*
la **culpa** *blame*
descansar *to rest*
destruir *to destroy*
estar muerto *to be dead (tired)*
grabar *to record (on tape)*
¡huy! *wow!*
llover (ue) *to rain*
nunca más *never again*
el **rayo** *lightning bolt*
tener la culpa *to be at fault*
la culpa la tuvo *the one to blame was . . .*
el **timbre** *doorbell*
la **tormenta** *storm*
¡uf! *ugh!*
la **verdad** *truth*
de verdad *in truth, really*

MEN'S	WOMEN'S
playera	bata
calzoncillos	playera
camiseta	sandalias
impermeable	impermeable
saco	

PRÁCTICA DEL VOCABULARIO

Make separate lists of all the items of clothing in this unit. Make a list for men's and women's clothing.

VAMOS A LEER

Antes de leer

Scan the selection briefly and try to find as many cognates as possible. Here are some hints:

1. Many Spanish and English words are similar in form and meaning. However, they are pronounced differently. Can you find two examples in the selection?

2. Some Spanish words ending in **-a, -e,** or **-o** have an English equivalent without the final vowel. There are at least three in the selection. Try to find them.

3. Many Spanish words ending in **-ia** have an English equivalent ending in -e. Find at least two examples in the selection.

Now make a list of the words you found and provide the English definitions.

Preparación para la lectura

Answer the following questions before reading.

1. Menciona dos o tres palabras en español que mucha gente que no habla español conoce.   uno, señorita, adiós, amigo, señor

2. Si buscas rápidamente en la Lectura, vas a encontrar algunas ciudades de los Estados Unidos que tienen nombres españoles. ¿Cuáles son?
Santa Fe, San Agustín, Los Angeles, San Francisco, Boca Ratón

3. ¿Qué otras ciudades con nombres españoles conoces?   Santa Bárbara, San Diego, San Antonio

4. ¿Qué crees que quiere decir *Sierra Nevada*?   Quiere decir montaña donde hay nieve.

5. ¿Puedes adivinar qué significan *emperador, símbolo, castillos, unidad monetaria* y *colonias*?   emperor, symbol, castles, currency, and colonies

6. ¿Por qué crees que Nuevo México se llama así?   Porque era parte de México.

7. ¿Sabes cuál es la ciudad más antigua del territorio de los Estados Unidos?
La ciudad más antigua es San Agustín en la Florida.

8. ¿Cómo crees que se llama ahora la antigua ciudad de Nuestra Señora de los Ángeles?   Se llama Los Ángeles.

España y los Estados Unidos

No es necesario estudiar español para saber un buen número de palabras en español. Palabras como **plaza, aficionado, sierra** y **rodeo** forman parte del lenguaje diario de los Estados Unidos desde hace muchos años. La historia y la cultura de los dos países tienen otras conexiones que muchas personas no conocen. ¿Sabes, por ejemplo, que algo tan norteamericano como el signo del dólar tiene origen español? La historia es muy interesante. Quizás puedes sorprender a algunos de tus amigos contándola.

En tiempos del emperador Carlos V, que fue también rey de España, se hicieron en el año de 1535 en México unas monedas° con el escudo° del emperador. Como símbolo de su gran poder,° le añadió a este escudo las dos columnas de Hércules, un héroe mitológico, con la inscripción *Plus Ultra* ("más allá"), referencia a sus colonias en la América. Esta moneda, como otras monedas españolas, también circuló en las colonias inglesas, que no tuvieron monedas hasta 1652.

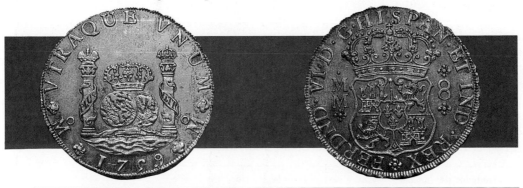

monedas   *coins; currency*   **escudo**   *coat of arms*   **poder**   *power*

Después de la independencia de los Estados Unidos, la moneda principal norteamericana fue el dólar. Esta moneda no era muy fuerte. Los hombres de negocios° prefirieron el *"Spanish pillars"* dólar, esto es, la moneda española de las dos columnas. Thomas Jefferson la propuso como unidad monetaria en los Estados Unidos en 1785 y así lo fue hasta 1857. Los primeros billetes de banco norteamericanos, en uso durante muchos años, tuvieron el escudo español con los castillos y los leones y con las dos columnas de Hércules. La inscripción *Plus Ultra* alrededor de° las columnas vino a ser° el signo $. Es conveniente recordar que el signo $ no significa solamente dólar norteamericano. En ocho países hispanoamericanos, como por ejemplo en México, Cuba y Colombia, representa la moneda nacional.

Otra gran influencia de España en los Estados Unidos está en los nombres de algunas ciudades como Los Ángeles, San Francisco, Amarillo, Las Vegas, Boca Ratón y muchas otras. También la influencia española es evidente en los nombres de varios estados que fueron antes territorios españoles. California era un lugar imaginario en un libro español de aventuras de 1510. Colorado recibió ese nombre por un río° de color rojo que los españoles exploraron (**colorado** es sinónimo de **rojo**). El nombre de la Florida viene de Pascua Florida *(Easter)*. Quiere decir *in full bloom*. En la Florida está San Agustín, la ciudad más antigua del territorio de los Estados Unidos. Fue fundada por Pedro Menéndez de Avilés en 1565, y en 1763 los españoles se la dieron a los ingleses a cambio de° La Habana, ciudad que ocuparon durante un ataque a la isla de Cuba.

Montana quiere decir *mountain* en español (sólo perdió la **ñ**, igual que la palabra **cabana**). **Nevada** quiere decir *covered with snow*. El nombre de **Oregon** posiblemente viene de una palabra española, **orejón,** que quiere decir "hombre de orejas° grandes". **Nuevo México** fue parte de México hasta 1848 y tiene otra de las ciudades más antiguas de los Estados Unidos, Santa Fe. El nombre de **Texas** era más largo, San Francisco de los Tejos. Los tejos eran los indios de la región.

Como puedes ver, la historia de España y de los Estados Unidos está íntimamente ligada.° En 1992, los Estados Unidos va a participar activamente en las celebraciones del 500 aniversario de la llegada de Colón a la América.

---

negocios *business*	**alrededor de** *around*	**vino a ser** *came to be*	**río** *river*
a cambio de *in exchange for*	**orejas** *ears*	**ligada** *linked*	

Actividad • Preguntas y respuestas  For answers, see p. T93.

Answer the following questions about the selection **España y los Estados Unidos.**

1. ¿En cuáles dos o tres estados de los Estados Unidos hay territorios que fueron antes de España?
2. ¿Por qué hay conexión entre la cultura de los Estados Unidos y la de España?
3. ¿Qué decidió el emperador Carlos V poner en su escudo?
4. ¿Quién es Hércules y qué representa?
5. Una parte del símbolo original del dólar son las dos columnas de Hércules. ¿Cuál es la otra?
6. ¿Cuándo hicieron sus monedas las colonias inglesas?
7. ¿Por qué tuvieron los primeros billetes de los Estados Unidos el escudo español de los castillos y los leones?
8. ¿Qué otra cosa tuvieron los españoles en ese escudo?
9. ¿Qué quiere decir *Florida*?
10. ¿Qué tienen en común San Agustín y Santa Fe?
11. ¿Qué otro nombre tuvo Texas?
12. ¿Cuál de los siguientes es buen título para esta Lectura?
    a. La historia del dólar
    b. La influencia española en los Estados Unidos
    c. Ciudades con nombres españoles

Actividad • ¡A ver el mapa! Answers will vary.

Take a look at a map of the United States and find seven more cities that have Spanish names. Find at least one in your state.

Actividad • Charla Answers will vary.

Tell a classmate why Thomas Jefferson allowed the Spanish pillars dollar to circulate in the United States. Ask a classmate the origin of the dollar sign and of its symbol.

UNIDAD 4 México lindo

Repaso

TEACHER-PREPARED MATERIALS
   Review 4   Map of Mexico,
      flashcards, magazine pictures,
      slides or pictures of the
      Zona Rosa

UNIT RESOURCES
Manual de actividades, Unit 4
Manual de ejercicios, Unit 4
Unit 4 Cassette
Transparency 10
Review Test 1

Unit 4 reviews functions, grammar, and vocabulary that the students have studied in Units 1–3. No new material is included. This unit provides communicative and writing practice in different situations; that is, it gives different applications and uses of the same material. If your students require further practice, you will find additional review exercises in Unit 4 of the **Manual de actividades** and the **Manual de ejercicios.** On the other hand, if your students have successfully mastered the material in Units 1–3, you may wish to omit parts of Unit 4. Some of the activities in this unit lend themselves to cooperative learning.

OBJECTIVE   To review communicative functions, grammar, and vocabulary from Units 1–3

CULTURAL BACKGROUND   Tourism is Mexico's most important source of income, and the country has many vacation areas. A lovely town near Mexico City, Valle de Bravo, seems to have been lifted from the mountains of Switzerland. It is a weekend resort town north of Toluca on a beautiful man-made lake, with trout streams, mountain lodges, and all the picturesque qualities of a colonial Mexican village. For a vacation in the sun, Mexico offers Cancún, Puerto Vallarta, Playa Careyes, Ixtapa, Zihuatanejo, Baja California, Cozumel, and a new area near Puerto Escondido and Huatulco. The Mexican government is planning several new tourist areas, realizing tourism is an important source of income for the country. There is an abundance of natural beauty in the country as well. Principally uninhabited areas, such as Copper Canyon and the Gulf Coast beaches are wonderful escapes.

MOTIVATING ACTIVITY   As a cultural review of Units 1–3, play a game in which you give the description of a place described in these units. Have the students form teams and identify it. If they identify the place correctly, give the team a point. Here are some of the examples:

> las ruinas cerca de Oaxaca (*Monte Albán*)
> el bosque tropical en Puerto Rico (*El Yunque*)
> una cascada en Venezuela (*Salto del Ángel*)

As a variation, allow the students in each team to identify the places described in Units 1–3 and to write the clues. The team that stumps the others wins extra points.

1 Una sorpresa

Introduce the selection by reading the opening paragraph to the students. Ask them to use context clues to determine the meaning of **extraña.**

Then point out on the map several towns or cities mentioned in the dialog, such as Oaxaca, Taxco, Puerto Vallarta, and Acapulco. Present the vocabulary items **estrella de mar** and **estrella de cine.** You may also wish to re-enter the preterit tense before presenting the dialog. After the students have role-played the dialog or have listened to it as you have read the dialog aloud or have played the cassette, ask the following or similar questions to check comprehension.

1. ¿Quiénes son Marcos y Cristina?
2. ¿Dónde se encontraron?
3. ¿Cuándo llegó Cristina?
4. ¿Qué lugares visitó Marcos?
5. ¿Qué hizo?
6. ¿Qué encontró Marcos?

SLOWER-PACED LEARNING   Distribute copies of the entire dialog from which you have deleted the preterit tense verb forms. Have the students fill in the missing verb forms as you dictate the dialog.

2 Actividad • Si no es así, ¿cómo es?

Allow the students to work through the sentences, correcting the false statements. When finished, ask them to compare their answers with those of a partner. Finally, review the entire activity with the class.

3 Actividad • Charla

Have the students create at least five questions to ask a partner about Marcos' and Cristina's trip. When finished, you may wish to play a round-robin during which student 1 will ask student 2 a question. Student 2 should respond and ask student 1 a question, and so on. Continue until all the students have had the opportunity to ask and answer the questions.

4 Actividad • ¡A escribir!

Have the students write the postcard in class or at home. Collect and correct their work. You may wish to display the postcards in the classroom.

5 Actividad • ¡La mía es mejor que la tuya!

Ask the students to choose a partner and alternate roles as they complete the activity. You may wish to call on volunteers to read the answers aloud.

SLOWER-PACED LEARNING   Have the students write out the sentences. To shorten the activity, assign two items to each row of students. Write the answers on the board or a transparency for correction.

6 Actividad • Ellos tuvieron que trabajar

Have the students work in pairs to complete this activity. When finished, review with the class while they have their books closed.

ANSWERS:
1. ¿Y Jorge? Fue director de una excursión.
2. ¿Y Susana? Fue guía de turistas.
3. ¿Y Carlos y tú? Fuimos empleados de una tienda.
4. ¿Y Estrella? Fue fotógrafa profesional.
5. ¿Y Raúl? Fue reportero de un periódico.
6. ¿Y Alberto? Fue profesor de karate.
7. ¿Y Julia y Andrés? Fueron vendedores de discos.

7 Actividad • ¡A completar!

Review the formation of adverbs with the students. Then have them complete the paragraph with the correct forms. When they have finished, have a transparency ready on which you have written the paragraph. Fill in the adverb forms as the students call them out.

8 Actividad • ¿Qué hacen?

Re-enter the present progressive, using flashcards or magazine pictures. Allow the students to complete the activity orally with a partner. When they have finished, ask them to write the sentences. As a review of the material, call on volunteers to write their sentences on the board or a transparency.

9 Actividad • ¡A escribir!

You may wish to assign this activity for homework. Mention that the ads may be illustrated. As a variation, the students may wish to present their ads orally to the class. You may wish to review command forms before they begin. Tell the students to use the hotel and tour brochures in the book as a guide.

10 SITUACIÓN • De compras en la Zona Rosa

Before reading the dialog, you may wish to show slides or pictures of the Zona Rosa in Mexico City. Review the names of items of clothing by using flashcards, your picture file, or by discussing articles of clothing being worn by members of the class. Have the students listen to the dialog as you read or play the cassette, or ask three students to role-play the dialog. Ask several questions to check comprehension.

SLOWER-PACED LEARNING   You may wish to work through the dialog a few lines at a time, asking questions after each section. Then allow the students time to read silently.

11 Actividad • Preguntas y respuestas

For writing practice, have the students write complete sentences. As a variation, you may wish to have them work with a partner to answer the questions. Review with the entire class.

12 Actividad • Charla

Have the students work with a partner to choose several items to "sell." Tell them to take turns playing the clerk and customer. When they have had time to practice, choose several pairs to act out their dialog for the class.

SLOWER-PACED LEARNING   Ask a volunteer to work with you to create a dialog. Then role-play the dialog to demonstrate a model for the class.

13 Actividad • Palabras y más palabras

Allow the students time to work through the activity. When they are finished, review with them the relationships of the words. You may then wish to play a vocabulary game with the words from Units 1–3.

You will hear Roberto's narration of his trip. The narration will be divided into three paragraphs. Each paragraph will be followed by several statements. If the statement is true, check **sí** on your answer sheet. If it is false, check **no.**

El verano pasado les pedí permiso a mis padres para visitar a mis amigos en México. Ellos lo pensaron unos días pero al fin me dieron permiso. Salí el quince de junio para pasar un mes en la capital. Visité muchos lugares de interés, pero lo mejor fue pasar tiempo con la familia de Luis Miguel Cuevas y su hermana menor Charín.

1. Roberto visitó a su familia en México. *no*
2. Luis Miguel tiene una hermana mayor. *no*
3. Los padres de Roberto no le dieron permiso inmediatamente. *sí*
4. Roberto pasó quince días en la capital. *no*

El primer día la familia Cuevas me llevó a ver las famosas pirámides de Teotihuacán. Subimos la pirámide del Sol y también la pirámide de la Luna. Fue fantástico ver una ciudad tan antigua y tan grande. Después comimos en un restaurante cerca de Teotihuacán y también visitamos un mercado donde compré unos regalos para mis amigos.

5. Roberto visitó las pirámides durante la primera semana. *sí*
6. Hay dos pirámides grandes en Teotihuacán. *sí*
7. La ciudad es antigua pero bastante pequeña. *no*
8. Fueron de compras y comieron antes de visitar Teotihuacán. *no*

La excursión más divertida fue a Acapulco. Pasamos cuatro días nadando, tomando el sol y divirtiéndonos mucho. Cuando llegamos al hotel, fuimos inmediatamente a la playa. ¡Cuánta gente!, pero la playa es muy hermosa. La primera noche fuimos a cenar y a bailar en un club muy elegante. ¡Qué pena que las vacaciones terminaron tan rápidamente y tuve que volver a casa!

9. Roberto y sus amigos pasaron un fin de semana en Acapulco. *no*
10. Roberto vio a muchas personas en la playa. *sí*
11. Al llegar al hotel salieron a comer y a bailar. *no*
12. Las vacaciones pasaron lentamente para Roberto. *no*

Now check your answers. *Read each paragraph and the statements again, and give the correct answers.*

Viñeta cultural 2

Los deportes

OBJECTIVE   To read in Spanish for cultural awareness

MOTIVATING ACTIVITY   Ask the students to name sports that are popular in the United States. Then ask them to identify which of these sports they think are also popular in Spain and Spanish America.

CULTURAL BACKGROUND   Spanish Americans play a great variety of sports. Many of these are played in the United States. Other sports, such as soccer, although known in the United States, are not as popular as they are in Spanish-speaking countries. Like many people in the United States, some Hispanics are just sports fans, while others actively participate in a wide variety of sports.

Interest in sports in Spanish America dates back to pre-Columbian times. The Mayas practiced a sport that was similar to a combination of volleyball and basketball. The object of the game was to throw a ball through a ring, without using the hands. These rings were usually made of stones. Among the Taino Indians of the West Indies, **juego de bates** was very popular and was played with two teams. The purpose of this game was to score a goal on the opponent's goal line. Some say that the modern game of baseball is derived from this Indian game, although it has never been proven.

From Spain comes another ancient sport, **jai alai,** which is also called **pelota vasca.** This game is played on a three-walled court called a **frontón.** The players use a curved **cesta,** also called a **canasta,** to catch and throw a very hard ball against the walls. It's been said that **jai alai** is the fastest game in the world, as well as being one of the most dangerous. This sport is very popular in Spain, Mexico, and South America. It is gaining more fans every year in the United States.

Soccer, or **fútbol** as it is called throughout the Hispanic world, is undoubtedly the most popular sport of the Spanish-speaking world. To many Spaniards and South Americans, soccer is more than a sport: it is a national passion.

Other sports popular in the Hispanic world are baseball—especially in the Caribbean basin—and basketball, volleyball, tennis, polo, cycling, boxing, yachting, swimming, horseback riding, car racing, as well as track and field. Spanish Americans are so enthusiastic about sports that it is said that every Hispanic is a sports fan.

You can proceed by reading the essay aloud or by playing the cassette, pausing to allow the students to relate the text to the photos. Have them look at the photograph at the top of page 138. Then ask whether they have heard of the young Argentine tennis player Gabriela Sabatini.

Write the following words on the board or a transparency.

fútbol	béisbol
básquetbol	volibol
tenis	polo

Call on the students to quickly identify the English meanings of these words. They should also be able to explain that the meanings of the words are readily identifiable because they are all cognates.

VIÑETA
CULTURAL

2

Page
139

Page
140–141

Pages
142-144

After the students have had a chance to look at the photographs and read the captions on page 139, inquire whether they have had the opportunity to play the sports depicted in the photographs. Then ask whether they have participated in any competitions. If they have, ask them to give a brief description of this to the class.

CULTURAL BACKGROUND   Explain to the students that the World Cup Soccer Championship is as popular in Spanish-speaking countries as the Olympic Games. It is played every four years in a different host country. Each country selects a national team to represent it during the games. The players on each team are usually professionals from regional teams throughout the country and must train together for several years before each world competition. Thousands of fans from all over the world attend the games to support their teams.

After reading the text on page 140 aloud or after playing the cassette, ask the students whether any of them has watched the World Cup on television or attended a professional soccer match. If they have, ask a volunteer to explain the game to the class.

As you continue to present the information on page 141, you may wish to ask the students to identify as many of the players as possible without looking at the captions. Then ask the students to name some of the Spanish-speaking baseball players who play for the American or National League in the United States. Write their names on the board.

Play the cassette or read aloud the text and the captions on pages 142 and 143 as the students follow along in their books. You may wish to discuss the Olympic Games with the students. Point out that the 1992 Olympics will be held in Barcelona, Spain.

Have the students look at the text, captions, and photos on page 144 as you play the cassette or read the text aloud. Ask them to identify the newest sports in the United States or in their own city and to explain why they think these sports would or would not be popular in Spain or Spanish America.

CHALLENGE   You may wish to ask the students to prepare an oral or written report about a sports figure of the Hispanic world.

SLOWER-PACED LEARNING   Ask each student to reread the essay and to make a list of the sports he or she plays. Each should also make a list of the sports he or she would like to play. Then have each student compare lists with those of another classmate.

México lindo

Repaso

1

Una sorpresa 📼

La verdad es a veces más extraña que la ficción. Marcos y Cristina, que son compañeros de clase en Los Ángeles, se encuentran de sorpresa en las pirámides de Teotihuacán, cerca de la capital de México.

MARCOS   Cristina, ¡qué sorpresa! ¡Cuánto me alegro de verte!
CRISTINA ¡Marcos! ¡Tú aquí! Nunca pude imaginar . . .
MARCOS   No me vas a creer. Ayer te escribí
          una tarjeta postal.
CRISTINA Y yo pensé que te fuiste a España
          cuando terminaron las clases.
MARCOS   ¿Quién te dijo eso?
CRISTINA Me lo dijo Esteban.
MARCOS   Oh, Esteban habla mucho. Nunca
          le dije mis planes. Bueno, y tú,
          ¿cuándo llegaste a México?

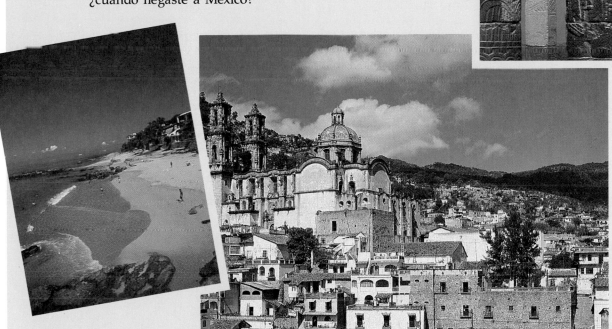

CRISTINA Llegué hace dos semanas. Regreso el jueves próximo.
MARCOS   ¿Y dónde estuviste?
CRISTINA ¡Oh! Estuve en muchos lugares. Visité dos ciudades coloniales, Taxco y Oaxaca.
          Después mi hermana mayor prefirió ir a Yucatán a ver las ruinas mayas.
          ¡Fabulosas! ¿Y tú?
MARCOS   Bueno, yo sólo vine a pasarla bien. Hicimos un viaje por la costa, Puerto Vallarta,
          Acapulco . . . Tú sabes, el sol, las playas . . . Nadé, pesqué y bailé todos los días.
CRISTINA ¿Te encontraste con alguna estrella de cine?
MARCOS   Sí, conocí a Bill Cosby y a Madonna.
CRISTINA ¿De verdad?
MARCOS   No, Tina, es una broma. Sólo encontré una estrella de mar. Es para ti . . . Es linda,
          ¿verdad?

México lindo   **133**

2 Actividad • **Si no es así, ¿cómo es?**

Change these statements, whenever necessary, to make them agree with the dialog in **Una sorpresa.**

1. Marcos fue a España.   Marcos fue a México.
2. Cristina dice que Esteban se lo dijo.   Es cierto.
3. Ella le escribió a Marcos ayer.   Él le escribió a Cristina ayer.
4. Esteban y Marcos llegaron hace dos semanas.   Cristina llegó hace dos semanas.
5. Las chicas prefirieron ver las ruinas mayas.   La hermana mayor de Cristina prefirió ver las ruinas mayas.
6. Marcos empezó por las ciudades coloniales.   Cristina empezó por las ciudades coloniales.
7. Cristina hizo un viaje por la costa.   Marcos hizo un viaje por la costa.
8. Ella viajó con su hermana gemela.   Cristina viajó con su hermana mayor.
9. Cristina y su hermana le dijeron una broma a Marcos.   Marcos le dijo una broma a Cristina.
10. Marcos le pidió una estrella de mar a Cristina.   Marcos le dio una estrella de mar a Cristina.

3 Actividad • **Charla**   Answers will vary. Possible answers are given.

Work with a partner. Ask each other about Marcos and Cristina's surprise meeting. You should ask at least five questions.   ¿Dónde se encontraron?   ¿Dónde viven Marcos y Cristina? ¿Qué hizo Marcos para divertirse?   ¿Dónde se encuentran las ruinas mayas?   ¿Cuándo regresa Cristina?

4 Actividad • **¡A escribir!**   Answers will vary.

Based on what Marcos told Cristina, try to imagine what kind of postcard he sent her. Then write it, making sure you include the date, the salutation, and the complimentary closing.

5 Actividad • **¡La mía es mejor que la tuya!**

Cristina and her sister often try to outdo each other. Work with a partner and play both roles. Here are some of the things you could discuss:

MODELO   calculadora
         Mi calculadora es mejor que la tuya.

cámara	fotografías	maleta	amigos
cartas	ropa	radio	bicicleta

Mi cámara es mejor que la tuya.
Mis fotografías son mejores que las tuyas.
Mi maleta es mejor que la tuya.
Mis amigos son mejores que los tuyos.
Mis cartas son mejores que las tuyas.
Mi ropa es mejor que la tuya.
Mi radio es mejor que el tuyo.
Mi bicicleta es mejor que la tuya.

6 Actividad • **Ellos tuvieron que trabajar**   For answers, see p. T95.

Some of Marcos's friends had to work during the summer. What did they do? Take turns asking and answering the questions with a partner. Follow the model.

MODELO   —¿Y Maricarmen?   —Fue camarera.

1. Jorge / director de una excursión
2. Susana / guía de turistas
3. Carlos y tú / empleados de una tienda
4. Estrella / fotógrafo profesional
5. Raúl / reportero de un periódico
6. Alberto / profesor de karate
7. Julia y Andrés / vendedores de discos

Actividad • ¡A completar! Answers will vary. Possible answers are given.

Using adverbs ending in **-mente,** say how people did things. Change the adjectives from the box into adverbs and use them as needed to complete the paragraph below. You may use an adverb more than once.

rápido	fantástico	alegre	desgraciado
frecuente	constante	afortunado	

Los muchachos planearon el viaje a México _____ . Les encantó la ciudad de México. Marcos salió con Cristina _____ . Fueron a muchas fiestas y bailaron _____ . Todos la pasaron _____ , pero también gastaron mucho dinero. Los padres de Marcos dicen que él tiene que ahorrar _____ , o que _____ no va a poder ir de vacaciones el año que viene. Cristina y Virginia van a trabajar parte del verano y van a ahorrar _____ . _____ a ellas no les gusta gastar dinero.

rápidamente/
frecuentemente
alegremente
fantásticamente
constantemente/
desgraciadamente
frecuentemente/
Afortunadamente

8

Actividad • ¿Qué hacen?

The members of your tour group are doing different things at the same time. Following the cues, say what everyone is doing.

MODELO   Diego / jugar al tenis
          Diego está jugando al tenis.

1. Tomás / escribir el diario del viaje
2. Estrella / conseguir un mapa
3. Jorge / cambiar cheques de viajero
4. Ana / preguntar cómo llegar al metro

5. Luis y Oscar / comprar billetes para el tren
6. Tú / mandar tarjetas postales
7. Susana y yo / cerrar las maletas
8. Diego y Andrés / leer la historia de los mayas

1. Tomás está escribiendo el diario del viaje.
2. Estrella está consiguiendo un mapa.
3. Jorge está cambiando cheques de viajero.
4. Ana está preguntando cómo llegar al metro.

5. Luis y Oscar están comprando billetes para el tren.
6. Tú estás mandando tarjetas postales.
7. Susana y yo estamos cerrando las maletas.
8. Diego y Andrés están leyendo la historia de los mayas.

9

Actividad • ¡A escribir! Answers will vary.

Write a short ad offering discounts for a tour of the Pirámide del Conejo or for a beach hotel in Acapulco named La Tortuga Verde. Offer things you would like to see or do at reduced prices. Use command forms.

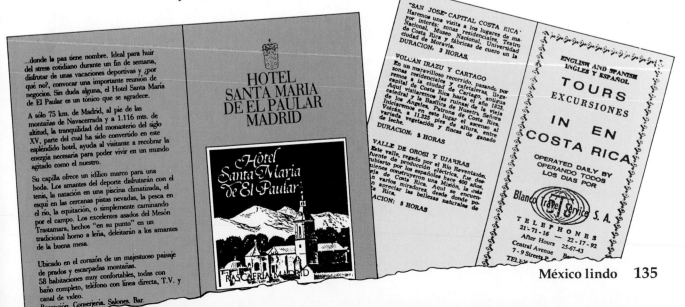

El último día antes de irse de la ciudad de México, Cristina y su hermana deciden ir de compras a la famosa Zona Rosa.

CRISTINA   ¿Me queda bien la falda azul?

VIRGINIA   Creo que es un poco grande. Te queda mejor la blanca.

CRISTINA   Señorita, si tiene la azul en una talla más pequeña que ésta, búsqueme una, por favor.

DEPENDIENTA   Sí, cómo no. Pruébese la negra, si quiere.

VIRGINIA   No, la negra no. Ésa me la llevo yo.

DEPENDIENTA   Bueno, venga conmigo a la caja, por favor.

VIRGINIA   Espere un momento. Estoy ayudando a mi hermana, esa chica que se está probando la falda azul.

DEPENDIENTA   Señorita, estamos ofreciendo grandes rebajas en blusas blancas de mangas largas. ¿Quiere verlas?

VIRGINIA   ¿Aceptan tarjetas de crédito?

DEPENDIENTA   Sí, ¡por supuesto!

CRISTINA   Vámonos, Virginia. Estamos gastando mucho dinero. No podemos comprar toda la tienda.

(Las chicas compran solamente la falda azul y la negra, y luego se van.)

11 Actividad • Preguntas y respuestas 🔲

Use the dialog in number 10 to answer the following questions. Use complete sentences.

1. ¿Qué se está probando Cristina?
2. ¿Por qué no le queda bien la azul?
3. ¿Es suya la falda negra o es de Virginia?
4. ¿Qué grandes rebajas está ofreciendo la tienda?
5. ¿Cómo quiere pagar Virginia?
6. ¿Cómo son las blusas?
7. ¿Por qué se van las chicas?
8. ¿Qué compran las chicas?

Cristina se está probando la falda azul.
No le queda bien porque es un poco grande.
La falda negra es de Virginia.
Están ofreciendo grandes rebajas en blusas.
Virginia quiere pagar con tarjeta de crédito.
Las blusas son blancas de manga larga.
Las chicas se van porque están gastando mucho dinero.
Las chicas compran la falda azul y la negra.

12 Actividad • Charla   Answers will vary.

With a partner, play the roles of a salesclerk and a customer, using the expressions and situations you have learned in Units 1–3. You could ask the clerk where the department you are looking for is located, how much the merchandise costs, and whether you are buying the item or find it too expensive

13 Actividad • Palabras y más palabras

Choose two words from each group that have something in common.

1. anuncios	recuerdos	saludos	anillos
2. olvidar	descansar	servir	atender
3. pez	bufandas	pescado	abrazos
4. sopa	supe	sabiendo	talla
5. sobrino	falda	cuñada	menor
6. conmigo	conejo	caballo	playera

14 Comprensión 🔲 For script, see p. T97.

Listen carefully to Roberto's narration of his trip. The narration will be divided into three paragraphs. Each paragraph will be followed by four true or false statements. If the statement is true, check **sí** on your answer sheet. If it is false, check **no.**

	1	2	3	4	5	6	7	8	9	10	11	12
Sí			✔		✔	✔				✔		
No	✔	✔		✔			✔	✔	✔		✔	✔

Viñeta cultural 2

Los deportes

En el mundo hispánico se practican gran cantidad (*large variety*) de deportes. Los hispanos siempre se han destacado (*have excelled*) en muchos de ellos, como por ejemplo, en el fútbol, el béisbol, el básquetbol, el volibol, el tenis, el polo, la natación (*swimming*), el ciclismo, la equitación (*horseback riding*), campo y pista (*track and field*) y muchos otros.

La joven tenista argentina Gabriela Sabatini es una de las más destacadas campeonas de tenis hoy día.

Todos los deportes que tienen que ver con los caballos, como el polo, son muy populares en la Argentina.

Los madrileños, aunque no tienen playas, son muy aficionados a la natación. Aquí podemos ver dos jóvenes nadando en una de las varias piscinas de la ciudad.

Uno de los deportes más populares en el mundo hispánico es el básquetbol, también llamado baloncesto. Por las tardes las canchas se llenan de jugadores.

Estos jóvenes practican la equitación (horseback riding) en España.

El volibol se está volviendo (is becoming) cada vez más popular en el mundo hispánico. Cada vez hay más campeonatos intercolegiales (intercollegiate championships).

El ciclismo (cycling) es un deporte muy popular en España, en el cual toda la familia puede participar.

Estas muchachas de Guatemala practican la arquería (archery). ¿Darán en el blanco (bull's-eye)?

Indudablemente *(Undoubtedly)*, el deporte más popular en España y Suramérica es el fútbol. Todas las semanas, miles de fanáticos llenan *(fill)* los gigantescos estadios *(stadiums)* y disfrutan *(enjoy)* intensamente de los emocionantes partidos. Dos países hispánicos, Argentina y Uruguay, han sido *(have been)* en dos ocasiones campeones mundiales *(world champions)* de fútbol y el jugador *(player)* argentino Diego Armando Maradona está considerado el mejor futbolista del mundo.

La Copa Mundial **(World Cup)** *de fútbol se jugó en México en 1986. El próximo campeonato será en Italia.*

Aquí podemos ver el monumental Estadio Azteca de México lleno a toda capacidad para un partido de la Copa Mundial. El estadio tiene cupo **(room)** *para 108,000 personas.*

El equipo de béisbol cubano está considerado como uno
de los mejores del mundo a nivel amateur.

En Venezuela el béisbol es tan popular como en los Estados Unidos.

Fernando Valenzuela, el
lanzador (pitcher) mexicano,
juega en Los Ángeles.

El deporte nacional de las islas del Caribe, sobre todo de Cuba, la República Dominicana y
Puerto Rico, es el béisbol. Este deporte también
se juega (is played) en Venezuela, Panamá, Nicaragua y México. Varias estrellas del béisbol,
como el mexicano Fernando Valenzuela y el cubano José Canseco, juegan en los Estados Unidos para equipos (teams) de las grandes ligas
(Major Leagues). Entre (Among) los miembros del
Salón de la Fama (Hall of Fame) figuran el
dominicano Juan Marichal y el puertorriqueño
Roberto Clemente.

El cubano José Canseco fue nombrado (was named) el
jugador más valioso de la Liga Americana por ser un
gran bateador (batter).

Sólo hay admiración cuando
se recuerda al gran pelotero
puertorriqueño (Puerto Rican),
Roberto Clemente.

Los atletas hispánicos también se han destacado en las olimpiadas. La isla de Cuba, por ejemplo, es el país hispánico que más medallas de oro, plata y bronce ha conquistado *(has won)* en boxeo, campo y pista y levantamiento de pesas *(weight lifting)*. A propósito *(Incidentally)*, las olimpiadas de 1992 se celebrarán en la ciudad española de Barcelona.

Pablo Morales, nacido en los Estados Unidos de padres cubanos, es ganador de una medalla olímpica en el relevo combinado (medley relay) *de natación* (swimming).

Aquí se ve el esfuerzo (effort) *y la determinación de Pablo Morales para ganar la medalla de oro para el equipo de los Estados Unidos.*

El clavadista (diver) *Roberto Camacho de España demuestra* (shows) *concentración, técnica y elegancia al ejecutar* (perform) *este clavado* (dive).

El famoso corredor cubanoamericano, Alberto Salazar, se prepara para el maratón de Boston.

Después de ganar el maratón de Boston, Alberto Salazar recibe su corona (crown) de campeón.

El equipo hípico (equestrian) de Guatemala participó en las competencias de salto de obstáculos (team jumping) de los Juegos Olímpicos.

El corredor (runner) cubano Alberto Juantorena ganó la medalla de oro en la carrera de 800 metros en los Juegos Olímpicos.

Cuba ha dado al deporte del boxeo muchos grandes boxeadores al nivel amateur. Aquí se ve a Teófilo Stevenson, boxeador de peso completo (heavyweight) que ganó tres medallas de oro para Cuba.

Los deportes 143

En los últimos años, deportes como el golf, la tabla vela *(windsurfing)* y el hockey sobre hierba *(field hockey)* han ganado *(have won)* muchos aficionados *(fans)* en el mundo hispánico. El jai alai, llamado también pelota vasca *(Basque ball)*, es un deporte que tiene su origen en la península ibérica y que cada día gana nuevos fanáticos en los Estados Unidos.

La afición *(enthusiasm)* de los hispanos por los deportes es tal que se puede decir que en cada hispano vive un deportista.

La campeona de golf mexicoamericana, Nancy López, ha ganado torneos **(has won tournaments)** *por todo el mundo. Es la única golfista que ha ganado cinco torneos consecutivos, y en 1985 la nombraron* **(named)** *"Woman Athlete of the Year".*

El deporte de tabla hawaiana **(surfing)** *cada día gana más popularidad entre la comunidad hispana.*

Jai alai quiere decir fiesta alegre. Es un juego de pelota veloz que requiere habilidad, buena condición física y gran concentración.

UNIDAD 5 Celebraciones y fiestas
Scope and Sequence

	BASIC MATERIAL	COMMUNICATIVE FUNCTIONS
SECTION A	Nuestras fiestas (A1) Los preparativos para la fiesta (A14)	**Socializing** • Extending an invitation • Congratulating someone **Exchanging information** • Expressing time (morning, afternoon, or evening) • Inquiring about age
SECTION B	¿Era verdad? (B1) Ya era tarde (B10)	**Exchanging information** • Describing events in the past **Expressing feelings and emotions** • Expressing intention
SECTION C	Hablando de la fiesta por teléfono (C1) ¿Cómo estaban mis amigos? (C10) Te lo agradezco (C18)	**Expressing feelings and emotions** • Expressing regret • Expressing how you feel about others and about yourself
TRY YOUR SKILLS	El Día de los Enamorados Dictado	

■ **Pronunciación**   (the letters **c, k, qu, s,** and **z**; vowels before **r**)
■ **¿Lo sabes?**   ■ **Vocabulario**

VAMOS A LEER	**Cuestión de opinión** (different points of view)

WRITING   A variety of controlled and open-ended writing activities appear in the Pupil's Edition. The Teacher's Notes identify other activities suitable for writing practice.

COOPERATIVE LEARNING   Many of the activities in the Pupil's Edition lend themselves to cooperative learning. The Teacher's Notes explain some of the many instances where this teaching strategy can be particularly effective. For guidelines on how to use cooperative learning, see page T13.

GRAMMAR	CULTURE	RE-ENTRY
Ordinal numbers (A10) The imperfect tense of regular verbs (A24)	Honoring Christopher Columbus in the New World Saint's Day in the Spanish- speaking world	Months of the year The infinitive after a preposition Numbers greater than 1,000
The imperfect tense forms of **ver, ir,** and **ser** (B7) Some uses of the imperfect tense (B13)	Celebrations in the Spanish-speaking world	Telling time
The imperfect and the preterit tenses contrasted (C6) Verbs ending in **-cer** and **-cir** (C20)	Teenage parties in Spanish-speaking countries	The imperfect tense of **estar** and **tener** The function "expressing emotions"

Recombining communicative functions, grammar, and vocabulary

Reading for practice and pleasure

TEACHER-PREPARED MATERIALS
Section A Pictures of a baseball player,
flashcards with names of the month
Spanish calendar, baby picture
Section B Toy telephones
Section C Pictures of people's faces
that show emotion

UNIT RESOURCES
Manual de actividades, Unit 5
Manual de ejercicios, Unit 5
Unit 5 Cassettes
Transparencies 11–13
Quizzes 10–12
Unit 5 Test

SECTION
A

OBJECTIVES **To socialize:** extend an invitation, congratulate someone; **to exchange information:** express time (morning, afternoon, and evening), inquire about age

CULTURAL BACKGROUND Spanish-speaking people have a great diversity of festivals and celebrations. Not only are there national holidays but also town festivities as well as family and personal celebrations. Many of the celebrations are religious; frequently the religious celebrations have an Indian or an African flair, especially in countries where indigenous customs are still evident or where there is a large black population.

Each town or city in Spain or Spanish America has a patron saint whom the people honor in week-long celebrations. On nearly every day of the year a celebration for a particular saint is held somewhere. Special church services, street fairs, dances, processions, parades, and parties are held to mark the occasion.

MOTIVATING ACTIVITY Discuss festivals and holidays with the students. Ask them to identify religious and national holidays in Spain and Spanish America. You may also have the students talk about the ways in which they celebrate national holidays.

A1

Nuestras fiestas

Before introducing the material in this section, discuss the most common holidays with the students. Include several national holidays of the United States. Re-enter the months of the year, and ask several students to identify their birth dates. Then have the students look at the lists on page 149 of the holidays celebrated in Spain and in Venezuela. Ask them to compare these holidays with those of the United States. You may want to review such words as **santo** and **Epifanía.**

Discuss the importance of Simón Bolívar in South America. Explain to the students that he was born in Caracas, Venezuela, and dedicated his life to free his country from the Spanish regime. He was known as **El Libertador** because he liberated Venezuela, Colombia, Bolivia, and Peru from the Spanish. The country of Bolivia is named in honor of Simón Bolívar. Play the cassette or read each section of the narrative aloud to the students, questioning them on the content. Mention the importance of the celebration of **carnaval** in many South American countries. Explain that it is similar to Mardi gras in New Orleans.

A2

Actividad • Preguntas y respuestas

You may wish to do this activity orally in class with books closed, or you may prefer to have each student work with a partner to complete the activity orally. Then review the answers with the entire class. You may also wish to have the students make up true or false statements about the content of the selection.

A3

Actividad • ¡A completar!

Allow each student to complete the activity with a partner. For writing practice, have them write the completed sentences. Review the answers with the class.

A4 Sabes que . . .

You may wish to discuss with the class the importance of the year 1992 and mention several celebrations to be held that year in Spain and in Spanish America. Also in 1992, the Summer Olympics will be held in Barcelona. The World's Fair will be held in Seville and replicas of the *Niña*, the *Pinta*, and the *Santa María* will sail to the site where Columbus arrived in the New World.

A5 Actividad • Entrevista

SLOWER-PACED LEARNING Have groups of students make calendars of any month. They should include all important dates for the month they choose, both for the United States and for Spanish-speaking countries.

A6 Actividad • ¿Qué dijo?

Call on volunteers to report their partner's responses. Encourage the students to listen carefully, and then ask them questions to check comprehension.

A7 SE DICE ASÍ

With books closed, present the expressions by inviting the students to various social functions. Allow them to respond as they wish. Encourage the students to ask questions, such as the time and place of the function. Then have them open their books and read the material.

A8 ¿RECUERDAS?

Ask the students to think of four events that will occur soon. Remind them to use the construction **ir** + **a** + *infinitive*. Give them an example, such as **Vamos a nadar la semana que viene.** Then ask several students to read their sentences aloud as you write them on the board or a transparency. Review the material in the text. Indicate that **acabar de** means *to have just:* **Acabo de hablar con Anita.** *I have just talked to Anita.* Then use magazine pictures to practice verbs that are followed by a preposition and an infinitive. For example, you may select a picture of a person playing baseball. Guide the students to use the verbs **aprender, comenzar, tratar,** and **terminar.**

> Aprendió a jugar al béisbol. Terminó de jugar al béisbol.
> Trata de jugar al béisbol. Comenzó a jugar al béisbol.

A9 Actividad • La fiesta

To check the answers, write the corrected sentences on a transparency. As a follow-up assignment, have the students write two original sentences for each verb phrase—one in the present and the other in the preterit.

A10 ESTRUCTURAS ESENCIALES

Point out that one of the most important uses of ordinal numbers is to rank the elements in a series or a group; for example, the best five students in the class: **Orlando es el primero, Ernesto es el segundo, Elena es la tercera, Josefa es la cuarta y Gustavo es el quinto.**

You may wish to write several numbers on the board or a transparency and ask the students to read them aloud. Then, using flashcards containing the names of the months, give a brief narration using ordinal numbers, such as the following:

> Enero es el primer mes del año.
> Febrero es el segundo mes del año.

SLOWER-PACED LEARNING   Introduce only three ordinal numbers at a time. Then ask the students to open their books and read the explanation about the numbers. You may guide them through the material using names of people or items in class. For example:

Susie es la primera persona en esta fila.
Susie y Ángela son las primeras personas en la fila.

A 11   Actividad • La liga de béisbol

Have the students rank the baseball teams listed in the activity. As a homework assignment, ask the students to list in order of importance the activities they have planned for next week. For example:

Primero, voy a estudiar para el examen de español.
Segundo, voy a ir a una fiesta.

A 12   SE DICE ASÍ

Write the expressions in the box on a transparency. Cover the English expressions and have the students read the sentences. Then ask them to identify the pattern when using **de** and **por.** Have the students open their books and confirm whether their original observations were correct.

A 13   Actividad • ¿Me dijiste cuándo?

Have several students write the sentences on the board. Ask other students to identify any mistakes and then correct their work.

A 14   SITUACIÓN • Los preparativos para la fiesta

You may wish to go over the new vocabulary and structures in the selection before starting the presentation. Then, tell the students to listen as you play the cassette or read the introduction and telephone conversation aloud. Have the students repeat after you, alternating choral and individual repetition to avoid boredom. In order to keep a fast tempo and maximum student attention, do not interrupt to explain grammar or vocabulary items. After you have finished, have the students read each paragraph silently and ask questions about the content. For cooperative learning, have pairs of students role-play Tere and Menchu's telephone conversation.

A 15   Actividad • ¡A ordenar!

You may wish to have each student compare his or her answers with those of a partner.

A 16   Actividad • ¡A escoger!

CHALLENGE   Have each student write five questions based on the events in A14. Then have the students exchange papers and answer each other's questions.

A 17   Actividad • Y tú, ¿qué crees?

You may wish to personalize the activity by allowing groups of two or three students to plan an ideal party for someone. They may decide what food they will serve, the activities they have planned, and whom to invite.

A 18   Actividad • Charla

Have each student ask and answer the questions with a new partner.

A 19 **SE DICE ASÍ**

Review the expressions in the box with the students. You may also wish to introduce the following popular birthday song, **Las mañanitas.**

> Éstas son las mañanitas que cantaba el Rey David.
> Y a las muchachitas se las cantamos así:
> Despierta, mi bien, despierta. Mira que ya amaneció;
> Ya los pajaritos cantan, la luna ya se metió.

A 20 **Comprensión**

Preparations are under way for the upcoming holiday celebrations. You will hear a short description followed by two statements. After listening to the description, decide if each of the statements is true **(verdadero)** or false **(falso)**. Check the appropriate space on your answer sheet. For example, you will hear: **Hoy vamos a comprar los regalos para papá. Mañana cumple cincuenta años.** You will also hear the statements: (a) **Ya compraron los regalos de papá.** (b) **Papá va a celebrar su cumpleaños mañana.** You should check **falso** to the first statement, because it is false. You should check **verdadero** to the second statement, because it is true.

Pronto tenemos vacaciones y además, vamos a celebrar la independencia. Creo que todos vamos al desfile y también vamos a la plaza para escuchar al presidente.

1. La independencia se celebra con una cena especial. *falso*
2. El presidente va a hablar en la plaza después del desfile. *verdadero*

El 24 de junio es el día de San Juan Bautista. En España se celebra con una gran fiesta porque es el santo del Rey Juan Carlos I.

3. Se celebra el día de San Juan Bautista durante el verano. *verdadero*
4. Es un día importante en España porque es el cumpleaños del rey. *falso*

El Día de la Raza es muy importante en las Américas con la excepción de los Estados Unidos. En ese día no se celebra sólo la llegada de Cristóbal Colón a este hemisferio, sino también la formación de la nueva raza americana.

5. Todos los países del hemisferio celebran el Día de la Raza. *falso*
6. El día celebra la llegada de Cristóbal Colón a las Américas. *verdadero*

En muchos pueblos de las Américas se celebra el Año Nuevo con una costumbre diferente. Por ejemplo, en algunos lugares, todos salen de la casa con una maleta y dan una vuelta a la cuadra para asegurar la buena suerte en el año que comienza.

7. El Año Nuevo se celebra de la misma manera en todas partes. *falso*
8. En la fiesta todos se van de casa con sus maletas. *verdadero*

La Nochebuena es una celebración de familia. En algunos países, la familia va a la iglesia a medianoche. Después regresan a la casa donde tienen una cena especial que dura hasta las cuatro o las cinco de la mañana.

9. Toda la familia celebra Nochebuena juntos. *verdadero*
10. Primero cenan y luego van a la iglesia. *falso*

Now check your answers. *Read each passage again and give the correct answer.*

A 21 **Sabes que . . .**

Bring a Spanish calendar to class or draw one on the board or a transparency. Remind the students that, according to such a calendar, the week starts on Monday, not on Sunday. Point out that for each day of the year there is a saint's day and give examples of how to name people born on some of the days, according to the calendar.

A 22 **Actividad • ¡Demasiadas cosas!**

Allow the students to work individually or in pairs to complete this activity. Review the answers with the class.

A 23 **Actividad • ¡A escribir!**

Ask each student to make plans, including the date, time, place, and purpose for a party he or she would like to have. Then have each student invite a partner to the party. Choose several pairs to role-play their dialogs for the class.

SLOWER-PACED LEARNING Brainstorm with the students about plans for a party. Review the elements of time, date, place, and purpose. Model a dialog with a student for the class. Then proceed as described.

A 24 **ESTRUCTURAS ESENCIALES**

You may wish to present the imperfect tense by showing the students one of your baby pictures. Use simple sentences to describe your age, what you were wearing, where you were living, and what you ate at that age. Write on the board: **Cuando yo tenía [tres] años . . .** Ask the students to add sentences to the description. Then ask the following or similar questions.

> Yo vivía en Chicago en 1973.   ¿Dónde vivías tú?
> ¿Qué comían ustedes?

Give examples and practice sentences with **-ar, -er,** and **-ir** verbs. Then have the students read the explanation in the book.

Ask the students to repeat as you write the examples on the board or a transparency. When most of the students understand the use of the imperfect and its structure, ask them to read with you the explanation in the book. Stress that the preterit and imperfect tenses are not interchangeable. Explain that the use of the imperfect is similar to the use of the present tense, but in the past. As the present tense may describe an action as it is going on in the present, the imperfect describes the action as it was going on in the past. For example, **Nosotros comemos en la cafetería a menudo. Nosotros comíamos en la cafetería a menudo. Mis padres viven en Boston. Mis padres vivían en Boston.**

A 25 **Actividad • ¡Todos hablaban al mismo tiempo!**

Collect and check the students' sentences or have them write the sentences on the board or a transparency.

A 26 **Actividad • ¿Y qué hacía Cecilia?**

SLOWER-PACED LEARNING For further practice, show the students pictures of two activities. Tell them to form one original sentence that describes the action in both pictures. For example, as you hold up a picture of a girl eating and a boy doing homework, say: **Carolina comía mientras Edmundo hacía la tarea.**

ANSWERS:
1. Lolita y Andrés discutían mientras Ofelia ayudaba a su mamá.
2. Irene y yo cocinábamos mientras Carlos lavaba los platos.
3. Pepe y tú preparaban la ensalada mientras Anita cortaba la cebolla.
4. Julia abría los paquetes mientras Georgina lavaba las uvas.
5. Jaime buscaba un cuchillo grande mientras Tomás sacaba la basura.
6. Cecilia ponía la mesa mientras Alberto compraba las flores.

A 27   **Actividad • Siempre lo mismo (o casi siempre)**

Prepare a transparency of the sentences, leaving blanks for the verb forms. Then call on students to complete the sentences as you or a volunteer fills in the answers.

A 28   **Actividad • Hace cinco años**

Ask each student to work with a partner to answer the questions. As a variation, you may have the students write the answers at home or in class in preparation for the written activity that follows. Call on volunteers to give their answers.

A 29   **Actividad • ¡A escribir!**

Ask the students to complete the essays, using the answers to their questions in A28 as a guide. Encourage them to include other information also.

CHALLENGE   Allow each student to illustrate his or her essay or to bring in a baby picture. Have each student use at least ten sentences to describe the person or event taking place in the illustration or photograph. Tell the students to use the imperfect tense in their descriptions.

OBJECTIVES   **To express feelings and emotions:** express intention; **to exchange information:** describe events in the past

CULTURAL BACKGROUND   One of the most important celebrations in Spanish-speaking countries is October 12, often called **el Día de la Raza, el Descubrimiento de América,** or **el Día de la Hispanidad.** Commemorated on that day is the spread of Spanish culture throughout the world, the unification of Spain, and the defeat of the Moors and the fall of Granada on the Iberian Peninsula in 1492. However, in Spanish America the celebration on October 12 stresses **el Descubrimiento de América** and the unification of the races.

MOTIVATING ACTIVITY   Have the students select three of their favorite holidays and describe how they celebrate each one.

B 1   **¿Era verdad?**

Set the scene of the narrative by playing the role of the narrator. Read the first section of the story aloud, making certain that the students understand when and where the story takes place. Call on two students to role-play the telephone conversation, using toy telephones. Then ask several questions to check comprehension. Continue reading aloud the final section of the narrative, stopping to question the students as needed. Ask the students to guess the equivalent of **el Día de los Inocentes** in English by using context clues.

B 2   **Actividad • Preguntas y respuestas**

With books closed, have each student answer the questions individually or with a partner. When they are finished, review the answers with the class.

ANSWERS:
1. Eran las cinco de la tarde. Era casi de noche.
2. No, hacía mucho frío.
3. Manolín iba a estudiar para un examen de química.
4. Sonó el teléfono.
5. Guille le dijo que cambiaron la fecha del examen.
6. Porque era una broma.
7. Va a hacerle una broma a Guille.
8. Celebran el Día de los Inocentes.

B3 Actividad • ¿Sí o no?

After the students have completed the activity, call on volunteers to read their answers aloud.

ANSWERS:
1. Guille sabía que no era martes 13.
2. Eran las cinco de la tarde.
3. Manolín no recuerda qué día era.
4. Es cierto.
5. Él estaba en su casa.
6. Cambiaron la fecha del examen.
7. Guille se reía.
8. Era una broma.

B4 Sabes que . . .

There are many celebrations during December and January in the Spanish-speaking world. Each country has its own special food, but a favorite in most of Spanish America is the **rosca de reyes.** It is served for **Epifanía** on January 6. It is a special loaf of sweet bread that is baked in the form of a wreath or a ring. Small gifts are placed inside. Usually one of the gifts is a china figure, often representing the Christ child. The bread is served to guests, and the person who receives the china figure must give a party for Candlemas (a church feast on February 2) or for Mardi gras, which is prior to Lent.

You may wish to discuss the information in the realia with the students. Point out that it is an advertisement for one of the many events held at Christmas in the Spanish world.

B5 Comprensión

> You will hear a series of invitations followed by an acceptance or a refusal. Listen to each invitation and decide whether it was accepted (**aceptó**) or turned down (**no aceptó**). Check the appropriate space on your answer sheet. For example, you will hear: **Oye, Marisol, ¿qué te parece si vamos al cine?** and the response: **Pues, chica, tengo que estudiar para los exámenes y si no estudio, no voy a pasar. De todos modos, muchas gracias.** Check the space labeled **no aceptó,** because the invitation was turned down.
>
> 1. —Aló, Marcos. Tengo dos boletos para el concierto del Miami Sound Machine. ¿Quieres ir?
>   —Claro que quiero ir. ¿A qué hora piensas salir?   *aceptó*
> 2. —Voy a dar una fiesta en casa este fin de semana. Quiero invitarte.
>   —¿Este fin de semana? ¡Qué lástima! Creo que tengo que trabajar. *no aceptó*
> 3. —José Luis y yo te necesitamos para el partido de béisbol esta tarde.
>   —Pues, ya saben cómo me gusta el béisbol. ¡Estupendo!   *aceptó*

4. —Maricarmen, tengo algo muy importante que preguntarte. ¿Quieres ir al baile conmigo?

—¡Qué sorpresa, Rafael! Me gustaría mucho ir contigo.   *aceptó*

5. —¿Quieres venir a la fiesta de cumpleaños de Eduardo?

—¡Ay! ¡Qué pena! Tengo que estudiar para un examen.   *no aceptó*

6. —Sara, el sábado vamos a nadar al lago. ¿Vas a venir con nosotros?

—Tú sabes que mi mamá no me permite ir al lago.   *no aceptó*

7. — Es el fin de semana. ¿Quieres hacer algo para divertirnos?

—Me gustaría pero tengo dolor de cabeza.   *no aceptó*

8. —Vicente y yo vamos a la biblioteca a estudiar. ¿Quieres venir con nosotros?

—¡Buena idea! Necesito un libro para la clase de historia.   *aceptó*

9. —Tengo el video de una película magnífica. ¿Quieres venir a mi casa a verla esta noche?

—¿Qué película? . . . Bueno, la verdad es que no importa. Me encantan todas las películas.   *aceptó*

10. —Jorge, ¿puedes ayudarme con las matemáticas? Podemos estudiar en mi casa si quieres.

—Lo siento, Gregorio. Tengo que ayudar a mi hermanito esta noche.   *no aceptó*

Now check your answers. *Read each exchange again and give the correct answer.*

B 6   SE DICE ASÍ

To practice expressing intentions, ask the students to think of three recent instances in which their plans were not carried out. Call on volunteers to write several of the examples on the board or a transparency.

B 7   ESTRUCTURAS ESENCIALES

Introduce the three irregular verbs in conversation form. Point out that they are the only irregular verbs in the imperfect tense. Stress that **ver** is accented on the **i** in all imperfect forms and that **ser** and **ir** are accented in the **nosotros** form. To re-enter the uses of **ser** to tell time, ask the students to recall at what time certain events happened yesterday.

Eran las ocho cuando fui a la escuela.
Era la una cuando almorzamos.

B 8   Actividad • Cuando yo era pequeño . . .

For writing practice, have each student describe him or herself as a child, using the questions as a guide.

B 9   Actividad • Los planes eran diferentes

Have the students work in pairs to supply the correct words and complete the sentences. The answers may also be written for homework.

B 10   SITUACIÓN • Ya era tarde

Have the students listen as you read the dialog aloud or play the cassette. Then call on pairs to role-play the dialog.

SLOWER-PACED LEARNING Distribute copies of the dialog in which you have left blanks for the forms of the imperfect tense. Have the students fill in the correct forms as you dictate the dialog.

B 11   Actividad • Preguntas y respuestas

Allow each student to work with a partner to complete the questions. Review with the class. As a variation, you may wish to have the students work alone and then review their answers with a partner.

B 12   Actividad • Todos tenían excusas

For cooperative learning, have the students form groups of two or three to think of six excuses for being unable to attend the picnic. Remind the students to use the imperfect tense.

CHALLENGE Ask several students to participate in an impromptu dialog in which all of them must give an excuse for not attending a function.

B 13   ESTRUCTURAS ESENCIALES

Read the explanation aloud to the students. For number 2, allow them to recall things they used to do often in the past. Stress that the imperfect is the ideal tense to use to reminisce and relive the past. Ask a few questions based on the students' real life experiences, such as **¿Dónde vivías cuando eras pequeño/a? ¿Cómo era tu casa?**

B 14   Actividad • ¿Qué hacían cuando se fue la luz?

Allow each student to work with a partner to decide what each person was doing when the lights went out.

SLOWER-PACED LEARNING As a follow-up, ask the students to select an event for discussion, such as a blackout, a major storm, or an important news announcement. You may wish to have them interview their parents or other family members and ask what they were doing when a major event occurred. Have the students report their findings to the class. For example:

> Cuando se murió el Presidente Kennedy, mi mamá estudiaba en la universidad.

B 15   Actividad • Siempre hacían lo mismo

Have each student complete the activity on paper and then exchange papers with a partner to correct their work.

B 16   Actividad • ¡A competir!

Assign this activity for homework. Select a few introductions to use to begin a class story. Call on volunteers to add details to the story.

SLOWER-PACED LEARNING Brainstorm several examples in class before allowing the students to work alone. Collect and review their introductions. You may wish to make transparencies of several introductions to show to the class.

B 17   Actividad • La persona ideal

Allow the students five minutes to complete the description of an ideal person. Ask them to work in pairs to discuss their favorite person.

SLOWER-PACED LEARNING   Create the beginnings of a description with the class that they may use as a model. Then have each student work with a partner to complete the activity.

B 18   ### Actividad • ¡Tenía mil planes!

Ask the students to think about a trip or another event that was canceled. Then ask each student to discuss the plans they had made with a partner.

B 19   ### SE DICE ASÍ

Point out that **había** is the imperfect tense form of **haber.** Use the form in a discussion of an event, such as a ball game that occurred recently at school. **Había mucha gente en el gimnasio el sábado. Había un locutor, dos equipos de béisbol y mucho ruido.**

B 20   ### Actividad • Ayer y hoy

Ask each student to complete the activity with a partner. You may wish to expand this activity, using magazine pictures as a stimulus for conversation.

CHALLENGE   After completing the activity, allow the students to write original stories. They should use the introductions they wrote for B16. Select and correct the stories, and make copies to create a booklet for each student. Use the stories to review the imperfect tense in Unit 8.

SECTION C

OBJECTIVES   **To express feelings and emotions:** express regret, express how you feel about others and about yourself

CULTURAL BACKGROUND   Teenagers' parties in Spanish-speaking countries are often informal and are usually held at home. Friends or relatives of the guests are always welcome. These parties are not only for the teenagers but for people of all ages. The adults, as well, are welcome to participate, dance, and enjoy the occasion. Even very young children are permitted to attend and join in the fun. A party in a Spanish-speaking country rarely begins on time. It is considered rude to arrive early or on time, because one may find the host or hostess in the midst of preparations.

MOTIVATING ACTIVITY   Have the students work together to plan a party. To encourage participation, ask the students questions, such as who will be invited, what kind of food will be served, what kind of music will be played, and which adults should be invited.

C1   ## Hablando de la fiesta por teléfono

You may wish to review new structures and vocabulary before starting the presentation. Play the cassette or read the introduction aloud. Have the students repeat after you, alternating choral and individual repetition to avoid boredom. In order to keep a fast tempo and maximum student attention, do not interrupt to explain grammar or vocabulary items. Select two students to play the roles of Rosita and Cecilia. Ask them to role-play the first part of the dialog. Then ask several questions to check comprehension before proceeding to the next section. Continue playing the cassette or reading the narrative in the second section. Pause after each description to ask questions.

C2 Actividad • Preguntas y respuestas

You may wish to do this activity orally in class with the books closed, or you may prefer to have each student work with a partner to answer the questions. Review the activity with the class when they finish.

ANSWERS:
1. Cecilia pensaba ir a la fiesta.
2. Cecilia no pudo ir.
3. La fiesta era de Conchita.
4. Rosita llegó temprano a la fiesta.
5. Estaban unos chicos, Miguel y Silvia.
6. Miguel y Silvia estaban bailando.
7. Conchita estaba en la cocina.
8. Sí, había mucha gente en la fiesta.

C3 Actividad • No es así

You may wish to have the students correct the statements orally as a class or in pairs. Prepare a transparency with the corrected sentences to help them check their work.

CHALLENGE Tell the students to write five original true or false statements. They should exchange papers and correct each other's sentences to make them agree with the dialog in C1.

ANSWERS:
1. No había mucha gente cuando Rosita llegó.
2. Miguel y Silvia bailaban.
3. Había mucha gente en la fiesta.
4. La mamá de Conchita preparaba unos platos.
5. Todos esperaban a Cecilia en la fiesta de Conchita.
6. La fiesta fue estupenda.

C4 Actividad • Charla

Have each student discuss the dialog with a partner. Then have a short class discussion about their opinions.

C5 Actividad • La mejor fiesta

Assign this activity for homework. The following day, allow the students to talk about their parties and to show photographs if they have them.

C6 ESTRUCTURAS ESENCIALES

Ask the students to think of moments when they were interrupted. For example, **Yo miraba la televisión cuando sonó el teléfono.** Write their sentences on the board or a transparency. Ask them to explain why one verb is in the preterit tense and the other is in the imperfect tense. Elicit that one verb describes a completed past action, while the other verb describes an action that was still in progress.

To practice the preterit and imperfect, use magazine pictures to stimulate conversation. For example, show a picture of a person running and call on a student to form a sentence, such as: **Él corría cuando vio un perro.**

You may wish to add that the imperfect tense uses adverbials that refer to indefinite duration or repetition, such as **todas las noches, frecuentemente, a menudo.** The preterit uses adverbials that refer to definite duration or repetition: **ese día, ayer, hoy, el año pasado.**

SLOWER-PACED LEARNING   You may wish to provide verbal and visual cues to help the students form sentences using the imperfect and preterit tenses. For example, as you hold up a picture of a girl talking on the telephone, say **tocar.** Then elicit a sentence from the students, such as **Ella hablaba por teléfono cuando alguien tocó a la puerta.**

C7   Actividad • El desfile

As a variation, write the paragraph on the board or a transparency, changing the verbs to their infinitive forms. Ask the students to complete the paragraph with the correct preterit and imperfect tenses of the verbs.

C8   Actividad • Y entonces, ¿qué pasó?

For cooperative learning, have the students form groups of two or three. Have each group complete the activity orally. Then call on members from each group to form a sentence with each item.

C9   Actividad • Hoy fue diferente

Ask the students to complete the sentences with the correct verb forms. Call on individuals to read their completed sentences aloud.

C10   SITUACIÓN • ¿Cómo estaban mis amigos?

Re-enter the forms of **tener** and **estar** in the imperfect tense. Also, re-enter the function "expressing emotions" with the two verbs from previous lessons by acting out situations in a game of charades. For example, as you frown and stomp your feet, elicit the expression **está furioso(a)** from the students. You may also wish to write the expressions on pieces of paper and then call on volunteers to select one and act out the emotion.

As a variation, distribute crayons and paper to the students. Explain that you are going to express two opposite emotions. The students should select any colors they wish and draw their interpretations of the emotions. Use the following or similar emotions.

estaba enamorado / estaba enojado
estaba feliz / estaba triste
estaba cansado / estaba alegre

Have students label their illustrations and discuss them. Then display the illustrations in the classroom.

C11   Actividad • ¿Cómo estabas tú?

Ask the students to work in pairs to complete the activity. When they have finished, review the sentences and responses with the entire class.

SLOWER-PACED LEARNING   Use magazine pictures of people whose faces show several of the expressions presented in C10, on page 175. Hold up each picture, and call on students to supply information about the person. For example, you may have a picture of a boy running to catch a bus. Ask the students the following or similar questions.

¿Qué está haciendo el muchacho? *(Está corriendo.)*
¿Por qué crees que está corriendo? *(Tiene prisa.)*

After you have practiced other expressions, repeat the procedure using the preterit and imperfect tenses.

▪ ¿Por qué corrió este muchacho? *(Tenía prisa.)*

C 12 SE DICE ASÍ

Write the Spanish sentences on the board. Ask the students to describe the differences between **ser** and **estar.** You may also wish to give the following or similar examples to illustrate the meanings.

> Mis hermanos ven el partido de béisbol todos los días. No me gusta el béisbol. Estoy aburrido.
> El vecino habla y habla y habla y no dice nada. El vecino es aburrido.
> Luis toma sus libros, abre la puerta y le dice adiós a su mamá. Luis está listo para salir.
> Anita recibe A en todas sus materias. Es una chica muy inteligente. Es muy lista.

To confirm the students' original observations, have them open their books and read the chart and the explanation of **ser** and **estar.**

C 13 Actividad • ¿Cuántos años tenías?

For cooperative learning, form groups of three to complete the activity. Ask each person in the group to take notes. Then call on volunteers to share the information with the class. To protect the privacy of each student, explain that they may give real or fictional responses.

SLOWER-PACED LEARNING   You may wish to have the students write the completed sentences on the board for correction by the class.

C 14 Actividad • ¿Por qué?

Permit the students to work in pairs to complete the activity orally. For writing practice, you may also wish to have each student combine the cues in each entry to form a sentence.

> comer / tener hambre
> Comí porque tenía hambre.

ANSWERS:
1. ¿Por qué compraste el saco?
   Compré el saco porque tenía dinero.
2. ¿Por qué vendiste la moto?
   Vendí la moto porque necesitaba dinero.
3. ¿Por qué fuiste a las ocho?
   Fui a las ocho porque no quería llegar tarde.
4. ¿Por qué bailaste?
   Bailé porque tenía ganas.
5. ¿Por qué llamaste a Ricardo?
   Llamé a Ricardo porque quería invitarlo.
6. ¿Por qué no pudiste entrar?
   No pude entrar porque eran las nueve.
7. ¿Por qué no llevaste la camisa azul?
   No llevé la camisa azul porque no me quedaba bien.

C 15 **Actividad • ¡Faltaban sólo dos días!**

Assign this activity for homework. Prepare a transparency to use in class for correction. Call on volunteers to read the answers aloud as you write them on the transparency.

SLOWER-PACED LEARNING   You may want to check comprehension of the paragraph by asking questions about content. Then have the students complete the activity in class.

C 16 **Comprensión**

You will hear a statement or a question followed by two responses. Choose the most appropriate response and check the space on your answer sheet. For example, you will hear: **Marcos estuvo cuatro horas afuera en la nieve.** You will also hear two responses: (a) **Tenía prisa.** (b) **Tenía frío.** You check **b,** because it is the appropriate response.

1. Elena no durmió en toda la noche.
   a. Tenía miedo. (√)
   b. Tenía sueño.
2. La temperatura estaba a cien grados hoy.
   a. Tenía calor. (√)
   b. Estaba enamorada.
3. Mi hermano rompió mi bicicleta nueva.
   a. Estaba enfermo.
   b. Estaba furioso. (√)
4. El profesor habló durante toda la clase, pero yo no entendí nada.
   a. Estaba aburrida. (√)
   b. Tenía calor.
5. Mañana Raúl tiene un examen de álgebra.
   a. Tiene que estudiar. (√)
   b. Está enamorado.
6. Martín acaba de ganar un millón de dólares.
   a. Tiene sueño.
   b. Tiene suerte. (√)
7. Son las ocho menos cinco y Elisa tiene clase en cinco minutos.
   a. Tiene miedo.
   b. Tiene prisa. (√)
8. Joaquín tiene una temperatura de 103 grados.
   a. Está furioso.
   b. Está enfermo. (√)
9. Mi prima tiene un novio nuevo.
   a. Está enamorada. (√)
   b. Tiene prisa.
10. Tengo mis maletas y mis boletos de avión.
    a. Estoy listo. (√)
    b. Tengo calor.

Now check your answers. *Read each statement again and give the correct answer.*

C17 Actividad • Yo iba a decirle a Alicia que . . .

Form cooperative learning groups of three to brainstorm logical reasons. Then call on individuals to give their excuses. You may also complete this activity as a game between teams of students in which the team with the most creative excuses wins.

C18 SITUACIÓN • Te lo agradezco

Play the cassette or read the dialog aloud, and ask the students to follow along in their books. Have the students repeat after you, alternating choral and individual repetition to avoid boredom. In order to keep a fast tempo and maximum student attention, do not interrupt to explain grammar or vocabulary items. Point out the problem that David has with the verb **agradecer.** Write several forms of the verb on the board, and ask the students to compare it to the verb **conocer.** Remind them about the stem change in the **yo** form. For cooperative learning, form groups of two to role-play the dialog.

C19 Actividad • Preguntas y respuestas

You may wish to do this activity with books closed. For further practice, you may add the following or similar questions.

¿Qué palabra no comprende David?
¿Qué le envió Sally a David?
¿Cuándo empezó Nora la carta?
¿Cómo expresa David su gratitud?

ANSWERS:
1. Nora y David esperan al profesor.
2. Sally es una amiga de ellos y le mandó a Nora un regalo de Navidad.
3. Nora le escribe una carta a Sally.
4. Nora quiere saber cómo se dice "te agradezco" en inglés.
5. No, porque no conoce la palabra "agradecer."

C20 ESTRUCTURAS ESENCIALES

Present the forms of the verbs ending in **-cer** and **-cir** to the class. Have the students practice the verbs in conversation. Ask the students to write the new verbs in the verb section of their notebooks.

C21 Actividad • Obedezcan las instrucciones

As a variation, distribute copies of the activity, leaving blanks as indicated. Dictate the sentences, and have the students fill in the blanks.

CHALLENGE Give pairs of students index cards on which you have described events and instructions for each speaker. The pairs of speakers must then create impromptu dialogs to match the situations.

C22 Actividad • Charla

Ask each student to work with a partner to practice the dialog as described. You may wish to call on volunteers to present their dialogs to the class.

C23 · Actividad · ¡A escribir!

Assign the activity for homework. Remind the students to use only the imperfect and the preterit tenses.

CHALLENGE Point out the new vocabulary to the students—**cortometraje,** *(short movie),* and **informes,** *(information).* You may wish to ask the students the following or similar questions based on the information contained in the realia.

> ¿Qué película daban en el cine La Independencia?
> ¿Quién era el director?
> ¿Qué día era?
> ¿A qué hora comenzaba la película?
> ¿Qué película daban en el Museo Tecnológico de la CFE?
> ¿Dónde queda el museo?
> ¿Dónde se puede llamar para pedir informes?
> ¿Qué daban en la embajada de España?
> ¿A qué hora?

TRY YOUR SKILLS

OBJECTIVES To recombine communicative functions, grammar, and vocabulary

CULTURAL BACKGROUND **El Día de los Enamorados** is celebrated in Spanish–speaking countries in much the same way as it is celebrated in the United States. It is also called **el Día de la Amistad** *(Friendship Day).* As a review of the cultural material from the unit, you may wish to discuss with the students several holidays celebrated in Spanish-speaking countries.

1 El Día de los Enamorados

Read the narrative aloud or play the cassette as the students follow along in their books. Discuss the illustration with them. Ask them to describe what each person was doing at the party.

2 Actividad · El catorce de febrero

SLOWER-PACED LEARNING For writing practice, have the students write complete sentences. You may wish to call on volunteers to write their answers on the board or a transparency.

ANSWERS:
1. En la fiesta de Carmela la gente bailó. La fiesta fue muy divertida.
2. Carmela invitó a muchos amigos y compañeros de clase.
3. Había mucha comida y cosas sabrosas.
4. José Gómez iba a venir temprano para ayudar a Carmela.
5. José no pudo venir temprano.
6. Su prima Marilú la ayudaba.
7. Ponían la mesa.
8. Tres parejas bailaban.
9. Cristina tocaba el piano. Eduardo tocaba la guitarra.
10. Sí, les gustó mucho.
11. Se fueron muy tarde.

3   **Actividad • ¡A escribir!**

Assign this activity for homework. Then collect and correct the papers. For oral practice, call on volunteers to talk about the parties they had attended, using their compositions as a guide.

SLOWER-PACED LEARNING   You may wish to write the following or similar questions on the board. Ask the students to use them as a guide to write their compositions.

> ¿Cuándo fue la fiesta?
> ¿Cuántas personas había?
> ¿Qué hacían?
> ¿Qué había de comer?
> ¿A qué hora fueron los invitados?

4   **Actividad • La fiesta de Navidad**

You may wish to prepare a transparency and then call on students to fill in the blanks with the correct prepositions.

5   **Actividad • Charla**

Have each student tell a partner about a nightmare or dream. You may wish to allow several volunteers to relate their experiences to the class.

6   **Actividad • ¿*De* la mañana o *por* la mañana?**

Instruct the students to choose between **de** and **por** to complete the sentences. Review the activity by writing the answers on the board or a transparency.

7   **Actividad • ¡Hoy no puedo estudiar!**

This activity may be completed in class or at home. If completed in class, write the opening portions of the sentences on the board or a transparency. Repeat each one several times, and allow the students to complete them with different phrases from the box.

8   **Dictado**

Write the following paragraph from dictation. First, listen to the paragraph as it is read to you. Then you will hear the paragraph again in short segments to allow you time to write. Finally, you will hear the paragraph a third time so that you may check your work. Let's begin.

> Cuando era niño *(pause)* me gustaban mucho las fiestas. *(pause)*
> En casa *(pause)* había muchas fiestas *(pause)* todos los meses. *(pause)*
> Mis padres me llevaban *(pause)* también a ver el desfile *(pause)* del
> Día de la Raza. *(pause)* Durante la Navidad *(pause)* siempre íbamos a
> cenar *(pause)* a casa de los abuelos.

PRONUNCIACIÓN

Review the letters **c** (before **a, o, u**), **k**, and **qu.** Tell the students that these three letters have the same sound, and that it is very similar to the English /k/ sound. Read the examples aloud and have students repeat after you.

Review the letters **c, s,** and **z.** You may also wish to point out the pronunciation of these letters in Spain. Practice the pronunciation of the words and sentences in the lists with the class by playing the cassette or reading them aloud. To practice the **c, s,** and **z,** you may wish to write the following tongue twister on the board and have each student practice the pronunciation with a partner.

> La feliz emperatriz despierta, reza sus
> oraciones y empieza a vestirse. La feliz
> emperatriz tiene una cruz de oro.
> Desayuna con arroz y azúcar.

Review the single **r** in the middle of a word. Ask the students to repeat the words after you. You may wish to have the students practice their pronunciation in pairs. Remind the students to assist and correct their partners' pronunciation when needed.

Actividad • Práctica de pronunciación

Discuss the linking of words in Spanish pronunciation. You may wish to have the students listen to a narrative and identify words that were linked together. You may also write several of the sentences from the narrative on a transparency and mark the links as the students listen. Practice the pronunciation of the sentences with the class.

¿LO SABES?

SECTION A

Have each student work with a partner to complete the activities and review the functions in this section. Call on several pairs to role-play the situation for the class.

SECTION B

Before the students complete the exercises, review the uses of the imperfect tense. For further practice with expressing intention, have the students discuss their plans for this school year.

SECTION C

Remind the students to be polite when expressing regret or declining an invitation. For additional practice expressing emotion, call on individuals to demonstrate an emotion as the other students try to identify it.

VOCABULARIO

To practice the vocabulary, you may wish to play the game **Lotería.** Prepare bingo grids. Select words from the vocabulary list, dividing them into six columns. Distribute the list to the students. Ask them to fill in the grid using words from each column. For example, words from column 1 of the list will be used in column 1 on the grid. Play several rounds of **Lotería** as you dictate the English definitions of the words in each column at random. Award points or small prizes to the winners.

PRÁCTICA DEL VOCABULARIO

Have the students complete the vocabulary practice at home. Call on volunteers to read their paragraphs aloud.

VAMOS A LEER

OBJECTIVE   To read for practice and pleasure

Antes de leer

You may wish to point out that **Había una vez . . .** is similar to *Once upon a time . . . .* Explain to the students that Spanish has many fables, such as the one in the book, that contain a moral at the end of the story. You may wish to add that many of the fables are very old and that the Arabs brought many of them to Spain from the Orient.

Before proceeding with the reading selection, you may wish to prepare a plot line, outlining the main ideas of the selection—the problems of the father and his son and the moral lesson that can be derived from the story. Prepare three or four guiding questions that elicit major ideas or aspects of the plot line.

Preparación para la lectura

Have the students answer the questions orally before reading the folk tale. You may wish to briefly discuss proverbs with the students.

ANSWERS:
1. *Answers will vary.*
2. *Answers will vary.*
3. lejísimo, muy lejos, bastante lejos, un poco lejos, nada lejos
4. *strange*
5. Si cada uno ve las cosas a su manera, entonces es muy difícil complacer a todo el mundo.

CUESTIÓN DE OPINIÓN

Review the introductory material with the students. Play the cassette or read the selection aloud as the students follow along in their books. You may wish to ask them to find specific information in each paragraph. Proceed one paragraph at a time, stopping to check for comprehension.

SLOWER-PACED LEARNING Divide the selection into several segments, and extend the reading over several days. Before beginning a new segment, review the previous material.

Actividad • Preguntas y respuestas

Have each student work with a partner and use the information in the reading selection to answer the questions. Review the answers with the entire class.

ANSWERS:
1. Necesitaba dinero para comprar abrigos para el invierno y los regalos de Reyes. Iba al mercado.
2. El burro nunca tenía prisa.
3. Encontraron primero a unas mujeres que ellos no conocían.
4. El hombre muy viejo.
5. Les compraron frutas.
6. El vendedor dijo "el mundo es muy extraño" porque el padre iba montado en el burro y el hijo iba caminando.
7. El primero significa *to want* y el segundo significa *to love*.
8. Desmontar significa "bajarse".
9. El hijo pensaba comprarle los cerdos a la mujer para después venderlos en el mercado.
10. a. *was saying*
11. *Answers will vary.*
12. Nadie quedó contento.

Actividad • A ordenar

Allow the students five minutes to complete the activity. You may wish to write the sentences on the board. Call on students to number the sentences in the correct order.

CHALLENGE Have the students write a complete paragraph using the numbered sentences. Encourage them to use connectors. When they are finished, have them read their paragraphs aloud to the class.

Actividad • Charla

For cooperative learning, ask the students to work in groups of three to retell the story. They may use their books for reference. They should also discuss the advantages and disadvantages of each decision the boy and his father made. Have each group take notes for use in a class discussion.

UNIDAD 5

Celebraciones y fiestas

Spanish-speaking teenagers, like their
American counterparts, love festivities
and celebrations. The Hispanic world has
many holidays, all celebrated uniquely,
and everybody enjoys them tremendously!

In this unit you will:

SECTION **A**	extend and accept an invitation . . . congratulate someone
SECTION **B**	express your intention . . . describe events in the past
SECTION **C**	express regret . . . express how you feel about others and about yourself
TRY YOUR SKILLS	use what you've learned
VAMOS A LEER	read for practice and pleasure

In the Spanish world, every occasion calls for a celebration. Most of these celebrations are family gatherings where young people and close relatives enjoy each other's company.

For teaching suggestions, see the Teacher's Notes preceding this unit (pp. T100–121).

A1   Nuestras fiestas 📼

Cumpleaños, aniversarios, graduaciones, bodas, nacimientos . . . siempre hay algo que celebrar en el calendario. La Navidad, el Año Nuevo, la Pascua, ¡cualquier motivo es bueno para pasar un buen rato con la familia y los amigos!

Fiestas equivalentes entre los Estados Unidos y el mundo hispánico

Año Nuevo	New Year's Day
Carnaval	Mardi Gras
Día de los Enamorados	St. Valentine's Day
Semana Santa	Holy Week
Pascua Florida	Easter; Passover
Día del Trabajo	Labor Day
Día de la Hispanidad	Columbus Day
Día de los Inocentes	April Fool's Day
Nochebuena	Christmas Eve
Navidad; Pascuas	Christmas
Fin de Año	New Year's Eve

Acabamos de escribir las tarjetas de Navidad y ya empezamos a ver a qué fiesta vamos a ir para el Fin de Año . . . y qué ropa vamos a llevar el Día de Año Nuevo. Además, pronto hay que hacer las listas de regalos para el Día de Reyes, el seis de enero.

Algunas fiestas importantes

En España

1º de enero	Año Nuevo
6 de enero	Epifanía (Día de Reyes)
1º de mayo	Día del Trabajo
24 de junio	San Juan y celebración del santo del rey
12 de octubre	Día de la Hispanidad
24 de diciembre	Nochebuena
25 de diciembre	Navidad
31 de diciembre	Fin de Año

En Venezuela

1º de enero	Año Nuevo
6 de enero	Día de Reyes
1º de mayo	Día del Trabajo
24 de junio	Batalla de Carabobo
5 de julio	Día de la Independencia
24 de julio	Aniversario del nacimiento de Bolívar
12 de octubre	Día de la Raza (Descubrimiento de América)
17 de diciembre	Aniversario de la muerte de Bolívar
24 de diciembre	Nochebuena
25 de diciembre	Navidad
31 de diciembre	Fin de Año

Luego tenemos que prepararnos para los desfiles de carnaval y pensar qué vamos a regalar el Día de los Enamorados.

Todavía no acabamos de celebrar ese día y ya tenemos que hacer planes para las vacaciones de primavera. ¿Quién va a venir a pasar unos días con nosotros? ¿Adónde vamos a ir con la familia para celebrar la Pascua?

Dentro de una semana las tiendas ya anuncian el Día de las Madres en mayo y el Día de los Padres en junio. En los Estados Unidos el Día del Trabajo es el primer lunes de septiembre, pero en el mundo hispánico es el primero de mayo. Por supuesto, en mayo tenemos que pensar qué vamos a hacer . . .

DÍA DE LAS MADRES

Entonces las agencias de viajes empiezan a anunciar los países maravillosos que podemos visitar en las vacaciones de verano.

Más tarde, en octubre, tenemos que decidir cómo vamos a celebrar el Día de la Raza. ¿Vamos a ir a un desfile? ¿Qué vamos a hacer?

Ya para esta fecha hay que volver a pensar en la Navidad. ¿A quién invitamos? ¿Qué regalos queremos recibir? Y, ¿dónde vamos a pasar las fiestas? ¿En nuestra casa? ¿En casa de los abuelos como el año pasado? ¿En casa de algún otro familiar? Bueno, muy pronto empezamos a contar los días que faltan y también a preparar las tarjetas que este año queremos mandar más temprano.

A2   Actividad • Preguntas y respuestas

Answer the questions according to the information in A1.

1. ¿Qué fiesta hay el primero de enero?
2. ¿Cuándo es el santo del rey de España?
3. ¿En qué mes celebra Venezuela su independencia?
4. ¿En qué estación del año llegó Colón a América?
5. ¿En qué fecha es el aniversario de la muerte de Bolívar?
6. ¿Qué celebran Venezuela y otros países hispánicos el 12 de octubre?
7. ¿Cuándo es el Día de Reyes?
8. ¿Cómo se llama *Columbus Day* en España?

1. El primero de enero es la fiesta de Año Nuevo.
2. El santo del rey de España es el 24 de junio.
3. Venezuela celebra su independencia el 5 de julio.
4. Colón llegó a la América en otoño.
5. El aniversario de la muerte de Bolívar es el 17 de diciembre.
6. Celebran el Día de la Raza.
7. El Día de Reyes es el 6 de enero.
8. En España *Columbus Day* se llama el Día de la Hispanidad.

A3   Actividad • ¡A completar!

Use the information in A1 to complete the following sentences.

1. El año comienza con el día de _____ . Año Nuevo
2. El Día del Descubrimiento de América también se llama _____ . el Día de la Raza
3. Hace casi _____ años que Colón llegó a América. quinientos
4. El 14 de febrero es el Día de los _____ . Enamorados
5. La Pascua Florida no es en otoño, es en _____ . la primavera
6. Para Navidad, les damos _____ a nuestros amigos. regalos

Celebraciones y fiestas   **151**

Todos los países hispánicos celebran el 12 de octubre, día en que Cristóbal Colón llegó a América. En 1492, Colón intentó llegar a las Indias Orientales *(East Indies)* y encontró un nuevo continente, "la tierra más hermosa que ojos humanos han visto *(have seen)."* Años después, Américo Vespucio, un marino *(navigator)* italiano, hizo un mapa del continente. Toda Europa comenzó a llamar América al nuevo continente.

El 12 de octubre es el Día de Colón en los Estados Unidos. En España y otros países lo llaman el Día de la Hispanidad. En algunos países hispánicos es el Día del Descubrimiento de América. En otros es el Día de la Raza. Ese día celebran la unión de las razas del viejo y del nuevo mundo.

Puede ser que algún otro navegante europeo llegara a América antes de Colón, pero son los viajes de Colón, auspiciados *(sponsored)* por los Reyes Católicos, Fernando e Isabel, los que abren las puertas del Nuevo Mundo a Europa, que hasta entonces desconocía su existencia. Con los viajes de Colón comienza la llegada de colonos europeos *(European colonists)* a América y el intercambio cultural y comercial, que serviría de base para lo que es América hoy día.

En honor a Colón, dos países de Centroamérica llaman colón a su moneda. Un puerto y una ciudad en esta región también se llaman así. Colombia, un país de Suramérica, la famosa universidad de Columbia en Nueva York y numerosas calles, plazas y parques honran a *(honor)* Colón. En 1992 se cumplen quinientos años del fabuloso encuentro de Europa y América, que tuvo consecuencias tan importantes. El mundo hispánico se prepara para una celebración monumental.

Actividad • Entrevista   Answers will vary.

How do you celebrate? Ask a classmate the following questions, and take notes.

1. ¿Cuál es tu fiesta favorita?
2. ¿Con quiénes celebras la fiesta?
3. ¿Cómo la celebras? ¿Con una cena? ¿Con un baile? ¿Con regalos?
4. ¿En qué estación del año es esa fiesta?
5. ¿Cómo celebras el Año Nuevo?
6. ¿Qué día es tu cumpleaños?
7. ¿Cómo celebras tu cumpleaños?

A6 **Actividad • ¿Qué dijo?**   Answers will vary.

Using your notes from A5, report to the class what your partner said.

A7 **SE DICE ASÍ**
Extending an invitation

Te llamaba para invitarte...	I was calling to invite you...
Quería invitarte...	I wanted to invite you...
¿Quieres ir a la fiesta?	Do you want to go to the party?
...a la graduación?	...to the graduation?
...al picnic?	...to the picnic?
...a la boda?	...to the wedding?

A8 **¿RECUERDAS?**
The infinitive after a preposition

Vamos a ir el primero de mayo.   *We are going to go on May first.*

You have already learned that in Spanish the infinitive is regularly used after a preposition. Other verbs that are followed by a preposition and an infinitive are:

aprender a	**Aprendí a** nadar.	*I learned to swim.*
comenzar a	Ella **comienza a** cantar.	*She begins to sing.*
empezar a	**¿Empiezas a** estudiar a las ocho?	*Do you start to study at eight o'clock?*
acabar de	**Acabo de** comprarte un calendario.	*I just bought you a calendar.*
tratar de	**Trato de** aprender a bailar.	*I am trying to learn to dance.*
terminar de	Ya **terminé de** leer.	*I already finished reading.*

Rewrite the following sentences to include the verbs in parentheses, making all other necessary changes. Follow the model.

> MODELO Mi clase celebra una fiesta española. (ir a)
> Mi clase **va a celebrar** una fiesta española.

1. Marisol prepara la paella.   (aprender a)
2. Andrés compra unos refrescos.   (ir a)
3. Nora ayuda a Marisol con la comida.   (empezar a)
4. Pepe pone la mesa.   (acabar de)
5. Marta sirve la comida.   (comenzar a)
6. Todos comen a las cuatro de la tarde.   (terminar de)
7. Todos pasan un buen rato.   (tratar de)

Marisol aprende a preparar la paella.
Andrés va a comprar unos refrescos.
Nora empieza a ayudar a Marisol con la comida.
Pepe acaba de poner la mesa.
Marta comienza a servir la comida.
Todos terminan de comer a las cuatro de la tarde.
Todos tratan de pasar un buen rato.

 ## ESTRUCTURAS ESENCIALES
Ordinal numbers

You have learned cardinal numbers in Spanish from 1 through 1,000. Here are the ordinal numbers from *first* through *tenth*.

1º	2º	3º	4º	5º
primero, -a	segundo, -a	tercero, -a	cuarto, -a	quinto, -a
6º	7º	8º	9º	10º
sexto, -a	séptimo, -a	octavo, -a	noveno, -a	décimo, -a

1. Ordinal numbers agree in gender and in number with the nouns to which they refer.

   el **primer** señor   los **primeros** señores
   la **primera** señora   las **primeras** señoras

2. Ordinal numbers usually precede the nouns they modify.

   el **cuarto** día   el **quinto** lugar
   la **cuarta** semana   la **quinta** posición

3. The ordinal numbers **primero** and **tercero** drop the final **o** when they precede a masculine, singular noun.

   el **primer** aniversario   el **primer** día
   el **tercer** jueves   el **tercer** mes

4. After *ten*, cardinal numbers are usually preferred.

   Luis XIV (Catorce)
   el siglo XX (veinte)

5. Notice that you use definite articles with ordinal numbers.

   Celebramos el Año Nuevo **el** primero de enero.

Actividad • La liga de béisbol

The national baseball championship is just around the corner. Rank the following teams according to their record for the season to see which teams qualify. Use ordinal numbers **primero, segundo,** and so on.

	EQUIPO	GANARON (Won)	PERDIERON (Lost)
cuarto	_____ Los Leones (The Lions)	35	15
noveno	_____ Los Atléticos (The Athletics)	18	32
octavo	_____ Los Pumas (The Panthers)	23	27
quinto	_____ Las Águilas (The Eagles)	32	18
décimo	_____ Los Vaqueros (The Cowboys)	9	41
sexto	_____ Los Tigres (The Tigers)	31	19
tercero	_____ Los Tiburones (The Sharks)	40	10
séptimo	_____ Las Estrellas (The Stars)	28	22
segundo	_____ Los Gemelos (The Twins)	41	9
primero	_____ Los Potros (The Colts)	42	8

A12

SE DICE ASÍ
Expressing time (morning, afternoon, or evening)

Fui ayer **por la mañana.**	I went yesterday morning.
Fui **a las diez de la mañana.**	I went at ten o'clock in the morning.
Vuelvo hoy **por la tarde.**	I'm returning this afternoon.
Vuelvo hoy **a las cuatro de la tarde.**	I'll be back today at four o'clock in the afternoon.
No voy **por la noche.**	I'm not going at night.
No voy **a las nueve de la noche.**	I'm not going at nine o'clock at night.

Remember to use **de** with a specific time. Use **por** when no hour is mentioned.

A13

Actividad • ¿Me dijiste cuándo?

Complete the following sentences with **de** or **por.**

1. Voy al cine __por__ la tarde.
2. Comimos en casa de abuela ayer __por__ la noche.
3. La fiesta de Maricarmen es a las cinco __de__ la tarde.
4. Carlos vino el día de Año Nuevo __por__ la noche.
5. El domingo __por__ la mañana sale el tren.
6. Ahora son las nueve __de__ la mañana.

Había que celebrar dos fiestas en la misma semana: el cumpleaños de Alicia, el 25 de junio, y el santo de Pablo, el 29 de junio. ¿Qué era mejor? ¿Hacer dos fiestas por separado o celebrar una sola para los dos? Había que decidir pronto.

Faltaban sólo dos semanas para el cumpleaños de Alicia y el santo de Pablo, y sus amigos todavía no sabían qué hacer. Había que pensar algo rápidamente. Decidieron reunirse todos en casa de María Elena para llegar a un acuerdo y preparar un plan.

Todos hablaban y discutían en voz alta, pero no se ponían de acuerdo. María Elena pensaba que era mejor hacer una sola fiesta. Pero nadie sabía qué día ni a qué hora debía ser. Al fin, después de discutir por un rato, decidieron hacer una sola fiesta.

Esa misma tarde empezaron a hacer las invitaciones por teléfono.

MENCHU ¿Teresita?

TERE Sí, . . . ¡Ah! ¿Eres tú, Carmenchu°?

MENCHU Sí, hija. Te llamaba para invitarte a la fiesta de cumpleaños que estamos preparando para Pablo y Alicia.

TERE Y, ¿cuándo es la fiesta?

MENCHU El viernes de la semana que viene, en casa de Luis. Va a ser una fiesta sorpresa para los dos juntos. Así que no puedes decir nada.

TERE ¿Una fiesta sorpresa? . . . Por supuesto que voy. Me encantan las fiestas sorpresa.

MENCHU ¡Qué bueno que puedes venir! . . . Todo el grupo va a estar allí. Por favor, Tere, ¿quieres traer tus casetes nuevos de Menudo?

TERE Sí, ¡cómo no!

MENCHU Bueno, Tere, hasta luego. Me quedan todavía muchas llamadas. Adiós.

TERE Hasta el viernes, Menchu, y gracias por la invitación.

(Menchu marca otro número.)

MENCHU ¿Andrés? . . .

°The name Carmen has several nicknames. In Spain, **Carmenchu** and **Menchu** are common.

A 15 Actividad • ¡A ordenar!

Number the following events in the proper sequence according to A14. Use ordinal numbers.

cuarto No se ponían de acuerdo.

tercero Los amigos de Pablo y Alicia discutían.

primero Había dos fiestas en la misma semana.

sexto Decidieron hacer una sola fiesta.

quinto Nadie sabía qué día debía ser la fiesta.

segundo Era necesario decidir pronto.

A 16 Actividad • ¡A escoger!

Choose the item that best completes each sentence according to A14.

1. El cumpleaños de Alicia y el santo de Pablo eran _____ .
   • la semana siguiente • en la misma semana • la semana pasada

2. Sus amigos no _____ qué iban a hacer.
   • escuchaban • sabían • discutían

3. Decidieron reunirse en casa de _____ .
   • María Elena • alguien • Menchu

4. Ellos no _____ mucho tiempo.
   • tenían • hablaban • había

5. Menchu tenía que hacer muchas _____ .
   • llamar • llamando • llamadas

6. La fiesta era _____ .
   • el martes • el jueves • el viernes

A 17 Actividad • Y tú, ¿qué crees? Answers will vary.

Express your opinion about the events in A14 by answering the questions below.

1. ¿Era mejor hacer dos fiestas? ¿Por qué?
2. ¿Era mejor preguntarles a Pablo y a Alicia?
3. ¿Crees que María Elena tenía razón?
4. ¿Cuál fue la decisión más importante?
5. ¿Por qué muchas veces es difícil llegar a un acuerdo?
6. ¿Crees que la fiesta iba a ser una sorpresa para Pablo y Alicia?

A 18 Actividad • Charla Answers will vary.

Get together with a classmate and take turns asking and answering the following questions.

1. ¿Ayudas a preparar fiestas a menudo?
2. ¿Vas a fiestas frecuentemente? ¿Quién las da?
3. ¿Cuál fue la última?
4. ¿Era una fiesta sorpresa? ¿Para quién?
5. ¿Quién hizo los preparativos?
6. ¿Cómo hicieron las invitaciones?
7. ¿Qué clase de fiesta era? ¿De cumpleaños? ¿De graduación?

SE DICE ASÍ
Congratulating someone; inquiring about age

¡Muchas felicidades!	Congratulations!
¡Feliz cumpleaños!	Happy birthday!
¿Cuántos años tienes?	How old are you?
¿Cuántos años cumples?	How old will you be?
¡Felicidades en el día de tu santo!	Congratulations on your saint's day!

Ask about age only among close friends.

A 20 Comprensión

For script, see p. T105.

Preparations are underway for the upcoming holiday celebrations. You will hear a short description followed by two statements. After listening to the description, decide if each statement is true **(verdadero)** or false **(falso)**. Check the appropriate space on your answer sheet.

MODELO —Hoy vamos a comprar los regalos para papá.
—Mañana cumple cincuenta años.

a. Ya compraron los regalos de papá.
b. Papá va a celebrar su cumpleaños mañana.

	a.	b.	1	2	3	4	5	6	7	8	9	10
Verdadero		✓		✓	✓			✓		✓	✓	
Falso	✓		✓			✓	✓		✓			✓

A 21 Sabes que . . .

En España y en Hispanoamérica, muchas personas celebran su cumpleaños y su santo el mismo día.

El calendario hispánico incluye el santoral, es decir, los nombres de los santos de cada día del año. Cuando un bebé nace *(is born)*, con frecuencia recibe el nombre de algún familiar. Algunas veces también recibe el nombre del santo del día. Entonces esa persona celebra su santo y su cumpleaños el mismo día.

A 22 Actividad • ¡Demasiadas cosas!

You need help organizing your calendar. Ask a classmate to help you put the following activities in order, using ordinal numbers. The first one is already completed.

____cuarto____ el viernes próximo, el cumpleaños de Alicia
____tercero____ pasado mañana, el santo de tío Pepe
__primero__ hoy, el último día de clases de la semana
____sexto____ el mes que viene, el picnic en la playa
____segundo____ mañana por la mañana, el santo de la profesora
____quinto____ el domingo de la semana próxima, las bodas de oro de los abuelos

A 23 Actividad • ¡A escribir!   Answers will vary.

Invite a friend to a party. Include all the necessary information, such as the date, time, location, and reason for having the party.

A 24 ESTRUCTURAS ESENCIALES
The imperfect tense of regular verbs

The imperfect tense and the present tense are very similar. The present tense describes an action as it is going on in the present. The imperfect tense describes the action as it was going on in the past. For example: "Mamá prepara la torta de cumpleaños." *Mom is preparing the birthday cake.* "Mamá preparaba la torta de cumpleaños." *Mom was preparing the birthday cake.*

In Spanish there are two simple past tenses to describe past actions and events. You have already learned one of these, the preterit tense.

The imperfect tense is another way of expressing the past. To form the imperfect tense, add the following endings to the verb stem.

hablar *to speak*		**comer** *to eat*		**vivir** *to live*	
hablaba	hablábamos	comía	comíamos	vivía	vivíamos
hablabas	hablabais	comías	comíais	vivías	vivíais
hablaba	hablaban	comía	comían	vivía	vivían

Ella **hablaba** rápido.   *She talked fast.*
Raúl **vivía** en México.   *Raúl was living in Mexico.*

1. All **-ar** verbs are regular in the imperfect tense. Notice that the **nosotros(-as)** form has a written accent.

   Nosotros siempre **celebrábamos** el santo de papá.   *We always celebrated Dad's saint's day.*
   Preparábamos la torta de cumpleaños.   *We used to prepare the birthday cake.*

2. The imperfect tense of both **-er** and **-ir** verbs uses the same set of endings. There is a written accent on the **í** in all of the endings.

   Anita **servía** la cena.   *Anita was serving dinner.*
   Tenía muchos invitados.   *She had many guests.*

3. Depending on the situation, there are several English equivalents for the Spanish imperfect tense.

   Discutían en voz alta.   ⎰*They were arguing loudly.*
                               ⎱*They used to argue loudly.*
                                They argued loudly.

Actividad • ¡Todos hablaban al mismo tiempo!   Answers will vary.

Everyone on the organizing committee was talking at once. Find out what each person said by choosing an element from each column. Use imperfect tense forms.

MODELO   Yo conversaba con Pepe.

Uds.	discutir	"¡Una sola fiesta!"
María Elena	decir	cómo preparar el postre
Ana y Luis	contestar	al mismo tiempo
el radio	explicar	una fiesta de carnaval
Menchu	gritar	"¡No hablen tan alto!"
Rita y tú	repetir	una pregunta
Cecilia	preguntar	la hora
Oscar y yo	anunciar	"¡Una fiesta sorpresa!"
Jorge	hablar	en voz alta
tú	llamar	a Menchu

A 26   Actividad • ¿Y qué hacía Cecilia?   For answers, see p. T107.

You and a group of friends got together to prepare for a party. Say what each person was doing. Use the conjunction **mientras** (while) to join your sentences.

MODELO   Rita / preparar el pan // Eva / poner el jamón
         Rita preparaba el pan mientras Eva ponía el jamón.

1. Lolita y Andrés / discutir // Ofelia / ayudar a su mamá
2. Irene y yo / cocinar // Carlos / lavar los platos
3. Pepe y tú / preparar la ensalada // Anita / cortar la cebolla
4. Julia / abrir los paquetes // Georgina / lavar las uvas
5. Jaime / buscar un cuchillo grande // Tomás / sacar la basura
6. Cecilia / poner la mesa // Alberto / comprar las flores

A 27   Actividad • Siempre lo mismo (o casi siempre)

Some people used to do the same things all the time. Complete each sentence with the appropriate verb form.

1. Juan siempre _____ té con limón. (tomar)   tomaba
2. Luisa _____ helado de fresa. (pedir)   pedía
3. A nosotros nos _____ las enchiladas. (gustar)   gustaban
4. A veces _____ pronto. (decidir)   decidían
5. Enrique nunca _____ tarde. (venir)   venía
6. Ellos _____ a menudo de la fiesta. (hablar)   hablaban
7. Rita no _____ carne, _____ vegetariana. (comer, ser)   comía / era
8. Carlos nunca _____ el postre. (hacer)   hacía

Actividad • **Hace cinco años** Answers will vary.

Five years ago you did things differently. You have changed, haven't you? Answer the following questions in complete sentences.

1. ¿Tenías muchos amigos? ¿Cuántos?
2. ¿Adónde te gustaba ir los sábados?
3. ¿Te gustaba la misma música? ¿Cuál era?
4. ¿Sabías bailar?
5. ¿Tenías algún animal? ¿Cuál?
6. ¿Dónde pasabas las vacaciones?
7. ¿Cuántos años tenías hace cinco años?
8. ¿Tenías novio(a)? ¿Cómo se llamaba?

A 29 Actividad • **¡A escribir!** Answers will vary.

In at least ten sentences, write a short essay describing your life five years ago. Use the imperfect tense.

I. Introducción: Lo que yo hacía hace cinco años
II. Desarrollo
   A. Las actividades de cada día
   B. Las actividades de la familia
   C. Los deportes que practicaba
   D. Las cosas que hacía con los amigos
III. Conclusión: En aquellos días, yo hacía muchas cosas . . .

Camisetas desde **995**

Pantalones desde **1.695**

ABIERTO HASTA LAS 9

HOY NIÑOS
La Mueca
presenta:
El mago de Oz
amiguito
TE INVITAMOS A DESCUBRIR
CUAL ES EL SECRETO DEL PAIS DE OZ
domingos 11h00
teatro
AGUIRRE Y CHILE   TELF. 320990

Isn't it exciting to get together with someone you haven't seen for awhile and reminisce about the past? Our lives are constantly changing, so it is nice to remember how things were some time ago.

B1   ¿Era verdad?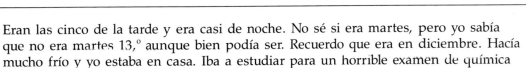

Eran las cinco de la tarde y era casi de noche. No sé si era martes, pero yo sabía que no era martes 13,° aunque bien podía ser. Recuerdo que era en diciembre. Hacía mucho frío y yo estaba en casa. Iba a estudiar para un horrible examen de química la semana siguiente. Entonces sonó el teléfono y contesté.

MANOLÍN   ¿Aló?
GUILLE   Manolín, es Guille. Tengo algo muy importante que decirte. Cambiaron la fecha del examen. Iba a ser la semana que viene y ahora el examen es mañana.

"¡No era verdad! ¡No podía ser verdad!" me dije. Miré sin querer el calendario enfrente de mí. Guille se reía en voz alta. De pronto me di cuenta: era una broma.

Tenía que pensar qué broma iba a hacerle yo a Guille. Tengo que decidirlo pronto, porque ya estamos a 20 de diciembre y el Día de los Inocentes es la semana que viene. . .

B2   Actividad • Preguntas y respuestas   For answers, see p. T108.

Answer the following questions according to B1.

1. ¿Qué hora era? ¿Era de día o de noche?
2. ¿Hacía calor?
3. ¿Qué iba a hacer Manolín?
4. ¿Qué pasó entonces?

5. ¿Qué le dijo Guille?
6. ¿Por qué se reía Guille?
7. ¿Qué va a hacer Manolín?
8. ¿Qué celebran la semana que viene?

°**Martes 13** is equivalent to Friday the 13th in English, a day considered by superstition to bring bad luck.

B3 Actividad • ¿Sí o no?   For answers, see p. T108.

Change these statements to make them agree with B1.

1. Guille sabía que era viernes.
2. Eran las cinco de la mañana.
3. Manolín no recuerda qué mes era.
4. Manolín iba a estudiar cuando sonó el teléfono.
5. Él estaba en el gimnasio.
6. Cambiaron la hora del examen.
7. Manolín se reía.
8. Era el Día de los Inocentes.

B4 Sabes que . . .   For information on how to present the realia, see p. T108.

El Día de los Inocentes es el 28 de diciembre. En ese día hacemos bromas a las personas que conocemos y a veces también a las que no conocemos. Es el equivalente al *April Fool's Day* en los Estados Unidos. Diciembre es un mes lleno de fiestas.

El 24 de diciembre es el día de Nochebuena, que es el día de la gran celebración en el mundo hispánico, en vez del día de Navidad. Para esa noche en todas las casas hispánicas la gente prepara una deliciosa cena con los variados platos de la cocina nacional. Muchas familias van a la Misa del Gallo *(Midnight Mass)* a las doce de la noche. El día 25 de diciembre, Navidad, es día de visitas y de reuniones familiares. Muchas familias, además del nacimiento *(Nativity scene)*, tienen un árbol de Navidad.

El 31 de diciembre, al oír las campanadas *(ringing of bells)* de las doce de la noche *(at the stroke of midnight)*, hay que comer una uva por cada campanada. ¡Esto trae buena suerte! ¡Música, ruido, alegría!

Las fiestas continúan. El 6 de enero es la Epifanía o el Día de Reyes, una alegre celebración infantil. La noche anterior, los niños escriben cartas a los Reyes Magos *(Three Wise Men)* y piden juguetes *(toys)* y regalos. Se van a dormir. Al otro día se levantan muy temprano para buscar sus juguetes. Y así terminan las fiestas de Navidad. ¡Hasta el próximo diciembre!

DE LOS NIÑOS PARA UN MUNDO FELIZ

UN SUEÑO DE NAVIDAD

85 niños cantando y soñando con la Navidad

Una obra de María Isabel Murillo

Un concierto espectacular donde la magia escénica se une a las voces infantiles acompañadas en vivo, por una orquesta sinfónica.

Teatro de Colsubsidio
ROBERTO ARIAS PEREZ
HOY
DOS FUNCIONES
3:00 y 7:00 P.M.
MAÑANA ULTIMAS FUNCIONES
11:00 A.M. y 3:00 P.M.
Boletería: Calle 26 No. 25-40 Tel: 2851826
Carrera 11 No. 66-70 Tel: 2356526
Informes en las taquillas del teatro

Un concierto de Navidad hecho realidad gracias a

C☐RPAVI   ☒ SKANDIA
Skandia Seguros de Colombia S.A.

FLOTA MERCANTE
GRANCOLOMBIANA

B5 Comprensión   For script, see p. T108–109.

You will hear a series of invitations followed by an acceptance or a refusal. Listen to each invitation and decide if it was accepted **(aceptó)** or turned down **(no aceptó).** Check the appropriate space on your answer sheet.

MODELO —Oye Marisol, ¿qué te parece si vamos al cine?
    —Pues, chica, tengo que estudiar para los exámenes y si no estudio, no voy a pasar. De todos modos, muchas gracias.

	0	1	2	3	4	5	6	7	8	9	10
Aceptó		✔		✔	✔				✔	✔	
No aceptó	✔		✔			✔	✔	✔			✔

SE DICE ASÍ
Expressing intention

Iba a ir a tu casa.	I was going to go to your house.
Iba a hacerlo ahora.	I was going to do it now.
Quería terminarlo.	I wanted to finish it.
Pensaba estudiar esta tarde.	I intended to study this afternoon.

B7 ## ESTRUCTURAS ESENCIALES
The imperfect tense forms of ver, ir, *and* ser

Only three verbs are irregular in the imperfect tense: **ver**, **ser**, and **ir**. The following chart shows the imperfect tense forms of these three verbs.

ver *to see*		ser *to be*		ir *to go*	
veía	veíamos	era	éramos	iba	íbamos
veías	veíais	eras	erais	ibas	ibais
veía	veían	era	eran	iba	iban

No **veía** ese programa.
Todos **íbamos** al cine.
Cuando **éramos** niños . . .

I didn't (usually) see that program.
We were all going to the movies.
When we were children . . .

Notice that the imperfect tense forms of **ser** and **ir** have a written accent only in the **nosotros(-as)** form.

B8 **Actividad • Cuando yo era pequeño . . .**   Answers will vary.

Do you remember when you were a child? What were you like? Get together with a classmate. Take turns asking and answering the following questions. Use masculine or feminine forms.

1. ¿Cómo eras cuando eras niño/a? ¿odioso o gracioso? ¿bonito o feo? ¿grande o pequeño? ¿alto o bajo? ¿atlético? ¿artístico?
2. ¿Eras un niño bueno o eras horrible?
3. ¿Eras bueno con los animales? ¿Eras cariñoso con tu familia?
4. ¿Eras generoso o egoísta con tus amigos?
5. ¿Ibas mucho al cine, al parque, a la playa? ¿Con quién ibas?
6. ¿Cómo eran tus amigos?
7. ¿Ibas a la cama temprano o tarde?
8. ¿Veías muchos programas de televisión? ¿Cuáles?
9. ¿Eran tus clases fáciles o difíciles? ¿Por qué?
10. ¿Cómo era tu escuela? ¿Grande o pequeña?

Actividad • Los planes eran diferentes

You were planning a party and all the plans had to be changed. Express what your intentions were by completing each sentence.

1. La fiesta es ahora a las siete. Antes _____ a las ocho.   era
2. Va a ser en casa de Ángela. Antes _____ a ser en casa de Celia.   iba
3. La fiesta es el viernes. Antes _____ el sábado.   era
4. Elena piensa que puede venir. Antes _____ que no _____ venir.   pensaba / podía
5. Conchita prepara la comida. Antes la _____ María Antonia.   preparaba
6. La fiesta es ahora hasta las diez. Antes _____ hasta las nueve.   era
7. Raúl compra los refrescos. Antes los _____ José.   compraba

B10   SITUACIÓN • Ya era tarde

Enrique vivía en Guadalajara, en casa de su abuelita doña Cecilia, cuando estudiaba en la secundaria.

ABUELA   ¿Había alguien en la puerta, Enrique?
ENRIQUE   Sí, abuela.
ABUELA   ¿Quién era?
ENRIQUE   Era Juan.
ABUELA   ¿Qué quería?
ENRIQUE   Saber cuál era la tarea de matemáticas.
Íbamos a estudiar juntos si teníamos tiempo.
ABUELA   ¿Y qué pasó?
ENRIQUE   Me dijo que no podía quedarse a estudiar
porque ya eran las nueve de la noche.

B11   Actividad • Preguntas y respuestas

Answer these questions about the preceding dialog.

1. ¿Con quién hablaba Enrique?
2. ¿Quién estaba en la puerta?
3. ¿Qué iban a hacer esa noche?
4. ¿Qué clase tenían juntos?
5. ¿Por qué Juan no podía estudiar con Enrique?
6. ¿Dónde estaba Enrique?
7. ¿Qué hora era?

1. Enrique hablaba con su abuela.
2. Juan estaba en la puerta.
3. Iban a estudiar juntos.
4. Tenían juntos la clase de matemáticas.   5. Porque no podía quedarse.   6. Estaba en casa de su abuela.
7. Eran las nueve de la noche.

Actividad • Todos tenían excusas   Answers will vary.

Rubén went to a picnic, but six of his friends could not go. Get together with a classmate and guess why not. Here are some ideas:

Enrique no podía ir porque tenía que estudiar (o tenía que bañar al perro, o iba a practicar en el coro o iba a otra fiesta).

Explain that the imperfect as a rule is related to another past event, since in most cases the action described by the imperfect is ongoing in relation to another past action.

ESTRUCTURAS ESENCIALES
Some uses of the imperfect tense

1. Use the imperfect tense to describe an event or an action that was in the process of happening in the past. The beginning and the end of the event or the action **are not** indicated.

¿Adónde **ibas** tan rápido?	*Where were you going so fast?*
Tenía que ir a casa.	*I had to go home.*
Un amigo me **esperaba.**	*A friend was waiting for me.*

2. Use the imperfect tense to express habitual actions (what used to happen) or repeated actions (what happened over and over) in the past. Again, the beginning and the end of the action **are not** indicated.

Yo la **veía** todos los domingos.	*I used to see her every Sunday.*
Yo **caminaba** a la escuela todos los días.	*I used to walk to school every day.*

3. Use the imperfect tense to describe states or conditions in the past.

Mi hermana Anita **era** alta y delgada. **Tenía** el pelo rubio.	*My sister Anita was tall and slim. She had blond hair.*
Ellos **estaban** cansados después de bailar tanto tiempo.	*They were tired after dancing for so long.*
Nuestra casa **era** muy grande y **estaba** en el campo.	*Our house was big and was in the country.*

Actividad • ¿Qué hacían cuando se fue la luz?   Answers will vary.

All of a sudden the lights went out in town. What was everyone doing at that moment? Using the phrases in the box, describe what each of the following people were doing.

la estudiante
los vecinos
la vendedora
el periodista
el músico
la camarera
mis hermanos
la abuela

atender al cliente   practicar la guitarra   servir el postre

mirar televisión   hacer la tarea   quitar la mesa

comprar un monedero   escribir para el periódico

Actividad • Siempre hacían lo mismo

We are all creatures of habit. Yesterday at the cafeteria, you
observed how people did the same things again and again. Complete
the paragraph using the appropriate form of the following verbs.

hablar   comer   tener   gustar
tomar   llamar   mirar   llegar

Antes de comer, Ángela siempre _____ un vaso de agua.   tomaba
Roberto _____ enchiladas todos los días. Luisa siempre _____   comía / llegaba
tarde. A Rafael no le _____ ser el primero. Gerardo   gustaba
nunca _____ dinero. Raquel _____ en voz alta y Ricardo   tenía / hablaba
la _____ sin decir nada. Fernando _____ con Trini y   miraba / hablaba
Manolo _____ a su novia por teléfono.   llamaba

B 16   **Actividad • ¡A competir!**   Answers will vary.

You have entered a short story contest. Your teacher tells you
that first you must set the scene in which the action will take
place. Write three possible introductions: one with the hour or
time of day, another with the season, and the other with the
date. Add weather conditions or other details to make your ideas
stand out. You could include phrases such as the following:

Era una noche fría de invierno . . .
Era el día de su cumpleaños . . .
Era el doce de octubre . . .
Eran casi las doce . . .
Era temprano y hacía buen tiempo . . .

B 17 Actividad • **La persona ideal** Answers will vary.

You went to a party and met your ideal person. Exchange ideas with a classmate about what the ideal person was like. Each of you should describe the person, using the imperfect. Include personality, age, clothing, and physical appearance.

B 18 Actividad • **¡Tenía mil planes!** Answers will vary.

You were hoping to take a trip but it had to be canceled. In five sentences, describe your plans to a classmate. Then reverse roles. Use the verbs in the box.

MODELO   Quería ir a la playa . . .

iba a	quería	tenía ganas de	tenía que	deseaba
trataba de	debía	me gustaba	pensaba	podía
creía que	esperaba	necesitaba	sabía que	era

B 19 SE DICE ASÍ
Describing events in the past

Había dos fiestas.	There were two parties.
Había poco tiempo.	There was little time.
Había muchos discos.	There were many records.

Había is the only imperfect form of **haber** that you will use. Note that it is equivalent to *there was* and *there were*.

Actividad • **Ayer y hoy**

Describe how many things there were yesterday and how many there are today.

AYER

HOY

MODELO

Ayer había seis latas de jugo.

Hoy hay dos.

1. Ayer había tres perros.

Hoy hay dos.

2. Ayer había cinco manzanas.

Hoy hay cuatro.

3. Ayer había tres lápices.

Hoy hay uno.

4. Ayer había un gato.

Hoy hay cinco.

Were you planning to go to a party, but you couldn't go? Wouldn't you like to find out something about it? Why don't you call someone who was there to get the scoop?

C1 Hablando de la fiesta por teléfono 📼

Cecilia quería ir a la fiesta, pero no pudo. Al fin llama por teléfono a Rosita para saber qué pasó. Rosita miraba fotos de la fiesta cuando sonó el teléfono.

ROSITA	¿Aló?
CECILIA	¿Rosita? Habla Cecilia. ¿Cómo estás?
ROSITA	Bien, ¿y tú? Pero, ¿qué te pasó el sábado? Te esperábamos en la fiesta de Conchita.
CECILIA	Ay, ¡qué pena! Lo siento, pero no pude ir. ¿Cómo estuvo la fiesta?
ROSITA	¡Buenísima! Cuando yo llegué, todavía no había mucha gente.
CECILIA	¿Llegó más gente después?
ROSITA	Claro, fue una fiesta estupenda. Saqué muchas fotos. Todo el mundo estaba allí. ¡Sólo faltabas tú!

Al día siguiente Cecilia pasó por casa de Rosita para ver las fotos. Mirando las fotos, Rosita le contaba a Cecilia lo que pasó en la fiesta . . .

Cuando llegué, unos chicos conversaban sentados en el sofá. Miguel y Silvia eran los únicos que bailaban entonces.

Conchita estaba en la cocina. Preparaba unos platos con su mamá y una amiga.

Aquí ya todas las parejas bailaban. La música era buenísima. Teníamos muchos discos. ¡Y mira cuánta gente había! Aquí Carmela está bailando con un chico muy guapo. No sé quién era, no lo conozco.

La mamá de Conchita servía la comida a los invitados. ¡Todo estaba riquísimo! Nos fuimos a casa tarde, cansados pero contentos.

For answers, see p. T112.

C2 **Actividad • Preguntas y respuestas**

Answer these questions according to Cecilia and
Rosita's conversation.

1. ¿Qué pensaba hacer Cecilia?
2. ¿Y qué pasó?
3. ¿De quién era la fiesta?
4. ¿Rosita llegó tarde o temprano a la fiesta?
5. ¿Quiénes estaban allí entonces?
6. ¿Qué hacían Miguel y Silvia?
7. ¿Dónde estaba Conchita?
8. ¿Había mucha gente en la fiesta?

C3 **Actividad • No es así** For answers, see p. T112.

Correct these statements to make them agree with
the information in C1.

1. Todo el mundo ya estaba allí cuando Rosita llegó.
2. Miguel y Silvia tocaban la guitarra.
3. Había muy poca gente en la fiesta.
4. La mamá de Conchita tocaba el piano.
5. Todos esperaban a Cecilia en la fiesta de Rosita.
6. La fiesta fue muy aburrida.

C4 **Actividad • Charla** Answers will vary.

Work with a partner. Ask each other's opinion regarding the dialog in C1.

1. ¿Crees que Cecilia quería ir a la fiesta? ¿Cómo lo sabes?
2. ¿Qué le pasó a Cecilia?
3. ¿Cuáles son tres cosas que confirman que la fiesta estuvo buenísima?
4. ¿Son Cecilia y Rosita buenas amigas? ¿Cómo lo sabes?
5. ¿Qué quieres saber de una fiesta cuando no puedes ir?

Think about the last party you went to. Organize your thoughts and prepare notes in Spanish. In five sentences, describe what was happening at the party. Here are some ideas:

la celebración
el tiempo
la hora
la fecha
la gente
la comida
la música
las sorpresas

C6 ESTRUCTURAS ESENCIALES
The imperfect and the preterit tenses contrasted

Comíamos cuando **llegaron.**   *We were eating when they arrived.*
　　imp.　　　　　　pret.

Hablaba con Luisa cuando **sonó** el teléfono.   *I was talking to Luisa when the telephone rang.*
　imp.　　　　　　　　　　pret.

The difference between the imperfect and the preterit tenses can be illustrated by the following diagram.

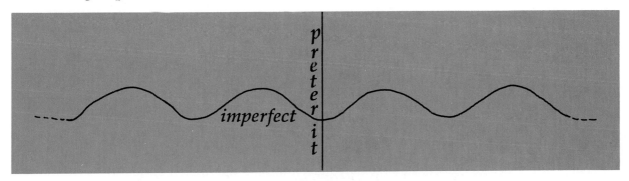

1. The continuous, moving line of the imperfect represents an action or event that was taking place in the past. We do not know when it began or ended.

　　Comíamos . . .   *We were eating . . .*
　　Hablaba con Luisa . . .   *I was talking to Luisa . . .*

2. The vertical line of the preterit tense reports what happened at a specific time in the past, since we know the beginning and end of the action.

　　. . . cuando llegaron.   *. . . when they arrived.*
　　. . . cuando sonó el teléfono. *. . . when the telephone rang.*

> Use the imperfect tense to express an event or action that was already going on when something else happened.

C7 Actividad • El desfile

Read the following paragraph. Then make two lists of verbs—one in the imperfect tense and one in the preterit tense.

Cuando llegamos al parque para ver el desfile del Día de la Raza, no llovía, pero hacía mucho calor. Juan dijo que iba a llover. De pronto cayó un aguacero muy fuerte, pero traíamos impermeables y paraguas. Luego salió el sol y pudimos ver el desfile.

Preterit	Imperfect
llegamos	llovía
dijo	hacía
cayó	iba
salió	traíamos
pudimos	

C8 Actividad • Y entonces, ¿qué pasó? Answers will vary.

From the box below, choose a logical ending for each numbered item. Join the two segments with **cuando**.

MODELO   Era temprano **cuando** llegué al baile.

1. No había mucha gente
2. Ellos bailaban
3. Tenía prisa
4. Ya estaba enferma
5. Tenía sueño
6. Iba a salir
7. Estaba cansada
8. Caminaba por el parque
9. La comida estaba lista

terminé el examen.

tomé el taxi.

entramos en la casa.

la fiesta empezó.

sonó el teléfono.

Alberto llegó con sus discos.

vi a Rosalía.

Conchita sirvió la comida.

fui a casa.

C9 Actividad • Hoy fue diferente

For some reason, people did things differently today from the way they used to. Complete the following sentences.

1. Carmencita nunca _____ postre y hoy comió dos.   comía
2. Luis antes _____ tarde y hoy llegó temprano.   llegaba
3. Juan Carlos siempre _____ refrescos y hoy tomó jugo.   tomaba
4. Andrés nunca _____ y hoy bailó con Ana.   bailaba
5. Rita antes _____ vegetariana, pero hoy comió carne.   era
6. Chela siempre _____ con su prima y hoy no vino.   venía
7. Gerardo nunca _____ suerte, pero hoy la tuvo.   tenía
8. Manolo _____ a su novia todos los días, pero hoy no la llamó.   llamaba
9. Rosalía siempre _____ mucho, pero hoy no comió nada.   comía
10. Leonardo nunca _____ nada, pero hoy compró unas sandalias.   compraba
11. Gonzalo siempre _____ al almacén, pero hoy no fue.   iba
12. Ramona nunca _____ nada, pero hoy le regaló un llavero a su papá.   regalaba

174   Unidad 5

Tenía calor.

Tenía frío.

Tenía sueño.

Tenía miedo.

Tenía prisa.

Tenía hambre.

Estaba enferma.

Estaba furioso.

Estaban enamorados.

Actividad • ¿Cómo estabas tú?

Suppose that the following events occurred. Explain how you reacted, using expressions from C10.

1. Querías ir a la fiesta y no pudiste.
2. Era tarde y no estabas lista.
3. Estabas en la playa al mediodía.
4. Estabas sin abrigo en las montañas.

5. Tu amigo te dijo que venía a las nueve y no vino.
6. Estudiaste hasta las dos de la mañana.
7. Ayer no almorzaste.
8. Alguien te mandó una tarjeta el 14 de febrero.

1. Estaba furioso(a).   2. Tenía prisa.
3. Tenía calor.   4. Tenía frío.

5. Estaba furioso(a).   6. Tenía sueño.
7. Tenía hambre.   8. Estaba enamorado(a).

C12 SE DICE ASÍ
Expressing how you feel about others and about yourself

Tere **estaba** aburrida.	Tere was bored.
Víctor **era** aburrido.	Víctor was boring.
Luis **estaba** listo.	Luis was ready.
Anita **era** lista.	Anita was smart.

Remember that **estar** is used for conditions subject to change or to signal a change from a previous condition°. **Ser** is used to express permanent qualities or conditions.

Answers will vary.

C13 Actividad • ¿Cuántos años tenías?

Do you remember when you did some things for the first time? Say how old you were then and where you were.

MODELO   viajar por avión
La primera vez que viajé por avión tenía cinco años y estaba en San Diego.

1. tomar un tren
2. ganar dinero
3. ir a un campamento de verano
4. pasar unos días con los abuelos
5. ir a un concierto
6. ir al teatro
7. asistir a un partido de fútbol
8. ir a una boda
9. bailar
10. montar a caballo o en bicicleta

°**Estar** is always used to express the condition of death, **estar muerto,** in contrast to the condition of life, **estar vivo.**

C14 Actividad • ¿Por qué? For answers, see p. T114.

C14 Actividad • ¿Por qué?

Explain why you did the following things. Follow the cues. Work with a partner and take turns.

MODELO   comer / tener hambre   —¿Por qué comiste?
— Comí porque tenía hambre.

1. comprar el saco / tener dinero
2. vender la moto / necesitar dinero
3. ir a las ocho / no querer llegar tarde
4. bailar / tener ganas
5. llamar a Ricardo / querer invitarlo
6. no poder entrar / ser las nueve
7. no llevar la camisa azul / no quedar bien (a mí)

C15 Actividad • ¡Faltaban sólo dos días!

You almost forgot Marisol's birthday. Send her a note to tell her what happened. Complete the note with the appropriate form of the verb in the preterit or imperfect tense.

Yo acababa de llegar a casa cuando _____ (empezar) a llover. El periódico _____ (estar) en la mesa y yo _____ (leer) la primera parte. _____ (haber) una foto de México. De pronto, _____ (pensar) en ti y en tu cumpleaños. ¡ _____ (ser) pasado mañana! Yo _____ (saber) que _____ (tener) tu dirección, pero _____ (buscar) y _____ (buscar) y no la _____ (encontrar). _____ (llamar) a Julia y ella me _____ (dar) tu dirección. Mientras te _____ (escribir), yo _____ (recibir) carta tuya. ¡Qué sorpresa!

empezó
estaba / leía
Había
pensé / Era
sabía / tenía
busqué / busqué / encontré
Llamé / dio
escribía / recibí

C16 Comprensión

For script, see p. T115.

You will hear a statement or a question followed by two responses. Choose the most appropriate response and check the space on your answer sheet.

MODELO   Marcos estuvo cuatro horas afuera en la nieve.
a. Tenía prisa.
b. Tenía frío.

	0	1	2	3	4	5	6	7	8	9	10
a.		✓	✓		✓	✓				✓	✓
b.	✓			✓			✓	✓	✓		

C17 Actividad • Yo iba a decirle a Alicia que . . .

Answers will vary.

Five friends were going to go to the school wrestling match but they could not go. Give five reasons why not.

MODELO   Alberto no pudo ir porque quería ir a una fiesta.

Celebraciones y fiestas   177

Nora y David conversan en la clase mientras esperan al profesor.

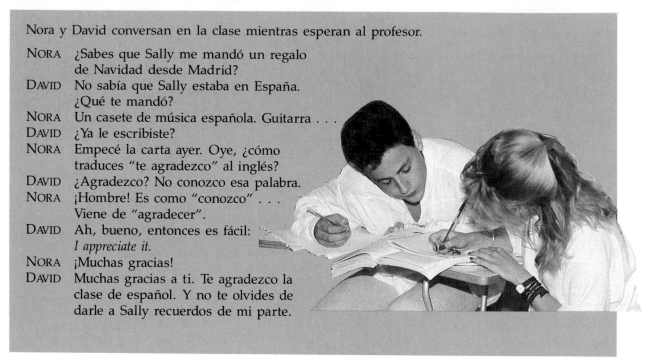

NORA ¿Sabes que Sally me mandó un regalo
de Navidad desde Madrid?

DAVID No sabía que Sally estaba en España.
¿Qué te mandó?

NORA Un casete de música española. Guitarra . . .

DAVID ¿Ya le escribiste?

NORA Empecé la carta ayer. Oye, ¿cómo
traduces "te agradezco" al inglés?

DAVID ¿Agradezco? No conozco esa palabra.

NORA ¡Hombre! Es como "conozco" . . .
Viene de "agradecer".

DAVID Ah, bueno, entonces es fácil:
I appreciate it.

NORA ¡Muchas gracias!

DAVID Muchas gracias a ti. Te agradezco la
clase de español. Y no te olvides de
darle a Sally recuerdos de mi parte.

C19 Actividad • Preguntas y respuestas   For answers, see p. T116.

Answer the questions according to the conversation between Nora and David.

1. ¿A quién esperan Nora y David?
2. ¿Quién es Sally y qué hizo?
3. ¿Qué hace Nora?
4. ¿Qué quiere saber Nora?
5. ¿Crees que David es hispano? ¿Por qué?

C20 ESTRUCTURAS ESENCIALES
Verbs ending in -cer *and* -cir

You have already learned the verb **conocer.** Notice that verbs ending in **-cer** and
-cir have an irregular **yo** form in the present indicative, just like **conocer.**

conocer	*to know*	traducir	*to translate*
conozco	conocemos	traduzco	traducimos
conoces	conocéis	traduces	traducís
conoce	conocen	traduce	traducen

1. Remember that the same irregularity of the **yo** form appears in the command forms.

Conozca a su país.	*Know your country.*
No **traduzcan,** por favor.	*Do not translate, please.*

2. Other verbs you know that follow this pattern are:

agradecer	*to appreciate*	**desaparecer**	*to disappear*	**obedecer**	*to obey*
aparecer	*to appear*	**parecer**	*to seem*	**ofrecer**	*to offer*

Les **ofrezco** veinte dólares por la guitarra.	*I offer them twenty dollars for the guitar.*
Aparezco cuando hay postre.	*I appear when there is dessert.*
Desaparezco cuando hay platos que lavar.	*I disappear when there are dishes to wash.*
Te lo **agradezco** mucho.	*I appreciate it a lot.*
Parece que Antonio **obedece** a su mamá.	*It seems that Antonio obeys his mother.*

C21 Actividad • Obedezcan las instrucciones

Complete the sentences with the correct forms of the verbs indicated on the left.

1. (conocer)   Si no _____ a Tere, te la presento.   conoces
2. (ofrecer)   Yo te lo _____ como un favor.   ofrezco
3. (parecer)   Debes descansar un rato. _____ cansado.   Pareces
4. (traducir)   ¿Cómo _____ tú la palabra "listo"?   traduces
   Depende. Si la uso con "estar", la _____ como   traduzco
   ready.
5. (obedecer)   Tener un perro y tener un gato son dos
   cosas diferentes. Mi perro me _____ a mí y yo _____ a
   mi gato.   obedece / obedezco

C22 Actividad • Charla   Answers will vary.

Someone invites you to a party, but you must refuse because you have something else to do. Be polite, excuse yourself, and thank your partner for the invitation. Then switch roles.

C23 Actividad • ¡A escribir!

Have you seen a good movie recently? Tell us about it in ten sentences. Remember to include the imperfect. Here are some hints: Answers will vary.
For information on how to present the realia, see p. T117.

   ¿Qué clase de película era?
   ¿Quiénes eran los actores? ¿Cómo eran?
   ¿Qué pasó en la película?
   ¿Cómo terminó?
   ¿Dónde daban la película?
   ¿Con quién fuiste?

1 El Día de los Enamorados 📼

Carmela Hernández daba una fiesta el Día de los Enamorados, la noche del catorce de febrero. Invitó a muchos amigos y compañeros de clase.

Había mucha comida y cosas sabrosas. José Gómez iba a venir temprano para ayudarle a Carmela con los preparativos, pero no pudo. Cuando José llegó con Carlos, Marilú, la prima de Carmela, ya la ayudaba a poner la mesa. Cristina tocaba el piano y Eduardo tocaba la guitarra. La música estuvo buenísima. La fiesta fue muy divertida, muchas parejas bailaron y todos regresaron a casa muy tarde.

2 Actividad • El catorce de febrero

Answer the following questions. Base your answers on Skills 1. For answers, see p. T117.

1. ¿Qué pasó en la fiesta de Carmela?
2. ¿A quiénes invitó?
3. ¿Qué cosas había?
4. ¿Quién iba a venir temprano? ¿Para qué?
5. ¿Qué pasó?
6. ¿Quién ayudaba a Carmela?
7. ¿Qué hacían?
8. ¿Cuántas parejas bailaban?
9. ¿Qué tocaba Cristina? ¿Y Eduardo?
10. ¿Les gustó la fiesta?
11. ¿Cuándo se fueron?

3 Actividad • ¡A escribir!   Answers will vary.

Write a brief description of a party you went to recently. Use **El Día de los Enamorados** in Skills 1 as a guide.

4 Actividad • La fiesta de Navidad

Everyone was helping at Tomás's home. Complete the following sentences with the preposition **a** or **de**.

1. Tomás acaba __de__ comprar el árbol de Navidad.
2. Nora comienza __a__ poner la estrella.
3. Andrés trata __de__ ayudar a Nora.
4. María Eugenia va __a__ preparar el postre.
5. Miguel empieza __a__ lavar la lechuga.
6. Bárbara y Débora aprenden __a__ servir la comida.
7. Todos van __a__ venir a la fiesta.

5 Actividad • Charla   Answers will vary.

Describe the setting of a dream or nightmare you had. Include what time of day it was, the day of the week, the weather conditions, the season, and where you were and what you were going to do at that moment.

6 Actividad • ¿De la mañana o por la mañana?

Complete the following sentences using **de** or **por.**

1. Tengo muchas cosas que hacer __por__ la mañana.
2. Voy a limpiar el acuario de las tortugas __por__ la tarde.
3. Paso la aspiradora a las nueve __de__ la mañana.
4. Preparo el desayuno __por__ la mañana.
5. Mi hermana Lucía hace la comida __por__ la noche.
6. Elena pone la mesa a las seis __de__ la tarde.
7. Luis lava los platos a las ocho __de__ la noche.

7 Actividad • ¡Hoy no puedo estudiar! Answers will vary. Possible answers are given.

You are trying to study but get interrupted constantly. Complete the sentences with an appropriate phrase from the box. Make any necessary changes.

tener que ir a la tienda

llegar mi amigo

venir visita

recibir una invitación para una fiesta

sonar el teléfono

empezar mi programa favorito

1. Iba a sacar el libro de biología cuando . . .
2. Quería estudiar la Unidad 3 cuando . . .
3. Necesitaba repetir la actividad cuando . . .
4. Tenía que estudiar para el examen, pero . . .
5. Iba a hacer una lista de las palabras difíciles, pero . . .
6. Estaba seguro de que no tenía amigos, pero . . .

1. Iba a sacar el libro de biología cuando sonó el teléfono. 2. Quería estudiar la Unidad 3 cuando llegó mi amigo. 3. Necesitaba repetir la actividad cuando vino visita. 4. Tenía que estudiar para el examen, pero tuve que ir a la tienda. 5. Iba a hacer una lista de palabras difíciles, pero empezó mi programa favorito. 6. Estaba seguro de que no tenía amigos, pero recibí una invitación para una fiesta.

8 Dictado 🗄 For script, see p. T118.

Copy the following paragraph to prepare yourself for dictation.

Cuando _____ niño me _____ mucho las fiestas. En casa _____ muchas fiestas todos los meses. Mis padres me _____ también a ver el _____ del Día de la Raza. _____ la Navidad siempre _____ a cenar a casa de los _____ .

Letters *c*, *k*, and *qu*

The Spanish letters **c** (before the vowels **a, o, u**), **k**, and **qu** are pronounced alike. The sound is produced in the same manner as the English *k* sound, but without a puff of air that usually accompanies it. Listen carefully and repeat the following words.

quitar	comer	sacar	caer	kilómetro	queso	esquiar
casa	taco	caloría	contigo	kilogramo	buscó	frecuente

Note that you do not pronounce the **u** in **que** and **qui.** It is silent.

Letters *c*, *s*, and *z*

The **s** sound in Spanish is represented by the letters **s, z,** and **c** followed by **e** and **i.** Remember that in Spanish America and parts of Spain the consonants **z** and **s** are pronounced alike. Listen carefully and repeat the following words and sentences.

necesita	zapato	sandalia	zona	cabeza	lápices	cine
Teresita	zapatilla	cero	azteca	hizo	azul	así

Quince veces busqué el queso.
No quiso obedecer.
Desapareció en el cine.
Ella empieza con los lápices azules.

The vowels before *r*

The pronunciation of a single **r** in the middle of a word is similar to the English *d* in *Eddy.* If you pay attention to the vowels and pronounce them openly, the pronunciation of the Spanish single **r** will almost take care of itself. For example, **Alberto:** make sure you say **Al-beh** (with a clear, open **e** sound) before you pronounce the **r** and the rest of the word. Listen carefully and repeat the following words.

Marta carta bailar Argentina cantar dar compartir
Norberto ver comer hacer hermano divertido perfecto
decidir ir decírselo aburrir servir Guadalquivir
enorme profesor director por corto tortilla
urgente Hurtado Úrsula sur eran surtido

Actividad • Práctica de pronunciación

You have surely noticed that Spanish speakers seem to "run words together." Practice linking these words by dividing them into syllables and not pausing between words.

Había alguien en la puerta.
¿Quién era? Era un hombre enorme.
No sé quién era. No iba a abrir.

Unos hablaban mientras otros discutían.
Nadie sabía a qué hora iba a ser.
¿Quién iba a hacer las invitaciones?

¿LO SABES?

Let's review some important points you've learned in this unit.

SECTION A

Answers will vary.

Can you describe how things used to be?
With a classmate, discuss five things you always did in elementary school.

Can you congratulate someone in Spanish?
Imagine that you are invited to a birthday party. Congratulate the person celebrating a birthday and ask how old he or she is.

Can you describe several events that were happening at the same time?
Talk about the last party you attended. Use **mientras** in your description.

Are you able to mention three Hispanic celebrations with their English equivalents?

SECTION B

Answers will vary.

Do you know how to discuss events in the past?
Describe three important events that happened to you. Here are some hints:
Cuando tenía . . .
Cuando era . . .
Nosotros vivíamos en . . .
Me gustaba . . .
Toda la familia iba . . .
Había . . .

Can you describe the plans you had?
List five New Year's resolutions that you made but were unable to carry out. Here are a few ideas:
Iba a ahorrar mucho dinero.
Tenía que aprender a bailar.
Quería ir a México.

SECTION C

Do you know how to decline an invitation and express regret? Answers will vary.
You received an invitation to a party and must decline. Work with a partner.

Can you describe how you felt in the following situations?
1. You jogged for three hours.
2. It was a very hot summer day.
3. Your girlfriend or boyfriend sent you a present.
4. You slept late and had to catch the bus for school.

1. Estaba cansado(a).
2. Tenía calor.
3. Estaba enamorado(a).
4. Tenía prisa.

VOCABULARIO

SECTION A

acabar *to finish*
el **aniversario** *anniversary*
anunciar *to advertise*
el **Año Nuevo** *New Year's Day*
así que *therefore*
la **boda** *wedding*
el **calendario** *calendar*
el **carnaval** *carnival; Mardi gras*
celebrar *to celebrate*
¿cuántos años cumples? *how old are you?*
¿cuántos años tienes? *how old are you?*
décimo, -a *tenth*
dentro de *within (a period of time)*
el **desfile** *parade*
el **Día de la Hispanidad** *Columbus Day*
el **Día de la Independencia** *Independence Day*
el **Día de la Raza** *Columbus Day*
el **Día de las Madres** *Mother's Day*
el **Día de los Enamorados** *Valentine's Day*
el **Día de los Inocentes** *Fool's Day*
el **Día de los Padres** *Father's Day*
el **Día de Reyes** *Epiphany (Day of the Three Wise Men)*
el **Día del Trabajo** *Labor Day*
la **Epifanía** *Epiphany*
discutir *to discuss*
durar *to last*
en voz alta *out loud*
la **fecha** *date*

¡felicidades en el día de tu santo! *congratulations on your saint's day!*
¡feliz cumpleaños! *happy birthday!*
el **Fin de Año** *New Year's Eve*
la **graduación** *graduation*
había que *it was necessary to*
inventar *to invent*
invitar *to invite*
la **llamada** *phone call*
llegar a un acuerdo *to come to an agreement*
¡muchas felicidades! *congratulations!*
el **nacimiento** *birth*
la **Navidad** *Christmas*
la **Nochebuena** *Christmas Eve*
noveno, -a *ninth*
octavo, -a *eighth*
pasar un buen rato *to have a good time*
la **Pascua Florida** *Easter; Passover*
por separado *separately*
por tanto *therefore*
los **preparativos** *preparations*
quedarse *to be left over*
quinto, -a *fifth*
reunirse *to get together*
el **santo** *saint's day; saint*
se ponían de acuerdo *came to an agreement*
la **Semana Santa** *Holy Week*
séptimo, -a *seventh*
sexto, -a *sixth*
¡silencio! *be quiet!*
la **torta** *cake*
  torta de cumpleaños *birthday cake*
traer *to bring*

SECTION B

aunque *although, even though*
había *there was; there were*
hacía frío *it was cold*
iba a ir *(I) was going to go*
juntos, -as *together*
la **lata** *can*
me di cuenta *I realized*
recordar (ue) *to remember*
se reía *(he) was laughing*
sonar (ue) *to ring*

SECTION C

agradecer *to thank; to be grateful*
al día siguiente *the following day*
al fin *finally*
buenísima, -o *very good*
desaparecer (zc) *to disappear*
enamorado, -a *in love*
estar aburrido, -a *to be bored*
estar listo, -a *to be ready*
furioso, -a *furious*
obedecer (zc) *to obey*
¡oye! *listen!*
la **pareja** *couple*
sacar fotos *to take pictures*
ser aburrido, -a *to be boring*
ser listo, -a *to be smart*
tener miedo *to be afraid*
tener prisa *to be in a hurry*
riquísimo, -a *very delicious*
traducir *to translate*
único, -a *only*

PRÁCTICA DEL VOCABULARIO   Answers will vary.

1. Find three words in the unit vocabulary that refer to important moments or celebrations. Use each word in a sentence.
2. Select your favorite holiday from the unit vocabulary list. Then write a short paragraph about it. Include at least five words from the list in your description.

VAMOS A LEER

Antes de leer

In Spanish, many narratives, folk tales, or legends begin with one of the following phrases: Había una vez . . . ; Cuentan que . . . ; Dicen que. . . .
These phrases give the story a sense of oral tradition. In many instances, stories that begin in this manner have been told for several generations.

Preparación para la lectura   For answers, see p. T120.

Before you read the following folk tale, answer these questions.
1. ¿Leíste cuentos y leyendas cuando eras niño? ¿Cuáles leíste?
2. ¿De qué habla el cuento? ¿Qué te dice el título?
3. Organiza las siguientes expresiones de más lejos a más cerca: *un poco lejos, bastante lejos, nada lejos, muy lejos, lejísimo.*
4. Conoces el verbo **extrañar** *(to miss)*, pero aquí **extraño** es un cognado, es decir, una palabra similar a su traducción al inglés. ¿Puedes adivinar qué significa?
5. Mira el último párrafo del cuento. Parecen dos proverbios, ¿verdad? ¿Qué relación hay entre la narración y ese párrafo?

Cuestión de opinión 📼

   Había una vez una familia que vivía en el campo. Faltaban pocos días para las grandes fiestas del pueblo y el padre decidió que era buen momento para vender uno de los burros° que tenía. Necesitaba dinero para comprar abrigos para el invierno y algunos regalos de Reyes.
   Todavía hacía muy buen tiempo y el hombre le preguntó a su hijo menor si quería ir con él al mercado. Al muchacho le gustaba mucho ir con su padre al mercado y hablar con la gente. Al día siguiente, salieron el hombre y su hijo con el burro, que se llamaba Cristóbal y nunca tenía prisa. Tenían bastante tiempo. El pueblo° estaba un poco lejos, pero era muy temprano.
   Cuando tenían hambre, paraban para comer unas uvas que llevaban. Caminando y caminando, encontraron° entonces a unas mujeres a quienes ellos no conocían. Oyeron que la tercera mujer dijo:

burros *donkeys*   **pueblo** *village*   **encontraron** *they met*

—¡Qué burros son! Con un burro tan bueno, ¡van caminando en vez de montar en el burro!

El padre pensó un momento y dijo: — Esa mujer tiene razón.

Y montó entonces a su hijo, que era un muchacho alto y fuerte°, en el burro. Siguieron su camino° y más tarde encontraron a un hombre muy viejo que dijo en voz alta:

—¡Qué hijo tan cruel! El pobre padre, que ya está viejo, va caminando y el hijo, tan joven y tan fuerte, va montado° en el burro. No hay justicia en este mundo.

El muchacho le dijo entonces a su padre: —Es verdad, tiene razón este hombre.— El padre respondió que él no estaba cansado, pero al fin, montó en el burro y el hijo caminó.

Los tres siguieron su camino por un rato. Entonces encontraron a dos vendedores que también iban al mercado. Les compraron unas frutas que vendían muy baratas con las últimas monedas que les quedaban. Cuando estaban a cierta distancia, oyeron que el vendedor que era más joven le dijo al otro:

—¡Qué padre tan cruel! Va tan cómodo° montado en el burro mientras que el pobre muchacho tiene que caminar. El mundo es muy extraño°.

---

fuerte *strong* **camino** *road* **montado** *on top of* **cómodo** *comfortable* **extraño** *strange*

El padre miró al hijo. No parecía que estaba cansado, pero él no quería ser un padre cruel. Él quería° mucho a su hijo.

—El vendedor tiene razón— dijo el padre. Y montó al muchacho en el burro también.

Ya se acercaba el mediodía° y hacía mucho calor cuando el padre y el hijo vieron una casa. En el jardín había una mujer muy vieja que le estaba dando° de comer a unos cerdos° muy gordos. Algunos no podían comer más y estaban descansando°.

Esta mujer, pensó el hijo, sabe cuidar a sus animales muy bien. Ya puede venderlos en el mercado a muy buen precio. Quizás°, después de vender el burro, podemos venir a comprarle los cerdos y llevarlos al mercado. Ya ella está muy vieja y el mercado está un poco lejos. Los dos podíamos ganar dinero de esa manera.

Y así pensaba el muchacho cuando vio que la mujer los miraba. Estaba furiosa. Entonces oyó que ella decía:

—¡Qué hombres más crueles! Dos hombres tan grandes y fuertes montados en un burro tan pequeño. ¡Pobrecito burro! Va a llegar muerto al mercado y nadie va a querer comprarlo.

El padre y el hijo estaban sorprendidos. Nunca pensaron en eso.

—Es verdad— dijo el hijo.

El padre lo miró en silencio y los dos desmontaron del burro y otra vez empezaron a caminar hacia el mercado, como antes.

Cada uno ve las cosas a su manera. ¡Qué difícil es complacer° a todo el mundo!

---

quería *loved*   **mediodía** *noon*   **estaba dando** *was giving*   **cerdos** *pigs*
estaban descansando *were resting*   **Quizás** *Maybe*   **complacer** *to please*

Actividad • Preguntas y respuestas

For answers, see p. T121.

Use the information in the reading selection to answer the following questions.

1. ¿Para qué necesitaba dinero el padre? ¿Adónde iba?
2. ¿Cómo era el burro?
3. ¿A quién encontraron primero?
4. ¿Quién dijo: "No hay justicia en este mundo"?
5. ¿Qué les compraron el padre y su hijo a los vendedores?
6. ¿Por qué dijo el vendedor: "El mundo es muy extraño"?
7. ¿Qué diferencia hay entre estos dos usos del verbo **querer?**
   No quería ser un padre cruel.
   Quería mucho a su hijo.
8. Si **descansar** es lo contrario de **cansar,** ¿qué crees que quiere decir **desmontar?**
9. ¿Qué plan tenía el muchacho para ganar más dinero?
10. En la oración "Entonces, oyó que ella decía", ¿cuál es el significado de **decía?**
    a. *was saying*   b. *said*   c. *used to say*   d. *would say*
11. ¿Tenían razón las tres personas que dieron su opinión? ¿Por qué?
12. ¿Qué pasó cuando ellos quisieron hacer lo que todo el mundo decía?

Actividad • A ordenar

¿Qué pasó primero?   Number the following sentences according to the order of events in **Cuestión de opinión.** Use ordinal numbers.

_____ Vieron a una mujer vieja que daba de comer a unos cerdos.   octavo
_____ Compraron unas frutas muy baratas.   séptimo
_____ El hijo montó en el burro.   cuarto
_____ Fueron al mercado a vender un burro.   segundo
_____ Encontraron a un hombre viejo.   quinto
_____ El padre montó en el burro.   sexto
_____ Le preguntó a su hijo si quería ir con él.   primero
_____ Encontraron a unas mujeres.   tercero
_____ La mujer estaba furiosa.   noveno
_____ El padre y el hijo se desmontaron del burro.   décimo

Actividad • Charla   Answers will vary.

Get together with a classmate and discuss the advantages and disadvantages of each decision as to who rode the donkey.

UNIDAD 6 **Para un cuerpo sano . . .**

Scope and Sequence

	BASIC MATERIAL	COMMUNICATIVE FUNCTIONS
SECTION A	**¡Suena el despertador!** (A1) **Cómo mantenerse en forma** (A9) **Partes del cuerpo** (A12)	**Exchanging information** • Talking about what one does every day • Describing emotion
SECTION B	**Un menú adecuado** (B1) **¡Qué malo es enfermarse!** (B7)	**Expressing feelings and emotions** • Asking and stating how one feels • Expressing sympathy
SECTION C	**Los chicos se preparan para el baile** (C1) **Cosméticos y artículos de tocador** (C7) **Preparándose para la fiesta** (C12)	**Exchanging information** • Discussing personal care and grooming • Discussing unplanned events **Socializing** • Paying compliments
TRY YOUR SKILLS	**Tu cuerpo** **Dictado**	

■ **Pronunciación** (letters **ll, y, p,** and **t**)
■ **¿Lo sabes?** ■ **Vocabulario**

VAMOS A LEER	**¿Te gustan las papas fritas?** (the origin of the potato)

WRITING A variety of controlled and open-ended writing activities appear in the Pupil's Edition. The Teacher's Notes identify other activities suitable for writing practice.

COOPERATIVE LEARNING Many of the activities in the Pupil's Edition lend themselves to cooperative learning. The Teacher's Notes explain some of the many instances where this teaching strategy can be particularly effective. For guidelines on how to use cooperative learning, see page T13.

GRAMMAR	CULTURE	RE-ENTRY
Reflexive pronouns (A4) The definite article with the parts of the body and with personal possessions (A14)	The Inca Empire A look at Lima, Peru	Indirect–object pronouns Names of clothing items and jewelry
Affirmative and negative expressions (B11) The preterit tense of **querer** and **poner** (B20)	Nutrition in Spanish America Native American foods discovered by the early Europeans Varieties of fruit from America	Names of foods Definite article with parts of the body Adjective and noun agreement The verb **gustar**
Verbs used with reflexive pronouns (C5) The present indicative tense of **traer** and **oír** (C19)	Spanish proverbs Grooming and fashion in Spanish America	Vocabulary for items of clothing The ordinal numbers Names of the parts of the body The verbs **tener** and **hacer**

Recombining communicative functions, grammar, and vocabulary

Reading for practice and pleasure

TEACHER-PREPARED MATERIALS
Section A Pictures of people doing various activities, exercise video, paper skeleton, pictures of people showing different emotions
Section B Pictures of food
Section C Pictures of clothing, toiletries, cosmetics, parts of the body; a bell

UNIT RESOURCES
Manual de actividades, Unit 6
Manual de ejercicios, Unit 6
Unit 6 Cassettes
Transparencies 14–16
Quizzes 13–15
Unit 6 Test
Midterm Test
Proficiency Test 1

SECTION

A

OBJECTIVES   **To exchange information:** talk about what one does every day, describe emotions

CULTURAL BACKGROUND   Peru is divided into three geographical regions: the Andes mountains in the central part of the country (**la Montaña** or **Altiplano**); the desert coastal area (**la Costa**) to the west of the Andes; and the tropical lowlands to the east of the mountains (**la Selva**). Each region has its distinctive climate and vegetation. Peru may have been settled as early as 18,000 years ago. One of the world's great civilizations, the Inca Empire, began with a Quechua tribe on the shores of Lake Titicaca in the twelfth century. The capital of the empire was the city of Cuzco, the residence of the **Inca,** which in the Quechua language was the title of the ruler. At the height of the expansion of the Inca Empire, its territory extended from south of Colombia to the north of Argentina and Chile. Extending from Cuzco in all directions, the **Inca** directed his people, the Quechua, to build a network of irrigation waterways, a system of roads, and splendid palaces and fortresses that can still be seen today. This empire disappeared shortly after the arrival of the Spaniards in 1532. The word *inca* refers to the Quechuan ruler and his family, while the common people were called the Quechua. The official language of Peru is Spanish, but in certain regions, like in the highlands of Peru and parts of Bolivia, Quechua, the Indian language, is also spoken. The majority of the population of Peru is either mestizo or Indian, and approximately 60% of the population lives in the **Altiplano.** Still today, several of the pre-Columbian celebrations are important festivities. For example, starting on June 24th, and ending a week later, Cuzco joyously celebrates the "Inti Raymi," or feast of the sun. This ancient festival consists of folk dancing, music, and processions of people dressed in native costumes.

MOTIVATING ACTIVITY   Have the students divide into groups of three. Instruct each group to make three or four suggestions for maintaining good health. You may wish to give them the following model sentence: **Es importante tomar ocho vasos de agua todos los días.** Allow the students to suggest physical activities as well as nutritious foods. You may also have each student make a poster using magazine pictures of sports, exercise, and nutritious foods to illustrate good health habits. Display the posters in the classroom.

A 1

¡Suena el despertador!

Tell the students to listen carefully as you read the selection aloud or play the cassette. Review the illustrations of Marisa's family one at a time. Read the segment of the selection that corresponds to each illustration, making the connection between the text and the illustrations. Have the students repeat the descriptions both chorally and individually. You may also wish to ask a few simple questions about what Marisa and her family are doing.

> ¿Quién duerme en su cuarto?
> ¿Cuándo se despierta Marisa?
> ¿Qué hace Ana?
> ¿Qué hace el papá de Marisa? ¿Y su mamá?

CHALLENGE   Ask the students to describe their daily schedules to the class, using reflexive pronouns.

A 2

Actividad • Ana no tiene prisa
Have each student work with a partner to choose the correct answer. They may refer to the illustration and information in A1 if necessary. Review the answers with the entire class.

A3 Sabes que . . .

Lima, the capital of Peru, derives its name from the river that flows through the city, the Rímac. Founded in 1535 by Francisco Pizarro, the conqueror of Peru, Lima is one of the oldest colonial cities in South America. Its university, **Universidad Mayor de San Marcos,** was founded in 1551, and is one of the oldest in the hemisphere. Next to modern highrises and shopping malls, one can still find examples of exquisite colonial architecture, such as **el Palacio de Torre Tagle** and **la Casa Aliaga,** the oldest continuously occupied house in the Americas. Built by Don Jerónimo de Aliaga in 1535, it is still inhabited, seventeen generations later, by members of the Aliaga family. Lima is a large and growing city of more than three million people. The city is rich in culture, history, and beauty. From June until September, Lima is blanketed by a mist called the **garúa.** The **garúa** is caused by the cold Humboldt current that flows north along the Peruvian coast. Although it almost never rains in Lima, the light mist gives a somber aspect to an otherwise lovely city known for its romantic balconies and colonial architecture.

A4 ESTRUCTURAS ESENCIALES

Introduce reflexive pronouns by showing pictures of people doing various activities. For example, show a picture of a girl combing her hair, and say: **Carmen se cepilla el pelo todos los días.** Have the students repeat chorally. Repeat the procedure with other verbs and reflexive pronouns presented in the selection. Then ask the students questions that require a response with a reflexive pronoun, such as **¿A qué hora te levantas?**

A5 Actividad • ¡A escoger!

Ask the students to write each sentence with the reflexive construction in their notebooks. Then, for writing practice, have them write original sentences.

A6 Actividad • ¿A qué hora?

Have each student work with a partner. Each partner will have the opportunity to act as the efficiency expert. Encourage each student to take notes on their partner's responses. Review the information with the class.

A7 Actividad • ¡Mucha gente!

For cooperative learning, have the students work in pairs. They should take turns asking and answering the questions. Each student should make sure that his or her partner can accurately form each sentence. You may wish to call on volunteers from each group to read their sentences aloud to the class.

A8 Actividad • ¡No me compré nada!

Before having the students complete this activity, you may wish to re-enter the indirect-object pronouns. Write the following or similar sentences on the board.

> Antonio se compró una raqueta.
> Antonio les compró una raqueta a sus primos.

Point out that **Antonio** is the subject of the first sentence. Because he bought the racket for himself, he is both the subject and the receiver of the action expressed by the verb **comprar,** which requires a reflexive construction. Have the students identify the subject and the receiver of the action in the second sentence. Stress the fact that they are different. **Antonio** is the subject, while the receiver of the action, **los primos,** is another person or persons. That is why they must use an indirect-object pronoun. Practice the indirect-object pronouns, using classroom objects. Then ask each student to complete the activity with a partner.

A 9 **SITUACIÓN • Cómo mantenerse en forma**

You may wish to introduce the selection by talking about exercise videos. Ask the students to talk about exercise videos they know about, or bring one to class if possible. Before reading, you may wish to prepare a transparency with a list of cognates the students might recognize in the article. Allow them to guess the meanings as you or a volunteer writes them next to the appropriate cognates. Ask the students to read the selection silently. You may use TPR (Total Physical Response) to demonstrate what is happening in the selection and to introduce new verbs. Review the selection by asking questions about the content and pointing out reflexive constructions. Then play the cassette or read the selection aloud.

You may wish to add that keeping in shape is very important to Spanish Americans. Point out the photographs of the gymnasium and the health food store at the top of the unit opener on pages 190–191. The following is a list of some of the new vocabulary contained in the realia on page 196. It may be useful for your students when discussing their health.

inscripción	*admission*	aprovechen	*to take advantage*
gratis	*free*	todo incluido	*everything included*
cupo	*capacity*	en pleno centro	*right downtown*
gordita	*chubby*	baño de vapor	*steam bath*
flaquito	*skinny*	adelgazante	*weight reducing*

A 10 **Actividad • Preguntas y respuestas**

Allow students to work in pairs or individually to answer the questions. Review with the class.

A 11 **Comprensión**

You will hear ten statements. Each statement describes two activities. If these activities are in logical order, check **sí** on your answer sheet. If not, check **no.** For example, you hear: **Yo me levanto y luego me despierto.** You place your mark in the row labeled **no,** since the activities are not in logical order.

1. Juan José se viste y se va al colegio. *sí*
2. Catalina se baña y se viste. *sí*
3. Yo sirvo el cereal y luego me preparo el desayuno. *no*
4. Carmen va a la cocina y se pesa. *no*
5. Mamá se acuesta tarde y se pone un vestido azul. *no*
6. Mi hermano se despierta temprano y se levanta inmediatamente. *sí*
7. Martín se cepilla los dientes y se levanta. *no*
8. Laura se lava la cabeza y se la seca. *sí*
9. Tomás se duerme cuando suena el despertador. *no*
10. Tú y yo preparamos el desayuno y nos servimos café con leche. *sí*

Now check your answers. *Read each statement again and give the correct answer.*

A 12   SITUACIÓN • Partes del cuerpo

Before discussing the names of the parts of the body, you may wish to make a movable figure to hang on the board. A paper skeleton could also be used. Remind the students that, in Spanish, the definite article is most often used with parts of the body and personal possessions instead of the possessive. For example: **Tengo las uñas muy sucias.** *(My nails are very dirty.)* **No sé dónde puse la camisa.** *(I don't know where I put my shirt.)*

As a comprehension check, read aloud several descriptions of faces and parts of the body. Have the students draw what you describe. Then have each student choose a partner with whom to compare drawings. Ask the students to write down the names of the parts of the body in the vocabulary section of their notebooks.

SLOWER-PACED LEARNING Introduce the names of four or five parts of the body each day for several days. Before introducing new words, re-enter the vocabulary learned previously.

A 13   Actividad • ¿Dónde te lo pones?

Before you complete this activity, you may wish to re-enter names of clothing items and jewelry. Then ask each student to work with a partner to complete the activity. For writing practice, have the students write complete sentences.

A 14   ESTRUCTURAS ESENCIALES

Introduce the reflexive pronouns and the definite article by writing the model sentences on the board or a transparency. Elicit from the students that no possessive adjective is needed because it is understood who the possessor is when the reflexive construction is used. Stress that the use of reflexive pronouns in Spanish is obligatory.

A 15   Actividad • ¡Qué frio!

Allow each student to choose a partner to complete the activity orally. For writing practice, the activity may be assigned for homework. Correct the sentences with the entire class.

A 16   Actividad • ¡Ay, qué dolor tengo!

For further practice with names of the parts of the body, ask the students to do a TPR (Total Physical Response) activity in which they carry out the following or similar commands.

> Cierren los ojos.
> Levanten el pie derecho.
> Toquen los dedos del pie izquierdo.
> No doblen las rodillas.
> Abran la boca.
> Agárrense la nariz.

A 17   SE DICE ASÍ

Bring to class magazine pictures of people participating in various activities, including pictures of people showing different emotions. Make a statement about each activity and about the reaction of the person shown. For example: **Cuando el muchacho juega al básquetbol, se pone contento.** Then have the students describe situations in which they feel happy, sad, furious, or nervous. Remind them to use the first person: **Me pongo. . . .**

CHALLENGE Make up situations about which the students will feel strongly. Present each situation to the class and call on volunteers to express how they feel about it. For example, **Tengo cinco exámenes en un día.** The response should be: **Me pongo nervioso.**

A 18 Actividad • ¿Cómo te pones tú si algo te pasa?

Allow the students to complete the activity orally or in writing. Review their reactions with the entire class. For further practice, read the following or similar statements aloud, and ask the students to react using **ponerse.**

> El profesor te da una "A" en la clase de álgebra.
> Acabas de perder tu calculadora.
> Comes quince helados en un día.
> Recibes rosas de un amigo o una amiga.
> El profesor dice que hay cuatro exámenes esta semana.
> Compras un coche nuevo.

A 19 Actividad • Para mantenerse en forma

Allow the students several minutes to read the statements and to correct them. Review by writing the sentences on the board or a transparency. For cooperative learning, ask the students to form groups of three. Each member of the group should make a list of the things he or she does to keep in shape. All the members should compile the lists into a new one. Then one student from each group should present the list to the class.

A 20 Actividad • Charla

Have each student choose a partner to take turns asking and answering questions, using the adjectives in the box. Then ask the students to share their findings with the class. For example: **Lisa se pone nerviosa cuando tiene un examen. Marcos también se pone nervioso cuando tiene un examen.**

A 21 Actividad • ¿Cómo es? ¿Qué hace?

You may wish to assign this as a writing activity after the students complete it orally. Have the students exchange papers to correct their work.

A 22 Actividad • Mi amigo el médico

For cooperative learning, have the students work in groups of three to create sentences that a doctor might say to patients. Ask the groups to list their sentences on the board or a transparency. As a variation, ask pairs of students to play the roles of patient and doctor. The "patient" should describe a symptom, and the "doctor" should offer a remedy.

> — Doctor, tengo dolor en un pie. —Pues, no camine tanto.
> — Doctor, siempre estoy cansada. —Pues, haga Ud. ejercicio.

A23 Actividad • ¡A escribir!

CHALLENGE   Tell the students to imagine they are listening to a conversation between two Spanish-speaking teenagers who are talking about normal routines they follow on school days and on summer days. For writing practice, have them write the conversation. Remind them to use as many reflexive verbs as possible. Call on volunteers to read their dialogs to the class.

OBJECTIVES   **To express feelings and emotions:** ask and state how one feels, express sympathy

CULTURAL BACKGROUND   Many differences in diet exist between the United States and Spanish America. In the United States people have a tendency, in recent times, to eat a more balanced diet and to avoid foods with a high caloric count. There has also been an increase in popularity of natural foods and the establishing of health food stores. In Spanish America, however, this awareness is not yet widespread. While Spanish Americans tend to eat a great deal of vegetables and fruits, they still love desserts and candy. Nutrition is a problem in many areas, not only because of the economic difficulties, but also because of the climate and the geography. In the highlands of Peru, for example, it is impossible to grow many vegetables except for tubers, such as potatoes. There is a lack of fresh green vegetables and fruits. For that reason, there are a number of health problems due to the lack of certain vitamins. While efforts are being made to correct the situation, it is often difficult to change traditions that have existed for hundreds of years.

MOTIVATING ACTIVITY   Write the following words on the board or a transparency as they appear below, but omit one or more words.

```
pesca d o
    l e che
   en s alada
manz a na
      y ogur
   j u go
  ma n tequilla
 poll o
```

Ask the students to complete the shopping list by adding the food items that are missing. They must add a word with a **u,** such as **fruta, jugo,** or **azúcar.** The letters, beginning with **d** in **pescado,** spell out the word **desayuno** vertically.

B1   Un menú adecuado

Before introducing the selection, write the following words on the board or a transparency.

dieta balanceada	régimen
alimentos	adelgazar
libras	

Ask the students to guess the meanings of the words as you use each one in a sentence which defines its meaning. You may wish to tell them that the words have to do with a diet. When the students have understood the new vocabulary, ask them to open their books. Play the cassette or read the introduction to the menu aloud. Continue with the rest of the menu, asking questions to check comprehension.

Before presenting the closing paragraph, write on the board or a transparency several other words, such as **calorías, tampoco, moderación, aumentar de peso, cuidarse, mantenerse,** and **médico.** Proceed as before, helping the students to guess the meanings of the words. Play the cassette or read the closing paragraph aloud.

SLOWER-PACED LEARNING   Re-enter several of the names of foods listed in the menu, using magazine pictures. You may want each student to make a collage with pictures of the foods labeled in Spanish. Display the collages in the classroom.

B 2   Actividad • Preguntas y respuestas

You may wish to do this activity orally in class with the books closed. As a variation, have the students make up original questions about the menu. Each student should choose a partner and answer one another's questions.

ANSWERS:
1. Sí, quiere decir que tu salud depende de lo que comes.
2. Marisa decide no comer carne con grasa, ni mantequilla ni azúcar.
3. Toma multivitaminas durante el desayuno.
4. Toma yogur con las fresas.
5. Marisa prefiere la leche descremada, porque no tiene grasa.
6. Come trocitos de apio y de zanahoria entre comidas.
7. Es bueno comer una ración de macarrones porque da más energía.

B 3   Actividad • ¡A completar!

Write the sentences on the board or a transparency. Call on volunteers to fill in the spaces with the appropriate words.

B 4   Sabes que . . .

You may wish to list on the board the following products from America that the Spaniards introduced to Europe.

maíz	*corn*
cacahuete	*peanut*
ají/chile	*green pepper/chili*
tomate	*tomato*
papa	*potato*
chicle	*gum*
vainilla	*vanilla*

You may also wish to add some of the products that the Spaniards brought to America.

naranjas	*oranges*
limones	*lemons*
aceitunas	*olives*
peras	*pears*
manzanas	*apples*
uvas	*grapes*

trigo	*wheat*
arroz	*rice*
caña de azúcar	*sugar cane*

You can ask the class if they can name any other products from America that were taken to Europe by the Spaniards, and any other products brought to America by the Spaniards.

B5 Comprensión

You will hear ten short conversational exchanges. If the second statement is a logical conclusion to the first, check **lógico** on your answer sheet. If it is not, check **ilógico.** For example, you will hear: **Ay, doctor. Siempre estoy cansado y no hago nada.** The response is: **Pues, haga ejercicio todos los días.** You check **lógico,** because it is a logical conclusion.

1. —Sólo duermo cuatro horas todas las noches.
   —Entonces, tiene que acostarse más tarde.   *ilógico*
2. —Yo quiero adelgazar unos diez kilos.
   —Entonces tiene que contar las calorías.   *lógico*
3. —Aumenté cuatro kilos durante mis vacaciones.
   —Pues, chica, come más helados y pasteles.   *ilógico*
4. —Creo que tengo el brazo roto, doctor.
   —Debes tomar té con limón.   *ilógico*
5. —Tengo catarro y dolor de garganta.
   —¿Por qué no tomas jugo de naranja?   *lógico*
6. —Mi hija quiere aumentar de peso.
   —Sírvale más postres y helados.   *lógico*
7. —Yo tengo dolor de cabeza.
   —Debes acostarte un rato a dormir.   *lógico*
8. —Gloria tiene dolor de estómago.
   —Puede tomar un refresco y comer una buena cena.   *ilógico*
9. —Quiero mejorar mi condición física.
   —Es una buena idea correr todos los días.   *lógico*
10. —Siempre tengo catarros y dolores de garganta.
    —Debes tomar multivitaminas y dormir ocho horas cada noche.   *lógico*

Now check your answers. *Read each exchange again and give the correct answer.*

B6 Actividad • ¡A escribir!

The students may complete this activity at home or in class. For cooperative learning, have groups of four read their menus aloud to each other for discussion and correction. Then call on a few volunteers to write their sample menus on the board or a transparency.

B7 SITUACIÓN • ¡Qué malo es enfermarse!

Play the cassette or read the selection aloud as the students follow along in their books. Then present new vocabulary, such as **dolor de garganta, dolor de cabeza,** and **fiebre.** You may also wish to borrow items from your school nurse to help you present several phrases. Items you might use include a thermometer, a medicine bottle, aspirin, and antacid tablets. If those items are not available, you may use magazine pictures of the items. Re-enter the use of the definite article with the parts of the body, using examples from the selection.

> Pepe tiene **el** brazo roto.
> Le duele **la** garganta.

B8 Actividad • ¿Sí o no?

Have the students correct the false statements. They may exchange papers to correct their work.

B9 SE DICE ASÍ

Read the expressions aloud to the students. Prepare index cards containing each of the following or similar ailments. **No me siento bien. Tengo catarro. Me duele el brazo. Tengo dolor de cabeza. Me siento mal. Ya tomé dos aspirinas. Me siento mejor.** Make copies of the cards so that there are enough for the entire class. Make sure that each student understands what is written on his or her card. Then call on volunteers to act out the expressions. Allow the class to guess what message each person is trying to convey.

B10 Actividad • ¡A escoger!

For cooperative learning, have the students work in pairs. One student will choose a statement about a health problem, eliciting sympathy from his or her partner. The other student will respond with an appropriate expression from the box. Then call on volunteers to role-play the exchange for the entire class.

CHALLENGE Have each student imagine that he or she is with a group of Spanish-speaking friends who do not speak English. Because of all the new foods the student has sampled and the number of desserts eaten, he or she is not feeling very well. Not only does the student feel sick but he or she has also injured a wrist. Unfortunately nobody has a dictionary. Have each student describe in Spanish each of the items below.

> a hot water bottle   a heating pad
> an ice pack   an elastic bandage
> heartburn

B11 ESTRUCTURAS ESENCIALES

To present the affirmative and negative expressions in Spanish, give an example of both in sentences. For example, hold out your hand and say: **¿Tengo algo en la mano? No, no tengo nada en la mano.** Then hold a pencil in your hand to elicit an affirmative response. Continue using examples based on classroom experiences. Ask the following questions: **Siempre hablamos español en clase, ¿verdad? Nunca hablamos inglés, ¿no es verdad? Tampoco llegamos tarde a clase, ¿verdad?** You can proceed asking questions: **¿Estudia alguien matemáticas? (física, química, alemán, francés. . .)** in order to elicit answers with **nadie** or **alguien.** Continue with a similar procedure to present the other expressions. Introduce the pronouns **alguno** and **ninguno** at the end of your presentation. Then read aloud the explanation in the book. After each explanation, repeat your presentation for practice. Ask the students to copy the words into the vocabulary sections of their notebooks.

B 12 Actividad • Por teléfono

For writing practice, have the students write the completed dialog in class or at home. You may wish to ask the students to exchange papers to correct the answers.

B 13 Actividad • ¡Te digo que no! 🔲

SLOWER-PACED LEARNING Ask the students to work in pairs to complete the activity. Tell them to use the model as a guide.

> ANSWERS:
> 1. ¿Tienes alguna foto para el periódico?
>   ¡No, no tengo ninguna!
> 2. ¿Invitas a alguien para mañana?
>   ¡No, no invito a nadie!
> 3. ¿Tienes alguna competencia pronto?
>   ¡No, no tengo ninguna!
> 4. ¿Quieres algo de la cafetería?
>   ¡No, no quiero nada!
> 5. ¿Quieres oír algún disco?
>   ¡No, no quiero oír ninguno!
> 6. ¿Estás enfadado con alguien?
>   ¡No, no estoy enfadado con nadie!
> 7. ¿Te duele algo?
>   ¡No, no me duele nada!
> 8. ¿Tomas alguna vitamina?
>   ¡No, no tomo ninguna vitamina!

B 14 Actividad • En la cocina 🔲

Re-enter adjective and noun agreement by using affirmative and negative expressions. Then have the students work in pairs to complete the activity. Remind them to use the correct gender and number in their answers.

B 15 Actividad • ¿Tienes alguna pregunta?

You may wish to provide a model by answering the first question before the students begin the activity. Call on volunteers to read their answers aloud.

B 16 Actividad • ¡Qué difícil es decidir! 🔲

SLOWER-PACED LEARNING You may wish to complete several exchanges with the class before you ask the students to work in pairs. Then call on individuals to write their exchanges on the board for correction.

CHALLENGE Ask the students to present impromptu dialogs in which they must role-play the situation described, using o. . .o and ni. . .ni.

B 17 Actividad • ¡A escribir!

Ask each student to make a list of real or imaginary students who are absent. Ask them to write complete sentences explaining why each person is absent.

B 18 ### Actividad • ¡La mejor dieta del mundo!

For cooperative learning, form groups of four to brainstorm ideas for the advertising agency. As a variation, have each group select an idea and present a television commercial to the class. The students may wish to use magazine pictures of nutritious foods to aid them in their presentations.

SLOWER-PACED LEARNING Provide Spanish magazine or newspaper advertisements for the students to use as models for writing original ads.

B 19 ### Sabes que . . .

Most people think that there is only one kind of tomato and only one kind of banana. In fact, there are as many kinds of bananas and tomatoes as there are apples. One variety of the tomato is the **tomatillo,** a small, green tomato-like fruit that has a distinctive flavor. It is often used for sauces. Bananas can be small, such as the **dominguín** or the **manzano,** which have a sharp flavor not unlike that of an apple. Bananas may also be large, such as the plantain which is normally used for cooking. A favorite dish, particularly in the Caribbean, is fried green plantains, called **tostones.** Spanish Americans consume large amounts of tropical fruits, such as **plátanos, piñas, mangos, papayas,** and many others with exotic names that are just now becoming popular in the United States, such as **chirimoyas.** These tropical fruits, in addition to having a high vitamin content, are very rich in fiber, which has been proven to be very good for the diet.

B 20 ## ESTRUCTURAS ESENCIALES

With books closed, present the preterit forms of the verbs **querer** and **poner,** using a conversational approach. Remind the students that **querer** means *to love* or *to want,* depending upon the context of the sentence. Point out the vowel change in all forms of the verbs:

▌ qu**e**rer qu**i**se   p**o**ner p**u**se

B 21 ### Actividad • ¿Querer o poner?

Have the students copy the paragraph and fill in each blank with the correct verb form. As a variation, call on a volunteer to write on the board or a transparency as the students dictate the sentences.

B 22 ### Actividad • Antes y después

You may wish to have the students complete this activity in class or at home. Review the answers with the class.

B 23 ### Actividad • Charla

For cooperative learning, form groups of three students to complete the activity. Tell them to take notes and report their findings to the class.

CHALLENGE Have each student imagine that he or she is a guest on a talk show. The topic of the day is wellness. You may wish to choose one student to play the role of the "expert" to give advice as the "audience" asks questions about health concerns.

B 24 ¿RECUERDAS?

Re-enter the verb **gustar,** using magazine pictures of food. Hold up a picture of an apple and say: **A mí me gustan las manzanas. ¿Te gustan?** Elicit the response: **Sí, a mí también me gustan.** Then introduce three new verbs, **doler, encantar,** and **importar,** by using them in sentences that illustrate their meanings. For example: **A mí me duele la cabeza.** Then, pointing at another student, ask: **¿y a él/ella?** Continue with other verbs: **¡A mí me encantan las manzanas! . . .¿y a él/ella?** Now read the explanation in the book with the students.

B 25 Actividad • No me importa

SLOWER-PACED LEARNING Prepare and distribute a handout of the paragraph in the book. Then dictate the paragraph to the students and have them fill in the blanks with the correct forms.

OBJECTIVES **To exchange information:** discuss personal care and grooming; **to express feelings and emotions:** pay compliments

CULTURAL BACKGROUND **"Seda y raso no dan estado, pero hacen al hombre autorizado."** This Spanish proverb means that one who dresses well will not be richer, nor will dressing well give a person status; but by dressing well, one will be better perceived, will find more opened doors, and may be considered for bigger and better things. Most Spanish-speaking teenagers (especially in Spanish America) live by this proverb. Good grooming habits and personal hygiene are extremely important to them.

MOTIVATING ACTIVITY Write the following list on the board or a transparency.

pantalón	falda	suéter
camisa	traje de baño	pantalón corto
vestido	traje	sombrero
corbata	chaqueta	zapatos
blusa		

Ask the students to read the list. Tell them to think of a system of categorizing clothing, such as men's, women's, or children's clothing, or clothing worn in a warm or cold climate. Each student may eliminate up to three items from the list so that the new list fits his or her system of categorizing.

C 1 Los chicos se preparan para el baile

Ask the students to follow along as you read the selection aloud or play the cassette. Then call for choral and individual repetition, alternating them to avoid boredom.

After presenting the material, introduce new vocabulary, such as **quitarse** and **ponerse.** Demonstrate to the class by putting on or removing a sweater or a jacket. Discuss with the students some of their preparations for a formal or informal party. Ask them to identify the type of clothing they would wear to each one. Re-enter the vocabulary of items of clothing, using magazine pictures and the clothing students are wearing.

C2 Actividad • ¿Qué pasó primero?

Re-enter the ordinal numbers. When the students have completed the activity, call on volunteers to read the sentences aloud in the correct order as you or a volunteer writes them on the board or a transparency.

C3 Actividad • Preguntas y respuestas

Have the students refer to C1 to answer the questions. For writing practice, have them write complete sentences.

CHALLENGE Begin the activity by listing the following useful vocabulary from the realia on the upper right, page 212, on the board or a transparency.

cosméticos	*cosmetics*	demostrador	*demonstrator*
marca	*brand*	maquillista	*make-up expert*
medicamento	*medicine*	peinado	*hairstyle*
anteojos		corte	*haircut*
espejuelos	*glasses*	gratis	*free*
gafas			
lentes			

Then ask the students the following or similar questions based on the information contained in the realia.

1. ¿Qué es la feria de la salud y la belleza?
2. ¿Qué se puede comprar allí?
3. ¿Qué otra cosa ofrecen?
4. ¿Hay algo para los animales?
5. ¿Cuánto cuestan los peinados y cortes?
6. ¿Dónde queda la tienda?

C4 Actividad • Charla

SLOWER-PACED LEARNING Have the students look carefully at the illustration. Call on volunteers to identify the items in the bedroom and the bathroom. Then form cooperative learning groups of three students. Have them describe what each boy in the illustration has done previously, what he is doing now, and what he will be doing. Call on members from each group to read their descriptions aloud.

C5 ESTRUCTURAS ESENCIALES

Review the reflexive pronouns introduced in A4 on p. T125. You may wish to write several sentences on the board or a transparency to review the structure. First, concentrate on verbs that express personal care and grooming. Write the list of verbs from number 1 on the board. Then, use a personalized question/answer drill, using students' real names: **Yo me peino todos los días, ¿y tú** *(student's name)?* Continue with number 2. Write the list of verbs on the board. Complete a personalized question/answer drill, using the students' real names: **¿Me enfado cuando ustedes no hacen la tarea? Y tú,** *(student's name),* **¿te alegras cuando puedes ir a una fiesta?** Finally, write the verbs from number 3 on the board and explain the change of meaning, using contrasting examples.

Me acuesto a las nueve de la noche. Mamá **acuesta** a mi hermanito a las ocho.
Me dormí enseguida. Mi tía Luisa **durmió** al bebé.

C6 Actividad • ¿Quién hace qué?

Before doing the activity, you may wish to review reflexive pronouns used with **mirar, servir, preparar,** and **lavar.** After the students have completed the activity, call on volunteers to read their answers aloud.

C7 SITUACIÓN • Cosméticos y artículos de tocador

Collect as many as possible of the items pictured in the book for a class demonstration. You may wish to use TPR (Total Physical Response) to introduce the vocabulary. For example, pretend that you are brushing your teeth, and identify the item as **un cepillo de dientes.** Do this with as many of the items as possible, having the students identify the items.

C8 Actividad • Uno no es del grupo

Have the students work in pairs. They should write their answers and then exchange papers with another pair for correction.

C9 Actividad • Dígame dónde

Re-enter the names of the parts of the body before completing the activity. Then ask the students to work in pairs to decide how to use the items or products listed. You may also expand the activity by including the names of other toiletries from C7.

SLOWER-PACED LEARNING Give half of the students magazine pictures of parts of the body, and give the other half pictures of cosmetics that are used on those parts of the body. Ask the students to find a person whose picture corresponds with theirs.

C10 Actividad • ¿Y tú?

Have each student ask and answer the questions with a partner. Then call on students to report their findings to the class.

CHALLENGE To further practice vocabulary, you may wish to ask the students to describe what the girl in the realia at the bottom of page 215 is doing.

C11 SE DICE ASÍ

Present the expressions in the box to the class. Then call on the students to form sentences using **romperse, perderse,** and **caerse.** Add that these types of expressions are very common in Spanish and that people use them frequently.

C12 SITUACIÓN • Preparándose para la fiesta

Play the cassette or read the dialog aloud, without any pauses. Then either play the paused version of the cassette or read the dialog aloud, pausing for student repetition. Initially, do not stop to explain grammar, vocabulary, or culture. This can follow later because students are already familiar with the words and expressions found in the dialog. Concentrate on the specific objectives of the presentation. Insist as much as possible on a normal delivery, giving special attention to correct linking and intonation. Then, practice the dialog chorally, insisting on maximum participation, alternating it with individual repetition to avoid monotony.

C13 Actividad • ¿Es cierto o no?

Do this activity with books closed. Write the statements on the board and have the students correct the false statements. For cooperative learning, form groups of two girls, and ask them to rehearse the dialog. Call on each to role-play the dialog in class.

C14 Actividad • Mientras tanto, ¿qué hacen los otros chicos?

Ask each student to complete the activity with a partner and to write the sentences. Then have them dictate the sentences as you or a volunteer writes them on the board or a transparency.

C15 Actividad • ¿Qué necesitas?

Ask the students to write the completed sentences at home or in class. As a variation, you may wish to form each sentence orally, inserting an incorrect item. The students must then name the correct item. For example, you say: **Para mirarte, necesitas un champú.** The students should respond: **¡No! Para mirarte, necesitas un espejo.**

> ANSWERS:
> 1. Para limpiarnos las uñas, necesitamos un cepillo de uñas.
> 2. Para secarte el pelo, necesitas una secadora.
> 3. Para cambiarse el color de los ojos, necesita lentes de contacto de color.
> 4. Para peinarse, necesita un peine.
> 5. Para afeitarse, necesitan una maquinilla de afeitar.
> 6. Para bañarme, necesito jabón.
> 7. Para maquillarse, necesitan maquillaje.
> 8. Para cepillarnos los dientes, necesitamos un cepillo de dientes.
> 9. Para cortarse el pelo, necesita una tijera.

C16 Actividad • ¡A escribir!

Ask the students to prepare the list of toiletries. Ask a boy and a girl to write the lists on the board. You may wish to play a game at this point. Begin by saying: **Voy de vacaciones y necesito llevar un cepillo de dientes.** Each student must then add an item after he or she recalls all the other items that have been named.

C17 SE DICE ASÍ

Read the list of compliments aloud to the class for pronunciation practice and write them on the board. Ask the students to walk around the room and practice paying each other compliments. Encourage them to respond to each compliment by saying **Muchas gracias, Muy amable,** or another appropriate response.

C18 Comprensión

> Marilú and Rogelio are preparing for a party. You will hear a statement followed by three possible responses. Choose the response that best completes each statement. For example, you will hear: **Acabo de lavarme la cabeza.** You will also hear the responses: (a) **Busco el perfume.** (b) **¿Tienes el jabón?** (c) **Necesito la secadora.** You check **c** on your answer sheet, because it best completes the first statement.

1. Quiero maquillarme.
   a. ¿Dónde está mi espejo? (√)
   b. ¿Tienes el desodorante?
   c. ¿Sabes dónde está el enjuague?
2. Rogelio va a cepillarse los dientes.
   a. Busca el enjuague.
   b. Necesita la maquinilla de afeitar.
   c. Busca la pasta y el cepillo de dientes. (√)
3. Marilú no puede ver lo que hace.
   a. Se pone el perfume.
   b. Se pone las lentes de contacto. (√)
   c. Se pone maquillaje.
4. Rogelio quiere peinarse.
   a. Busca el cepillo y el peine. (√)
   b. Busca la secadora.
   c. Busca el cepillo de uñas.
5. Marilú va a pintarse las uñas.
   a. Quiere esmalte. (√)
   b. Quiere colorete.
   c. Quiere espejo.
6. Mamá, voy a bañarme.
   a. ¿Dónde está la pasta de dientes?
   b. ¿Dónde está el lápiz labial?
   c. ¿Dónde está el jabón? (√)
7. Rogelio acaba de afeitarse.
   a. Se pone perfume.
   b. Se pone loción de afeitar. (√)
   c. Se pone enjuague.
8. Marilú quiere lavarse el pelo.
   a. Necesita desodorante.
   b. Necesita polvo.
   c. Necesita champú y enjuague. (√)
9. Marilú se ve muy pálida porque estaba enferma.
   a. Debe ponerse colorete. (√)
   b. Debe ponerse esmalte.
   c. Debe ponerse lápiz labial.
10. Rogelio va a afeitarse.
    a. Se compra una secadora.
    b. Se compra crema de afeitar. (√)
    c. Se compra maquillaje.

Now check your answers. *Read each sentence again and give the correct answer.*

C19 **ESTRUCTURAS ESENCIALES**

Re-enter several verbs, such as **tener** and **hacer,** in conversational situations. Then introduce **traer,** using context clues to demonstrate its meaning. Use the verb in all forms of the present indicative tense in conversation, having students participate in the discussion. Use the same procedure to introduce **oír** and **caer.** When finished, ask the students to recall the forms of the verbs. Stress that the **yo** forms are similar to those of **tener** and **hacer.**

C20 **Actividad • ¿Cierto o falso?**

Ask the students to read the sentences and to correct the false statements. Review the answers with the entire class.

C21 Actividad • ¿Qué oyes?

Ask the students to write the sentences, using **oír.** Call on individuals to write the sentences on the board or a transparency for correction.

C22 Actividad • ¡A escribir!

Ask the students to prepare the activity for homework. Review with the class by making a composite list the next day. You may wish to collect and correct the sentences.

C23 Actividad • Una dieta balanceada

Have the class identify the items in the illustrations. Allow each student to complete the activity with a partner. Call on several pairs to read their sentences aloud.

TRY
YOUR
SKILLS

OBJECTIVE   To recombine communicative functions, grammar, and vocabulary

CULTURAL BACKGROUND   Although sports clubs are common in Latin America and Spain, often they have been oriented more toward social interaction than toward fitness. Today, more people are becoming aware of the importance of exercising and eating the right foods. Sports and exercise are common elements in most curriculums in Spanish and Spanish-American high schools. Elementary students are taught the importance of good nutrition and good grooming.

1   **Tu cuerpo**

Allow the students to work in groups of two or three to talk about their routines. Call on volunteers to talk about how they take care of themselves.

2   **Actividad • Cuando suena el despertador**

Remind the students to use reflexive verbs. Have each student exchange papers with a partner to compare morning activities.

3   **Actividad • ¿Me pongo contento o furioso?**

Have each student take notes on what his or her partner said. Call on volunteers to describe at least six things that make them happy or angry.

4   **Actividad • En el mercado**

Have each student prepare a shopping list. You may wish to set up the classroom as a grocery store. For cooperative learning, have the students take turns role-playing customer and vendor. Have them discuss the nutritious foods on their lists and foods they would like to prepare.

5   **Actividad • ¿Quién está enfermo?**

Have each student write the excuses and choose the one they feel is best. Then call on students to dictate the excuses as you or a volunteer writes them on the board or a transparency. Have the class choose the best excuse.

6   **Actividad • ¡Vamos a la tienda!**

Have each student work with a partner to complete the activity. Each student should write the answers to be handed in for correction.

7   **Dictado**

> Write the following paragraph from dictation. First, listen to the paragraph as it is read to you. Then you will hear the paragraph again in short segments, with a pause after each segment to allow you time to write. Finally, you will hear the paragraph a third time so that you may check your work. Let's begin.
>
>   El baile era a las ocho. *(pause)* Me bañé y me afeité. *(pause)* Me miré en el espejo *(pause)* y me peiné dos veces. *(pause)* Me vestí *(pause)* y me puse la corbata nueva. *(pause)* Llamé a Rafa por teléfono. *(pause)* Me dijo *(pause)* que tenía dolor de garganta, *(pause)* pero que iba a ir *(pause)* sin falta. *(pause)* Miré el reloj. *(pause)* Eran las ocho y cinco. *(pause)* Era tarde. *(pause)* Salí corriendo.

PRONUNCIACIÓN

Play the cassette or read the explanation and sentences aloud. Review the pronunciation of the **y** and the **ll.** You may wish to explain to the students that they will hear varied pronunciations of the letters, depending upon whom they meet from the Spanish-speaking world. Allow the students to practice saying the sentences aloud. Remember that these drills are strictly for practicing sounds and not for conveying a message, thus, student's attention span is short. Present the **p** and **t** sounds. Tell the students that when they pronounce these letters, they should feel no puff of air as they hold their hand in front of their mouths.

Actividad • Práctica de pronunciación

Play the cassette or read the sentences aloud. Then call on volunteers to read the sentences aloud. Allow each volunteer to finish his or her sentence before you correct any pronunciation errors.

¿LO SABES?

Allow students to complete each of the exercises orally. Each student may work with a partner and then participate in a review with the entire class. You may wish to review some of the activities in the earlier sections.

Ask the students to write the menus on the board. Discuss the items with the class.

To practice expressing sympathy and expressing how they feel physically, have the students work in groups of three to ask and answer questions about how they feel.

Combine the last two activities by creating questions with the pronouns **algo, alguien, algún,** and **algunas.** Ask the students to respond negatively with the appropriate pronouns and adjectives.

For additional practice discussing grooming, have each student imagine that he or she will be going to a prom. Ask each to name things he or she does to get ready. Then have each student make believe he or she is at the dance, and pay compliments to the other students.

VOCABULARIO

To practice the unit vocabulary and the previously learned vocabulary, you may wish to play a game of Scrabble® with the students. You will need to have prepared letter "tiles" cut from index cards. Assign each letter a point value, with lower values given to letters used more frequently and higher values given to letters used less frequently. Draw a Scrabble® board on the chalkboard, shading respective squares on the board. Assign the shaded squares the appropriate double or triple values. Write the message **"nutrición"** on the middle of the board. The day of the game, group the students into teams of three or four. Give each team four consonants and three vowels. Have the teams take turns building words using the letters of the word you have written. Allow each team to create as many words as they can, using tape to attach the letters to the board. Tell them that all words must connect to a word already on the board. After each team takes its turn, have one of the members replace their used letters, choosing vowels for vowels and consonants for consonants. The team with the most points wins.

VAMOS A LEER

Antes de leer

You may wish to prepare a brief outline of the story, highlighting the main ideas. Then ask some questions that elicit major points of the story that can be grasped from your outline and a brief scanning of the reading selection. You may also wish to prepare a handout of Pablo Neruda's poem **"Oda a las papas fritas"** and read it aloud to the class. Have the students listen carefully for onomatopoetic words.

Preparación para la lectura

Before the students read the selection, have them answer the questions orally. You may also wish to form groups to answer the questions and review the answers with the class.

¿TE GUSTAN LAS PAPAS FRITAS?

Play the cassette or have the students read the selection silently. Encourage them to guess the meanings of the new words by using context clues. As you proceed, ask questions to check comprehension.

Actividad • Preguntas y respuestas

Allow the students to work in groups of three or four to answer the questions. Have them refer to the reading selection if necessary. You may wish to discuss with the class what they found interesting about the reading selection.

ANSWERS:
1. Porque no había papas en Europa.
2. El Imperio Inca estaba en los Andes.
3. Los indios cultivaban la papa.
4. Dejaban las papas fuera de la casa toda la noche para congelarlas. A la mañana siguiente, con el calor del sol, las papas se descongelaban. Entonces, con los dedos de la mano les extraían el agua.
5. Los españoles encontraron la batata en las islas del Caribe.
6. Otro producto que se menciona en la lectura es el tomate.
7. Sir Walter Raleigh llevó la papa a Irlanda para combatir el hambre.
8. Porque la reina comió las hojas de la planta.
9. Porque se decía que era un alimento diabólico porque la Biblia no lo menciona.
10. Parmentier, un biólogo francés, descubrió que la papa era rica en nutrición.
11. Se inventaron en Bélgica y se comen con mayonesa.
12. La papa resolvió el problema de alimentar al pueblo de una manera barata y nutritiva.

Actividad • Defensores de la papa

Write on 3 × 5 index cards the names of the people or groups of people mentioned in the reading selection. For cooperative learning, form groups of three or four. Then give one of the cards to each group in the class. Each group must find out what the person or group of people listed did to promote the potato. Then call on a volunteer from each group to read the information aloud.

Actividad • Familia de palabras

Allow the students to complete the activity at home or in class. Review with the entire class.

UNIDAD **6**

Para un cuerpo sano . . .

It is important to think about yourself —
what you do every day, how you keep
yourself in shape, the foods you eat, and
the image you portray. Of course, young
Hispanic Americans share your interests
and concerns about these topics.

In this unit you will:

SECTION A	talk about what you do every day . . . discuss how you keep yourself in shape
SECTION B	discuss food and nutrition . . . talk about health
SECTION C	discuss personal care and grooming . . . pay compliments
TRY YOUR SKILLS	use what you've learned
VAMOS A LEER	read for practice and pleasure

191

SECTION A

talking about what you do every day . . . discussing how you keep yourself in shape

Daily exercise and good grooming habits will help you feel good about yourself, give you self-confidence, and help you make a better impression wherever you go.

A1 ¡Suena el despertador! 📼

Estamos en una casa de Lima, la capital del Perú. Es temprano por la mañana . . . Marisa duerme en su cuarto. Se despierta cuando suena el despertador. Ana también se levanta . . . pero se acuesta otra vez. Su papá se cepilla los dientes. Su mamá se pesa. Su hermano mayor se baña, se viste y se pone los zapatos. Su hermano menor se desayuna y se va para la escuela.

La familia de Marisa se mantiene en forma de diferentes maneras. Marisa se levanta temprano. Antes de ir a la escuela, corre media hora todos los días. Sus padres juegan al tenis. Su hermano mayor va al gimnasio a hacer ejercicios y su hermano menor practica la lucha libre. Su hermana Ana prefiere nadar tres veces por semana en la piscina de la escuela.

Actividad • Ana no tiene prisa

Choose the most logical answer to each question. Refer to A1 as needed.

1. ¿Qué hace Marisa cuando suena el despertador?
   a. Se despierta.   b. Se viste.   c. Se acuesta.
2. ¿Por qué se acuesta otra vez su hermana Ana?
   a. No oye el despertador.   b. Quiere dormir un poco más.
   c. No tiene ganas de desayunar.
3. ¿Qué hace la mamá de Marisa cuando se levanta?
   a. Se pesa.   b. Se despierta.   c. Se pone los zapatos.
4. Para mantenerse en forma, ¿qué hacen los padres de Marisa?
   a. Corren.   b. Hacen ejercicio.   c. Juegan al tenis.
5. ¿Quién se levanta temprano para correr?
   a. Marisa   b. su hermano mayor   c. su hermana Ana

A3   Sabes que . . .

Lima, la capital de Perú, es una ciudad de contrastes (contrasts). Fundada (founded) en 1535 por el conquistador Francisco Pizarro, todavía conserva bellas casas de arquitectura colonial y numerosas iglesias y palacios de estilo barroco (baroque) en la parte antigua de la ciudad. Junto a estas muestras (samples) de esplendor colonial se puede ver (one can see) la ciudad moderna, con grandes centros comerciales, tiendas por departamentos y sus plazas y avenidas con bellos edificios modernos. Lima también tiene excelentes museos, donde se pueden ver joyas y objetos de la época precolombina. La universidad de San Marcos, una de las más antiguas del hemisferio, fue fundada en 1551.

A reflexive construction such as **Anita se baña** (*Anita bathes herself*) consists of a
reflexive pronoun, **se** (*herself*), and a verb, **baña** (*bathes*). The subject, **Anita,** is both
the performer and the receiver of the action.

Anita se baña.   Anita baña al perro.

Use reflexive pronouns whenever the same person performs and receives the action
of the verb. With the exception of **se,** reflexive pronouns have the same forms as
the direct- and indirect-object pronouns. The following chart shows the reflexive
pronouns.

Subject Pronoun	Reflexive Pronoun	**bañarse** *to bathe (oneself)*	
Yo	**me**	baño.	*I bathe (myself).*
Tú	**te**	bañas.	*You bathe (yourself).*
Ud.			*You bathe (yourself).*
Él	**se**	baña.	*He bathes (himself).*
Ella			*She bathes (herself).*
Nosotros	**nos**	bañamos.	*We bathe (ourselves).*
Vosotros	**os**	bañáis.	*You bathe (yourselves).*
Ellos Ellas Uds.	**se**	bañan.	*They bathe (themselves).* *You bathe (yourselves).*

1. Reflexive pronouns are placed immediately before the conjugated verb except in
   affirmative commands. For an affirmative command, the reflexive pronoun is
   attached to the command.

   Marisa **se** despierta.   *Marisa wakes up.*
   ¡Despiérten**se**!   *Wake up!*

2. In the progressive construction, reflexive pronouns are either attached to the
   end of the **-ndo** form or placed in front of the verb **estar.**

   Anita está vistiéndo**se**. ⎫
   Anita **se** está vistiendo. ⎬   *Anita is getting dressed.*

Point out the use of
the written accent in
affirmative commands
with the reflexive
pronoun attached,
and in the progressive
construction with the
pronoun attached:
"¡Despiértense!, Anita
está vistiéndose."

3. In verb + infinitive constructions, reflexive pronouns are either attached to the infinitive or placed before the conjugated verb.

> Luis va a bañar**se.** }
> Luis **se** va a bañar. }   *Luis is going to take a bath.*

4. Many Spanish verbs can be made reflexive with the aid of a reflexive pronoun. Contrast the two sentences, pointing out the change of meaning.

> Yo llamo a Juan.   *I call Juan.*
> Yo **me** llamo Juan.   *My name is Juan. (I call myself Juan.)*

A5   Actividad • ¡A escoger!   Sentences that contain reflexive constructions are underlined. All other answers will vary.

Choose the sentence that has a reflexive construction and write it on a separate sheet of paper. Then write another sentence with the reflexive construction.

> MODELO   **a.** <u>Me lavo</u> las manos.   *Me lavo la cabeza.*
>   **b.** Lavo una camisa.

1. a. Ella no duerme al niño.
   b. Elisa no <u>se duerme</u>.
2. a. <u>Ella se va ahora</u>.
   b. Ella va a la escuela.
3. a. <u>¡Báñense!</u>
   b. ¡Bañen al gato!

4. a. <u>Me sirvo</u> el jugo de naranja.
   b. <u>¿Te sirvo</u> la leche?
5. a. <u>Me compré</u> un disco.
   b. Le compré un regalo.
6. a. <u>Me corté</u> con un cuchillo.
   b. Corté el pan.

A6   Actividad • ¿A qué hora?   Answers will vary.

An efficiency expert is helping you manage your time. Answer the following questions about your daily schedule.

1. ¿A qué hora te acuestas?
2. ¿Te duermes rápidamente? ¿A qué hora te duermes?
3. ¿Te despierta tu mamá o tienes un despertador?
4. ¿Cuándo te levantas?
5. ¿Te acuestas más tarde en el fin de semana?
6. ¿A qué hora te levantas los sábados y los domingos?
7. ¿Cuánto tiempo necesitas para bañarte? ¿Y para vestirte?
8. ¿Te bañas por la mañana o por la noche?

1. ¿Cuándo se baña Toni?
   Cuando nosotros nos vestimos.
2. ¿Cuándo se lava la cabeza Laura?
   Cuando Carmen se va a la cocina.

A7   Actividad • ¡Mucha gente!

During the summer, you and all of your cousins are staying at your grandparents' beach house. There are so many people that everybody has to take turns in the morning. Work with a partner and take turns asking and answering the questions.

> MODELO   Tomás / cepillarse los dientes   —¿Cuándo se cepilla los dientes Tomás?
>   Nicolás / levantarse   —Cuando Nicolás se levanta.

1. Toni / bañarse
   nosotros / vestirse
2. Laura / lavarse la cabeza
   Carmen / irse a la cocina
3. ¿Cuándo se despiertan Luis y Raúl?
   Cuando el despertador se cae.

3. Luis y Raúl / despertarse
   el despertador / caerse
4. Tú y yo / prepararse el desayuno
   los abuelos / hacerse el café
4. ¿Cuándo nos preparamos el desayuno tú
   y yo? Cuando los abuelos se hacen el café.

A8   Actividad • ¡No me compré nada!

Everybody went shopping and you want to know who bought what for whom.
Take turns with a partner asking and answering the questions. Follow the model.

> MODELO   (papá) un paraguas   — ¿Papá se compró un paraguas?
>   a mamá   — No, le compró un paraguas a mamá.

1. (ustedes) dos camisas
   al abuelo

   ¿Ustedes se compraron dos camisas? No, le compramos dos camisas al abuelo.

2. (tú) un cinturón de cuero
   a Eduardo

   ¿Te compraste un cinturón de cuero? No, le compré un cinturón de cuero a Eduardo.

3. (Elena) una revista
   a su hermana

   ¿Elena se compró una revista? No, le compró una revista a su hermana.

4. (Juan) un radio
   al tío Pepe

   ¿Juan se compró un radio? No, le compró un radio al tío Pepe.

A9   SITUACIÓN • Cómo mantenerse en forma

For information on how to present the realia, see p. T126.

¡Al fin Alicia encontró lo que buscaba! En una revista vio un anuncio de Isabel Palacios, la famosa estrella de cine. Anunciaba un video para hacer ejercicios en casa. Alicia sabía que nunca iba a ir a un gimnasio todos los días, pero en casa . . . no tenía excusa. Así que pidió el video rápidamente por correo, antes de cambiar de opinión.

El video acaba de llegar. Alicia se pone muy contenta. Está lista para empezar.

" . . . hasta tocar los dedos del pie derecho con la mano izquierda . . . uno dos, uno dos, . . . " La música ayuda. Alicia hace ejercicios aeróbicos. ¡Cómo se divierte! Baila, corre, se acuesta, se levanta. ¡Ay, cómo se cansa! Se siente débil. Después de un rato, se aburre. Necesita descansar. Es el primer día. No se preocupa. ¡Ya se siente con más energía! ¡Eso era lo que ella necesitaba!

INSCRIPCION Y CURSO
GRATIS
CUPO LIMITADO

GORDITAS, FLAQUITOS
FLAQUITAS, GORDITOS
APROVECHEN SUS VACACIONES
• Gimnasia rítmica • fisicoculturismo •
sauna • cámara • aromática • masajes.
Todo incluido en un gran programa.
GIMNASIO LOS TIBURONES
Avda. Cra. 68 N° 70-A-15. Tel: 2507220.

CENTRO DE GIMNASIA Y ESTETICA
Ladybel
EN PLENO CENTRO. MODERNO SALON DE
GIMNASIA Y ESTETICA CORPORAL
EXCLUSIVO PARA DAMAS
• GIMNASIA DIRIGIDA Y RITMICA • GIMNASIA PASIVA
• APARATOS • BAÑOS DE VAPOR Y SAUNA FINLANDESA
• PARA REBAJAR, REDUCIR O FORTALECER
• ESPECIAL DESPUES DEL PARTO
TRATAMIENTOS ESPECIALES
CONTRA CELULITIS Y FLACIDEZ; PARA MOLDEAR LA FIGURA
ABDOMEN, CINTURA, ESPALDAS, CADERAS, MUSLOS
O BRAZOS - ES IDEAL PARA: BUSTO, ROSTRO
Y DESPUES DEL PARTO
Horario Corrido para Damas inscritas de lunes a viernes
de 9 a 8 P.M - NUEVAS INSCRIPCIONES PREVIA CITA
Av Urdaneta, Pelota a Punceres, Residencias 26 Piso 12
Frente Edificio Protexo, lado Hotel Tiuna
TELEFONO 561.5936

LUZCA
UNA
FIGURA

GIMNASIO
NUEVA GRANADA
GIMNASIA ADELGAZANTE
CULTURA FISICA
(PESAS)
MASAJE
Y
SAUNA
Av. Nva. Granada
Fte. Correo
Telf.
62.4649

196   Unidad 6

A10 Actividad • Preguntas y respuestas

Use the information in A9 to answer the following questions.

1. ¿Qué buscaba Alicia?   Alicia buscaba un video para hacer ejercicio en casa.
2. ¿Quién era Isabel Palacios?   Isabel Palacios era una famosa estrella de cine.
3. ¿Qué hizo Alicia antes de cambiar de opinión?   Pidió el video rápidamente por correo.
4. ¿Por qué era mejor para ella hacer ejercicio en casa?   Porque sabía que nunca iba a ir a un gimnasio.
5. ¿Cómo estaba Alicia cuando llegó su video?   Alicia estaba muy contenta.
6. ¿Qué le ayuda a hacer los ejercicios?   La música le ayuda a hacer los ejercicios.

A11 Comprensión For script, see p. T126.

You will hear ten statements about daily activities. If they are in logical order, check **sí** on your answer sheet. If they are not, check **no**.

MODELO   Yo me levanto y luego me despierto.

	0	1	2	3	4	5	6	7	8	9	10
Sí		✔	✔				✔		✔		✔
No	✔			✔	✔	✔		✔		✔	

A12 SITUACIÓN • Partes del cuerpo

1. la cara
2. la boca
3. el pelo
4. el bigote
5. la frente
6. la nariz
7. los labios
8. el brazo
9. las uñas
10. los dedos
11. el hombro
12. el cuello
13. la cabeza
14. la oreja
15. los ojos
16. el pie
17. los dedos
18. el tobillo
19. la rodilla
20. la pierna
21. la cintura
22. la espalda
23. la muñeca
24. el cuerpo

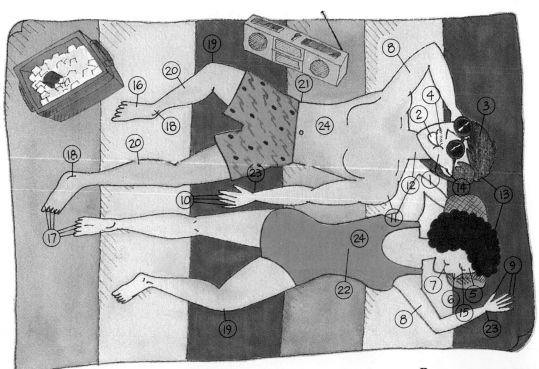

A 13 Actividad • ¿Dónde te lo pones?

Say on what part of the body people wear the following items.

MODELO: Ana se pone la bufanda en el cuello.

1. José se pone el reloj en la muñeca.   2. Pepe se pone la corbata en el cuello.   3. Marco se pone el cinturón en la cintura.   4. Ana se pone el sombrero en la cabeza.   5. Cristina se pone las medias en los pies.   6. Maribel se pone los aretes en las orejas.   7. Ana se pone los guantes en las manos.   8. María se pone los zapatos en los pies.

A 14 ESTRUCTURAS ESENCIALES

The definite article with the parts of the body and with personal possessions

Andrés **se** lava **la** cara.	*Andrés washes his face.*
Yo **me** cepillo **los** dientes.	*I brush my teeth.*
Ana **se** pone **la** blusa roja.	*Ana puts on her red blouse.*
Él **se** lava **las** manos.	*He washes his hands.*

In Spanish, reflexive pronouns and definite articles are often used with parts of the body, articles of clothing, and personal possessions, while English uses possessive adjectives.

A 15 Actividad • ¡Qué frío!

After the wrestling match at school, everybody prepares to go home. It is cold outside. Say what everyone is doing. Follow the model.

MODELO   Cristina / abrigo   Cristina se pone **el** abrigo.

1. Salvador / sombrero   Salvador se pone el sombrero.
2. Yo / abrigo   Yo me pongo el abrigo.
3. Tú y Alberto / guantes   Tú y Alberto se ponen los guantes.
4. Cecilia / suéter   Cecilia se pone el suéter.
5. Nosotros / botas   Nosotros nos ponemos las botas.
6. Arturo / chaqueta   Arturo se pone la chaqueta.

A16 Actividad • ¡Ay, qué dolor tengo!

Now it's time for the school wrestling team to go home. Everybody is aching. Say what is bothering each member of the team.

> MODELO Roberto / mano
> Roberto tiene dolor en la mano.

1. Andrés / rodilla — Andrés tiene dolor en la rodilla.
2. Luis / cuello — Luis tiene dolor en el cuello.
3. David / tobillo — David tiene dolor en el tobillo.
4. Víctor / brazo — Víctor tiene dolor en el brazo.

5. Manolo / oreja — 5. Manolo tiene dolor en la oreja.
6. Raúl y Esteban / muñeca — 6. Raúl y Esteban tienen dolor en la muñeca.
7. Jorge / cuerpo — 7. Jorge tiene dolor en el cuerpo.
8. Pepe y Rafael / espalda — 8. Pepe y Rafael tienen dolor en la espalda.

A17 SE DICE ASÍ
Describing emotions

You may wish to add that "tan" and "muy" are often used with these expressions: "Tomás se puso *muy* contento." "Anita se pone *tan* nerviosa cuando llega tarde."

Se pone furioso(a).	He (she) gets furious.
Se pone triste.	He (she) gets sad.
Se pone contento(a).	He (she) gets happy.
Se pone nervioso(a).	He (she) gets nervous.

Note that Spanish expressions with **ponerse** often correspond to English *get* + adjective.

A18 Actividad • ¿Cómo te pones tú si algo te pasa?

If the following events occur, what would be a logical reaction? Choose from the items in the box. Follow the model.

> MODELO Papá me dice que la casa nueva tiene piscina.
> Me pongo contento(a).

1. Juan come algo en la calle que no está bueno.
2. Ellos no sabían que había examen.
3. Tomás saca "A" en todas las materias.
4. Miguel recibe una mala noticia.
5. Ahora comemos menos y hacemos ejercicio.
6. Una persona se lleva tu dinero.

1. Se pone enfermo. 2. Se ponen nerviosos. 3. Se pone contento.
4. Se pone triste. 5. Nos ponemos delgados. 6. Me pongo furioso.

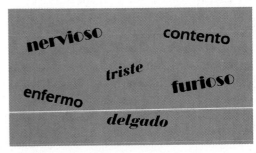

nervioso   contento
triste
enfermo   furioso
delgado

A19 Actividad • Para mantenerse en forma

Rewrite the sentences that do not offer healthful advice.

1. Levántense siempre tarde. — Levántense siempre temprano.
2. Hagan ejercicio.
3. Duerman poco. — Duerman lo suficiente.
4. Acuéstense temprano.
5. No tomen agua. — Tomen agua.

6. Pésense frecuentemente.
7. No se preocupen demasiado.
8. No practiquen deportes. — Practiquen deportes.
9. Coman menos vegetales. — Coman más vegetales.
10. Descansen si están cansados.

Actividad • Charla Answers will vary.

¿Cuándo te pones contento(a)? Get together with a classmate and ask each other about situations that make you happy, sad, and so on. Use the verb **ponerse** in reflexive constructions and choose words from the box below to describe how you feel. Use masculine or feminine forms.

A 21 **Actividad • ¿Cómo es? ¿Qué hace?**

You are invited to spend a week at your friend's home. Since you haven't met every member of your friend's family, you would like to find out something about each one. Get together with a classmate and play both roles. Follow the cues.

MODELO los abuelos / mantenerse en forma — ¿Qué hacen los abuelos?
— Se mantienen en forma.

1. Luis y Carlos / levantarse temprano
2. Patricia / no preocuparse por nada
3. Oscar / irse a la playa los sábados
4. la tía Tula / acostarse muy tarde
5. el tío Julián / aburrirse siempre en el campo
6. Pablo / no cansarse nunca
7. Estela / divertirse con todo

1. ¿Qué hacen Luis y Carlos? Luis y Carlos se levantan temprano. 2. ¿Cómo es Patricia? Patricia no se preocupa por nada. 3. ¿Qué hace Oscar? Oscar se va a la playa los sábados. 4. ¿Qué hace la tía Tula? La tía Tula se acuesta muy tarde. 5. ¿Cómo es el tío Julián? El tío Julián se aburre siempre en el campo. 6. ¿Cómo es Pablo? Pablo no se cansa nunca. 7. ¿Cómo es Estela? Estela se divierte con todo.

A 22 **Actividad • Mi amigo el médico** Answers will vary.

Your friend, who is a pre-med student, wants to know some useful phrases in Spanish. Come up with six phrases a doctor might find useful when talking to a patient. Include some command forms.

MODELO Abra la boca, por favor.

A 23 **Actividad • ¡A escribir!** Answers will vary.

Compare what you do on a summer day with what you do on a school day. Use as many reflexive verbs as you can. Write at least six or eight sentences.

Keeping yourself healthy requires a lot of care. There is an old proverb that says: **"Dime lo que comes y te diré quién eres."** *("You are what you eat.") It is a very truthful proverb since what you eat will reflect on how you feel.*

B1

Un menú adecuado

¿Tienes una dieta balanceada? ¿Comes alimentos que son buenos para ti? Vamos a ver el régimen de Marisa. Ella quiere estar fuerte, pero quiere adelgazar cinco libras porque aumentó de peso un poco durante las vacaciones.

DIETA BALANCEADA

Desayuno:
media toronja (sin azúcar)
cereal de trigo con leche y fruta
té con limón
multivitaminas

Almuerzo:
pequeña porción de pescado o de carne sin grasa
ensalada de lechuga y tomate (sin aceite)
fruta fresca

Comida:
un cuarto de pollo
una papa pequeña (sin mantequilla)
ensalada de espinacas (sin aceite)
fresas con yogur

Entre comidas (a escoger uno):
trocitos de apio y de zanahoria
palomitas de maíz
un vaso de leche descremada
una limonada

Cuando hay competencia deportiva, añadir una ración
de macarrones o fideos. Da más energía para competir.

Marisa ahora cuenta las calorías. No come mantequilla ni tampoco carne con grasa. Come con moderación y por supuesto, no come nada con azúcar. No quiere aumentar más de peso. Tiene que cuidarse. Marisa quiere mejorar su condición física y mantenerse en forma. Su médico le recomienda un buen régimen y ejercicio.

Actividad • Preguntas y respuestas  For answers, see p. T130.

Use the information in B1 to answer the following questions.

1. ¿Crees que "eres lo que comes"? ¿Qué quiere decir eso?
2. ¿Cuáles son las tres   cosas que Marisa decide no comer?
3. ¿Cuándo toma multivitaminas?
4. ¿Qué toma con las fresas en vez de crema de leche?
5. ¿Qué tipo de leche prefiere Marisa? ¿Por qué?
6. ¿Cuándo come trocitos de apio y de zanahoria?
7. ¿Por qué es bueno comer una ración de macarrones cuando hay competencia?

B3   Actividad • ¡A completar!

Complete these statements with the information from B1.

1. Es importante tener una dieta _____ . balanceada
2. Marisa come media toronja sin _____ . azúcar
3. El postre de Marisa es _____ . fruta fresca
4. Medio pollo es más que un _____ de pollo. cuarto
5. Marisa come apio y _____ . zanahoria
6. Marisa puede comer palomitas de maíz por la noche o _____ comidas. entre

B4 Sabes que . . .

Muchos productos que hoy comemos todos los días no se conocían en Europa antes de la llegada de Colón a América. Por ejemplo, el maíz *(corn)* era y es el alimento principal en muchas regiones de América. Cuando Colón llegó a América, el maíz era desconocido en Europa.

El chocolate era una bebida muy popular entre los aztecas y los mayas. Era tan valioso *(valuable)* que lo usaban como moneda. De México, los españoles lo llevaron a España y pasó después a toda Europa.

Antes de la llegada de Colón, los indios de varias regiones comían maní o cacahuete *(peanuts)* y preparaban sus alimentos con ají o chile *(green pepper or hot pepper)* y tomate. Hoy día el chile es un ingrediente principal en muchos platos de la cocina internacional. El tomate es importante en la preparación de varias comidas, especialmente en la cocina italiana. Otro alimento indispensable para la alimentación en muchos países es la papa. Los españoles encontraron la papa en el Perú, y de allí pasó a Europa.

El chicle *(chewing gum)*, producto de El Salvador y Guatemala, no es un alimento. Se obtiene de la savia *(sap)* de un árbol. Por razones misteriosas, millones de personas tienen fascinación con este producto. ¡Lo mastican *(chew)* a todas horas! No podríamos terminar sin mencionar esos sabrosos helados y batidos *(milk shakes)* con sabor a vainilla que se hacen con otro producto nativo de América: la vainilla.

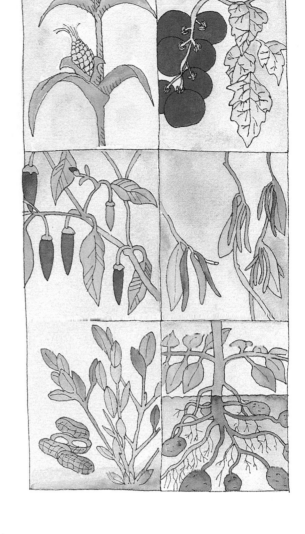

B5 Comprensión   For script, see p. T131.

Listen to the following conversations. If the advice is logical, check **lógico** on your answer sheet. If it is not, check **ilógico.**

MODELO —Ay, doctor, siempre estoy cansado y no hago nada.
—Pues haga ejercicio todos los días.

	0	1	2	3	4	5	6	7	8	9	10
Lógico	✔		✔			✔	✔	✔		✔	✔
Ilógico		✔		✔	✔				✔		

B6 Actividad • ¡A escribir!   Answers will vary.

Write a menu for someone who wants to gain weight. Include those names of foods you have already learned or those you research. Use magazine pictures or drawings of popular foods from Spanish America or Spain to illustrate your menu. Include at least seven main courses in the menu.

Esta semana la clase de español está medio vacía. Casi todo el mundo está enfermo. Bueno, todo el mundo no. La mayoría de mis amigos se enfermaron y nuestro profesor, el señor Orozco, se siente mal también.

Juan tiene catarro.

Pepe está en el hospital. Tiene un brazo roto.

Alicia tiene dolor de garganta.

El señor Orozco tiene dolor de cabeza.

Gloria tiene dolor de estómago y toma su medicina.

Cecilia tiene dolor en la rodilla.

Juan se enfermó hoy. Tiene un poco de fiebre. Pepe tuvo un accidente y tiene el brazo derecho roto. Alicia tiene gripe. Le duele la garganta. El señor Orozco no se siente bien. Tiene dolor de cabeza y va a tomar dos aspirinas. Gloria comió mucho. Tiene dolor de estómago y va a tomar su medicina. Cecilia también tuvo un accidente. Le duele la rodilla. . . .Y yo, ¿qué tengo? Pues, yo no tengo nada.

Actividad • ¿Sí o no?

Correct the following sentences according to the information in B7.

1. Pepe tiene catarro.   Pepe tiene un brazo roto. / Juan tiene catarro.
2. Alicia está en el hospital.   Alicia tiene dolor de garganta. / Pepe está en el hospital.
3. El señor Orozco tiene un poco de fiebre.   El señor Orozco tiene dolor de cabeza.
4. Cecilia tiene un brazo roto.   Cecilia tiene dolor en la rodilla.
5. A mí me duele la garganta.   Yo no tengo nada.

B9 **SE DICE ASÍ**
Asking and stating how one feels
Expressing sympathy

Point out that these expressions can also be used with "muy," "mucho," "tan," or "tanto." "Me siento *muy* bien." "Me siento *mucho* mejor."

Me siento bien (mal).	I feel good (bad).
Me siento mejor.	I feel better.
Tengo dolor de...	I have a pain...
Me duele...	My ... hurts.
Lo siento (mucho).	I am (very) sorry.
¿Cómo te sientes?	How do you feel?
¿Qué tienes?	What's wrong?
¡Qué lástima!	How awful!
¡Cuida tu salud!	Take care of your health!

B10 **Actividad • ¡A escoger!**   Answers will vary. Possible answers are given.

Choose the correct response from the box for each of the
following statements. You may use responses more than once.

1. Hoy no me siento bien.
2. Creo que me voy a enfermar.
3. Los niños están en el hospital.
4. Creo que tengo fiebre.
5. Luis tiene un brazo roto.
6. El Sr. Orozco tiene gripe.

1. ¿Qué tienes? 2. ¡Cuida tu salud! 3. Lo siento
mucho. 4. ¡Cuida tu salud! 5. ¡Cuánto lo siento!
6. ¡Qué lástima!

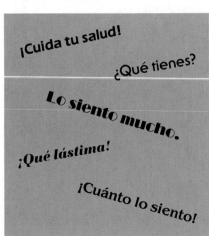

¡Cuida tu salud!
¿Qué tienes?
Lo siento mucho.
¡Qué lástima!
¡Cuánto lo siento!

The following chart shows the most commonly used affirmative and negative expressions. You already know most of them. The words in the *Negative* column are the opposite of those in the *Affirmative* column.

Affirmative		*Negative*	
algo	*something, anything*	**nada**	*nothing, not anything*
alguien	*someone, anyone*	**nadie**	*nobody, no one*
alguno(-a)		**ninguno(-a)**	
algún	*any, some*	**ningún**	*none, not any*
algunos(-as)			
siempre	*always*	**nunca**	*never*
también	*also, too*	**tampoco**	*neither, not either*
o . . . o	*either . . . or*	**ni . . . ni**	*neither . . . nor*

1. Place affirmative words and expressions either before or after the verb.

   Siempre como media toronja. ⎱
   Como **siempre** media toronja. ⎰   *I always eat half a grapefruit.*

   ¿Alguien desayunó? ⎱
   ¿Desayunó **alguien?** ⎰   *Did anyone have breakfast?*

2. Sentences using a negative word can occur in two forms.
   a. The negative word appears before the verb.

   Hoy **tampoco** me levanté tarde.   *Today I didn't get up late either.*
   Nunca servimos postre.   *We never serve dessert.*
   Nadie descansó.   *No one rested.*

   b. The negative expression appears after the verb. Add **no** before the verb.

   Hoy **no** me levanté tarde **tampoco.**   *Today I didn't get up late either.*
   No servimos postre **nunca.**   *We never serve dessert.*
   No descansó **nadie.**   *No one rested.*

   ATENCIÓN: Notice that Spanish often uses double negatives.

   No compramos **nada.**   *We don't buy anything.*
   No tengo **ninguno.**   *I don't have any.*

3. **Alguno** and **ninguno** drop the **-o** and add an accent before a masculine singular noun: **algún, ningún.** The feminine forms are **alguna** and **ninguna.** **Alguno(-a)** has plural forms, but **ninguno(-a)** is only used in the singular.

   ¿Tienes **alguna** medicina para la gripe?   *Do you have any medicine for the flu?*
   No tengo **ningún** dolor, ni fiebre tampoco.   *I don't have any pain or fever either.*

4. Answering a question with a negative expression will sometimes require a triple negative in the answer.

   ¿Quieres comer **algo?**   *Do you want to eat something?*
   No, no quiero comer **nada.**   *No, I don't want to eat anything.*

   ¿Qué prefieres, limonada o jugo?   *What do you prefer, lemonade or juice?*
   Gracias, **no** quiero **ni** limonada **ni** jugo.   *Thank you, I want neither lemonade nor juice.*

Actividad • Por teléfono

Susana and Carmencita are talking on the phone. Complete their conversation with the words **alguien** or **nadie,** whichever is appropriate.

—Hola, Susana. ¿Hay _____ en tu casa?   alguien
—No, Carmencita. No hay _____ .   nadie
—¿No hay _____ en la casa?   nadie
—Sí, hay _____ . ¡Estoy yo!   alguien
—Ay . . . Oye, ¿sabes si van a cambiar la fecha de la competencia?
—No, yo no sé tampoco. _____ me dijo que iban a cambiarla,   Alguien
   pero creo que _____ sabe nada todavía.   nadie
—Debes llamar a _____ . Tere va a competir.   alguien
—Ahora no puedo llamar a _____ más. Me voy a la   nadie
   piscina a practicar porque a esta hora no hay _____ .   nadie

B 13   Actividad • ¡Te digo que no!   For answers, see p. T133.

Your friend Esteban is in a bad mood today and says *no* to everything. Get together with a classmate and ask each other the following questions according to the model.

MODELO   escribir algo   — ¿Escribes algo, Esteban?
                          — ¡No, no escribo nada!

1. tener alguna foto para el periódico
2. invitar a alguien para mañana
3. tener alguna competencia pronto
4. querer algo de la cafetería

5. querer oír algún disco
6. estar enfadado con alguien
7. doler algo
8. tomar alguna vitamina

1. ¿Quieres algún sandwich?
2. ¿Hay algunos huevos en el refrigerador?
3. ¿Tienes algún queso?

B 14   Actividad • En la cocina

Today your friend is sick and alone. You offer some help and ask a few questions. Change the questions, using the words in parentheses. Follow the model.

MODELO   ¿Tomaste alguna merienda? (desayuno)
         ¿Tomaste algún desayuno?

1. ¿Quieres algunas frutas? (sandwich)
2. ¿Hay alguna carne en el refrigerador? (huevos)
3. ¿Tienes algunas papas? (queso)
4. ¿Quieres algunos trocitos de zanahoria? (apio)
5. ¿Prefieres alguna sopa? (yogur)
6. ¿Tienes que tomar alguna medicina? (jugo o té)
7. ¿Necesitas alguna revista? (música)

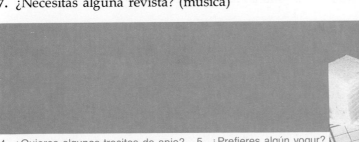

4. ¿Quieres algunos trocitos de apio?   5. ¿Prefieres algún yogur?
6. ¿Tienes que tomar algún jugo o té?   7. ¿Necesitas alguna música?

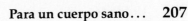

Para un cuerpo sano...   207

Actividad • ¿Tienes alguna pregunta?

Respond to each question by choosing the appropriate answer from the box.

1. ¿Compraste algunas papas? Sí, algunas.
2. ¿Viste a alguien en el mercado? No, a nadie.
3. ¿Tienes algo de comer? No, nada.
4. ¿Tienes fresas para el postre? No, ninguna.
5. ¿Y yogur? Tampoco.
6. ¿Hay alguien en la cocina? No, nadie.
7. ¿Está alguien cocinando? Sí, algunos chicos.
8. ¿Comes macarrones a menudo? No, casi nunca.

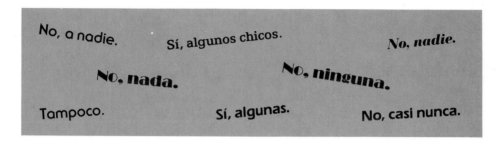

No, a nadie.   Sí, algunos chicos.   No, nadie.

No, nada.   No, ninguna.

Tampoco.   Sí, algunas.   No, casi nunca.

B 16 **Actividad • ¡Qué difícil es decidir!**

Fernando cannot make up his mind. This irritates his older brother who shares his room. With the help of a classmate, play both roles. Follow the model.

MODELO   bañarse, vestirse / lavarse la cara
— ¡O te bañas o te vistes!
— Ni me baño ni me visto. Me lavo la cara.

1. irse hoy, irse mañana / irse el martes
2. arreglar el cuarto, limpiar el baño / poner la mesa
3. ponerse los zapatos, ponerse las botas / ponerse los tenis
4. acostarse, levantarse / dormirse otra vez
5. pesarse, cepillarse los dientes / lavarse la cabeza
6. entrar, salir / quedarse aquí

1. ¡O te vas hoy o te vas mañana! Ni me voy hoy ni me voy mañana. Me voy el martes. 2. ¡O arreglas el cuarto o limpias el baño! Ni arreglo el cuarto ni limpio el baño. Pongo la mesa.   3. ¡O te pones los zapatos o te pones las botas! Ni me pongo los zapatos ni me pongo las botas. Me pongo los tenis.   4. ¡O te acuestas o te levantas! Ni me acuesto ni me levanto. Me duermo otra vez.   5. ¡O te pesas o te cepillas los dientes! Ni me peso ni me cepillo los dientes. Me lavo la cabeza.   6. ¡O entras o sales! Ni entro ni salgo. Me quedo aquí.

B 17 **Actividad • ¡A escribir!** Answers will vary.

It was reported that five students in your class were sick today. Name each one and explain what illness they had. Hint: **Adolfo no vino a clase porque tenía gripe.**

B 18 **Actividad • ¡La mejor dieta del mundo!** Answers will vary.

Your brother works for a Spanish agency that writes commercials for television. He wants your ideas for an ad about a new health diet. Give him at least five suggestions.

Sabes que . . .

La piña crece muy bien en Hawaii, pero es una fruta americana. Los españoles la llevaron a España y de ahí pasó al resto del mundo.

La papaya es una fruta tropical maravillosa. Se originó en la América Central y de ahí pasó a otras regiones. Cientos de años antes de Colón ya la cultivaban en Perú. Es una fruta muy fresca y rica en vitaminas. Tiene cualidades medicinales extraordinarias.

El aguacate (*avocado*) gana popularidad todos los días y la guayaba (*guava*) también. Antes de llegar los españoles, los aztecas cultivaban estas dos frutas y muchas otras que todavía no son populares en los Estados Unidos.

Entre las más populares frutas tropicales están el plátano (*banana*) y el mango. No son nativas de América. El plátano se originó en la India y el mango en el Asia. Los españoles trajeron (*brought*) el plátano a la América en el siglo XVI y el mango en el XVIII.

B 20 **ESTRUCTURAS ESENCIALES**
The preterit tense of querer *and* poner

The preterit forms of **querer** and **poner** are irregular.

querer	*to want*	poner	*to put*
quise	quisimos	puse	pusimos
quisiste	quisisteis	pusiste	pusisteis
quiso	quisieron	puso	pusieron

Anita no **quiso** comprar la piña.
Anita did not want to buy the pineapple.

Puse las papas y los macarrones en la cocina.
I put the potatoes and the macaroni in the kitchen.

B 21 Actividad • ¿Querer o poner?

Fill in the blanks with the correct form of **querer** or **poner** as needed.

—¿Supiste dónde _____ la moto tus amigos? pusieron
—No, no supe dónde la _____ . pusieron
—¿Y dónde la _____ poner tu hermano? quiso
—Él la _____ enfrente de la casa. puso
—¿Por qué no _____ la tuya enfrente de la casa? puso/pusiste
—Porque no _____ . quiso/quise

B 22   Actividad • Antes y después

Manolito did not take good care of himself, but now he does. Help describe the situation by completing the sentences.

ANTES

1. Siempre se enfermaba.
2. Se acostaba muy tarde.
3. No dormía bien.
4. Se despertaba cansado.
5. Y se volvía a acostar.
6. Nunca se vestía rápido.
7. Se dormía a veces en la clase.
8. Siempre tenía catarro.
9. Nunca se divertía.
10. No se sentía bien.

DESPUÉS

1. Ahora no se _____ nunca.   enferma
2. Ahora se _____ mucho más temprano.   acuesta
3. Ahora _____ toda la noche.   duerme
4. Siempre se _____ contento y con energía.   despierta
5. Ahora no _____ a acostarse.   vuelve
6. Ahora se _____ en diez minutos.   viste
7. No se _____ nunca en clase.   duerme
8. No _____ catarro nunca.   tiene
9. Ahora se _____ mucho más.   divierte
10. Ahora se _____ lleno de energía.   siente

B 23   Actividad • Charla   Answers will vary.

With a classmate, talk about at least four health habits you both would like to improve. Take turns.

MODELO: Me acostaba muy tarde antes, pero entonces estaba muy cansado por la mañana. Ahora me voy a acostar temprano todos los días . . .

B 24   ¿RECUERDAS?
The verb gustar

1. As you recall, **gustar** is used only in the third person singular and plural: **gusta/gustan.**
   A mí me **gusta** mucho ir al centro comercial.   *I like to go to the mall.*
   A Elena le **gustan** los vegetales.   *Elena likes vegetables.*
2. The verb agrees with the subject of the sentence. The subject is often found at the end of the sentence.
   Me **gustan los vegetales.**   *I like vegetables.*
   No me **gusta el yogur.**   *I don't like yogurt.*
3. The verbs **doler** (*to hurt; to ache*), **encantar** (*to love*), and **importar** (*to matter*) follow the same pattern as the verb **gustar.**
   Me **encantan** las zanahorias.   *I love carrots.*
   A Rita le **duele** la cabeza.   *Rita has a headache.*
   Me **importa** mucho comer bien.   *It's important to me to eat well.*

B 25   Actividad • No me importa

Complete the following paragraph with the correct forms of **gustar, doler, encantar,** and **importar.**

Me _____ mucho sacar buenas notas. En otras palabras, no me _____ sacar malas   importa / gusta
notas. A casi todos mis amigos les _____ sacar buenas notas, pero a algunos no   importa
les _____ estudiar. A todos nos _____ pasear o ir al centro comercial. Nos _____ los   gusta / encanta / gustan
helados también. Nos _____ los refrescos, especialmente cuando vamos a la playa.   encantan
Hoy todos fueron menos yo. Me quedé en casa porque me _____ la cabeza.   dolía

discussing personal care and grooming . . . paying compliments

Personal care and grooming are very important in Hispanic America. People are not as casual about how they dress. Young men often wear a coat and tie, and young women take a great deal of interest in their personal appearance.

C1 Los chicos se preparan para el baile

Esta noche es la fiesta de Trini. Son ya las cinco de la tarde y todos los chicos se preparan para salir. Hay prisa, emoción y alegría en el aire. Raquel se prueba un vestido amarillo. Se mira en el espejo. Le pregunta a su mamá cómo le queda. No está contenta. Se quita el vestido. ¿Quizás el azul? Se lo pone. Se vuelve a mirar en el espejo. ¡Ahora sí! Sólo falta hacer algo. Se ríe contenta y corre hasta la sala. Raquel le enseña el vestido a su mamá, le trae una tijera y le pregunta una cosa. Tiene el pelo un poco largo sobre los ojos. La mamá le dice que no está tan largo, pero, si quiere, se lo puede cortar. Raquel toma la tijera y se corta el pelo un poco. ¡Ahora todo está perfecto!

Susana se pinta los ojos y luego se pinta las uñas.

Mientras tanto, ¿qué hacen los otros chicos?

Trini se pone la base y luego se pinta los labios.

Amalia se peina.

El hermano de Trini se limpia los dientes y luego se afeita.

C2 Actividad • ¿Qué pasó primero?

Use the information in C1 to number the following events in the correct order.

__4__ Raquel se quita el vestido.
__2__ Se mira en el espejo.
__8__ Ahora todo está perfecto.
__7__ Se corta un poco el pelo.
__1__ Raquel se prueba un vestido.
__6__ Corre hasta la sala.
__5__ Se pone el vestido azul.
__3__ Le pregunta a su mamá cómo le queda.

For information on how to
present the realia. see p. T136

C3 Actividad • Preguntas y respuestas

2. Le pregunta a su mamá cómo le queda.
Answer each question about the situation in C1.

1. ¿Qué se prueba Raquel? Raquel se prueba un vestido amarillo.
2. ¿Qué le pregunta ella a su mamá?
3. ¿Qué vestido se pone entonces? Se pone el vestido azul.
4. ¿Y qué hace después? Se vuelve a mirar en el espejo.
5. ¿Por qué corre hasta la sala?
6. ¿Quién se ríe? Raquel se ríe.
7. ¿Cómo tiene el pelo Raquel? Raquel tiene el pelo un poco largo.
8. ¿Qué hacen Trini y su hermano?
9. ¿Qué hace Susana? Susana se pinta los ojos y las uñas.

5. Corre hasta la sala para enseñarle el vestido a su mamá.
8. Trini se maquilla y se pinta los labios. Su hermano se limpia los dientes y se afeita.

FARMEXPO

F·A·R·M·E·X·P·O
La feria de la salud y la belleza

VENGA HOY !!

¡Exhibición y venta para toda la familia!

- Cosméticos de las principales marcas
- Medicamentos
- Anteojos, lentes y artículos ópticos
- Literatura e información sobre salud y belleza
- Equipo médico
- Servicios para la salud y la belleza
- Productos veterinarios

Y MUCHO MAS!

Demostradores y maquillistas! Estilistas! Peinados y cortes gratis! Todo sobre salud y belleza! Grandes ofertas!

NO SE LO PIERDA!

Muy cerca... a350 mts. norte del Hotel Irazú, o por La Uruca, frente a Canada Dry, en las instalaciones de la Liga de la Caña.

C4 Actividad • Charla   Answers will vary.

The two young people in the illustration are getting ready for a party. Describe what they may be doing. Use at least five sentences in your descriptions.

ESTRUCTURAS ESENCIALES
Verbs used with reflexive pronouns

Point out that a verb is called reflexive when the subject does something to himself or herself, either directly or indirectly: "Elena se peina". "Luis se compra una camisa". After the explanation you may wish to do a personalized question/answer drill: "¿Te peinas por la mañana? ¿y ustedes?" "¿Te afeitas todos los días? ¿y él?" "¿Se alegran ustedes cuando sacan buenas notas? ¿y ella?"

1. Verbs that express personal care and grooming are used with a reflexive pronoun when the same person performs and receives the action of the verb. Similar constructions are used in English, but in English the reflexive pronoun is often omitted.

peinarse	Roberto se peina.	*Roberto combs his hair.*
afeitarse	Julián se afeita.	*Julián shaves (himself).*
lavarse	Elena se lava las manos.	*Elena washes her hands.*

2. Many Spanish verbs that express feelings, emotions, and memories are used with reflexive pronouns.

alegrarse	*to become happy*		**acordarse**	*to remember*
enfadarse ⎫			**sentirse**	*to feel*
enojarse ⎭	*to get angry*		**olvidarse**	*to forget*
enamorarse	*to fall in love*		**enfermarse**	*to get sick*
divertirse	*to have a good time*			

No **me acuerdo** dónde vive Roberto.   *I don't remember where Roberto lives.*
Se divirtieron mucho en la fiesta de Elenita.   *They had a good time at Elenita's party.*
Él **se enamoró** de Susana el verano pasado.   *He fell in love with Susana last summer.*

Notice that these Spanish verbs do not correspond to English reflexive verbs. They are often equivalent to *to get* or *to become.*

3. Some Spanish verbs change their meaning when they are used with reflexive pronouns.

Used with reflexive pronouns		*Used without reflexive pronouns*	
acostarse	*to go to bed*	**acostar**	*to put to bed*
dormirse	*to fall asleep*	**dormir**	*to sleep*
irse	*to leave, to go away*	**ir**	*to go*
ponerse	*to put on*	**poner**	*to put, to place*
llamarse	*to be called*	**llamar**	*to call*

Ella **se llama** María.   *Her name is María.*
Ella **llamó** a Carolina.   *She called Carolina.*
Tomás **se acostó** tarde anoche.   *Tomás went to bed late last night.*
Tomás **acostó** a su hermanito.   *Tomás put his little brother to bed.*

Actividad • **¿Quién hace qué?**   Answers will vary. Possible answers are given.

Make two logical sentences with each of the words below. Only one of the sentences should be a reflexive construction. Follow the model.

MODELO   probar(se)   Ana se prueba el vestido.
                              Ana prueba la sopa.

1. dormir(se)   3. servir(se)   5. poner(se)
2. mirar(se)   4. preparar(se)   6. lavar(se)

1. Ana se duerme a las diez. Ana duerme en el cuarto de su hermana.   2. Ana se mira en el espejo. Ana mira la televisión.   3. Ana se sirve la sopa. Ana le sirve la sopa a su novio.   4. Ana se prepara para el viaje. Ana prepara la comida.   5. Ana se pone los zapatos. Ana pone la mesa.   6. Ana se lava las manos. Ana lava el coche.

LÁPIZ LABIAL

LÁPIZ PARA LOS OJOS

POLVO

COLORETE

MAQUILLAJE, BASE

PEINE

SECADORA

CEPILLO PARA EL PELO

ESMALTE

LENTES DE CONTACTO DE COLORES

CHAMPÚ Y ENJUAGUE

PASTA DE DIENTES

CEPILLO DE DIENTES

ESPEJO

TIJERA

ENJUAGUE PARA LA BOCA

CREMA Y LOCIÓN PARA LA PIEL

LIMA DE UÑAS

TALCO

CUCHILLAS

PERFUME

JABÓN

JABÓN O CREMA DE AFEITAR

MÁQUINA DE AFEITAR ELÉCTRICA

MAQUINILLA DE AFEITAR

LOCIÓN DE AFEITAR

DESODORANTE

BOTELLA DE AGUA DE COLONIA

C8 Actividad • Uno no es del grupo

Which object does not belong in each group?

1. pasta de dientes   polvo   enjuague   cepillo de dientes
2. agua de colonia   loción   espejo   perfume
3. crema de afeitar   jabón   lima   champú
4. cuchilla   tijera   cepillo   maquinilla de afeitar
5. secadora   cremas   peine   champú
6. esmalte de uñas   desodorante   colorete   lápiz labial

C9 Actividad • Dígame dónde

Say for what part of the body you use the following products.

MODELO   lápiz labial
         Uso el lápiz labial en los labios.

1. lentes de contacto
2. cepillo
3. maquillaje
4. crema de afeitar
5. perfume
6. enjuague

1. Uso las lentes de contacto en los ojos.
2. Uso el cepillo en el pelo.
3. Uso el maquillaje en la cara.
4. Uso la crema de afeitar en la cara.
5. Uso el perfume en el cuerpo.
6. Uso el enjuague en la boca.

C10 Actividad • ¿Y tú?   Answers will vary.

Get together with a classmate and ask each other when you do the following things.

MODELO   ponerse   ¿Cuándo te pones polvo?
                   Me pongo polvo antes de salir.

1. secarse el pelo
2. pintarse las uñas
3. afeitarse
4. ponerse maquillaje
5. limpiarse las uñas con cepillo
6. pintarse los labios
7. ponerse perfume o colonia
8. mirarse en el espejo
9. cepillarse el pelo
10. cortarse las uñas

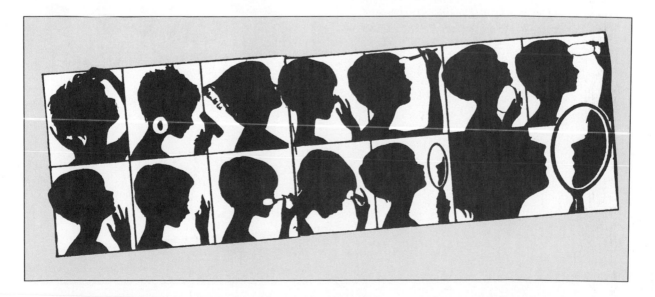

SE DICE ASÍ
Discussing unplanned events

Explain that these types of sentences are extremely common in the Hispanic world. They are used when the identity of the subject is unknown or not important. They are also used when the subject wants to shed responsibility for what happened.

¿Me prestas tu espejo?	Will you lend me your mirror?
No puedo. El espejo se rompió.	I can't. The mirror broke.
Luis, ¿dónde está el reloj que compré?	Luis, where is the watch that I bought?
Ay, se perdió ayer.	Oh, it got lost yesterday.
Antonio, ¿qué pasó?	Antonio, what happened?
Nada, la taza se cayó.	Nothing, the cup fell down.

Unplanned or involuntary events can be expressed by: **se** + a verb in the preterit. The verb will be in the third person singular if the subject is singular, and in the third person plural if the subject is plural.

C12 SITUACIÓN • Preparándose para la fiesta

Pilar y Alicia conversan frente al espejo. Se arreglan el pelo, se maquillan un poco y esperan a Fernando que va a llevarlas a una fiesta.

PILAR Oye, ¿me prestas la lima de uñas?

ALICIA Sí, como no, pero está un poco vieja. No está muy buena. Aquí está la tijerita también.

PILAR Gracias. Me gusta mucho el color de tu lápiz labial. Te queda muy bien.

ALICIA Y a mí me gusta tu perfume. ¿Cómo se llama?

PILAR "Imaginación." Me lo regaló Fernando.

ALICIA ¿El hermano de Cristina? No sabía que él se preocupaba de esas cosas.

PILAR Estuvo en mi fiesta de cumpleaños . . .

ALICIA Ay, no veo nada con tan poca luz. ¿Tienes un espejito? El mío se perdió.

PILAR Ay, no. El mío se rompió esta mañana. ¡Ahora voy a tener siete años de mala suerte!

ALICIA ¡Huy! Ésos son muchos años. Tú no crees en eso, ¿verdad?

C13 Actividad • ¿Es cierto o no?

Change the sentences to make them agree with C12.

1. Pilar y Alicia están en la cocina.
2. Van a ir a una fiesta con Fernando.
3. La lima es nueva.

4. El perfume se llama Fantasía.
5. Fernando es el primo de Cristina.
6. El espejito de Alicia se rompió.

1. Pilar y Alicia están frente al espejo. 2. Es cierto. 3. La lima está un poco vieja. 4. El perfume se llama "Imaginación". 5. Fernando es el hermano de Cristina. 6. El espejito de Alicia se perdió.

C14 Actividad • Mientras tanto, ¿qué hacen los otros chicos? Answers will vary.

Look at each illustration and describe what the people are doing.

1.

2.

3.

4.

5.

6.

7.

8.

C15 Actividad • ¿Qué necesitas? For answers, see p. T138.

Say what these people need in order to do the following things.

MODELO   mirarse / tú   Para mirarte, necesitas un espejo.

1. limpiarse las uñas / nosotros
2. secarse el pelo / tú
3. cambiarse el color de los ojos / ella
4. peinarse / él
5. afeitarse / ellos

6. bañarse / yo
7. maquillarse / ustedes
8. cepillarse los dientes / tú y yo
9. cortarse el pelo / él

C16 Actividad • ¡A escribir!   Answers will vary.

You have been invited to a friend's home for a week. Make a list of the toiletries you need to take along.

C17 SE DICE ASÍ
Paying compliments

¡Qué linda estás hoy!	You look so cute today!
¡Qué vestido más elegante!	What an elegant dress!
¡Qué bien bailas!	You're such a good dancer!
¡Qué simpática eres!	You're so nice!
¡Qué guapo estás!	You look so handsome!
¡Estás a la última moda!	You look so fashionable!
¡Qué bien te queda!	That looks great on you!
¡Cuánto me alegro!	I'm so glad!
¡Qué alegría verte!	It's great to see you!
¡Qué bien luces!	You look great!

C18 Comprensión   For script, see p. T138–139.

Marilú and Rogelio are preparing for a party. You will hear a statement about a problem followed by three possible solutions. Choose the best solution and check the appropriate space on your answer sheet.

MODELO   Acabo de lavarme la cabeza.
        a. Busco el perfume.
        b. ¿Tienes el jabón?
        c. Necesito la secadora.

	0	1	2	3	4	5	6	7	8	9	10
a.		✓			✓	✓				✓	
b.				✓				✓			✓
c.	✓		✓			✓		✓			

ESTRUCTURAS ESENCIALES

The present indicative tense of **traer** *and* **oír**

traer	to bring
traigo	traemos
traes	traéis
trae	traen

oír	to hear
oigo	oímos
oyes	oís
oye	oyen

1. You have already learned that several verbs, like **traer,** add a **g** in the first person singular of the present indicative—for example, **tener: tengo; hacer: hago; venir: vengo; caer: caigo.** All other forms of the present indicative tense of these verbs are regular.

   Yo les **traigo** el perfume. *I bring you the perfume.*
   Rosita **se cae** en la nieve. *Rosita falls in the snow.*

2. The verb **oír** is irregular.

   ¿Oyes la música? *Do you hear the music?*
   No, no **oigo** nada. *No, I can't hear anything.*

C20 Actividad • ¿Cierto o falso?

Some statements are true, and others are not. Correct the false statements.

1. Si la botella de perfume se cae, se rompe.   Es cierto.
2. Primero viene el enjuague y después el champú.   Primero viene el champú y después el enjuague.
3. Tengo las lentes de contacto amarillas.   Tengo las lentes de contacto verdes.
4. Cuando vengo a la playa, traigo cremas para la piel.   Es cierto.
5. Pongo la cuchilla en la crema de afeitar.   Pongo la cuchilla en la maquinilla de afeitar.
6. Le traigo la pasta de dientes para bañarse.   Le traigo la pasta de dientes para limpiarse los dientes.

C21 Actividad • ¿Qué oyes?

After the picnic, your friends sit on the grass to rest. Many of them have radios. What are they listening to?

   MODELO: el señor Díaz / noticias   El señor Díaz oye las noticias.

1. Paco y Luis / música mexicana   Paco y Luis oyen música mexicana.
2. Yo / entrevista con un atleta   Yo oigo la entrevista con un atleta.
3. Adolfina / concierto de guitarra   Adolfina oye un concierto de guitarra.
4. Nosotros / juego de fútbol   Nosotros oímos el juego de fútbol.
5. Ustedes / el noticiero   Ustedes oyen el noticiero.
6. Tú / música popular   Tú oyes música popular.

C22 Actividad • ¡A escribir!   Answers will vary.

Make a list of ten things you do to prepare for a party. Include grooming and makeup.

C23 Actividad • Una dieta balanceada

There is a health fair at school. Your friends want to organize a picnic. Get together with a classmate and ask what people are bringing. Take turns answering, and add some details of your own.

MODELO — ¿Quién trae la fruta fresca? Mariana
— Mariana trae naranjas, fresas y melocotones.

Mariana

1. yo

2. Felipe

3. Cecilia

4. Rafael y María

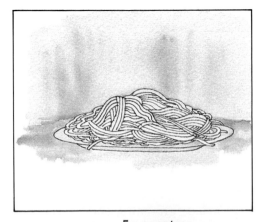

5. nosotros

6. tú

1. ¿Quién trae la ensalada? Yo traigo la ensalada.   2. ¿Quién trae el agua mineral? Felipe trae el agua mineral.   3. ¿Quién trae la sopa? Cecilia trae la sopa.   4. ¿Quién trae el pollo? Rafael y María traen el pollo.   5. ¿Quién trae los macarrones? Nosotros traemos los macarrones.   6. ¿Quién trae los trocitos de apio? Tú traes los trocitos de apio.

1   Tu cuerpo   Answers will vary.

Discuss with a classmate the ways in which both of you take care of your health. What time do you go to bed and wake up? Do you exercise, jog, or practice a sport frequently? How often do you brush your teeth and your hair? What do you eat or avoid eating? When do you weigh yourself?

2   Actividad • Cuando suena el despertador   Answers will vary.

Write a list of six things you do in the morning to get ready for school. Write them in the order you do them.

3   Actividad • ¿Me pongo contento o furioso?   Answers will vary.

Tell a classmate what makes you happy and what makes you angry. Take turns.

4 Actividad • En el mercado   Answers will vary.

When you go shopping, what do you and the members of your family buy that is nutritious?

5 Actividad • ¿Quién está enfermo?   Answers will vary.

Explain to a classmate five common excuses the members of your team give when they are absent.

6 Actividad • ¡Vamos a la tienda!

There are many products in the store, but what you are looking for is always in another department. For each numbered entry, find two articles that are usually found on the same shelf.

1. cuchillas   colorete   secadora   maquinilla de afeitar
2. polvo   talco   desodorante   cepillo
3. esmalte de uñas   peine   enjuague   lápiz labial
4. agua de colonia   perfume   pasta de dientes champú
5. maquinilla   jabón   base   maquillaje
6. tijerita   crema de afeitar espejo   lima

7 Dictado   For script, see p. T141.

Copy the following paragraph to prepare yourself for dictation.

El ____ a las ocho. Me bañé y ____ . Me miré en el espejo y ____
dos veces. Me vestí y me puse ____ . Llamé a Rafa por teléfono.
____ que tenía ____ , pero que iba a ir ____ . Miré el reloj.
Eran las ____ . Era tarde. Salí ____ .

Letters *ll* and *y*

1. In Spanish, **ll** is a letter by itself. The letter **ll** in Spanish has a sound similar to the English *y* in the word *yet.* Read and repeat the following words.

    sello   amarillo   toalla   cuello   rodilla   cepillar

2. The letter **y** is also pronounced like *y* in *yet* when used before a vowel. Read and repeat the following words and sentences.

    yo   playa   desayunar   ayudar   ayer   oye   ya   tuyo

    El auto amarillo iba por la calle.
    Oye, la toalla que tienes en el cuello no es tuya.
    Ayúdame a cepillar el caballo.
    Yo desayuno con Yeyo y Yara.

Letters p and t

1. The Spanish **p** is produced by bringing the lips together in a similar way you do to produce the English *p* sound, but without the puff of air that usually accompanies the English *p.*

    Pepe   popular   poco   peso
    peces   peor   pronto   posible

2. The Spanish *t* is pronounced by placing the tongue against the upper teeth. Again, there is no puff of air as in the English *t.*

    todo   tonto   ratón   tormenta
    tanto   tomar   tuyo   artículo

3. Compare these sounds:

    Pepe — *pep*   té — *tea*   tú — *two*   come — *come*

    Pepe es poco popular.
    ¡Tantos tontos toman té!
    Come un taco con pocas calorías.

Actividad • Práctica de pronunciación

Listen to the following sentences and repeat.

    Juanillo tiene las rodillas y los tobillos sucios.
    Ayer yo desayuné con Yolanda en la playa.
    Ponga el pie en el zapato para ver si es su talla.
    Toma la toronja entera que te quité esta tarde.
    Cuarenta calorías para comenzar no es mucho, ¿verdad?

¿LO SABES?

Let's review some important points you've learned in this unit.

SECTION A

Answers will vary.

Can you talk about your daily routine?
Say what you do to get ready for school every day, using reflexive constructions.

Do you know how to use the verbs *comprar, dormir, poner,* and *caer* in reflexive constructions?

Are you able to discuss how you keep in shape?
Say what you and three relatives or friends do to keep in shape.

Can you name most of the parts of the body?
Use them in sentences and use the articles correctly.

Can you talk about your emotions?
Say what makes you angry, happy, sick, and worried.

SECTION B

Answers will vary.

Can you talk about food and nutrition?
Discuss a balanced menu, things you should eat or should avoid in order to be healthy, and a diet to gain weight and another to lose weight.

Are you able to talk about your aches and pains when you are not feeling well?
Tell a classmate about your latest illnesses.

Can you ask about other people's health, express concern, and wish them well?
Ask four classmates how they feel. After they respond, express concern and wish them well.

Do you know how to use double negatives correctly?
Write five sentences with **nada, nadie, ningún, ninguna,** and **tampoco.**

Can you ask questions with *algo, alguien, algún,* and *algunas?*

SECTION C

Answers will vary.

Can you talk about personal care and grooming?
Make a list of five things you do when going to a party or a special date and five things you do every day before going to school.

When you receive an invitation, how can you decline courteously?
Explain why you cannot accept three invitations.

Can you talk about cosmetics and toiletries?
Mention ten beauty and grooming aids you use regularly.

Do you know how to pay compliments?
Think of five compliments you could give your date at the dance.

VOCABULARIO

SECTION A

aburrirse *to get bored*
acostar(se) (ue) *to lie down; to go to bed*
bañar(se) *to bathe (oneself)*
el bigote *moustache*
la boca *mouth*
el brazo *arm*
cansarse *to get tired*
la cara *face*
cepillar(se) *to brush*
la cintura *waist*
cortar(se) *to cut (oneself)*
el cuello *neck*
el cuerpo *body*
débil *weak*
el dedo de la mano *finger*
el dedo del pie *toe*
el despertador *alarm clock*
despertar(se) (ie) *to wake up*
los dientes *teeth*
divertirse (ie) *to have fun*
dormir (ue) *to fall asleep*
la energía *energy*
la espalda *back (of the body)*
la estrella de cine *movie star*
la frente *forehead*
el gimnasio *gym*
la gripe *flu*
el hombro *shoulder*
los labios *lips*
levantarse *to get up*
la lucha libre *wrestling*
la manera *way; manner*
mantenerse *to keep in shape*
mejorar *to improve*
la muñeca *wrist*
la nariz *nose*
el ojo *eye*
la oreja *ear*
el pelo *hair*
pesar(se) *to weigh (oneself)*
el pie *foot*
la pierna *leg*
ponerse *to put on; to wear*
ponerse furioso, -a *to get furious*
ponerse triste *to get sad*
preferir (ie) *to prefer*
preocupar(se) *to worry*
la rodilla *knee*
sano, -a *healthy*
sentirse (ie) *to feel*
el tobillo *ankle*
la uña *nail*
vestir (i) *to dress*
vestirse (i) *to get dressed*

SECTION B

el accidente *accident*
adecuado, -a *adequate*
adelgazar *to become thin; to lose weight*
alguien *someone*
algún (m.) *any; some*
el alimento *food*
el apio *celery*
la aspirina *aspirin*
aumentar de peso *to gain weight*
la caloría *calorie*
carne sin grasa *lean meat*
el catarro *head cold*
competir (i) *to compete*
¡cuánto me alegro! *I am so happy!*
¡cuida tu salud! *take care of your health!*
la dieta balanceada *balanced diet*
doler (ue) *to hurt; to ache*
el dolor de garganta *sore throat*
el dolor de estómago *stomach ache*
enfermar(se) *to become ill*
las espinacas *spinach*
el estómago *stomach*
los fideos *noodles*
la fiebre *fever*
fresco, a *fresh*
la garganta *throat*
la grasa *fat*
la mayoría de *the majority of*
la leche descremada *skim milk*
la libra *pound*
la limonada *lemonade*
los macarrones *macaroni*
el médico *doctor*
medio, -a *one half*
la moderación *moderation*
la multivitamina *multivitamin*
ninguno, -a *none*
o . . . o *either . . . or*
las palomitas de maíz *popcorn*
la porción *portion*
¿qué tienes? *what's wrong with you?*
quitarse *to take off*
la ración *portion*
recomendar (ie) *to recommend*
el régimen *diet plan*
roto, -a *broken*
la salud *health*
sentir(se) (ie) bien *to feel good*
sentir(se) (ie) mal *to feel bad*
tampoco *neither*
la toronja *grapefruit*
el trigo *wheat*

vacío, -a *empty*
el yogur *yogurt*
la zanahoria *carrot*

SECTION C

acordarse (ue) *to remember*
afeitar(se) *to shave*
el agua de colonia *cologne*
alegrarse *to get happy*
los artículos de tocador *toiletries*
la base *foundation (makeup)*
la botella *bottle*
el cepillo *brush*
el colorete *rouge; blush*
la crema de afeitar *shaving cream*
la cuchilla *razor blade*
el champú *shampoo*
el desodorante *deodorant*
enamorarse *to fall in love*
el enjuague *hair rinse*
el enjuague para la boca *mouthwash*
enfadarse *to get angry*
enojarse *to get angry*
el esmalte de uñas *nail polish*
el espejo *mirror*
el jabón *soap*
el lápiz labial *lipstick*
el lápiz para los ojos *eyeliner*
lavar(se) la cabeza *to wash one's hair*
la lente de contacto *contact lens*
la lima de uñas *nail file*
la loción *lotion*
el maquillaje *makeup*
maquillar(se) *to apply makeup*
la maquinilla de afeitar *razor*
oír *to hear*
olvidarse *to forget*
la pasta de dientes *toothpaste*
peinar(se) *to comb (one's hair)*
el peine *comb*
perder (ie) *to lose*
se perdió *it got lost*
el perfume *perfume*
pintar(se) *to apply makeup*
el polvo *powder*
preocupado, -a *worried*
preparar(se) *to get ready*
prestar(se) *to loan*
reír(se) *to laugh*
¡qué bien luces! *you look great!*
quizás *maybe; perhaps*
romper(se) *to break*
la secadora *hair dryer*
la suerte *luck*
el talco *dusting powder; talcum powder*
la tijera *scissors*

VAMOS A LEER

Antes de leer

1. You can often understand unknown words by identifying their endings and recognizing their similarities. Can you guess the meanings of the following words by using this strategy?

    exploradores   conquistadores   trabajadores   *explorers, conquistadors, and workers*

2. Many words that refer to science and technology are cognates. Can you find two of them in the reading selection?   **análisis** and **biólogo**

Preparación para la lectura

Answer the following questions before reading.

1. ¿Cuántas clases de papas conoces?   *Answers will vary.*
2. En muchas competencias de lucha libre, la dieta la noche anterior es una papa cocida. ¿Sabes si esa dieta es para aumentar de peso?   *No, da energía.*
3. ¿Sabes de dónde llegaron a Europa el maíz, el aguacate, los frijoles, los tomates, el chocolate, la vainilla y la piña?   *Llegaron de las Américas.*
4. Mira rápidamente la Lectura. Busca cinco palabras que no conoces, pero que puedes comprender porque tienen cognados en inglés.   *leyenda, diabólico, balcón, demostró, islas*
5. Si **congelar** quiere decir *to freeze*, ¿sabes qué quiere decir **descongelar**?   *to thaw*
6. ¿Puedes buscar rápidamente en la Lectura los nombres en español de dos países europeos?   *Inglaterra y Francia*
7. ¿Cuál crees que es el tema principal de esta Lectura?
    a. Los viajes de Cristóbal Colón
    b. La historia de la papa
    c. La papa es un alimento barato y nutritivo

¿TE GUSTAN LAS PAPAS FRITAS?

Cristóbal Colón nunca comió papas fritas. ¿Sabes por qué? Porque no había papas en esa época. Es decir, no había papas en Europa. No se conocían. Sólo había papas en la región de los Andes, en el Imperio Inca. Pero Colón nunca llegó hasta los Andes. Otros exploradores y conquistadores llegaron a esas montañas más tarde. Había allí una civilización sorprendente. El tesoro° más importante que los españoles encontraron no fue el oro ni la plata. Fue la humilde° papa.

Los incas tenían muchas variedades de papas. Primero, eran muy chiquitas°. Se cree que los indios ya cultivaban la papa por lo menos 750 años antes de Cristo. Seguramente tú piensas que las papas deshidratadas° son un invento de la tecnología moderna. Pues bien, parece que no.

Los incas tenían un sistema muy ingenioso. Dejaban las papas fuera de° la casa toda la noche para congelarlas°. A la mañana siguiente, con el calor del sol, las papas se descongelaban. Entonces, los incas, con los dedos de la mano, les extraían el agua (a veces también lo hacían con los pies, como se hace con las uvas para hacer vino). Despues molían° las papas y las convertían en harina.° De esta manera tenían comida todo el año.

---

tesoro *treasure*   **humilde** *humble*   **chiquitas** *very small*   **papas deshidratadas** *instant (dehydrated) potatoes*   **fuera de** *outside*   **congelarlas** *to freeze them*   **molían** *used to grind* **harina** *flour*

La papa también se llama **patata.** Papa es el nombre en quechua, que es el idioma de los incas. Cuando Cristóbal Colón llegó a la América, descubrió en las islas° del Caribe una papa dulce° que los españoles llamaron **batata.** Ésta se hizo° popular. Cuando llegó la papa a Europa, por unos años había confusión y la llamaron **patata.** Sin embargo en la América todavía se usa el nombre de papa que le dieron los incas.

Sir Walter Raleigh llevó la papa a Irlanda para combatir el hambre. Una de las muchas leyendas de la papa cuenta que cuando él le llevó unas papas a la reina Isabel de Inglaterra°, ella dijo que eran horribles . . . Como eran algo nuevo que nadie conocía, ¡la reina comió las hojas° de la planta, no las papas!

La papa no se hizo popular. En Escocia° se dijo que era un alimento diabólico° porque la Biblia no la menciona. Otros países, como Francia, la consideraron venenosa°.

En 1750, el rey Federico el Grande ordenó el cultivo de la papa en su reino°. Tuvo que salir al balcón° de su palacio comiendo papas para convencer al pueblo° de que no eran malas para la salud. Algo similar ocurrió cien años después en Inglaterra con el tomate, otro producto del Nuevo Mundo.

La ciencia entonces tuvo que salir en defensa de° la papa. Un biólogo francés, llamado Parmentier, hizo un análisis químico y demostró° que la papa era rica en nutrición. Como era fácil de cultivar, podía ayudar a combatir el hambre en Europa. El biólogo francés no inventó las papas fritas. En realidad dicen que las papas fritas no son francesas sino belgas°. Pero allí no se comen con salsa de tomate. ¿Sabes con qué se comen? ¡Con mayonesa!

Papas Fritas

islas *islands*	**dulce** *sweet*	**se hizo** *became*	**Inglaterra** *England*	
hojas *leaves*	**Escocia** *Scotland*	**diabólico** *diabolic*		
venenosa *poisonous*	**reino** *kingdom*	**balcón** *balcony*		
al pueblo *people*	**salir en defensa de** *to go out in the defense of*			
demostró *demonstrated*	**belgas** *from Belgium*			

Así es que la humilde papa de los incas tuvo la oportunidad de cambiar para muchos el curso de la historia. La revolución industrial creó° muchas ciudades con grandes masas de trabajadores. La papa resolvió el problema de alimentar al pueblo de una manera barata y nutritiva. En 1845, cuando una enfermedad° atacó las papas en Irlanda, había tanta hambre que miles° de hombres y mujeres salieron del país en busca de una vida mejor. ¿Y sabes adónde emigraron? A los Estados Unidos.

Cuando comes una hamburguesa con unas sabrosas papas fritas, piensa en esta historia y cuéntasela a tus amigos.

creó   *created*   **enfermedad**   *disease*   **miles**   *thousands*

Actividad • Preguntas y respuestas For answers, see p. T143.

Use the information in the reading selection to answer the following questions.

1. ¿Por qué Cristóbal Colón nunca comió papas fritas?
2. ¿Dónde estaba el Imperio Inca?
3. ¿Quiénes cultivaban las papas?
4. ¿Cómo hacían los incas papas deshidratadas?
5. ¿Dónde encontraron los españoles las batatas o papas dulces?
6. ¿Qué otro producto del Nuevo Mundo se menciona en la Lectura?
7. ¿Para qué llevó Sir Walter Raleigh la papa a Irlanda?
8. ¿Por qué no le gustaron las papas a la reina?
9. ¿Por qué no se hizo popular la papa en Escocia?
10. ¿Quién descubrió que la papa era rica en nutrición?
11. ¿Dónde se inventaron las papas fritas y cómo se comen allí?
12. ¿Qué gran problema resolvió la papa?

Actividad • Defensores de la papa

Explain what these people did for the potato.

- Colón
- los conquistadores
- los indios suramericanos
- Parmentier
- Sir Walter Raleigh
- la reina Isabel
- Federico el Grande

1. Colón descubrió una papa dulce en el Caribe llamada batata. 2. Los conquistadores llegaron a los Andes donde se cultivaba la papa. 3. Los indios suramericanos cultivaban la papa y tenían muchas variedades. 4. Parmentier fue un biólogo francés que descubrió el valor nutritivo de la papa. 5. Sir Walter Raleigh llevó la papa a Irlanda. 6. La reina Isabel comió las hojas de la planta y no las papas. 7. Federico el Grande tuvo que salir al balcón de su palacio comiendo papas para convencer al pueblo de que no eran malas para la salud.

Actividad • Familia de palabras

Which words from the same family as the ones listed below can you find in the reading selection?

1. sorpresa — sorprendente
2. enfermo — enfermedad
3. defender — defensa
4. trabajar — trabajadores
5. rey — reina
6. química — químico
7. alimento — alimentar
8. nutrición — nutritiva

UNIDAD 7 La tecnología y el progreso
Scope and Sequence

	BASIC MATERIAL	COMMUNICATIVE FUNCTIONS
SECTION A	Cómo usar la computadora (A1)	**Expressing feelings and emotions** • Expressing displeasure **Persuading** • Directing others to do something • Asking for help
SECTION B	El mundo del futuro (B1)	**Persuading** • Giving advice using proverbs **Exchanging information** • Expressing time factors
SECTION C	¿Qué haríamos sin la tecnología? (C1) ¿Qué haríamos con la tecnología del futuro? (C15) Una planta nuclear (C22)	**Expressing attitudes and opinions** • Expressing logical conclusions **Persuading** • Requesting favors or asking for help
TRY YOUR SKILLS	El consejo estudiantil Dictado	

■ **Pronunciación** (letters ñ, h, and ch)
■ **¿Lo sabes?**   ■ **Vocabulario**

VAMOS A LEER	**Un mundo diferente** (a look at modern technology)

WRITING   A variety of controlled and open-ended writing activities appear in the Pupil's Edition. The Teacher's Notes identify other activities suitable for writing practice.

COOPERATIVE LEARNING   Many of the activities in the Pupil's Edition lend themselves to cooperative learning. The Teacher's Notes explain some of the many instances where this teaching strategy can be particularly effective. For guidelines on how to use cooperative learning, see page T13.

GRAMMAR	CULTURE	RE-ENTRY
Affirmative familiar commands: **tú** form (A7) Irregular verbs in the familiar **tú** command (A11) Position of pronouns with affirmative **tú** commands (A15)	A Mexican astronaut Technology and change An important radio telescope in Arecibo, Puerto Rico	The verbs **apretar, encender,** and **traer**
The future tense (B5) Irregular verbs in the future tense (B12)	Higher education in Latin America and Spain The educational system in Chile	Names of professions and trades
The Spanish conditional tense (C6) Irregular verbs in the conditional tense (C9)	New discoveries in technology Observatories in Latin America Spanish-speaking Nobel Prize winners	Future tense forms of irregular verbs Spanish names of foods

Recombining communicative functions, grammar, and vocabulary

Reading for practice and pleasure

Section A Diagram of a computer
Section B Map of Chile, poster board, strips of paper, magazines
Section C Pictures of modes of transportation, cue cards for C16, pictures of food, signs for C23
Try Your Skills Poster board

Manual de actividades, Unit 7
Manual de ejercicios, Unit 7
Unit 7 Cassettes
Transparencies 17–19
Quizzes 16–18
Unit 7 Test

SECTION

A

OBJECTIVES **To express feelings and emotions:** express displeasure; **to persuade:** direct others to do something, ask for help

CULTURAL BACKGROUND   Point out the photograph on page 231 of Rodolfo Neri Vela to the students. Explain that Rodolfo Neri Vela was born in 1952 in Chilpancingo, Mexico. He took the master's program in science at the University of Essex in England, where he specialized in telecommunications systems. He received a doctoral degree in electromagnetic radiation from the University of Birmingham, England. Neri was chosen by the Mexican government to deploy the Morelos communication satellite into space. In 1986, Neri joined the crew of NASA's Shuttle Mission 61B as a payload specialist. He became the first Spanish American to travel into space. You may also wish to tell the students that the large, beautiful photograph on page 230 is of the planetarium located in Buenos Aires, Argentina.

MOTIVATING ACTIVITY   Divide the class into groups of two or three. Write the word **tecnología** on the board or a transparency. Tell the students that they must see how many words they can derive from that word in five minutes. Have one person in each group write down the words. The following are a few of the words they will find: **técnico, técnicamente, técnica, tecnicismo.**

A1   # Cómo usar la computadora

When presenting the dialog in class, insist on a normal delivery, approximating that of a native speaker as much as possible. You may wish to first model each exchange and then call for choral and individual repetition. After the students have practiced the dialog once, you may ask them to listen again and to repeat the exchanges with their books closed in order to help their auditory memory. Try to alternate choral and individual repetition to avoid boredom. For cooperative learning, form groups of two or three and have each group role-play the dialog.

   In order to keep a fast tempo and maximum student attention, do not interrupt to explain grammar or vocabulary items once you start reading the dialog. Explanations should be given either before or after the presentation. Concentrate on the specific objectives of the activity in progress, which are mainly to develop oral production in terms of accurate pronunciation, stress, and intonation, and to develop an auditory memory in the foreign language.

   After presenting the dialog, introduce several new vocabulary items relating to computers, such as **impresor, pantalla, base de datos, disquete,** and **teclear.** Use a computer or a diagram of a computer to introduce the new words. You may wish to explain that the word **computadora** is used in most Spanish-American countries. In Spain and in a few other Spanish-speaking countries, the word **ordenador** is also used. Point out that **informática** is the equivalent of *computer sciences.* You may also add that many Spanish words used in relation to computer science are derived from English.

A2   ## Actividad • Preguntas y respuestas

You may wish to do this activity orally in class with books closed.

CHALLENGE   Ask the students the following questions based on the realia on pages 232 and 233.
   Referring to the realia at the upper right of page 232, ask:

   1. ¿Qué te descubre la Academia Colón?
   2. ¿Qué cursos ofrece?
   3. ¿Cómo son los grupos?

   4. ¿Cómo son los horarios?
   5. ¿Cuántas academias hay?

Referring to the realia at the lower right on page 232, you may ask:

   1. ¿Qué cursos ofrecen?
   2. ¿A qué edad se puede comenzar?
   3. ¿Es necesario tener transporte?

Referring to the realia on page 233 on the upper left side, ask:

   1. ¿Cuánto cuestan los cursos de un día?
   2. ¿A qué hora empiezan y a qué hora terminan?
   3. ¿Qué cursos ofrecen?

A3   Sabes que . . .

You may wish to tell the students about the radio telescope located in
Arecibo, Puerto Rico, which is one of the world's largest and most important
radio telescopes. Built in 1963, it is considered to be the radio telescope that
has the greatest range into space. Cables support the 500-foot antenna above
the reflector, which is 1,000 feet in diameter.

A4   SE DICE ASÍ

Read aloud the expressions in the box to the class. Have the students create
exchanges that contain at least one of the expressions. You may also wish to
add several responses that the students may include in their dialogs, such as
¡Pobrecita!, Comprendo muy bien, Estoy en las mismas, and **De acuerdo.**
Then call on pairs to role-play the original dialogs in class.

A5   Actividad • ¿Qué me cuentas?

For cooperative learning, form groups of two or three students to discuss
the questions. Remind the students to take notes in order to share the
information with the class at a later date. You may wish to write several of
the students' comments on the board or a transparency to aid comprehension
and to encourage further discussion.

A6   Comprensión

You will hear ten short exchanges. If the second speaker gives good
advice, check **¡qué bueno!** on your answer sheet. If not, check **¡qué horror!**
For example, you will hear: **Esta computadora me está volviendo loco.** You
will also hear the response: **Chico, ten un poco de paciencia.** You check
¡qué bueno!, since the advice is good.

   1. —No sé nada de este vocabulario.
      —Entonces escucha una vez más este casete.   *¡qué bueno!*
   2. —¡Ay, cómo me duelen los ojos!
      —¿Por qué no lees una revista?   *¡qué horror!*
   3. —Mamá, me duele el estómago.
      —Pues, come más despacio, niño.   *¡qué bueno!*
   4. —No sé qué hacer, Pepe. Tengo cinco exámenes esta semana.
      —Amigo, toma las cosas con calma.   *¡qué bueno!*
   5. —Señor Fernández, la semana pasada me rompí la pierna.
      —Pues, camina media hora todos los días.   *¡qué horror!*
   6. —Este cuarto es un desastre. ¡Qué sucio!
      —¡Limpia el cuarto ahora!   *¡qué bueno!*

7. —Tengo mucho frío.
   —Entonces, abre la ventana.   *¡qué horror!*
8. —Necesito leer cien páginas esta noche.
   —Apaga la televisión y empieza a leer.   *¡qué bueno!*
9. —Mi amiga Marisol sólo habla español.
   —Pues, háblale en inglés.   *¡qué horror!*
10. —Martín, ayúdame a preparar la cena.
    —Pues, saca la basura.   *¡qué horror!*

Now check your answers. *Read each exchange again and give the correct answer.*

A 7   ESTRUCTURAS ESENCIALES

To practice the familiar commands, use TPR (Total Physical Response). Call on students to carry out the following or similar instructions in class. Use only vocabulary and commands that the students are familiar with.

Abre el libro.
Cierra la puerta.
Saca una hoja de papel.
Abre la ventana.

Write the model sentences on the board. Call on the students to identify the verbs in each sentence and explain how the familiar commands are formed. Then have them open their books to read the information in the chart to confirm whether their observations were correct.

A 8   Actividad • La mandamás

Ask the students to work in pairs to complete the activity. For writing practice, have them write complete sentences. Review the activity by calling on individuals to read the sentences aloud.

A 9   Actividad • El abuelo

Allow the students to complete this activity orally or in writing. Review with the entire class.

CHALLENGE   Ask the students to make additional lists of good advice for better health and a long life. Write the suggestions on the board.

ANSWERS:
1. Toma las cosas con paciencia.
2. Cena temprano todas las noches.
3. Come poco y lentamente.
4. Bebe solamente agua o jugo de frutas variadas.
5. Practica algún deporte.
6. Camina veinte minutos todos los días.
7. Trabaja bien.
8. Descansa los fines de semana.

A 10   Actividad • Pidiendo permiso

CHALLENGE   Allow the students to write questions that they will use in class to ask permission. Have them move about the room asking permission of other students, who should respond with a command form. As a follow-up activity, you may wish to play **Simón dice.**

A 11 ESTRUCTURAS ESENCIALES

Present the irregular command forms by writing the infinitives of the verbs on the board or a transparency. Present two or three verbs at a time. Give the command form as you underline or point to the infinitive. Have each student give the same or a slightly altered command to another student. For example:

> Di tu nombre.
> Di tu dirección.
> Di el nombre de tu mejor amigo.

Ask the students to write the infinitives and the command forms in the verb section of their notebooks.

A 12 Actividad • ¡Órdenes, órdenes y más órdenes!

Have each student complete the activity with a partner. Encourage the students to add original commands, using the irregular verbs from A11.

ANSWERS:
1. —Di dónde vas a comprar la computadora.
   —Sí, te digo dónde voy a comprar la computadora.
2. —Ve a comprarla ahora.
   —Sí, voy a comprarla ahora.
3. —Ten cuidado de no perder el dinero.
   —Sí, tengo cuidado de no perder el dinero.
4. —Sé amable con el dependiente.
   —Sí, soy amable con el dependiente.
5. —Sal de la tienda temprano.
   —Sí, salgo de la tienda temprano.
6. —Ven a casa inmediatamente.
   —Sí, voy a casa inmediatamente.
7. —Pon la computadora en tu cuarto.
   —Sí, pongo la computadora en mi cuarto.
8. —Haz tu tarea en la computadora.
   —Sí, hago la tarea en la computadora.

A 13 Actividad • Cómo usar la computadora

After the students have completed the activity in writing, call on individuals to read aloud a command. Then have each student exchange papers with a partner to correct the work. You may also use this activity as a quiz.

A 14 Actividad • Ven a mi casa

Have the students work in pairs. Tell them to use the verbs in the box to explain to each other where they live and how they get from their house to the nearest computer store. One partner can draw a map while the other partner gives the directions.

A 15 ESTRUCTURAS ESENCIALES

Present the pronouns and their positions by acting out commands with direct objects, using the students' real names and classroom situations.

> (*Name of student*), tráeme el libro.
> (*Name of student*), pon los lápices en la mesa.
> (*Name of student*), abre tu cuaderno.

Repeat each command, exchanging the direct object for a pronoun.

> Tráeme el libro. Tráemelo.
> Pon los lápices en la mesa. Ponlos en la mesa.
> Abre tu cuaderno. Ábrelo.

Write on the board the following or a similar list of common verbs with direct objects. Ask the students to give the commands with the pronouns attached.

> Escribe tu nombre.
> Abre la ventana.
> Compra el libro.
> Haz la tarea.
> Apaga la luz.
> Juega al básquetbol.

SLOWER-PACED LEARNING   Write the phrases on the board or a transparency. Ask the students to write the commands with the pronouns attached. You may wish to explain that if there is more than one syllable in the verb, it is necessary to write an accent over the second-to-last syllable before adding the pronoun.

A 16   Actividad • El invitado

CHALLENGE   Have the students expand on the activity. Have pairs of students create impromptu dialogs using command forms and pronouns. They may wish to present the dialogs to the class.

A 17   Actividad • El instructor de computadoras

Before completing this activity, you may wish to re-enter several verbs, such as **apretar, encender,** and **traer.** Ask each student to work with a partner to complete the activity.

A 18   Actividad • Charla

For cooperative learning, form groups of three or four students to discuss computers. Each group should select a speaker to represent the group.

A 19   Actividad • ¡A conversar!

Have each student work with a partner. Tell the students to take turns discussing their problems and giving advice. Then have each pair present an impromptu dialog. Remind them to use **tú** commands.

SECTION B

OBJECTIVES   To persuade: give advice using proverbs; **to exchange information:** express time factors

CULTURAL BACKGROUND   Chile's tradition for excellence in the educational field is one that dates back many years. Chile is, for example, considered the first Spanish American nation to have granted degrees in law and medicine to women during the 1880's. In modern times, Chile's educational system has been noted as one of the most outstanding in Spanish America. This is evident by its literacy rate, which exceeds ninety percent in the urban areas and which is almost eighty percent in the rural sectors. There are four levels of educational instruction: preschool, basic, middle, and superior—equivalent to kindergarten, primary, secondary, and college in the United States. Many Chilean schools, especially private schools, offer bilingual education, generally in English and Spanish.

MOTIVATING ACTIVITY Allow pairs of students to discuss their future plans using **ir + a +** *infinitive.* If the students do not know what they plan to do in the future, let them express what their interests are. You may wish to write the names of several professions on the board for reference during the discussion.

B1   El mundo del futuro

Locate Chile and its capital, Santiago, on the map. Play the cassette or read the interviews aloud as the students read along in their books. Insist on a normal delivery, approximating that of a native speaker. Call for choral and individual repetition, alternating them to avoid boredom. After you have gone over the interviews once, you may have the students listen and repeat again, this time with books closed. Now call on volunteers to read the interviews aloud. Personalize the information in the interviews by asking the students what they plan to do after graduation from high school. Then ask the students to express their opinions about the future plans of the students that are presented in the book. Ask them to compare their goals with those of the students from Chile, and to point out the similarities and differences.

B2   Actividad • Preguntas y respuestas

SLOWER-PACED LEARNING Have the students refer to the interview in B1 to answer the questions. Call on volunteers to read the answers aloud.

B3   Sabes que . . .

Students in Spanish America have several choices after completing secondary school. Depending on their means or goals, they may try to find a job immediately, or they may enroll in a vocational program, a technological school, or a university to complete a professional degree. The majority of students try to enroll in a school near their home, since they will be living at home. If there are no vocational or technological schools or universities in their hometown, they will go to another town and live in a boarding house while attending school, because most higher-learning institutions in Spanish America do not have dormitories. You may wish to mention that the majority of the public schools in Spanish America and Spain are free, and most universities and colleges only charge a minimal fee.

B4   SE DICE ASÍ

Have the students select their favorite proverbs, or have them create their own. Ask them to write the proverbs on poster board and illustrate them any way they wish. Then ask each student to explain why he or she chose the proverb. Display the posters in class.

B5   ESTRUCTURAS ESENCIALES

Present the future tense forms. Write the verb forms on the board and ask the students to read the explanation in the book to confirm their observations. Point out that in Spanish **ir + a +** *infinitive* or the present tense used with a time expression are commonly used to refer to future actions.

> Voy a ir a la playa el domingo.
> Tengo clase esta tarde.

You may wish to add that in Spanish the future tense is generally used for emphatic contexts or for future plans, predictions, or resolutions. Stress that all forms of the future tense are accented, with the exception of the **nosotros** form. Review the **Atención** and contrast the English and Spanish examples, stressing that the Spanish future tense is not used to express willingness.

B 6   Comprensión

You will hear ten conversational exchanges. If the second statement is a logical conclusion to the first, check **lógico** on your answer sheet. If it is not, check **ilógico.** For example, you will hear: **A José le encantan las computadoras.** You will also hear the response: **José estudiará informática en la universidad.** You check **lógico** because it is a logical conclusion.

1. —Anita toca muy bien el piano.
   —Anita será una pianista famosa en el año 2000. *lógico*
2. —Mamá invitó a diez personas a cenar el domingo.
   —Mamá comprará mucha ropa en el almacén. *ilógico*
3. —Mi hermano estudia tres idiomas.
   —Tu hermano será intérprete. *lógico*
4. —A Carmen le gusta trabajar con los niños.
   —Carmen será secretaria. *ilógico*
5. —Mamá sabe que todos tenemos mucha hambre hoy.
   —Mamá cocinará algo delicioso para la cena. *lógico*
6. —Acabamos de cenar y lavar los platos.
   —Entonces comeremos el postre. *ilógico*
7. —Papá, llegaron los Hernández de visita.
   —Pues, les prestaremos el abrigo. *ilógico*
8. —Vamos a tener un picnic mañana, ¿no?
   —Sí, y tu hermana preparará unos bocadillos. *lógico*
9. —Estamos estudiando la séptima lección.
   —Pronto empezaremos la segunda lección. *ilógico*
10. —Mario recibió cinco cartas hoy.
    —Las contestará muy pronto. *lógico*

Now check your answers. *Read each statement again and give the correct answer.*

B 7   Actividad • La fiesta

As a variation, call out a name from the list and have the students suggest a task from the box for that person. To personalize the activity you may call out some of the students' names.

B 8   Actividad • A completar

Have each student choose a partner. Have the partners take turns reading each sentence aloud and supplying the missing preterit and future tense forms of the verbs in parentheses.

B 9 ## Actividad • Dentro de diez años . . .

This activity uses the future tense to refer to future plans or predictions. Ask the students to work in pairs or in groups of three to discuss what their lives will be like in ten years. Ask each student to take notes on his or her partner's comments. Discuss the results with the class, encouraging participation from everyone.

CHALLENGE   You may wish to ask the students to write a composition, outlining what they will be doing after college.

B 10 ## SE DICE ASÍ

Write the expressions on the board and read them aloud as the students follow along in their books. Give an example using each expression, such as **Miguel hizo la tarea en un abrir y cerrar de ojos.** You may also ask the students questions, such as **¿Juegas al tenis?** Elicit the response: **Juego a menudo** or **Juego de vez en cuando.** Ask the students to write the expressions in their notebooks.

B 11 ## Actividad • Charla

Have each student talk to a partner, using the questions as a guide. Ask each student to take notes on what his or her partner said. Tell the students to be prepared to report their findings to the class.

B 12 ## ESTRUCTURAS ESENCIALES

Use the same procedure as presented in B5 on pages T151 and T152. Introduce only two or three verbs at a time. Ask the students to write them in the verb section of their notebooks.

B 13 ## Actividad • El profesor Recio

CHALLENGE   Prepare a handout of the activity to use for dictation of the sentences. Have the students fill in the appropriate verb forms. Then have each student exchange papers with a partner to correct the sentences. As a homework assignment, ask the students to write ten original sentences, using the new verb forms and giving their predictions for the future.

B 14 ## Actividad • El fin de semana

Write each student's name on a small strip of paper. Give each student a strip of paper and have him or her pair up with the person indicated. Tell each pair to discuss and write down their plans for the weekend. Call on volunteers to read the plans aloud to the class.

B 15 ## Actividad • Combinación

ANSWERS:
Una secretaria escribirá muchas cartas.
Un cocinero preparará una paella muy sabrosa.
Un dependiente ayudará a los clientes.
Una ingeniera construirá un transbordador espacial.
Una profesora explicará la lección.
Un médico atenderá a personas enfermas.
Una guía de turistas irá en una excursión.

After the students have completed the activity, form cooperative learning groups of three or four and assign an ad to each group. Each group should study its ad and explain the contents to the class. They may use the vocabulary in the Reference section of their books and a dictionary to identify any unfamiliar words. Take into account the level of complexity when assigning the ads. They are listed here in order of complexity, starting with the most difficult: **médico, secretaria ejecutiva, ingeniero electrónico, profesores(as), ayudantes de cocina.**

B 16   Actividad • Expresa tu opinión

Allow the students time to review the questions and to form their own opinions. Tell them to prepare for a class discussion. Call on individuals to express their opinions.

CHALLENGE   Ask the students to research the discovery made by scientists in Chile of Supernova 1987A. Have them discuss how modern technology made this discovery possible.

B 17   Actividad • ¡A escribir!

This activity uses the future tense to express plans and resolutions. It may be completed in class or at home. Have the students write complete sentences using the future tense. You may wish to call on volunteers to write their resolutions on the board or a transparency.

B 18   Actividad • El reportero

Re-enter the names of trades and professions. Then divide the class into groups of three or four students. Each student will take a turn acting as the reporter. The "reporter" should ask: **¿Qué serás en el futuro?** The other students should respond by stating the name of a profession. You may wish to take a poll from the groups to identify the most popular profession.

B 19   Actividad • ¿Qué crees tú?

Ask each student to choose a partner to complete the questionnaire. Remind the students to use the future tense in their answers. Have each student take notes on what his or her partner said. Then have a class discussion to compare the answers.

B 20   Actividad • Charlemos

CHALLENGE   Have the students cut out magazine pictures that illustrate what they think they might be doing in five years. Each student should make a collage and take notes, using the questions as a guide. Call on each student to explain his or her collage to the class. For example, a student may cut out a picture of Plácido Domingo and say: **Dentro de cinco años seré cantante.** Encourage the other students to ask questions of each person presenting his or her collage.

B 21   Actividad • ¡A escribir y a conversar!

Assign this activity for homework. Suggest that the students use their answers to the questions in B20 as a guide. For oral practice, have them read their compositions aloud.

SECTION C

OBJECTIVES To express attitudes and opinions: express logical conclusions; **to persuade:** request favors or ask for help

CULTURAL BACKGROUND   There are a number of important observatories and telescopes in Spanish America. It was at Las Campanas Observatory in northern Chile that the exploding star, Supernova 1987A, was discovered. The largest reflecting optical telescope in the Southern Hemisphere is located at the Cerro Tololo Observatory in La Serena, Chile. The telescope was used by astronomers to take the first photographs of 47 Tucanae, one of the brightest masses of stars known to man. Other important observatories in Spanish America are located in Bosque Alegre, Argentina; Baja California, México; and Cerro La Silla, Chile.

MOTIVATING ACTIVITY   Write a list of professions and trades on the board. Ask the students to talk about the qualifications for each item, such as schooling, interests, and skills.

médico	plomero
programador de	mecánico
computadoras	secretaria
contador	dentista
veterinario	profesor

Have the students use the future tense when discussing the professions and trades. For example, they may say: **Para ser mecánico, estudiaré matemáticas.**

C1   ¿Qué haríamos sin la tecnología?

Before presenting the selection, introduce the new vocabulary. Write the cognates **campo de la medicina, curar,** and **industria** on the board, and ask the students to identify their meanings. Then write the words **viaje, viajero, agencia de viajes,** and **cheques de viajero** on the board. Ask the students to define them and explain that **viajar** is a verb. Have them guess its meaning. Finally, point out that **fabricar** is a false cognate. Use the word in a sentence that illustrates its meaning, such as **La compañía Reebok fabrica zapatos de tenis.**

Draw the students' attention to the title of the selection, and encourage them to guess the meaning and the tense of the verb. You may wish to present the **yo** form of the conditional tense. Explain that the verbs that are irregular in the future tense have the same stem as those in the conditional tense. Play the cassette or read the selection aloud. Discuss each caption as you read. Ask the students to compare the information in the selection with situations that are common today. You may also have them use magazine pictures to compare past and present modes of travel.

SLOWER-PACED LEARNING   You may wish to prepare a handout of the selection with verbs and other words deleted. Dictate the material to the students and ask them to fill in the blanks. For correction, allow each student to exchange papers with a partner.

C2   Actividad • ¡A escoger!

SLOWER-PACED LEARNING   Have the students work in pairs to choose the option that best completes the sentence. They may refer to the selection in C1 if they have difficulty. They should first complete the activity orally and then in writing.

C3 Sabes que . . .

Among the scientists who have won the Nobel Prize, three Spanish-speaking men can be noted. Bernardo Alberto Houssay, an Argentinian physiologist, was the first Spanish American to receive the Nobel Prize in a scientific field. Houssay earned the Nobel Prize in medicine and physiology in 1947 for his demonstration of the complex interlocking of hormonal effects. Severo Ochoa, a Spanish-speaking biologist, became the first scientist to produce RNA in the laboratory. In 1959 Ochoa won the Nobel Prize for medicine and physiology for his outstanding discoveries in the field of RNA research. Luis W. Álvarez, a Mexican American, won the Nobel Prize for Physics in 1968 for his studies and discoveries about molecules.

C4 Comprensión

Your principal is discussing the plans for your school and expresses some problems. Each problem will be followed by three possible solutions suggested by different people. Choose the most appropriate solution and place a check in the corresponding box on your answer sheet. For example, you will hear: **El colegio es muy viejo.** You will also hear the responses: (a) **Buscaría nuevos profesores.** (b) **Construiría un colegio nuevo.** (c) **Gastaría más dinero en deportes.** You check **b** because it is the most appropriate solution.

1. Pocos estudiantes comen en la cafetería.
   a. Los estudiantes podrían comer fuera.
   b. Los cocineros deberían preparar mejores comidas. (√)
   c. Cerraría la cafetería.
2. Los estudiantes no llegan a tiempo al colegio.
   a. Los estudiantes tendrían que llegar más temprano. (√)
   b. Cambiaría los relojes.
   c. Compraría más libros y mapas.
3. La última vez que compramos libros fue en 1975.
   a. Pediría libros nuevos. (√)
   b. Vendería libros nuevos.
   c. Compraría libros viejos.
4. No hay mucho interés en los deportes.
   a. Trataría de crear entusiasmo entre los estudiantes. (√)
   b. Buscaría un equipo de fútbol.
   c. Compraría uniformes nuevos.
5. La tecnología es muy importante para los estudiantes de hoy.
   a. Prestaría más atención a los estudiantes.
   b. Compraría más computadoras. (√)
   c. Mandaría muchas cartas de recomendación.
6. Los administradores no saben lo que ocurre en las clases.
   a. Saldría del colegio con frecuencia.
   b. Visitarían las clases con frecuencia. (√)
   c. Vería más televisión.
7. Los libros de la biblioteca son viejos. Están en malas condiciones.
   a. Seleccionaría nuevos libros. (√)
   b. Pondría a más estudiantes a estudiar en la biblioteca.
   c. Permitiría más juegos en la biblioteca.
8. La clase de español quiere hacer un viaje a México.
   a. Hablaría con la Oficina de Turismo del Ecuador.
   b. Buscaría un agente de viajes para arreglar el viaje. (√)
   c. Diría que no es necesario hablar español.

9. Las clases son muy grandes.
  a. Pondría más estudiantes en cada clase.
  b. Compraría más mesas para estudiantes.
  c. Pondría un límite al número de estudiantes en cada clase.   (√)
10. Muchos estudiantes quieren estudiar idiomas.
  a. Buscaría más profesores.   (√)
  b. Vendería los libros viejos.
  c. Compraría un edificio más grande.

Now check your answers. *Read each statement and the responses again and give the correct answer.*

SLOWER-PACED LEARNING   You may wish to do the listening comprehension exercise after C6, **Estructuras esenciales.**

C5   ## SE DICE ASÍ

Have the students complete this activity with books closed. Write the expressions on the board. Review the meanings with the students. As a homework assignment, allow them to write two original sentences for each expression. Review the sentences on the board or a transparency the following day.

C6   ## ESTRUCTURAS ESENCIALES

Present the **yo** form of the conditional tense with the students. You may wish to begin a conversation by writing the following sentence on the board: **Si yo tuviera un millón de dólares, yo....** Explain the meaning of the fragment, and call on each student to complete the sentence using a verb in the conditional tense. Present all the verb forms by asking the students questions, such as **¿Qué comprarían ustedes?** or **José iría a Acapulco de vacaciones, ¿dónde irían María y Mario?** Explain that the conditional tense corresponds to *would* + *verb* in English. Review the explanations in the book, stressing that a written accent is required on the **i** of every verb form.

C7   ## Actividad • ¿Qué haríamos?

Have the students complete the activity orally in pairs. For writing practice, have them write original sentences using the verbs in parentheses.

  ANSWERS:
  1. Isabel estudiaría más cursos de matemáticas.
  2. María Elena y Matilde tomarían una clase de programación.
  3. Jaime le pediría una carta al profesor.
  4. Mi hermano sacaría mejores notas que antes en todos sus cursos.
  5. Leonardo hablaría con el secretario de la escuela.
  6. Sarita trataría de ir a la universidad para pedir información.
  7. Ricardo y Roberto prestarían más atención en clase.
  8. Además de español, Eugenio aprendería otro idioma.

C8   ## Actividad • Mis excusas para el sábado

For cooperative learning, ask the students to form groups of three to complete the activity. For oral practice, have each group present an impromptu dialog. Encourage the students to be as imaginative as possible in creating their excuses.

C9   ## ESTRUCTURAS ESENCIALES

Before presenting the irregular verbs in the conditional tense, you may wish to re-enter the same verbs in the future tense. Stress that the stems will remain the same in the conditional tense. Review three or four verbs at a time, breaking for conventional practice between presentations. Review the explanation and the information in the chart. For additional practice, you may wish to assign an oral presentation to the class. Have the students speak about designing their own houses or rooms using the conditional tense. Give the students a model sentence, such as **Mi casa ideal tendría seis piscinas.** Suggest a minimum of eight sentences in the conditional tense. The students may also wish to use magazine pictures in their presentations.

C 10   Actividad • Charlemos un poco

Have pairs of students take turns asking and answering the questions. Encourage them to take notes on responses to share with another classmate.

C 11   Actividad • La mala suerte de Eugenio

Ask the students to complete the paragraph with the correct forms of the verbs in the conditional tense. When finished, ask them to read the paragraph again for comprehension.

As a variation, you may wish to write the paragraph on the board with the verb forms deleted. Dictate the paragraph to the students, allowing them to complete the sentences with the correct forms of the verbs.

SLOWER-PACED LEARNING   To check comprehension, ask the following questions.

1. ¿Adónde iba Eugenio?
2. ¿Qué le dijo el empleado a Eugenio?
3. ¿A qué hora llegó el avión?
4. ¿Qué hizo al llegar a Cincinnati?
5. ¿Qué les dijo Eugenio a sus primos?

C 12   Actividad • Los sueños de cada uno

Assign this activity for homework. Have each student write original sentences to give to a partner in class the next day. Partners must correct each other's work.

C 13   Actividad • El viernes por la noche

CHALLENGE   Have the students work in groups of three. Then ask several groups to present an impromptu conversation based on the questions they have just answered.

C 14   Actividad • ¡A escribir y a hablar!

Before assigning this activity, you may wish to review with the students the information in C6 and C9. Then ask them to complete the activity in class or at home. Have each student read his or her composition to the class.

C 15   SITUACIÓN • ¿Qué haríamos con la tecnología del futuro?

Before reading the narrative, introduce the new vocabulary. Use pictures to present the words, such as **cortar el césped, cosecha, misiones espaciales, investigaciones submarinas,** and **plantas nucleares.** Have the students identify cognates, such as **robots, labores domésticas, trasplantes de órganos, medicina,** and so on.

Have the students read each numbered item silently. Then play the cassette or read the statements aloud and have the students follow along in their books. Ask questions to check comprehension. As a practice to aid comprehension, prepare a summary of the selection with words or phrases missing and ask the students to complete the sentences with the correct words or phrases from memory or from the unit vocabulary list.

C 16   **Actividad • ¿Es cierto o no?**

You may wish to complete the activity with books closed or allow the students to read each sentence and decide whether it is true or false. Ask them to correct the false statements. Review the answers with the class.

SLOWER-PACED LEARNING   To check comprehension, call on students to summarize the selection by explaining each numbered item in their own words. Use cue cards with key words or phrases contained in the selection to guide the students.

C 17   **SE DICE ASÍ**

Present the expressions for requesting favors or help with books closed by requesting favors from the students. For example, call on a student and say: **¿Serías tan amable de traerme tu libro?** Then have the students read the expressions in the book.

C 18   **Actividad • El camarero amable**

SLOWER-PACED LEARNING   Re-enter the Spanish names of foods, using magazine pictures. For cooperative learning, have the students suggest ideas for a menu as you write the words on the board or a transparency. Allow the students to pretend they are in a restaurant. Have pairs take turns role-playing the server and customer. They should use the conditional tense when ordering or asking a question. Choose several pairs to role-play their dialogs for the class.

C 19   **Actividad • Charla**

Instruct the students to work in pairs to complete the activity. For writing practice, ask them to write a paragraph, using their answers to the questions as a guide.

C 20   **Actividad • Mi persona ideal**

For cooperative learning, form groups of three or four to discuss the questions. Each member of the group should give an opinion about his or her ideal person. Have each group compile the qualities and describe the person to the rest of the class.

C 21   **Actividad • ¡A escribir!**

For writing practice, have the students form the same groups as in C20 and use their answers to write two or three paragraphs. Have one member of each group take notes while the other members contribute information. All the members should help in revising the final composition. Have groups exchange papers for correction.

C22 SITUACIÓN • Una planta nuclear

Play the cassette or read the vocabulary aloud and have the students repeat after you. Explain that many of the words are cognates. Ask the students to point out words that are similar to words in English. Explain that knowing this vocabulary will help them complete the activity in C23. Write the Spanish words on the board and ask the students to give the English equivalents with their books closed.

C23 Actividad • Minidebate

Place five large signs around the classroom. Label the signs **Muy de acuerdo, De acuerdo, Neutral, En desacuerdo,** and **Muy en desacuerdo.** Tell each student to decide which sign best describes his or her feelings about the use of nuclear energy and to form a group with other students at that sign. Have each group discuss the advantages and disadvantages of nuclear energy. Ask a volunteer from each group to be prepared to tell the entire class why the group believes as they do. Then allow the students to begin the debate. You should act as a "moderator" and remind them that only one person may talk at a time.

C24 Actividad • ¡A escribir!

Assign the composition to be completed in class or at home. It should be at least three paragraphs in length. Collect and grade the papers.

TRY YOUR SKILLS

OBJECTIVE To recombine communicative functions, grammar, and vocabulary

CULTURAL BACKGROUND You may wish to explain to the students that elections in Spanish America are not computerized as they are in the United States. Although the technology is available, the high cost of computers prevents most countries from using them for elections. Instead, voters fill out ballots, seal them, and place them in voting boxes. Then government-appointed vote counters usually tally the votes and announce the winners.

1 El consejo estudiantil

Ask the students to prepare their campaign promises. Encourage them to use the conditional tense. If necessary, review the conditional endings and give an example, such as **Yo les daría una hora para almorzar a los estudiantes.** Allow the students to use posters to illustrate their messages if they wish. Have several students read aloud their lists of campaign promises.

2 Actividad • El vicepresidente

Allow the students to create their questions either in class or at home. Then ask pairs to interview each other and report their findings to the class.

3 Actividad • Los candidatos

After the students have thought of their slogans, call on pairs to present their campaign ideas to the class.

4 **Actividad • La elección**

Remind the students to use the conditional tense when talking about what they would do to win the next election. For example, **Trabajaría más para ganar la próxima elección.**

5 **Actividad • ¿Qué les dices tú?**

Review the familiar commands with the class. Have the students take turns giving and taking orders.

6 **Actividad • Dando órdenes**

After the students have completed the activity, write additional questions on the board or a transparency. Have the students use command forms to respond. Some examples are as follows:

> ¿Escribo las cartas? Sí, escríbelas.
> ¿Llamo a Hilda? Sí, llámala.
> ¿Vendo la bicicleta? Sí, véndela.

7 **Actividad • Después de mi graduación**

For writing practice, have the students write complete sentences. Then have each student tell a partner his or her future plans. Suggest that the students use the future or the conditional tense.

8 **Actividad • El presidente de los Estados Unidos**

For further practice, have the students write five complete sentences using the conditional tense.

9 **Dictado**

Write the following paragraph from dictation. First, listen to the paragraph as it is read to you. Then you will hear the paragraph again in short segments, with a pause after each segment to allow you time to write. Finally, you will hear the paragraph a third time so that you may check your work. Let's begin.

Cada uno de nosotros (*pause*) tendrá que prepararse (*pause*) para el mundo del futuro (*pause*) porque la gente no podrá vivir (*pause*) sin los adelantos tecnológicos (*pause*). Si todos nosotros (*pause*) podremos prepararnos bien, (*pause*) entonces, sabremos más, (*pause*) saldremos adelante y (*pause*) haremos un mundo mejor (*pause*) para nosotros y para los que (*pause*) vendrán después.

PRONUNCIACIÓN

Review the pronunciation of the words containing the letters **h** and **ñ**. You may wish to dictate several familiar words for spelling practice. Continue with the letter **ch,** reminding the students not to emit a puff of air when pronouncing this sound. Play the cassette or read aloud the words and sentences, and have the students repeat after you.

Actividad • Trabalenguas fácil

Have the students practice the tongue twister with a partner. Call on volunteers to read the tongue twister aloud.

¿LO SABES?

After the students express their displeasure about one of the suggested items, have each of them ask a partner for help. The partner should make suggestions using the command form. Then ask the students to switch roles.

> STUDENT A Estoy harto de esta computadora. Por favor, ayúdame.
> STUDENT B Ten paciencia. Saca el manual y léelo con cuidado.

Allow the students to write the sentences and paragraph as indicated. Ask volunteers to write their sentences on the board or a transparency for correction. Then call on students to express orally how often or how quickly they do each of the activities listed in the book.

After the students have completed the first activity in pairs, have them form cooperative learning groups. They should discuss each of the situations and be prepared to share the information with the other groups.

VOCABULARIO

You may wish to play a vocabulary game. Write a sentence on a transparency or the board and cover each letter. Call on a student to name a letter of the alphabet. If the student names a letter contained in the sentence, he or she has the opportunity either to guess the message or to name another letter. If the student does not name a letter contained in the sentence, another student gets a turn.

PRÁCTICA DEL VOCABULARIO

Have each student complete the activity at home or in class with a partner. Call on volunteers to describe the innovations.

VAMOS A LEER

OBJECTIVE   To read for practice and pleasure

Antes de leer

Tell the students to look at the illustrations and try to guess the topic of the reading selection. Have them answer the questions orally.

You may wish to discuss a few of the great inventions of the turn of the century. Mention Alexander Graham Bell, who invented the telephone in 1876. Explain how much telephones have changed. Talk a little about Thomas Edison and the invention of the electric light and the gramophone. Compare the gramophone with modern CD players. Discuss the Wright Brothers, the pioneers of aviation. Bring magazine pictures of their first flight and compare their airplane to a modern jet. Point out that most people take for granted the enormous progress in the twentieth century.

Ask the students to scan the reading. Then ask some questions that make the students aware of the contrast between past and present.

Preparación para la lectura

Ask the students to prepare a list of the technology they think their parents had. List their findings on the board and add to the list if necessary. Proceed with number 2. Ask the students to identify as many cognates as they can find by scanning the reading. Write them on the board. Then call on students to answer number 3 and identify the topic of the reading selection. Have them answer numbers 4 and 5 orally.

UN MUNDO DIFERENTE

Have the students read each paragraph silently. Discuss each paragraph, asking the students questions to check comprehension. Finally, play the cassette or read the selection aloud as the students follow along in their books. After the reading, you may wish to ask some questions eliciting predictions about the future from the students.

Actividad • Preguntas y respuestas

Allow each student to complete this activity with a partner. Check the answers with the entire class.

Actividad • ¿Qué uso?

You may wish to divide the class into teams for competition. Have each group write and hand in their answers. Read each question aloud and then write the answer on the board or a transparency. The team with the most correct answers wins.

Actividad • Charla

Ask the students to work in groups of three to complete the activity. When they are finished, call on individuals to give their descriptions to the class.

UNIDAD 7

La tecnología y el progreso

In Spanish America, very much like in the
United States, young people are interested in
the future and in progress. However, since
there are fewer opportunities for employment
after graduation, students have to be more
careful in deciding what they are going to
study. This important decision is usually
made with the help of their parents.

In this unit you will:

SECTION A	express displeasure and ask for help . . . direct others to do something
SECTION B	advise others . . . describe your plans for the future . . . express time factors
SECTION C	inquire whether something is considered possible or impossible . . . request favors or help
TRY YOUR SKILLS	use what you've learned
VAMOS A LEER	read for practice and pleasure

231

SECTION A

expressing displeasure and asking for help . . . directing others to do something

Learning how to use a computer may be frustrating. It takes patience and the ability to follow instructions carefully. You must take each step at a time.

A1   Cómo usar la computadora°

Lucho Chávez está sentado en su cuarto frente a la computadora, pero tiene problemas y llama a su hermana mayor, Consuelo. Ella estudia informática en la universidad de Santiago, Chile, y toma varias clases de programación.

LUCHO   Chelo, por favor, ayúdame.
CHELO   Dime, ¿qué te pasa?
LUCHO   Pues que esta computadora me tiene hasta la punta de los pelos . . . No está funcionando bien. Tecleo y no sale nada en la pantalla. Creo que hay un problema en la base de datos.

INFORMÁTICA
Academias
COLON

Te descubre un nuevo mundo

• CURSOS DE BASIC, COBOL, PASCAL, RPG II, GRABACION DE DATOS, T. TEXTOS, BASE DE DATOS Y ANALISIS.

• GRUPOS REDUCIDOS. LA MEJOR RELACION CALIDAD-PRECIO. HORARIOS COMPATIBLES (MAÑANA, TARDE, NOCHE O SABADO) EN LAS MAS AMPLIAS INSTALACIONES. 12 AÑOS DE EXPERIENCIA. ORDENADORES IBM S/34 PC IBM.

• NUEVOS CURSOS: MASTER INFORMATICO (2 años).

ANTES DE DEDICIRTE VISITANOS. INFORMACION Y RESERVAS EN:

Plaza de España, 12 (Esquina Ferraz) Tf. 241 83 00-247 54 93
Paseo Delicias, 31 (Metro Atocha) Tf. 228 02 75-468 71 93
Y en Valencia Gran Via Marqués del Turia, 8 Tf. 373 73 55

NIÑOS
CURSOS DE VACACIONES
EN COMPUTADORES
I.B.M.
Edad: 5 años en adelante. Con o sin transporte.
Escoja su horario
UNIVERSITARIO: Curso para todos los lenguajes. ASICO: Cra. 5ª N° 18-57, piso 2°. Tel: 2431852.

CHELO   A ver . . . vuelve al menú. Teclea de nuevo . . . No, así no. Borra. Comienza otra vez y haz todo de nuevo.
LUCHO   No . . . hazlo tú.
CHELO   Mira, cálmate. Ten un poco de paciencia. A ver, abre el cajón del escritorio, saca el manual, léelo bien y aprende las instrucciones. Ahora, aprieta el botón y pon otro disquete.

°Some Spanish-American countries use **el computador** for the word *computer* while most other countries use **la computadora.**

(Después de unos minutos)

LUCHO
Mira, Chelo, ¡qué bien funciona! Y el impresor es estupendo.

CHELO
Ya ves que con paciencia puedes aprender muy bien.

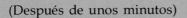

CLASES DE COMPUTADORA
EN ESPAÑOL

University of Miami
School of Business
P.O. Box 248505
Coral Gables, FL 33124

Dr Micro Lo quiere a Ud.

Cursos de Un Dia 9am-5pm $135

LLAME AL

- Introducción a Micro-computadoras
- Introducción a Word Perfect
- Introducción a dBase III
- Introducción a Lotus

529-3999
Para Folleto

Clases de Noche tambien disponibles

ESTUDIE CONTABILIDAD EN UN CENTRO ESPECIAZADO CURSOS EXCLUSIVAMENTE PRACTICOS CALCULADORAS ULTIMO MODELO PARA EL USO DE LOS ALUMNOS.

ARCHIVO Y KARDEX EN SOLAMENTE TRES MESES PUEDE Ud. GRADUARSE DE KARDISTA. ¡CLASES PRACTICAS!

CURSOS DE COMPUTACION LABORATORIO PARA LAS PRACTICAS CON COMPUTADORAS ULTIMO MODELO

ESCUELA PROFESIONAL DE INFORMATICA
EPI

- INFORMATICA BASICA, COBOL, BASIC.
- MS-DOS
- TRATAMIENTO DE TEXTOS

PREPARACIÓN PARA LAS OPOSICIONES DE LA ADMINISTRACIÓN DEL ESTADO, MODALIDAD B

Alcala, 55 - 1º D
Metro BANCO (Junto a Cibeles)
Tel. 43168 98 - 28014 MADRID

For information on how to present the realia, see p. T146.

A2 Actividad • Preguntas y respuestas

Answer the following questions according to A1.

1. ¿Qué hace Lucho en su cuarto? Lucho está sentado frente a la computadora.
2. ¿Por qué llama a su hermana? Llama a su hermana porque tiene problemas con la computadora.
3. ¿Qué estudia Chelo en la universidad? Chelo estudia informática.
4. ¿Por qué dice Lucho que la computadora lo tiene hasta la punta de los pelos? Porque no está funcionando bien.
5. ¿Qué saca Lucho del cajón del escritorio? Lucho saca el manual.
6. ¿Qué le dice él a Chelo después de leer las instrucciones? Le dice a Chelo que la computadora funciona muy bien.
7. ¿Qué piensa Lucho del impresor? Piensa que el impresor es estupendo.
8. ¿Qué le dice Chelo a Lucho al final? Chelo le dice que con paciencia puede aprender muy bien.

La tecnología y el progreso   **233**

Nuestras vidas han cambiado *(have changed)* mucho en los últimos veinte años. Muchos descubrimientos y productos que no existían antes, ahora están en todas partes. Los vemos tan frecuentemente que no nos damos cuenta *(we don't realize)* de lo nuevo que son. Para dar un ejemplo, las calculadoras de bolsillo *(pocket calculators)* se empezaron a hacer populares en 1971 y hoy día millones de personas las usan diariamente.

En el mundo hispánico la tecnología también está cambiando muchas cosas aunque los países hispánicos no están tan adelantados *(advanced)* como los Estados Unidos en este aspecto. En los últimos tiempos se puede apreciar el progreso, y ya se fabrican *(are manufactured)* equipos electrónicos en muchos países de Latinoamérica y España.

A4 SE DICE ASÍ
Expressing displeasure and asking for help

Estoy harto de (caminar).	I am sick and tired of (walking).
Me estoy volviendo loca.	I am going crazy.
Me tiene hasta la punta de los pelos.	I'm fed up with it.
Por favor, ayúdame.	Help me, please.
¿Me puedes dar una mano?	Can you give me a hand?

Actividad • ¿Qué me cuentas?   Answers will vary.

Now is your chance to tell your classmates about some of the things that upset you. Answer the following questions.

1. ¿De qué estás harto(a)?
2. ¿Qué te tiene hasta la punta de los pelos?

3. ¿Qué te está volviendo loco(a)?
4. Cuando pides ayuda, ¿qué dices?

A6   **Comprensión**   For script, see p. T147–148.

Two friends are discussing problems. If the second speaker gives good advice, check **¡qué bueno!** on your answer sheet. If not, check **¡qué horror!**

MODELO   — Esta computadora me está volviendo loco.
          — Chico, ten un poco de paciencia.

	0	1	2	3	4	5	6	7	8	9	10
¡Qué bueno!	✔	✔		✔	✔		✔		✔		
¡Qué horror!			✔			✔		✔		✔	✔

A7   **ESTRUCTURAS ESENCIALES**
     Affirmative familiar commands: **tú** *form*

Carmita, **lleva** los libros a la biblioteca.
Ahora no puedo, Tere. Los llevo mañana.

Carmita, take the books to the library.
I can't now, Tere. I'll take them tomorrow.

Tomás, **abre** el cajón y **saca** las revistas.
Está bien.

Tomás, open the drawer and take out the magazines.
Okay.

Gabriela, **trae** el manual de la computadora.
No puedo. No sé dónde está.

Gabriela, bring the computer manual.
I can't. I don't know where it is.

1. For most regular and irregular verbs, the affirmative **tú** command has exactly the same form as the third person singular of the present indicative.

2. Use familiar commands with people you normally address as **tú.**

3. The following chart lists some very important verbs you will be using with the **tú** form to give familiar commands in this unit.

Before starting the familiar commands, review the uses of the familiar form *"tú"*. After you have gone through the examples, and covered explanation 1, tell the students that the context, and the intonation will tell them whether the form is a command or the present indicative. Give contrasting examples, both orally and in writing.

Verb	*Third person singular Present indicative*	*Familiar command* **tú** *form*
hablar	Ella **habla** español.	**Habla** español.
comer	Luis **come** queso.	**Come** queso.
abrir	Elena **abre** el refrigerador.	**Abre** el refrigerador.
sacar	Gerardo **saca** la basura.	**Saca** la basura.
llevar	Luisa **lleva** el libro.	**Lleva** el libro.
pedir	Tomás **pide** la revista.	**Pide** la revista.
traer	José **trae** al perro.	**Trae** al perro.

A8 Actividad • La mandamás

Because of your good grades, your teacher has allowed you to give instructions to your classmates for one day. Each person in the class must carry out your instructions. Follow the model, using the real names of your classmates.

> MODELO   escribir el ejercicio en la pizarra
>   Hilda, escribe el ejercicio en la pizarra.

1. apagar la luz
2. abrir la ventana
3. hablar español
4. sacar la basura
5. limpiar la sala de clase
6. recitar un poema en español
7. leer la revista en voz alta
8. cantar una canción en español

1. Raúl, apaga la luz. 2. Susana, abre la ventana. 3. Felipe, habla español. 4. Roberto, saca la basura. 5. Ramón, limpia la sala de clase. 6. Patricia, recita un poema en español. 7. Lupe, lee la revista en voz alta. 8. Ana, canta una canción en español.

A9 Actividad • El abuelo  For answers, see p. T148.

Here is your grandfather's advice to you on how to live a long and healthy life. Complete each of his suggestions using the familiar command form of the verb in parentheses. Follow the model.

> MODELO   (vivir) una vida tranquila.
>   Vive una vida tranquila.

1. (tomar) las cosas con paciencia.
2. (cenar) temprano todas las noches.
3. (comer) poco y lentamente.
4. (beber) solamente agua o jugo de frutas variadas.
5. (practicar) algún deporte.
6. (caminar) veinte minutos todos los días.
7. (trabajar) bien.
8. (descansar) los fines de semana.

Actividad • Pidiendo permiso

Your parents are away for the weekend and your older sister or brother has been left in charge. Pair up with a classmate and ask permission to do a number of things. Follow the model.

MODELO   ¿Puedo hablar por teléfono?
    Sí, habla por teléfono.

1. ¿Puedo comprar una calculadora?   Sí, compra una calculadora.
2. ¿Puedo estudiar mañana?   Sí, estudia mañana.
3. ¿Puedo beber un refresco?   Sí, bebe un refresco.
4. ¿Puedo preparar el desayuno?   Sí, prepara el desayuno.
5. ¿Puedo jugar con mis amigos?   Sí, juega con tus amigos.
6. ¿Puedo comer en la cafetería con José y Charo?   Sí, come en la cafetería con José y Charo.
7. ¿Puedo volver tarde de la cafetería?   Sí, vuelve tarde de la cafetería.
8. ¿Puedo traer a mis amigos a casa?   Sí, trae a tus amigos a casa.

A 11   ESTRUCTURAS ESENCIALES
Irregular verbs in the familiar **tú** *command*

Eight Spanish verbs are irregular in the affirmative command of the **tú** form.

decir	**di**	**Di** cuál es tu problema.
hacer	**haz**	**Haz** los ejercicios.
poner	**pon**	**Pon** los libros allí.
ir	**ve**	**Ve** a la esquina.
salir	**sal**	**Sal** de aquí ahora mismo.
ser	**sé**	**Sé** más amable.
tener	**ten**	**Ten** más paciencia.
venir	**ven**	**Ven** a mi casa esta noche.

A 12   Actividad • ¡Órdenes, órdenes y más órdenes! For answers, see p. T149.

Team up with another student in class who will play the role of a family member and give you orders. Answer affirmatively. Then switch roles.

MODELO   (ir) _____ a la clase de programación todos los días.
    — Ve a la clase de programación todos los días.
    — Sí, yo voy a la clase de programación todos los días.

1. (decir) _____ dónde vas a comprar la computadora.
2. (ir) _____ a comprarla ahora.
3. (tener) _____ cuidado de no perder el dinero.
4. (ser) _____ amable con el dependiente.
5. (salir) _____ de la tienda temprano.
6. (venir) _____ a casa inmediatamente.
7. (poner) _____ la computadora en tu cuarto.
8. (hacer) _____ tu tarea en la computadora.

Actividad • Cómo usar la computadora

Take the role of the instructor and give advice on how to use the computer. Follow the model.

MODELO   (escuchar) _____ bien mis consejos.
         Escucha bien mis consejos.

1. (poner)   _____ atención. Pon
2. (buscar)   _____ el manual. Busca
3. (leer)   _____ bien el manual. Lee
4. (aprender)   _____ las instrucciones. Aprende
5. (mirar)   _____ la pantalla. Mira
6. (estudiar)   _____ el menú. Estudia
7. (tener)   _____ cuidado al teclear. Ten
8. (seguir)   _____ el programa. Sigue
9. (sacar)   _____ el disquete. Saca
10. (apagar)   _____ la computadora. Apaga

A 14   Actividad • Ven a mi casa   Answers will vary.

Your friend wants to know how to get to the new computer store. Ask where your friend lives and give directions from his or her house to the store. The verbs in the box should be helpful.

MODELO   Sal de tu casa y ve hasta la calle . . .

seguir	quedar		caminar
		venir	
llegar	salir		preguntar
doblar	estar	dar	ir

A15 ESTRUCTURAS ESENCIALES
Position of pronouns with affirmative **tú** *commands*

Review the two pronoun groups in Unit 2, C6 for position of object pronouns attached to a command.

Tráeme el libro y los lápices.
¿Los platos? **Ponlos** en la mesa.
¿La basura? **Sácala** por la noche.
Lávate las manos antes de comer.
¿Las flores? **Póntelas** en el pelo.

Bring me the book and pencils.
The dishes? Put them on the table.
The garbage? Take it out at night.
Wash your hands before eating.
The flowers? Put them in your hair.

Indicate that accent marks are added to keep the original stress on verbs of more than one syllable.

Direct and indirect objects, as well as reflexive pronouns, are always placed after an affirmative command and attached to it, forming one word. Accent marks are used only to keep the original stress.

A16 Actividad • El invitado

You and your best friend have invited your computer instructor to dinner. She is about to arrive and there are still a few things to do. Your friend asks you for instructions. Follow the model.

> MODELO ¿Paso la aspiradora en la sala?
> Sí, pásala.

1. ¿Apago el televisor? Sí, apágalo.
2. ¿Saco los refrescos del refrigerador? Sí, sácalos.
3. ¿Les echo hielo a los vasos? Sí, échales hielo.
4. ¿Me lavo las manos? Sí, lávatelas.
5. ¿Pongo la mesa? Sí, ponla.
6. ¿Traigo la sal? Sí, tráela.
7. ¿Corto el pan? Sí, córtalo.
8. ¿Me peino y me pongo la corbata? Sí, péinate y póntela.
9. Aquí está la profesora, ¿abro la puerta? Sí, ábrela.

A17 Actividad • El instructor de computadoras

Pair up with another student. You have just purchased a computer and since you are not too familiar with it, you ask your classmate for help. Follow the model.

> MODELO ¿Enciendo la computadora?
> Sí, enciéndela.

1. ¿Traigo el manual? Sí, tráelo.
2. ¿Leo las instrucciones? Sí, léelas.
3. ¿Aprieto el botón? Sí, apriétaio.
4. ¿Miro la pantalla? Sí, mírala.
5. ¿Toco esa tecla? Sí, tócala.
6. ¿Pido la información? Sí, pídela.
7. ¿Consigo un disquete nuevo? Sí, consíguelo.
8. ¿Pongo ese disquete en la computadora?
   Sí, ponlo.

A18 Actividad • Charla   Answers will vary.

Now is your chance to talk about computers and express your opinion.

1. ¿Por qué es importante tomar cursos de programación de computadoras? Explícalo.
2. ¿Estás tomando algún curso de programación? ¿Qué haces en el curso?
3. Di algunos usos de la computadora.
4. Hay mucha gente que tiene una computadora en casa. Explica para qué la usan.
5. ¿Cómo te puede ayudar una computadora?

A19 Actividad • ¡A conversar!   Answers will vary.

Pair up with a classmate and pretend that he or she is having problems using the computer. Your classmate will tell you some of the problems and you will offer your advice.

advising others . . . describing your plans for the future . . . expressing time factors

It is very important to plan what to do after graduation—you might be doing it for a long time. Try to plan for the future and don't leave it all to chance.

B1

El mundo del futuro

Antes de terminar el curso, los estudiantes de la clase de español de la escuela secundaria Bernardo O'Higgins, en Santiago de Chile, escriben composiciones sobre sus planes para el futuro. He aquí algunas de ellas.

Yo iré a la universidad y tomaré varios cursos de programación, porque la informática es la llave del futuro, y muy pronto no podremos vivir sin una computadora. Tendré que prepararme bien para el futuro, porque algún día quiero casarme y tener familia. Como dice el viejo proverbio: "Más vale precaver que tener que lamentar."

Horacio Camacho

Después de graduarme, aprenderé inglés en la universidad. Los idiomas serán muy importantes en el futuro porque cada día nos ponemos en contacto con más gente de otros países. Además, con los adelantos tecnológicos, pronto podremos estar en un país extranjero de otro continente en un par de horas.

Teresa Elvira Gutiérrez

Mi hermano y yo estudiaremos ingeniería espacial, porque la carrera espacial sin duda continuará. En el futuro las naciones construirán más transbordadores y estaciones espaciales. Pronto no podremos vivir sin los adelantos tecnológicos. Nosotros soñamos con dar un viaje a un planeta lejano.

Miguel Merino

1. La escuela se llama Bernardo O'Higgins.
2. La escuela queda en Santiago de Chile.

3. La llave del futuro será la informática.
4. El proverbio es "Más vale precaver que tener que lamentar".
5. Porque cada día nos ponemos en contacto con más gente de otros países.

B2 Actividad • Preguntas y respuestas

Use the information in B1 to answer the following questions.

1. ¿Cómo se llama la escuela adonde van los chicos?
2. ¿Dónde queda la escuela?
3. Según Horacio, ¿cuál será la llave del futuro?
4. ¿Cuál es el proverbio que escribe Horacio?
5. Según Teresa ¿por qué serán muy importantes los idiomas en el futuro?
6. ¿Con qué sueñan Miguel y su hermano?

6. Miguel y su hermano sueñan con dar un viaje a un planeta lejano.

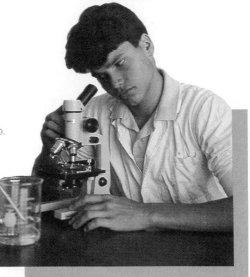

B3 Sabes que . . .

Tanto en la América hispana como en España, las carreras universitarias de ciencias, tales como programación, ingeniería o medicina, se consideran muy importantes por lo necesarias que son para el progreso y adelanto de los países y por las ventajas económicas que ofrecen. Sin embargo, más aún que en los Estados Unidos, las carreras llamadas de artes y letras (*liberal arts*) son también populares. Muchos estudiantes se matriculan (*enroll*) en ellas. La mayoría de las universidades son gratis y ofrecen diversidad de carreras. Aún las universidades privadas son mucho más económicas que las de los Estados Unidos.

B4 SE DICE ASÍ
Giving advice using proverbs

Point out that proverbs are a very important part of Spanish culture, and that people use them frequently in conversation to convey an idea or a point of view, and to give advice.

Más vale pájaro en mano que ciento volando.	A bird in the hand is worth two in the bush.
Más vale precaver que tener que lamentar.	An ounce of prevention is worth a pound of cure.
Del dicho al hecho hay un gran trecho.	It's easier said than done.
En boca cerrada no entran moscas.	Silence is golden.
Más vale tarde que nunca.	Better late than never.

ESTRUCTURAS ESENCIALES
The future tense

You may wish to point out that the Spanish future tense is used to anticipate future events, or to describe conjecture or probability: "Papá ganará más dinero y viviremos mejor." "¿Qué hora será? María estará en casa ahora." Stress that **ir a** + infinitive or the present tense are most often used in Spanish to express future time. Go over the **Atención** in class with the students.

The Spanish future tense is the equivalent of English *will* or *shall* plus a verb. The following chart shows how to form the future tense of regular **-ar, -er,** and **-ir** verbs.

FUTURE TENSE

tomar *to take*	**aprender** *to learn*	**vivir** *to live*
tomar**é**	aprender**é**	vivir**é**
tomar**ás**	aprender**ás**	vivir**ás**
tomar**á**	aprender**á**	vivir**á**
tomar**emos**	aprender**emos**	vivir**emos**
tomar**éis**	aprender**éis**	vivir**éis**
tomar**án**	aprender**án**	vivir**án**

Teresa Elvira **tomará** clases de programación.
Teresa Elvira will take computer programming classes.
Aprenderé inglés.
I'll learn English.
Viviremos en una ciudad muy moderna.
We'll live in a very modern city.

1. Notice that the infinitive is used as the stem for regular verbs in the future.
2. The endings are the same for all three conjugations.
3. Notice the accent on the last syllable, except in the **nosotros** form.
   llamaremos   aprenderemos   subiremos
4. As you have already learned, Spanish also uses the present tense with a time expression or the verb **ir** + **a** + *infinitive* to express future actions.
   Vamos a ir al cine **mañana.**
   We are going to go to the movies tomorrow.
   ¿Tienes clase de informática **esta tarde?**
   Do you have computer science class this afternoon?

ATENCIÓN: Do not use the future tense to express willingness. In Spanish, to be willing to do something is expressed with the verb **querer.**
   ¿Quieres traerme el libro?   *Will you bring me the book?*

Comprensión For script, see p. T152.

Listen to the following predictions. If the prediction is logical, check **lógico** on your answer sheet. If it is not, check **ilógico.**

MODELO — A José le encantan las computadoras.
— José estudiará informática en la universidad.

	0	1	2	3	4	5	6	7	8	9	10
Lógico	✔	✔		✔		✔			✔		✔
Ilógico			✔		✔		✔	✔		✔	

Actividad • La fiesta   Answers will vary. Possible answers are given.

Your class is planning a party and everyone must pitch in. Follow the model and choose activities for each person.

MODELO   ¿Y Charo?
             Comprará los refrescos.

1. ¿Y Chelo?
2. ¿Y Clemencia?
3. ¿Y Salvador?
4. ¿Y Ramón y Tito?
5. ¿Y Héctor?

6. ¿Y Teresita y Angelita?
7. ¿Y tú y tus amigos?
8. ¿Y tú?
9. ¿Y Ernestico?
10. ¿Y Manolo?

1. Limpiará la casa.   2. Traerá los discos.   3. Cocinará la comida.   4. Quitarán la mesa.   5. Servirá la comida.   6. Lavarán los platos.   7. Prestaremos el estéreo. 8. Sacaré la basura.   9. Tocará la guitarra. 10. Preparará los bocadillos.

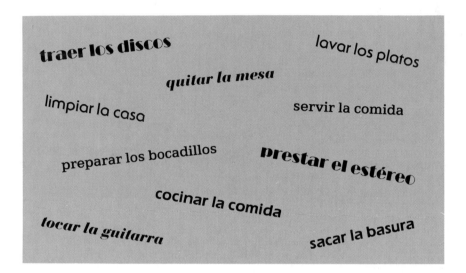

traer los discos   lavar los platos
quitar la mesa
limpiar la casa   servir la comida
preparar los bocadillos   prestar el estéreo
cocinar la comida
tocar la guitarra   sacar la basura

B8   Actividad • A completar

Your friends want to know about some of the things you and your family did in the past, and what all of you are planning to do in the future. Follow the model.

MODELO   Ayer papá (llegar) llegó temprano del trabajo,
             pero mañana llegará tarde.

1. Anoche mamá (hablar) _____ con mi tía Luisa y mañana   habló
   _____ con mi tía Carmen.   hablará
2. El año pasado mis hermanos (aprender) _____ español   aprendieron
   y el año que viene _____ francés.   aprenderán
3. La semana pasada mi hermana y yo (estudiar) _____   estudiamos
   la séptima lección, y la próxima semana _____   estudiaremos
   la octava lección.
4. Ayer yo (comer) _____ en el restaurante El Sol y   comí
   mañana _____ en La Marina.   comeré
5. El verano pasado nuestros primos (ir) _____ a   fueron
   Viña del Mar, pero este verano _____ a Puerto Montt.   irán

Actividad • Dentro de diez años . . .   Answers will vary.

Pair up with a classmate and discuss how life will be for each of you ten years from now. You may react affirmatively or negatively. Choose verbs from the list below, and use the model as a guideline.

> MODELO — Dentro de diez años **seré** astronauta y
> **viajaré** por el espacio . . .

comprar
ganar
recibir
casarse
conocer
escribir
ser
estar
viajar
vivir

B10   **SE DICE ASÍ**
Expressing time factors

en un par de horas	in a couple of hours
en un dos por tres	in a jiffy
a la carrera	in a hurry
en un abrir y cerrar de ojos	in a second; in a flash
dentro de un rato	in a while
de vez en cuando	once in a while
a menudo	often

B11   **Actividad • Charla**   Answers will vary.

Answer the following questions.

1. ¿Qué puedes hacer en un abrir y cerrar de ojos?
2. ¿Cuándo comes a la carrera?
3. ¿Haces la tarea de español en un dos por tres o te toma un par de horas?
4. ¿Puedes decir dos cosas que haces de vez en cuando?
5. ¿Vas al cine a menudo? ¿Cuándo?

ESTRUCTURAS ESENCIALES
Irregular verbs in the future tense

In Spanish, only a few verbs are irregular in the future tense. For these verbs, form the future tense by adding the future endings to the irregular stems.

IRREGULAR FUTURE STEMS

Infinitive		Stem	Ending
1.	decir hacer	dir- har-	
2.	haber querer saber poder	habr- querr- sabr- podr-	**-é** **-ás** **-á** **-emos**
3.	salir poner venir tener valer	saldr- pondr- vendr- tendr- valdr-	**-éis** **-án**

The endings are the same for regular and irregular verbs.

No **podremos** viajar a otros planetas.   *We won't be able to travel to other planets.*
Saldremos con Inés y su mamá.   *We'll go out with Inés and her mother.*

Notice that in the first category, **c** + vowel are dropped. In the second category, the infinitive ending, **-er,** loses the **e.** In the third category, the vowel of the infinitive ending is replaced by **d.**

B 13   Actividad • El profesor Recio

Your teacher has invited Dr. Recio, a noted scholar, to your class. Complete his predictions for the future, using the future tense of the verbs in parentheses.

1. Los robots (hacer) _____ casi todos los trabajos.   harán
2. La gente (salir) _____ más temprano del trabajo.   saldrá
3. Nuestro planeta (tener) _____ más gente.   tendrá
4. Muchos extranjeros (venir) _____ a nuestro país.   vendrán
5. Las personas (poder) _____ viajar rápidamente.   podrán
6. Nosotros (poner) _____ un astronauta en Venus.
7. Las personas (saber) _____ más idiomas.
6. pondremos   7. sabrán

Actividad • **El fin de semana**   Answers will vary.

Get together with a classmate and discuss your plans for the weekend. Each plan must contain at least three verbs in the future. Report to the class what your partner said. Follow the model.

MODELO   Este fin de semana iré al cine el viernes por la
noche, me levantaré a las once de la mañana el sábado
y saldré con mis amigos el domingo.

Actividad • Combinación For answers, see p. T153.

Say what these people are going to do today. Match each person with his or her job description.

1	2
una secretaria	explicar la lección
un cocinero	ayudar a los clientes
un dependiente	construir un transbordador espacial
una ingeniera	escribir muchas cartas
una profesora	atender a personas enfermas
un médico	ir en una excursión
una guía de turistas	preparar una paella muy sabrosa

SECRETARIA EJECUTIVA
INGLÉS - ESPAÑOL

Importante empresa privada dedicada a la fabricación de computadores personales, requiere Secretaria Ejecutiva, que reúa los siguientes requisitos:

– Dominio del inglés
– Buena presencia
– Disponibilidad inmediata

Las interesadas deberán presentarse portando su currículum vitae a partir del día lunes 30 en horas de oficina, en **Los Colibríes 104 San Isidro**. (Alt. Cdra. 9 Av. Aramburú).

MEDICO

Empresa Minera del sector privado requiere los servicios de un Médico para cubrir una vacante en el Hospital de su Asiento Minero, ubicado en la sierra norte a 6 horas de distancia de la ciudad de Lima.

REQUISITOS
— Titulado y colegiado.
— Experiencia mínima 2 años de preferencia en campamento minero.
— Disponibilidad inmediata.
— Soltero.

SE OFRECE
— Alojamiento gratuito en la Unidad Minera.
— Alimentación subvencionada.

Los interesados se servirán presentarse el día lunes 30 de noviembre en Av. República de Chile Nº 498, Jesús María, portando currículum vitae.

INGENIERO ELECTRONICO

Importante Empresa en Telecomunicaciones requiere para su Departamento Técnico: 1 Ingeniero Electrónico.

REQUISITOS:
* Recién egresado de Universidades U.N.I.; Ricardo Palma
* Conocimiento básico de inglés
* Experiencia en telefonía (no imprescindible)

SE OFRECE:
* Remuneración de acuerdo a calificaciones
* Posibilidad de desarrollo profesional
* Seguro médico familiar y otros beneficios

Enviar Currículum Vitae al **APARTADO 10309**, indicando pretensiones de sueldo.

AYUDANTES DE COCINA

Requisitos:
● Edad entre 25 y 35 años
● De preferencia casados
● Experiencia mínima tres años en cocina internacional
● Con disponibilidad de horario de 7 a 17 horas

SOLICITAMOS SOLICITAMOS
PROFESORES(AS)
ESPECIALISTAS EN BASIC
(SE VALORARA TAMBIEN LOGO Y PASCAL)

Requisitos:
● Titulados o con estudios equivalentes
● Experiencia docente

Ofrecemos:
– Altos ingresos según aptitudes
– Horario flexible
– Amplio desarrollo profesional

Presentarse lunes y martes, de 9.00 a 14.00 y de 16.00 a 19.00 horas, en ADOLFO PRIETO NUMERO 1634, colonia Del Valle

For information on how to present the realia, see p T154

Actividad • Expresa tu opinión Answers will vary.

It is now time to express your own opinion by answering the following questions and stating your reasons for your answers.

1. ¿Cuál será la llave del futuro?
2. ¿Por qué serán muy importantes los idiomas en el futuro?
3. ¿Crees que la carrera espacial continuará?
4. ¿Piensas que habrá en el futuro muchos adelantos espaciales?
5. ¿Piensas que pronto muchas personas darán viajes a planetas lejanos? ¿Adónde viajarán?

B17 Actividad • ¡A escribir! Answers will vary. Possible answers are given. Estudiaré más. No hablaré tanto en clase. Ayudaré más en la casa. Escribiré más a mi abuela. Aprenderé a nadar.

Last year you made a list of New Year's resolutions. Do you remember them? You may not have followed many of them, but this coming year will be a different story. Write ten resolutions for the New Year using the future tense. Then read them aloud to the class.

B18 Actividad • El reportero

Get together with a classmate. One student will be a reporter and interview the other. Discuss your future plans following the model. Switch roles.

> MODELO   piloto / dentro de diez años
> Dentro de diez años seré piloto.

astronauta / dentro de quince años   Dentro de quince años seré astronauta.
jugador de béisbol / después de terminar la escuela secundaria   Después de terminar la escuela secundaria seré jugador de béisbol.
médica famosa / dentro de veinte años   Dentro de veinte años seré una médica famosa.
atleta / en unos diez años   En unos diez años seré atleta.
gerente / después de graduarme de la universidad   Después de graduarme de la universidad seré gerente.
actor de televisión / dentro de dos años   Dentro de dos años seré actor de televisión
modelo / pronto   Pronto seré modelo.
estrella de rock / el año que viene
El año que viene seré estrella de rock.

B19 Actividad • ¿Qué crees tú? Answers will vary.

Pair up with a classmate and ask each other the following questions. Be prepared to support your answers.

1. ¿Cuál país estará en primer lugar en la carrera espacial en el año 2000?
2. ¿Qué película ganará el Oscar este año?
3. ¿Quién será el próximo presidente de los Estados Unidos?
4. ¿Podrás votar en las próximas elecciones para presidente?
5. ¿En qué año te graduarás de la escuela?

Actividad • Charlemos   Answers will vary.

Tell the class what you think your life will be like five years from now by answering the following questions.

1. Después de la graduación, ¿estudiarás o trabajarás?
2. ¿A qué universidad irás? ¿Qué trabajo tendrás?
3. ¿Qué carrera estudiarás?
4. Si no piensas ir a la universidad, ¿qué harás?
5. ¿Te casarás o no?
6. Si piensas casarte, ¿con quién te casarás?
7. Si te casas, ¿cuántos hijos tendrás?
8. ¿Dónde vivirán tú y tu familia?
9. Si piensas hacer un viaje, ¿a qué países viajarás?
10. ¿Qué harás con tu dinero?

B 21   Actividad • ¡A escribir y a conversar!   Answers will vary.

Prepare a brief composition in Spanish about your future career. The following suggestions might help you with this task.

   I. Introducción
      A. Si termino la secundaria con buenas notas, mi carrera será . . .
      B. Por qué estudiaré esa carrera
  II. Desarrollo
      A. Descripción de la carrera
      B. ¿Dónde la estudiaré? (nombre de la universidad)
      C. ¿Es una carrera fácil o difícil?
      D. ¿Cuántos años tomará?
 III. Conclusión: Lo que haré con mi carrera

Then, present your composition orally in class.

inquiring whether something is considered possible or impossible . . . requesting favors or help

We all try to predict what the future has in store for us, and we like to express what we would do if. . . . Also, we often need to ask somebody to help us.

C1 ## ¿Qué haríamos sin la tecnología?

1. Nosotros no podríamos viajar frecuentemente y los viajes tomarían mucho tiempo.

2. Las industrias fabricarían muy pocos productos. Muchas de ellas hasta cerrarían sus puertas. De hecho, muchos quedarían sin trabajo.

3. Todos trabajaríamos más horas. Solamente saldríamos de vez en cuando y tendríamos menos tiempo libre.

4. Los artículos costarían más. Habría menos productos en el mercado y muy pocas personas tendrían coches, calculadoras o computadoras.

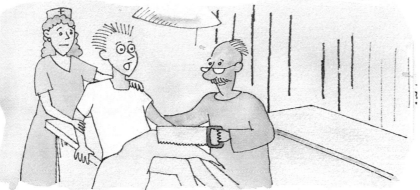

5. Habría menos adelantos en el campo de la medicina. Los médicos sabrían menos sobre el ser humano y tendrían más dificultades en curar a los enfermos. Por lo tanto, la gente viviría menos tiempo.

C2   Actividad • ¡A escoger!

For each numbered sentence, choose the statement that best completes the idea stated in C1.

1. Sin la tecnología, las industrias
   • fabricarían muchos productos.   • <u>fabricarían pocos productos.</u>
   • saldrían de vez en cuando.
2. Sin la tecnología, los médicos
   • <u>sabrían menos.</u>   • tendrían pocas dificultades.   • curarían a muchos enfermos.
3. Gracias a la tecnología,
   • podríamos viajar lentamente.   • <u>viajaríamos frecuentemente.</u>
   • los viajes tomarían mucho tiempo.
4. Sin la tecnología, los artículos
   • saldrían a menudo.   • <u>costarían más.</u>   • costarían menos.
5. Sin la tecnología,
   • <u>trabajaríamos más horas.</u>   • tendríamos mucho tiempo libre.
   • trabajaríamos menos horas.

Son muchos los descubrimientos y adelantos en el mundo durante los últimos veinticinco años. Uno de los más importantes, que ya se ve en todo el mundo hispánico, es la aplicación médica del láser. Con la ayuda del láser se tratan *(are treated)* muchas enfermedades que antes necesitaban operaciones quirúrgicas *(surgical)*.

En la industria de alimentos se encuentran toda clase de alimentos precocidos *(precooked)* y congelados *(frozen)*, listos para el horno de microondas *(microwave oven)*. En el mundo hispánico están teniendo un gran éxito y los hay en todas partes. Por supuesto en los países hispánicos existe también la preocupación por la salud y por mantenerse en forma. El culturismo *(body building)*, la gimnasia y los maratones populares están de moda.

Por último, uno de los descubrimientos más populares es el disco compacto. En muchas partes estos discos están reemplazando *(replacing)* los viejos discos o casetes. El sonido de estos discos es estupendo y ocupan poco espacio.

C4   Comprensión   For script, see p. T156–157.

Your principal is discussing the plans for your school and mentions some problems. After each problem, you will hear three possible solutions suggested by different people. Choose the most appropriate solution and place a check in the corresponding box on your answer sheet.

MODELO   El colegio es muy viejo.

    a. Buscaría nuevos profesores.
    b. Construiría un colegio nuevo.
    c. Gastaría más dinero en deportes.

	0	1	2	3	4	5	6	7	8	9	10
a.			✓	✓	✓			✓			✓
b.	✔	✓				✓	✓		✓		
c.										✓	

SE DICE ASÍ
Expressing logical conclusions

	por lo tanto	as a result; therefore
	de hecho	as a matter of fact
	a la corta o a la larga	sooner or later
	por consiguiente	consequently; thus

C6 ESTRUCTURAS ESENCIALES
The Spanish conditional tense

You may wish to point out that the conditional is used to describe intent or to indicate probability or conjecture.
"Ellos irían al cine ayer."
"¿Dónde viviría Luis antes de mudarse aquí?"

Conditional tense		
trabajar	comer	vivir
trabajaría	comería	viviría
trabajarías	comerías	vivirías
trabajaría	comería	viviría
trabajaríamos	comeríamos	viviríamos
trabajaríais	comeríais	viviríais
trabajarían	comerían	vivirían

1. The conditional, like the future, uses the infinitive as the stem. It has only one set of endings for all three conjugations.

Yo **trabajaría** en una tienda, pero no tengo tiempo.
I would work at a store, but I don't have time.

Ellos **comerían** en ese restaurante, pero no tienen dinero.
They would eat at that restaurant, but they don't have money.

Nosotros **viviríamos** en California ahora, pero papá no quiso aceptar el trabajo.
We would live in California now, but Dad didn't want to accept the job.

2. Notice that all forms have an accent on the **í** of the ending.
3. The Spanish conditional tense is equivalent to *would* + infinitive. The verb **deber** in the conditional is equivalent to *should*.

Yo **trabajaría** en el programa espacial de los Estados Unidos.
I would work in the United States space program.

Comeríamos antes de ir a clase, pero no tenemos tiempo.
We would eat before going to class, but we don't have time.

Ella **viviría** cerca de Cape Canaveral, pero hace mucho calor allí.
She would live close to Cape Canaveral, but it is very hot there.

Debería estudiar más.
I should study more.

ATENCIÓN: The Spanish conditional tense, like the English, is also used in polite terms to soften a request.

¿**Podrías** traerme la libreta?
Could you bring me the notebook?

¿**Podrías** hacerme un favor?
Could you do me a favor?

¿**Serías** tan amable de ayudarme?
Would you be kind enough to help me?

C7 Actividad • ¿Qué haríamos? For answers, see p. T157.

The following high school students want to go to college. What would each of them do in order to be accepted? Change the verb in parentheses to the conditional tense.

> MODELO Pancho (ir) a clase todos los días.
> Pancho iría a clase todos los días.

1. Isabel (estudiar) más cursos de matemáticas.
2. María Elena y Matilde (tomar) una clase de programación.
3. Jaime le (pedir) una carta al profesor.
4. Mi hermano (sacar) mejores notas que antes en todos sus cursos.
5. Leonardo (hablar) con el secretario de la escuela.
6. Sarita (tratar) de ir a la universidad para pedir información.
7. Ricardo y Roberto (prestar) más atención en clase.
8. Además de español, Eugenio (aprender) otro idioma.

C8 Actividad • Mis excusas para el sábado   Answers will vary.

Team up with two classmates. Each of them will invite you to do something this Saturday. Tell them that you would like to accept their invitations, but you must decline. Offer the reasons for refusing. Follow the model.

> MODELO jugar al béisbol
> ¿Quieres jugar al béisbol conmigo el sábado?
> Gracias. Jugaría contigo, pero tengo que estudiar.

1. estudiar
2. visitar a Juan
3. comer en la cafetería
4. tomar el sol en la playa
5. correr en el parque
6. estudiar en la biblioteca
7. dar un paseo
8. ir de compras

The same verbs that are irregular in the future tense are irregular in the
conditional tense. For these verbs, the conditional tense is formed by adding the
conditional endings to an irregular stem.

Irregular Conditional Stems

	Infinitive	Stem	Ending
1. {	decir	dir-	
	hacer	har-	
2. {	haber	habr-	–ía
	querer	querr-	–ías
	saber	sabr-	–ía
	poder	podr-	–íamos
3. {	salir	saldr-	–íais
	valer	valdr-	
	poner	pondr-	–ían
	venir	vendr-	
	tener	tendr-	

Notice that the endings are the same for regular or irregular verbs. Also notice
that the stems are the same as the future tense stems.

Yo **compraría** una computadora.	*I would buy a computer.*
Costaría mucho dinero.	*It would cost a great deal of money.*
Nosotros **hablaríamos** con él.	*We would talk to him.*
Carlos y Pedro **harían** los programas.	*Carlos and Pedro would create the programs.*

C10 **Actividad • Charlemos un poco** Answers will vary.

Pair up with another classmate and ask each other the following questions.

1. ¿Con quién saldrías este fin de semana?
2. ¿Qué harías con cien dólares en el bolsillo?
3. ¿Qué cursos tendrías que tomar para graduarte de la escuela?
4. ¿Qué podrías hacer después de aprender español?
5. Ahora eres un estudiante de secundaria, pero, ¿qué
   querrías ser en el futuro?

C11 Actividad • La mala suerte de Eugenio

Complete the following paragraph with the correct conditional forms
of the verbs in parentheses.

La semana pasada Eugenio compró un billete para viajar a
Cincinnati. Al llegar al mostrador, un empleado le informó que
(tener) que pagar más por el billete y también le indicó que el vuelo   tendría
no **(salir)** hasta las seis. Cuando el avión salió del aeropuerto, Eugenio   saldría
creyó que **(poder)** llegar a tiempo a Cincinnati, pero el avión no llegó   podría
hasta las diez de la noche. Al llegar a Cincinnati, Eugenio llamó a
casa de sus primos y le dijeron que **(ir)** a buscarlo en cinco minutos,   irían
pero ellos llegaron muy tarde. Cuando Eugenio los vio, les dijo que
no **(volver)** a viajar más por esa compañía. ¡Pobre Eugenio!   volvería

C12 Actividad • Los sueños de cada uno

By replacing the blanks with the correct forms of the conditional tense, you will
find out the dreams of the following people.

1. Antonio (viajar) _____ a España y (aprender) _____ español.   viajaría / aprendería
2. Rosaura (ser) _____ ingeniera y (construir) _____ muchos   sería / construiría
   rascacielos.
3. Federico y su hermano (vivir) _____ en Colorado y (esquiar) _____   vivirían / esquiarían
   todos los inviernos.
4. Alberto (tomar) _____ muchas clases de computación y   tomaría
   (saber) _____ usar las computadoras perfectamente.   sabría
5. Manuel (ser) _____ presidente y (decir) _____ muchas cosas   sería / diría
   al país.
6. Cuco y Alfonso (jugar) _____ al béisbol para los Medias   jugarían
   Rojas de Boston y (tener) _____ mucho dinero.   tendrían
7. Beto (estudiar) _____ ingeniería espacial y (hacer) _____   estudiaría / haría
   muchos transbordadores espaciales.

C13 Actividad • El viernes por la noche   Answers will vary.

Pair up with a classmate and ask what he or she would like to do this coming Friday evening.

1. ¿Irías al cine conmigo el viernes por la noche?
2. ¿Con quién más querrías ir al cine?
3. ¿Qué película verías?
4. ¿Te gustaría comer en una cafetería después del cine? ¿Dónde?
5. ¿Qué más harías?
6. ¿A qué hora volverías a casa?

C14 Actividad • ¡A escribir y a hablar!   Answers will vary.

Imagine that you have inherited a million dollars. Write a brief composition describing what you would do with the money, and then tell the class.

C15 SITUACIÓN • ¿Qué haríamos con la tecnología del futuro?

1. Nosotros nos libraríamos de muchas labores domésticas, porque los robots cortarían el césped, limpiarían la casa y hasta cocinarían. Además, podrían arreglar muchas cosas en la casa.

2. Las industrias gozarían de grandes ventajas, porque usarían los robots para hacer labores muy peligrosas. Éstos podrían trabajar en investigaciones submarinas, plantas nucleares y misiones espaciales.

3. Gracias a los adelantos médicos, la gente viviría muchos años porque la medicina progresaría mucho. Los médicos harían trasplantes de órganos y las operaciones serían muy fáciles con la ayuda de rayos láser.

4. Las personas irían de un continente a otro en pocos minutos porque los aviones viajarían a miles de millas por hora.

5. Habría una revolución agrícola, porque los científicos producirían frutas y legumbres que serían resistentes a las enfermedades y a los cambios del tiempo. Por lo tanto, habría más cosechas y menos hambre en el mundo.

C16 Actividad • ¿Es cierto o no?

Use the information in C15 to decide whether each statement is true or false. Correct the false statements.

1. Las labores domésticas serían más fáciles.   Es cierto.
2. Los trabajos serían muy peligrosos.   No, los trabajos serían menos peligrosos.
3. Los médicos harían las operaciones más fácilmente.   Es cierto.
4. Las personas podrían viajar frecuentemente.   Es cierto.
5. Los viajes tomarían mucho tiempo.   No, los viajes tomarían poco tiempo.
6. Tendríamos menos cosechas.   No, tendríamos más cosechas.

C17 SE DICE ASÍ
Requesting favors or help

Stress the importance of the conditional to express polite requests in Spanish.

¿Serías tan amable de . . . ?	Would you be nice enough to . . . ?
¿Podrías hacerme el favor de . . . ?	Could you do me a favor . . . ?
¿Querrías decirme (darme, prestarme, etc.) . . . ?	Would you tell me (give me, lend me, etc.) . . . ?
¿Me podrías ayudar (prestar, decir, etc.) . . . ?	Could you help me (lend me, tell me, etc.) . . . ?
¿Tendrías la bondad de . . . ?	Would you be so kind as to . . . ?

C18 Actividad • El camarero amable

Pair up with a classmate and imagine that one of you is a waiter or a waitress and the other one is a customer who asks for the following items. Remember to be very polite or you might be replaced by a robot! Follow the model.

> MODELO ¿Podría traerme el menú?
>   Sí, se lo traigo ahora mismo.

3. Sí, se lo digo ahora mismo.
4. Sí, se los enseño ahora mismo.
5. Sí, se la traigo ahora mismo.

1. ¿Podría servirme el agua?
2. ¿Podría darme la sal?
3. ¿Querría decirme qué postres hay?
4. ¿Querría enseñarme los postres?
5. ¿Podría traerme la cuenta?
6. ¿Querría darme una servilleta?

6. Sí, se la doy ahora mismo.

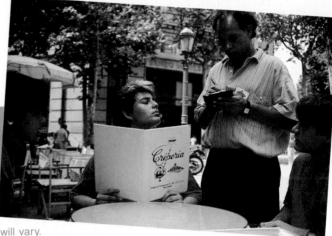

C19 Actividad • Charla   Answers will vary.

Answer the following questions concerning your future career.

1. ¿Qué tipo de trabajo te gustaría? ¿Qué crees que podrías hacer?
2. ¿Dónde buscarías trabajo y qué harías para encontrarlo?
3. ¿Cuántas horas podrías trabajar y a qué hora entrarías y saldrías del trabajo?
4. ¿Cuánto querrías de sueldo? ¿Qué harías con el dinero?

C20 Actividad • Mi persona ideal   Answers will vary.

Answer the following questions concerning your ideal friend.

1. ¿Cómo sería esta persona?
2. ¿Sería norteamericano(a) o de otro país?
3. ¿Qué edad tendría?
4. ¿De qué color tendría el pelo?
5. ¿Cómo sería su personalidad?
6. ¿Cuál sería su profesión?
7. ¿Hablaría muchos idiomas? ¿Cuáles?
8. ¿Sería inteligente?
9. ¿Sabría muchas cosas? ¿Cuáles?
10. ¿Le gustaría la música, el arte o las ciencias?
11. ¿Le gustaría leer muchos libros?
12. ¿Le gustarían los deportes o las fiestas?
13. ¿Tendría mucho o poco dinero?
14. ¿Cuál sería su pasatiempo favorito?

C21 Actividad • ¡A escribir!   Answers will vary.

Now put together all your answers from C20. Add the necessary connecting words, such as **y, en,** or **entonces,** and you will have a brief composition about your ideal person.

The following vocabulary will help you prepare for a lively debate in C23.

el átomo *atom*	los residuos radioactivos *radioactive waste*	conservar *to preserve*
la energía nuclear *nuclear energy*	la bomba atómica *atomic bomb*	el suministro *supply*
la planta nuclear *nuclear plant*	la guerra nuclear *nuclear war*	la fuente de energía *source of energy*
el reactor nuclear *nuclear reactor*	la prueba nuclear *nuclear test*	duradero *lasting*
la precipitación radioactiva *radioactive fallout*	la contaminación *pollution*	el peligro *danger*
la radiación *radiation*	la contaminación ambiental *environmental pollution*	el medio ambiente *environment*
el desastre nuclear *nuclear disaster*		

Actividad • Minidebate   Answers will vary.

The class will be divided into small groups. Each group will discuss the advantages and disadvantages of nuclear energy and should report its conclusions to the class. Use the vocabulary in C22 and the lists below to help you prepare for this debate.

Desventajas de la energía nuclear
1. los posibles desastres y explosiones en las plantas nucleares
2. la precipitación radioactiva
3. el problema de los residuos nucleares
4. la contaminación de los mares y la tierra

Ventajas de la energía nuclear
1. una fuente de energía barata para la industria
2. menos contaminación ambiental
3. conservación de recursos naturales
4. electricidad a un precio más económico

You may also want to bring magazine or newspaper clippings or other materials to illustrate your views. You and the members of your group should get together and discuss your points of view and how you are going to present them in the debate. You may take notes, but your group presentation should be oral. A spokesperson from each group should present the group's point of view, and in turn, may call on other members for support.

C24   Actividad • ¡A escribir!   Answers will vary.

Using the following outline, write a composition about modern technology.

  I. Introducción: La tecnología en el mundo de hoy
 II. Desarrollo
     A. Las ventajas de la tecnología
     B. Las desventajas de la tecnología
III. Conclusión: La tecnología en el mundo de hoy (no) es necesaria porque . . .

1 El consejo estudiantil   Answers will vary.

Imagine that you are a candidate for student council president. List ten things you
will do if elected.

2 Actividad • El vicepresidente   Answers will vary.

Let's see if someone in class shares your ideas. Team up with another student and
ask ten questions about what he or she will do if elected vice-president.

3 Actividad • Los candidatos   Answers will vary.

Now prepare a **lema** for your campaign and tell the class what both of you will do
if elected president and vice-president.

4 Actividad • La elección   Answers will vary.

Suppose you were not elected. Show your disappointment and discuss what you
would like to do to win the next election.

5 Actividad • ¿Qué les dices tú?

In Spanish, tell your partner to follow the suggestions below.

1. speak slowly   Habla lentamente.
2. open the window   Abre la ventana.
3. be good   Sé bueno.
4. eat slowly   Come lentamente.
5. go to the board   Ve a la pizarra.

6. bring the bicycle   Trae la bicicleta.
7. serve breakfast   Sirve el desayuno.
8. be patient   Sé paciente.
9. sleep late   Duerme tarde.
10. do homework   Haz la tarea.

6 Actividad • Dando órdenes

Answer each question with the affirmative **tú** command. Use pronouns.

1. ¿Bebo un refresco?   Sí, bébelo.
2. ¿Saco al perro?   Sí, sácalo.
3. ¿Pongo el disquete?   Sí, ponlo.
4. ¿Tomo notas?   Sí, tómalas.
5. ¿Escribo la carta y el poema?   Sí, escríbelos.

6. ¿Leo el manual?   Sí, léelo.
7. ¿Digo la verdad?   Sí, dila.
8. ¿Me levanto temprano?   Sí, levántate temprano.
9. ¿Toco la guitarra?   Sí, tócala.
10. ¿Hago ejercicio?   Sí, hazlo.

7 Actividad • Después de mi graduación   Answers will vary.

Tell your classmates five different things you would like to do after graduation. Use complete sentences.

8 Actividad • El presidente de los Estados Unidos   Answers will vary.

Tell the class five different things you would do if you were president of the United States.

9 Dictado   For script, see p. T161.

Get ready to complete the following paragraph from dictation.

_____ uno de nosotros _____ que prepararse
_____ porque la gente no _____ vivir sin los
adelantos _____ . Si todos nosotros _____ ,
entonces, _____ más, _____ adelante y _____
para nosotros y para los que _____ después.

Letter *ñ*

The sound of the Spanish **ñ** has no exact equivalent in English. It is similar to the combination *n* + *y* in *canyon*, or the *g* + *n* in *filet mignon*, an expression of French origin. Listen carefully and repeat the following words and sentences.

mañana	España	uñas	bañar
señor	enseñar	compañero	año

El señor Peña enseña mañana.
En la cabaña hay un pañuelo de España.
El año que viene comeremos piña.

Letter *h*

In Spanish, the letter **h** is silent. Listen carefully and repeat the following words and sentences.

Horacio	ahora	hambre	habrá
hora	horario	hacer	haber

Horacio hace el horario ahora.
La hija y el hijo de Horacio hacen helado.
Hablan del hermano de Héctor.

Letter *ch*

In Spanish, the letter **ch** is pronounced like the English letters *ch* in the word *much*. Listen carefully and repeat the following words and sentences.

Lucho	mucho	chiquito	chica
Chávez	Camacho	muchacha	churros

Lucho Chávez come muchos churros.
Chelo es la chica que escribe cheques.
Lucho charla con Chelo y toma chocolate.

Actividad • Trabalenguas fácil

Practice the following tongue twister.

> María Chucena su choza techaba y un techador
> que por allí pasaba le preguntó:
> — ¿Qué techas María Chucena?
> ¿Techas mi choza o techas la ajena?
> — Ni techo tu choza ni techo la ajena.
> Yo techo la choza de María Chucena.

¿LO SABES?

Let's review some of the points you've learned in this unit.

SECTION A

Answers will vary.

Are you able to express yourself in Spanish when you are disappointed?
Form five sentences showing your dissatisfaction or annoyance with someone or with something. Then ask for help. Here are some ideas:
  You bought a new television set and you can't make it work.
  You are having problems with your motorcycle.
  Your portable radio is old, and it is not working well.

Can you give commands in Spanish to others?
Make a list of the six most common commands you receive from your parents.

SECTION B

Answers will vary.

Can you say what you will do tomorrow?
Write five sentences in Spanish indicating what you will do tomorrow.

Do you know how to express your predictions for the future in Spanish?
Using your imagination, write a paragraph predicting at least five different things that will happen in the future.

Are you able to discuss how often or how quickly you can do something?
Explain how often you do the following activities.
  1. pasear por el parque
  2. andar en bicicleta
  3. cortar el césped
Now explain how quickly you do each of the following things.
  1. hacer la tarea
  2. arreglarse para salir
  3. salir de la escuela por la tarde

SECTION C

Answers will vary.

Are you able to express logical conclusions in Spanish?
Pair up with a partner and discuss your Spanish course, following the model.
  A la corta o a la larga tendremos que estudiar más.

Do you know how to express what you would do in each of the following situations?
  1. You were accepted to a well-known college in Spain.
  2. You needed to raise your grade point average to graduate.
  3. You made the basketball and swim teams, but you could only participate in one sport.
  4. You visited friends in Madrid and got lost.

When you receive an invitation, how would you politely decline that invitation by expressing other obligations?
Pair up with a classmate who will invite you to do five different things.
Tell him/her that you would like to do those things, but you have other plans.

Can you ask somebody to help you in Spanish?
Ask a classmate to help you with your computer. Then ask two other classmates to do you a favor.

VOCABULARIO

SECTION A

apretar (ie) *to press*
la **base de datos** *data base*
borrar *to erase*
el **botón** *button*
el **cajón** *drawer*
calmar(se) *to calm (oneself)*
dar una mano *to lend a hand*
el **disquete** *disk*
el **escritorio** *desk*
estar harto de . . . *to be sick and tired of . . .*
funcionar *to work; to operate*
hasta la punta de los pelos *fed up*
el **impresor** *printer*
la **informática** *data processing*
inmediatamente *immediately*
el **manual** *manual*
el **menú** *menu (computer)*
la **pantalla** *screen*
la **programación** *computer programming*
el **progreso** *progress*
teclear *to type*
la **tecnología** *technology*
tener paciencia *to be patient*
la **universidad** *university*
volverse loco, -a *to go crazy*

SECTION B

a la carrera *in a hurry*
el **adelanto tecnológico** *technological advance*
la **carrera** *career*
casarse *to get married*
el **continente** *continent*
de vez en cuando *once in a while*
dentro de un rato *in a while*
en un abrir y cerrar de ojos *in a second, in a flash*
en un dos por tres *in a jiffy*
en un par de horas *in a couple of hours*
he aquí *here is; here are*
el **idioma** *language*
la **ingeniería espacial** *aerospace engineering*

lamentar *to regret*
lejano, -a *distant*
la **llave** *key*
la **nación** *nation*
el **país extranjero** *foreign country*
poner(se) en contacto *to get in touch (with)*
precaver *to take precautions*
el **proverbio** *proverb*
soñar (ue) *to dream*
el **transbordador espacial** *space shuttle*

SECTION C

a la corta o a la larga *sooner or later*
agrícola *agricultural*
el **átomo** *atom*
la **bomba atómica** *atomic bomb*
el **campo de la medicina** *medical field*
el **césped** *lawn, grass*
cortar el césped *to mow the lawn*
la **científica** *scientist (f.)*
el **científico** *scientist (m.)*
conservar *to preserve*
la **contaminación** *pollution*
la **contaminación ambiental** *environmental pollution*
la **cosecha** *harvest, crop*
curar *to cure*
de hecho *as a matter of fact*
el **desastre** *disaster*
la **dificultad** *difficulty*
duradero, -a *lasting*
la **energía nuclear** *nuclear energy*
fabricar *to manufacture; to construct*
la **fuente** *source*
gozar de *to enjoy*
la **guerra** *war*
la **industria** *industry*
la **labor** *labor; work*
labores domésticas *household chores*
librar(se) *to free (oneself)*
la **libreta** *notebook*

¿me podrías dar (decir, prestar) . . . ? *could you give me (tell me, lend me) . . . ?*
la **medicina** *medicine*
el **medio ambiente** *environment*
la **milla** *mile*
la **misión espacial** *space mission*
la **operación** *operation; surgery*
el **peligro** *danger*
peligroso, -a *dangerous*
la **planta nuclear** *nuclear plant*
¿podrías hacerme el favor de . . . ? *could you do me a favor and . . . ?*
por consiguiente *consequently; thus*
por lo tanto *as a result; therefore*
la **precipitación radioactiva** *radioactive fallout*
producir *to produce*
progresar *to progress, to advance*
la **prueba** *test*
¿querrías decirme (darme, prestarme) . . . ? *would you tell me (give me, lend me) . . . ?*
la **radiación** *radiation*
radioactivo *radioactive*
el **rayo láser** *laser beam*
el **reactor nuclear** *nuclear reactor*
los **residuos radioactivos** *radioactive waste*
resistente *resistant*
la **revolución agrícola** *agricultural revolution*
¿serías tan amable de . . . ? *would you be nice enough to . . . ?*
submarino, -a *underwater*
el **suministro** *supply*
¿tendrías la bondad de . . . ? *would you be so kind as to . . . ?*
el **trasplante de órgano** *organ transplant*
la **ventaja** *advantage*
viajar *to travel*

PRÁCTICA DEL VOCABULARIO

1. Review the unit vocabulary list and find at least six names of technological innovations. La base de datos, el disquete, el impresor, el menú, la informática, ingeniería espacial.
2. Now write a sentence describing the particular use of each innovation. Answers will vary.

VAMOS A LEER

Antes de leer

1. Remember that many scientific and technical words are cognates. In the reading selection you will find cognates that are easily identifiable, such as **existir** and **órganos.** You will also find others that are more difficult to identify, such as **acostumbrar, monstruos,** and **pasajeros.** What do they mean?   *accustom, monsters, passengers*
2. Once in a while you will come across a false cognate — that is, a Spanish word that may look like an English word, but has a different meaning. What do you think is the definition of the word **realizar?**   *to fulfill*

Preparación para la lectura

Answer the following questions before reading.

1. Antes no había en el mundo luz eléctrica, automóviles, televisión ni teléfono. ¿Qué adelantos tecnológicos tuvieron tus padres que no tuvieron tus abuelos?   la televisión
2. ¿Y qué adelantos tienes tú que no tuvieron tus padres?   videos
3. Mira rápidamente la Lectura. ¿De qué se trata?   La tecnología cambia el mundo.
4. Sabes que lo contrario de *aparecer* es *desaparecer.* ¿Sabes cuál es la relación entre *posible* e *imposible; cómodo* e *incómodo*?   Son antónimos.
5. Busca rápidamente en la Lectura en qué año tuvimos las primeras calculadoras pequeñas.   Desde 1971.

UN MUNDO DIFERENTE

Hace veinte años el mundo era diferente. La tecnología moderna nos ha acostumbrado a muchas cosas que no existían antes. ¿Cómo podíamos vivir entonces? ¿Podríamos ahora vivir sin ellas? Es difícil imaginar la vida sin todos estos adelantos. Aquí hay sólo unos ejemplos.

LOS TRASPLANTES

Los hombres que no tenían suficiente pelo empezaron a hacerse trasplantes, pero el pelo no crecía° normalmente. Cuando el doctor Barnard trasplantó un corazón° humano por primera vez en 1967 y trató de hacerlo funcionar, esto parecía imposible. Hoy se hacen trasplantes de toda clase de órganos, algunos artificiales.

LA CALCULADORA Y EL RELOJ DIGITAL

Antiguamente había que pasar mucho tiempo para sumar, restar, multiplicar y dividir. Desde 1971, una calculadora de bolsillo° puede dar las respuestas en un instante. En la misma fecha, apareció el reloj digital y pronto los dos se combinaron, añadiéndosele° después el calendario y el despertador.

---

no crecía *did not grow*   **corazón** *heart*   **bolsillo** *pocket*   **añadiéndosele** *adding on*

EL JUMBO 747

El avión gigante° hizo su primer vuelo en 1970.
Al principio se pensó que íbamos a tener cabinas
cómodas° con camas para dormir. ¡Había tanto
espacio! Pero resultó más importante reducir el
precio de los boletos°. Estos monstruos del espacio
pueden transportar 490 pasajeros. Después vino
el Concorde, el avión más rápido, que cruza el
Atlántico en menos de tres horas.

LA MICROCOMPUTADORA

Las primeras microcomputadoras de 1971
eran muy diferentes de las computadoras
profesionales y domésticas que tenemos ahora.
Éstas nos trajeron° además una gran variedad
de juegos de video como el "comecocos"°.

LAS LENTES DE CONTACTO

Para todo el mundo que usa lentes de cristal,
las lentes de contacto blandas° representan una
verdadera revolución. Las primeras eran duras°
e incómodas°. Ahora casi no se sienten. Puedes
enseñar° tus lindos ojos y ver bien al mismo
tiempo. Y si siempre soñaste con° tener los ojos
azules, verdes o color violeta, ahora puedes
realizar tu sueño.

---

gigante	*giant*	**cómodas**	*comfortable*	**boletos**	*tickets*	**trajeron**	*brought*	**"comecocos"**	*Pac-man*	**blandas** *soft*
duras	*hard*	**incómodas**	*uncomfortable*	**enseñar**	*to show*	**soñaste con**	*dreamed of*		

LA VIDEOCASETERA

Antes de 1969 no existía. Hoy es posible ver en cualquier momento muchas películas viejas y nuevas, el programa de televisión que no pudiste ver porque fuiste a una fiesta, un concierto de música o instrucciones para preparar una paella.

LA ANTENA PARABÓLICA

Los programas de televisión de los canales locales ya no eran interesantes. La comunicación mundial por medio de satélites nos trajo° la posibilidad de ver toda la televisión del mundo. Y llegaron las parabólicas° que nos permiten ver los programas de otras ciudades lejanas.

EL CONTESTADOR AUTOMÁTICO

¿Te gusta hablar con una máquina°? ¿No? A nadie le gusta, pero es mucho mejor que tener que repetir la llamada una y otra vez y no encontrar a la persona que buscas. Ahora con una llamada es suficiente. Y si estás muy ocupado° y no puedes ir al teléfono, puedes recibir el mensaje y llamar más tarde. ¡Nunca pierdes una invitación!

---

trajo *brought*   **parabólicas** *satellite dishes*   **máquina** *machine*   **ocupado** *busy*

NUEVOS DEPORTES

No es fácil inventar un deporte nuevo. Pero la tabla vela entró en los Juegos Olímpicos por primera vez en 1984. Comenzó en las playas de Australia y pronto se hizo popular. Requiere, además de mucha práctica, una tabla hawaiana° donde vas de pie, una vela° triangular de lindos colores que se dirige° con las manos, y no tenerle miedo al agua fría.

Actividad • Preguntas y respuestas

Answer the following questions about **Un mundo diferente.**

1. ¿Por qué era el mundo diferente hace veinte años?
2. ¿Qué es lo nuevo en un reloj digital?
3. ¿Cómo cambió nuestra vida la calculadora de bolsillo?
4. ¿Cuál es el avión más grande hasta ahora? ¿Y el más rápido?
5. ¿Cuál es la diferencia?
6. ¿Cómo son las nuevas lentes de contacto?
7. ¿Es una buena idea cambiar el color de los ojos de acuerdo con la ropa que llevas? ¿Por qué?
8. ¿Qué ventajas tiene el contestador automático?
9. ¿Dónde comenzó la tabla vela? ¿Por qué es necesario no tener miedo al agua fría?

1 Porque hay muchas cosas hoy día que no existían antes.   2. Tiene la hora y el minuto exacto.   3. No tenemos que pasar mucho tiempo para sumar, restar, multiplicar y dividir.   4. El avión más grande es el Jumbo 747. El avión más rápido es el Concorde.   5. El avión más grande lleva más pasajeros y es más económico.   6. Las nuevas lentes de contacto son blandas.   7. *Answers will vary.*   8. El contestador automático tiene la ventaja de que no se tiene que repetir la llamada muchas veces.   9. La tabla vela comenzó en Australia. Cuando aprendes a usar la tabla vela, te caes al agua muchas veces.

Actividad • ¿Qué uso?

What technological advance is useful in the following situations?

1. Me estoy bañando y suena el teléfono.   Uso el contestador automático.
2. Quiero saber cuánto cuestan tres relojes a $9.75 cada uno.   Uso la calculadora de bolsillo.
3. Se me cae el pelo.   Necesito un trasplante de pelo.
4. Quiero ir a París lo más rápidamente posible.   Voy en el Concorde.
5. No escribo claramente y tengo que presentar un informe.   Uso una microcomputadora.
6. No veo bien. No me gusta usar lentes de cristal.   Uso las lentes de contacto.
7. Los programas de televisión locales son muy tontos.   Busco una buena película y la pongo en mi videocasetera.

Actividad • Charla   Answers will vary.

With a classmate, discuss how life used to be without modern technology. How did students get to school? What did people do without television? How long did it take to visit a relative or a friend who lived in another state?

---

tabla hawaiana   *surfboard*   **vela**   *sail*   **se dirige**   *is steered*

UNIDAD **8** Las fiestas son
para divertirse

Repaso

TEACHER-PREPARED MATERIALS
Review 8   Map of Bolivia,
   magazine pictures of
   chocolate cake, chicken
   sandwiches, enchiladas

UNIT RESOURCES
Manual de actividades, Unit 8
Manual de ejercicios, Unit 8
Unit 8 Cassette
Transparency 20
Review Test 2

Unit 8 reviews functions, grammar, and vocabulary that the students have
studied in Units 5–7. No new material is included. This unit provides
communicative and writing practice in different situations; that is, it gives
different applications and uses of the same material. If your students require
further practice, you will find additional review exercises in Unit 8 of the
Manual de actividades and the **Manual de ejercicios.** On the other hand, if
your students have successfully mastered the material in Units 5–7, you may
wish to omit parts of Unit 8. Some of the activities in this unit lend
themselves to cooperative learning.

OBJECTIVE   To review communicative functions, grammar, and vocabulary
from Units 5–7

CULTURAL BACKGROUND   One of the most important celebrations in
Spanish America is a girl's fifteenth birthday. A party given in honor of the
quinceañera is usually very formal and elaborate. Preparations take several
months, because many guests are invited, and there is an abundance of
food, decorations, and music. The **quinceañera** wears a beautiful formal
gown and is escorted by a young man called **compañero de baile** or **pareja.**
The party begins with the girl dancing with her father, then with her
brothers, and finally with her guests.

MOTIVATING ACTIVITY   Tell the class to imagine that several Bolivian
students are coming to visit. They would like to meet some American
students, have fun, and perhaps teach their peers some Spanish. You may
wish to locate Bolivia on the map for the students. Suggest to the students
that they plan a welcoming party. Have them brainstorm ideas about
location, food, and entertainment, including such details as name tags. You
may wish to write their ideas on the board or a transparency. If possible, hold
an actual party at school and call on volunteers to act as Bolivian students.

1

¡A dieta!

Before the students read the selection, you may wish to discuss diets with
the students. They may suggest several foods that help people lose or gain
weight. You may also quickly review the foods mentioned in the dialog,
using magazine pictures. Play the cassette or read the dialog aloud. Then
call on volunteers to role-play the dialog. To check comprehension, call on
students to retell the events of the dialog in their own words.

2   Actividad • Preguntas y respuestas

Have the students work in pairs to complete the activity. They should take turns asking and answering the questions.

As a variation, have the students write true or false statements. They should exchange papers and correct the false statements.

3   Actividad • ¡A escoger!

For writing practice at home or in class, instruct the students to select the correct word to complete each sentence and then write the completed sentences. Review the answers with them. You may wish to use this activity or a similar one as a practice quiz.

4   Actividad • ¿Qué escribías en tu diario?

Assign this activity for homework. Tell the students that their diary entries may be real or imaginary. They should use the questions as a guide. Then call on volunteers to read their entries aloud to the class.

CHALLENGE   For additional practice describing details, ask the students to complete the following activity. They should imagine that they were on a plane en route from Madrid to Málaga. A woman suddenly seized the plane and forced the pilot to land in Toledo. After the plane landed, she fled into a crowd. The police are now looking for her. For cooperative learning, form groups of three. Have the groups write descriptions of the skyjacker using the imperfect tense and descriptive adjectives.

5   Actividad • ¡Ayúdame, por favor!

Re-enter the familiar **tú** command before the students complete the activity. For writing practice, have them write the answers in complete sentences. Then have them exchange papers to correct their work.

6   Actividad • Charla

You may wish to review the names of the parts of the body, names of toiletries, and reflexive pronouns with the students before they complete the activity. Have each student work with a partner to describe what each person did before the party. For further practice, have the students describe things they did to get ready for school. Remind them to use reflexive pronouns when necessary.

7   Actividad • ¿Quién se va de viaje?

Have the students complete the activity orally or in writing. Call on individuals to read the sentences aloud as you or a volunteer writes them on the board.

8   SITUACIÓN • ¡Qué pena!

Before presenting the letter, you may wish to re-enter the irregular verb **venir** in the preterit tense (Unit 3, C9), in the future tense (Unit 7, B5), and in the conditional tense (Unit 7, C6). Play the cassette or read the letter aloud. To check comprehension, ask the following or similar questions.

1. ¿Por qué dejó la nota Marta?
2. ¿Qué hará desde el aeropuerto?

3. ¿Por qué Marta no puede ir a visitar a Laura?
4. ¿Qué promete Marta?

9 Actividad • Dime cuándo

CHALLENGE   Have each student write a note to a friend who was not at home when he or she went to visit. They should write at least six sentences and use the conditional, future, and preterit tenses.

10 Actividad • Querida Marta . . .

Assign this activity to be completed at home. Collect and correct the papers. You may also wish to compose a sample note that contains the students' most common errors and write it on the board or a transparency. Have the students point out the mistakes and suggest ways to correct the note.

11 Actividad • ¡A escribir!

For cooperative learning, have the students work in groups of four. When the groups have finished, call on a member from each group to read the list aloud as you or a volunteer writes it on the board or a transparency. Then compare all the plans for the party and have the class prepare a master list.

12 Actividad • Palabras y más palabras

SLOWER-PACED LEARNING   Complete the activity orally. Ask the students to explain the reason for not including the words that they have omitted.

13 Comprensión

You will hear Arturo's description of his trip to Spain. It consists of three paragraphs, each followed by four statements. After listening to each paragraph, decide if the statements are true (**verdadero**) or false (**falso**). Check the appropriate space on your answer sheet.

Recuerdo mi primer viaje a España. Fui con un grupo de estudiantes y al llegar a Madrid estaba lloviendo mucho. El primer día perdimos cuatro maletas en el aeropuerto. Fue un problema horrible porque todos nos mojamos en la lluvia y cuatro personas no tenían ropa seca al llegar al hotel.

1. El viaje fue con un grupo de profesores.   *falso*
2. Perdieron unas maletas al llegar.   *verdadero*
3. Hacía muy buen tiempo en Madrid.   *falso*
4. El problema fue que no podían cambiarse la ropa al llegar al hotel.
   verdadero

La primera noche salimos a comprar unas tarjetas postales para escribirles a nuestros amigos en casa. Luego decidimos buscar un restaurante porque teníamos hambre. Ese mismo día, Diana cumplía 17 años y cuando vimos que vendían flores en la esquina, Rolando me dijo, —¡Cómprale unas rosas!

5. Buscaron tarjetas postales para mandárselas a los amigos.
verdadero
6. Decidieron comer en una cafetería. *falso*
7. Diana celebraba el día de su santo. *falso*
8. Los dos muchachos le compraron flores a Diana. *verdadero*

Al día siguiente nos levantamos temprano porque íbamos a hacer una excursión al Palacio Real, La Puerta del Sol y el museo de El Prado. A Sara le gustaba mucho el arte y estaba muy entusiasmada. El profesor tenía dos cámaras y siempre buscaba la foto perfecta de todo el grupo y decidió sacar una delante del Palacio.

9. Se levantaron tarde el primer día. *falso*
10. Visitaron tres lugares de interés el primer día. *verdadero*
11. A Sara le gustaba ver las cosas antiguas. *falso*
12. El profesor sacaba muchas fotos. *verdadero*

Viñeta cultural 3

Lugares de interés

OBJECTIVE To read in Spanish for cultural awareness

MOTIVATING ACTIVITY You may wish to compare **Viñeta cultural 3** with **Viñeta cultural 1.** First, use the transparencies of the maps (Transparencies 31, 31A, 32, 32A, 33, 33A, 34, 34A, 35, 35A) or a map of the world to show that the Hispanic world is very extensive and is composed of many different countries. Explain to the students that all these countries have something in common—the Spanish language—but that they also have a great diversity, not only of ethnic groups, as they learned in **Viñeta cultural 1,** but also of landscape, architecture, and their conception of the arts.

CULTURAL BACKGROUND Point out to the students that Spain is very diverse because each ethnic group that settled in the Iberian Peninsula left its imprint. The diversity is even greater in Spanish America because of its enormous territorial extension and its pre-Columbian cultures. In many countries, the ruins of pre-Columbian civilizations are found next to structures built by the Spaniards in styles predominant in Spain at that time.

Explain to the students that many of the fortifications that remain from the past throughout the Spanish world, in cities such as St. Augustine in Florida, Cartagena in Colombia, La Habana in Cuba, and San Juan in Puerto Rico, were constructed by order of King Charles III of Spain. Fortifications were built specifically for the purpose of protecting coastal towns from pirate attacks, and as a protection against English invasions.

Page 278

As you play the cassette or read aloud the text and captions on page 278, have the students follow along in their books. Point out the photograph of the Alcázar in Segovia on the bottom left side of the page. Explain to the students that the Spanish monarchs have changed capital cities several times. Segovia and Toledo were once capitals of Spain. It was not until King Philip II, great-great-grandson of the **Reyes Católicos** (the *"Catholic Kings"*), that Madrid became the official capital in 1561.

Draw the students' attention to the photograph of the statue of **Cristóbal Colón,** and stress the enormous importance of **Colón** and of the Catholic Kings, Fernando and Isabella. There might have been other navigators who arrived in America before **Cristóbal Colón,** but he was the person responsible for creating a bridge between America and Europe. The Catholic Kings had the foresight that no other monarch in Europe had to back **Colón** in his enterprise. Make the students aware that Europeans had no idea of the existence of the Americas and thought at first that they had found a new route to the Indies. With **Cristóbal Colón's** discovery, a whole new world was revealed.

Page 279

Now, as you read the text aloud or play the cassette, have the students look at the photos, text, and captions on page 279. Point out the photograph on the upper right side of the page. Explain to the students that it is a statue of Philip III and is located in the **Plaza Mayor** in Madrid.

Page 280

After the students have silently read the text and captions on page 280, you may wish to add that the **Prado** museum contains one of the largest art collections in the world. The bulk of it represents the collections of the Spanish monarchs, starting with the Catholic Kings. Explain to the students that the monarchs collected not only Spanish paintings, but art from all over Europe. For example, Fernando and Isabella, the Catholic Kings, favored

Page
281

Page
282

Page
283

Page
284

Flemish paintings, while the Emperor Charles V preferred Italian art and made Titian his official painter. Charles V's son, Philip II, preferred the Dutch painter Hieronymus Bosch (called **Bosco** in Spanish), while Philip IV named Velázquez as his court painter. King Charles IV's favorite artist was Goya.

As you read the text and captions aloud on page 281, or play the cassette, ask the students to follow along in their books. Explain to the students that many of the pre-Columbian cities, such as Tenochtitlán (Mexico City) and Cuzco, were larger than most European cities at the time.

Continue reading the text and captions aloud on page 282 or playing the cassette. You may wish to add that Machu Picchu is located high in the Andes mountains. For that reason, it was not found until early in the twentieth century. There had always been talk of a legendary lost city of the Incas, but it was not until 1911 that the American archeologist H. A. Bingham discovered it.

Point out to the students the photograph on the bottom right side of page 282. Explain to them that Lima, the capital of Peru, was founded by Francisco Pizarro in 1535 and is one of the most beautiful cities in South America. The **Universidad Mayor de San Marcos,** which is located in Lima, was founded in 1551 and is one of the oldest universities in America.

After the students have had the opportunity to read the captions and look at the photographs on page 283, you may wish to tell them that Venezuela has beautiful beaches on the Caribbean Sea and that Venezuela and Colombia were once part of the **Virreinato de Nueva Granada** during colonial times. Point out that the city of Cartagena in Colombia was one of the most important Spanish ports in America and that it was attacked by pirates and the English Navy during the Spanish-English wars. For that reason it was fortified during the times of King Charles III of Spain. Point out to the students the photograph of the Spanish fort of **El Morro** in Puerto Rico and explain that it is an example of the forts built to protect all the important Spanish coastal cities from attack.

Have the students follow along in their books as you read aloud the text and the captions on page 284 or play the cassette. Point out to the students the photographs of Caracas (upper right side of page) and Cuzco (lower left side of page). Ask them to compare the view of Caracas with the view of Cuzco. Explain that modern cities, such as Caracas, Bogotá, Buenos Aires, and Montevideo, are cities equal to, or perhaps more interesting than, New York or London. In cities such as Cuzco, the Spanish world is gifted not only with modern cities, but also with gems of colonial architecture that seem to have been forgotten by time.

UNIDAD 8

Las fiestas son para divertirse

Repaso

1

¡A dieta! 📼

Las comidas y los dulces se ponen de moda en las celebraciones
y las fiestas, pero las personas que están a dieta no deben caer en
la tentación. En la fiesta de Laura había muchas cosas de comer.

ELENITA   Eduardo, mira como hay cosas sabrosas en la mesa.

EDUARDO   Sí, ¿te gustaría probar la torta de chocolate?

ELENITA   Ay, sí, ¡cómo me gustaría! . . . pero estoy a dieta.

EDUARDO   Un pedacito no te hará aumentar mucho.

ELENITA   ¡Qué tentación! Bueno, un pedacito nada más.

*(Elenita come un poco, camina un poco y de pronto se encuentra con
dos amigas.)*

JOSEFINA
Y ELISA   ¡Hola, Elenita! ¡Cuánto tiempo sin verte!

ELENITA   ¡Qué sorpresa! No sabía que estaban aquí . . . y tu hermano
Tomás, ¿cómo está?

ELISA   Está muy bien, pero no pudo venir a la fiesta.

(Las muchachas se acercan a la mesa y miran los platos que hay.)

JOSEFINA   ¡Mira, Elenita! ¡Qué bocadillos de pollo tan sabrosos!
Prueba uno.

ELENITA   Bueno, uno sólo, . . . y esas enchiladas tan sabrosas. ¡Tráeme una!

(Josefina le trae una enchilada.)

ANITA   Y tú, ¡come la torta de chocolate! ¡Está tan rica!

(Las muchachas comen alegremente cuando Eduardo se acerca y . . .)

EDUARDO   Pero, Elenita, ¿no estabas a dieta?

ELENITA   Eduardo, ¡por favor! Tú siempre con tus cosas.

EDUARDO   Sí, pero no estoy a dieta como tú.

JOSEFINA
Y ELISA   Vamos, ¡no discutan ahora! Las fiestas son para divertirse.

EDUARDO   Elenita, ¿me perdonas?

ELENITA   Por supuesto . . . si me sacas a bailar.

EDUARDO   Mira, están tocando nuestra canción favorita. ¿Bailamos ahora?

Las fiestas son para divertirse   **273**

2 Actividad • Preguntas y respuestas

Answer each of the following questions in complete sentences.

1. ¿Quién estaba a dieta?   Elenita estaba a dieta.
2. ¿Qué le dijo Eduardo a Elenita?   Eduardo le dijo que un pedacito no la haría aumentar mucho.
3. ¿Con quién se encontró Elenita?   Elenita se encontró con dos amigas.
4. ¿Quién no pudo venir?   Tomás no pudo venir a la fiesta.
5. ¿Qué probó Elenita?   Elenita probó un bocadillo de pollo.
6. ¿Para qué son las fiestas?   Las fiestas son para divertirse.
7. ¿Quién saca a bailar a Elenita?   Eduardo saca a Elenita a bailar.

3 Actividad • ¡A escoger!

Choose the correct word in parentheses to complete each sentence.

1. Eduardo (probó, probaba) la torta de chocolate.
2. Elenita (estuvo, estaba) a dieta.
3. No (vio, veía) a sus amigas desde hacía mucho tiempo.
4. Tomás no (pudo, podía) venir a la fiesta.
5. Ellas (comieron, comían) cuando él se acercó.
6. Oyeron que (tocaron, tocaban) su canción favorita.

4 Actividad • ¿Qué escribías en tu diario?   Answers will vary.

Prepare an entry for your diary describing the last party you attended. Use the
preterit and the imperfect tenses. Here are some hints.

¿A qué hora llegaste? ¿Y los otros invitados?
¿Cuánta gente había? ¿Quién no estaba?
¿Qué pasó?
¿Bailaste? ¿Con quién? ¿Y los demás?
¿Qué había de comer?
¿A qué hora terminó la fiesta?

5 Actividad • ¡Ayúdame, por favor!

You are getting things ready for a party and your friends are helping you. Tell
them what to do.

MODELO   Evelio / comprar los refrescos.
         Evelio, compra los refrescos, por favor.

1. Alicia / traer las flores   Alicia, trae las flores, por favor.
2. Víctor / poner un casete   Víctor, pon un casete, por favor.
3. Rosalía / contestar el teléfono   Rosalía, contesta el teléfono, por favor.
4. Antonio / volver a abrir la puerta   Antonio, vuelve a abrir la puerta, por favor.
5. Silvia / hacer los bocadillos   Silvia, haz los bocadillos, por favor.
6. Tere / empezar a servir la comida   Tere, empieza a servir la comida, por favor.

Using the illustrations as clues, describe what each person did before the party.
Follow the model.

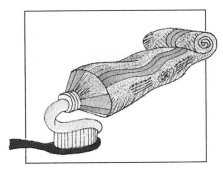

MODELO   la señora Gómez
La señora Gómez se cepilló los dientes.

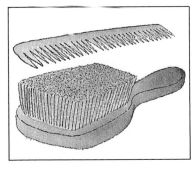

1. Elisa

2. Laura

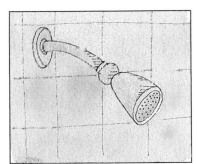

3. Toni

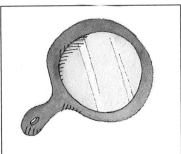

4. Eduardo

5. María Isabel

6. César

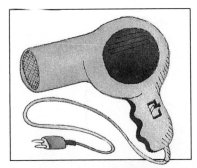

7. el señor Díaz

1. Elisa se bañó.   2. Laura se lavó el pelo.   3. Toni se cepilló y se peinó
el pelo.   4. Eduardo se miró en el espejo.   5. María Isabel se pintó los
labios.   6. César se lavó las manos.   7. El señor Díaz se secó el pelo.

7 Actividad • ¿Quién se va de viaje?

While at a party, you love to chat with your friends. Complete the following sentences with the correct form of the verb in parentheses.

1. Marta (irse) de viaje mañana.   Marta se va de viaje mañana.
2. Elenita (servirse) toda la tortilla anoche.   Elenita se sirvió toda la tortilla anoche.
3. Yo quise (ponerse) a dieta todos los días.   Yo quise ponerme a dieta todos los días.
4. Tú no (quedarse) en casa el sábado pasado.   Tú no te quedaste en casa el sábado pasado.
5. David (enfermarse) anoche.   David se enfermó anoche.
6. Los niños (dormirse) temprano todas las noches.   Los niños se duermen temprano todas las noches.
7. Nosotros (prepararse) más enchiladas.   Nosotros nos preparamos más enchiladas.

8 SITUACIÓN • ¡Qué pena!

Laura went shopping for the party. When she came back, she found this note on the door.

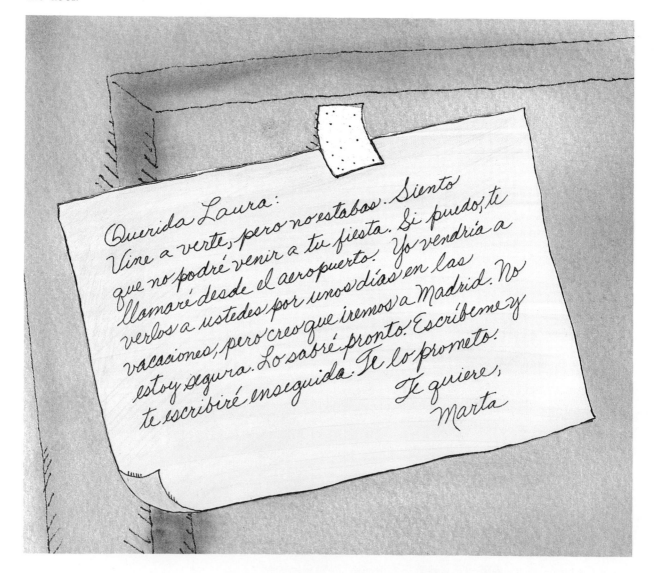

Querida Laura:
Vine a verte, pero no estabas. Siento que no podré venir a tu fiesta. Si puedo, te llamaré desde el aeropuerto. Yo vendría a verlos a ustedes por unos días en las vacaciones, pero creo que iremos a Madrid. No estoy segura. Lo sabré pronto. Escríbeme y te escribiré enseguida. Te lo prometo.
Te quiere,
Marta

Actividad • Dime cuándo

Looking at Marta's note, find two actions that have already happened; two that are happening in the present; two that will happen in the future; and two that might happen.

Past	Present	Future	Might happen
Vine a verte	No estoy segura	No podré venir	Yo vendría
No estabas	Te lo prometo	Te escribiré	Si puedo, te llamaré

10 ## Actividad • Querida Marta . . .   Answers will vary.

Write to Marta. Imagine you are Laura, and comment on Marta's note. Do not forget to tell her how the party was.

11 ## Actividad • ¡A escribir!   Answers will vary.

Your cousin comes to the city unexpectedly and you want to give a party. You have only one day to prepare. What would you do? Make a list of the things you would do. Here are some hints:

¿A quién invitarías?
¿Qué prepararías de comida? ¿de bebida?
¿Dónde sería la fiesta?
¿Qué música pondrías?
¿Qué más harías?

12 ## Actividad • Palabras y más palabras

Choose a word that is not related to the others from each group.

1. graduaciones — aniversarios — bodas — carnavales
2. noveno — séptimo — cuarto — cuatro
3. pierna — régimen — espalda — cintura
4. sabía — esperaba — iba — celebro
5. afeitarse — cepillar — bañarse — vestirse
6. nadie — algo — alguien — algunos
7. secadora — desodorante — peine — enjuague
8. jabón — nariz — ojos — boca
9. espinacas — zanahorias — apio — almuerzo
10. llegará — iré — era — abriré
11. artículo — progreso — ádelanto — tecnología
12. Teresita — Saulito — Manuel — Angelita

13 ## Comprensión   For script, see p. T166–167.

You will hear Arturo's description of his trip to Spain. It consists of three paragraphs, each followed by four statements. After listening to each paragraph, decide if the statements are true (**verdadero**) or false (**falso**). Check the appropriate space on your answer sheet.

	1	2	3	4	5	6	7	8	9	10	11	12
Verdadero		✔		✔	✔			✔		✔		✔
Falso	✔		✔			✔	✔		✔		✔	

Lugares de interés

El mundo hispánico le ofrece al viajero todo lo que podría interesarle. En España, por ejemplo, se encuentra la ciudad de Segovia, famosa por su acueducto romano. Este acueducto, que mide *(measures)* 2,500 pies de largo y 85 de alto, todavía abastece de *(supplies)* agua a la ciudad. Otros lugares de interés para el viajero son las catedrales de León, Barcelona, Burgos, Toledo y Sevilla que son muestras *(samples)* incomparables de la arquitectura gótica.

La estatua de Cristóbal Colón domina (dominates) *el sector portuario* (harbor area) *en la ciudad de Barcelona, España.*

El acueducto romano de Segovia

El Alcázar, castillo histórico y legendario, fue una vez residencia de los Reyes Católicos. Está en Segovia, España.

La Catedral de Barcelona, ejemplo del estilo gótico en España

En la región de Andalucía, al sur de España, es donde verdaderamente se puede apreciar el esplendor de la España musulmana. Los palacios árabes de La Alhambra y El Generalife, en las afueras de Granada, son verdaderas joyas *(jewels)* arquitectónicas y la torre *(tower)* de La Giralda también posee una belleza inigualable *(unequalled)*.

Madrid, la capital de España, es una ciudad de incomparable belleza. La Plaza Mayor fue una vez el centro de la ciudad y aún hoy día su arquitectura barroca atrae *(attracts)* los visitantes. El Palacio Real es otra muestra de la arquitectura barroca.

La Giralda en Sevilla fue construida por los árabes en el siglo XII. Hoy día es la torre de la Catedral de Sevilla.

La Plaza Mayor, Madrid, España

El Palacio Real de Madrid ha sido asiento **(the seat)** *de la monarquía española desde el siglo XVIII.*

Los jardines del Generalife en Granada cuentan con múltiples fuentes **(fountains)** *que refrescan el ambiente* **(environment)**.

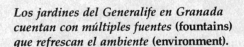

El palacio morisco **(Moorish)** *de La Alhambra es una de las joyas arquitectónicas de Granada.*

En los museos de Madrid, incluyendo El Prado, se pueden ver cuadros *(paintings)* de grandes maestros *(masters)* españoles, tales como El Greco, Velázquez, Goya y Picasso.

El Prado, uno de los más grandes museos del mundo, contiene una vasta colección de obras (works) de arte.

Velázquez: "La reina Isabel, esposa del rey Felipe IV"

El Greco: "El entierro del Conde de Orgaz"

Goya: "La Maja y los embozados"

En Hispanoamérica también se encuentran lugares de interés. En México, a lo largo de la península de Yucatán, así como también en Guatemala y en Honduras, se pueden ver numerosas ruinas de ciudades precolombinas, tales como Uxmal, Chichén Itzá, Tikal Copán. Todas ellas son ejemplos de la magnífica civilización maya.

Mercado Libertad en Guadalajara, México

Ruinas de la gran civilización maya, en Palenque, México

El Museo de Arte Popular en Mérida posee bellas muestras de tejidos (samples of hand-woven fabrics).

Una vista de Mérida en Yucatán

Impresionante perspectiva de la Casa de las Monjas en Uxmal

Uno de los lugares más interesantes de toda Hispanoamérica es la ciudad inca de Machu Picchu en Perú. Situada en la cordillera (mountain range) de los Andes, Machu Picchu es una de las más impresionantes muestras de la civilización inca.

El mercado del Sol en Pisac, Perú

Ruinas de Machu Picchu, la ciudad perdida de los incas que fue descubierta (was discovered) por el arqueólogo norteamericano H. A. Bingham en 1911.

Una vista de la Plaza de Armas en Lima, Perú

Cuando se habla de bellezas naturales *(natural beauty)*, pocos lugares en el mundo se pueden comparar con las mundialmente conocidas *(world renowned)* playas hispánicas y las cristalinas aguas del Caribe.

El Morro en San Juan, fuerte defensor de la isla de Puerto Rico

Disfrutando de un día de playa en Caraballeda, Venezuela

Este velero (sailboat) *se acerca a una de las bellas playas de Santo Domingo.*

Pescadores (Fishermen) *en el puerto de Campeche, México*

Debido (*Due to*) a sus lugares de gran valor cultural, al igual que a sus bellezas naturales, el mundo hispánico sigue siendo (*continues to be*) un mundo de gran interés para el viajero.

Montevideo, en Uruguay, cuenta con hermosas avenidas y numerosos restaurantes.

Vista del Capitolio de Caracas, Venezuela. Una pintura (painting) panorámica representando la Batalla de Carabobo cubre la cúpula (dome) del Capitolio. Esta batalla (battle) fue una importante victoria en la guerra (war) de la independencia contra los españoles.

Cuzco, antigua capital de los incas, en el Perú

Un día placentero en la bella isla de Puerto Rico. Al fondo puede verse el castillo del Morro.

UNIDAD 9
La juventud

286

In this unit you will learn about the many different ways in which Spanish-speaking teenagers have fun. Are they very different from yours? Read on and meet Narciso and his friends as they enjoy themselves.

UNIDAD 10
La ciudad y el campo

330

City life and country life . . . two different styles of living. In this unit you will learn about Argentina and its capital, Buenos Aires. You will also meet several teenagers and learn what they like best about living in the big city or in the great outdoors.

UNIDAD 11
¡Qué bonita es Barcelona!

366

In this unit you will travel to Barcelona, Spain, one of the most beautiful port cities on the Mediterranean. You will learn about Barcelona and the Catalonians as you join Isabel, Jimmy, and Víctor while they tour the city.

UNIDAD 12
La última reunión

406

Preparations are being made for the last get-together of the school year. Join these students as they talk of the year they've spent together, and about their plans for the summer.

UNIDAD 9 La juventud
Scope and Sequence

	BASIC MATERIAL	COMMUNICATIVE FUNCTIONS
SECTION A	**Narciso el bello** (A1) **En la verbena** (A12) **Practicando la tabla vela** (A15) **Divirtiéndose en la playa** (A19)	**Exchanging information** • Reporting what others say **Persuading** • Asking for help or giving a warning
SECTION B	**Mi mejor amiga** (B1) **Leyendo los anuncios clasificados** (B15) **Los oficios** (B20)	**Expressing feelings and emotions** • Expressing amazement and pity • Expressing desire **Socializing** • Writing salutations and complimentary closings for business letters
SECTION C	**La carta del gerente** (C1) **La entrevista** (C9)	**Socializing** • Congratulating someone • Writing common introductions for business letters **Persuading** • Directing others to tell someone else to do something
TRY YOUR SKILLS	**Los clasificados** **Dictado**	

■ **Pronunciación**   (letter **d,** contrasting the sounds of the Spanish **t** and **d**)
■ **¿Lo sabes?**   ■ **Vocabulario**

VAMOS A LEER	**La entrevista** (tips for a successful interview)

WRITING   A variety of controlled and open-ended writing activities appear in the Pupil's Edition. The Teacher's Notes identify other activities suitable for writing practice.

COOPERATIVE LEARNING   Many of the activities in the Pupil's Edition lend themselves to cooperative learning. The Teacher's Notes explain some of the many instances where this teaching strategy can be particularly effective. For guidelines on how to use cooperative learning, see page T13.

GRAMMAR	CULTURE	RE-ENTRY
The superlative construction (A9)	The fairs of Spain	The indicative mood Comparisons with **más** and **menos** The use of the preterit and imperfect tenses
Irregular forms of comparatives and superlatives (B5) The Spanish subjunctive mood (B10) The subjunctive to express demands, wishes, and requests (B13) Present subjunctive of some irregular verbs (B17)	Household chores in Spanish-speaking countries	The **yo** form of irregular verbs in the present indicative
Irregular verbs and verbs ending in **-car, -gar,** and **-zar** in the present subjunctive (C5) Indirect commands (C15)	Summer vacation and the youth of Spanish America	Expressing sympathy Telling time Vocabulary for items of clothing Command forms Conditional tense Numbers

Recombining communicative functions, grammar, and vocabulary

Reading for practice and pleasure

TEACHER-PREPARED MATERIALS
Section A Magazine pictures of a fair or carnival, of four boys, of emergency situations
Section B The classified section of a Spanish newspaper, magazine pictures of people at work

UNIT RESOURCES
Manual de actividades, Unit 9
Manual de ejercicios, Unit 9
Unit 9 Cassettes
Transparencies 21–23
Quizzes 19–21
Unit 9 Test

UNIDAD

9

A1–2

OBJECTIVES **To exchange information:** report what others say; **to persuade:** ask for help or give a warning

CULTURAL BACKGROUND A **verbena** can be described as a night festival on the eve of a religious holiday. In Spain, **verbenas** are open-air festivals and are most popular during the summer months. They include fireworks, music, and traditional dances and costumes. The **verbena de la Paloma,** a well-known Spanish festival, is celebrated on the eve of August 14th in honor of the **Virgen de la Paloma,** patron saint of Madrid. To mark the occasion, windows and balconies in the populous Paloma quarter are decorated with flowers, ribbons, and ornamental tapestries. In Spanish America the **verbenas** are not necessarily connected with religious holidays. They can celebrate many other events and are often held to help raise money for charity. They usually have booths where one can purchase items, play games, or buy something to eat.

MOTIVATING ACTIVITY Ask the students to discuss any festivals held in their area. Encourage them to talk about why the festival is celebrated and to describe the kinds of food, music, rides, and games that can be found at a festival.

A1

Narciso el bello

Introduce the dialog by describing a **verbena.** You may wish to compare the Spanish celebration to a fair or a carnival in the United States. Point out that a **verbena** is sometimes held in conjunction with a saint's day, normally the patron saint of the town.

To present new vocabulary, such as **la verbena, el pulpo,** and **tirar al blanco,** bring in magazine pictures of a fair or carnival. Identify each item and ask the students to repeat after you.

While presenting and practicing the dialog in class, try to keep a fast tempo in order to maintain as much of the students' attention as possible. Insist on a normal delivery—as close as possible to that of a native speaker. Particular attention should be given to the linking of words, syllable length, and intonation. You may wish to play the cassette or read the dialog aloud. Then have the students role-play the dialog for the class. Ask several questions to check student comprehension.

After practicing the dialog, you may also wish to explain briefly the Greek legend of Narcissus (**Narciso** in Spanish). Narcissus was a beautiful youth who fell in love with his own reflection in the waters of a pond. When he fell in the pond and drowned, he was transformed into the narcissus flower (daffodil). Explain to the students that it is from this legend that we derive the English word *narcissism* and the Spanish word **narcisismo.**

A2

Actividad • Preguntas y respuestas

You may wish to do this activity with books closed. For cooperative learning, have the students work in pairs. They should take turns asking and answering the questions. Tell the students that they may refer to A1 if necessary.

SLOWER-PACED LEARNING Have the students complete the activity orally and then assign it as a written activity in class or at home.

A3 Sabes que . . . 📼

Many festivals are held in Spain and Spanish America. Each city has a patron saint whose feast "day" is sometimes celebrated in a week-long festival. A Spanish celebration that is widely known abroad is the festival of San Fermín. San Fermín was a Spanish martyr from Pamplona, a town in northeastern Spain. Spaniards and thousands of foreign visitors celebrate San Fermín on July 7th with a week of festivities. Each morning for seven days the bulls are run from their pens in the outskirts to the bullring located in the center of the city. People run this course alongside the bulls, challenging fate. Until recently, women were barred from the running, but since the mid 1980s, some women have also run.

A4 SE DICE ASÍ

Reinforce the information in the chart with a personalized activity. You may begin with a statement, such as **La gente dice que el ejercicio es necesario.** Then ask a student **¿Qué crees tú?** Then randomly ask individuals, **¿Qué dijo** (student's name) **del ejercicio?**

A5 Comprensión 📼

> You will hear a series of ten statements. Decide if each statement represents an event that is occurring now (**ahora**), in the past (**pasado**), or in the future (**futuro**). Mark the appropriate space on your answer sheet. For example, you will hear: **Nosotros estamos planeando una fiesta para el sábado.** You should place a check mark in the row labeled **ahora,** because the event is happening now.
>
> 1. Le pedí permiso a mamá para salir esta noche.   *pasado*
> 2. Mis amigos irán a Chile durante sus vacaciones en diciembre.   *futuro*
> 3. Mi hermano me dice que va al partido de fútbol esta noche.   *ahora*
> 4. El profesor viajará a Argentina durante las vacaciones del verano.   *futuro*
> 5. Llegarás a las ocho, ¿verdad?   *futuro*
> 6. Ellos salieron con sus amigos ayer por la tarde.   *pasado*
> 7. Yo escribí una carta a mi amigo Rafael.   *pasado*
> 8. El año que viene nosotros nos graduaremos del colegio.   *futuro*
> 9. La chica más bonita es la que está al lado de Roberto.   *ahora*
> 10. Tendrás que estudiar mucho para los exámenes de fin de año.   *futuro*
>
> Now check your answers. *Read each statement again and give the correct answer.*

A6 ¿RECUERDAS?

Review with the students the explanation and examples in the chart. Then ask them to think of other examples for each tense of the indicative mood. Call on volunteers to write their sentences on the board or a transparency. Review the sentences with the class.

A7 Actividad • ¡A completar!

For writing practice, have the students copy the paragraph. They should fill in the blanks with the correct form of the verb.

SLOWER-PACED LEARNING   Tell the students to write the paragraph as you dictate it to them and to fill in the missing verb forms. Read the paragraph again and have them correct their work.

A 8   Actividad • ¿Qué me cuentas?

Have each student choose a partner. Instruct the students to ask each other the questions and remind them to take notes. Then you may wish to ask each student to report the information to the class or to another student. Circulate through the class to monitor the students' progress.

A 9   ESTRUCTURAS ESENCIALES

To introduce the superlative, choose several students of varying heights to stand in front of the class. Point to the tallest student and ask: **¿Es alto/a** *(student's name)*? and elicit the response: **Sí, es alto/a.** Then point to the shortest student and ask: **¿Es bajo/a** *(student's name)*? Finally, point to the tallest person and say: *(Student's name)* **es el/la más alto/a del grupo.** Point to the shortest person and say: *(Student's name)* **es el/la más bajo/a del grupo.** Use the superlative in several other examples, perhaps with magazine pictures to assist you. You may wish to call on volunteers to make up a few original sentences.

You may wish to re-enter the comparative construction: **más** + *adjective* or *adverb* + **que.** Using the same pictures you used to discuss the superlative, select two people or objects and compare them. For example, **Juan es más alto que Alicia.** Then call on students to make their own comparisons.

A 10   Actividad • El sabelotodo

SLOWER-PACED LEARNING   Before the students begin the activity, read the model aloud. Then, using magazine pictures of four different boys, point to one of the pictures and say: **Narciso es el más guapo del grupo.** Then have each student work with a partner to complete the activity. You may wish to call on volunteers to write their answers on the board or a transparency.

A 11   Actividad • Mi familia

Allow the students to interview each other. To safeguard privacy, remind them that they may answer the questions with real or imaginary information. Ask them to report their findings to the class.

CHALLENGE   For writing practice, you may wish to have the students write a short paragraph about the person they interviewed, using the answers to the questions as a guide.

A 12   SITUACIÓN • En la verbena

Before presenting the new vocabulary, you may wish to begin with a brief discussion about carnivals and fairs. Explain that most Spanish-American countries use the word **la rueda giratoria** for *Ferris wheel.* In Spain it is called **la noria.** **El coche de topetazos** (bumper cars) is also called **los carros locos** in Spanish America. Then copy the illustration onto a transparency, and cover the captions. Introduce the vocabulary, working with two or three words or phrases at a time. You may wish to play the cassette and have the students repeat the words for pronunciation practice. After you have presented the material, you may use the illustration or the transparency in a vocabulary quiz.

A 13 Actividad • **Descripción del dibujo**

Ask the students to answer the questions by themselves. Remind them that they may refer to A12 as necessary. You may wish to call on students to read their answers aloud as you or a volunteer writes them on the board or a transparency. Have the students exchange papers to correct each other's work.

A 14 Actividad • **¿Qué te gusta a ti?**

Have the students work in pairs to answer the questions. For writing practice, have them write complete sentences in class or at home.

A 15 SITUACIÓN • **Practicando la tabla vela**

Discuss the photographs before reading the selection with the class. You may wish to have a copy of the selection prepared for a cloze procedure.

To check comprehension, you may wish to ask the following or similar questions.

1. ¿Adónde fueron los muchachos?
2. ¿Por qué fueron a la caseta?
3. ¿Cómo era el día?
4. ¿Por qué alquilaban el equipo temprano?

A 16 Actividad • **¿Es así o no es así?**

Ask the students to read the statements and to correct the false items.

CHALLENGE   Have the students write original true or false statements. Have them exchange papers to correct each other's statements.

A 17 Actividad • **Mi primo Alfredo**

Before you complete this activity, you may wish to re-enter the use of the preterit and the imperfect tenses. Remind the students that the imperfect describes an action in progress at some time in the past. The preterit describes a completed action. For writing practice, have the students write the completed paragraph at home or in class. You may wish to call on a volunteer to read it aloud to the class.

A 18 Actividad • **¡A escribir y a hablar!**

Before beginning, you may wish to brainstorm ideas with the class to stimulate creativity. Allow the students to complete their compositions in class to enable you to supervise and correct as they write.

For cooperative learning, form groups of two or three. Ask each group to prepare a report and to bring five or more photographs, magazine pictures, or illustrations to class. Remind the students to use the preterit and imperfect tenses. Then call on the groups to present their reports to the class. After each presentation, you may wish to ask questions.

A 19 SITUACIÓN • **Divirtiéndose en la playa**

Present the new vocabulary, such as **pescar un resfriado, ¡auxilio! ¡socorro!, echar al agua,** and **el mástil** by using the corresponding photographs in the book as visual reinforcement. Finally, play the cassette or read the selection aloud, and ask questions to check comprehension.

A 20   Actividad • Combinación

Have the students use the information in A19 to complete the activity. After matching the elements from each column, ask the students to place the sentences in the correct order of occurrence. Then have each student exchange papers with a partner for correction.

A 21   Actividad • ¿Adónde fuiste?

Have each student work with a partner to complete the activity. Encourage each student to add his or her own examples.

SLOWER-PACED LEARNING   Do several exchanges with the class before allowing the students to complete the activity with a partner. You may also wish to elicit from the students the Spanish names of leisure-time activities and write the names on the board. The students may use them to guide their conversation.

A 22   Actividad • ¿Qué hacen o qué hicieron?

For writing practice, have the students write complete sentences at home or in class. You may wish to tell them that they should use the present, the progressive, or the preterit tense, and that they may use each element more than once. Remind them to add any missing words needed to complete the sentences. Call on volunteers to write their sentences on the board or a transparency for correction.

A 23   SE DICE ASÍ

Introduce the expressions in the box, using magazine pictures that show emergency situations or by using realia that is associated with emergencies. For cooperative learning, divide the class into groups of three or four and give each group a magazine picture. Tell each group to write a short dialog, using the picture and the words from the box as a guide. Have each group role-play its dialog for the class.

A 24   Actividad • ¡Auxilio!

CHALLENGE   Have each student write five original sentences in Spanish about emergency situations that would require one of the responses in A23. Then ask each student to exchange papers with a partner and respond to each other's situations with the correct expression.

A 25   Actividad • El héroe

You may wish to re-enter the preterit and imperfect forms of the irregular verbs in the paragraph before doing the activity. Then ask the students to complete the paragraph with the correct forms of the verbs in parentheses.

SLOWER-PACED LEARNING   Make a list of correct verb forms, in scrambled order, and allow the students to choose the appropriate answer for each blank. Prepare a transparency of the paragraph. Then write the correct answers as volunteers call them out.

A 26 **Actividad • ¿Adónde vamos?**

For cooperative learning, form groups of four students to complete the activity. Tell the students to imagine that each group is going on a trip. The members of the group should agree on the place, the date, the time, the method of transportation, and so on. Groups may use pictures to illustrate their planned trips. Then call on each group to describe its plans to the class.

A 27 **Actividad • Composición dirigida**

SLOWER-PACED LEARNING You may wish to have the students prepare a poster or a collage of pictures to describe their hobbies or interests. Ask them to write a caption for each of the pictures.

SECTION B

OBJECTIVES **To express feelings and emotions:** express amazement and pity, express desire; **to socialize:** write salutations and complimentary closings for business letters

CULTURAL BACKGROUND Most families in Spain do not employ live-in or full-time maids. However, housekeepers are still available, and they are more common than in the United States.

MOTIVATING ACTIVITY Have the students think about the times when they had chores to do before they were allowed to leave the house. Ask them whether they have ever helped a friend with chores or whether a friend has ever helped them.

B 1

Mi mejor amiga

Play the cassette or read the dialog aloud. Have the students follow along in their books as they listen. Write the following new vocabulary on the board or a transparency: **la terraza, insistir, aconsejar, imaginarse,** and **tender la ropa.** Explain that some of these words are cognates, and have the students guess their meaning. If they have difficulty, use each word in a sentence. Now model each exchange, calling for choral and individual repetition. It is best to have the students listen and then repeat without reading the exchange from the book. Alternate choral and individual repetition to avoid boredom. Insist on a natural delivery paying particular attention to correct linking, rhythm, and intonation.

Then call on two volunteers to role-play the dialog for the class. Finally, you may wish to write the following or similar true or false statements on the board or read them aloud. Ask the students to correct the false statements.

> Claudia no puede ir a la playa porque tiene que estudiar.
> Claudia necesita que su hermana la ayude con su tarea.
> Su papá quiere que prepare unos bocadillos.
> Claudia está enfadada.
> Su papá quiere que limpie la sala.
> Su mamá quiere que Claudia lave la ropa.
> Diana va a ayudar a Claudia con el trabajo.

B 2 **Actividad • ¡A escoger!**

For writing practice, have the students write complete sentences at home or in class. You may also wish to call on volunteers to read their answers aloud for oral practice.

B3 Actividad • Preguntas y respuestas

You may wish to do this activity with books closed. You may prefer to have the students answer the questions the day after the presentation of the dialog, following a brief review of the dialog in class.

B4 Sabes que . . .

Read the cultural note aloud, pausing to ask some questions to check students'comprehension. Point out that in the Spanish world family ties are very strong and that everybody cooperates and helps. In many instances, grandparents live with a married son or daughter and help with household chores and babysitting for the grandchildren, especially now that more married women have jobs. Also, Spanish families often live in the same neighborhood as their relatives, so they can more easily help each other.

B5 ESTRUCTURAS ESENCIALES

Review the comparative forms with the students, beginning with **mejor, peor, mayor,** and **menor.** In order to present the grammar in context, ask several students to name the month and year in which they were born. Write the dates on the board or a transparency. Then ask the students to select two people and compare their ages using **mayor que** and **menor que.** For example: **Patrick es mayor que Mary. Mary es menor que Patrick.**

You may wish to point out that **mejor** and **peor** are adverbs similar to **más** and **menos;** the others are adjectives.

The adjective **grande** changes to **gran** when used before a masculine or feminine singular noun. When used before a noun, **gran** generally means *great.* The full form is used before plural nouns: **un gran actor; unos grandes actores.**

Review with the class the remaining information in the chart and the explanation. Read the examples aloud and have the students repeat. Then call on volunteers to use the irregular forms in sentences.

B6 Actividad • Charla

Have pairs of students take turns asking and answering the questions. Remind the students that they may respond to the questions with real or imaginary information.

CHALLENGE   For cooperative learning, form groups of three to select ten people whom they would classify as **El/la más bueno(a) del mundo.** Discuss the selections with the class, and ask the students in each group to explain the reasons for their choices. For example: **La Madre Teresa es la persona más buena del mundo porque ayuda a mucha gente.**

B7 Actividad • Una encuesta

Have each student work with a partner to complete the activity. Tell them to take notes and to be prepared to support their choices. You may wish to make a large chart on a transparency. Call on volunteers to call out their choices as you or a volunteer writes them on the transparency.

B 8   SE DICE ASÍ

Review the expressions in the chart with the students. To practice expressing amazement and pity, have the students respond to the following or similar situations.

> No hay examen mañana.
> Hoy vamos a tener una fiesta en la clase.
> Linda está en el hospital.
> Tenemos que cancelar el partido de fútbol.

B 9   Actividad • ¡No me digas!

Have each student choose a partner. Each student should make up three statements to tell his or her partner. The partner should respond with an appropriate expression from the box in B8.

B 10   ESTRUCTURAS ESENCIALES

Begin your presentation of the Spanish subjunctive by giving a series of easily understood commands, such as these statements:

> Abre las ventanas.
> Escribe tu nombre en la pizarra.
> Cierra la puerta.

You may also wish to use the **usted** form of the command. Ask the students to comment on what you were saying. Then make the following statements:

> Quiero que abras las ventanas.
> Necesito que escribas tu nombre en la pizarra.
> Prefiero que cierres la puerta.

Now, using TPR (Total Physical Response), say and perform these sentences and then write them on the board.

> Abro las ventanas.
> Escribo mi nombre en la pizarra.
> Cierro la puerta.

Compare both groups of sentences to reinforce the explanation in number 1 on page 304.

Try to elicit the idea that you are trying to get people to do things. Point out that the statement, which uses the subjunctive, is essentially the same request as the command, but less direct.

Now review the explanation below the title, *Use of the Spanish subjunctive.* Discuss the chart on page 305, stressing that there are two sentences with two verbs, joined together with **que.** Explain that the verb **quiere** in the main clause is in the present indicative, while the verb **estudie** in the subordinate clause is in the present subjunctive. Point out both subjects: **La profesora** in the main clause and **Jorge** in the subordinate clause. Indicate that someone, **la profesora** in this case, wants someone else, **Jorge,** to do something. Indicate to the students that what the professor wants, **que Jorge estudie más,** has not yet taken place and that it only represents the wishes of the professor.

Continue with a guided question/answer drill using real-life classroom situations; for example: **Quiero que** (*student's name*) **abra el libro a la página 305.** Then ask another student: (*student's name*), **¿qué quiero yo?** and elicit the response: **Ud. quiere que** (*student's name*) **abra el libro a la página 305.**

B 11   Actividad • Adela y sus hermanos

CHALLENGE   As a variation, ask the students to take turns playing the role of Adela. Have them instruct other class members to complete a variety of tasks.

ANSWERS:
1. Adela quiere que Pedro y Pablo barran su cuarto.
2. Adela quiere que Juan compre la leche.
3. Adela quiere que Alejandro abra las ventanas de la cocina.
4. Adela quiere que Ada pase la aspiradora por toda la casa.
5. Adela quiere que Arnaldo limpie la sala.
6. Adela quiere que Domingo y Diego corten el césped.
7. Adela quiere que Mariana cocine el pollo.
8. Adela quiere que todos ayuden en casa.

B 12   Comprensión

Mr. Chávez has many things for his students to do. He names a task and then asks a student to carry out his instructions. If the instructions match the task, check **sí** on your answer sheet. If they do not, check **no**. For example, you will hear: **Necesito mandar muchas cartas. Rafael, quiero que escribas estas cartas en la computadora.** You should place your check mark in the row labeled **sí**, because the instructions match the task.

1. Debemos comprar más papel.
   María Elena, recomiendo que estudies estos papeles.   *no*
2. No conocemos estas palabras.
   José Luis, quiero que estudies el vocabulario.   *sí*
3. Siempre vienes tarde a la clase.
   Raimundo, te aconsejo que llegues a tiempo.   *sí*
4. Mañana hay un examen.
   Sugiero que trabajen en la tienda esta noche.   *no*
5. Hace mucho frío, ¿no les parece?
   Quiero que cierren las ventanas.   *sí*
6. Ahora vamos a ver una película.
   Necesito que apagues las luces.   *sí*
7. Vamos a tener un examen de vocabulario.
   Quiero que abran los libros a la página cincuenta y seis.   *no*
8. Ustedes van a buscar información sobre México para un proyecto nuevo.
   Sugiero que vayan al gimnasio a buscar los libros.   *no*
9. El examen va a ser muy largo.
   Sugiero que estudien esta noche.   *sí*
10. Esta clase está muy sucia.
    Recomiendo que limpien la clase antes de salir.   *sí*

Now check your answers. *Read each statement again and give the correct answer.*

B 13   ESTRUCTURAS ESENCIALES

Review the functions of the subjunctive with the students. Stress the fact that there must be two different subjects for the subjunctive to be used. One subject in the main clause who wants another subject in the subordinate clause to carry out his or her wishes. Write the examples on the board, highlighting each subject with a different color chalk.

Indicate that if both clauses have the same subject, the indicative is used. Go over the examples in the **Atención,** pointing out the infinitives.

Have each student write eight sentences, using eight of the twelve verbs from the list in item 3. The students must relay a wish, demand, or request to a member of their family or to a friend. Collect and correct the sentences, or ask volunteers to write their sentences on the board for correction.

B 14 **Actividad • Nuestros profesores**

Ask the students to complete the sentences with the correct forms of the subjunctive. You may wish to call on volunteers to write their answers on the board or a transparency for correction.

ANSWERS:
1. El director quiere que yo escuche sus consejos.
2. La profesora de español desea que tú hables español.
3. La señorita Ortiz pide que nosotros aprendamos dos idiomas.
4. El señor López aconseja que los chicos escriban cartas a varias universidades.
5. La profesora de matemáticas nos aconseja que tomemos un curso de álgebra.
6. El supervisor insiste en que ellos no coman en clase.
7. El doctor Recio prohibe que ustedes corran por el pasillo.
8. La señora Murphy quiere que él lea la lectura.

B 15 **SITUACIÓN • Leyendo los anuncios clasificados**

Before presenting the selection, bring the classified section of a Spanish newspaper to class. Have the students skim the employment section of the classified ads and find jobs that they would find suitable. Call on volunteers to give general descriptions of the jobs. Then, have two students reenact the dialog, substituting the jobs for others found in the ads.

Introduce the new vocabulary, such as **la solicitud de empleo, la ferretería, solicitar, el plomero, la cañería,** and **el sueldo.** Then read the selection aloud or play the cassette. Ask whether anyone in the class would like either of the jobs described in the selection and why or why not. You may also wish to call on volunteers to role-play David and Daniel's conversation for the class.

SLOWER-PACED LEARNING   You may wish to provide students with the following or a similar worksheet to complete as they listen to the selection.
1. David Alvarado es estudiante de _____ .
2. Él quiere conseguir _____ .
3. Necesitan un empleado joven para trabajar por las _____ .
4. David decide consultar con su _____ .
5. David va a escribir una carta al señor _____ .

B 16 **Actividad • ¿Es cierto o no?**

CHALLENGE   Have the students make up their own true or false statements. Then have them exchange papers to correct the false statements.

B 17 **ESTRUCTURAS ESENCIALES**

Re-enter the irregular verbs by eliciting from the students the **yo** form of the verbs in the indicative. Continue your presentation, expressing wishes, commands, or requests, and by incorporating the new verbs. Encourage the students to listen carefully to the verb forms as you read them aloud.

> Quiero que me digas la verdad.
> Necesito que hagas la tarea.
> Prefiero que salgan temprano.

Finally, ask each student to write in his or her own words a rule on the formation of the irregular verbs in the subjunctive.

B 18 Actividad • Los padres de Lolita y Lilita

For writing practice, have the students write the completed sentences.

CHALLENGE   Write several sentences that are similar to those in the activity on a transparency. Then, with books closed, ask the students to fill in the blanks with the correct subjunctive forms of the verbs in parentheses.

B 19 Actividad • Combinación

Ask the students to form as many sentences as possible by combining the elements in the box. Tell them that they may use each item more than once. Review the sentences on the board or a transparency.

B 20 SITUACIÓN • Los oficios

Present the names of the trades by having the students look at the illustrations with the captions covered. Ask the students to describe what each person in the illustration does at his or her job. Practice the new vocabulary by using magazine pictures depicting people engaged in those trades in the book.

CHALLENGE   Bring the classified section of a Spanish newspaper and ask the students to find an ad for each of the trades listed. You may wish to display the ads on the bulletin board.

B 21 Actividad • Combinación

Assign this activity to be completed in class. For writing practice, have the students write the completed sentences.

B 22 Actividad • ¡A escribir!

Assign the activity for homework or to be completed with a partner. Ask the students to write the ads on 3 × 5 cards or poster board. They may wish to use magazine pictures to help illustrate the ads. Remind the students to use the subjunctive.

> Necesito que la cocinera *prepare* dos comidas al día.
> Quiero que la intérprete *hable* dos idiomas.
> Deseo que el plomero *sepa* arreglar baños.

Review the advertisements with the class.

CHALLENGE   Bring classified ads from Spanish newspapers, photocopy and number the ads, and distribute them to the class. Prepare a guided question/answer drill using the realia and the students' real names.

> (Student's name), ¿qué solicitan en el anuncio número uno?
> Solicitan una cocinera que trabaje de lunes a viernes.

SLOWER-PACED LEARNING   You may wish to discuss the ads with the students before completing the activity to help them incorporate ideas from ads into their task. Tell the students that **ojo,** many times written **¡ojo!,** in this context means *Attention!;* It is used to attract attention. Students should use verbs, such as **solicitar, necesitar, querer, buscar.** Have each student begin his or her ad with the name of the trade, continue with the requirements for the job, and end the ad with the information related to salary and the phone number or address.

B 23 **SE ESCRIBE ASÍ**

Review the form of a business letter with the students. You may wish to create a model letter using some of the expressions in the box to guide the students in B24.

B 24 **Actividad • ¡A escribir!**

Ask the students to write a letter in class. Circulate around the classroom to give advice. Tell them to use a salutation and complimentary closing from B23 and the vocabulary section at the end of the unit on page 325 as a guide. You may wish to display the corrected letters or make copies of them for the class to read.

OBJECTIVES **To socialize:** congratulate someone, write common introductions for business letters; **to persuade:** direct others to tell someone else to do something

CULTURAL BACKGROUND Part-time employment and summer jobs for Spanish-speaking youth are almost nonexistent. In recent years the economy has had a hard time supporting the adults. Underemployment is a fact of life in most countries. Spain's rate of unemployment is approximately thirty percent. For that reason, most available jobs go to adults who support families. However, it is possible that a young person be given a job in a family business.

MOTIVATING ACTIVITY Ask the students to describe their after-school job or recent summer job. Allow them to discuss the questions they were asked in their interview, the work they did, the money they earned, and what they learned on the job. If they have not had a job, allow them to talk about the job they would like to have.

C 1   **La carta del gerente**

Before reading the letter with the students, ask the students to scan it for cognates. Ask them to call out the cognates they have found or to write them on the board. Then write the following questions on the board or a transparency. Ask the students to listen carefully for the answers to these questions.

> ¿Cuál es la fecha de la carta?
> ¿Cuándo tiene la cita David?
> ¿Cómo son las recomendaciones de su antiguo jefe?
> ¿Cuándo necesitan que trabaje David?
> ¿Cuáles son tres cualidades que debe tener el candidato?

Now play the cassette or read the letter aloud to the students. Then allow them to read silently. You may wish to ask for choral and individual repetition of the letter while you read it aloud a second time.

C2 **Actividad • Preguntas y respuestas**

You may wish to have the students complete this activity orally with books closed, or you may allow them to complete the answers to the questions with a partner. Review the answers with the entire class.

C3 **Sabes que . . .**

Spanish-speaking students generally have little time or opportunity to work during the school year. Most Spanish-American schools have two sessions each day; thus students attend classes during most of the day, often carrying as many as ten to twelve subjects in a semester. Since final examinations are critical to continuation in school, and in many countries students who do not pass must leave, there is greater emphasis on passing grades.

C4 **SE ESCRIBE ASÍ**

Review the expressions in the box with students. Using a transparency, write a brief business letter and omit the date, salutation, introduction, and complimentary closing. Ask the students to supply the missing information.

C5 **ESTRUCTURAS ESENCIALES**

Present the verb forms, using a conversational approach. Encourage the students to respond to your questions, using the subjunctive in their responses. Examples are as follows:

> Quiero que le des el libro a Marta.
> Necesito que vayas a la pizarra.
> Es importante que sepas estas palabras para mañana.
> Es necesario que estés aquí mañana.

Write the verbs with orthographic changes on a transparency or on the board. To expand, introduce other verbs that form the same pattern, such as the following:

> explicar   organizar   marcar   merecer
> alcanzar   pagar   buscar   ofrecer
> llegar   cargar   alzar

C6 **Actividad • El gerente**

For writing practice, have the students complete the activity for homework. Collect and correct the sentences.

C7 **Comprensión**

You are working for a relative who owns a small business. Listen to each statement and decide if it describes a quality you would be looking for in a new employee. If the statement describes a favorable quality, check **sí** on your answer sheet. If it does not, check **no.** For example, you will hear: **Deseamos que siempre llegue a tiempo.** You should place your mark in the row labeled **sí,** because it is a favorable quality.

1. Preferimos que sepa muy poco de computadoras.   *no*
2. Queremos que no tenga recomendaciones.   *no*
3. Necesitamos que hable muy bien el español.   *sí*

4. Preferimos que conozca los productos. *sí*
5. Deseamos que no coloque las cosas con cuidado. *no*
6. Necesitamos que no sepa nada de matemáticas. *no*
7. Queremos que siempre llegue tarde. *no*
8. A veces necesitamos que trabaje horas extras. *sí*
9. Preferimos que sepa manejar un coche. *sí*
10. Deseamos que no tenga licencia de manejar. *no*

Now check your answers. *Read each statement again and give the correct answer.*

C 8 Actividad • Charla

CHALLENGE   Divide the class into groups of three or four students. Each group may call on a volunteer to be interviewed by the group. Have the students write the questions or cues on cards to use for their conversation. They may use the questions as a guide. Finally, after each group has completed its interview, you may wish to call on a few volunteers to role-play an interview for the class.

C 9 SITUACIÓN • La entrevista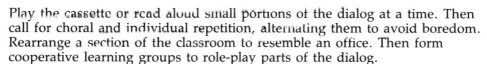

Play the cassette or read aloud small portions of the dialog at a time. Then call for choral and individual repetition, alternating them to avoid boredom. Rearrange a section of the classroom to resemble an office. Then form cooperative learning groups to role-play parts of the dialog.

C 10 Actividad • Preguntas y respuestas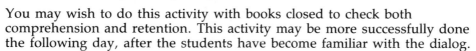

You may wish to do this activity with books closed to check both comprehension and retention. This activity may be more successfully done the following day, after the students have become familiar with the dialog.

C 11 SE DICE ASÍ

Read the expressions in the chart aloud to the class. Write the following or similar sentences on index cards and distribute them to the students.

> Acabo de recibir una A en español.
> Mi hermano dijo que ganamos la lotería.
> Mamá dijo que vamos a Buenos Aires para las vacaciones.
> Hoy es mi cumpleaños.
> Me dieron el trabajo.

Call on a student to read his or her sentence aloud. Then ask another student to respond, using one of the expressions in the chart. Include a few disappointing situations to re-enter the expressions of sympathy, such as **¡Qué horror! ¡Lo siento mucho! ¡No me digas! ¿Qué paso?**

> Saqué mala nota en el examen de álgebra.
> No puedo ir a la fiesta porque tengo que trabajar.
> Mi perro está enfermo.

C 12 Actividad • La entrevista

You may wish to combine activities C12 and C13 to complete the interview. Have pairs of students take turns imagining that they are presently employed but are looking for other jobs. Ask them to define their present job and to describe the type of jobs they are looking for. After several minutes of practice, choose several pairs to role-play the interview for the class. Encourage the class to listen to each interview and decide whether or not each person should get the job.

C13 Actividad • Más preguntas

Follow the procedure as described in C12. You may wish to re-enter the vocabulary for items of clothing, for telling time, and numbers.

C14 Actividad • La solicitud de empleo

You will find the application in copying master form on page 33 of the Teacher's Resource Materials. Have the students work individually. Tell them that they may use real or imaginary information to complete the application.

C15 ESTRUCTURAS ESENCIALES

Present this material using TPR (Total Physical Response). Give indirect commands to the students, using students' real names and incorporating real classroom situations.

> José, dígale a David que cierre la puerta.
> Anita, pídale a Pablo que le preste un lápiz.
> Martín, dígale a Rafael que abra su libro.

Encourage the students to carry out the instructions they are given. Ask them to generalize about the structures they have heard and also about the verb forms. Then read aloud the examples and explanations in the book.

C16 Actividad • El tímido

SLOWER-PACED LEARNING You may wish to re-enter the command forms with the students before they complete the activity. Write the sentences on the board or a transparency. Call on volunteers to read the sentences aloud. Have the students write the sentences in their notebooks.

C17 Actividad • En mi trabajo

Have the students work in pairs to complete the activity. They should take turns giving instructions. For writing practice, have the students write the completed sentences.

C18 Actividad • Están ocupados

For cooperative learning, have the students form groups of three. Groups should complete the activity by following the model. Ask the students to take turns playing each role. Then call on members of each group to role-play the dialog for the class.

C19 Actividad • Charla

Before you begin the activity, you may wish to re-enter the conditional tense with the students. Then ask each student to complete the activity with a partner. Remind the students to use interview techniques and job application procedures to ask and answer the questions.

C20 Actividad • Composición

For cooperative learning, divide the class into groups of four. Have each group create a list of admirable qualities for an employee to have. Then, using the outline as a guide, ask each group to describe its ideal candidate to the class. You may wish to write names of different professions or trades on the board or a transparency and have the class decide which candidate is most suitable for each job.

CHALLENGE For writing practice, have the students write compositions about their favorite job candidates.

TRY
YOUR
SKILLS

OBJECTIVE To recombine communicative functions, grammar, and vocabulary

CULTURAL BACKGROUND You may wish to point out that in many Spanish-speaking countries, a classified advertisement for a job may often include specific requirements, such as age, marital status, and physical appearance. It is not uncommon to find companies that request a potential employee to be between the age of 25 to 35, married (or single), and male (or female).

1 Los clasificados

Before the students complete the activity, call on volunteers to read aloud the newspaper ads. You may wish to tell them that **mesero(-a)** is another word for **camarero(-a)** or **mozo(-a).** Then have each student select the profession or trade that interests them most. Tell them to use poster board, magazine pictures, and anything else that will help them to design an ad. Remind the students that the ad must be in Spanish. You may wish to display the ads in the classroom.

You may wish to give the class useful vocabulary from the ads.

empresa	company
reemplazo de vacaciones	vacation replacements
dactilógrafa	typist
casilla	box
mesero / camarero	waiter
de preferencia	preferable
con disponibilidad	available
promedio	average
ingresos	income, earnings
cajera	cashier
media jornada	part time
redacción	editing, writing
para postular	to request
pretensiones	expectations
¿Se muda?	Are you moving?
destapamos	we unclog
corregimos	we correct
aumentamos	we increase

2   Actividad • El comparativo y el superlativo

For writing practice, ask the students to write at least five sentences, using the adjectives that are given. When they have finished, call on volunteers to read their sentences aloud as you or a volunteer writes them on the board or a transparency.

3   Actividad • El pretérito y el imperfecto

Review the formation of the preterit and imperfect tenses. You may wish to write the paragraph on the board or a transparency. Then call on volunteers to supply the correct form of the preterit or the imperfect. When the paragraph is completed, call on a volunteer to read it aloud.

SLOWER-PACED LEARNING   Have the students copy the sentences from their books, leaving spaces for the verbs. Then tell them to close their books. Read the sentences aloud with the correct verb forms in place. The students should write the missing verb forms on their papers as they hear them.

4   Actividad • Yo quiero que . . .

Allow each student to work with a partner to complete the activity. For writing pratice, have the students write what they tell their partners. You may wish to remind the students of the formation of the subjunctive and the syntax of the sentence: *verb in the indicative* + **que** + *verb in the subjunctive.*

5   Actividad • Aquí mando yo

CHALLENGE   Choose several class members to give their commands as indirect commands, encouraging the recipients to respond appropriately.

6   Actividad • Los datos personales

Have each student prepare his or her résumé at home. In order to safeguard the privacy of the students, tell them that they may include real or imaginary information.

CHALLENGE   You may also wish to have the students play the roles of employer and applicant, using the résumés as a guide. Call on two students at a time. Allow the student playing the role of the employer to review the "applicant's résumé" before the interview begins.

7   Actividad • Una carta

Assign the business letter for homework. You may wish to review with the students the proper form for the letter and the various expressions they will need to use.

8   Dictado

Write the following paragraph from dictation. First, listen to the paragraph as it is read to you. Then, you will hear the paragraph again in short segments, with a pause after each segment to allow you time to write. Finally, you will hear the paragraph again a third time so that you may check your work. Let's begin.

Ayer, la mamá de Caridad le dijo: *(pause)* "Cari, necesito que vayas a la tienda", *(pause)* y ella le contestó, *(pause)* "¡Mamá, estás loca! *(pause)* Yo no puedo ir a la tienda *(pause)* porque Eduardo y Carmen quieren que *(pause)* yo vaya a su casa ahora mismo *(pause)* para ir al cine". *(pause)* La mamá de Caridad *(pause)* se enfadó con ella y le dijo, *(pause)* "Cari, te aconsejo que no me hables así *(pause)* y ahora te prohibo que vayas *(pause)* al cine con ellos".

PRONUNCIACIÓN

Read the explanation and words aloud or play the cassette. You may wish to point out the pronunciation of the intervocalic **d** as in the word **estudio.** Allow each student to practice saying the words aloud with a partner as you circulate through the room to check for correct pronunciation and make suggestions. You may wish to prepare flashcards with words containing the different **d** and **t** sounds. As you show a card to the class, pronounce the word and call on volunteers to repeat after you. Explain to the students that in Spanish, word boundaries cannot be recognized in spoken language because the chain of speech is divided into evenly timed syllables. That is why, in many instances, the consonant **d** at the end of a word will be linked with a following vowel to form a syllable and then it will be pronounced. For example: **La ciudad está de fiesta.**

Actividad • Práctica de pronunciación

Have the students listen and repeat as you play the cassette or read the sentences aloud. Each student in the class should have the opportunity to read a sentence aloud. As a variation, discuss with the students what the general pronunciation problems were with the class as a whole instead of correcting each student individually.

¿LO SABES?

SECTION A

To review the superlative, emergency expressions, and the imperfect and preterit verb forms, you may wish to write a group essay with the class. On the board or a transparency write the first sentence of the essay, such as: **Había una vez una muchacha interesantísima que vivía en un pueblecito español. Era una noche oscura y tormentosa . . .** Call on volunteers to add to the story. Remind them to include phrases with superlatives, emergency expressions, and imperfect and preterit verbs. When the students have finished writing the essay, you may correct it with the entire class.

SECTION B

To review expressions of surprise and pity, have the students respond to various statements, such as: **Ayer gané la lotería.** They should respond: **¡Qué suerte!** or **¡No me digas!** To practice addressing a business letter, divide the class into groups of four and have each group write a short letter, using the correct salutations and complimentary closings. Review the letters with the class.

SECTION C

Have the students work in groups to interview prospective job candidates. Choose several groups to role-play for the class. Then allow the class to ask questions. You may also wish to play the role of interviewer in order to provide input and to extend the conversation. You may prompt, expand, or offer help as needed.

VOCABULARIO

To practice the vocabulary for occupations, you may wish to play a game called **¿Qué soy?** Call on a volunteer to be "it." Make a sign bearing the name of a specific occupation from the vocabulary list. Place the sign, which the student cannot see, on his or her back. The student with the sign asks **sí** or **no** questions to the other students until he or she identifies the correct occupation.

¿Arreglo coches?
¿Hablo muchos idiomas?
¿Entrego cartas?

Call on students to take turns being "it."

VAMOS A LEER

OBJECTIVE   To read for practice and pleasure

Antes de leer

Have the students scan the selection to find examples that contain the suffixes. Write the words on the board. Then call on volunteers to give other examples.

Preparación para la lectura

Call on volunteers to answer the first four questions. Then allow the students time to answer the last three questions individually.

LA ENTREVISTA

Read the selection aloud or play the cassette. Then call on volunteers to read the different segments of the selection. You may wish to discuss with the students what they would or wouldn't do during an interview, whether they agree with the reading selection, and what kind of profession they would or wouldn't like to have.

Actividad • Preguntas y respuestas

For writing practice, have the students answer the questions in complete sentences for homework. You may wish to call on volunteers to pronounce the words in question 6. Also have each student compare his or her list of cognates from question 8 with a partner.

Actividad • Familia de palabras

Divide the class into groups of four students. Then allow each group ten minutes to find words related to those in the list. The group with the most words wins. You may wish to review the words with the class.

Actividad • ¡A escribir!

Have each student pair up with a partner to prepare a list of the techniques for an interview. Allow the partners to practice interviewing each other. Call on volunteers to present their interviews to the class.

La juventud

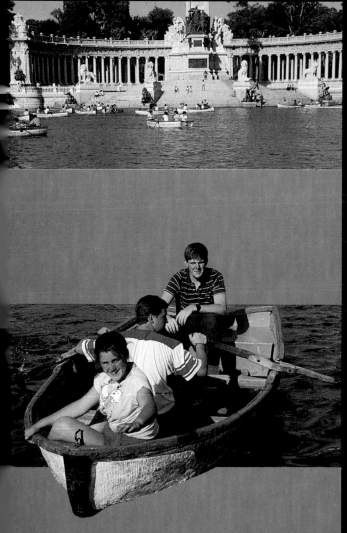

Young people in the Hispanic world have similar ambitions, needs, and means of entertaining themselves as their peers in the United States. Although there may be cultural differences, the Hispanic teens think and act just like teenagers everywhere.

In this unit you will:

SECTION A	report what somebody said . . . ask for help or give a warning
SECTION B	express amazement and pity . . . make comparisons . . . express needs and desires
SECTION C	congratulate someone . . . direct others to tell someone else to do something
TRY YOUR SKILLS	use what you've learned
VAMOS A LEER	read for practice and pleasure

SECTION A

reporting what somebody said . . . asking for help or giving a warning

Fairs in Spanish-speaking countries are similar to those in the United States. Everyone enjoys the wild rides, the candied apples, and having a great time with friends.

A1

Narciso el bello

En casi todos los pueblos de España siempre hay un festival o una verbena adonde va todo el mundo. Aquí estamos en una verbena. Veremos qué pasa . . . Narciso Domínguez es el muchacho más guapo y más popular de la escuela. Todas las chicas siempre quieren salir con él. Hoy hay mucha gente en la verbena de San Juan.

MARÍA ELENA   Mira, Pili, allí veo a Narciso . . . ¡qué guapo es! Fíjate, está comprando las entradas para montar en el pulpo. Estoy segura de que se sentará aquí con nosotras.

PILAR   No, no lo creo porque ahí está Lolita Martorell. Mi hermano me dijo que él antes salía con Silvia, pero dicen que ahora está saliendo con Lolita.

MARÍA ELENA   Pues mira, ya se sentaron juntos. Ay, ésa es la chica más antipática del mundo.

(Carmen y sus amigas también ven a Narciso y a Lolita.)

CARMEN   Miren, chicas. Allí está Narciso.
CLARA   Sí, ya lo vimos, pero está con Lolita. Compraron churros y se los están comiendo juntos.

ADA   Y ahora Narciso va a tirar al blanco y ella está a su lado.
SILVIA   ¡Bah! Algún día se dará cuenta de que nosotras somos mucho más atractivas que Lolita.
CARMEN   ¡Ay, pero qué bello es . . . !

A2   Actividad • Preguntas y respuestas

Use the information in A1 to answer the following questions.

1. ¿Por qué todas las chicas siempre quieren salir con Narciso?   Porque es el muchacho más guapo y más popular de la escuela.
2. ¿Dondé están los chicos?   Los chicos están en la verbena de San Juan.
3. ¿De qué está segura María Elena?   María Elena está segura de que Narciso se sentará con ellas.
4. ¿Con quién salía Narciso antes?   Narciso antes salía con Silvia.
5. ¿Con quién está saliendo ahora?   Ahora está saliendo con Lolita.
6. ¿Quiénes se sentaron juntos en el pulpo?   Lolita y Narciso se sentaron juntos.
7. ¿Qué dice María Elena de Lolita?   Ella dice que es la chica más antipática del mundo.
8. ¿Qué dice Silvia?   Silvia dice que algún día se dará cuenta de que ellas son mucho más atractivas que Lolita.

Las romerías son muy populares en España, y
los españoles con cualquier pretexto inventan
una. Las ferias hispánicas se parecen un poco
a las ferias de los Estados Unidos y también
son muy populares. Hay muchos espectáculos,
juegos y lugares para comer y divertirse.

Además, cada pueblo español tiene un
santo patrón. El santo tiene un día que se
celebra con una fiesta. En la víspera *(eve)* hay
una verbena o fiesta nocturna. La romería es
la peregrinación *(pilgrimage)* a la tumba *(tomb)*
o iglesia del santo. La gente pasa el día al aire
libre comiendo y bailando.

Por diez días Pamplona celebra la fiesta de
San Fermín. Todos los años, el 7 de julio, la
ciudad se llena de turistas. Vienen a ver a los
jóvenes correr por la calle delante de los toros
(bulls). ¡Qué alboroto *(confusion)*!

A4 SE DICE ASÍ
Reporting what others say

Mi hermano me dijo que...	My brother told me ...
Alguien me dijo que...	Somebody told me ...
La gente dice que...	People say ...
Dicen que...	They say ...

To report what somebody said, you can name your source or begin the sentence
with **alguien** or **la gente**. You may also use the verb in the third person plural
with no subject expressed.

A5 Comprensión For script, see p. T173.

Listen carefully to the following ten statements. Decide if each statement
represents an event that is occurring now **(ahora),** in the past **(pasado),** or in the
future **(futuro).** Mark the appropriate space on your answer sheet.

MODELO   Nosotros estamos planeando una fiesta para el sábado.

	0	1	2	3	4	5	6	7	8	9	10
Ahora	✔			✔						✔	
Pasado		✔					✔	✔			
Futuro			✔		✔	✔			✔		✔

A6 ¿RECUERDAS?
Review of the Spanish indicative mood

Anita **estudia** en la escuela secundaria.	*Anita is in high school.*
Luis y José **van** a la playa todos los días.	*Luis and José go to the beach every day.*
Tomás **comió** en el restaurante El Sombrero la semana pasada.	*Tomás ate at El Sombrero restaurant last week.*
Adela y Lupe **van a ir** a España en el verano.	*Adela and Lupe are going to Spain during the summer.*
Jorge **está hablando** por teléfono.	*Jorge is talking on the phone.*
Yo **llegaré** a las ocho.	*I'll be here at eight.*
Ella **iría** de compras, pero no tiene dinero.	*She would go shopping, but she has no money.*
Salían juntos todas las tardes.	*They went out together every evening.*

All the sentences above are in the Spanish indicative mood. Remember that the Spanish indicative mood is used to describe or report what is happening either in the past, the present, or the future. That is, it expresses facts, or something factual and definite. The tense indicates when the action happened. For example, a verb in the present tense indicates that the action is happening now, while a verb in the preterit tense indicates a past action.

A7 Actividad • ¡A completar!   Some answers will vary. Possible answers are given.

Change the verb in parentheses to the correct indicative tense form (present, preterit, imperfect, or future).

El año pasado yo (estudiar)_____ español en la clase del señor Domínguez. La   estudié
clase (ser)_____ muy grande porque (tener)_____ muchos estudiantes. Este año yo   era / tenía
(estar)_____ en la clase de la señorita Taylor. La clase (ser)_____ muy pequeña, pero   estoy / es
también (ser)_____ muy interesante. Ahora nosotros (escribir)_____ composiciones.   es / escribimos
A mí me (gustar)_____ mucho las composiciones. El año que viene nosotros   gustan
(graduarse)_____ de la escuela y yo (ir)_____ a la universidad y también   nos graduaremos / iré
(tomar)_____ muchos cursos de español.   tomaré

A8 Actividad • ¿Qué me cuentas?   Answers will vary.

Team up with another student and ask each other the following questions.

1. ¿Estás trabajando en algún lugar? ¿Dónde?
2. ¿Cuándo fue la última vez que fuiste de compras con tus amigos?
3. ¿Con quién salías antes y cómo era esa persona?
4. ¿Con quién estás saliendo ahora y cómo es esa persona?
5. ¿Qué hiciste anoche?
6. ¿Qué harás este fin de semana?
7. ¿Cómo se llamaba tu profesor(a) de español el año pasado y cómo se llama tu profesor(a) de español este año?
8. ¿Qué planes tienes para las vacaciones del verano?
9. ¿Cuáles son tus planes para después de la graduación?

ESTRUCTURAS ESENCIALES
The superlative construction

The Spanish superlative is equivalent to *the . . . -est* or *the most*, as in *the prettiest girl* or *the most beautiful garden*. It also expresses the other extreme, as in *the least beautiful garden*. To form the Spanish superlative, follow the chart.

el, la, los, las (+ noun) +	más *or* menos	+ adjective + de

Ana María es **la** estudiante **más** inteligente **de** la clase.
Ana María is the most intelligent student in the class.

¿Quiénes son **los** estudiantes **menos** atentos **de** la escuela?
Who are the least attentive students in school?

Narciso es **el más** guapo **de** todos.
Narciso is the most handsome of all.

ATENCIÓN: Notice that **de** is equivalent to *in* or *of* in English.

A10 Actividad • El sabelotodo *The know-it-all*

There is always a know-it-all in every group. Play the role of the know-it-all by following the model.

MODELO Narciso es un estudiante guapo. (el grupo)
Narciso es el estudiante más guapo del grupo.

1. Silvia es una chica bonita. (la clase)   Silvia es la chica más bonita de la clase.
2. La tercera lección es una lección muy fácil. (el curso)   La tercera lección es la lección más fácil del curs
3. Daniel y Ricardo son jugadores altos. (el equipo)   Daniel y Ricardo son los jugadores más altos del equ
4. Romualdo es un dependiente amable. (la tienda)   Romualdo es el dependiente más amable de la tiend
5. Bruno no es un estudiante inteligente. (la escuela)   Bruno es el estudiante menos inteligente de la esc
6. Yo soy un muchacho atlético. (el pueblo)   Yo soy el muchacho más atlético del pueblo.
7. Alejandra y yo somos unas personas simpáticas. (el país)   Alejandra y yo somos las personas más simpáticas del país.

A11 Actividad • Mi familia   Answers will vary.

Get together with a classmate and ask the following questions about each other's real or imaginary family.

MODELO ¿Quién es la persona más alta de tu familia?
Mi hermano Rafael es la persona más alta de mi familia.

1. ¿Quién es la persona más simpática de tu familia?
2. ¿Quién es la persona más artística de tu familia?
3. ¿Quiénes son las personas más fuertes de tu familia?
4. ¿Cuál de tus hermanos es el más delgado?
5. ¿Quién es la persona más joven de tu familia?
6. ¿Quién es la persona más guapa de la familia?

1. la montaña rusa
2. la rueda giratoria
3. el tiro al blanco
4. el pulpo
5. el coche de topetazos

6. el tiovivo
7. la rifa
8. la churrería
9. la taquilla
10. el rifle

11. el muñeco

bajarse   *to step down*
subirse   *to get on*
marearse   *to get dizzy (motion sickness)*
sacarse la rifa   *to win the raffle*

Actividad • Descripción del dibujo

After looking at the illustration in A12, answer the following questions.

1. ¿Dónde se pueden comprar los billetes? Los billetes se pueden comprar en la taquilla.
2. ¿Qué están haciendo los chicos en la montaña rusa? Los chicos se están subiendo en la montaña rusa.
3. ¿Qué le pasó a la chica que se bajó del pulpo? La chica se mareó.
4. ¿Por qué está contento el chico que tiene el muñeco? Porque se sacó la rifa.
5. ¿Qué está haciendo el chico que tiene el rifle? El chico está en el tiro al blanco.
6. ¿Qué comen los dos niños? Los dos niños comen churros.

A14 Actividad • ¿Qué te gusta a ti? Answers will vary.

It is now time to talk a bit more about yourself by answering the following questions.

1. ¿Cuándo fue la última vez que fuiste a una verbena?
2. ¿Fuiste solo o con alguien más?
3. ¿Te gustaría ir de nuevo a una verbena? ¿Por qué?
4. ¿En cuál de los juegos te diviertes más?
5. ¿Cuál de ellos es el que te gusta menos?
6. ¿Te sacaste algo en alguna rifa? ¿Qué te sacaste?
7. ¿Qué cosas comes cuando vas a una verbena?

A15 SITUACIÓN • Practicando la tabla vela

El sábado pasado Ricardo, Daniel, Pedro y Rodrigo fueron a la Costa Brava a practicar la tabla vela.

Al llegar a la playa, estacionaron sus motos frente al muro y fueron a la caseta a alquilar el equipo.

34234

Había mucha gente en la playa. Era un día hermoso y el mar estaba en calma.

Como no hacía mucho viento, el día estaba perfecto para los principiantes de tabla vela. Había muchos principiantes ese día, y todos alquilaban el equipo temprano para aprovechar el tiempo.

A16 Actividad • ¿Es así o no es así?

Decide whether each statement is true or false according to A15. Correct the false statements.

1. El sábado pasado los chicos fueron a la playa a practicar béisbol.

   El sábado pasado los chicos fueron a la Costa Brava a practicar la tabla vela.

2. Ellos fueron en bicicleta.   Ellos fueron en moto.

3. Ellos estacionaron sus motos frente a la caseta.

   Ellos estacionaron sus motos frente al muro.

4. Los chicos fueron al muro a alquilar el equipo.

   Los chicos fueron a la caseta a alquilar el equipo.

5. Era un día hermoso y el mar estaba en calma.

   Es cierto.

6. El día estaba perfecto para los principiantes porque hacía mucho viento.

   El día estaba perfecto para los principiantes porque no hacía mucho viento.

Actividad • Mi primo Alfredo

Change the verb in parentheses to the correct form of either the preterit or imperfect tenses.

Mi primo Alfredo (ir) a un festival en la Costa Brava y (estar) allí por tres días. fue / estuvo
En el festival mi primo (conocer) a una chica que (ser) alta y morena, y que (tener) conoció / era / tenía
los ojos azules. Ella (llamarse) Ester y (ser) de Israel. Alfredo y Ester (montar) en se llamaba / era / montaron
la montaña rusa y después (ir) al tiovivo. Ellos (divertirse) mucho y la (pasar) de fueron / se divirtieron /
lo mejor. pasaron

A18
Actividad • ¡A escribir y a hablar! Answers will vary.

Imagine that you were either at the beach or at a carnival last Saturday and you want to tell the class about it. Prepare a report, using both the preterit and the imperfect, and then be prepared to read your composition aloud in class.

A19
SITUACIÓN • Divirtiéndose en la playa

Pedro y Rodrigo practicaron la tabla vela por mucho rato. Al terminar de practicar la tabla vela, cargaron la vela y Rodrigo la enrolló en el mástil.

Luego fueron a la playa y se reunieron con Daniel, Ricardo y los demás del grupo, menos Andrés que no pudo ir porque pescó un resfriado.

Algunos de ellos jugaban al fútbol y otros conversaban cuando, de repente, Aurelio y sus primos agarraron a Mati, que gritaba "¡Auxilio! ¡Socorro!," y la echaron al agua. Todos pasaron un día magnífico.

A 20 Actividad • Combinación

Explain who completed each action in A19 by matching the elements in each box.

Andrés	enrolló la vela en el mástil
Pedro y Rodrigo	se reunieron con los demás
Rodrigo	echaron a Mati al agua
Algunos de los chicos	pescó un resfriado
Aurelio y sus primos	jugaban al fútbol

1. Andrés pescó un resfriado.   2. Pedro y Rodrigo se reunieron con los demás.
3. Rodrigo enrolló la vela en el mástil.   4. Algunos de los chicos jugaban al fútbol.
5. Aurelio y sus primos echaron a Mati al agua.

Actividad • ¿Adónde fuiste? Answers will vary.

Ask your partner where he or she went last weekend and why. Switch roles.

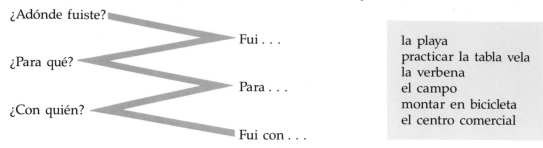

¿Adónde fuiste?

¿Para qué?

¿Con quién?

Fui . . .

Para . . .

Fui con . . .

la playa
practicar la tabla vela
la verbena
el campo
montar en bicicleta
el centro comercial

A 22 **Actividad • ¿Qué hacen o qué hicieron?**

Choosing elements from each column, write eight sentences telling when and what
each person is doing or did.

Andrés	estar	la verbena	ahora
Elena	sentarse	la tabla vela	el sábado pasado
Gerardo	comer	montar en el pulpo	a menudo
Gabriel	ir	el cine	de vez en cuando
Delia y Lola	alquilar	comer churros	todos los lunes
Los muchachos	estacionar	la cafetería	la semana pasada
Ernestina y Claudia	cargar	la rueda giratoria	el mes que viene
Tú	montar	la moto	los domingos

Answers will vary. Possible answers are given.
Andrés va al cine a menudo.   Elena está comiendo churros ahora.   Gerardo carga la tabla vela los domingos.
Gabriel está montando en el pulpo ahora.   Delia y Lola comieron churros la semana pasada.   Los muchachos
se sientan en la rueda giratoria todos los lunes.   Ernestina y Claudia comerán en la cafetería el mes que viene.
Tú estacionaste la moto el sábado pasado.

A 23 **SE DICE ASÍ**
Asking for help or giving a warning

¡Auxilio!	Help!
¡Socorro!	Help!
¡Fuego!	Fire!
¡Cuidado!	Watch out!
¡Alto!	Stop!

These expressions can be very helpful in an emergency.

A 24 Actividad • ¡Auxilio! Answers will vary. Possible answers are given.

Read each emergency situation below and choose an appropriate response from A23.

1. Someone was running away with your school bag. ¡Alto!
2. There was a fire in the chemistry lab. ¡Fuego!
3. Your friend was about to step in a puddle. ¡Cuidado!
4. You were windsurfing and noticed a shark in the water. ¡Socorro!

A 25 Actividad • El héroe

Complete the following paragraph with the correct forms of the preterit or imperfect tenses.

El sábado por la mañana yo (ir) _____ con mi perro a la playa. (Ser) _____ un   fui / Era
día hermoso, y (haber) _____ mucha gente en la playa cuando todos (oír) _____ un   había / oímos
grito de ¡Auxilio! ¡Socorro! Yo (ver) _____ que los gritos (ser) _____ de una muchacha   vi / eran
que (estar) _____ en el agua y que no (saber) _____ nadar. Por un momento no   estaba / sabía
(saber) _____ qué hacer, pero inmediatamente yo (echarse) _____ al agua y   supe / me eché
(nadar) _____ hacia donde (estar) _____ ella. Entonces, yo la (agarrar) _____ por el   nadé / estaba / agarré
pelo y la (llevar) _____ hasta la playa. Yo (ponerse) _____ muy contento porque le   llevé / me puse
(poder) _____ salvar la vida.   pude

A 26 Actividad • ¿Adónde vamos? Answers will vary.

Work with two or three classmates. Imagine that you are going out together. Decide where you are going, what you are going to do, and on what day and at what time you are meeting. Report your plans to the class.

¿Qué día?   ¿Qué van a hacer?
¿Con quién?
¿A qué hora?   ¿Cómo van a ir?   ¿Adónde?

A 27 Actividad • Composición dirigida Answers will vary.

Prepare a description in Spanish of your favorite hobby. Use the following outline as a guide.

    I. Introducción
       A. Mi pasatiempo favorito es . . .
       B. Cómo aprendí ese pasatiempo
       C. Fue fácil o difícil de aprender
   II. Desarrollo
       A. Por qué lo practico
       B. Dónde lo practico
       C. Cuándo lo practico
       D. Cómo lo practico
  III. Conclusión: Me gusta ese pasatiempo porque . . .

Wouldn't it be great if you could do everything you always wanted to do? Unfortunately, that is not possible. Now and then it's necessary to cancel your plans and lend a helping hand.

B1

Mi mejor amiga 📼

La pobre Claudia Acosta quiere ir a la playa el sábado, pero tiene tantas cosas que hacer que no va a poder ir. De pronto, suena el teléfono.

CLAUDIA Diga.
  DIANA Hola, Claudia. Te habla Diana, ¿cómo te va?
CLAUDIA ¡Muy mal! Ay, Diana, tengo tanto trabajo que no puedo más.
  DIANA ¡Qué barbaridad! ¿Qué te pasa?
CLAUDIA Imagínate, quería ir a la playa con el grupo, pero mi hermana necesita que yo la ayude con la tarea.
  DIANA Eso no te va a tomar tanto tiempo, Claudia.

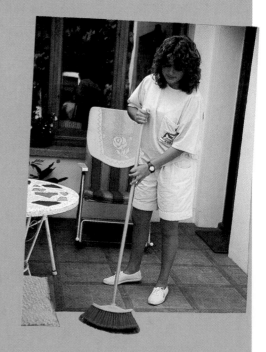

CLAUDIA Pero es que papá quiere que yo barra la terraza y que prepare unos bocadillos para la merienda. Mamá insiste en que yo lave y tienda la ropa. Con tantas cosas, no sé qué voy a hacer.
  DIANA Mira, no te enfades. Te aconsejo que tomes las cosas con calma. Ahora mismo voy para tu casa a ayudarte.
CLAUDIA Gracias, Diana. Ya veo por qué eres mi mejor amiga.

B2   Actividad • ¡A escoger!

Use the information in B1 to help you choose the most appropriate ending for each of the following sentences.

1. Claudia no va a poder ir a la playa porque
   • suena el teléfono.   • tiene cosas que hacer.   • Diana la va a ayudar.
2. Claudia quería ir a la playa con
   • unos amigos.   • Diana.   • su hermana.
3. Claudia recibe una llamada por teléfono de
   • Diana.   • su hermana.   • su mamá.
4. La hermana de Claudia necesita que ella
   • barra la terraza.   • tienda la ropa.   • la ayude con la tarea.
5. El papá de Claudia quiere que ella
   • lave la ropa.   • vaya a la playa.   • prepare unos bocadillos.

B3   Actividad • Preguntas y respuestas

Answer the following questions according to B1.

1. ¿Adónde quiere ir Claudia el sábado?
2. ¿Qué dice Claudia cuando Diana le llama por teléfono?
3. ¿En qué insiste la mamá de Claudia?
4. ¿Qué le aconseja Diana a Claudia?
5. ¿Quién va a ayudar a Claudia?
6. ¿Por qué Diana es la mejor amiga de Claudia?

1. Claudia quiere ir a la playa.   2. Claudia le dice a Diana que tiene tanto trabajo que no puede más.   3. La mamá de Claudia insiste en que lave y tienda la ropa.   4. Diana le aconseja que tome las cosas con calma. 5. Diana va a ayudar a Claudia.   6. Porque Diana la ayuda.

En la mayoría de los países hispánicos, hasta hace relativamente poco tiempo, era fácil encontrar personas que hacían el servicio doméstico y aún se pueden encontrar sirvientes más fácilmente que en los Estados Unidos. Sin embargo, mucha gente que antes hacía el servicio doméstico, hoy día encuentra trabajo en fábricas, oficinas y otros lugares donde reciben un sueldo *(salary)* más alto y trabajan menos horas al día. Por esta razón y porque además, la esposa trabaja fuera de la casa en muchas familias hispánicas, es necesario dividir las labores domésticas entre todos los miembros de la familia. Los jóvenes tienen que ayudar a los padres y a los abuelos con parte de las tareas de la casa.

B5   ESTRUCTURAS ESENCIALES
Irregular forms of comparatives and superlatives

Spanish, like English, has some irregular comparatives and superlatives.

You may wish to point out that the superlative of adverbs is expressed:
verb + (más / menos / mejor / peor)
"Pedro es el que escribe más claramente." "Ana es la muchacha que baila mejor."

Adjectives	Regular	Irregular	
bueno(a)	**más** bueno(a)	**mejor**	*better, best*
malo(a)	**más** malo(a)	**peor**	*worse, worst*
grande	**más** grande	**mayor**	*bigger, biggest*
viejo(a)	**más** viejo(a)		*older, oldest*
pequeño(a)	**más** pequeño(a)	**menor**	*smaller, smallest*
joven	**más** joven		*younger, youngest*

1. **Más bueno** and **más malo** are usually used to refer to moral qualities or conduct.

| Cristina es **más mala** amiga **que** Angélica. | *Cristina is a worse friend than Angélica.* |
| Teresa es **la más buena de** todas mis amigas. | *Teresa is the best of all my friends.* |

2. Use **mejor** and **peor** to refer to general qualities.

Mi tabla vela es **peor que** la tuya.	*My windsurfing board is worse than yours.*
Estas fresas son **mejores que** las de Toni.	*These strawberries are better than Toni's.*
Sí, pero éstas son **las mejores del** pueblo.	*Yes, but these are the best in town.*

3. **Más grande** and **más pequeño** are used to refer to size.

Esta camisa es **más grande que** aquélla.	*This shirt is bigger than that one.*
Mi casa es **más pequeña que** la tuya.	*My house is smaller than yours.*
La montaña rusa de la Ciudad de México es **la más grande de** todo el país.	*The roller coaster in Mexico City is the biggest in the country.*

4. Use **mayor** or **menor** to refer to age.

Josefina es **mayor que** Ana.	*Josefina is older than Ana.*
Roberto es **menor que** Ángel.	*Roberto is younger than Ángel.*
Eduardo es **el menor de** la familia.	*Eduardo is the youngest in the family.*

B6 **Actividad • Charla** Answers will vary.

Team up with another student and ask each other the following questions.

1. ¿Qué personas de tu familia son mayores que tú?
2. ¿Quién de tu familia es menor que tú?
3. ¿Quién es la persona mayor de tu familia?
4. ¿Quiénes son los mejores atletas de tu escuela?
5. ¿Quién es el mejor de tus amigos?
6. Para ti, ¿quién es la persona más buena del mundo?

B7 **Actividad • Una encuesta** Answers will vary.

Make a survey of restaurants, current movies, and television programs in your home town. Select at least four items from each category and rate them according to the classifications listed in the chart.

	bueno(a)	malo(a)	el/la mejor	el/la peor
restaurante				
película				
programa de televisión				

viernes

CINE

Los aventureros: Vuelve una interesante comedia romántica con un joven Alain Delon, un justo Lino Ventura y la atractiva Joanna Shimkus, dirigidos por Robert Enrico. (Premier, Corrientes 1565).

Sibaris RESTAURANT. **HOY**

FESTIVAL DE PAELLAS
todas nuestras especialidades.
Disfrute música en vivo con el grupo:
VIDA NUEVA y
SANGRE JOVEN (Yahuarusyna)
8 de Julio 540 Miraflores — Telf. 43

TV abierta

sábado

Canal 2: "Jefe", largometraje norteamericano con Alain Delon y Mireille Darc (00.20).
ATC: "Dinero fácil", con Paul Newman (foto) y Lee Marvin. Presenta Salvador Sammaritano "Aquel cine" (14.00).
Canal 11: "El archivo de Odessa", film de espionaje con Jon Voight y Maximilian Schell (22.00).

ATC: "La dama de las botas rojas", producción franco - española de Jean Louis Buñuel, con Catherine ...uve, José ...stán (foto) ...nando Rey ...0).
...l 11: "La ...handra", ... Anthony ...n, Claudia ...linale y ...co Nero ...00).

La juventud 303

SE DICE ASÍ
Expressing amazement and pity

¡Qué suerte!	How lucky!
¡Qué lástima!	What a pity!
¡Qué pena!	What a shame!
¡Qué horror!	How horrible!
¡Qué barbaridad!	How terrible!
¡No me digas!	You don't say!

B9 **Actividad • ¡No me digas!**   Answers will vary. Possible answers are given.

Use the appropriate expression from B8 to respond to each of the following statements.

1. ¡Antonio comió doce bocadillos de jamón!   ¡Qué barbaridad!
2. Roberto está en el hospital.   ¡Qué lástima!
3. Encontré el anillo que perdí hace una semana.   ¡Qué suerte!
4. El tornado destruyó las casas.   ¡Qué horror!
5. Fui a Washington y conocí al Presidente.   ¡No me digas!

B10 **ESTRUCTURAS ESENCIALES**
The Spanish subjunctive mood

1. You have already learned that the indicative mood is used to express or describe events that are real, factual, and definite. In this unit you will begin to use the Spanish subjunctive to express what you would like others to do and what others may want you to do.

2. To form the present subjunctive tense of regular **-ar, -er,** and **-ir** verbs, add the following endings to the **yo** form of the present indicative after dropping the **-o.**

You may wish to point out that *-ar* verbs have subjunctive endings beginning with *e*, and that both *-er* and *-ir* verbs have subjunctive endings beginning with *a*.

Infinitive	Yo form Present Indicative	Stem of yo form	Present Subjunctive -ar	-er	-ir
estudiar **aprender** **abrir**	estudio aprendo abro	estudi- aprend- abr-	estudie estudies estudie estudiemos estudiéis estudien	aprenda aprendas aprenda aprendamos aprendáis aprendan	abra abras abra abramos abráis abran

Notice that regular **-er** and **-ir** verbs have the same endings in the present subjunctive tense.

Use of the Spanish subjunctive

The Spanish subjunctive is normally used in subordinate clauses, that is, in compound sentences with two verbs and two subjects.

subject +	verb in indicative	+	que	+ subject +	verb in subjunctive

La profesora **quiere que** Jorge **estudie** más.   *The teacher wants Jorge to study more.*
Pres.   Con-   Pres.
Ind.   nector   Subj.

1. The two clauses above are joined together with **que.**
2. Notice that the subjunctive appears in the clause after **que:**
     . . . **que** Jorge **estudie** más.

ATENCIÓN: The verb in the main clause is in the present indicative:
     La profesora **quiere** que . . .

B 11   Actividad • Adela y sus hermanos    For answers, see p. T180.

Because Adela's mother is sick, Adela is in charge of the house. Here are some of the things she wants to tell her brothers and sisters to do. Help her out by following the model.

   MODELO   Ana María / lavar los platos
            Adela quiere que Ana María lave los platos.

1. Pedro y Pablo / barrer su cuarto
2. Juan / comprar la leche
3. Alejandro / abrir las ventanas de la cocina
4. Ada / pasar la aspiradora por toda la casa
5. Arnaldo / limpiar la sala
6. Domingo y Diego / cortar el césped
7. Mariana / cocinar el pollo
8. Todos / ayudar en casa

B 12   Comprensión   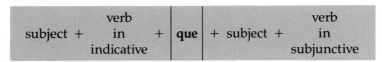 For script, see p. T180.

Mr. Chávez has many things for his students to do. He names a task and then requests a student to carry out his instructions. If the instructions match the task, check **sí** on your answer sheet. If they do not, check **no.**

   MODELO   Necesito mandar muchas cartas.
            Rafael, quiero que escribas estas cartas en la computadora.

	0	1	2	3	4	5	6	7	8	9	10
Sí	✔		✔	✔		✔	✔			✔	✔
No		✔			✔			✔	✔		

B13 ESTRUCTURAS ESENCIALES

The subjunctive to express demands, wishes, and requests

Point out that indirect commands can be expressed in many different ways. Go over the list of verbs used to express them. Indicate that some are more polite than others, just like in English.

When you want to express demands, wishes, and requests, you need to use the present subjunctive in the subordinate clause.

Roberto necesita que **tú** le prestes el libro.   *Roberto needs that you lend him the book.*
Luisa desea que **sus amigos** hablen en español.   *Luisa wishes that her friends speak Spanish.*
La **profesora** quiere que **Elena** estudie más.   *The teacher wants that Elena study more.*

1. All of the Spanish sentences above have two clauses. Each clause has a different subject, because there is a person in the main clause who wants someone else in the subordinate clause to do something.
2. The subjunctive follows **que**.
3. Here are some important verbs you may use to express demands, wishes, and requests.

querer	*to want*	**permitir**	*to permit*
aconsejar	*to advise*	**recomendar**	*to recommend*
mandar	*to command*	**esperar**	*to hope*
pedir	*to ask*	**desear**	*to wish*
necesitar	*to need*	**insistir (en)**	*to insist*
prohibir	*to prohibit*	**sugerir**	*to suggest*

ATENCIÓN: If there is only one subject in the sentence, **que** is not used and the second verb is an infinitive.

Roberto **necesita leer** el libro.   *Roberto needs to read the book.*
Luisa **desea hablar** español.   *Luisa wishes to speak Spanish.*
La profesora **quiere estudiar** más.   *The teacher wants to study more.*

B14 Actividad • Nuestros profesores ▭ For answers, see p. T181.

The faculty members have something to say to the students. You can find out what they want by following the model.

MODELO   La señorita Banks prohibe que nosotros (beber)
                  refrescos en clase.
              La señorita Banks prohibe que nosotros bebamos
                  refrescos en clase.

1. El director quiere que yo (escuchar) sus consejos.
2. La profesora de español desea que tú (hablar) español.
3. La señorita Ortiz pide que nosotros (aprender) dos idiomas.
4. El señor López aconseja que los chicos (escribir) cartas a varias universidades.
5. La profesora de matemáticas nos aconseja que (tomar) un curso de álgebra.
6. El supervisor insiste en que ellos no (comer) en clase.
7. El doctor Recio prohibe que ustedes (correr) por el pasillo.
8. La señora Murphy quiere que él (leer) la lectura.

David Alvarado es estudiante de secundaria. Está leyendo los clasificados en el periódico porque quiere conseguir un trabajo por las tardes. Así podrá ahorrar dinero y comprarse la moto que vio el otro día.

JOVEN

Necesitamos empleado joven para trabajar por las tardes en ferretería. Preferimos alguien con experiencia. Para solicitud de empleo, escriba a Mateo Hernández, Gerente, Ferretería La Llave, Apartado postal 354, Granada.

AYUDANTE DE PLOMERO

Solicitamos ayudante de plomero con experiencia en arreglar cañerías para trabajar por las tardes. Buen sueldo. Llame al 68523.

(Después de leer los clasificados, David decide consultar con su hermano Daniel.)

DAVID   *(mostrándole los clasificados)*   ¿Qué te parecen estos trabajos? Son los únicos que hay por las tardes. ¿Qué debo hacer? Necesito que me aconsejes.

DANIEL   Te aconsejo que le hagas una carta al gerente de la ferretería y que le digas que te interesa el trabajo . . . tú no sabes nada de plomería.

DAVID   Tienes razón. Hoy mismo le escribo una carta al señor Hernández.

B 16   Actividad • ¿Es cierto o no?

Correct the following sentences so they agree with the information in B15.

1. David Alvarado es estudiante de la universidad.
2. David quiere conseguir un trabajo para comprarse una tabla vela.
3. Mateo Hernández es el dependiente de la ferretería.
4. La ferretería necesita un empleado joven para trabajar por las noches.
5. David decide hablar con su papá.
6. David sabe mucho de plomería.

1. David Alvarado es estudiante de secundaria. 2. David quiere conseguir un trabajo para comprarse una moto. 3. Mateo Hernández es el gerente de la ferretería. 4. La ferretería necesita un empleado joven para trabajar por las tardes. 5. David decide hablar con su hermano. 6. David no sabe nada de plomería.

ESTRUCTURAS ESENCIALES
Present subjunctive of some irregular verbs

Many verbs that you have learned are irregular in the present indicative. However, notice that they form the present subjunctive in the same way as the regular **-ar,** **-er,** and **-ir** verbs. That is, they add the regular subjunctive endings to the **yo** stem of the present indicative.

Verb	**Yo** *form*	*Stem*	*PRESENT SUBJUNCTIVE*
decir	digo	dig-	di**ga**, di**gas**, di**ga**, di**gamos**, di**gáis**, di**gan**
hacer	hago	hag-	ha**ga**, ha**gas**, ha**ga**, ha**gamos**, ha**gáis**, ha**gan**
oír	oigo	oig-	oi**ga**, oi**gas**, oi**ga**, oi**gamos**, oi**gáis**, oi**gan**
poner	pongo	pong-	pon**ga**, pon**gas**, pon**ga**, pon**gamos**, pon**gáis**, pon**gan**
salir	salgo	salg-	sal**ga**, sal**gas**, sal**ga**, sal**gamos**, sal**gáis**, sal**gan**
tener	tengo	teng-	ten**ga**, ten**gas**, ten**ga**, ten**gamos**, ten**gáis**, ten**gan**
traer	traigo	traig-	trai**ga**, trai**gas**, trai**ga**, trai**gamos**, trai**gáis**, trai**gan**
venir	vengo	veng-	ven**ga**, ven**gas**, ven**ga**, ven**gamos**, ven**gáis**, ven**gan**

B 18 Actividad • **Los padres de Lolita y Lilita**

Lolita y Lilita are twin sisters with very strict parents. Find out what their parents tell them and complete the sentences with the correct forms of the verbs in parentheses.

1. Queremos que ustedes siempre (decir) _____ la verdad. digan
2. Lolita, ¡te prohibimos que (ver) _____ esa película! veas
3. Les sugerimos que (tener) _____ cuidado con esos chicos. tengan
4. Lilita, te recomendamos que no (venir) _____ tarde del cine. vengas
5. Les pedimos a ustedes que nos (prestar) _____ atención. presten
6. Insistimos en que las dos (oír) _____ nuestros consejos. oigan
7. Lolita, no te permitimos que (salir) _____ con Carlitos. salgas
8. Lilita, te recomendamos que (hacer) _____ tus tareas todos los días. hagas

B 19 Actividad • **Combinación** Answers will vary.

Combine elements from each column to form nine sentences. Follow the model.

MODELO   Yo necesito que tú estudies conmigo.

Ella	aconsejar		Ud.	venir temprano a clase
Mis padres	querer		mis amigos	manejar con cuidado
Tu hermana	desear		nosotros	salir con ella
Tú	esperar		yo	ver ese programa
Mi tío	prohibir	que	mi primo	trabajar en su tienda
Adela	necesitar		Elena	llamar a la casa
Los muchachos	insistir (en)		la directora	hacer la cena temprano
La profesora	sugerir		los alumnos	traer la tarea
Don Alonso	recomendar		los sobrinos	salir temprano

cocinero

dependiente

mecánico

plomero

camarera

cartero

jardinero

intérprete

carpintero

cajera

B 21 Actividad • Combinación

Join the elements in the two boxes to form ten logical sentences. Use B20 as a guide.

una cocinera	vender artículos
una intérprete	hacer una mesa
una cajera	arreglar el carro
un plomero	tener que saber idiomas
un cartero	reparar las cañerías
un jardinero	entregar las cartas
una dependienta	servir la comida
una camarera	contar el dinero
un mecánico	cortar el césped
un carpintero	preparar la comida

Una cocinera prepara la comida
Un intérprete tiene que saber idiomas.
Una cajera cuenta el dinero.
Un plomero repara las cañerías.
Un cartero entrega las cartas.
Un jardinero corta el césped.
Una dependienta vende artículo
Una camarera sirve la comida.
Un mecánico arregla el carro.
Un carpintero hace una mesa.

B 22 Actividad • ¡A escribir!   Answers will vary.

Prepare five classified ads to place in the newspaper. Here are some of the people you might be looking for in your ads. Each ad should be about two lines.

una cocinera
una intérprete
un carpintero
una dependienta
un camarero
un mecánico

For information on how to present the realia, see p. T182.

B 23 SE ESCRIBE ASÍ
Salutations and complimentary closings for business letters

Saludos		Despedidas	
Distinguida señora:	Dear Madam:	Muy agradecido por su atención,	Very grateful for your attention,
Estimado señor:	Dear Sir:	Atentamente,	Very truly yours,
Muy señores míos:	Gentlemen:	Suyo afectísimo,	Cordially,
Muy señor nuestro:	Dear Sir:		

B 24 Actividad • ¡A escribir!   Answers will vary.

Imagine that you have just read the classified ads and found a job that sounds interesting. Write a letter inquiring about the job. Be sure to include your qualifications.

310   Unidad 9

congratulating someone . . . directing others to tell someone else to do something

Going on an interview for a summer or part-time job can be nerve-racking. You must be confident in your abilities and have a positive attitude. So, don't worry beforehand. You may get the job and then congratulations will be in order.

C1   La carta del gerente

Después de varios días, el cartero le entrega una carta a David. Al mirar el remitente, David ve que es una carta del señor Hernández. Abre el sobre, saca la carta y comienza a leerla.

Ferretería La Llave
Apartado postal 354
Granada, España

17 de octubre

Sr. David Alvarado
Avenida Cristóbal Colón 11
Granada, España

Estimado Sr. Alvarado,

Acusamos recibo de su carta del tres del presente y nos es grato informarle que le concederemos una entrevista el día 25 del presente a las diez de la mañana. Creemos que Ud. es uno de los mejores candidatos para el puesto y las recomendaciones del señor Joaquín Blanco, su antiguo jefe, son magníficas.

En cuanto a sus preguntas sobre el puesto, queremos que el candidato sea puntual y que esté disponible por las tardes. También necesitamos que el candidato conozca los productos y los coloque con cuidado en los estantes. Por último, deseamos que atienda cortésmente a los clientes, les dé buen servicio y sepa operar la caja. Le adjunto una solicitud de empleo. Haga favor llenarla y traerla el día de la entrevista.

Atentamente,

Mateo Hernández

Mateo Hernández, Gerente

Actividad • Preguntas y respuestas

Use the information in C1 to answer the following questions.

1. ¿Quién le entrega la carta a David? El cartero le entrega la carta a David.
2. ¿De quién es la carta? La carta es del señor Hernández.
3. Según el señor Hernández, ¿quién es uno de los mejores candidatos para el puesto? David es uno de los mejores candidatos para el puesto.
4. ¿Para cuándo es la entrevista de David? La entrevista de David es el día 25 a las diez de la mañana.
5. ¿Quién es Joaquín Blanco? Joaquín Blanco es el antiguo jefe de David.
6. ¿Qué le adjunta el señor Hernández con su carta? Le adjunta una solicitud de empleo.
7. ¿Qué cualidades quiere el gerente que el candidato tenga? Quiere que el candidato sea puntual, que esté disponible por las tardes, que conozca los productos y los coloque con cuidado y que atienda cortésmente a los clientes.

C3 Sabes que . . .

En el mundo hispánico no es común que los estudiantes de secundaria trabajen durante el verano o después de clase. No hay tantos trabajos disponibles para los jóvenes como en los Estados Unidos, y muchos de los trabajos que hay los toman personas mayores.

Muchos jóvenes pasan las vacaciones de verano con sus padres o familiares en el campo, en la playa o en alguna otra ciudad. Si no tienen familiares en esos lugares o no pueden ir, se quedan en casa con la familia.

Algunos jóvenes, especialmente en los últimos años, tratan de encontrar trabajo en el verano para ahorrar dinero y poder comprarse algo costoso (expensive), como una bicicleta nueva o una motocicleta. Muchos de los jóvenes que trabajan, en general, lo hacen en el negocio de sus padres o de algún otro familiar.

C4 SE ESCRIBE ASÍ
Common introductions for business letters

Acusamos recibo de su carta...	We acknowledge receipt of your letter...
En relación con su carta del...	Regarding your letter dated...
Nos es grato informarle...	We are pleased to inform you...
Por medio de la presente tenemos el gusto de comunicarle...	Hereby we are pleased to inform you...
Sentimos comunicarle...	We regret to inform you...

ESTRUCTURAS ESENCIALES

Irregular verbs and verbs ending in -car, -gar, and -zar in the present subjunctive

A. The following verbs are irregular in the present subjunctive.

dar	estar	ir	saber	ser
dé	esté	vaya	sepa	sea
des	estés	vayas	sepas	seas
dé	esté	vaya	sepa	sea
demos	estemos	vayamos	sepamos	seamos
déis	estéis	vayáis	sepáis	seáis
den	estén	vayan	sepan	sean

Mi mamá quiere que Luisa le **dé** los libros a mis primos.

My mother wants Luisa to give the books to my cousins.

La profesora insiste en que **estemos** en clase temprano.

The professor insists that we be in class early.

Tomás, necesito que **vayas** a la tienda y compres huevos.

Tomás, I need you to go to the store and buy eggs.

Mis padres esperan que nosotros **sepamos** cómo hacer la tarea.

My parents hope that we know how to do the homework.

Tía Luisa desea que Anita **sea** más cariñosa.

Aunt Luisa wishes that Anita were more affectionate.

B. You have already studied the verbs ending in **-car, -gar,** and **-zar** in the preterit tense. These verbs have the same changes in all forms of the present subjunctive.

explicar	entregar	comenzar
explique	entregue	comience
expliques	entregues	comiences
explique	entregue	comience
expliquemos	entreguemos	comencemos
expliquéis	entreguéis	comencéis
expliquen	entreguen	comiencen

1. Verbs ending in **-car** change **c** to **qu** before **e** in all forms of the present subjunctive.

explicar → explique

Él quiere que tú **expliques** los ejercicios.   *He wants you to explain the exercises.*

2. Verbs ending in **-gar** change **g** to **gu** before **e** in all forms of the present subjunctive.

entregar → entregue

El gerente quiere que nosotros **entreguemos** la solicitud.

The manager wants us to hand in the application.

3. Verbs ending in **-zar** change from **z** to **c** in all forms of the present subjunctive.

comenzar → comience

Yo quiero que usted **comience** a trabajar mañana.   *I want you to start working tomorrow.*

C6 Actividad • El gerente

The store manager wants each of the employees to do something at the store. Follow the model.

> MODELO Ana / llegar temprano
> El gerente quiere que Ana llegue temprano.

1. Gloria / ser atenta con los clientes
2. Domingo y Danilo / llegar temprano al trabajo
3. Tú y yo / ir a la oficina
4. Carlos y Miguel / saber los precios de los artículos
5. Dorotea / entregar la solicitud de empleo
6. Manolo / buscar la carta de David
7. Usted / dar una vuelta por la tienda
8. Tú / conocer a los otros empleados
9. Luis / no hablar con la secretaria
10. Tomás y Elena / ser puntuales
11. Gerardo / escribir la recomendación
12. La nueva empleada / escribir los anuncios
13. El joven / operar la caja
14. La dependienta / no hablar tanto por teléfono
15. El candidato / llegar temprano a la cita
16. El señor Gómez / explicar el horario nuevo

1. El gerente quiere que Gloria sea atenta con los clientes. 2. El gerente quiere que Domingo y Danilo lleguen temprano al trabajo. 3. El gerente quiere que tú y yo vayamos a la oficina. 4. El gerente quiere que Carlos y Miguel sepan los precios de los artículos. 5. El gerente quiere que Dorotea entregue la solicitud de empleo. 6. El gerente quiere que Manolo busque la carta de David. 7. El gerente quiere que usted dé una vuelta por la tienda. 8. El gerente quiere que tú conozcas a los otros empleados. 9. El gerente quiere que Luis no hable con la secretaria. 10. El gerente quiere que Tomás y Elena sean puntuales. 11. El gerente quiere que Gerardo escriba la recomendación. 12. El gerente quiere que la nueva empleada escriba los anuncios. 13. El gerente quiere que el joven opere la caja. 14. El gerente quiere que la dependienta no hable tanto por teléfono. 15. El gerente quiere que el candidato llegue temprano a la cita. 16. El gerente quiere que el señor Gómez explique el horario nuevo.

C7 Comprensión

For script, see p. T184–185.

You are working for a relative who owns a small business. Listen to each statement and decide if it describes a quality you would be looking for in a new employee. If the statement describes a favorable quality, check **sí** on your answer sheet. If it does not, check **no**.

> MODELO Deseamos que siempre llegue a tiempo.

	0	1	2	3	4	5	6	7	8	9	10
Sí	✔			✔	✔				✔	✔	
No		✔	✔			✔	✔	✔			✔

C8 Actividad • Charla

Answers will vary.

Pair up with another student and imagine that you both have jobs. Ask each other the following questions.

1. ¿Dónde trabajas tú?
2. ¿Cómo se llama tu jefe?
3. ¿A qué hora quiere que tú llegues al trabajo?
4. ¿A qué hora permite que ustedes salgan del trabajo?
5. ¿Qué cosas necesita tu jefe que ustedes hagan en el trabajo?
6. ¿Cómo quiere que ustedes sean en el trabajo?
7. ¿Qué prefiere que ustedes sepan?
8. ¿Qué les aconseja a ustedes?

314 Unidad 9

El día 25, David llega a la Ferretería La Llave para su cita con el señor Hernández.
Una recepcionista lo atiende.

DAVID	Buenos días, señorita. Soy David Alvarado y tengo una cita con el señor Hernández.
RECEPCIONISTA	Sí, un momento *(llamando por teléfono al señor Hernández)*. Señor Hernández, aquí está David Alvarado.
SR. HERNÁNDEZ	*(hablando por teléfono)* Pídale que me traiga la solicitud y dígale que pase a mi despacho.

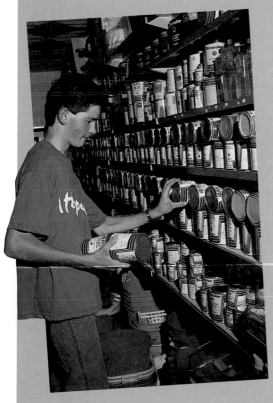

(En el despacho del señor Hernández)

SR. HERNÁNDEZ	Pase, joven, y siéntese.
DAVID	Muchas gracias.
SR. HERNÁNDEZ	*(mirando la solicitud)* Estoy muy satisfecho con sus referencias y su solicitud, pero ¿por qué dejó su trabajo en la ferretería El Águila?
DAVID	Porque ese trabajo era solamente durante el verano. ¿Podría decirme a qué hora empieza el trabajo y a qué hora termina?
SR. HERNÁNDEZ	Empieza a las cuatro y termina más o menos a las siete. ¿Tiene otra pregunta sobre el puesto?
DAVID	Sí, ¿cuánto es el sueldo?
SR. HERNÁNDEZ	El sueldo es de seis mil pesetas a la semana. ¿Alguna otra pregunta?
DAVID	No, gracias, no tengo más preguntas.
SR. HERNÁNDEZ	¡Felicitaciones! El puesto es suyo.

C10   Actividad • Preguntas y respuestas

Use the information in C9 to answer the following questions.

1. ¿Con quién tiene la entrevista David?   David tiene la entrevista con el señor Hernández.
2. ¿Quién atiende a David al llegar a la ferretería?   La recepcionista atiende a David.
3. ¿Con qué está satisfecho el señor Hernández?   El señor Hernández está satisfecho con sus referencias y su
4. ¿Por qué dejó David su trabajo en El Águila?   Porque ese trabajo era solamente durante el verano.   solicitud.
5. ¿A qué hora comienza y termina el trabajo?   El trabajo comienza a las cuatro y termina a las siete.
6. ¿Qué le dice el señor Hernández a David al final de la entrevista?   Le dice: ¡Felicitaciones! El puesto es suyo.

C11   SE DICE ASÍ
Congratulating someone

Te felicito.	I congratulate you.
¡Enhorabuena!	Congratulations!
¡Felicitaciones!	Congratulations!
¡Felicidades!	Congratulations!

C12   Actividad • La entrevista   Answers will vary.

Choose a partner. Then take turns playing the role of a personnel manager. Ask and answer the following questions.

1. ¿Cómo se llama Ud.?
2. ¿Dónde vive?
3. ¿Dónde trabajó antes?
4. ¿Por qué dejó ese trabajo?
5. ¿Por qué quiere trabajar aquí?
6. ¿Podría darme algunas referencias?
7. ¿Qué experiencia tiene para este trabajo?
8. ¿Cuándo puede empezar el trabajo?

Answers will vary.
C13   Actividad • Más preguntas

You will now ask the "personnel manager" a number of questions and he or she will answer you.

1. ¿De qué hora a qué hora es el trabajo?
2. ¿Qué cosas tengo que hacer en el trabajo?
3. ¿Quién es el gerente?
4. ¿Qué tipo de ropa tengo que traer al trabajo?
5. ¿Dan vacaciones en el trabajo?
6. ¿Cuándo quiere que comience a trabajar?
7. ¿Cuánto es el sueldo?

Imagine that you are looking for a job and that you need to fill out a job application. Copy and complete the following application correctly.

SOLICITUD DE TRABAJO

Puesto que desea _____   Sueldo que desea _____

Horas de trabajo   ☐ Tiempo completo   ☐ Mañanas   ☐ Tardes

Apellidos	Nombre

Dirección (calle, ciudad, zona postal)	Teléfono

Fecha de nacimiento   Día ___ Mes ___ Año ___   Sexo ☐ M ☐ F

Tiempo en la escuela		Nombre y dirección de la escuela	Año de graduación
de	a		
Mes Año	Mes Año	Escuela secundaria o vocacional	

Tiempo en el trabajo		Puesto actual	Descripción del trabajo
de	a		
Mes Año	Mes Año		

Tiempo en el trabajo		Último puesto	Descripción del trabajo
de	a		
Mes Año	Mes Año		

Fecha _____   Firma _____

ESTRUCTURAS ESENCIALES
Indirect commands

To give an indirect command, use:

> **que** + **(lo)** + subjunctive + subject

Que trabaje Isabel.	*Let Isabel work.*
Que lo aprendan ellos.	*Let them learn it.*
Que se bañe Miguel.	*Let Miguel take a bath.*

1. Indirect commands usually give an order or instruction to a person who is to convey it to a third party.
2. Notice that the verb is in the third person singular or plural.
3. Object pronouns and reflexive pronouns precede the verb. To form a negative statement, **no** also comes before the verb: **Que *no* vayan al cine.**

C16 Actividad • El tímido *The shy one*

Pair up with a classmate and imagine you are the manager of a hardware store. Give indirect orders to your employees, following the model.

> MODELO   pasar al despacho (Elena)
> Que Elena pase al despacho.

1. traer la solicitud (Evaristo) Que Evaristo traiga la solicitud.
2. empezar mañana (Ramiro) Que Ramiro empiece mañana.
3. hablar en español (Graciela) Que Graciela hable en español.
4. ser más rápido (ellos) Que ellos sean más rápidos.
5. traer la cuenta (Tomás y Raúl) Que Tomás y Raúl traigan la cuenta.
6. esperar un momento (Clarisa) Que Clarisa espere un momento.
7. ir a la caja (David) Que David vaya a la caja.
8. colocar los productos en los estantes (Ana y María) Que Ana y María coloquen los productos en los estantes.

C17 Actividad • En mi trabajo

You got a job and you have been working for three months. Your boss is so pleased with you that he now depends on you to tell others what to do. Pair up with a partner. Repeat the instructions to your partner, who will convey them to a co-worker.

> MODELO   Dígale a Alejandro que (ayudar) a los clientes.
> Dígale a Alejandro que ayude a los clientes.
> Alejandro, ayude a los clientes.

1. Pídale a Luisa que (ser) más amable con los clientes.
2. Dígale a Pablo que siempre (entrar) a las ocho.
3. Recomiéndeles a Belinda y a Melba que (venir) más temprano al trabajo.
4. Aconséjele a Carmen que (conocer) la mercancía.
5. Prohíbale a Cándido que (salir) temprano del trabajo.
6. Dígales a Eduardo y a María que (limpiar) la tienda.
7. Ordénele a Silvia que (ir) al banco.
8. Pídale a Luisa que (trabajar) más.

1. Pídale a Luisa que sea más amable con los clientes. Luisa, sea más amable con los clientes.   2. Dígale a Pablo que siempre entre a las ocho. Pablo, entre siempre a las ocho.   3. Recomiéndeles a Belinda y a Melba que vengan más temprano al trabajo. Belinda y Melba, vengan más temprano al trabajo.   4. Aconséjele a Carmen que conozca la mercancía. Carmen, conozca la mercancía. 5. Prohíbale a Cándido que salga temprano del trabajo. Cándido, no salga temprano del trabajo.   6. Dígales a Eduardo y a María que limpien la tienda. Eduardo y María, limpien la tienda.   7. Ordénele a Silvia que vaya al banco. Silvia, vaya al banco.   8. Pídale a Luisa que trabaje más. Luisa, trabaje más.

C18 Actividad • Están ocupados   Answers will vary.

You ask the manager about the instructions you need to give to the new employees. But when you ask them to do something, they always seem too busy. Choose two classmates and follow the model.

MODELO

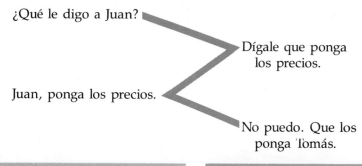

¿Qué le digo a Juan?

Dígale que ponga los precios.

Juan, ponga los precios.

No puedo. Que los ponga Tomás.

Esteban	llegar temprano
los jóvenes	sentarse y esperar
Luis	arreglar la vitrina
Carlota	sacar la basura
el señor Gómez	operar la caja
Carolina y Héctor	mostrar la mercancía
señorita Méndez	atender a los clientes

C19 Actividad • Charla   Answers will vary.

Pair up with a classmate and ask each other the following questions.

1. ¿Qué harías para buscar trabajo?
2. ¿Cómo te prepararías para una entrevista?
3. ¿A quién pondrías tú como referencia?
4. ¿Con quién te gustaría tener la entrevista?
5. ¿Qué harás si no te dan el trabajo?

C20 Actividad • Composición   Answers will vary.

You are competing for a job, and you believe you are the right person. Write a letter explaining why you are that person, taking into account the following suggestions.

I. Introducción
   A. Yo soy la persona ideal porque . . .
   B. Mis intereses son . . .

II. Desarrollo
   A. Mi experiencia para el trabajo
   B. Mis años de estudio en la escuela
   C. Los idiomas que hablo
   D. Mis referencias
   E. Otra información importante

III. Conclusión
   A. Mis cualidades personales son . . .
   B. Quiero que . . .

For information on how to present the realia, see p. T187.

1 Los clasificados

Answers will vary.

Use what you have learned in this unit and the advertisements below as models to write a classified ad in Spanish for one of the following professions or trades.

secretaria	vendedor	arquitecto
mesero	programadora	ingeniero
recepcionista	cajero	plomero

IMPORTANTE EMPRESA
NECESITA
PARA REEMPLAZO
DE VACACIONES
SECRETARIAS-DACTILOGRAFAS
ENVIAR CURRICULUM Y FOTOGRAFIA A:
SECTEMP 29
CASILLA 13-D STGO.

IMPORTANTE INSTITUCION FINANCIERA
SOLICITA
PARA SUS COMEDORES DE EJECUTIVOS
M E S E R O S

Requisitos:
- Edad entre 25 y 35 años
- De preferencia casados
- Experiencia mínima de dos años en puesto similar
- Con disponibilidad de horario de 7 a 17 horas

Recepcionista

Nuestro cliente, importante empresa industrial del país, necesita contratar recepcionista de alto nivel.

Debe poseer, como requisito indispensables, excelente presencia, experiencia en atención de público de central telefónica. Edad entre 25 y 35 años.

Se invita a las interesadas que verdaderamente cumplan con los requisitos, a postular al cargo enviando sus antecedentes con fotografía reciente a casilla 50080.

B&B Auditores e Ingenieros Consultores.
Bakovic y Balic

Miembros Int'l Council
EW
Ernst & Whinney

VENDEDORES(AS)
Con experiencia a nivel ejecutivo, promedio de ingresos de $400,000 a $500,000 mensuales, entre sueldo y comisiones, edad de 25 a 40 años y buena presentación
DURANGO 263, 6o. piso, colonia Roma, D.F.

AA
SE SOLICITA
AA
CAJERA ADMINISTRATIVA
Con 1 año mínimo de experiencia. SAN LUIS TLATILCO No. 34, fraccionamiento Parque Industrial Naucalpan, Edo. de México. 576-68-55

BUSCAMOS PROGRAMADORES(AS)
De buena presencia para promoción de sistemas computacionales.
NUEVA YORK 57 PISO 2

2 Actividad • El comparativo y el superlativo   Answers will vary.

Compare the shops in your town, the movies now playing at the local cinema, and several famous actors or actresses. Use the comparative and superlative forms of the following adjectives.

bueno   malo   pequeño   mayor   menor

3 Actividad • El pretérito y el imperfecto

Complete the following paragraph, using the correct form of either the preterit or the imperfect tenses.

La semana pasada yo (salir) _____ a dar un paseo por la ciudad. Yo (querer) _____   salí / quería
ir a la verbena de San Juan, pero nadie (querer) _____ ir conmigo. Mientras   quiso
(caminar) _____ por las calles de la ciudad, (pensar) _____ en mi amiga Aleida.   caminaba / pensé
Yo (pensar) _____ regresar a casa cuando (oír) _____ la voz de Aleida. Ella   pensaba / oí
(traer) _____ un vestido muy hermoso. Yo la (invitar) _____ a beber un refresco y   traía / invité
después nosotros (ir) _____ a la verbena de San Juan. Nosotros (montar) _____ en   fuimos / montamos
el pulpo, (comer) _____ muchos churros y (divertirse) _____ mucho.   comimos / nos divertimos

4 Actividad • Yo quiero que . . .   Answers will vary.

You and a friend are planning a surprise party for your Spanish teacher. Tell your friend at least five things you want him or her to do. Then your friend should tell you what he or she wants you to do.

5 Actividad • Aquí mando yo   Answers will vary.

Today is the day of the surprise party. You need to get everything organized before your Spanish teacher arrives, but the people you need are not there. Give ten indirect commands to ten of your classmates.

6 Actividad • Los datos personales   Answers will vary.

You are applying for a job at a store in a shopping mall. Write a brief résumé in Spanish, listing in outline form the most important details of your education and work experience. Use the following résumé as a guide.

La carta solicitando trabajo debe ir con los datos personales, tales como los estudios y la experiencia de trabajo. Por ejemplo:

John Castagno
345 W. 89 Street
New York, NY 10024
Teléfono: (212) 618-2828

INFORMACIÓN

Nacimiento:	10 de septiembre de 1970
Ciudadanía:	Estados Unidos
Estado civil:	Soltero
Salud:	Excelente

ESTUDIOS

3 de junio de 1988
Graduado de la escuela secundaria
Escuela Secundaria Simón Bolívar
Caracas, Venezuela

HONORES

Primero de la clase
Medalla de oro en español
Miembro de la Sociedad Hispánica

EXPERIENCIA DE TRABAJO

Verano de 1988:	Supermercado La Abundancia: cajero
Verano de 1987:	Agencia de viajes Las Maravillas: guía de turistas
Verano de 1986:	Cine Rex: cajero en la taquilla

REFERENCIAS

Le envío con la carta las referencias de mis jefes en los tres empleos.

7 Actividad • Una carta   Answers will vary.

Write a business letter in Spanish inquiring about a job. Use the appropriate salutation, introduction, and complimentary closing. Be sure to include your résumé with the letter.

8 Dictado   For script, see p. T188.

Copy the following paragraph to prepare yourself for dictation.

Ayer la mamá de ____ le ____: "Cari, necesito que ____ a la ____," y ella le contestó, "¡Mamá, estás loca! Yo no puedo ir ____ porque Eduardo ____ que yo ____ a su casa ahora mismo para ____ al ____." La mamá ____: "Cari, te ____."

Letter *d*

1. The Spanish consonant **d** has two different sounds, depending on its position. After a pause and after the letters **n** or **l**, the Spanish **d** has a sound similar to the English **d.** Listen to the following words and repeat.

día	comprando
montando	dónde
Daniel	Domínguez
Rolando	diálogo

2. The Spanish consonant **d** at the end of a word is often not pronounced unless the following word starts with a vowel. Listen to the following words and repeat.

ciudad	verdad	actualidad	Madrid
amistad	dificultad	virtud	calidad

3. In all other positions the sound of **d** is similar to the *th* sound of *they.* Listen carefully and repeat the following words and sentences.

Eduardo	pesada
Rodrigo	estudio
verdadero	helado
ayudar	educación

Eduardo Domínguez está comprando demasiado.
Daniel decide ayudar a Rolando.

Contrasting the sounds of the Spanish *t* and *d*

Listen carefully and repeat the following sentences.

Debo tener diez tarjetas de cumpleaños.
El dependiente tiene mucho trabajo.
David practica la tabla vela todos los domingos.
Don Diego, tenemos el gusto de darle el puesto.

Actividad • Práctica de pronunciación

Listen carefully and repeat the following sentences.

Maldonado le dio dinero a don Diego.
Todos los días Daniel daba un paseo con Cándido.
Dolores le dijo adiós a su ciudad.
Secreto de dos, lo sabe Dios.
Después de cada día, nadie decía nada.

¿LO SABES?

Let's review some important points you've learned in this unit.

SECTION A

Answers will vary.

Are you able to talk about the best things in your life?
Discuss your favorite people, sports, and activities with a partner.

Do you know how to ask for help or warn others in an emergency?
Use a Spanish exclamation or expression for each of the following situations.
1. A fire is burning out of control.
2. A child is running in front of a car.
3. You are trapped in a locked room.
4. Someone is stealing your wallet.

Can you narrate a story in Spanish in the past?
Write a story in Spanish describing something that happened to you in the past.

SECTION B

Answers will vary.

Do you know how to express surprise or pity in Spanish?
React to each of the following statements.
1. Gané un premio en la rifa.
2. El fuego destruyó la casa de Jorge.
3. Lucía no puede ir a la verbena.
4. Hubo un accidente y murió mucha gente.

Do you know how to properly address a business letter?
Write three different salutations.

SECTION C

Answers will vary.

Do you know how to conduct interviews in Spanish?
Get together with three classmates and interview them for a job. Select the most qualified person based on the interview, and congratulate him or her.

Can you give an indirect command in Spanish?
Excuse yourself from doing certain things by saying who should do them.

VOCABULARIO

SECTION A

agarrar *to grab*
alquilar *to rent*
¡alto! *stop!*
atractivo, -a *attractive*
¡auxilio! *help!*
bajarse *to step down*
bello, -a *beautiful*
cargar *to carry*
la **caseta** *booth*
el **coche de topetazos** *bumper car*
¡cuidado! *watch out!*
la **churrería** *churro store*
darse cuenta de que *to realize that*
echar al agua *to throw in the water*
en calma *calm*
enrollar *to roll up*
el **equipo** *equipment*
estacionar *to park*
el **fuego** *fire*
marearse *to get dizzy*
el **mástil** *mast*
la **montaña rusa** *roller coaster*
el **muro** *outside wall*
pescar un resfriado *to catch a cold*
ponerse contento, -a *to become happy*
popular *popular*
el **pulpo** *octopus; amusement park ride*
la **rifa** *raffle*
el **rifle** *rifle*
la **rueda giratoria** *Ferris wheel*
sacarse la rifa *to win the raffle*
sentarse (ie) *to sit*
¡socorro! *help!*
subirse *to get on*
la **tabla vela** *windsurfing*
la **taquilla** *ticket booth*
el **tiovivo** *merry-go-round*
tirar al blanco *to shoot at a target*
el **tiro al blanco** *shooting gallery*
la **verbena** *fair; carnival*

SECTION B

aconsejar *to advise*
el **anuncio clasificado** *classified ad*
arreglar *to fix*
atentamente *cordially*
el **ayudante** *assistant*
la **cajera** *cashier (f.)*
el **cajero** *cashier (m.)*
la **cañería** *pipe*
el **carpintero** *carpenter*
el **cartero** *mail carrier*
la **cocinera** *cook (f.)*
el **cocinero** *cook (m.)*
consultar *to consult*
distinguida señora *dear madam*
esperar *to hope*
estimado señor *dear sir*
la **ferretería** *hardware store*
imaginarse *to imagine*
insistir (en) *to insist*
interesar *to be interested in*
el **intérprete** *interpreter*
mandar *to command; to send*
mayor *bigger; older*
    el mayor *biggest; oldest*
el **mecánico** *mechanic*
mejor *better*
    el mejor *best*
menor *smaller; younger*
    el menor *smallest; youngest*
mostrar (ue) *to show*
muy señor nuestro *dear sir*
muy señores míos *gentlemen*
¡no me digas! *you don't say!*
peor *worse;* **el peor** *worst*
la **plomería** *plumbing*
el **plomero** *plumber*
prohibir *to forbid*
¡qué barbaridad! *How terrible!*
¡qué horror! *how horrible!*
¡qué suerte! *how lucky!*
solicitar *to apply*
la **solicitud de empleo** *job application*
sugerir (ie) *to suggest*
suyo afectísimo *sincerely yours*
el **sueldo** *salary*
tender la ropa *to hang clothes*
tener razón *to be right*

la **terraza** *terrace*
tomar las cosas con calma *to take things calmly*

SECTION C

acusar recibo de *to acknowledge receipt of*
adjuntar *to enclose*
el **apartado postal** *post office box*
la **caja** *cash register*
el **candidato** *candidate*
la **cita** *appointment*
colocar *to place*
conceder *to grant*
cortésmente *courteously*
la **cualidad** *quality*
del presente *of this month*
el **despacho** *office*
disponible *available*
en cuanto a *in regard to*
en relación con *regarding*
¡enhorabuena! *congratulations!*
entregar *to deliver*
el **estante** *shelf*
¡felicitaciones! *congratulations!*
informar *to inform*
la **jefa** *boss (f.)*
el **jefe** *boss (m.)*
llenar *to fill (out)*
más o menos *more or less; so so*
nos es grato informarle *we are pleased to inform you*
operar *to operate*
por medio de la presente *hereby*
por último *finally*
el **puesto** *position; job*
puntual *punctual*
la **recepcionista** *receptionist*
la **recomendación** *recommendation*
el **remitente** *sender*
el **responsable** *the person in charge*
sacar *to take out*
satisfecho, -a *satisfied*
sentimos comunicarle *we regret to inform you*
el **sobre** *envelope*
tenemos el gusto de comunicarle *we are pleased to inform you*

VAMOS A LEER

Antes de leer

There are many suffixes commonly found in Spanish. Three familiar suffixes are
-dad (*-ity*), **-able** (*-ble*), and **-mente** (*-ly*). For each of these suffixes, find at least one
word in the reading selection. *-dad* personalidad   *-able* razonable   *-mente* rápidamente

Preparación para la lectura   Some answers will vary. Possible answers are given.

Answer the following before reading.

1. ¿Qué sabes de las entrevistas de trabajo? ¿Tuviste una recientemente?
2. ¿Cómo te fue? ¿Lo conseguiste?
3. ¿Qué aprendiste en esa entrevista?
4. ¿Piensas trabajar en el verano o en las Navidades?
5. Mira rápidamente la Lectura. ¿De qué trata la segunda parte de la Lectura?   Como proyectar tu imagen.
6. Encuentra en la primera parte cinco palabras que no conocías pero que puedes
   entender por el contexto o porque son cognados.
7. Tú conoces la expresión "estoy muerto". ¿Puedes adivinar qué quiere decir "te
   estás muriendo de miedo"?   *You are scared to death.*

La entrevista

¡El sueño° de tu vida! El trabajo que tú más
querías, pero que nunca pensaste que ibas a
conseguir. Y te han llamado° para una entrevista, ¡mañana!

Tú sabes que los primeros tres minutos
serán decisivos. La primera impresión es muy
importante. Tú sabes que la persona que te va
a entrevistar quiere descubrir cuáles son tus
puntos fuertes y tus puntos débiles. Después
te va a comparar con los otros candidatos. Y
tú te estás muriendo de miedo. ¿Qué puedes
hacer?

Necesitas preparar un plan para conseguir
lo que quieres. Creo que te puedo ayudar.
Aquí está el plan.

A. Antes de la entrevista es bueno saber algo
más de la compañía, de los diferentes productos que fabrican o de los servicios que ofrecen
a los clientes. Por ejemplo, si la compañía tiene
varias sucursales°, sería bueno saber si hay
más de una cerca de tu casa. Quieres dar la
impresión de ser una persona bien informada.

Luego debes pensar si el trabajo es apropiado para ti. ¿Tienes alguna experiencia o
cualidad en tu favor? ¿Es razonable° pensar
que puedes tener éxito° en ese trabajo?
¿Puedes aprender lo que no sabes rápida-

---

sueño *dream*   **han llamado** *have called*   **sucursales** *branches*   **razonable** *reasonable*   **éxito** *success*

mente? ¿Tienes la personalidad que se necesita?

Después de analizar el trabajo y tu capacidad para hacerlo, pregúntate: "¿En qué puedo ser útil° a mi jefe? ¿Con qué puedo contribuir° a la compañía?" Entonces, ya estás listo para pensar en la segunda parte de tu tarea, la entrevista, sin olvidar el objetivo principal: conseguir el trabajo.

B. La imagen que tú proyectas es muy importante. Te recomiendo que te vistas sencillamente,° sin ningún extremo; zapatos limpios° (no tenis); posiblemente corbata si eres muchacho o falda si eres muchacha (no jeans). En el mundo de los negocios, estar elegante significa vestirse con moderación. Córtate el pelo, si te hace falta.° Si usas maquillaje, no exageres.

Durante la entrevista, cuida tus movimientos. Siéntate con buena postura, sin rigidez. Es mejor no hablar en voz alta, ni tampoco en voz muy baja. Sonríe°, pero no demasiado. Te aconsejo que practiques tus movimientos frente al espejo antes de la entrevista, o mejor aún, con un amigo o amiga. Tu objetivo es parecer amable y responsable.

útil *useful*   **contribuir** *contribute*   **sencillamente** *simply*   **limpios** *clean*   **te hace falta** *you need to*
sonríe *smile*

Al igual que tú proyectas una imagen, la persona que te entrevista te proyecta la suya. Observa la expresión de su cara y su manera de hablar. Mira lo que hay en su oficina y en su escritorio. ¿Qué te dice? Si la persona que te entrevista parece impaciente o mira el reloj, quizás tus respuestas son muy largas o inadecuadas. O tal vez es hora de despedirte. Te recomiendo que observes a tu entrevistador y que trates de actuar en armonía.

Escucha las preguntas con cuidado. Asegúrate° de que has entendido° y pregunta si es necesario. Es mejor establecer un diálogo natural desde el comienzo. Da solamente la información necesaria. Evita palabras o detalles negativos. Recuerda siempre tu razón para estar allí.

¿Recuerdas cuál es?

¡Buena suerte!°

---

asegúrate *make sure*   **has entendido** *have understood*   **razón** *reason*   **buena suerte** *good luck*

Actividad • Preguntas y respuestas

Answer the following questions about the reading selection.

1. ¿Por qué son importantes los primeros tres minutos de una entrevista? *Porque la primera impresión es muy importante.*
2. ¿Qué quiere saber tu entrevistador? *El entrevistador quiere saber cuáles son tus puntos fuertes y tus puntos débiles.*
3. La primera parte (A) de tu tarea tiene tres secciones que se refieren a tres temas diferentes. ¿Cuáles son? *Son: saber algo de la compañía, pensar si el trabajo es apropiado para ti y analizar en qué puedes contribuir a la compañía.*
4. ¿A qué se refiere la parte B?
   a. Estar elegante significa vestirse con moderación
   b. La imagen que tú proyectas
   c. Practica tus movimientos frente a un espejo
5. Por el contexto, ¿qué significa la palabra **fabrican** (página 326, Sección A, línea 3)? *Fabricar significa to make, to manufacture.*
6. Hay cognados fáciles de comprender pero difíciles de pronunciar. Repite **exagerar, postura, rigidez** y **establecer.**
7. ¿Puedes adivinar qué quieren decir **inadecuada, inútil** e **impaciente?** *inadecuada: inadequate; inútil: useless; impaciente: impatient*
8. Haz una lista de cognados de la Lectura. Vamos a ver quién de tu clase encuentra más cognados. *For answers, see below.*
9. En conclusión, ¿cuál es el objetivo principal de esta entrevista? *El objetivo principal de esta entrevista es conseguir el empleo.*

Actividad • Familia de palabras

In the reading selection you will find words that belong to the same word family as those listed below. See how many you can find.

1. soñar *sueño*
2. razón *razonable*
3. fábrica *fabricar*
4. entrevista *entrevistar*
5. información *informada*
6. maquillar *maquillaje*
7. persona *personalidad*
8. comienzo *comenzar*

Actividad • ¡A escribir! *Answers will vary.*

Prepare a list of things you should do or shouldn't do during a job interview. Then discuss it with a partner.

8. Possible answers: impresión — *impression;* importante — *important;* persona — *person;* descubrir — *to discover;* puntos — *points;* candidatos — *candidates;* preparar — *to prepare;* plan — *plan;* compañia — *company;* diferentes — *different;* productos — *products;* servicios — *services;* ofrecer — *to offer;* clientes — *clients;* informada — *informed;* apropiado — *appropriate;* experiencia — *experience;* cualidad — *quality;* favor — *favor;* razonable — *reasonable;* rápidamente — *rapidly;* personalidad — *personality;* analizar — *analyze;* contribuir — *contribute;* parte — *part;* objetivo — *objective;* imagen — *image;* movimiento — *movement;* información — *information;* recomendar — *recommend;* proyecta — *project*

UNIDAD 10 La ciudad y el campo
Scope and Sequence

	BASIC MATERIAL	COMMUNICATIVE FUNCTIONS
SECTION A	Una gran ciudad (A1) En camino a la panadería (A12)	**Exchanging information** • Reporting, describing, and narrating • Describing things you have done in the past
SECTION B	¡Qué bonito es el campo! (B1) La granja (B15)	**Expressing feelings and emotions** • Expressing your likes and dislikes **Persuading** • Warning others to refrain from doing something
SECTION C	Nuestro planeta (C1) ¿El campo en peligro o el mundo en peligro? (C12)	**Expressing attitudes and opinions** • Expressing obligation or necessity **Expressing feelings and emotions** • Expressing doubt, disbelief, or denial
TRY YOUR SKILLS	¿Qué ha pasado? Dictado	

■ **Pronunciación** (letter **x** and linking)
■ **¿Lo sabes?** ■ **Vocabulario**

VAMOS A LEER	**Las culturas hispanoamericanas** (the music, dance, and crafts of Spanish America)

WRITING A variety of controlled and open-ended writing activities appear in the Pupil's Edition. The Teacher's Notes identify other activities suitable for writing practice.

COOPERATIVE LEARNING Many of the activities in the Pupil's Edition lend themselves to cooperative learning. The Teacher's Notes explain some of the many instances where this teaching strategy can be particularly effective. For guidelines on how to use cooperative learning, see page T13.

GRAMMAR	CULTURE	RE-ENTRY
The present perfect tense (A6) Stem-changing verbs in the preterit tense (A17)	Argentina and its people The similarities between the United States and Argentina	Seasons and months of the year
Negative familiar commands (B8) Some irregular past participles (B18)	The Spanish origin of some American words from the West The **charro** from Mexico and the **gaucho** from Argentina	Names of popular animals and common pets
The subjunctive to express doubt, disbelief, or denial (C8) The use of **se** for indefinite subjects (C14)	Protecting the environment of Spanish America The city of Buenos Aires	Regular verb forms of the present subjunctive The indicative mood

Recombining communicative functions, grammar, and vocabulary

Reading for practice and pleasure

TEACHER-PREPARED MATERIALS
Section A Map of South America, globe, picture of a theater
Section B Map of Argentina, magazine pictures of animals and plants.
Section C Magazine pictures showing pollution of rivers, oceans and cities, including, if possible, Mexico City.

UNIT RESOURCES
Manual de actividades, Unit 10
Manual de ejercicios, Unit 10
Unit 10 Cassettes
Transparencies 24–26
Quizzes 22–24
Unit 10 Test

OBJECTIVES To exchange information: report, describe, and narrate; describe things you have done in the past

CULTURAL BACKGROUND Explain to the students that Argentina is divided into twenty-two provinces, a federal territory (Tierra del Fuego, the Argentine Antarctic zone, and the South Atlantic islands), and a federal district (Buenos Aires). You may wish to point out that Argentina is often compared to the United States for many reasons, such as the geography (central plains or **pampas,** the mountains to the west), the variety of climates, the products, and the high number of immigrants to the country. About 35 percent of the population of Argentina is of Italian origin, 28 percent is of Spanish origin, and the remaining population is of English, German, Yugoslavian, and Russian descent.

MOTIVATING ACTIVITY Locate Argentina on a map of South America. Ask the students to locate its major cities. Some topics for student research include General José de San Martín, the **gaucho,** the Argentine soccer teams, or the music of Argentina (the **tango** as well as the music from the Northwest mountain regions).

A 1   Una gran ciudad

Before beginning the letter, prepare several advance organizers. Be sure to point out the photographs and the geographical location of Buenos Aires on the **Río de la Plata.** Using a globe, locate the Southern and Northern Hemispheres. Explain that Argentina is located in the Southern Hemisphere; therefore, the seasons are the reverse of those in the United States. When it is summer in the United States, it is winter in Argentina and vice-versa.

Introduce the letter, explaining that it is written by an exchange student who is living in Buenos Aires. Then tell the students that they already know many of the words in the letter and that some of the new vocabulary items are cognates. Ask them to scan the letter and make a list of all the cognates they can find. Then call on volunteers to read their lists aloud, as you write them on the board. Tell the students to read the letter silently and try to guess the meanings of new words by using context clues.

Present the new vocabulary that the students were not able to decode by using pictures or by defining each word using synonyms. You may also wish to re-enter the seasons and months of the year in relation to the Southern Hemisphere. Then read the letter aloud or play the cassette as the students follow along in their books. In presenting the letter in class, try to keep a fast tempo in order to get as much student attention as possible. Insist on a normal delivery, as close as possible to that of a native speaker. Particular attention should be given to linking of words, syllable length, and intonation. You may prefer to read small portions of the letter first and then call for choral and individual repetition, alternating them to avoid boredom.

SLOWER-PACED LEARNING Read a paragraph of the letter at a time. Then ask several questions to check comprehension. After reading the entire letter, call on students to recall information about Buenos Aires.

A2   Actividad • Preguntas y respuestas

You may wish to have the students complete this activity with books closed. For writing practice, have the students write complete sentences when answering the questions. Ask them to exchange papers to correct their work.

A3 **Actividad • Veamos las diferencias**

For cooperative learning, ask the students to form groups of two or three. Each group should write down at least three statements of opinion and three factual statements that are found in Lorenzo's letter. Allow five minutes for the groups to finish compiling their lists. Then call on members of each group to read the statements aloud as you or a volunteer writes them on the board. Each member of the group should be prepared to explain why the statements express facts or opinions.

A4 **Sabes que . . .**

After reading the information about Argentina aloud or playing the cassette, you may wish to lead a discussion about the similarities between Argentina and the United States. The territory of Argentina is about three million square kilometers—an area roughly the size of the territory east of the Mississippi River in the United States. Point out that Argentina's current agricultural diversity is the result of its climate and soil as well as the contribution of its immigrants. For example, Italian immigrants contributed to the country's thriving wine industry. Russian immigrants grew the first sunflowers in 1890. You may also wish to explain the tremendous population growth of Argentina. In 1816, there were about .5 million Argentines. In 1895, there were 4 million. Between 1857 and 1939, over 3.5 million immigrants settled there.

A5 **SE DICE ASÍ**

Read the expressions in the box aloud to the students. Explain that these are some of the phrases most commonly used to report, describe, or narrate. For cooperative learning, form groups of three or four. Ask the students in each group to prepare a narration, using each of these beginning phrases. Then call on a volunteer from each group to read the narration aloud to the class.

A6 **ESTRUCTURAS ESENCIALES**

Using magazine pictures, prepare a narration of the accomplishments—real or imaginary—you have achieved or are still working to achieve. Use the present perfect tense of verbs that are most common to the students' vocabulary. Then using the **tú** form of the verb, ask the students whether or not they have accomplished the same things. Encourage the students to respond with the present perfect tense form of the verb. After they are familiar with the new tense, ask the students to generalize about its formation. Then ask the students to follow along in their books as you read aloud the information in the chart and the explanation. Pay special attention to 5, stressing that unlike English, Spanish present perfect can refer to definite past time.

A7 **Actividad • ¡Ay, qué cansados estamos!**

Have the students combine one element in each column to form eight sentences. Ask them to write the completed sentences. Then, using pictures of the places mentioned in the activity, complete the activity orally. For example, as you hold up a picture of a park, ask the student: **¿Has jugado en el parque?** The students should respond negatively or affirmatively, using the words **siempre** or **nunca: Siempre he jugado en el parque. Nunca he jugado en el parque.**

A 8 Actividad • Un día de mala suerte

Ask the students to complete the sentences with the correct form of the verb **haber.** Review the answers by writing them on the board. Remind the students that the form of **haber** may never be separated from the past participle.

A 9 Actividad • ¿Ha pasado algo?

Have each student select a partner with whom to complete the activity. As a variation, ask the students to repeat the activity and answer the questions affirmatively.

SLOWER-PACED LEARNING Ask the students to write the sentences before they complete the activity orally.

ANSWERS:
1. ¿Han pasado el día en casa?
   No, no hemos pasado el día en casa.
2. ¿Han llegado cartas de la Argentina?
   No, no han llegado cartas de la Argentina.
3. ¿Has tenido noticias de Lorenzo?
   No, no he tenido noticias de Lorenzo.
4. ¿Ha comprado helado mamá?
   No, mamá no ha comprado helado.
5. ¿Han traído el refrigerador?
   No, no han traído el refrigerador.
6. ¿Ha prestado el coche tío Enrique?
   No, tío Enrique no ha prestado el coche.

A 10 Comprensión

Trini and David are reporting to their teacher about a project they were assigned to complete. If it went well, check **¡estupendo!** on your answer sheet. If not, check **¡qué malo!** For example, you will hear: **Hemos podido terminar sólo una parte del proyecto.** Because the project was not finished, you should check **¡qué malo!** on your answer sheet.

1. Pero he encontrado muchísimos libros y artículos para el proyecto. *¡estupendo!*
2. Y luego el perro de Trini se comió todos los papeles. *¡qué malo!*
3. Entonces he escrito la información otra vez con la ayuda de David. *¡estupendo!*
4. El lunes he sacado copias de tres artículos muy buenos. *¡estupendo!*
5. ¡Trini! Nos ha llamado tres veces la señora de la biblioteca para pedirnos que devolvamos los libros. *¡qué malo!*
6. Y cuando fuimos a la biblioteca para devolverlos, de repente me dije,"¡Ay, David, has olvidado un libro en casa!" *¡qué malo!*
7. Afortunadamente hemos tenido buena suerte con la señora porque nos dio permiso para sacar los libros de nuevo. *¡estupendo!*
8. Y ayer hemos decidido trabajar toda la noche para terminar el proyecto para mañana. *¡estupendo!*
9. No hemos tenido la oportunidad de usar la computadora en toda la semana. *¡qué malo!*
10. Pero papá nos ha prometido que esta noche podemos usarla para terminar. *¡estupendo!*

Now check your answers. *Read each exchange again and give the correct answer.*

A 11   **Actividad • Y ahora, tú**

Ask the students to interview someone in class with whom they have not worked very often. You may wish to have them complete two interviews. As a variation, ask volunteers to choose secret identities and then play the roles of guests in the class. The other students must interview each "guest," using the questions as a guide.

A 12   **SITUACIÓN • En camino a la panadería** 🔲

Show the students a transparency of the illustration with the vocabulary items omitted. Point out the various locations indicated on the map and have the students repeat the names after you. Ask them about the meanings in Spanish, using the following or similar questions.

> ¿Qué compras en una librería?
> ¿Qué compras en un supermercado?
> ¿Por qué vas a la tintorería?
> ¿Por dónde cruzas un río?

Play the cassette or read the paragraph aloud to the students. You may wish to ask the following questions to check comprehension.

> ¿Qué quiere la mamá de Marisol?
> ¿Qué ocurrió mientras Marisol fue a la panadería?
> ¿Por qué está molesta su mamá?

CHALLENGE   To expand vocabulary, you may wish to ask the students questions about other kinds of stores, including a **zapatería, cafetería, sombrerería,** and **frutería.** Read each of the following tasks aloud and ask the students where they would go to carry out the task.

> comprar pan dulce
> comprar un diccionario
> pedir prestada una novela
> comprar café
> encontrarse con los amigos
> comprar una camisa nueva
> arreglar el reloj
> cruzar el puente

A 13   **Actividad • En la ciudad**

Have the students complete the paragraph with the appropriate words. After reviewing the answers with the class, you may wish to call on students to retrace Marisol's steps. Using the map, ask the students to recall each place where Marisol stopped. You may also ask questions to check comprehension.

> ¿Por qué fue a la biblioteca?
> ¿Por qué fue a la librería?
> ¿Qué quería su hermano?
> ¿Por qué fue a la tienda El Elegante?

A 14   **Actividad • ¡A escribir!**

Set a five-minute time limit for the students to write the sentences. Ask each student to exchange sentences with a partner for correction. Then select several students to read their sentences aloud.

A 15 Actividad • ¿Has vivido alguna vez en una ciudad?

Allow each student to choose a partner with whom to complete the activity. Encourage the students to answer in complete sentences and to take notes on the responses. Review the questions and answers with the class. You may wish to choose a pair of students to conduct a model interview for the entire class.

A 16 Actividad • La carta

Ask the students to write their letters in class in order for you to help them with any difficulties. Encourage them to combine sentences to lengthen their responses. Collect and correct the papers.

A 17 ESTRUCTURAS ESENCIALES

Present the forms of the stem-changing verbs in the preterit tense through conversation. You may wish to use the following or a similar conversation.

TEACHER	No dormí bien anoche. Y tú (Sergio), ¿dormiste bien?
SERGIO	Sí, dormí bien.
TEACHER	Sergio durmió bien. Y tú (Carolina), ¿dormiste bien?
CAROLINA	Sí, dormí bien.
TEACHER	Sergio y Carolina durmieron bien. ¿Quién no durmió bien?
ARTURO	Yo no dormí bien.
TEACHER	Nosotros no dormimos bien.

Ask the students to recall the verb forms as you write them on the board or a transparency. Continue with the other model verbs. When all the verbs have been presented, read aloud the chart and the explanation in the book. Point out that **-ar** and **-er** verbs have no stem changes in the preterit tense.

A 18 Actividad • Todo fue diferente

Review the stem-changing verbs in the preterit tense by allowing the students to describe events that occurred within the last two days. You may wish to review the verb endings with the class. Then ask the students to work in pairs to complete the activity orally before you ask them to write the responses.

POSSIBLE ANSWERS:
1. Pepito siempre se acuesta temprano, pero ayer se acostó tarde.
2. Marilú nunca me despierta, pero ayer me despertó.
3. Ella prefiere nadar en el mar, pero ayer prefirió nadar en la piscina.
4. Yo nunca encuentro nada en la calle, pero ayer encontré dinero.
5. Enrique se siente bien hoy, pero anoche se sintió mal.
6. Los domingos ellos almuerzan con los tíos, pero ayer almorzaron con nosotros.
7. Hoy pienso que era fácil, pero ayer pensé que era muy difícil.
8. Ada habla a menudo por teléfono, pero ayer no habló con nadie.
9. Ernesto estudia todas las tardes, pero ayer no estudió.

A 19 Actividad • Cuéntame qué pasó

Ask the students to complete the activity for homework. Review the answers with the entire class. You may wish to write the forms on the board or a transparency.

SLOWER-PACED LEARNING   Have the students write the paragraph, leaving spaces for the verbs in parentheses. Read the paragraph aloud and have the students fill in the missing verbs.

 Actividad • ¡A escribir!

As a variation, ask each student to select a city in Spain or Spanish America that he or she would like to visit. Each student should write a composition based on that city. Encourage the students to use brochures or encyclopedias to include specific information about the city. They may also include photographs or illustrations of places of interest within the city.

SECTION B

OBJECTIVES   To express feelings and emotions: express your likes and dislikes; **to persuade:** warn others to refrain from doing something

CULTURAL BACKGROUND   The gaucho is an Argentine folk figure whose existence has been romanticized in much the same way as that of the nineteenth century American cowboy. Many gauchos are mestizos, descendants of the Indians and the Spanish. Although few in number, they still live and work on the ranches that dot the pampas. Much of their folklore and tradition has been lost, but their spirit and lifestyle remain. The gaucho wears a poncho, **bombachas** (knee-length pants that resemble long bloomers), knee-high boots, and a flat-brimmed hat. He carries a large knife called a **facón,** which is often worn in the back of a silver-studded belt called a **rastra.** Some of the traditional gaucho songs and poems are widely sung or recited in Argentina, and its literature contains a great deal of folklore concerning the gaucho, such as José Hernández's epic poem, *"Martín Fierro,"* and Ricardo Güiraldes's novel, *Don Segundo Sombra.*

MOTIVATING ACTIVITY   Have the students compare the gaucho with the American cowboy. Ask them to compare their ways of life today and their ways of life in the past. How has technology changed their lives?

B1   **¡Qué bonito es el campo!**

Locate the province of La Pampa on a map of Argentina. In Spanish, explain that La Pampa is an agricultural region and that the word **pampas** means *plains* in Quechua, one of the Indian languages. You may wish to allow the students to work in groups of two or three to prepare a list of ten items they might find in the country and a list of what they will not find, such as **un metro, un cine, un supermercado moderno.** Call on members of each group to name items from the lists and write them on the board.

Follow the same procedure as described in A1 on page T194. Then introduce the new vocabulary by using magazine pictures of the animals and insects mentioned in the letter, such as fly, bee, mouse, bull, rooster, horse, and mosquito. Point out that **quince días** is the equivalent of *two weeks* in English. Play the cassette or read the letter aloud as the students follow along in their books. When finished, ask them to add items mentioned in the letter to the lists on the board.

Unidad 10   Teacher's Notes   T199

B2 Actividad • Preguntas y respuestas

You may wish to have the students complete this activity orally with books closed. For writing practice, ask them to write the answers. Review the answers with the class.

ANSWERS:
1. Raquel fue a visitar a sus abuelos.
2. Fue con sus padres y su amiga Paula.
3. La estancia queda en La Pampa.
4. Paula le escribe a su amigo Juan Manuel.
5. Piensa que el campo tiene muchas cosas buenas y le encanta estar allí.
6. Los abuelos de Raquel le dicen a Paula que no deje la puerta del gallinero abierta, que no se bañe en el lago y que no coma tantos duraznos.
7. Han comido legumbres y carnes frescas.
8. Paula no le tiene miedo a los ratones, las moscas, las abejas y los mosquitos.

B3 Actividad • ¡A escoger!

Have the students complete the activity without referring to Lorenzo's letter. If they have difficulty, return to the letter and review the information with the class to check comprehension.

B4 Actividad • Los animales y los insectos del campo

Allow ten minutes for the students to walk around the room and ask several classmates the questions. Each student should ask at least three questions to three different classmates. Then call on volunteers to give the answers they received. You may wish to ask them to use the following model:

> María dijo que le gustan todos los animales.
> Toni dijo que hay muchos mosquitos en el verano.
> Sergio dijo que prefiere vivir en la ciudad porque hay muchas cosas que puede hacer.

B5 Actividad • Cuentos de animales

Have each student choose a partner with whom to share his or her story. For writing practice, you may ask each student to write the story at home after he or she tells it. If so, collect and correct the stories. You may also want to make a book with illustrations and a table of contents of all the corrected stories. Brainstorm with the students for ideas for the title of the book, and then place the book in the classroom library for the students to read.

B6 SE DICE ASÍ

Using magazine pictures of items you like and dislike, present the expressions in the book. For example, hold up a picture of a pizza and exclaim: **¡Cómo me gusta!** Hold up a picture of a polluted city and say: **¡Qué asco!** Be sure to use the appropriate facial expressions and gestures to accompany each expression. Then hold up the same or other pictures and ask the students to respond, expressing their likes and dislikes.

B 7 Actividad • ¿Cuál es tu reacción?

Have each student take turns reading the statements to his or her partner. Each student must respond accordingly.

CHALLENGE Ask the students to make up three new situations. They should choose new partners and respond to each other's statements.

B 8 ESTRUCTURAS ESENCIALES

To introduce the negative familiar commands, tell the students that you are going to give them some advice. Read the following or similar commands aloud and ask the students to listen carefully to the verb forms in order to make generalizations about them.

> No duermas en la clase.
> No comas tanto azúcar.
> No uses drogas.
> No bebas demasiado café.
> No vengas tarde a la escuela.

Ask the students to make generalizations about what they have heard. Then have them read the information in the book to verify their observations. To practice the new forms, ask the students to offer advice to their classmates. You may wish to write several of their suggestions on the board or a transparency.

B 9 Actividad • ¿Qué hago?

Instruct each student to chose a partner. One partner will ask the questions, and the other partner will respond with a negative command. You may wish to have each student ask five questions and then switch roles.

B 10 Actividad • En la hacienda

CHALLENGE Choose several pairs of students to role-play a dialog in which the host or hostess must explain to the guests the reasons for not allowing them to do the requested items. They may add any additional questions.

> ¿Puedo dormir aquí? No duermas aquí, mejor duerme allá.
> Aquí hay muchos mosquitos.

B 11 Actividad • ¿Qué les digo?

Have the students respond to each problem by offering good advice. They should use the negative familiar command form of the verb in their responses.

B 12 Actividad • Por favor, no cambies de opinión

SLOWER-PACED LEARNING Allow the students to write their answers first. Instruct them to select a partner. When they are finished, review orally. You may wish to give the students other examples of commands to which they will respond with the negative form.

> Cómpramelo.
> Mándaselos.
> Escríbenoslas.
> Búscamela.
> Cántanoslas.
> Recógeselo.

B 13   Actividad • ¡A escribir!

Allow the students to make their lists and to share the information with the class.

CHALLENGE   To expand the activity, ask each student to think of advice that he or she would give to a good friend. Have each student write six affirmative sentences and six negative ones. Write the following or similar examples on the board for the students to use as a model.

> Di la verdad.
> No repitas chismes.
> Di cosas buenas de tus amigos.
> No pidas dinero prestado.

B 14   Comprensión

You will hear a statement followed by a command. If the command is a logical response to the statement, check **lógico** on your answer sheet. If not, check **absurdo.** For example, you will hear: **Hace mucho calor.** You will also hear the response: **No abras las ventanas.** You should mark the box labeled **absurdo** because the response was not logical.

1. Ese caballo es muy malo.
   Pues no lo montes.   *lógico*
2. La leche está mala.
   Pues, no la bebas.   *lógico*
3. Los duraznos son buenos para la salud.
   No los comas.   *absurdo*
4. Voy a sacarte una foto.
   Sonríe.   *lógico*
5. Estoy muy cansada.
   Pues no te duermas.   *absurdo*
6. Tenemos clase a las siete y media de la mañana.
   No te levantes temprano.   *absurdo*
7. Están entrando mosquitos.
   No abras la puerta.   *lógico*
8. Quiero hablar con Esperanza.
   No la llames.   *absurdo*
9. Me gustaría ver a mi tío.
   No lo visites.   *absurdo*
10. Enrique no ha llegado todavía.
    Pues no lo esperes.   *lógico*

Now check your answers. *Read each exchange again and give the correct answer.*

B 15   SITUACIÓN • La granja

Use magazine pictures or a transparency made from the illustration in the book to present the farm vocabulary. Ask the students to talk about the contents of the illustration, using the vocabulary. You may also wish to re-enter the names of pets and other animals that they learned in Unit 2, B8, pages 66–67. Then ask the following or similar comprehension questions.

¿En qué estación aramos la tierra?
¿Qué nos da la vaca?
¿Qué animal come maíz?
¿De qué hacemos el pan?

CHALLENGE   After presenting the new vocabulary, you may wish to expand by completing an enriching activity. Explain to the class that you have received a call from a local farm. The farmers are very worried because nobody seems to be buying the meat and dairy products that the animals produce. Ask the students, as "expert biologists," to invent a new, more interesting animal. Have the students work in groups of three or four. Each group must describe this animal, its habitat, food, habits, and other special features. Write the following or similar questions on the board. You may also wish to have the students draw the animals.

¿Cómo es?
¿Cómo se parece a otros animales?
¿Qué come?
¿Dónde vive?
¿Es grande o pequeño?
¿Cuáles son sus hábitos?
¿Qué produce?

B 16   **Actividad • ¡A completar!**

Ask the students to complete the sentences with the appropriate words. Review the answers with the entire class.

The students may be interested in learning the sounds these animals make in Spanish. Write the following list of animals and their sounds on the board and present them to the class.

la oveja:	beee, beee
la vaca:	muuu, muuu
el gallo:	quiquiriquí
la gallina:	clo, clo
el pollito:	pío, pío
el gato:	miau
el pato:	cuac, cuac
el perro:	guau, guau

B 17   **Sabes que . . .**

In Mexico, a **charro** is an expert horseman. The typical and traditional clothes of a **charro** consist of a large wide-brimmed hat, tight pants, short jacket, a bow, and a whip. The **charros** are well-known in Mexico for maintaining the tradition of the **charrería** by holding elaborate shows and rodeos to exhibit their talents. They are usually well-off and demonstrate this by wearing their clothes adorned with silver and gold. Their saddles also are often made of the finest leather and silver. All **charros** belong to the **Asociación Nacional de Charros.**

B 18   **ESTRUCTURAS ESENCIALES**

Present the irregular past participles by using them in sentences. Explain that these irregular forms must be memorized and are very important because they are very useful verbs that the students will need to use often. Remind the students to use the helping verb **haber** when using the present perfect tense.

B 19 Actividad • ¿Qué ha hecho Rogelio?

Ask the students to work in pairs to complete the activity. One student should ask the question and the other should respond negatively. Then have the students switch partners and tasks.

CHALLENGE Have the students make up their own cues based on the model. Then they should ask other classmates the questions and elicit their responses.

| ir a la China | ¿Has ido a la China?
No, nunca he ido a la China.

B 20 Actividad • En la estancia del abuelo

SLOWER-PACED LEARNING Write the conversation on the board or a transparency, including the spaces for the past participles. Then fill in the blanks as the students dictate the correct forms of the verbs.

B 21 Actividad • Conversaciones sobre animales

Have the students complete the conversation in pairs. As a follow-up activity, ask them to prepare a few lines about the animal they would like to be. **Si tú fueras animal, ¿qué serías? ¿Por qué?**

B 22 Actividad • ¡A escribir!

Have each student complete the composition at home. Collect and correct the papers.

SECTION C

OBJECTIVES **To express attitudes and opinions:** express obligation or necessity; **to express feelings and emotions:** express doubt, disbelief, or denial

CULTURAL BACKGROUND The city of Buenos Aires is divided into various sections. Each section is known for something special. San Telmo, for example, is the site of a flea market held every Sunday. A visit reveals many of the treasures of the past, items typical of the Argentina of the past century. A section of the city called La Boca is perhaps the most colorful. Located near the port, it is the area in which many Italian immigrants settled. It derives its name from its location at the mouth of the Riachuelo *(Little river)*, a short course of water that flows into the Río de la Plata. Recently, La Boca has been in the news because of its soccer team, the Boca Juniors, home team of Diego Maradona. Maradona is considered to be the best soccer player in the world. Another area, Recoleta, is known for its boutiques, high-rise apartments, and sidewalk cafés. It is also the home of the **Cementerio del Norte,** burial place of many of Argentina's wealthiest families. Eva Perón is buried in this cemetery. The areas of Palermo and Belgrano are northern suburbs and are mostly residential in nature. Each area is different and is accessible by bus or by the subway system, the **subte,** which is short for **subterráneo,** meaning *underground.*

MOTIVATING ACTIVITY Write the word **contaminación** on the board. Discuss some of the problems or causes of pollution with the students. You may wish to ask them to think of ways to correct the problem. An example of a recent campaign against pollution in Mexico City states: **Camine, no contamine.** Write this on the board and use it as a model for the students to use in their discussion. You may also wish to add some of the following examples.

> Tome el autobús en vez de manejar el coche.
> Use menos gasolina.
> Use menos electricidad.
> Use menos productos plásticos.

C1   Nuestro planeta

Begin your presentation of the selection with a discussion of the major problems a city faces every day. Read the selection aloud or play the cassette. You may wish to divide it into sections to facilitate comprehension. Then call for choral and individual repetition, alternating them to avoid boredom. Ask questions to check comprehension after each section.

You may also wish to prepare questions or facts that the students must answer or find as they read.

> ¿Cuándo comenzó la revolución industrial?
> ¿Qué problema se ha presentado en las ciudades después
>   de la revolución industrial?
> Encuentra dos maneras en que la gente puede ayudar a salvar
>   nuestras ciudades de la contaminación.

Then relate the information found in the selection to the real-life situation in the students' hometowns. Ask the students to make a list of five problems in their city. For cooperative learning, they may work in groups of two or three. After eight minutes, ask each group to share its ideas with the class. You may wish to ask a volunteer to write the items on the board to stimulate further discussion. Finish by asking the students to brainstorm ideas that will correct the problems they have mentioned.

C2   Actividad • Preguntas y respuestas

Allow each student to work with a partner to complete the activity. Review the answers with the class in discussion format.

C3   Actividad • ¡Qué confusión!

Designate a time limit of ten minutes for the students to complete the activity. Then ask volunteers to write the sentences on the board.

C4   Actividad • Charla

Assign the questions to the students for homework. Review with the class after each student has had the opportunity to share the information with a partner. For writing practice, you may wish to ask the students to write short essays based on the answers to the questions.

C5   Sabes que . . .

You may wish to add information about the Coto de Doñana in Huelva, Andalucía, Spain. The Coto is home to many kinds of flora and fauna, particularly migratory birds that spend the summer in northern Europe and stop over in Coto on their way to Africa, where they spend the winter. You may also wish to discuss the various groups that support the protection of the environment in the United States, such as the Audubon Society, the Sierra Club, and Greenpeace.

C6 SE DICE ASÍ

Present the expression **hay que . . .** to the students. Read the sentences in the chart aloud. Then allow the students to make statements about the environment and solutions to the problems, using **hay que** . . . .

C7 Actividad • ¿Qué hay que hacer?

Ask the students to complete the activity in pairs. Then call on pairs to read their solutions aloud.

CHALLENGE After completing the activity, ask the students to write a list of five original problems. Each student should exchange papers with a partner and find a solution to each other's problems.

C8 ESTRUCTURAS ESENCIALES

Before presenting the subjunctive to express doubt, disbelief, or denial, you may wish to quickly re-enter the present subjunctive verb forms. Then read aloud several of the following or similar sentences that refer to real-life situations using the students real names.

> Dudo que Juan juegue al básquetbol.
> No es cierto que sirvan filete mignon en la cafetería.
> No creo que Elisa gane la lotería.

Encourage the students to make similar statements. You may initiate the response by making a factual statement and asking the students to give their opinions, expressing doubt.

> TEACHER Anita tiene una vaca.
> STUDENT Dudo que Anita tenga una vaca.

After several models have been given, write a few examples on the board. Ask the students to generalize about the structures, the content, and the meaning. Then introduce the students to the material in the text. Indicate that when expressing doubt and using the subjunctive, the subjects of both clauses can be the same or different. Give examples of both cases.

> Dudo que pueda dar la clase mañana.
> Dudo que Anita pueda venir a clase mañana.

Remind them that when no doubt, disbelief, or denial is expressed, the indicative mood is used. Review the sentences in the text that are examples of the indicative mood. Ask the students to change them to state disbelief, denial, or doubt.

> Yo sé que Marcela está en la estancia.
> No creo que Marcela esté en la estancia.

C9 Actividad • El tío de Victoria

SLOWER-PACED LEARNING You may wish to ask the students to write the responses at home or in class. Review the sentences by having volunteers write the sentences on the board for correction.

C10 Actividad • Juanita Calamidad

Allow ten minutes for each student to work with a partner and to prepare a dialog based on one of the situations mentioned. Instruct the students to write at least six lines in which they must try to instill confidence in their partners or attempt to persuade them.

STUDENT 1   Creo que puedes ganar el premio.
STUDENT 2   No es cierto. No creo que pueda ganar.
STUDENT 1   Pero tú juegas muy bien.
STUDENT 2   Creo que Sandra juega mejor que yo.
STUDENT 1   Dudo que Sandra pueda ganar. Eres la mejor.
STUDENT 2   Sí, tienes razón. ¡Soy la campeona!

Choose several pairs to present their dialogs to the class.

ANSWERS:
1. No creo que pueda ganar el premio.
    No seas tonto. Yo creo que lo puedes ganar.
2. No creo que Ramona pueda ir mañana al concierto.
    No seas tonta. Yo creo que ella puede ir al concierto.
3. No creo que papá me dé permiso para ir al cine.
    No seas tonto. Yo creo que él te da permiso.
4. No creo que sepa la lección de español.
    No seas tonto. Yo creo que la sabes.
5. No creo que Andrés venga a cenar con nosotros.
    No seas tonta. Yo creo que viene.
6. No creo que ella me invite a ir al teatro.
    No seas tonto. Yo creo que te invita.
7. No creo que Rigoberto recuerde las respuestas.
    No seas tonta. Yo creo que las recuerda.
8. No creo que Marisa esté lista para la fiesta.
    No seas tonta. Yo creo que está lista.
9. No creo que nosotras podamos salvar las ciudades.
    No seas tonta. Yo creo que las salvamos.
10. No creo que Juan Manuel le escriba a ella.
    No seas tonto. Yo creo que le escribe.

C11   Comprensión

You will hear two political candidates discuss important issues concerning conservation. If they are in favor of protecting the environment, check **de acuerdo** on your answer sheet. If they don't believe there is a problem, check **se opone**. For example, you will hear: **Dudo que tengamos que ahorrar energía eléctrica.** You should place a mark in the box marked **se opone** because the candidate does not believe there is a problem.

1. Creo que debemos buscar otras formas de energía para el futuro.   *de acuerdo*
2. Pienso que el aire de las ciudades está contaminado.   *de acuerdo*
3. No tenemos que preocuparnos por ahorrar petróleo.   *se opone*
4. No es cierto que haya demasiado tráfico en las ciudades.   *se opone*
5. Creo que es la responsabilidad de todos proteger el medio ambiente.   *de acuerdo*
6. Dudo que podamos hacer algo para limpiar el aire de las ciudades.   *se opone*
7. No pienso que el problema sea tan grave.   *se opone*
8. Creo que pueden evitarse muchos problemas si caminamos en vez de usar los coches.   *de acuerdo*
9. Dudo que las ciudades sean demasiado grandes.   *se opone*

10. Creo que el gobierno debe controlar más el uso de productos químicos en el agua.   *de acuerdo*

Now check your answers. *Read each statement again and give the correct answer.*

C 12   SITUACIÓN • ¿El campo en peligro o el mundo en peligro?

Ask the students to follow along in their books as you play the cassette or read aloud the statements about our environment. After you have checked comprehension, instruct the students to work in groups to rank each of the eight problems mentioned in the selection from the most serious to the least serious. Discuss the ratings with the class and the reasons for them. Remember, there are no right or wrong answers; but encourage each group to defend its opinions as much as possible.

C 13   Actividad • Preguntas y respuestas

You may wish to write the questions on the board or a transparency and ask the students to complete the activity with books closed. Have them answer the questions in complete sentences. Review the answers quickly.

C 14   ESTRUCTURAS ESENCIALES

Review the expressions with **se** with the students. Then read the explanation and examples aloud as the students follow along in their books. To practice the new structure, ask the students to make three original signs to post in the classroom. Encourage them to make the signs relay a positive message. Use the following or similar models.

> ¡Aquí se habla español!
> Se solicitan sonrisas.

C 15   Actividad • Mi amigo el artista

SLOWER-PACED LEARNING   You may want to do the activity orally with the students. Give them several additional situations to complete for extra practice.

> Nosotros solicitamos una secretaria bilingüe.
> La compañía fabrica televisores aquí.
> El periódico necesita periodista.

C 16   Actividad • Dime cómo se hace

Have the students select one or two items and complete the instructions. You may wish to ask them to prepare a demonstration and instruct class members on how to make something. Tell them to give the instructions orally, using the **se** construction, in a minimum of ten sentences. The following topics may also be suggested.

> Cómo se hace un taco.
> Cómo se escribe una carta.
> Cómo se preparan las palomitas de maíz.
> Cómo se hace la leche con chocolate.

You may wish to videotape the presentations.

C 17 **Actividad • ¡A escoger!**

Ask the students to complete the activity for homework. Arrange the signs on a bulletin board or use them in classified ads in a newspaper that you might produce as a class project. Use articles about conservation from a newspaper, and include students' opinions.

Tell the students to use the information found in the realia as a model to write their advertisements. You may also wish to refer to the procedure dealing with realia described in Unit 9, B22, page T182–183. Most of the terms and expressions in the realia are either cognates or have already been introduced. New vocabulary:

Primera planta	*Ground floor*	base	*foundation*
semisótano	*half basement*	terreno	*lot*
frente	*front*		

C 18 **Actividad • ¿Cómo se escribe?**

Allow several minutes for the students to organize the instructions in logical order. Review by writing them on the board or a transparency.

C 19 **Actividad • ¡A escribir!**

You may wish to ask the students to complete the activity in essay form. For additional topics, you might add the following items.

diez maneras de mejorar la vida en la ciudad
diez maneras de mejorar el ambiente
diez maneras de conservar la energía

TRY YOUR SKILLS

OBJECTIVE   To recombine communicative functions, grammar, and vocabulary

CULTURAL BACKGROUND   In recent years, Spanish America has become aware and concerned not only about pollution, but also about preserving the environment. In many countries, including Costa Rica, Ecuador, Chile, and Argentina, extensive areas have been dedicated as national parks to preserve the habitat of endangered species, as well as plants and trees. At last, Brazil became aware of the potential world catastrophe that threatens if the destruction of the Amazon jungle continues. As a result, its president has initiated legislation to preserve the zone. However, the influx of population to the cities creates serious problems, not only of providing homes for many people, but increased air pollution, garbage collection and disposal, and growth of industrial waste.

1

¿Qué ha pasado?

You may wish to complete the first caption with the students, which they can follow as a model. Then have the students complete the activity in pairs. Review the answers with the class.

CHALLENGE   To expand the activity, bring magazine pictures to the class. Ask the students to make up their own captions, using the present perfect tense.

2 **Actividad • No recuerdo bien**

Ask the students to complete the activity orally or in writing. Have each student exchange papers with a partner and correct each other's sentences.

3   Actividad • La competencia

After the students have written their ideas for five projects, you may wish to begin a class discussion to decide the ten most important projects for their city or town. Write the topics on the board and have the students place the projects in order of importance.

4   Actividad • No digas quién te lo dijo

Allow the students time to complete the activity as stated. Then encourage them to pass on information they have heard in school. Start the process with the following or similar statements.

> Se dice que no va a haber vacaciones este año.
> La gente dice que la otra secundaria es mejor que ésta.

5   Actividad • Protegiendo el planeta

For cooperative learning, form groups of three or four students. Have the students take turns asking and answering the questions. When the groups have finished, ask the students to summarize what they have learned from each other.

6   Actividad • Mi pueblo

Have the students draw the map as homework. Then ask the following or similar questions to a few students about their maps.

> Si estoy en la librería y necesito ir a la biblioteca, ¿cómo iría?
> ¿Cómo voy de la panadería a la tintorería?
> ¿Puedes decirme cómo ir al supermercado? Estoy en el centro comercial.

7   Actividad • ¿Estás de acuerdo o no?

Ask the students to work in pairs to complete the activity. Then call on volunteers to express their points of view.

8   Dictado

Write the following paragraph from dictation. First, listen to the paragraph as it is read to you. Then you will hear the paragraph again in short segments, with a pause after each segment to allow you time to write. Finally, you will hear the paragraph a third time so that you may check your work. Let's begin.

> Hay gente que no cree *(pause)* que el problema de nuestro planeta *(pause)* sea un problema grave. *(pause)* Sin embargo, *(pause)* muchos científicos están muy preocupados *(pause)* con la contaminación del aire, *(pause)* del agua y de los bosques. *(pause)* Se ha logrado la solución *(pause)* de muchos problemas. *(pause)* Ahora todos tenemos que resolver *(pause)* el problema de la contaminación.

PRONUNCIACIÓN

Review the sound of the letter **x** with the students. Ask them to repeat each word after you. You may wish to add that most words that start with **x** are of Indian origin. In these words the **x** is usually pronounced like the Spanish **s**; for example: **Xochimilco**.

Continue with the linking exercise and the pronunciation practice. Have the students listen carefully as you read the sentences aloud or play the cassette.

¿LO SABES?

Review quickly the present perfect tense with the students. Then ask them to complete the first part of the section. Review by asking each student to share his or her comments with a partner. Summarize by asking the students to share their ideas with the class. You may wish to write several of the comments on the board. Complete the next exercise, allowing the students to form five questions. Allow time for them to complete the answer process. Finally, ask the students to work in pairs to complete a short dialog in which the items mentioned are included. Choose several pairs of students to present their mini-dialogs to the class.

To practice expressing likes and dislikes, ask each student to work with a classmate and exchange commands. Then assign the poster for homework. Ask the class to choose the posters they like most for placement around the school.

Ask the students to complete the first part of the section, writing five instructions. Review by asking them to write their sentences on the board. Continue with the section by beginning a short conversation on ways to save the world from pollution. Next ask the students to become fashion commentators to explain what is in or out of style this season. Give them model sentences. Finally, to practice expressing doubt or disbelief, instruct the students to make five predictions.

VOCABULARIO

To practice the vocabulary, you may wish to play the game **Mi secreto.** Ask each student to select a vocabulary item from the unit list. Have each student write the title **Mi secreto** on a piece of cardboard or stiff paper (8 × 10), followed by at least five clues that describe the item. Call on a student to show the card and read his or her clues to the class. The class should take turns guessing what it is. The student who correctly identifies the item then has the opportunity to show his or her card and read the clues.

PRÁCTICA DEL VOCABULARIO

As a variation, you may ask the students to make lists of vocabulary items in semantic groupings. Each student should make one list of words for animals, one for cities, and one for words dealing with the environment.

VAMOS A LEER

OBJECTIVE   To read for practice and pleasure

Antes de leer

Before presenting the reading selection, prepare an outline of the most important ideas in the selection, and the conclusions that can be derived from them, in order to help the students with the activity. Also prepare some questions that elicit major points of the selection.

Have the students write their lists of words and the topic of the paragraph. They should keep them in their notebooks to save until after they have finished reading the selection.

Preparación para la lectura

Ask the students to answer the questions orally. As a variation, they may also complete the activity in pairs.

LAS CULTURAS HISPANOAMERICANAS

Read the introductory paragraph aloud or play the cassette as the students follow along in their books. You may wish to ask a few questions before continuing to the other sections of the reading selection. Work through the reading material in small sections. Introduce the sections by discussing musical instruments common to Spanish America, singers, or other topics of information found in the selection. Allow the students to read the material silently. If you have Spanish folk music available, play excerpts of a few songs in order for the students to hear the different types of music. The popular song by Simon and Garfunkel, "El cóndor pasa," based on an Inca folk melody, is a very good example to play for the students. You may wish to assign reports to students who would like to earn extra credit.

Actividad • ¿Cuántas palabras sabes?

Ask the students to return to their lists of words in their notebooks from the **Antes de leer** activity and to identify the meanings of the unfamiliar words. Encourage them to define the words by using context clues or identifying the word as a cognate.

Actividad • Preguntas y respuestas

Have the students work in pairs to answer the questions. Then review the answers with the class.

Actividad • ¿A qué se refiere?

CHALLENGE You may wish to have the students write original descriptions of items described in the reading selection. Each student may exchange papers with a classmate to identify the items being described.

Actividad • Charla

This is an optional activity. The students may enjoy collecting music from Spain and Spanish America. They can bring the cassettes or records to class to show how music varies from country to country.

UNIDAD 10

La ciudad y el campo

In Spanish-speaking countries, life in the city varies greatly from life in the country. Although the city offers all the modern conveniences, it is often overpopulated, causing overcrowding, pollution, and traffic congestion. Country life offers tranquillity and a more relaxed atmosphere, but perhaps a more rugged life style. Which do you prefer?

In this unit you will:

SECTION A	report, describe, and narrate . . . describe things you have done in the past
SECTION B	express your likes and dislikes . . . warn others to refrain from doing something
SECTION C	express obligation or necessity . . . express doubt, disbelief, or denial
TRY YOUR SKILLS	use what you've learned
VAMOS A LEER	read for practice and pleasure

SECTION A

reporting, describing, and narrating . . . describing things you have done in the past

Argentina is the second-largest country in South America, and Buenos Aires is its largest city and capital. Argentina is an urban country with almost eighty percent of its population living in cities or towns. One out of every three Argentines lives in Buenos Aires!

For additional background on Buenos Aires, see p. T194.

A1

Una gran ciudad

Querida Marisa,

Te escribo desde la Argentina. He estado en Buenos Aires por seis meses y me ha fascinado la ciudad. Me siento ya un poco Argentino. Sé que no has estado aquí, pero quiero que vengas y te voy a decir por qué.

La capital de la Argentina, Buenos Aires, es una gran ciudad con muchos rascacielos. Tiene casi tantos habitantes como Nueva York, pero es más extensa. Está en el hemisferio sur. Eso quiere decir que cuando en los Estados Unidos es invierno, en la Argentina es verano. Así que te aconsejo que traigas tu traje de baño si piensas venir en diciembre.

Te mando unas fotos. Quiero que veas qué linda es la ciudad. Y, ¿qué he encontrado aquí tan especial? Pues, una gran variedad. Los habitantes de Buenos Aires se llaman porteños. Muchos de los porteños son descendientes de inmigrantes europeos y muchos de ellos llegaron de Italia a partir de 1880.

En Buenos Aires hay muchas actividades culturales y más de 120,000 estudiantes universitarios. Estoy seguro de que te gustaría pasear por la avenida más ancha del mundo, que se llama Nueve de Julio, o ir de compras por la calle Florida.

El fútbol es una pasión nacional aquí. Los argentinos también juegan mucho al tenis y al polo. Y como sabes, Buenos Aires es la cuna del tango. Tienes que pedirles a tus padres que te traigan de vacaciones. Sé que todos se van a divertir. Además, tengo muchas ganas de verte.

Muchos saludos,

Lorenzo

A2 Actividad • Preguntas y respuestas 📼

Answer the following questions according to Lorenzo's letter to Marisa.

1. ¿Desde dónde escribe Lorenzo?
2. ¿Cuál es la capital de la Argentina?
3. ¿Cuánto tiempo ha estado Lorenzo en Buenos Aires?
4. ¿Por qué debe traer Marisa su traje de baño en diciembre?
5. ¿Cuándo es invierno en la Argentina? ¿Por qué?
6. ¿Qué aprendiste de la avenida Nueve de Julio?
7. ¿Cuál es el deporte favorito?
8. ¿Por qué debe ir Marisa a Buenos Aires, según Lorenzo?

1. Lorenzo escribe desde la Argentina.
2. La capital de la Argentina es Buenos Aires. 3. Lorenzo ha estado en Buenos Aires por seis meses. 4. Porque es verano en la Argentina. 5. El invierno en la Argentina es cuando en los Estados Unidos es verano. Porque la Argentina está en el hemisferio sur. 6. Que la avenida nueve de julio es la avenida más ancha del mundo. 7. El deporte favorito es el fútbol. 8. Marisa debe ir a Buenos Aires porque se va a divertir y porque Lorenzo tiene muchas ganas de verla.

A3 Actividad • Veamos las diferencias

Answers will vary.

From Lorenzo's letter in A1, list three statements of fact and three statements of opinion.

No fue hasta 1860 que el presidente de la Argentina, Santiago Derqui, decretó *(decreed)* que el gobierno usaría el nombre de República Argentina para todos los documentos y actos oficiales. Hasta esa fecha la Argentina había tenido varios nombres, entre ellos el de Virreinato del Río de la Plata, durante su época colonial.

Durante el período colonial, la población creció *(population grew)* muy lentamente, y estaba formada en su mayoría por indios y españoles. A partir de 1816, cuando la dominación española terminó, comenzó a aumentar la población. La Argentina y los Estados Unidos tienen un desarrollo parecido con respecto a la formación de su población, ya que ambos son países de inmigrantes. La Argentina multiplicó su población diez veces en un siglo *(century)*. Aproximadamente el 35 por ciento de todos los argentinos es de descendencia italiana, y el 28 por ciento de descendencia española. El resto de la población está formado por inmigrantes de otros países.

Reporting, describing, and narrating

The present perfect is often used in Spanish to describe and narrate past events, especially if more than one person is included.

He visto . . .	I have seen . . .
Hemos visitado varios . . .	We have visited many . . .
Me siento muy contento de . . .	I feel very happy . . .
Quiero que veas . . .	I want you to see . . .
Hay pocas actividades . . .	There are few activities . . .
Estoy seguro de que . . .	I am sure that . . .

A6 ESTRUCTURAS ESENCIALES
The present perfect tense

Indicate that the simple present tense can also be used in this context: "Ha trabajado allí desde hace mucho tiempo." "Trabaja allí desde hace mucho tiempo." The present perfect also describes completed events in the past that have been ongoing up to the present: "Hemos comido en ese restaurante muchas veces durante este mes." Time expressions that help extend the action into the present are often used: "esta semana, este año, en los últimos meses, en estos días," and so forth.

The present perfect is a compound tense. It is made up of a helping verb and a main verb. It is formed by using the present tense form of the verb **haber** *(to have)* as a helping verb, followed by the past participle of the main verb.

Regular Past Participle Endings		
-ar verbs	habl	**-ado**
-er verbs	corr	**-ido**
-ir verbs	viv	**-ido**

1. The past participle of all regular **-ar** verbs ends in **-ado: hablado.**
2. The past participle of all regular **-er** and **-ir** verbs ends in **-ido: corrido, vivido.**

Present Perfect	
he hablado	**hemos** hablado
has corrido	**habéis** corrido
ha vivido	**han** vivido

3. Notice that the helping verb **haber** *(to have)* changes form to agree with the subject, but the past participle of the main verb always remains the same.

Ella **ha decidido** ir a Buenos Aires.	*She has decided to go to Buenos Aires.*
Ellos **han vivido** en Buenos Aires.	*They have lived in Buenos Aires.*

4. In Spanish, the past participle of the main verb cannot be separated from the helping verb.

Siempre he vivido en Buenos Aires.	
He vivido **siempre** en Buenos Aires.	*I have always lived in Buenos Aires.*

5. The uses of the Spanish present perfect are very similar to those of the English present perfect, except that in Spanish the present perfect can refer to a specific point in the past.

Ayer **he hablado** con Lolita.	*Yesterday I talked to Lolita.*
Ella **ha trabajado** en la escuela.	*She has worked at the school.*
Roberto no **ha llamado** todavía.	*Roberto has not called yet.*
Luisa y Toni **han ido** al cine varias veces.	*Luisa and Toni have gone to the movies several times.*

A7 Actividad • ¡Ay, qué cansados estamos! Answers will vary.

Everybody has had a busy day. See what each person has done by combining elements from each column. Let's see how many logical sentences you can form.

Luis		trabajado	en el partido
Teresita	he	jugado	en el teatro
yo	has	ayudado	en el jardín
nosotros	ha	caminado	en la cocina
Paco y Luz	hemos	bailado	en el parque
tú	han	gritado	en la ciudad
ustedes		paseado	en la oficina

A8 Actividad • Un día de mala suerte

Today was a bad day. Complete the sentences with the correct form of **haber.**

1. Clara _____ perdido su libro. ha
2. Yo _____ quemado el pan. he
3. Nadie _____ llamado por teléfono. ha
4. Los niños _____ llorado todo el día. han
5. Héctor _____ chocado la moto. ha
6. Hoy no _____ ocurrido nada. ha

A9 Actividad • ¿Ha pasado algo?

For answers, see p. T196.
Suppose you are back from school and want to
know what went on at home during the day.
Get together with a classmate and follow
the model. Take turns.

> MODELO Tomás / llamar
> — ¿Ha llamado Tomás?
> — No, no ha llamado.

1. Uds. / pasar el día en casa
2. cartas / llegar de la Argentina
3. Tú / tener noticias de Lorenzo
4. Mamá / comprar helado
5. (ellos) / traer el refrigerador
6. tío Enrique / prestar el coche

A10 Comprensión For script, see p. T196.

Trini and David are reporting to their teacher about a project they were assigned to
complete. If it went well, check **¡estupendo!** on your answer sheet. If not, check
¡qué malo!

> MODELO Hemos podido terminar sólo una parte del proyecto.

	0	1	2	3	4	5	6	7	8	9	10
¡Estupendo!		✔		✔	✔			✔	✔		✔
¡Qué malo!	✔		✔			✔	✔		✔		

A11 Actividad • Y ahora, tú Answers will vary.

Answer the following questions about yourself.

1. ¿Vives en la ciudad o en el campo?
2. ¿Has vivido alguna vez en otra ciudad? ¿Cuál?
3. ¿Has visitado otro estado? ¿Cuál? ¿Por cuánto tiempo?
4. ¿Has visitado algún otro país? ¿Cuál? ¿Cuándo?
5. De todos los lugares que has visitado, ¿cuál te ha gustado más? ¿Por qué?

SITUACIÓN • En camino a la panadería

La mamá de Marisol quiere que ella vaya a comprar el pan para el desayuno, pero en el camino, Marisol pasa por muchos lugares y hace muchas cosas. Cuando regresa, ya todos han desayunado . . . ¡sin pan! Y su mamá está muy enojada.

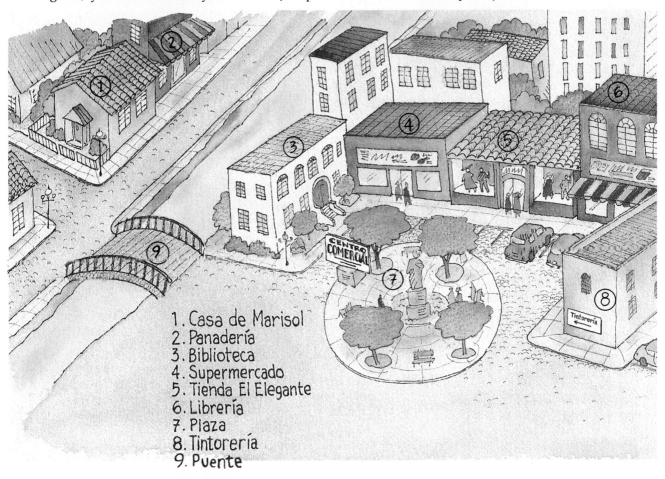

1. Casa de Marisol
2. Panadería
3. Biblioteca
4. Supermercado
5. Tienda El Elegante
6. Librería
7. Plaza
8. Tintorería
9. Puente

A 13 Actividad • En la ciudad

Complete the following paragraph and you'll find out why Marisol was late.

La mamá de Marisol quiere que ella vaya a la _____ de la esquina a comprar pan fresco para el desayuno. Marisol prefiere ir al _____ del _____ que está al cruzar el _____ . Su hermana Coralia necesita que ella le traiga un libro de la _____ y, si no lo encuentra, que lo compre en la _____ . Además, su hermano Ignacio le pidió que le compre el periódico *La Nación* y que le lleve una camisa a la _____ . Marisol también quiere pasar por la _____ El Elegante para ver la última moda. Cuando Marisol regresa con el pan, ya todos _____ y su mamá está muy _____ .

panadería
supermercado
centro comercial
puente / biblioteca
librería
tintorería
tienda
han desayunado / enojada

A 14 Actividad • ¡A escribir!   Answers will vary.

Write five sentences that describe five different things you have done or have bought at your favorite shopping mall recently. Use the present perfect tense.

Actividad • ¿Has vivido alguna vez en una ciudad?   Answers will vary.

Answer the following questions about life in a city. If you have never lived in a city, base your answers on a city where you would like to live.

1. ¿Cómo se llama la ciudad?
2. ¿Cuántos años has vivido en esa ciudad?
3. ¿Qué has hecho para divertirte en la ciudad?
4. ¿Qué lugares has visitado?
5. ¿Qué cosas te han gustado de la ciudad?
6. ¿Qué cosas no te han gustado?
7. ¿Cómo ha sido tu vida en esa ciudad?

Actividad • La carta   Answers will vary.

Write a letter to a friend, describing life in a big city. Base your letter on the answers in A15. Do not forget to add the necessary connectors, such as **y, luego, además, también, después,** and so on.

ESTRUCTURAS ESENCIALES   You may wish to review the uses of the preterit tense (Unit 1)
Stem-changing verbs in the preterit tense   at this time, and to contrast them with the uses of the present perfect.

There are some Spanish verbs that have vowel changes in the preterit tense. The infinitive form of all of these verbs ends in **-ir.**

Infinitive Ending	Verb	Stem Changes	Preterit Tense
-ir	dormir	**o** to **u**	dormí, dormiste, d**u**rmió, dormimos, dormisteis, d**u**rmieron
	sentir	**e** to **i**	sentí, sentiste, s**i**ntió, sentimos, sentisteis, s**i**ntieron
	pedir	**e** to **i**	pedí, pediste, p**i**dió, pedimos, pedisteis, p**i**dieron

1. Verbs like **dormir** change **o** → **u** in the **Ud., él, ella,** and **Uds., ellos, ellas** forms of the preterit. All other forms do not change.

   Nora se **durmió** en el sofá.   *Nora fell asleep on the sofa.*

2. Verbs like **sentir** and **pedir** change **e** → **i** in the **Ud., él, ella,** and **Uds., ellos, ellas** forms of the preterit. All other forms do not change.

   Ella se **sintió** muy bien.   *She felt very well.*
   Tomás **pidió** tortilla a la española.   *Tomás asked for the Spanish omelette.*

ATENCIÓN: The stem changes **e** → **ie** and **o** → **ue** in the present indicative do not occur in the preterit tense.

   Me **despierto** temprano todos los días.   *I wake up early every day.*
   Ayer me **desperté** tarde.   *Yesterday I woke up late.*
   Vuelven tarde de la escuela.   *They come back late from school.*
   Volvieron a comprar pan.   *They came back to buy bread.*

A 18 Actividad • **Todo fue diferente** For answers, see p. T198.

Complete the following sentences by repeating the verb in the preterit tense. Add additional information as needed.

MODELO   Marisol siempre pide jamón en el desayuno, pero ayer. . . .
Marisol siempre pide jamón en el desayuno, pero ayer no lo pidió.

1. Pepito siempre se acuesta temprano, pero ayer. . . .
2. Marilú nunca me despierta, pero ayer. . . .
3. Ella prefiere nadar en el mar, pero ayer. . . .
4. Yo nunca encuentro nada en la calle, pero ayer. . . .
5. Enrique se siente bien hoy, pero anoche. . . .
6. Los domingos ellos almuerzan con los tíos, pero ayer. . . .
7. Hoy pienso que era fácil, pero ayer. . . .
8. Ada habla a menudo por teléfono, pero ayer. . . .
9. Ernesto estudia todas las tardes, pero ayer. . . .

A 19 Actividad • **Cuéntame qué pasó**

Complete the following paragraph about Trini with the correct preterit forms of the verbs in parentheses.

El sábado pasado mi hermana Trini ____ (pedir) permiso para ir al cine con Lupe.   pidió
Mamá no le ____ (dar) permiso y Trini ____ (sentir) mucho no poder ir. Su amiga   dio / sintió
Lupe lo ____ (sentir) también. Trini y yo vimos televisión por un rato, pero Trini   sintió
tenía sueño y ____ (dormirse) en la silla. Al otro día, Trini ____ (levantarse)   se durmió / se levantó
temprano, ____ (vestirse) y llamó a Lupe por teléfono. Lupe le ____ (decir) que   se vistió / dijo
ella y sus primos ____ (divertirse) mucho.   se divirtieron

A 20 Actividad • **¡A escribir!**   Answers will vary.

Prepare a brief composition in Spanish about a plan to visit a big city. The following suggestions might help you.

  I. Introducción
    A. La ciudad que quiero visitar
    B. Por qué me gusta esa ciudad
 II. Desarrollo
    A. Adónde quiero ir
    B. Qué quiero hacer
    C. Lugares interesantes que quiero ver
III. Conclusión
    A. Cuándo voy a ir
    B. Por cuánto tiempo

The pampas is the economic heart of Argentina. Because of its rich soil and mild climate, it is considered to be one of the richest agricultural areas in the world. It is also the home of the gaucho, the "cowboy of the pampas."

For additional background on La Pampa, see p. T199.

B1   ¡Qué bonito es el campo!

Adrián y Mercedes Lombardi van con su hija Raquel a visitar a los padres de Mercedes, que viven en una estancia en La Pampa. Raquel quería quedarse en Buenos Aires, pero sus padres insistieron en que todos tenían que ir a ver a los abuelos. Ella invitó a su amiga Paula a acompañarla. Ya en la estancia, Paula le escribe a su amigo Juan Manuel sobre la vida en el campo.

> Querido Juan Manuel,
>
> Ya llevo quince días aquí en la estancia. Como sabes, Raquel no quería venir. Pero la verdad es que hemos pasado unos días maravillosos. Al principio, los abuelos de Raquel se enfadaban a veces y nos decían: "Chicas, no se acerquen al toro. Muchachas, no monten solas a caballo. Niñas, no se acuesten tan tarde".
>
> A mí me decían: "Paula, no dejes la puerta del gallinero abierta que se salen las gallinas. No te bañes en el lago. No comas tantos duraznos que te vas a enfermar". Pero poco a poco nos hemos acostumbrado a la vida del campo y a las cosas de los abuelos, que muchas veces tienen razón.
>
> La verdad es que el campo tiene muchas cosas buenas y me encanta estar aquí. En la estancia no habrá las comodidades de la ciudad, pero no hay contaminación, ni problemas de tránsito, ni ruido. Aquí sólo se respira aire puro y sólo se comen legumbres y carnes frescas.
>
> Como sabes, me gustan mucho los animales...¡hay tantos aquí! Y aunque hay moscas, abejas y mosquitos, y a veces hasta ratones, ya no les tengo tanto miedo como antes.
>
> Bueno, Juan Manuel, ya te contaré más la próxima vez.
>
> Hasta pronto,
>
> Paula

B2 Actividad • Preguntas y respuestas

Use the information in B1 to answer the following questions.

For answers, see p. T200.

1. ¿A quién fue a visitar Raquel?
2. ¿Con quién fue?
3. ¿Dónde queda la estancia?
4. ¿A quién le escribe Paula?
5. ¿Qué piensa ella de la vida del campo?
6. ¿Qué le dicen a Paula los abuelos de Raquel?
7. ¿Qué han comido allí?
8. ¿A qué ya no le tiene miedo Paula?

B3 Actividad • ¡A escoger!

Choose the most appropriate answer based on the information from B1.

1. Adrián y Mercedes Lombardi van a visitar a los padres de
   • Adrián. • Paula. • Mercedes.
2. Paula le escribe a
   • Adrián. • Mercedes. • Juan Manuel.
3. Paula ya lleva _____ en la estancia.
   • diez días • quince días • dos meses
4. En el campo hay mucho
   • tránsito. • aire puro. • ruido.
5. A Paula le gustan
   • los animales. • los ratones. • los mosquitos.

B4 Actividad • Los animales y los insectos del campo

Answer the following questions about your preferences.

1. ¿Cuál prefieres, la ciudad o el campo? ¿Por qué?
2. ¿Tienes amigos que viven en el campo?
3. ¿Los visitas alguna vez?
4. ¿Te gustan los animales? ¿Cuáles?
5. ¿Qué animales hay donde tú vives?
6. ¿Hay muchos mosquitos durante el verano? ¿En el invierno?
7. ¿Le tienes miedo a algún animal? ¿A cuál?
8. ¿Cuál es el animal que más te gusta?
9. ¿Cuál es el que menos te gusta?
10. ¿Te gustaría bañarte en un lago?
11. ¿Crees que te acostumbrarías al campo? ¿Por qué?
12. ¿Cuáles son tres cosas buenas que tiene el campo?

B5 Actividad • Cuentos de animales   Answers will vary.

Do you have a favorite animal story you would like to share? Get together with a classmate and tell each other about a frightening or humorous encounter with an insect or other animal.

B6 SE DICE ASÍ
Expressing your likes and dislikes

¡Me encanta!	I love it!
¡Cómo me gusta!	I like it a lot!
¡Cómo me divierto!	I'm having so much fun!
¡No hay nada igual!	There is nothing like it!
¡Cómo lo odio!	How I hate it!
¡Qué asco!	How disgusting!

B7 Actividad • ¿Cuál es tu reacción?   Answers will vary. Possible answers are given.

How do you react to the following situations? Use the expressions in B6 to respond to each statement.

1. Te dicen que vas a ir de vacaciones a Buenos Aires.   ¡Me encanta!
2. Hay un mosquito en la leche.   ¡Qué asco!
3. Tu hermana te dice que hoy hay helado de fresa.   ¡Cómo me gusta!
4. Te preguntan si te gusta el campo.   ¡Me encanta!
5. Alguien quiere saber si te gusta la ciudad.   ¡No hay nada igual!
6. Hoy hay un buen partido de fútbol.   ¡Cómo me gusta!

ESTRUCTURAS ESENCIALES
Negative familiar commands

Review affirmative familiar commands (Unit 7) at this time, together with the negative commands that require use of the subjunctive.

No olvides las botas.   *Don't forget your boots.*
No bebas esa agua.   *Don't drink that water.*
No escriban en la mesa.   *Don't write on the table.*

1. To form the negative familiar **tú** command, simply use **no** and the **tú** form of the present subjunctive.

   No **te bañes** en el lago.   *Don't swim in the lake.*
   No **duermas** tanto.   *Don't sleep so much.*
   No **comas** tantos duraznos.   *Don't eat so many peaches.*

2. For the negative plural familiar command, use the **Uds./ellos/ellas** form of the present subjunctive, just like the formal commands that you learned in Unit 3.

   No **vengan** tarde.   *Don't come late.*
   No **monten** a caballo solas.   *Don't ride a horse alone.*

3. Notice that **no** is placed before the verb.
4. Use the familiar negative commands only with someone you address as **tú**.

Actividad • ¿Qué hago?

Your kid brother always wants to do the wrong things at the wrong time. Work with a partner and answer negatively to each of the questions below.

1. ¿Cuido los conejos? No, no los cuides.
2. ¿Me acerco al toro? No, no te acerques.
3. ¿Visito a la vecina? No, no la visites.
4. ¿Traigo los duraznos? No, no los traigas.
5. ¿Cierro la puerta? No, no la cierres.

6. ¿Despierto al abuelo? No, no lo despiertes.
7. ¿Monto a caballo? No, no lo montes.
8. ¿Corro hasta la casa? No, no corras.
9. ¿Dejo salir las gallinas? No, no las dejes salir.
10. ¿Me acuesto tarde? No, no te acuestes tarde.

B10 Actividad • En la hacienda

Answers will vary. Possible answers are given. 1. No te bañes ahora, mejor báñate después. 2. No te sientes aquí, mejor siéntate allí. 3. No uses ese teléfono, mejor usa éste. 4. No almuerces en el jardín, mejor almuerza en la cocina. 5. No juegues con el gato y el perro, mejor juega con el gato. 6. No des de comer a las gallinas, mejor da de comer a los pavos.

Imagine that you are spending a few days in the country. Ask your host or hostess if you can do each of the following things. Get together with a classmate and switch roles.

> MODELO   ¿Puedo dormir aquí?   No duermas aquí, mejor duerme allí.

1. ¿Puedo bañarme en el lago ahora?
2. ¿Puedo sentarme aquí?
3. ¿Puedo usar ese teléfono?
4. ¿Puedo almorzar en el jardín?
5. ¿Puedo jugar con el gato y el perro?
6. ¿Puedo dar de comer a las gallinas?

B11 Actividad • ¿Qué les digo?

People often ask you for advice. Explain to them how they can change things for the better.

> MODELO   Ella se pone furiosa si llegamos tarde.
>   Pues, no lleguen tarde.

1. Nos sentimos cansados si corremos mucho.   Pues, no corran mucho.
2. Cuando quitamos el aire acondicionado, tenemos calor.   Pues, no quiten el aire acondicionado.
3. El abuelo se enfada si montamos solas a caballo.   Pues, no monten a caballo solas.
4. Si abrimos la puerta, entran los mosquitos.   Pues, no abran la puerta.
5. Si comemos tantos duraznos, nos vamos a enfermar.   Pues, no coman tantos duraznos.
6. Si nos levantamos muy temprano, despertamos a los abuelos.   Pues, no se levanten muy temprano.

B12 Actividad • Por favor, no cambies de opinión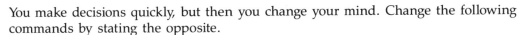

You make decisions quickly, but then you change your mind. Change the following commands by stating the opposite.

> MODELO   Tráemelo.   No me lo traigas.

1. Dímelo.
2. Póntelo.
3. Dáselo.
4. Házmelo.
5. Óyelo.
6. Véndeselos.

1. No me lo digas.
2. No te lo pongas.
3. No se lo des.
4. No me lo hagas.
5. No lo oigas.
6. No se los vendas.

B13 Actividad • ¡A escribir!   Answers will vary.

Make a list of six things you would like your friend not to do.
   Here are some ideas:
      No vengas tarde.
      No hables mal de mis amigos.

B14 Comprensión   For script, see p. T202.

You will hear a statement followed by a command. If the command is a logical response to the statement, check **lógico** on your answer sheet. If not, check **absurdo**.

> MODELO   —Hace mucho calor.
>   —No abras las ventanas.

	0	1	2	3	4	5	6	7	8	9	10
Lógico		✔	✔		✔			✔			✔
Absurdo	✔			✔		✔	✔		✔	✔	

SITUACIÓN • La granja 🔲

① la oveja	⑤ el gallo	⑨ la hierba	⑬ el prado	⑰ arar la tierra
② la vaca	⑥ el cerdo	⑩ el cielo	⑭ el trigo	⑱ sembrar
③ el pato	⑦ el ganado	⑪ las nubes	⑮ el maíz	⑲ el campesino
④ el pavo	⑧ el burro	⑫ el huerto	⑯ las semillas	

Actividad • ¡A completar!

Use the illustration in B15 to help you complete the following sentences.

1. El pan es de _____ , y las tortillas mexicanas son de _____ . trigo / maíz
2. Las _____ nos dan lana. ovejas
3. Hay muchas _____ en el cielo. nubes
4. Los _____ están nadando en el lago. patos
5. El ganado come _____ . hierba
6. Un campesino _____ y el otro _____ las semillas. ara / sembrar
7. En el _____ hay muchas legumbres. huerto
8. El _____ y las gallinas comen maíz. gallo

Los españoles trajeron los caballos a la América. Muchas de las palabras que tienen que ver con el caballo y el ganado en inglés vienen del español, como *lariat, lasso, rodeo, corral, hacienda* y *palomino.* En la Argentina el caballo fue muy importante para cruzar las pampas y en la industria ganadera. La Argentina es uno de los principales exportadores de carne del mundo. Sin embargo, en las regiones andinas, el animal más valioso no es el caballo, ni el burro, ni la mula, sino la llama. En la América hay varios equivalentes del *cowboy.* Dos de ellos son **el gaucho** en la Argentina y **el charro** en México.

B 18 ESTRUCTURAS ESENCIALES
Some irregular past participles

The following verbs that you have learned have irregular past participles.

Antonio no ha **vuelto** todavía.	*Antonio has not returned yet.*
Has **escrito** muchas cartas.	*You have written many letters.*
No he **visto** a Luisa hoy.	*I have not seen Luisa today.*

Infinitive	Past Participle
abrir	**abierto**
decir	**dicho**
escribir	**escrito**
hacer	**hecho**
poner	**puesto**
romper	**roto**
ver	**visto**
volver	**vuelto**

B 19 Actividad • ¿Qué ha hecho Rogelio? 📼

Rogelio never tells you whether he did something or not. You have to ask him. Work with a classmate and take turns playing both roles. Follow the model.

MODELO   hacer las compras   —¿Has hecho las compras?
—No, todavía no las he hecho.

1. ver a tus primos   ¿Has visto a tus primos? No, todavía no los he visto.
2. escribir la carta   ¿Has escrito la carta? No, todavía no la he escrito.
3. volver a llamar por teléfono   ¿Has vuelto a llamar por teléfono? No, todavía no he vuelto a llamar por teléfono.
4. poner el dinero en el banco   ¿Has puesto el dinero en el banco? No, todavía no lo he puesto.
5. hacer la cama   ¿Has hecho la cama? No, todavía no la he hecho.
6. lavar el coche   ¿Has lavado el coche? No, todavía no lo he lavado.
7. decir la verdad   ¿Has dicho la verdad? No, todavía no la he dicho.
8. ir a la estancia   ¿Has ido a la estancia? No, todavía no he ido.
9. beber el jugo   ¿Has bebido el jugo? No, todavía no lo he bebido.
10. abrir el gallinero   ¿Has abierto el gallinero? No, todavía no lo he abierto.

B 20   Actividad • En la estancia del abuelo

Choose the appropriate verbs in the box to complete the following conversation between Raquel and her grandfather. Make any necessary changes.

—¿Ya te lo han _____ , abuelo?   dicho
—No, ¿qué pasó?
—Alguien ha _____ la puerta del   abierto
gallinero y el gallo se fue.
—¿Quién ha _____ eso?   hecho
—Ay, no sé.
—¿Y el gallo no ha _____ todavía?   vuelto
—No, nadie lo ha _____ .   visto

decir
abrir
hacer
ver   volver

B 21   Actividad • Conversaciones sobre animales   Answers will vary.

Pair up with a classmate and talk about one of the following topics.

1. ¿Has montado a caballo alguna vez? ¿Dónde? ¿Te gustó? ¿Es difícil? ¿Por qué?
2. ¿Te has vestido de animal para una fiesta? ¿Qué animal escogiste? ¿Por qué?
3. ¿Has comido pato alguna vez? ¿Dónde? ¿Te gustó? ¿Lo comerías otra vez?
4. ¿Qué animal has tenido? ¿Quién te lo dio? ¿Lo tienes todavía?
5. ¿Qué otro animal preferirías tener? ¿Por qué? ¿Sabes cuidarlo?
6. ¿Has pasado vacaciones en el campo? ¿Dónde? ¿Cómo fueron? ¿Viste muchos animales interesantes?

B 22   Actividad • ¡A escribir!   Answers will vary.

If you live in a city, describe in eight sentences a visit—real or imaginary—to the countryside. If you live in the country, describe a real or imaginary trip to the city. Then read your description aloud to the class.

SECTION
C
expressing obligation or necessity . . . expressing doubt, disbelief,
or denial . . . stating rules or regulations

*Whether you live in the city or country, you will have to think about how to save our planet.
We should all help to protect our environment. How can you help?*

C1   Nuestro planeta

¿Vivían tus abuelos en la ciudad o en el campo?
¿Y dónde vives tú? Es probable que si tú vives en
la ciudad, tus abuelos vivieron en el campo. En
los últimos ciento cincuenta años, muchas
personas se han mudado o emigrado a las
grandes ciudades en busca de una vida mejor.
La revolución industrial, que comenzó a finales
del siglo pasado, ha creado grandes centros de
trabajo. Pero, la solución de un problema a veces
crea otro problema que hay que resolver. ¿Qué ha
pasado en las ciudades después de la revolución
industrial?

1. En poco espacio hay demasiados coches,
fábricas, edificios y personas.
2. El número de habitantes aumenta cada vez
más.
3. Las industrias crean centros de trabajo,
pero también crean contaminación. Por tanto,
aumentan los desperdicios de toda clase. La
tierra se contamina. El aire se hace impuro.

¿Qué se puede hacer para salvar nuestras
ciudades? Algunas personas no creen que el
gobierno deba controlar y decidirlo todo. Otros
piensan que sí. Sea como sea, la responsabilidad
es de todos, y no tenemos mucho tiempo. En
muchas ciudades el cielo ha perdido su color
azul. Ya no pueden verse las estrellas. El aire
está tan sucio que casi no se puede respirar.
¿Cómo podemos ayudar?

1. Evita gastar gasolina. Si puedes caminar o ir en bicicleta, no uses el coche.
Así también se evitan los embotellamientos.
2. No fumes.
3. Ahorra energía eléctrica y petróleo. Dudo que necesites tantos aparatos
eléctricos o productos plásticos como la industria produce.
4. Apoya leyes que ayuden a proteger el ambiente en las ciudades.

C2 Actividad • Preguntas y respuestas

Answer the following questions according to the information in C1.

1. ¿Por qué se han mudado tantas personas a la ciudad?
2. ¿Qué cambios trajo la revolución industrial a las ciudades?
3. ¿Qué ha pasado con el número de habitantes?
4. ¿Por qué se hace el aire impuro?
5. ¿Qué puedes hacer para ahorrar gasolina?
6. ¿Cómo puedes ahorrar energía eléctrica?
7. ¿De qué otra manera puedes proteger el ambiente?
8. ¿De quién es la responsabilidad?

1. Porque buscan una vida mejor.   2. La revolución industrial trajo cambios que crearon contaminación en los centros de trabajo.   3. El número de habitantes ha aumentado.   4. Porque las industrias contaminan el aire.   5. Puedes caminar o ir en bicicleta.   6. No tener tantos aparatos eléctricos o productos plásticos.   7. Puedes proteger el ambiente apoyando leyes que protegen el ambiente.   8. La responsabilidad es de todos.

C3 Actividad • ¡Qué confusión!

Reorder the words to form logical sentences.

1. en / impuro / es / ciudades / el / muchas / aire   En muchas ciudades el aire es impuro.
2. centros / de / hay / trabajo / grandes   Hay grandes centros de trabajo.
3. fábricas / demasiados / hay / coches / y   Hay demasiados coches y fábricas.
4. ya / azul / es / cielo / no / el   El cielo ya no es azul.
5. no / coche / si / caminar / uses / el / puedes   Si puedes caminar no uses el coche.
6. industrias / muchos / las / desperdicios / producen   Las industrias producen muchos desperdicios.

C4 Actividad • Charla   Answers will vary.

Now it's your turn to express your opinion. What do you think?

1. ¿Dónde vivían los padres de tus abuelos?
2. ¿Crees que la gente encuentra una vida mejor en la ciudad? ¿Por qué?
3. ¿Qué te gusta de la ciudad? ¿Qué es lo que no te gusta?
4. ¿Cómo se pueden evitar los embotellamientos?
5. ¿Conoces otros problemas de las grandes ciudades?
6. ¿Crees que el gobierno debe atender a los problemas de la ciudad? ¿Por qué?

El hombre, a veces por codicia *(greed)* y otras por negligencia, abusa de los recursos naturales o contamina el ambiente. La tecnología moderna puede causar grandes daños *(harm)* al ambiente. Olvidamos que viajamos por el espacio en nuestra nave espacial, la Tierra. Hay que cuidarla mejor.

Los defensores del ambiente convencieron a los gobiernos de la importancia de conservar extensos territorios libres de la intervención humana. Con la creación de los parques nacionales, los científicos pueden estudiar la naturaleza en estado primitivo y observar la interdependencia entre las plantas y los animales.

Los países hispanos tienen importantes parques nacionales. Costa Rica reserva el cuatro por ciento de su territorio a este proyecto. El ambiente de las islas Galápagos ahora está seguro. El Ecuador las declaró parque nacional. Otros ejemplos notables de protección del ambiente son el Parque Nacional de Manú en el Perú, y El Yunque en Puerto Rico.

C6 SE DICE ASÍ
Expressing obligation or necessity

Hay que controlar la contaminación.	We must control pollution.
Hay que limpiar el aire.	We must clean our air.
Hay que ahorrar gasolina y petróleo.	One has to save gas and oil.

Actividad • ¿Qué hay que hacer?

Answers will vary. Possible answers are given.
1. Hay que caminar más. 2. Hay que trabajar más.
3. Hay que descansar. 4. Hay que comer.
5. Hay que ir en carro.
6. Hay que pasar las leyes para protegerlas.

Find a logical solution. Follow the model.

MODELO Hay demasiados coches. Hay que tomar el tren.

1. La gasolina está muy cara.
2. Queremos ganar dinero.
3. Estamos cansados.

4. Tenemos hambre.
5. No podemos ir en moto.
6. Las ciudades están en peligro.

Contrast the use of "creer" and "no creer." *"Anita no cree que pueda venir."* Anita doubts that she can come. *"Anita cree que puede venir."* Anita thinks she can come. Some verbs and expressions used to show doubt, disbelief, or denial are: dudar, negar, no creer, no es cierto, no estar seguro.

C8 ESTRUCTURAS ESENCIALES
The subjunctive to express doubt, disbelief, or denial

Dudo que Tomás **sea** rico.
José **no cree** que **pueda** ir a la estancia.
No es cierto que ellos **sepan** montar a caballo.

I doubt that Tomás is rich.
José doesn't think he'll be able to go to the ranch.
It's not true that they know how to ride a horse.

1. The subjunctive is used after **que** when the first part of the sentence expresses doubt, uncertainty, or disbelief

Ana **no cree** que él **viva** en esa ciudad.   *Ana doesn't believe he lives in that city.*

2. When the first part of the compound sentence denies what is said after **que,** the subjunctive is used.

No es cierto que ella **venga** hoy.   *It's not true that she is coming today.*

3. Notice that the subjects of both clauses can be the same or different.

ATENCIÓN: When no doubt, disbelief, or denial is expressed and the subject is sure of the facts, the indicative is used.

Yo **sé** que Raquel **está** en la estancia.
Juan Manuel **cree** que **puede** ir a Buenos Aires.
Es cierto que ellas **son** las campeonas.

I know that Raquel is at the ranch.
Juan Manuel thinks he can go to Buenos Aires.
It's true that they are the champions.

C9 Actividad • El tío de Victoria   Answers will vary. Possible answers are given.

Victoria has organized a recital at her home and her uncle will play the violin. Many of her friends are not coming. Her cousin does not believe their excuses and tells her so. Use **no creo que, dudo que,** and **no es cierto que.**

MODELO Gil / tener mucho trabajo
— Dudo que Gil tenga mucho trabajo.

1. Gaby / estar enferma   Dudo que Gaby esté enferma.
2. Julián / salir con su novia   No creo que Julián salga con su novia.
3. Antonia y su esposo / llegar mañana   No es cierto que Antonia y su esposo lleguen mañana.
4. Miguel / estar en la estancia   Dudo que Miguel esté en la estancia.
5. Las gemelas / ir a otra fiesta   No es cierto que las gemelas vayan a otra fiesta.
6. Guille / cambiar de opinión   No creo que Guille cambie de opinión.
7. César / trabajar esta noche   Dudo que César trabaje esta noche.

Actividad • Juanita Calamidad For answer, see p. T207.

You have a friend who is always afraid things are going to turn out badly. Try to give him or her confidence. Get together with a classmate and take turns playing both roles. Follow the model.

> MODELO yo / pasar el examen
> —No creo que pase el examen.
> —No seas tonta. Yo creo que pasas.

1. yo / poder ganar el premio
2. Ramona / ir mañana al concierto
3. papá / darme permiso para ir al cine
4. yo / saber la lección de español
5. Andrés / venir a cenar con nosotros
6. ella / invitarme a ir al teatro

7. Rigoberto / recordar las respuestas
8. Marisa / estar lista para la fiesta
9. nosotros / poder salvar las ciudades
10. Juan Manuel / escribirle a ella

Comprensión For script, see p. T207–208.

You will hear two political candidates discuss important issues concerning conservation. If they are in favor of protecting the environment, check **de acuerdo** on your answer sheet. If they don't believe there is a problem, check **se opone**.

> MODELO Dudo que tengamos que ahorrar energía eléctrica.

	0	1	2	3	4	5	6	7	8	9	10
De acuerdo		✔	✔			✔			✔		✔
Se opone	✔			✔	✔		✔	✔		✔	

Si pronto no cuidamos nuestro planeta, estaremos en peligro. Hay que aprender de las lecciones del pasado. No cierres los ojos para no ver lo que está pasando.

1. El hombre ha cortado los árboles para tener más tierra para arar, pero sin árboles hay erosión. La erosión hace la tierra pobre.

2. Todos los años la expansión industrial destruye bosques tropicales en el Brasil que equivalen al área de California.

3. Especies de animales, como el elefante, la ballena y la pantera, están en peligro de extinción.

4. Los insecticidas matan muchos animales e insectos útiles.

5. Los desperdicios que la industria produce van por el aire y por el agua de país a país. Nadie se salva. El planeta es uno.

6. La lluvia ácida destruye los bosques y los peces en los lagos y en los ríos.

7. Las plantas nucleares producen grandes cantidades de desperdicios radioactivos que nadie quiere tener cerca.

8. Toda clase de fertilizantes e insecticidas contaminan las aguas de los ríos y de los mares. Y el agua limpia es indispensable para la vida.

Éstos son los problemas que tú y los jóvenes de tu generación van a ayudar a resolver. ¿Has pensado en eso alguna vez?

C13   Actividad • Preguntas y respuestas

Answer each question based on the information in C12.

1. ¿Para qué se cortan los árboles?
2. ¿Qué pasa cuando no hay árboles?
3. ¿Qué tienen en común el elefante y la ballena?
4. ¿Por qué ningún país se salva de la contaminación?
5. ¿Qué hace la lluvia ácida?
6. ¿Qué producen las plantas nucleares?
7. ¿Quiénes van a tener que resolver los problemas de la contaminación?

5. La lluvia ácida destruye los bosques y los peces en los lagos y en los ríos.   6. Las plantas nucleares producen grandes cantidades de desperdicios radioactivos.   7. Los jóvenes de esta generación.

1. Se cortan los árboles para tener más tierra.   2. Cuando no hay árboles, la erosión hace la tierra pobre.   3. Tienen en común que están en peligro de extinción.   4. Porque los desperdicios que la industria produce van por el aire y por el agua de país a país.

ESTRUCTURAS ESENCIALES
The use of se *for indefinite subjects*

In Spanish it is very common to use a construction with the reflexive pronoun **se** in sentences where the subject is indefinite. The construction is as follows:

> **se** + verb + rest of sentence

Se habla español.	*Spanish is spoken.*
Se escribió un libro muy bueno.	*A good book was written.*
Se venden zapatos baratos.	*Inexpensive shoes for sale (are sold).*

1. Notice that the verb immediately follows **se.**
2. There are only two verb forms used in this construction. Use the third person singular form of the verb if the object is singular. Use the third person plural if the object is plural.

Se alquilan bicicletas.	*They rent bicycles.*
Se necesita carpintero.	*Carpenter needed.*

3. The most common English equivalents of this construction are *one, you, people, they,* and *it.*

En la clase de Español **se trabaja** mucho.	*One works a lot in Spanish class.*
Se come bien en esta cafetería.	*You eat well in this cafeteria.*

4. In Spanish, a construction with **se** is used to state rules, regulations, or to prepare signs and advertisements.

Se prohibe fumar.	*No smoking.*
Se arreglan coches.	*Car repair.*
Se solicita plomero.	*Plumber wanted.*
Se buscan empleados.	*Now hiring.*

C15 Actividad • **Mi amigo el artista**

A friend of yours is an artist who makes signs. Help finish the work faster by explaining what signs to make according to the following situations.

> MODELO La joyería acepta tarjetas de crédito.
> Se aceptan tarjetas de crédito.

1. Queremos comprar discos viejos.   Se compran discos viejos.
2. Manolo tiene que vender su moto.   Se vende moto.
3. El papá de Rubén necesita una secretaria.   Se necesita una secretaria.
4. El restaurante busca un cocinero.   Se busca un cocinero.
5. La panadería no acepta cheques.   No se aceptan cheques.
6. Necesitamos periódicos viejos.   Se necesitan periódicos viejos.

C16 Actividad • **Dime cómo se hace**   Answers will vary.

Give instructions on how to do the following things.

1. ¿Cómo se hace una limonada?
2. ¿Cómo se empieza una carta?
3. ¿Cómo se va a la cafetería que queda cerca de la escuela?
4. ¿Cómo se cocina una hamburguesa?

For information on how to present the realia, see p. T209.

C17 Actividad • ¡A escoger! Answers will vary.

Prepare signs or classified ads by choosing elements from the following boxes.
Form at least five sentences.

C18 Actividad • ¿Cómo se escribe?

Your sister has all the instructions to write a letter in Spanish, but she doesn't
know how to arrange them in a logical fashion. Help her reorganize the following
instructions.   c., a., f., b., e., d.

a. Se pone la dirección a la izquierda.
b. Se escribe el mensaje o texto.
c. Se escribe la fecha a la derecha.
d. Se pone el nombre de la persona que escribe (la firma).
e. Se añade la despedida.
f. Se escribe el saludo.

C19 Actividad • ¡A escribir! Answers will vary.

Make a list of ten things you can do to help improve your environment.

La ciudad y el campo 355

1 ¿Qué ha pasado?

Use the illustrations to help you complete the captions. Use the present perfect tense.

1. . . . y estoy muy cansado.

He caminado mucho.

2. . . . y sacamos buenas notas.

Hemos estudiado toda la semana.

3. . . . y ahora me duele la garganta.

He hablado por tres horas.

4. . . . y ahora estamos a dieta.

Hemos comido mucho.

5. . . . y ahora no tengo dinero.

He comprado muchas cosas.

6. . . . y por eso están contentos.
. . . y por eso están tristes.

Han ganado el partido. Han perdido el partido.

2 Actividad • No recuerdo bien

A friend of yours does not remember details very well and gets the information all mixed up. Provide the correct information.

> Modelo Ellas se enfermaron ayer. (tú)
> Tú te enfermaste ayer.

1. Rafa se durmió mirando televisión. 2. Tu primo se vistió enseguida. 3. Yo me sentí mal. 4. Alberto pidió limonada. 5. Nosotros nos aburrimos mucho. 6. Ana perdió el dinero. 7. Leonardo no comió mucho.

1. Tú te dormiste mirando televisión. (Rafa)
2. Yo me vestí enseguida. (tu primo)
3. Juan se sintió mal. (yo)
4. Nosotros pedimos limonada. (Alberto)
5. Luis se aburrió mucho. (nosotros)
6. Los chicos perdieron el dinero. (Ana)
7. Ellos no comieron mucho. (Leonardo)

3 Actividad • La competencia   Answers will vary.

Your group is competing for first place in a recycling project. You are on the committee. Think of five projects your group can start, using **Hay que.**

4 Actividad • No digas quién te lo dijo

People have told you things and you want to repeat them, but without revealing the source. Be general and use a **se** construction, **dicen que . . . ,** or **la gente dice que. . . .**

1. Cristina dice que el jueves no hay examen.   Se dice que el jueves no hay examen.
2. Mario cree que Leonor está enferma.   Se cree que Leonor está enferma.
3. Laura piensa que los chicos van a terminar el proyecto.   Se piensa que los chicos van a terminar el proyecto.
4. Las gemelas piensan que ella rompió la libreta.   Se piensa que ella rompió la libreta.
5. Las chicas creen que Luis perdió el dinero.   Se cree que Luis perdió el dinero.
6. Tomás dice que el profesor prohíbe comer churros.   Se dice que el profesor prohíbe comer churros.

5   Actividad • Protegiendo el planeta   Answers will vary.

Are you part of the problem or are you part of the solution? With a classmate, take turns asking and answering the following questions.

1. ¿Has tratado de usar objetos de papel, en vez de objetos de plástico?
2. Para salvar los árboles, ¿usas papel reprocesado?
3. ¿Caminas algunas veces para ahorrar gasolina?
4. ¿Ayudas a alguien a dejar de fumar?
5. ¿Tiras en la calle o en la hierba botellas de refrescos?
6. ¿Cuidas de no usar más agua o electricidad de la que necesitas?

6   Actividad • Mi pueblo   Answers will vary.

Draw a map of a real or imaginary town or city. Label each of the following places.

supermercado	panadería
biblioteca	librería
centro comercial	tintorería

7   Actividad • ¿Estás de acuerdo o no?   Answers will vary.

Express your points of view. Use **creo que** plus the indicative if you agree with the statement. Use **no creo que** plus the subjunctive if you disagree.

MODELO   Es peligroso acercarse al toro.
Yo creo que es peligroso acercarse al toro.
No creo que sea peligroso acercarse al toro.

1. Los árboles son necesarios.
2. La vida en el campo es mejor.
3. Las plantas nucleares son buenas.
4. La lluvia ácida destruye los bosques.
5. Se debe evitar gastar gasolina.
6. Los chicos ahorran más energía que las chicas.
7. El número de habitantes disminuye cada año.
8. No hay desperdicios.
9. El aire de las ciudades es muy puro.
10. En el campo no hay las comodidades de la ciudad.
11. Los alumnos tienen más cuidado con el ambiente que los profesores.
12. En la ciudad hay muchos problemas de tránsito.

8   Dictado   For script, see p. T210.

Complete the following paragraph from dictation.

Hay gente que no cree que el problema de nuestro planeta _____ .
Sin embargo, muchos científicos _____ con la _____ , _____ y
de los bosques. Se ha _____ la solución de _____ . Ahora _____
que _____ el problema de la _____ .

Letter *x*

1. The Spanish **x** has a sound similar to *ks* in English.

    taxi   máximo   examen   tóxico   exagerar
    exactamente   explicar   extranjero

2. In certain words of Mexican origin, the **x** is sometimes pronounced like the Spanish **j.**

    mexicano   México   texano   Oaxaca

El mexicano del taxi exagera.
Perdí mi sombrero texano en Oaxaca.
El profesor texano dio un examen extraordinario.
Xavier exige que expresemos nuestra opinión.

Linking

As you know, in Spanish the words in a sentence are not pronounced in isolation, but joined together. Special care must be taken not to shorten any syllables and to pronounce all the vowels in a clear and distinct way. However, remember that when a word ends in a vowel and the following word starts with the same vowel, you only pronounce the vowel once: **la Argentina = largentina.**

Te escribo desde la Argentina.
Está en el hemisferio sur.
Nos hemos acostumbrado a la vida del campo.
¿Vivían tus abuelos en la ciudad o en el campo?

Actividad • Práctica de pronunciación

Listen carefully to the following sentences and then repeat.

Marisa te escribió varias cartas desde la Argentina.
A Xavier le gustaría pasear por Oaxaca.
Sara y Tere corren detrás del toro.
¡Caramba, era el primo de Victoria!
Prefiero tomar un taxi a México.

¿LO SABES?

Let's review some important points you've learned in this unit.

Can you talk about things that have happened in the past?
It has been a great day. Say what has happened in five sentences.

Do you know how to ask *"Have you ever . . ."* **in Spanish?**
Prepare five questions to ask a classmate. Then answer your classmate's questions.

Can you use stem-changing verbs you know in the preterit?
Ask your neighbor whether he had a good time at your farm, if he slept enough, and how he felt in the morning.

Do you know how to express likes and dislikes?
Imagine that you're babysitting. There are five things you don't want the child to do. Tell the child what these things are. Then express how pleased or displeased you are when the child obeys you or not.

Can you tell others not to do something?
Prepare a poster warning people to refrain from damaging the environment. Give at least five warnings.

Do you know how to express obligation?
Make a list of five things one must do to save our world from pollution.

Do you know how to say in general what people are doing, saying, selling, and buying?
Explain what is no longer fashionable, using the phrase **Ya no se usa(n). . . .**
Refer to long or short hair, wide or narrow skirts, jeans, colors, and so on. List five or six items.

Can you express doubt or disbelief?
Make five statements about the future. These should express doubt, such as: **No creo que vaya a llover.**

Do you know how to say what the rules are?
If you go to the park or the beach, you often see a sign with a long list of things that cannot be done there. What does it say? Write five of the restrictions in Spanish.

VOCABULARIO

SECTION A

a partir de *as of*
la **actividad cultural** *cultural activity*
ancho, -a *wide*
la **biblioteca** *library*
el **campo** *country*
la **capital** *capital*
el **centro comercial** *shopping center*
la **cuna** *cradle*
descendiente *descendant*
estar enojado, -a *to be angry*
el **estudiante universitario** *college student*
europeo, -a *European*
extenso, -a *extensive*
fascinar *to fascinate*
el **habitante** *resident*
el **hemisferio** *hemisphere*
el **inmigrante** *immigrant*
la **librería** *bookstore*
nacional *national*
la **panadería** *bakery*
la **pasión** *passion*
la **plaza** *square*
el **polo** *polo*
porteño, -a *person from Buenos Aires*
el **puente** *bridge*
el **supermercado** *supermarket*
el **tango** *tango*
la **tintorería** *dry cleaning store*

SECTION B

la **abeja** *bee*
abierto, -a *open*
acompañar *to accompany*
el **aire puro** *pure air*
al principio *at the beginning*
arar la tierra *to plow the land*
el **burro** *donkey*
la **campesina** *country dweller (f.)*
el **campesino** *country dweller (m.)*
el **cerdo** *pig*
el **cielo** *sky*
¡cómo lo odio! *how I hate it!*

¡cómo me divierto! *I'm having so much fun!*
¡cómo me gusta! *I like it a lot!*
dicho *said; expressed*
el **durazno** *peach*
escrito *written*
la **estancia** *cattle ranch*
la **gallina** *hen*
el **gallinero** *chicken coup*
el **gallo** *rooster*
el **ganado** *cattle*
la **granja** *farm*
hecho *made; done*
la **hierba** *grass*
el **huerto** *fruit and vegetable garden*
llevo . . . aquí *I have been here for . . .*
el **maíz** *corn*
maravilloso, -a *marvelous*
¡me encanta! *I love it!*
la **mosca** *fly*
el **mosquito** *mosquito*
¡no hay nada igual! *there's nothing like it!*
la **nube** *cloud*
la **oveja** *sheep*
el **pato** *duck*
el **pavo** *turkey*
el **prado** *meadow*
puesto *put; placed*
¡qué asco! *how disgusting!*
respirar *to breathe*
roto, -a *broken*
sembrar *to plant*
la **semilla** *seed*
la **Tierra** *Earth*
el **toro** *bull*
la **vaca** *cow*
visto *seen*
vuelto *returned*

SECTION C

a final de *by the end of*
el **ambiente** *environment*
el **aparato eléctrico** *appliance*
apoyar *to support*
aumentar *to increase*
la **ballena** *whale*

la **cantidad** *amount*
el **centro de trabajo** *work place*
contaminar *to pollute*
crear *to create*
el **desperdicio** *waste*
el **edificio** *building*
el **elefante** *elephant*
el **embotellamiento** *traffic jam*
emigrar *to emigrate*
en busca de *in search of*
equivaler *to be equivalent*
la **erosión** *erosion*
el **espacio** *space*
la **especie** *species*
evitar *to avoid*
la **expansión** *expansion*
la **fábrica** *factory*
la **falta de** *lack of*
el **fertilizante** *fertilizer*
fumar *to smoke*
la **gasolina** *gasoline*
gastar *to use up*
la **generación** *generation*
impuro, -a *not pure*
indispensable *essential*
el **insecticida** *insecticide*
la **lección** *lesson*
la **ley** *law*
limpio, -a *clean*
la **lluvia ácida** *acid rain*
matar *to kill*
mudar(se) *to move*
la **necesidad** *need*
la **pantera** *panther*
el **petróleo** *oil*
proteger *to protect*
radioactivo, -a *radioactive*
resolver (ue) *to solve*
la **responsabilidad** *responsibility*
la **revolución industrial** *industrial revolution*
salvar *to save*
sea como sea *whatever it may be; anyway*
el **siglo** *century*
sucio, -a *dirty*
tropical *tropical*
útil *useful*

PRÁCTICA DEL VOCABULARIO

1. How many names of animals can you find in the unit vocabulary? Name two insects.
2. From the vocabulary list above, make a list of all the places that are often located in a shopping center. la librería, la panadería, el supermercado, la tintorería

---

1. el burro, el cerdo, la gallina, el gallo, la oveja, el pato, el pavo, el toro, la vaca, la ballena, el elefante y la pantera
Two insects: el mosquito, la abeja

VAMOS A LEER

Antes de leer

Rapidly scan the reading selection paragraph by paragraph. After you finish, write down what you think the reading is about. Then go back and write a list of words whose meaning you can guess and a list of words that you don't know.

Preparación para la lectura

1. *Answers will vary.* 2. *Answers will vary.* 3. generaciones - *generations,* melodía - *melody,* tradicional - *traditional,* identidad - *identity* 4. riqueza - *riches,* herencia - *heritage,* región - *region,* bambú - *bamboo,* humano - *human* 5. Quieren decir *sound* y *tombs.*

Answer the following questions before reading the selection.

1. ¿Conoces algo de música hispanoamericana? ¿De qué país?
2. ¿Conoces algún baile latino? ¿Cuál?
3. De una mirada rápida vas a encontrar cognados fáciles como *generaciones, melodía, identidad* y *tradicional.* ¿Te puedes imaginar qué significan?
4. ¿Puedes encontrar otros cinco cognados?
5. Hay cognados que son difíciles. ¿Te puedes imaginar qué quieren decir *sonido* y *tumbas*?

Las culturas hispanoamericanas

¿Has bailado un tango o salsa alguna vez, o el jarabe tapatío°? ¿O has oído a Linda Ronstadt cantar los corridos° mexicanos que su padre le cantaba? La música es el puente más directo entre culturas distintas. La música popular pronto pasa de moda,° pero cuando una melodía va de padres a hijos por varias generaciones, se convierte en música tradicional. Como muchas otras, esta tradición no debe perderse. Forma parte de nuestra identidad, más que las fechas de batallas y otros sucesos° históricos. Además de tratar de preservar el mundo físico en que vivimos, debemos de preservar la riqueza° de culturas. Sus orígenes a veces se pierden en el misterio de los siglos. Veamos algunos ejemplos.

La música

Quizás los instrumentos musicales más antiguos que se conocen en la América son de la región de los Andes. Flautas de bambú,° de varias formas y tamaños, invitan a bailar con su ritmo irresistible o atraen° con un sonido melancólico que imita el sonido del viento en las montañas.

---

jarabe tapatío *Mexican hat dance* **corridos** *ballads* **pasa de moda** *is no longer fashionable or popular*
sucesos *events* **riqueza** *richness* **flautas de bambú** *bamboo flutes* **atraen** *they attract*

El instrumento más popular es la quena, parecida a la flauta dulce°. Originalmente se hacía de hueso° de llama y a veces de fémur humano.° Otro instrumento popular es el charango, una guitarra muy pequeña. Antiguamente se hacía del carapacho° del armadillo. Los jóvenes de hoy mantienen vivas las antiguas melodías incas. Una de ellas llegó al *hit parade* de los Estados Unidos hace unos años. Se llama "El cóndor pasa". ¿La has oído?

El baile

Algunos bailes antiguos también se han preservado. El baile era ceremonial. Servía para comunicar al ser humano° y su mundo natural con los dioses° y el mundo sobrenatural. Más tarde descubrieron que era divertido y se inventaron más bailes. El Ballet Folklórico de México, por ejemplo, es una institución que trae a la vida bailes de muchas regiones, no sólo el jarabe tapatío y la bamba. La zarzuela española, que es una comedia con música y bailes folklóricos, vuelve a estar de moda. Y se puede ver en Albuquerque, San Antonio, Chicago, Nueva York y Miami. Compañías de baile de lugares tan distantes como Puerto Rico y las Filipinas reviven° la herencia° española en sus danzas.

---

flauta dulce *recorder*   **hueso** *bone*   **fémur humano** *thigh bone*   **carapacho** *hard shell*
ser humano *human being*   **dioses** *gods*   **reviven** *revive*   **herencia** *heritage*

Tejidos a mano°

Hay muchas y bellas artesanías° en nuestras tierras. Una de las artesanías más interesantes es la de los tejidos, tanto mayas como incas. Las mujeres mayas de Guatemala, por ejemplo, hacen tejidos a mano de gran belleza° con diseños geométricos o de animales, en colores brillantes. En la región andina,° tanto hombres como mujeres, hilan la lana° mientras conversan o caminan. Los hombres se tejen sus propios ponchos de lana de alpaca, animal nativo de la región. En otras partes del mundo, los tejidos se hacen a máquina, pero no pueden compararse en calidad y belleza. Éste es un arte que no debe perderse.

Tejidos a mano *Hand-woven fabrics*   **artesanías** *arts and crafts*   **belleza** *beauty*
región andina *Andean region*   **hilan la lana** *spin wool*

Actividad • ¿Cuántas palabras sabes?

After reading the selection carefully, return to your lists of words from **Antes de leer,** and try to identify the meaning of each one by the way it is used in the sentence. You will be surprised by how many words you already know. Use a dictionary or the footnote translations to help you identify the more difficult ones.

Actividad • Preguntas y respuestas

Use the information you found in the reading selection to answer the following questions.

1. ¿Cuál es el puente más fácil entre dos culturas diferentes?
2. ¿Qué es la música tradicional?
3. ¿Cómo es la música de los Andes?
4. ¿De qué se hacía la quena o flauta?
5. ¿Para qué servían los bailes ceremoniales?
6. ¿Qué es una zarzuela?

1. La música es el puente más directo entre dos culturas diferentes.   2. Es la música que pasa de padres a hijos por generaciones.   3. Es una música de sonido melancólico que imita el sonido del viento en las montañas. 4. La quena o flauta se hacía de hueso de llama y a veces de fémur humano.   5. Para comunicar al ser humano y su mundo natural con los dioses y el mundo sobrenatural.   6. La zarzuela es una comedia con música y bailes folklóricos.

Actividad • ¿A qué se refiere?

Read the following descriptions and identify the items being described.

1. Baile mexicano que se baila alrededor de un sombrero.   Jarabe tapatío.
2. Canciones que cantaba el padre de Linda Ronstadt.   Corridos mexicanos.
3. El instrumento musical más popular de los Andes.   La quena.
4. Guitarra pequeña que se hacía del carapacho del armadillo.   El charango.
5. Puente entre las culturas de Puerto Rico y las Filipinas.   Las compañias de baile que reviven la herencia española en sus danzas.

Actividad • Charla   Answers will vary.

Prepare a list of the songs or dances you know from Spanish America or Spain. Get together with a classmate and compare the lists.

UNIDAD 11 ¡Qué bonita es Barcelona!
Scope and Sequence

	BASIC MATERIAL	COMMUNICATIVE FUNCTIONS
SECTION A	**Un viaje a Barcelona** (A1) **Haciendo los preparativos** (A14)	**Expressing feelings and emotions** • Expressing emotions **Expressing and finding out moral attitudes** • Expressing agreement or lack of preference • Expressing approval or satisfaction with emphasis
SECTION B	**En el hotel** (B1) **¿Qué hacemos en Barcelona?** (B12)	**Expressing attitudes and opinions** • Expressing what is needed or expected • Expressing probability or denial **Persuading** • Making suggestions
SECTION C	**En Barcelona** (C1) **Saludos desde Barcelona** (C13)	**Socializing** • Attracting attention **Expressing feelings and emotions** • Expressing uncertainty
TRY YOUR SKILLS	**En la agencia de viajes** **Dictado**	

■ **Pronunciación** (letters **b** and **v**, and intonation)
■ **¿Lo sabes?**   ■ **Vocabulario**

VAMOS A LEER	**Panorama de España** (the varied regions of Spain)

WRITING   A variety of controlled and open-ended writing activities appear in the Pupil's Edition. The Teacher's Notes identify other activities suitable for writing practice.

COOPERATIVE LEARNING   Many of the activities in the Pupil's Edition lend themselves to cooperative learning. The Teacher's Notes explain some of the many instances where this teaching strategy can be particularly effective. For guidelines on how to use cooperative learning, see page T13.

GRAMMAR	CULTURE	RE-ENTRY
The use of the subjunctive to express feelings and emotions (A7) The use of the subjunctive to express the indefinite (A17)	Learning about Catalonia, Spain	Demonstrative adjectives and pronouns
The use of the subjunctive in impersonal expressions (B5) Softened commands (B15)	Vacationing in Spain A visit to Montjuich, Spain Exploring Barcelona	The present subjunctive verb forms
The expression ¡ojalá! (C6) The subjunctive with **tal vez** and **quizás** (C17)	**La sardana:** A folk dance from Catalonia	The indicative mood

Recombining communicative functions, grammar, and vocabulary

Reading for practice and pleasure

TEACHER-PREPARED MATERIALS
Section A A map of Spain
Section B A map of Barcelona
Section C A map of the world

UNIT RESOURCES
Manual de actividades, Unit 11
Manual de ejercicos, Unit 11
Unit 11 Cassettes
Transparencies 27–29
Quizzes 25–27
Unit 11 Test

UNIDAD 11

A1–3

SECTION A

OBJECTIVES **To express feelings and emotions:** express emotions; **to express and find out moral attitudes:** express agreement or lack of preference, express approval or satisfaction with emphasis

CULTURAL BACKGROUND Barcelona, Spain's second largest city, stretches between the Pyrenees and the Mediterranean Coast. The oldest part of the city is built on a small hill called **Monte Taber.** Roman walls that surround this section are still visible. In the center of the city stands the cathedral, built between 1289 and 1450. Cutting through the modern area of Barcelona is a wide avenue called **Las Ramblas,** which leads from the **Puerta de la Paz** to the **Plaza de Cataluña. Las Ramblas,** lined with benches and enormous trees, is well known not only for its bird and flower vendors but also for its distinct charm.

In 1992, Barcelona, the rest of Spain, and certainly all the Americas will celebrate the five hundredth anniversary of the discovery of America. It was in Barcelona where Columbus informed Queen Isabella of the new lands he had seen. In celebration of this anniversary, replicas of Columbus's ships will sail from Barcelona.

MOTIVATING ACTIVITY Tell the students to imagine that they are planning a trip to Barcelona. You may wish to ask the students what they would like to see, what they would like to learn, and what they would like to eat.

A1 Un viaje a Barcelona

To create a cultural setting for **Un viaje a Barcelona,** point out the city of Barcelona on a map of Spain or on Transparencies 34 and 34A. You may wish to discuss additional cultural information about Barcelona and Catalonia. For example, discuss the Catalonian movement for independence from Spain, their language **(catalán),** and their love of music, particularly of choral singing, which is very important in northern Spain. Discuss the fact that a replica of Columbus's flagship is anchored in the harbor. You may also wish to include information concerning the architectural work of Gaudí, such as **el Parque Güell, la iglesia de la Sagrada Familia,** and other buildings located around the city. Mention that along each block of **Las Ramblas** there are stalls and vendors offering products, such as books, birds and small animals, flowers, and so on.

Present the new vocabulary and expressions to the students, such as **graduarse, las olimpiadas, el boleto, molestar,** and **¿qué hay de nuevo?** Then read the dialog and introduction aloud or play the cassette. For cooperative learning, divide the class into groups of four. Each student may choose the role he or she wants to play. After each group practices reading the dialog, call on groups to role-play for the class.

A2 Actividad • Preguntas y respuestas

You may wish to have the students complete this activity orally with books closed, or you may ask the students to work with partners to answer the questions. Remind them that they may refer to Al as necessary. For writing practice, assign this activity as written homework.

A3 Actividad • ¿Es cierto o no?

CHALLENGE Have each student write ten false statements and exchange papers with a partner. You may wish to call on individuals to read a false statement aloud and ask another student to correct it.

A4 Sabes que . . .

You may wish to read the cultural note aloud or play the cassette as the students follow along in their books. Then write the new vocabulary on the board and ask the students to identify other words that they may have difficulty understanding. To check comprehension, you may wish to ask the following or similar questions.

1. ¿Qué cosa tienen los catalanes que es diferente del resto de España?
2. ¿Qué era Cataluña durante la Edad Media?
3. ¿En qué consiste la autonomía de Cataluña?
4. ¿Qué les informó Cristóbal Colón a los Reyes Católicos en Barcelona?

A5 SE DICE ASÍ

Read the phrases in the box aloud as the students follow along in their books. You may wish to give an example of each of the phrases, such as **¡Cuánto me alegro de que estés aquí!** or **Siento tanto que mi amigo esté triste.** Explain to the students that verbs that are used to express emotions always take the subjunctive if the subjects of both clauses are different.

A6 Actividad • La excursión de la clase

For writing practice, have the students write the completed sentences. You may wish to call on volunteers to write their answers on the board or a transparency. Have the students correct their work.

ANSWERS:
1. Nos sorprende mucho que Ernesto no compre los refrescos.
2. ¡Cuánto me alegro de que Elenita pueda ir a la excursión!
3. Están tan contentos de que nosotros los invitemos a la excursión.
4. Luisa siente tanto que Miguel no traiga los folletos de la agencia de viajes.
5. Me molesta que Juan y Lucía no ayuden con los preparativos.

A7 ESTRUCTURAS ESENCIALES

Introduce the material by reading aloud several sentences that include the model verbs. You may wish to use the activity as an occasion to give a pep talk to the students or to praise them for their work. For example:

Me alegro de que Uds. tengan buenas notas.
Espero que aprendan mucho español.
Me encanta que sean tan listos y que estén preparados.
Lamento que no los pueda llevar a España.

You may wish to use the contents of your picture file to stimulate some of the conversations. Allow the students to make generalizations about the types of verb forms they hear. You may ask them to write the sentences they hear before you request the generalizations. Once they have expressed their ideas, review the material in the text. Ask the students to form sentences, using each of the verbs. For example:

Me alegro de que Rafael reciba una A.
Me enfada que no estudien tanto.
Espero que podamos viajar a México.

Stress that the subject in the main clause must be different from the subject in the subordinate clause. Write an example on the board, such as **Me sorprende que tú no tengas dinero.** Point out both subjects. Then write a sentence containing one subject, such as **Me sorprende no tener dinero.** Explain to the students that because there are two different subjects in the first sentence, the verb in the subordinate clause, **tengas,** is in the present subjunctive tense. In the second sentence, because there is only one subject, the verb **tener** is in the infinitive.

A 8 Actividad • Combinación

For cooperative learning, divide the class into groups of three or four. Tell each group that it must see how many sentences the members can form in five minutes. The group that forms the most sentences may write them on the board or a transparency.

A 9 Actividad • En el aeropuerto

SLOWER-PACED LEARNING You may wish to review some of the subjunctive verb forms before the students begin the activity. Instruct them to complete the sentences according to the model. Review the activity with the entire class.

A 10 Actividad • ¡A conversar!

Ask the students to work in pairs. Explain that they must express their likes and dislikes about traveling, using the present subjunctive. Then have the students complete a survey of the class to find out the three things they like or dislike most about traveling.

A 11 SE DICE ASÍ

Read the expressions aloud to the class. You may wish to use each of the expressions in a sentence. For example, say to the class, **Dicen que no dan buena comida en este restaurante, pero tengo tanta hambre que no me importa.** After you have given several examples, ask the students to generalize about the statements. Once they understand the idea, give them a variety of suggestions and allow them to respond appropriately, either positively, negatively, or with indifference.

A 12 Actividad • Me da igual

Before beginning the activity, you may wish to re-enter the demonstrative adjectives and the demonstrative pronouns. Have pairs of students express agreement or lack of preference by using the demonstrative pronouns in conversations. Select a student to demonstrate the following or a similar exchange with you.

> TEACHER ¿Qué prefieres, este libro o aquél?
> STUDENT Me da igual.
> TEACHER ¿Quieres sentarte en esta silla o en ésa?
> STUDENT No me importa.

A13 Comprensión

You will hear ten exchanges among several people. Each exchange will express approval or disapproval. If the people are pleased, check **¡fantástico!** on your answer sheet. If not, check **¡qué horror!** For example, you will hear: **¿Qué te parece la idea de visitar Barcelona?** You will also hear the response: **Me encanta que podamos conocer esa ciudad.** You place your check mark in the row labeled **¡fantástico!** because the person expressed approval.

1. ¿Qué piensas de los precios en este hotel?
   Me sorprende que las habitaciones sean tan horribles y tan caras.
   ¡qué horror!
2. ¿Te parece bueno el menú de este restaurante?
   Me enoja que no sirvan paella.   *¡qué horror!*
3. No puedo creer que no haya taxis a estas horas.
   Temo que tengamos que caminar hasta el hotel.   *¡qué horror!*
4. El museo está cerrado los lunes.
   Lamento que no podamos ver las pinturas de Picasso.
   ¡qué horror!
5. Vamos a esa agencia de viajes.
   Me gusta que la agente allí sea tan amable.   *¡fantástico!*
6. Las habitaciones no tienen aire acondicionado.
   Me molesta que no tengan aire acondicionado porque hace mucho calor.   *¡qué horror!*
7. El banco cierra a la una, pero tengo tiempo para sacar dinero.
   Me encanta que tengas suficiente dinero para pagar la comida.
   ¡fantástico!
8. El avión va a llegar a tiempo al aeropuerto internacional de Madrid.
   Me alegro que lleguemos a tiempo porque nos espera María Elena.
   ¡fantástico!
9. Adiós, amigos. Nos vemos pronto.
   Espero que tú y Vicente tengan un buen viaje.   *¡fantástico!*
10. Las habitaciones no estarán listas hasta las tres de la tarde.
    Lamento que no podamos dormir un rato.   *¡qué horror!*

Now check your answers. *Read each exchange again and give the correct answer.*

A14 SITUACIÓN • Haciendo los preparativos

Before presenting the dialog, introduce the new vocabulary, such as **ida y vuelta, la pandilla, entusiasmado, vuelo sin escala, la tarifa especial, ¡bárbaro!, la reservación, el aire acondicionado,** and **la habitación.** You may wish to write the words on the board or a transparency. After you play the cassette or read the dialog aloud, call for choral and individual repetition, alternating them to maintain student interest. Then call on five volunteers to role-play the dialog. You may wish to mention that the Hotel Montserrat was probably named after the famous Monastery of Montserrat in Barcelona.

A15 Actividad • Preguntas y respuestas

You may wish to read the questions aloud and ask the students to answer them orally in class with books closed, or you may assign them as written homework. For correction, ask the students to exchange papers with a classmate.

ANSWERS:
1. Los chicos van a la agencia de viajes a comprar los boletos.
2. Araceli Valdés es la propietaria de la agencia.
3. Araceli les consigue un vuelo sin escala con una tarifa especial.
4. El vuelo cuesta $480 por persona, ida y vuelta.
5. Regresan el catorce de agosto.
6. El grupo necesita habitaciones que tengan baño privado y aire acondicionado.
7. El hotel se llama Montserrat.
8. Es un hotel de tres estrellas.
9. Araceli les desea un feliz viaje.

A 16 SE DICE ASÍ

Read the expressions in the box aloud to the students. Make statements that might require these types of responses and have the students respond, using the expressions. For example, you say *(student's name),* **la escuela te quiere mandar a Barcelona.** Elicit the response: **¡Regio!** or **¡Maravilloso!** Then ask the students to make similar statements to other members of the class. Some of these expressions, such as **¡Regio!, ¡De película!,** and **¡Bárbaro!** are more regional or colloquial than the others.

A 17 ESTRUCTURAS ESENCIALES

Explain to the class that you are looking for someone to help you with your work. Provide the following or similar examples that follow the model.

> Busco una persona que sepa español.
> Necesito un estudiante que pueda trabajar los sábados.
> Quiero una persona que prefiera trabajar los fines de semana.
> Busco una persona que pueda usar una computadora.

You may write the sentences on the board or a transparency. Ask the students to generalize about the use of the subjunctive. When finished, have them make up a list of five qualifications needed for someone who works in an import-export office.

> Buscamos una persona que sea bilingüe.
> Necesitamos una persona que pueda escribir a máquina.

You may also wish to add a guided question-and-answer drill, using contextual situations.

> TEACHER Busco un estudiante que sepa escribir español. ¿Qué busco yo?
> STUDENT Ud. busca un estudiante que sepa escribir español.
> TEACHER Espero que Uds. saquen buenas notas en la prueba de mañana. ¿Qué espero yo?
> STUDENT Ud. espera que nosotros saquemos buenas notas en la prueba de mañana.

Point out to the students that when they are discussing something definite, specific, and certain, they must use the indicative mood. Review the examples included in number 2, contrasting the use of the definite article **el** to express something definite with the use of the indefinite article **un** to express something indefinite.

A 18   **Actividad • ¡A completar!**

CHALLENGE   After the students have completed the activity, have them write five new sentences using the subjunctive to express the indefinite.

A 19   **Actividad • ¿Y tú qué piensas?**

Have each student choose a partner. Partners should take turns interviewing each other, using the questions as a guide. Tell each student to take notes on his or her partner's responses. Then call on volunteers to report the information to the class.

A 20   **Actividad • Mi mundo de fantasía**

Allow the students to work in groups of two or three to write six sentences that describe their fantasy world. Ask each group to write its sentences on the board for review, or have groups present their ideas orally to the class. Encourage the students to listen carefully and tell them you will question them about the content of the presentations. When they have finished, ask the following types of questions.

¿Quién quiere que el mundo esté en paz?
¿Quién busca un lugar que sea hermoso?

A 21   **Actividad • En la agencia de viajes**

Allow the students to work in pairs to prepare a dialog that they will present in class. You may wish to instruct them to include a specific number of conversational exchanges, perhaps ten, and to include questions and answers about flights, costs, hotels, tours, weather, and clothing required. Ask the students to role-play the dialogs for the class.

A 22   **Actividad • ¡A escribir y a hablar!**

Assign the project for presentation two or three days later. Allow the students time to work in class. Provide assistance as they present the material. You may wish to record the presentations for easier grading and for providing feedback to the students about their progress.

SECTION **B**

OBJECTIVES   **To express attitudes and opinions:** express what is needed or expected, express probability or denial; **to persuade:** make suggestions

CULTURAL BACKGROUND   Antonio Gaudí (1852–1926) was a famous Catalonian architect, sculptor, and ceramic artist. He is recognized as being ahead of his time because of his daring ideas for the design of public buildings and private homes. For his patron, Count Güell, he built **el Palacio Güell** and a fabulous park for children, called **el Parque Güell.** He began working on his most famous building, **la iglesia de la Sagrada Familia,** in 1881. The building is still unfinished. In addition to **el Parque Güell,** Gaudí also built **la Casa Milá** and **la Casa Batló** in Barcelona.

MOTIVATING ACTIVITY   Have the students research information about Barcelona. Ask them to be prepared to discuss the different sites they would like to see if they were to go there.

B 1   En el hotel

Before presenting the dialog, you may wish to read the opening paragraph aloud and review the events that took place in the previous dialogs—A1 on pages 368–369 and A14 on page 374. Then play the cassette or read small portions of the dialog aloud. Call for choral and individual repetition, alternating them to maintain student interest. When you have completed the presentation, you may wish to call on students to role-play parts of the dialog. Ask them to bring in props, such as a suitcase, keys, passports, and a record book.

CHALLENGE   You may wish to incorporate the realia into your presentation of the dialog. Explain to the students that Barcelona is a very important tourist center in Spain and must accommodate a large number of tourists on widely varying budgets. Barcelona, like the rest of Spain, has many different kinds of hotels.

Ask the students to look at the realia on page 377 and to find as many cognates as possible. You or a volunteer may write the words on the board as the students read them aloud. Add any words the students might have missed. Then have the students practice the pronunciation of the cognates, contrasting the Spanish with the English pronunciation.

Now ask the students to read the realia silently. Then call on volunteers to explain in their own words each item listed. Encourage them to use context clues to comprehend any new vocabulary. List on the board all of the words and expressions the students did not know.

B 2   Actividad • Preguntas y respuestas

Allow the students to work in pairs. Have them refer to the dialog in B1 to use as a guide.

B 3   Sabes que . . .

After presenting the information in the cultural note, you may wish to add that there are many historical buildings and monuments in disrepair in Spain. The government has been restoring many of these buildings and turning them into inns or **paradores,** for example, the **Parador Nacional de la Arruzafa** in Córdoba. **Paradores** are hotels in which the architecture and style of the historical buildings have been preserved and which are usually furnished in either period furniture or reproductions. Recently rates have increased considerably and are now equal to those of first-class hotels.

B 4   SE DICE ASÍ

Read the expressions aloud to the students. Then have each student practice using the expressions with a partner.

B 5   ESTRUCTURAS ESENCIALES

Stress to the students that it is necessary to have a subject expressed (or understood) in the clause after **que** in order to use the subjunctive. If no subject is expressed, neither the subjunctive nor **que** is used. Contrast the following or similar examples.

Es importante que tú vayas a España.
Es importante ir a España.

Point out that most of these expressions express doubt, emotion, or attitudes about something. After presenting the explanation and examples in number 1, write the impersonal expressions in number 2 on the board or a transparency. Read them aloud to the students.

Have the students practice these expressions by conducting brief question/answer drills, using real-life situations and addressing the students by name. Ask the questions in the indicative mood and have the students respond using the subjunctive mood.

(Hiding a book or other classroom object)
TEACHER (*Student's name*), ¿es fácil encontrarlo?
STUDENT Sí, es fácil que yo lo encuentre.
TEACHER (*Two students' names*), ¿es mejor tener exámenes los domingos?
STUDENT No, no es mejor que tengamos exámenes los domingos.

Re-enter the use of the Spanish subjunctive, presented on pages 304–305. Review the **-ar, -er,** and **-ir** verb endings and remind the students of the formula: *verb + subjunctive + verb.*

B6 Actividad • ¡Es increíble!

SLOWER-PACED LEARNING Have the students copy the sentences from their books, leaving spaces for the verbs. Then tell them to close their books. Read the sentences aloud with the correct form of the verb and have the students fill in the blanks.

B7 Actividad • Combinación

Ask the students to write a sentence for each of the impersonal expressions. Call on volunteers to write sentences on the board for review and correction.

B8 Actividad • Antes de dar un viaje

Call on students to complete the activity orally using impersonal expressions from the box. You or a volunteer may write the sentences on the board or a transparency for correction.

POSSIBLE ANSWERS:
1. Antes de dar un viaje, es importante que ustedes hagan reservaciones en un hotel.
2. Antes de dar un viaje, es preciso que Julio Mario tenga su pasaporte listo.
3. Antes de dar un viaje, es probable que los turistas consigan una tarifa especial.
4. Antes de dar un viaje, es necesario que tú llegues a tiempo al aeropuerto.
5. Antes de dar un viaje, es indispensable que nosotros leamos algo sobre el país que pensamos visitar.
6. Antes de dar un viaje, es mejor que uno no traiga muchas maletas.

B9 Comprensión

You will hear ten statements or questions each followed by a comment. If the comment is logical, check **lógico** on your answer sheet. If not, check **ilógico**. For example, you will hear the statement: **No podemos salir después de las seis.** You will also hear the comment: **Es dudoso que salgamos antes de las diez.** You place your check mark in the row labeled **ilógico,** because the comment is illogical.

1. Debemos estudiar para el examen de mañana.
   No es probable que tengamos examen pronto.   *ilógico*
2. ¡Ay! ¡Qué calor hace!
   Es mejor que abramos las ventanas.   *lógico*
3. El coche tiene poca gasolina.
   Es preciso que le pongamos gasolina.   *lógico*
4. La clase está completamente llena. No hay más espacio.
   Es fácil que admitan más estudiantes.   *ilógico*
5. Quedan solamente tres boletos para el concierto.
   No es necesario que compremos los boletos hoy.   *ilógico*
6. Rafael no puede salir para México hoy.
   Es dudoso que llegue a la ciudad de México esta tarde.   *lógico*
7. ¿Dónde puedo comprar un boleto de avión?
   Es mejor que vayas a una agencia de viajes.   *lógico*
8. ¿Qué necesito para viajar de California a Nueva York?
   Es importante que tengas un pasaporte.   *ilógico*
9. Juan me dice que tus tíos salen para Madrid mañana.
   Sí, es cierto que salen de viaje mañana.   *lógico*
10. Javier y Vicente siempre llegan tarde.
    Es dudoso que ellos estén en el aeropuerto a tiempo.   *lógico*

Now check your answers. *Read each exchange again and give the correct answer.*

B 10   **Actividad • Cosas esenciales**

Have each student choose a partner. Have partners take turns asking and answering the questions. You may also wish to call on the students at random to answer the questions.

B 11   **Actividad • ¡A escribir!**

Tell the students to scan the realia and make a list of all the cognates they can find. Have them begin with **Hotel Alfonso XIII,** continue with **Hotel Residencia Carmen,** and end with **Hotel Bonaire.** Then call on the students to read their lists aloud as you or a volunteer writes them on the board. Now ask the students to read the realia silently, using context clues to identify unfamiliar words. They should prepare a second list of words they cannot identify and add them to the ones on the board.

Now ask each student to make a list of favorable features of a hotel, such as the following.

un exquisito hotel de la más fina tradición
112 habitaciones lujosamente amuebladas
aire acondicionado en todo el hotel
restaurante
categoría de cuatro estrellas
situado en la zona más céntrica
seis salas de conferencia
una playa de blanca y limpia arena

Now tell each student to select a name and a location for his or her hotel. Then guide the students in writing their brochures, following the style of the realia and starting with the following or similar expressions:

un magnífico hotel . . .
un hotel muy grande, que tiene . . .
situado en el . . .

For cooperative learning, divide the class into groups of three or four students. Instruct the groups to design a travel brochure for any hotel in the world, real or imaginary. Remind them that they must imagine that they are the owners of the hotels. Encourage them to use magazine pictures or photographs to help them present their brochures to the class.

B 12   SITUACIÓN • ¿Qué hacemos en Barcelona?

You may wish to mention that Barcelona is surrounded by mountains and **el Tibidabo** is 1,745 feet high. Montjuich is a hill that rises from the sea, with beautiful terraced gardens, statues, amusement park, and an open-air theatre. There, one can also find two palaces that house the Museum of Fine Arts of Catalonia and the Museum of Archeology.

Now play the cassette or read the dialog aloud as the students follow along in their books. You may wish to call for choral or individual repetition, alternating them to maintain student interest. Then call on volunteers to role-play the dialog.

B 13   Actividad • ¡A escoger!

Have the students choose the correct answer for each item. Review the answers with the class.

B 14   Sabes que . . .

Visitors to the area of Montjuich find it worthwhile to visit **El Pueblo Español,** a Spanish village that was built for the World's Fair of 1929. Two palaces that now house the museums were built especially for the fair. The village is made up of replicas of many different examples of architecture from different regions of Spain.

B 15   ESTRUCTURAS ESENCIALES

Present several "let's" commands. Instruct the students to use **vale** as a response if they agree. If they do not, they must make another suggestion. When they have understood the new structure, read the explanation and examples aloud as the students follow along in their books. Point out that when object pronouns are attached to the command form, an accent mark must be placed over the syllable that is stressed. Also point out that in cases where the verb is reflexive, the first **s** is eliminated: **vámonos, sentémonos, comprémonos.** Review the information in number 3 quickly. Explain that object pronouns are used with command forms mainly in writing and are not often heard in spoken language.

B 16   Actividad • Esto tiene que cambiar

Allow the students to work in pairs to complete the activity. Review the answers with the entire class. Then ask the students to close their books. Make a statement and ask them to change it to a "let's" command. Continue by asking the students to make suggestions about activities they would enjoy doing.

B 17 Actividad • Sigamos al líder

After choosing a partner, have each student take turns asking and answering the questions.

B 18 Actividad • ¡A escribir y a hablar!

Allow the students to complete the activity in essay form. When they have finished, you may wish to ask them to present the information to the class in the form of advertisements or commercials for television.

SECTION C

OBJECTIVES **To socialize:** attract attention; **to express feelings and emotions:** express uncertainty

CULTURAL BACKGROUND In medieval times, the cathedral was usually the center of the town. As the city grew, it evolved around the cathedral, with the streets radiating out like the spokes of a wheel. That is one of the differences between European cities and American cities. In many instances, American cities such as Washington, D.C. or the borough of Manhattan in New York City follow a gridiron plan. European cities, such as Barcelona, tend to follow a radial plan. Some cities had more than one center, for example, a royal palace and a city hall. **El Barrio Gótico** in Barcelona is a good example of the radial plan because it evolved around the cathedral. This section of the city is very picturesque and one of Barcelona's main tourist attractions.

MOTIVATING ACTIVITY Ask the students to make a list of places they would like to visit and learn about, preferably in Spanish-speaking countries. You may wish to provide the class with a map of the world. Ask them to state reasons for their choices. You may wish to give them an example, such as: **Me gustaría ir a Perú para conocer Machu Picchu** or **Tengo ganas de ir a Barcelona porque quiero visitar El Barrio Gótico.**

C 1 En Barcelona

Discuss the photographs that accompany the basic dialog. These photos are very important because they serve as a basis for the dialog and offer a visual support of what is being said. Ask the students to relate their impressions of **El Barrio Gótico.** Have them review what thay have learned about Barcelona. Ask them to discuss **El Tibidabo** and the attractions they might find there. Now read the dialog aloud, relating the photos to the text by stopping to refer to each photo in relation to what you are reading. Then call for choral and individual repetition of the dialog, alternating them to maintain student interest. Ask several students to read the dialog aloud after you have presented it. Discuss the basic content of the dialog after you have allowed the students to read it a second time. Ask several questions to check comprehension.

C 2 Actividad • ¿Es cierto o no?

Have the students correct the false statements. They may exchange papers to correct their work.

C 3 Actividad • Preguntas y respuestas

You may wish to complete the activity orally with books closed.

SLOWER-PACED LEARNING   Have each student work with a partner to complete the activity. Remind the students to refer to the dialog if necessary.

C4   **Sabes que . . .**   🔲

Ask the students to read the cultural note silently. They should try to guess the meaning of unfamiliar words, using the general sentence context to help them. Explain the meanings of any words or expressions the students may not be able to identify.

C5   **SE DICE ASÍ**

Explain to the students that the expressions in the box are used to attract someone's attention. They may be used at the beginning of a statement or alone. You may wish to point out that **¡Oigan!** is used in an informal situation, usually among friends. In a more formal situation, **Escuchen, por favor** should be used. You may wish to have the students practice the expressions in small groups.

C6   **ESTRUCTURAS ESENCIALES**

Introduce **ojalá** by describing some upcoming activities. For example:

> Vamos a tener una fiesta el sábado. ¡Ojalá que no llueva!
> Anita sale para Madrid el viernes. ¡Ojalá que tenga un buen viaje!
> Uds. van a tener un examen pronto. ¡Ojalá que estudien mucho!

You may wish to mention that the word **ojalá** comes from Arabic and means: *"May Allah grant."* Also mention that **ojalá** is always followed by a verb in the subjunctive. You may wish to mention that many Spanish words come from Arabic, such as **alcalde** *(mayor)*, **alcoba** *(alcove)*, **almohada** *(pillow)*, **alfombra** *(carpet)*, **naranja, albaricoque** *(apricot)*, **alcázar** *(fortress)*, **Gibraltar, aljava** *(quiver)*, and **alacena** *(cupboard)*.

C7   **Actividad • ¡Ojalá!**   🔲

Instruct the students to work in pairs to complete the activity orally.

SLOWER-PACED LEARNING   Review the subjunctive verb forms with the students. Then, after completing the activity orally, have the students write the completed sentences.

C8   **Comprensión**   🔲

Sometimes people have difficulty understanding instructions. You will hear ten short conversational exchanges. If the person has understood correctly, check **sí** on your answer sheet. If not, check **no.** For example, you will hear: **Debemos llegar a las seis.** You will also hear the response: **Te dije que es importante que salgas a las seis.** You place your mark in the row labeled **no,** since the person did not understand the instruction.

1. Puedo comer frutas, ¿verdad?
   Te prohibo que comas más verduras.   *no*
2. Víctor está enfermo, ¿no?
   Es una lástima que esté enfermo.   *sí*
3. ¡No puede llover el sábado!
   ¡Oh, no! Ojalá que no llueva.   *sí*

Unidad 11   Teacher's Notes   T227

4. Mamá, voy a salir con Quique.
   Te dije que no te permito que salgas ahora. *sí*
5. Vas a llegar a tiempo al colegio, ¿no?
   Ojalá que salga a buena hora. *sí*
6. Hace mucho frío. ¿Dónde está tu suéter?
   Quieres que me ponga el abrigo, ¿verdad? *no*
7. Tenemos que comprar los boletos para Madrid.
   ¿Prefieres que vayamos a la agencia de viajes? *sí*
8. Alicia va a Costa Rica y no habla mucho español.
   Es indispensable que estudie el idioma. *sí*
9. Tengo mucha hambre. ¿Qué hay de comer?
   ¿Quieres que apague la televisión? *no*
10. Podemos considerarte para el puesto de secretaria.
    Entonces es indispensable que llene la solicitud de empleo. *sí*

Now check your answers. *Read each exchange again and give the correct answer.*

C9 Actividad • Nuestros deseos

Before asking students to begin the activity, brainstorm with them several things they wish might happen. Then allow them to work in pairs. You may wish to ask the students to write two or three of their wishes on paper. Collect the papers and read several aloud to the class. Encourage the students to identify the author of each wish.

C10 Actividad • El señor Carpineto

Instruct the students to write the paragraph and to fill in the blanks with the correct forms of the verbs. Remind them of the various forms of each verb to be used, and that directly after a preposition or another verb, they must use an infinitive. For correction, prepare a transparency of the activity and ask the students to dictate the sentences with the correct verb forms.

C11 Actividad • ¿Qué pasa?

Ask the students to state what is happening in each illustration. For writing practice, have them write the sentences on the board or a transparency. Correct the sentences with the help of the entire class.

C12 Actividad • ¡Cuéntame de ti!

As a variation, instruct the students to form groups of three. Tell groups to write ten characteristics of a good friend. When the groups have finished (within a time limit of ten to twelve minutes), review the characteristics and ask the students to choose the ten they consider the most important.

C13 SITUACIÓN • Saludos desde Barcelona

Play the cassette or have the students read the postcards silently. Discuss the content of each one. Ask them to summarize in their own words the most important facts they have learned. Call on volunteers to present their summaries orally to the class.

C 14   Actividad • **Preguntas y respuestas**

Do this activity orally with books closed.

SLOWER-PACED LEARNING   Instruct the students to answer the questions in complete sentences. You may wish to allow them to work in pairs. Review the answers with the entire class.

> ANSWERS:
> 1. Los jóvenes les escriben postales a sus familiares, a Vicente y a su profesora, la señora Morse.
> 2. Isabel pudo ver toda la ciudad.
> 3. A Beatriz le gustó la iglesia de la Sagrada Familia y el parque de Montjuich.
> 4. Visitaron El Pueblo Español.
> 5. Las playas de la Costa Brava son bellísimas.
> 6. La sardana es el baile típico de Cataluña.
> 7. A los jóvenes les encanta la comida catalana.
> 8. Todas las noches caminan por Las Ramblas.

C 15   Actividad • **¡A escoger!**

Ask the students to complete the activity as though it were a short quiz. Review the answers with the class.

C 16   **Sabes que . . .**

The **sardana** is a folk dance characteristic of the region of Catalonia, Spain. The dance probably originated hundreds of years ago. The **sardana** is made up of complex steps that change according to the music. The **sardanistas** join hands to form a circle and move to the rhythm of the music played by an eleven-person orchestra, called a **cobla.** The **cobla** is made up of cornets, trombones, a double bass, and small percussion instruments.

C 17   **ESTRUCTURAS ESENCIALES**

Discuss the meanings of **tal vez** and **quizás.** Explain that these expressions are used to refer to possibilities.

> Es posible que vayamos a México. Tal vez vayamos a México.
> Es posible que visite Barcelona. Quizás visite Barcelona.

Ask the students to generalize about the meanings of the sentences and of the two new expressions. When they understand the structure, review the material in the text.

C 18   Actividad • **Tal vez**

Write the model on the board and read it aloud to the students. Then have the students complete the activity orally, using the cassette or calling on individual students.

     You may also prefer to have each student complete the activity with a partner. Review the answers with them when they have finished. Then present the following questions and ask the students to respond using **quizás** or **tal vez.**

> ¿Vamos a dar un viaje a México?
> ¿Quién va a ganar el partido de béisbol esta semana?
> ¿Uds. van a tener un examen pronto?

C19 Actividad • Quizás

You may wish to do this activity orally, using the cassette or calling on individual students to form the sentences with **quizás.** For writing practice, have the students complete the activity on paper. Correct the sentences by asking volunteers to write them on the board. Review with the entire class. Ask them then to use **tal vez** or **quizás** to form three sentences about the future, perhaps about things they would like to see happen in their school or community within the next ten years. Review the expressions in a general discussion with the class. Write some of the suggestions on the board or a transparency.

C20 Actividad • ¡A escribir tarjetas postales!

Assign the activity for homework. If you have contact with another Spanish teacher in your school or in another school, ask the students to exchange the postcards they have written in Spanish.

C21 Actividad • Repasando lo que he aprendido

Before the students begin the activity, you may wish to re-enter the indicative mood. Remind the students that the indicative mood is used to describe events that are real, factual, and definite. Write a few examples on the board.

For writing practice, have the students write the completed paragraph. You may wish to copy the paragraph onto the board or a transparency and to call on volunteers to give their answers. Once the paragraph is completed, read it aloud to the class.

C22 Actividad • ¡A escribir y a hablar!

Complete the writing activity in class. Provide suggestions and help as needed. Collect and correct the papers. You may wish to ask the students to prepare oral presentations based on their descriptions.

· TRY
YOUR
SKILLS

OBJECTIVE   To recombine communicative functions, grammar, and vocabulary

CULTURAL BACKGROUND   Allow the students to make statements about what they have learned about Barcelona. You may wish to make a list of the statements on the board or a transparency.

1 En la agencia de viajes

For cooperative learning, have the students work in groups to prepare a short skit for the class. Remind them that the scene takes place in a travel agency. Two students should play the roles of the tourist and the travel agent. Encourage them to use the vocabulary they learned in Sections A, B, and C. Finally, call on volunteers to present their dialogs to the class.

SLOWER-PACED LEARNING   Before the students begin the activity, review the information in the map. Point out the location of each of the numbered items. Then ask each student to work with a partner and write an original dialog, using the information in the map. You may also wish to refer the students to the dialog in A14 on page 374 to use as a model.

2 Actividad • Mi familia y yo

Instruct the students to complete the sentences. Then permit them to share their comments with partners. Ask for volunteers to share their ideas with the class as a review. Remind the students that they must use the subjunctive when forming the sentences and that the word **que** will appear in each sentence.

3 Actividad • Buscando algo perfecto

Allow the students to work in pairs to write at least five sentences. You may wish to suggest that they cut out magazine pictures of hotels, stores, and restaurants to accompany their sentences.

4 Actividad • El premio

Brainstorm with the entire class the commands that will lead to receiving the award. Write the suggestions on the board or a transparency.

5 Actividad • Mis recomendaciones para un viaje

Allow the students to work independently to make the suggestions. Call for volunteers to write their best suggestions on the board. Correct their work.

6 Actividad • El lugar donde vivo

Ask each student to prepare a brochure or a one-page advertisement to be placed in a newspaper, advertising the benefits of living in their city or town. You may wish to display the brochures in the classroom.

UNIDAD

SKILLS 7

7 **Dictado**

Write the following paragraph from dictation. First, listen to the paragraph as it is read to you. Then you will hear the paragraph again in short segments, with a pause after each segment to allow you time to write. Finally, you will hear the paragraph again a third time so that you may check your work. Let's begin.

Me alegra mucho que *(pause)* Isabel, Beatriz y Víctor vayan a Barcelona *(pause)* porque es una ciudad muy bonita. *(pause)* Allí podrán ver El Tibidabo *(pause)* y El Pueblo Español. *(pause)* Espero que también *(pause)* den un paseo por Las Ramblas. *(pause)* Es una lástima que *(pause)* Vicente no vaya a Barcelona con ellos.

PRONUNCIACIÓN

Play the cassette or read the explanations aloud. Review the pronunciation of the letters **b** and **v.** Remind the students that both letters are pronounced the same. The difference is the hard or soft sound as indicated by the two groups of words. These letters should never be pronounced like the English *v.* Allow the students to practice pronouncing the words and sentences.

Actividad • Práctica de pronunciación

Read the sentences aloud to the students. Then call on volunteers to read one sentence at a time. Correct their pronunciation when necessary.

¿LO SABES?

SECTION A

As a variation, have the students work in groups of three to write short dialogs between a travel agent and two customers. The travel agent should ask one customer about the accommodations he or she would like and the second customer should make suggestions. Each group should present its dialog to the class.

SECTION B

Instruct the students to prepare notes on various places to visit in their hometown. Allow them to form groups of four in order to make suggestions and come to a consensus. Review the lists with the entire class. To practice the subjunctive, ask the students to write a list of suggestions on how to improve their proficiency in Spanish.

SECTION C

Ask the students to suggest five recommendations concerning improvements needed to their school, using **ojalá.** Discuss their ideas.

Continue by having the students write three sentences using **tal vez** and three using **quizás.** Review the material on the board or a transparency. Finally, ask the students to write postcards about their imaginary trips to Barcelona.

VOCABULARIO

You may wish to play the game **Santo y seña** to practice the unit vocabulary. Divide the class into two teams. Ask each team to select a contestant. The contestants should sit in front of the room, facing their teammates and having their backs to the chalkboard. You or a volunteer should write a word from the unit vocabulary on the board so that all but the contestants can see it. The object of the game is for one of the two contestants to guess the word (before the other contestant is able to guess it) from clues provided by his or her teammates. Clues must be single words in Spanish and may be synonyms or antonyms or any word that the contestants might associate with the word on the board. A team member must raise his or her hand and be called upon before giving the one-word clue. Each team must take turns providing clues to its contestant. A correct guess on the first turn is worth ten points. The number of points decreases by one with each incorrect guess.

PRÁCTICA DEL VOCABULARIO

Ask each student to make a list of all the unit vocabulary items that have to do with travel. Then instruct each student to write a short paragraph about a real or an imaginary trip to a place of his or her choice.

As a variation, have each student make a list of all the nouns, adjectives, and verbs in the unit vocabulary list.

VAMOS A LEER

OBJECTIVE   To read for practice and pleasure

Antes de leer

Have the students skim the reading selection to see how many cognates they can find. You may also wish to have them write any vocabulary items they don't understand. Review the words by writing them on the board or a transparency.

Preparación para la lectura

Call on the students to answer the questions orally.

PANORAMA DE ESPAÑA

To create a cultural setting for the reading selection, point out the various regions and cities on Transparencies 34 and 34A or on a map of Spain. Then play the cassette or read the selection aloud, pausing after each section to discuss the content. If possible, have the students bring in books or travel brochures containing photographs of the various regions in Spain.

You may wish to bring a copy of *Cuentos de La Alhambra* by Washington Irving to the class to read a couple of paragraphs aloud to the students.

Actividad • Preguntas y respuestas

Have the students work with a partner to answer the questions. For writing practice, have them write complete sentences. Remind the students to refer to the reading selection, if necessary.

ANSWERS:
1. La capital de España está en la región de Castilla.
2. Porque sus murallas son del siglo once.
3. La ciudad más turística de España es Toledo.
4. El Greco era un pintor.
5. Los catalanes hablan catalán. Los vascos hablan euskera.
6. En la región de Andalucía hay muchas flores en las ventanas.
7. La ciudad turística de Toledo está cerca de Madrid.

Actividad • ¿Cuál es la ciudad o región?

SLOWER-PACED LEARNING   Write the activity on the board or a transparency. Then call on volunteers to match the city or region to the correct description. If the students are unsure of the answers, review the selection.

Actividad • ¡A escoger!

CHALLENGE   Have each student write five additional questions based on the reading selection. Then have the students exchange papers to answer one another's questions.

Actividad • Charla

This is an optional activity. Divide the class into groups of three or four students to discuss which places they would like to visit in Spain.

UNIDAD 11

¡Qué bonita es Barcelona!

Traveling to a foreign city can be nerve-racking and at the same time very rewarding. If the place happens to be Barcelona, you will be exposed to one of the oldest civilizations in Europe as well as one of the most beautiful ports on the Mediterranean Sea. You will also profit by meeting young Catalonians and by experiencing the life and culture of this magnificent city.

In this unit you will:

SECTION A	express emotions . . . express agreement or lack of preference . . . express approval
SECTION B	express what is needed or expected . . . express probability or denial . . . make suggestions
SECTION C	attract attention . . . express uncertainty
TRY YOUR SKILLS	use what you've learned
VAMOS A LEER	read for practice and pleasure

SECTION A

expressing emotions . . . expressing agreement or lack of preference . . . expressing approval or satisfaction

Planning a trip is exciting, but it requires the cooperation of everyone. Where do you want to go? What do you want to see? How long can everyone stay?

A1

Un viaje a Barcelona

Isabel, Jimmy, Beatriz y Víctor son cuatro compañeros de clase que se acaban de graduar de la escuela secundaria. Han ahorrado dinero durante todo el año para ir de viaje a España con los padres de Isabel, quienes han prometido llevarlos a todos por haber sacado buenas notas. Jimmy y Víctor están de visita en casa de Isabel cuando entra Beatriz.

BEATRIZ   Hola, ¿qué hay de nuevo? Me alegro de que ya estén planeando el viaje. ¿Por fin, han decidido adónde iremos?

JIMMY   Víctor quiere que vayamos a Madrid, pero yo espero que podamos ir a Barcelona.

BEATRIZ   Sí, la profesora dijo que era una de las ciudades más bonitas de España. ¿No se acuerdan? Además allí se celebrarán las próximas olimpiadas.

VÍCTOR   ¿Qué crees tú, Isabel?

ISABEL   Mamá teme que no haya tiempo para visitar las dos ciudades. Recuerden que sólo tenemos dos semanas.

VÍCTOR   Bueno, en ese caso me da igual . . . Isabel, vamos a decirle que preferimos ir a Barcelona.

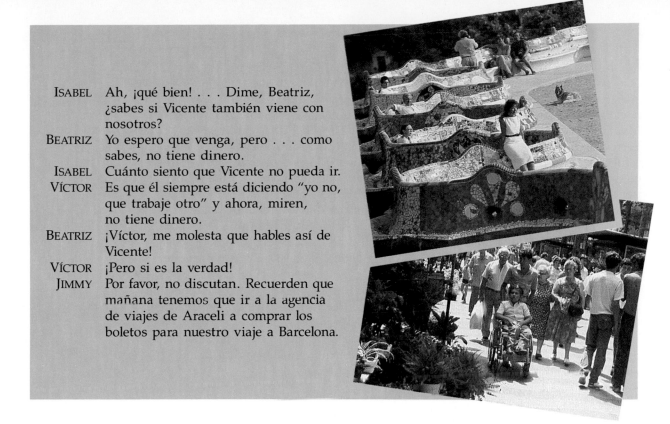

ISABEL   Ah, ¡qué bien! . . . Dime, Beatriz, ¿sabes si Vicente también viene con nosotros?

BEATRIZ   Yo espero que venga, pero . . . como sabes, no tiene dinero.

ISABEL   Cuánto siento que Vicente no pueda ir.

VÍCTOR   Es que él siempre está diciendo "yo no, que trabaje otro" y ahora, miren, no tiene dinero.

BEATRIZ   ¡Víctor, me molesta que hables así de Vicente!

VÍCTOR   ¡Pero si es la verdad!

JIMMY   Por favor, no discutan. Recuerden que mañana tenemos que ir a la agencia de viajes de Araceli a comprar los boletos para nuestro viaje a Barcelona.

A2   Actividad • Preguntas y respuestas

Use the information in A1 to answer the following questions.

1. ¿Quiénes son Isabel, Jimmy, Beatriz y Víctor?   Son cuatro compañeros de clase que se acaban de graduar de la escuela secundaria.
2. ¿Con quiénes van ellos en el viaje?   Van con los padres de Isabel.
3. ¿De qué se alegra Beatriz?   Beatriz se alegra de que ya estén planeando el viaje.
4. ¿Qué dijo de Barcelona la profesora?   La profesora dijo que era una de las ciudades más bonitas de España.
5. ¿Qué ciudades quieren visitar los chicos?   Los chicos quieren visitar Madrid y Barcelona.
6. ¿Qué teme la mamá de Isabel?   La mamá de Isabel teme que no haya tiempo para visitar las dos ciudades.
7. ¿Por qué no puede ir Vicente?   Vicente no puede ir porque no tiene dinero.
8. ¿Qué es lo que siempre está diciendo Vicente?   Vicente siempre está diciendo "yo no, que trabaje otro".
9. ¿Dónde van a comprar los boletos para el viaje?   Van a comprar los boletos para el viaje en la agencia de viajes de Araceli.

A3   Actividad • ¿Es cierto o no?

Decide whether each statement is true or false according to A1. Correct the false statements.

1. Los chicos se acaban de graduar de la universidad.
2. Los padres de Isabel les han prometido llevarlos a Chile.
3. Jimmy y Víctor están en la escuela.
4. Las próximas olimpiadas se celebrarán en Madrid.
5. Los chicos han ahorrado dinero porque quieren trabajar.
6. A Víctor le da igual ir a Barcelona o a Madrid.
7. Los cuatro compañeros van de viaje a Barcelona.

1. Los chicos se acaban de graduar de la escuela secundaria. 2. Los padres de Isabel les han prometido llevarlos a España. 3. Isabel, Jimmy, Beatriz y Víctor estaban en la misma escuela. 4. Las próximas olimpiadas se celebrarán en Barcelona. 5. Los chicos han ahorrado dinero porque quieren viajar. 6. Es cierto. 7. Es cierto.

Cataluña, una de las regiones más ricas de España, es como un país dentro de otro país. Los catalanes tienen su idioma, sus costumbres y sus tradiciones propias. ¿Por qué? Pues porque durante la Edad Media (*Middle Ages*) Cataluña era una nación aparte. Su influencia militar y mercantil (*trade*) se extendía por todo el mar Mediterráneo desde Valencia hasta Grecia. En 1469 Isabel de Castilla se casó con Fernando de Aragón. Al unirse los reinos de Castilla y de Aragón, Cataluña pasó a formar parte de España. Para mantener su identidad, los catalanes insistieron en conservar su idioma y sus leyes. En 1978 España dio autonomía a Cataluña, y así pueden elegir (*elect*) su gobierno local y decidir muchas cuestiones, entre ellas, asuntos mercantiles, educacionales, de la industria y de la vivienda (*housing*).

Cataluña es una región industrializada con mucho progreso y una economía dinámica. Cataluña es también una región muy hermosa. Tiene bellas playas en la Costa Brava y montañas preciosas. Es una de las regiones más turísticas de España.

Barcelona es la capital de Cataluña y su ciudad más importante. Es interesante destacar (*to note*) que fue en Barcelona hace casi quinientos años donde Cristóbal Colón le informó a los Reyes Católicos, Isabel y Fernando, que había llegado a la India, pues Colón no sabía que esas tierras eran la América. En Barcelona existe una réplica de una de las carabelas (*ships*) de Colón. También hay un monumento en su honor.

SE DICE ASÍ
Expressing emotions

¡Cuánto me alegro de que...!	I am so happy that...!
¡Estoy muy contento de que...!	I am so pleased that...!
Me sorprende mucho que...	It surprises me a lot that...
Siento tanto que...	I am sorry that...
Me molesta que...	It bothers me that...

To express how you feel about someone or something, use the subjunctive after **que**.

A 6 Actividad • La excursión de la clase  For answers, see p. T217.

Your friends and you are planning the class trip. Pair up with a classmate and discuss how you feel about how things are going. Follow the model.

MODELO   Estamos contentos...
Daniel / poder traer su radio
Estamos contentos de que Daniel pueda traer su radio.

1. Nos sorprende mucho...
Ernesto / no comprar los refrescos
2. ¡Cuánto me alegro...!
Elenita / poder ir a la excursión
3. Están tan contentos...
nosotros / invitarlos a la excursión
4. Luisa siente tanto...
Miguel / no traer los folletos de la agencia de viajes
5. Me molesta...
Juan y Lucía / no ayudar con los preparativos

A 7 ESTRUCTURAS ESENCIALES
The use of the subjunctive to express feelings and emotions

Use the subjunctive after **que** whenever the main sentence expresses feelings or emotions, such as hope, pleasure, surprise, regret, fear, or anger.

Me alegro de que ya **estén** planeando el viaje.
I'm glad that you are already planning the trip.

Me sorprende que no **tengas** dinero para el viaje.
It surprises me that you do not have money for the trip.

1. Notice that the subject in the sentence after **que** must be different from the subject in the main clause.

2. Here are some common verbs used to express feelings or emotions in Spanish.

esperar *to hope*	**enojarse** *to be angry*
temer *to fear*	**sorprender** *to surprise*
lamentar *to regret*	**sentir** *to regret*
molestar *to bother*	

ATENCIÓN: If the subject of the two clauses is the same, the second verb will be an infinitive. **Que** is usually dropped.

(yo siento –
yo no puedo)

Yo siento no **poder** ir a Barcelona con ustedes.
I am sorry that I can't go to Barcelona with you.

Actividad • Combinación   Answers will vary.

Combine an element from each column to form complete sentences.

Sentimos		tú	no poder ir a Barcelona
Me enoja		Beatriz	no comprar los boletos
Nos encanta		Jimmy y Víctor	ir a la agencia de viajes
Temen	que	el avión	salir tarde
Le sorprende		los viajes	costar tan caros
Me gusta		la agente	no dar la información
Él espera		Vicente y yo	volver pronto del viaje
Ellos lamentan		yo	no llegar a tiempo al aeropuerto

A9   Actividad • En el aeropuerto

Imagine that you are at the airport and things are not going well. Express your reactions by following the model.

MODELO   Me enoja / tú / no mirar los horarios
Me enoja que tú no mires los horarios.

1. Me sorprende / el avión / no llegar a tiempo   Me sorprende que el avión no llegue a tiempo.
2. Me molesta / los niños / estar gritando   Me molesta que los niños estén gritando.
3. Lamento / el piloto / no hablar español   Lamento que el piloto no hable español.
4. No me gusta / tú / no tener paciencia   No me gusta que tú no tengas paciencia.
5. Me enoja / nosotros / no ir a Barcelona   Me enoja que nosotros no vayamos a Barcelona.
6. Siento / las maletas / no estar aquí   Siento que las maletas no estén aquí.
7. Temo / nosotros / perder el avión   Temo que nosotros perdamos el avión.
8. Espero / el próximo viaje / ser mejor   Espero que el próximo viaje sea mejor.

A10   Actividad • ¡A conversar!   Answers will vary.

Pair up with a classmate and tell each other three things that you like and three things that you dislike about traveling. Use the present subjunctive.

MODELO   Siento que tengamos que esperar tanto.

A11   SE DICE ASÍ
Expressing agreement or lack of preference

No me importa.	I don't care.
Me da igual.	It's the same to me.
Me da lo mismo.	It's the same to me.
Como quieras.	As you wish.
De acuerdo.	Okay.

Actividad • **Me da igual** Answers will vary. Possible answers are given.

Complete the following conversation by using the expressions in A11.

TOMÁS Víctor, ¿quieres ir a El Sombrero o a El Marino?
VÍCTOR _____. Me da igual.
  (En el restaurante)
TOMÁS ¿Nos sentamos en esta mesa o en aquélla?
VÍCTOR _____. Como quieras.
TOMÁS ¿Quieres comer paella o enchiladas?
VÍCTOR _____. No me importa.
TOMÁS ¿Qué prefieres, agua mineral o un refresco?
VÍCTOR _____. Y de postre, ¿te gusta el bizcocho de fresas o el
  de chocolate? Me da igual.
TOMÁS _____. Me da lo mismo.
  (Después de comer)
TOMÁS ¿Pagamos la cuenta?
VÍCTOR _____. De acuerdo.

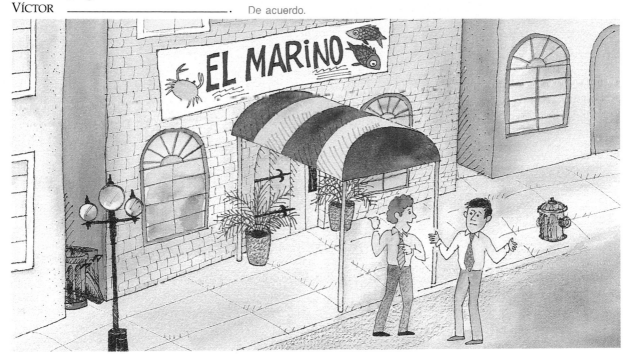

A13 Comprensión For script, see p. T219.

You will hear ten exchanges between several people. Each exchange will express
approval or disapproval. If the people are pleased, check **¡fantástico!** on your
answer sheet. If not, check **¡qué horror!**

MODELO —¿Qué te parece la idea de visitar Barcelona?
  —Me encanta que podamos conocer esa ciudad.

	0	1	2	3	4	5	6	7	8	9	10
¡Fantástico!	✔					✔		✔	✔	✔	
¡Qué horror!		✔	✔	✔	✔		✔				✔

Al día siguiente el grupo va a la agencia de viajes Universal para comprar los boletos. Allí los atiende Araceli Valdés, la propietaria.

ARACELI   Hola, ¿qué dice la pandilla? ¿Cómo está Ud., Sra. Vélez?
           Ya me han dicho que piensan ir de viaje este verano.
SRA. VÉLEZ Sí, Araceli. Estamos muy entusiasmados con nuestro viaje a
           Barcelona. ¿Qué vuelo nos puedes conseguir que no cueste mucho?
JIMMY   Buscamos un vuelo que sea sin escala.
SRA. VÉLEZ Silencio, Jimmy, deja trabajar a Araceli.
ARACELI   *(mirando la computadora)* Aquí les
           tengo un vuelo sin escala con una
           tarifa especial de $480.00 por
           persona, ida y vuelta. Es una
           ganga, pero tienen que salir antes
           del 15 de julio.
VÍCTOR   ¡Bárbaro! Danos los boletos ahora
           mismo.
SRA. VÉLEZ Está bien Araceli. Reserva los pasajes
           para el 30 de junio y el regreso para
           el catorce de agosto.
ARACELI   Sra. Vélez, ¿quiere que les haga
           reservaciones en un hotel?
SRA. VÉLEZ Sí, necesitamos tres habitaciones que
           tengan baño privado.
ISABEL   Araceli, por favor, preferimos que las
           habitaciones tengan aire
           acondicionado.
ARACELI   *(tecleando)* Bueno, les he conseguido
           tres habitaciones con aire
           acondicionado y baño privado en el
           hotel "Montserrat". Es un hotel de
           tres estrellas y está muy céntrico.
           ¿Algo más?
SRA. VÉLEZ No, Araceli. Muchas gracias, muy
           amable.
ARACELI   De nada. ¡Feliz viaje!

A 15 Actividad • Preguntas y respuestas  For answers, see p. T219– 220.

Refer to the dialog in A14 to answer the following questions.

1. ¿A qué van los chicos a la agencia de viajes?
2. ¿Quién es Araceli Valdés?
3. ¿Qué vuelo les consigue Araceli?
4. ¿Cuánto cuesta el vuelo?
5. ¿Cuándo regresan?

6. ¿Qué clase de habitaciones necesita el grupo?
7. ¿Cómo se llama el hotel que les ha conseguido Araceli?
8. ¿De cuántas estrellas es?
9. ¿Qué le desea Araceli al grupo?

SE DICE ASÍ
Expressing approval or satisfaction with emphasis

¡Maravilloso!	Marvelous!
¡Fantástico!	Fantastic!
¡Regio!	Great!
¡Fabuloso!	Fabulous!
¡Magnífico!	Super!
¡De película!	Out of this world!
¡Bárbaro!	Awesome!

A 17 ESTRUCTURAS ESENCIALES
The use of the subjunctive to express the indefinite

1. Use the subjunctive after **que** to express something that is indefinite.

   Quiero una habitación que **tenga** baño privado.
   I want a room that has a private bathroom.

   Busco un restaurante que **sirva** comida catalana.
   I am looking for a restaurant that serves Catalonian food.

   ATENCIÓN: Notice the use of the indefinite article (**un, una**).

2. If the main clause refers to something definite, specific, and certain, the indicative is used.

   Quiero la habitación que **tiene** baño privado.
   I want the room that has a private bathroom.

   Busco el restaurante que **sirve** comida catalana.
   I am looking for the restaurant that serves Catalonian food.

   ATENCIÓN: Notice the use of the definite article (**el, la**).

You may write the following on the board:
Main clause   Subordinate clause
"Quiero una habitación que tenga baño privado."
          something in-   verb
          definite or   in the
          nonexistent   subjunctive
"Quiero la habitación que tiene baño privado."
          specific   verb
          room   in Ind.
You may wish to ask the students to provide other examples, and write them on the board.

A 18 Actividad • ¡A completar!

Complete each sentence with the correct form of the verb in parentheses.

1. Quiero una habitación que (tener) ____ aire acondicionado.   tenga
2. Busco un vuelo que (ser) ____ sin escala.   sea
3. Quiero dos habitaciones que (tener) ____ vista a la calle.   tengan
4. Buscamos un amigo que (querer) ____ ir con nosotros.   quiera
5. ¿Sabes dónde está el guía que (hablar) ____ español?   habla
6. Necesito ir a una agencia de viajes que (vender) ____ boletos baratos.   venda
7. Busco a un secretario que (llegar) ____ a tiempo.   llegue
8. Quiero cenar en el restaurante que (servir) ____ platos mexicanos.   sirve

A 19 Actividad • ¿Y tú qué piensas?   Answers will vary.

Express your opinion about traveling by answering the following questions.

1. ¿Qué te gusta hacer cuando estás de vacaciones?
2. ¿Qué países te gustaría visitar? ¿Por qué?
3. ¿Cómo preferirías viajar a esos países?
4. ¿Por qué es importante hacer reservaciones en un hotel?
5. ¿Por qué es bueno conseguir una tarifa especial?
6. Quieres hacer un viaje a un país extranjero, pero no tienes dinero. ¿Qué harías tú?

A 20 Actividad • Mi mundo de fantasía   Answers will vary.

Get together with two of your classmates. Each of you will create your own fantasy world. Here is a hint:

> Busco un lugar que sea hermoso, donde no haya contaminación y donde pueda ser muy feliz . . .

A 21 Actividad • En la agencia de viajes   Answers will vary.

Work with a partner and play the roles of a travel agent and a client. The "client" should ask questions about his or her travel arrangements. The "travel agent" should make suggestions and answer the "client's" questions. Use A14 as a guide.

A 22 Actividad • ¡A escribir y a hablar!   Answers will vary.

Write about a real or imaginary trip you plan to take. Use the following suggestions to develop it.

    I. Introducción: Tu viaje a . . .
        A. ¿Por qué quieres dar el viaje?
        B. ¿Qué lugares visitarías?
        C. ¿Por qué visitarías esos lugares?
        D. ¿Irías solo o con un grupo?
   II. Desarrollo
        A. ¿Cuánto costaría el viaje?
        B. ¿Cómo conseguirías el dinero?
        C. ¿Qué cosas te molestan en un viaje?
        D. ¿Qué tipo de hotel buscas?
        E. ¿Qué clase de vuelo te interesa?
        F. ¿Aprenderías el idioma del país?
  III. Conclusión
        A. Lo que espero aprender en el viaje
        B. Todo lo que me va a gustar del viaje

Now present your composition orally in class.

Arriving at a city such as Barcelona can be confusing at first. But once you check into your hotel, you are ready for an exciting adventure.

B1

En el hotel 📼

Una semana después de comprar los boletos, los padres de Isabel y los muchachos llegan a Barcelona. Pasan por la aduana y después toman un taxi que los lleva al hotel.

EN BARCELONA
HOTEL DUQUES DE BERGARA
★★★★

● **EL MÁS CÉNTRICO**
(Por estar en la plaza de Cataluña.)
● **EL MÁS NUEVO**
(Por haberse inaugurado en octubre de 1987.)
● **EL MÁS BONITO**
(Por estar ubicado en un palacete modernista.)
● **EL MÁS PERSONALIZADO**
(Por el trato humano que nos permite dar sus 56 habitaciones.)
● **EL MÁS MODERNO**
(Por TV mando distancia, antena parabólica, 4 canales música, aire acondicionado, mini-bar, ascensor panorámico, etc.).

C/ BERGARA, 11 (JUNTO A LA PLAZA DE CATALUÑA)
Tel. 93/ 301 51 51. Télex 98718-APRO. Fax 93/ 418 51 57

(En la recepción del hotel los atiende el recepcionista.)

RECEPCIONISTA   Buenos días. ¿En qué puedo servirles?

SR. VÉLEZ   Buenos días. Tenemos reservaciones a nombre de Luis y María Eugenia Vélez.

Hotel a su medida

Alójese en el Hotel que mejor se adapte a su gusto y posibilidades. En Viajes Melia, gracias al sistema ME-[...]ectado con las principales cadenas [...]tra amplia red de oficinas propias en [...]tranjero, podemos proporcionarle la [...]ión sobre precios, situación, cali[...] cada Hotel.

PASE PARA ABORDAR
BOARDING PASS

VUELO / FLIGHT   FECHA / DATE
TRANSITO   ASIENTO / SEAT No.
DESTINO / DESTINATION

ROGAMOSLE PASAR DE INMEDIATO A LA SALA

PLEASE PROCEED AT ONCE TO GATE

RECEPCIONISTA   *(mirando la lista y luego, sacando las llaves del casillero)*   Aquí están las llaves. Ahora es importante que Uds. firmen el registro y me entreguen los pasaportes.

JIMMY   ¿Por qué es necesario que le entreguemos los pasaportes?

RECEPCIONISTA   Porque es preciso que les tome las señas. Después los pueden recoger aquí.

SR. VÉLEZ   ¿Quién se encarga del equipaje?

RECEPCIONISTA   Ahora mismo vendrá el botones. Él se encargará del equipaje. Sus habitaciones están en el quinto piso. Pueden tomar el ascensor que está a la derecha del vestíbulo.

EL GRUPO   Muchas gracias, señor.

RECEPCIONISTA   *(sonriéndose y mirando a los chicos)* Estoy aquí para servirles en cualquier cosa que necesiten, ¿vale?

1. El grupo llega a Barcelona una semana después de comprar los boletos.
2. Toman un taxi para ir al hotel.
3. Los padres de Isabel se llaman Luis y María Eugenia Vélez.

4. Les pide que firmen el registro y entreguen los pasaportes.
5. Porque es preciso que les tome las señas.
6. El botones se encargará del equipaje.

B2 **Actividad • Preguntas y respuestas**

Use the information from the dialog in B1 to answer the following questions.

1. ¿Cuándo llega el grupo a Barcelona?
2. ¿Qué toman ellos para ir al hotel?
3. ¿Cómo se llaman los padres de Isabel?
4. ¿Qué les pide el recepcionista?
5. ¿Por qué es necesario que le entreguen los pasaportes al recepcionista?
6. ¿De qué se encargará el botones?
7. ¿En qué piso están las habitaciones?
8. ¿Dónde está el ascensor?

7. Las habitaciones están en el quinto piso.
8. El ascensor está a la derecha del vestíbulo.

B3 **Sabes que . . .**

Para unas vacaciones inolvidables (*unforgettable*) pocos lugares superan (*surpass*) a España. ¡Cómo cambia el escenario, las comidas y las costumbres! El gobierno sabe que el turismo es muy importante y ofrece lo mejor a precios muy razonables.

Agencias del gobierno controlan los precios de hoteles y restaurantes de acuerdo a categorías específicas. La categoría se determina por medio de estrellas. Cinco estrellas es la más alta distinción. Muy pocos establecimientos la obtienen. Los precios aumentan con las estrellas. Hay hoteles, hostales, pensiones (*bed and breakfasts*) y refugios. Los refugios están situados en las montañas para la conveniencia de los amantes de la naturaleza (*nature lovers*).

El gobierno administra los albergues (*lodges*) nacionales que se llaman paradores. Son hoteles de gran categoría. Los paradores están en los lugares apartados (*separated*) de todas las regiones en monumentos históricos, castillos, conventos y palacios. Tienen todas las comodidades modernas y los precios son muy razonables.

Iberotel en la Costa del Sol

Si busca algo más allá de las 4 estrellas...

El Iberotel Atalaya Park es un cuatro estrellas con un servicio eficiente y flexible que satisface n creces todas las ecesidades de sus ntes. Y eso, créanos, nota.

★★★★
Atalaya Park

Marbella-Estepona
Tel. (952) 78.01.50
Sra. Pilar Herrera

iberotel
La cadena creada
por amor al ocio

PARADOR NACIONAL DE LA ARRUZAFA CORDOBA

¡BUENOS DIAS!
¡BON JOUR!
¡GOOD MORNING!

B4 **SE DICE ASÍ**
Expressing what is needed or expected

Es importante que firmen el registro.	It is important that you sign the record book.
Es necesario que le entreguemos los pasaportes.	It is necessary that we give her the passports.
Es preciso que les tome las señas.	It is essential that he take down your personal descriptions.

B5 ESTRUCTURAS ESENCIALES
The use of the subjunctive in impersonal expressions

1. The subjunctive is used after impersonal expressions that indicate doubt, necessity, probability, denial, and uncertainty when the clause after **que** has a subject expressed or understood.

Es importante que **tú tengas** reservaciones.	*It is important that you have reservations.*
No es necesario que **(Ud.) compre** los boletos hoy.	*It is not necessary that you buy the tickets today.*
Es mejor que **Luis y Víctor vayan** a casa.	*It is better that Luis and Víctor go home.*

2. Here are some of the most common impersonal expressions used in Spanish:

Es difícil	*It is difficult*	**Es imposible**	*It is impossible*
Es dudoso	*It is doubtful*	**Es probable**	*It is probable*
Es fácil	*It is easy*	**Es increíble**	*It is incredible*
Es mejor	*It is better*	**Es una lástima**	*It is a pity*
Es indispensable	*It is indispensable*	**Es preciso**	*It is essential*

ATENCIÓN: The indicative is used after impersonal expressions that convey certainty.

Es cierto que Isabel **está** en Barcelona.	*It is true that Isabel is in Barcelona.*
Es verdad que ellos **tienen** reservaciones.	*It is true that they have reservations.*
Es seguro que ellos **van** a Madrid.	*It is certain that they are going to Madrid.*

B6 Actividad • ¡Es increíble!

Complete the following sentences with the subjunctive or indicative, as appropriate.

1. Es difícil que tú (poder) graduarte.   Es difícil que tú puedas graduarte.
2. Es cierto que Inés (estar) en España.   Es cierto que Inés está en España.
3. Es fácil que Ricardo (tener) veinticinco pesos.   Es fácil que Ricardo tenga veinticinco pesos.
4. Es increíble que el coche (gastar) tanta gasolina.   Es increíble que el coche gaste tanta gasolina.
5. Es probable que ellos (llamar) por teléfono.   Es probable que ellos llamen por teléfono.
6. Es mejor que tú (venir) por la mañana.   Es mejor que tú vengas por la mañana.
7. Es seguro que Juan (sacar) buena nota en el examen.   Es seguro que Juan saca buena nota en el examen.
8. Es verdad que abuelita (llegar) esta noche.   Es verdad que abuelita llega esta noche.

B7 Actividad • Combinación   Answers will vary.

By combining elements from each column, form eight sentences. Follow the model.

MODELO   Es difícil que yo viaje a Barcelona.

Es imposible que	el grupo	estar	pronto del viaje
Es probable que	yo	dar	reservaciones
Es dudoso que	tus amigos	llegar	al aeropuerto a la una
Es necesario que	Víctor y yo	regresar	de su viaje el lunes
Es mejor que	Orlando y tú	pedir	información sobre Barcelona
Es fácil que	la pandilla	salir	en Puerto Rico
Es verdad que	Javier y Vicente	tener	un viaje a Chile
Es seguro que	Isabel y Beatriz	volver	en ese vuelo

B8 Actividad • Antes de dar un viaje   Answers will vary. For possible answers, see p. T223.

Araceli, the owner of a travel agency, is offering valuable advice to prospective travelers. Find out what she has to say. Follow the model, use an impersonal expression from the box, and begin each sentence with: **Antes de dar un viaje. . . .**

MODELO   Ud. (comprar) los boletos.
Antes de dar un viaje, es importante que Ud.
compre los boletos.

1. Uds. (hacer) reservaciones en un hotel.
2. Julio Mario (tener) su pasaporte listo.
3. Los turistas (conseguir) una tarifa especial.
4. Tú (llegar) a tiempo al aeropuerto.
5. Nosotros (leer) algo sobre el país que pensamos visitar.
6. Uno no (traer) muchas maletas.

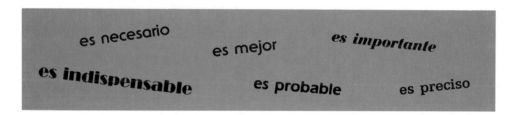

es necesario   es mejor   es importante
es indispensable   es probable   es preciso

B9 Comprensión   For script, see p. T223–224.

You will hear a statement or a question followed by a comment. If the comment is logical, check **lógico** on your answer sheet. If the response is not logical, check **ilógico.**

MODELO   —No podemos salir después de las seis.
—Es dudoso que salgamos antes de las diez.

	0	1	2	3	4	5	6	7	8	9	10
Lógico			✔	✔			✔	✔		✔	✔
Ilógico	✔	✔			✔	✔			✔		

B10 Actividad • Cosas esenciales   Answers will vary. Possible answers are given.

Pair up with a classmate and ask each other for advice. Follow the model.

MODELO   ¿Qué es importante en el mundo del futuro?
Es importante que estudies informática.

1. ¿Qué es necesario para dar un viaje?   Es necesario que lleves una maleta.
2. ¿Qué es preciso para sacar buenas notas?   Es preciso que estudies mucho.
3. ¿Qué es indispensable para hablar español?   Es indispensable que practiques con tus amigos.
4. ¿Qué es necesario para visitar un país extranjero?   Es necesario que tengas tu pasaporte.
5. ¿Qué es importante para conseguir un buen trabajo?   Es importante que te gradúes de la universidad.

Imagine that you are the owner of a hotel. Write a brief brochure advertising your hotel. Pattern your brochure after the models below. Include at least five features of the hotel.

For information on how to present the realia, see p. T224.

HOTEL
ALFONSO XIII
SEVILLA

HOTEL
ALFONSO XIII
SEVILLA

Un exquisito hotel de la más fina tradición. Un monumento inspirado en lo mejor del arte cerámico. Orgullo de Andalucía.

Todos estos elogios describen sólo en parte la majestuosa belleza del Hotel Alfonso XIII, el cual, desde su inauguración en 1928, ha mantenido su conocida reputación de ser el mejor en su clase. Visitantes de la Realeza, Aristócratas, Jefes de Estado, estrellas de cine y teatro, autores y artistas han acreditado su historia.

El suntuoso esplendor de su interior y la tradicional perfección del servicio, aseguran un inmejorable nivel de calidad y confirman su bi merecida fama.

En el exterior, la mágica ciudad de Sevilla of toda su belleza y tesoros históricos.

Situado en el corazón de la ciudad.
112 habitaciones dobles lujosamente amuek
y 18 habitaciones individuales, todas con l
completo, teléfono con línea directa, radio
y mini bar.
Suite Real. 18 Suites Junior.
Aire acondicionado en todo el hotel.
Recepción. Conserjería. Salones. Bares.
Restaurante.
Peluquería. Boutiques.
6 salas de conferencias/banquetes cor
personas.
. Jardines.
parcamiento.

esto
es vida

Lewicz

**HOTEL
GERIATRICO,
HAY UNO SOLO.**

• Terapia ocupacional • Reposo
controlado • Sala de cine • TV color
• Juegos • Excursiones
• Kinesiolog
• Pedicur
• 700
s/hr
de
pv
pe

H

(a 2 c

Tel:

Antillas Holandesas
BONAIRE
La Isla
Excepcional

Excepcionalmente limpia, excepcionalmente amigable, unos paisajes
excepcionales, y unas aguas y una vida
marina excepcionalmente bellas
que la colocan entre los tres primeros
lugares del mundo con las más
perfectas condiciones para gozar del
buceo.
   El Hotel Bonaire y el Casino cuentan
con 145 habitaciones, repartidas en
once edificios separados, diseminados
en 12 acres de terreno costero, y una
playa de blanca y limpia arena, con
transparentes y cristalinas aguas, lo ideal
para nadar, bucear ...o simplemente para
tomar el sol.
   La navegación a vela y los acuaplanos
son gratis...al igual que el tenis durante

el día y el
tarifas sor
desde $3
dos perse
   Hotel
para la D
Excepc
   Para
comuni

HOTEL RESIDENCIA CARMEN

Categoría 4 estrellas. Situado en la zona más céntrica, amplia y
comercial de Granada.
208 habitaciones con terrazas, vistas panorámicas de la Alhambra, Albayzin y Sierra Nevada. Suntuosas suites. 400 plazas.
Aire acondicionado, teléfono, megafonía, T.V., boutique, souve-
nirs, cajas de seguridad y garaje.

Sala de Juntas   Salle de Conférence   Meeting room

**HOTEL
BONAIRE** AND CASINO

Todos descansan el primer día. Al día siguiente, mientras los padres de Isabel van de compras, el grupo se reúne en el vestíbulo del hotel.

JIMMY   Bueno, primero tomemos el desayuno.
VÍCTOR   Sí, tomémoslo ahora mismo.
BEATRIZ   Espérense, sentémonos aquí y
    discutamos lo que vamos a hacer hoy.
ISABEL   De acuerdo. Vamos al Museo de Arte.
JIMMY   No vayamos allí. Primero veamos El Tibidabo.
VÍCTOR   No, nada de eso, visitemos Montjuich.
BEATRIZ   Miren, mejor hablemos con el conserje
    y pidámosle su opinión.
JIMMY   Buena idea, pero desayunemos primero.

(Después de desayunar, todos van al buró del conserje.)

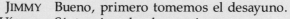

VÍCTOR   Buenos días, señor. ¿Podría
    recomendarnos algunos lugares que
    deberíamos visitar en Barcelona?
CONSERJE   Cómo no. Primero les recomiendo
    que den un paseo a pie por el Barrio
    Gótico, que es muy pintoresco, y
    luego por la tarde, les recomiendo
    que vayan a Montjuich. Más tarde,
    les aconsejo que den un paseo por
    Las Ramblas.
BEATRIZ   Muchas gracias, y ahora . . .
    ¡a conocer Barcelona!

EXCURSIONES RADIALES BARCELONA

EXCURSIONES	SALIDA DEPART	PESETAS	FRECUENCIA
Visita Ciudad Mañana	09,30	1.900	DIARIAS TODO EL AÑO / DAILY ALL YEAR / QUOTIDIENNE TOUT E L'ANNÉE
Visita Ciudad Tarde (GAUDI y PICASSO)	15,30	2.300	
Montserrat Medio día Mañana	09,30	2.750	
Montserrat Medio día Tarde	15,30	2.750	1/4 al 30/9
Gala en Scala Con cena	20,00	7.000	DIARIA (Excepto Domingos, Festivos y Lunes) DAILY (Except Sundays, Holidays and Mondays) QUOTIDIENNE (Excepte Jours de Fête, Dimanches et Lundis) GIORNALIERA (Meno Domenica, Lunedi e Festivo)
Gala en Scala Con consumición	20,00	4.000	
Panorámica de noche y flamenco	22,00	3.900	Diario excepto domingos y festivos Daily excepting sundays and holidays Journalier, à l'exception rien dimanalua y jours de fête
Noche Flamenca Con cena	20,00	6.400	
Costa Brava	09,00	4.800	1/5 al 30/9 Diario excepto domingos Daily excepting sundays Journalier, à l'exception des dimanches
Toros Sombra	A confirmar	5.000	Domingos y días de Corrida. En Temporada Sundays and bullfight days. In season Dimanches et jours de «corrida». En saison
Toros Sol		4.200	
Andorra 1 Día Con almuerzo	06,30	5.000	Lunes-Miércoles-Viernes Monday-Wednesday-Friday Lundi-Mercredi-Vendredi
Andorra 1 Día Sin almuerzo		3.900	

Con la garantía de **JULIATOURS**

B 13 Actividad • ¡A escoger!

Choose the ending that best completes the sentence, according to the information in B12.

1. Los jóvenes se reúnen en
   • la recepción.   • la habitación.   • el vestíbulo.
2. Jimmy dice:
   • tomemos el desayuno.   • vamos al Museo de Arte.   • visitemos Montjuich.
3. Los chicos piden la opinión
   • del recepcionista.   • del conserje.   • de Beatriz.
4. Isabel quiere ir
   • al Museo de Arte.   • a El Tibidabo.   • a Montjuich.
5. El conserje recomienda que por la tarde
   • visiten el Museo de Arte.   • vayan a Montjuich.   • vayan a El Tibidabo.

El Montjuich es una colina *(hill)* desde la cual puede verse la ciudad de Barcelona. En una de las laderas *(sides)* está la Plaza España con réplicas de las distintas regiones del país. ¡Qué variedad de pueblos! La Feria Mundial de 1929 se celebró en este lugar y los pabellones *(pavilions)* son los restos de este evento. Detrás de la plaza hay una fuente luminosa. Desde allí los turistas tienen una vista fabulosa de la ciudad. En lo alto de la otra ladera hay un castillo y también un jardín precioso, un estadio y el teatro griego. En el verano ofrecen obras clásicas. De este lado de la colina está el Miramar con una vista maravillosa del mar y de la ciudad.

B15 ESTRUCTURAS ESENCIALES
Softened commands

1. To make a suggestion similar to English *Let's . . .* , Spanish uses **ir a** + an infinitive construction.

Vamos a estudiar.	*Let's study.*
Vamos a comer.	*Let's eat.*
Vamos a abrir la tienda.	*Let's open the store.*

2. Another way of suggesting politely is to use the **nosotros(as)** form of the present subjunctive as a command.

Estudiemos.	*Let's study.*
Comamos.	*Let's eat.*
Abramos la tienda.	*Let's open the store.*

3. Remember that when object pronouns are used with command forms, the object pronouns are placed immediately after the verb and are written as a single word. Notice that an accent is added to keep the stress on the same syllable.

Estudiemos la lección.	**Estudiémosla.**
Comamos el almuerzo.	**Comámoslo.**
Abramos la tienda.	**Abrámosla.**

You may wish to mention that some of the first person plural forms of the commands with pronouns attached are not often used in speech. For example, it is more common to say *Comamos el almuerzo* than *Comámoslo,* which would sound stilted.

B 16 Actividad • Esto tiene que cambiar

Change each sentence to a softened command by following the model.

MODELO Vamos a cambiar impresiones sobre Barcelona.
Cambiemos impresiones sobre Barcelona.

1. Vamos a leer un libro sobre Barcelona.   Leamos un libro sobre Barcelona.
2. Vamos a tomar el desayuno ahora mismo.   Tomemos el desayuno ahora mismo.
3. Vamos a comprar los boletos en la agencia.   Compremos los boletos en la agencia.
4. Vamos a hablar con el conserje.   Hablemos con el conserje.
5. Vamos a visitar el Museo de Arte.   Visitemos el Museo de Arte.
6. Vamos a escribir una tarjeta postal.   Escribamos una tarjeta postal.
7. Vamos a trabajar para ahorrar dinero.   Trabajemos para ahorrar dinero.
8. Vamos a aprender más acerca de Barcelona.   Aprendamos más acerca de Barcelona.

B 17 Actividad • Sigamos al líder

Work with a classmate and ask each other the following questions. Follow the model.

1. Sí, entreguemos las maletas.   2. Sí, vayamos a la sala de espera.   3. Sí llamemos a nuestros amigos.   4. Sí, comamos algo.   5. Sí, cambiemos los cheques de viajero.   6. Sí, compremos algo para leer en el avión. 7. Sí, consigamos un periódico en español.   8. Sí, sentémonos a esperar el vuelo.   9. Sí, escribamos unas tarjetas postales.   10. Sí, subamos al avión.

MODELO ¿Comemos en la cafetería?
Sí, **comamos** en la cafetería.

1. ¿Entregamos las maletas?
2. ¿Vamos a la sala de espera?
3. ¿Llamamos a nuestros amigos?
4. ¿Comemos algo?
5. ¿Cambiamos los cheques de viajero?

6. ¿Compramos algo para leer en el avión?
7. ¿Conseguimos un periódico español?
8. ¿Nos sentamos a esperar el vuelo?
9. ¿Escribimos unas tarjetas postales?
10. ¿Subimos al avión?

B 18 Actividad • ¡A escribir y a hablar!   Answers will vary.

Prepare a description in Spanish of a hotel where you would like to stay. Here are some suggestions.

I. Introducción
   A. Mi hotel favorito se llama . . .
   B. ¿Está en un lugar céntrico?
   C. ¿Cuántas veces he estado en ese hotel?
II. Desarrollo
   A. ¿Cómo es el hotel?
   B. ¿Es caro o barato?
   C. ¿Cómo son las habitaciones?
   D. ¿Cómo son sus empleados?
   E. ¿Tiene restaurante?
   F. ¿Qué otras cosas tiene el hotel?
III. Conclusión
   A. Me gusta ese hotel porque . . .
   B. Tengo planes de volver a quedarme . . .

attracting attention . . . expressing uncertainty

When traveling, it is best to schedule your plans carefully and not try to see everything in one day. This way you can enjoy your vacation and wisely make use of your time.

C1 En Barcelona

Los cuatro compañeros comienzan su paseo
por el Barrio Gótico.

VÍCTOR ¡Qué interesante es este barrio! Es tan
antiguo y tiene casas tan pintorescas.
ISABEL Sí, y fíjense qué estrechas son
estas calles.
BEATRIZ Y, ¿dónde está Jimmy?
VÍCTOR Está en la Catedral. Tú sabes que él
siempre está sacando fotos.
ISABEL Ojalá que se apure.
VÍCTOR Sigamos con nuestro paseo y
esperémoslo más adelante.
ISABEL Un momento, allí viene.
BEATRIZ Oigan, sentémonos en esta fuente a
descansar un poco.
ISABEL Sí, y luego compremos unos helados
en el carrito . . . ¡Huy, qué sabrosos
están!

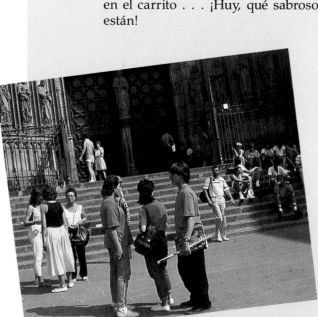

Después de terminar su paseo por el Barrio
Gótico, los muchachos se detienen en
la Plaza de Cataluña.

BEATRIZ Miren, es mejor que almorcemos ahora.
VÍCTOR Sí, porque es necesario que lleguemos
temprano al parque de diversiones de
El Tibidabo.
ISABEL ¿Qué les parece ese café al aire libre?
(leyendo el menú) Pidamos algo ligero,
demos un paseo por Las Ramblas y esta
noche pidámosles a papá y a mamá que
nos lleven a cenar a un restaurante
catalán.
TODOS De acuerdo.

Actividad • ¿Es cierto o no?

Decide whether each statement is true or false, according to C1. Correct
the false statements.

1. Los jóvenes comienzan su paseo por Montjuich.   Los jóvenes comienzan su paseo por el Barrio Gótico.
2. El Barrio Gótico es muy moderno.   El Barrio Gótico es muy antiguo.
3. Jimmy nunca saca fotos.   Jimmy siempre saca fotos.
4. Los helados están sabrosos.   Es cierto.
5. Es necesario que los chicos lleguen temprano al Museo de Arte.   Es necesario que los chicos lleguen temprano al parque de diversiones de El Tibidabo.
6. Los chicos almuerzan en un café al aire libre.   Es cierto.

C3 Actividad • Preguntas y respuestas

Use the information in C1 to answer the following questions.

1. ¿Cómo son las casas del Barrio Gótico?   Las casas del Barrio Gótico son pintorescas.
2. ¿Cómo son sus calles?   Las calles son estrechas.
3. ¿Qué está haciendo Jimmy en el interior de la Catedral?   Jimmy está sacando muchas fotos.
4. ¿Dónde se sientan a descansar los jóvenes?   Los jóvenes se sientan a descansar en una fuente.
5. ¿Qué van a comprar ellos en el carrito?   Ellos van a comprar unos helados.
6. ¿Dónde se detienen después de terminar su paseo?   Se detienen en la Plaza de Cataluña.
7. ¿En qué lugar almuerzan?   Almuerzan en un café al aire libre.
8. ¿Qué van a hacer por la noche?   Les van a pedir a los padres que los lleven a cenar a un restaurante catalán.

Barcelona es una ciudad culta y alegre, populosa y elegante. Tiene bellas secciones modernas y barrios antiguos, llenos de historia. Uno de los sectores más conocidos es la vieja ciudad que incluye el Barrio Gótico y los pintorescos barrios de artesanos. En el Barrio Gótico queda la Catedral, construida a fines del siglo XIII. En la Plaza de San Jaime se encuentran la iglesia de San Jaime, el Ayuntamiento *(City Hall)* y el Palacio de la Generalitat, que es la sede *(seat)* del gobierno.

Barcelona es también la ciudad natal *(native)* de Antonio Gaudí (1852–1926), el famoso arquitecto catalán que construyó el parque Güell, la iglesia de la Sagrada Familia y muchos otros edificios en la ciudad.

C5 SE DICE ASÍ
Attracting attention

Un momento...	One moment...
Un minuto...	One minute...
Escuchen, por favor.	Listen, please.
¡Oigan!	Listen!
¡Miren!	Look!

ESTRUCTURAS ESENCIALES
The expression ¡Ojalá . . . !

¡**Ojalá** que **vayan** a Barcelona!   *If only they could go to Barcelona!*
¡**Ojalá** que **se apure**!   *I hope he hurries!*

The expression ¡**Ojalá!** came into Spanish from the Arabic, and it means
if only or *I hope*. ¡**Ojalá!**, with or without **que**, is usually followed by the present
subjunctive and it expresses a wish that refers to something that may happen in
the future.

C7   Actividad • ¡Ojalá!

Juan is planning a trip to Barcelona with his friends. Follow the model to find out
what he hopes will happen.

     MODELO   ¡Ojalá que nosotros (poder) ir en el verano!
                  ¡Ojalá que nosotros podamos ir en el verano!

1. ¡Ojalá que Luisa (poder) ir a Barcelona!
2. ¡Ojalá que mis amigos (ir) también conmigo!
3. ¡Ojalá que tú (hacer) pronto las reservaciones!
4. ¡Ojalá que el hotel (tener) aire acondicionado!
5. ¡Ojalá que el hotel (estar) céntrico!
6. ¡Ojalá que nosotros (comer) en un restaurante catalán!
7. ¡Ojalá que Lucho y Chela (dar) un paseo por el Barrio Gótico!
8. ¡Ojalá que el conserje (hablar) español!
9. ¡Ojalá que no (llover) durante nuestro viaje!
10. ¡Ojalá que el grupo (volver) pronto del viaje!

1. ¡Ojalá que Luisa pueda ir a Barcelona!
2. ¡Ojalá que mis amigos vayan también conmigo! 3. ¡Ojalá que tú hagas pronto las reservaciones!
4. ¡Ojalá que el hotel tenga aire acondicionado! 5. ¡Ojalá que el hotel esté céntrico! 6. ¡Ojalá que nosotros comamos en un restaurante catalán!
7. ¡Ojalá que Lucho y Chela den un paseo por el Barrio Gótico! 8. ¡Ojalá que el conserje hable español!
9. ¡Ojalá que no llueva durante nuestro viaje! 10. ¡Ojalá que el grupo vuelva pronto del viaje!

C8   Comprensión   For script, see p. T227–228.

Sometimes people have difficulty understanding instructions. You will hear ten
short conversational exchanges. If the person has understood correctly, check **sí** on
your answer sheet. If not, check **no.**

     MODELO   —Debemos llegar a las seis.
                  —Te dije que es importante que salgas a las seis.

	0	1	2	3	4	5	6	7	8	9	10
Sí			✔	✔	✔	✔		✔	✔		✔
No	✔	✔					✔			✔	

C9   Actividad • Nuestros deseos   Answers will vary.

Pair up with a classmate. Tell each other five things you wish would happen, using
¡**Ojalá que . . . !**

C10 Actividad • El señor Carpineto

Mr. Carpineto is a high school Spanish teacher. Here is what he says about his
students. Complete the paragraph with the correct form of the verb in parentheses.

Soy profesor de español de una escuela secundaria. Me alegra (tener)_____   tener
muchos estudiantes. Yo siempre les aconsejo que (estudiar)_____ y (aprender)   estudien
_____ mucho, porque es necesario que ellos (prepararse)_____ para el futuro.   aprendan / se preparen
A mí me alegra mucho que (escuchar)_____ mis consejos. ¡Ojalá que todos   escuchen
los profesores (poder)_____ tener estudiantes que (ser)_____ tan buenos como   puedan / sean
los míos!

C11 Actividad • ¿Qué pasa?

Look at each illustration and explain what is going on. Follow the model.

MODELO   El papá quiere / los chicos / barrer la terraza
          El papá quiere que los chicos barran la terraza.

1. La mamá insiste en / los niños / comer la comida   La mamá insiste en que los niños coman la comida.

2. Es importante / Vicente / llenar la solicitud de empleo   Es importante que Vicente llene la solicitud de empleo.

3. El entrenador se alegra de / el equipo / ganar el partido   El entrenador se alegra de que el equipo gane el partido.

4. Isabel duda / Víctor / estar enfermo   Isabel duda que Víctor esté enfermo.

5. ¡Ojalá! / nosotros / ir al baile   ¡Ojalá que nosotros vayamos al baile!

C12 Actividad • ¡Cuéntame de ti!   Answers will vary.

Work with a partner. Ask each other the following questions.

1. ¿Crees que es importante tener muchos amigos? ¿Por qué?
2. ¿Les das consejos a tus amigos? ¿Qué les aconsejas?
3. ¿Te enojas fácilmente? ¿Con quién? ¿Por qué?
4. Por lo general, ¿cuáles son las cosas que te molestan a ti?
5. ¿Cuáles son algunas cosas que te alegran a ti?

Durante sus vacaciones en Barcelona, los chicos les escriben unas postales a sus familiares, a Vicente y a su profesora, la señora Morse.

ALBERGUE DE CARRETERA · TORDESILLAS
Serie M
N.º 7

Queridos padres,
¿Cómo están? Todos estamos muy bien y divirtiéndonos mucho en Barcelona. Me gustó mucho la iglesia de la Sagrada Familia y el parque de Montjuich. En Montjuich, visitamos el Pueblo Español que contiene réplicas de todas las regiones de España. Les escribiría más, pero no tengo tiempo. Muchos cariños.
Beatriz

DIRECCIÓN GENERAL DE EMPRESAS Y ACTIVIDADES TURÍSTICAS — ESPAÑA

Ediciones ___. Paseadom, 26. Barcelona. Printed in Spain.

Sr. y Sra. Villarreal
250 Woodland Avenue
Austin, Texas 78741

Querido Vicente,
La estamos pasando de lo mejor en Barcelona. Es una ciudad muy grande y muy hermosa. Fuimos al Tibidabo y desde allí pudimos ver toda la ciudad. Es una lástima que no estés aquí con nosotros. Quizás algún día puedas visitar Barcelona. Te extrañamos mucho.
Isabel

Nº 173
PIRINEU CATALÀ
Esglesia romànica de Santa Maria de Taüll (S. XII)

Ediciones Sicilia · ZARAGOZA

Vicente Gonzáles
512 Windsor Rd.
Austin, Texas
78703

USA

Depósito Legal Z. 43.394 XXII

BARCELONA
La Sagrada Familia
Arquitecto: Gaudí

Estimada Sra Morse
Saludos desde Barcelona.
Nos gusta mucho esta ciu
dad y sobre todo nos
encanta la comida cata
lana, especialmente la
zarzuela de mariscos y
la sopa payés. Todas
las noches caminamos
por las Ramblas. Ojalá
algún día volvamos a
Barcelona. Hasta pronto
    Jimmy

Sra. Louise Morse
2086 Rothington Rd.
Austin, Texas
        78726
    U.S.A.

Wertcrom, S. A

Depósito Legal. B. 27.947. - XXVII

Querido Hermano;
Te envío esta postal desde
Barcelona. Hemos recorrido
la ciudad y hasta visitamos
varias playas de la Costa
Brava. Son bellísimas, pero
el agua estaba muy fría.
Hemos aprendido a hablar
un poco de Catalán y
tal vez aprendamos a bailar
la Sardana, el baile típico
de Cataluña. Pronto estaremos
de vuelta.
            un abrazo,
                Héctor

N.º 145 PIRINEO ARAGONES (Huesca)
Puerto de Somport. Alt. 1640 m.
Frontera Franco-Española
Frontière Franco-Española
Frontier Franco Española
                    1880

Carlos Hinajosa

320 Santa Maria St.

Austin, Texas 78733

Depósito Legal B. 19951 VIII

C14 Actividad • Preguntas y respuestas   For answers, see p. T229.

Use the information in C13 to answer the following questions.

1. ¿A quiénes les escriben postales los jóvenes?
2. ¿Qué pudo ver Isabel desde El Tibidabo?
3. ¿Qué le gustó a Beatriz?
4. ¿Qué visitaron ellos en Montjuich?

5. ¿Cómo son las playas de la Costa Brava?
6. ¿Qué es la sardana?
7. ¿Qué les encanta a los jóvenes?
8. ¿Qué hacen ellos todas las noches?

C15 Actividad • ¡A escoger!

Use the information in C13 to select the most appropriate word or words to complete each sentence.

1. La señora Morse es la _____ de los jóvenes.
   • mamá   • profesora   • guía
2. Barcelona es una ciudad _____ .
   • pequeña   • hermosa   • fea
3. La Sagrada Familia es una _____ .
   • iglesia   • catedral   • cafetería
4. Los jóvenes han aprendido un poco de _____ .
   • español   • inglés   • catalán
5. Los compañeros han aprendido a _____ .
   • bailar la sardana   • cantar la sardana   • hablar la sardana

C16 Sabes que . . .

La sardana es el baile típico de Cataluña y se baila en todas las celebraciones. Los domingos, después de ir a la iglesia, la gente se reúne en la plaza de la Catedral. Todos, jóvenes y viejos, hombres y mujeres forman círculos y bailan la sardana.

Este baile es muy antiguo. Los círculos humanos celebran el triunfo del sol sobre la oscuridad (*darkness*) de la noche. Los antiguos griegos establecieron colonias en lo que es hoy Cataluña. Se cree que ellos introdujeron este baile en la región.

ESTRUCTURAS ESENCIALES
The subjunctive with **tal vez** *and* **quizás**

Tal vez ellos **vayan** a Barcelona. *They might go to Barcelona.*
Quizás visiten Madrid. *They might visit Madrid.*

Tal vez and **quizás** *(perhaps, maybe)* are two Spanish expressions that are followed by the subjunctive when the speaker wishes to convey doubt or uncertainty.

C18 Actividad • Tal vez

Change the following statements to express doubt or uncertainty by using **tal vez**. Follow the model.

MODELO Lolita habla catalán.
Tal vez Lolita hable catalán.

1. Víctor y Beatriz comen en un café al aire libre. Tal vez Víctor y Beatriz coman en un café al aire libre.
2. Isabel visita El Pueblo Español. Tal vez Isabel visite El Pueblo Español.
3. (Nosotros) escribimos postales desde Barcelona. Tal vez nosotros escribamos postales desde Barcelona.
4. Jimmy y tú pasean por Las Ramblas. Tal vez Jimmy y tú paseen por Las Ramblas.
5. (Tú) compras los boletos en la agencia de viajes. Tal vez tú compres los boletos en la agencia de viajes.
6. Nuestro abuelo lee un libro sobre Barcelona. Tal vez nuestro abuelo lea un libro sobre Barcelona.
7. Los padres de Carmen son catalanes. Tal vez los padres de Carmen sean catalanes.
8. Los muchachos van al teatro del Liceo en Barcelona. Tal vez los muchachos vayan al teatro de Liceo en Barcelona.

C19 Actividad • Quizás

Change the following statements to express doubt or uncertainty by using **quizás**. Follow the model.

MODELO Lilita va a la Costa Brava.
Quizás Lilita vaya a la Costa Brava.

1. Jimmy trae la cámara. Quizás Jimmy traiga la cámara.
2. Vicente se siente enfermo. Quizás Vicente se sienta enfermo.
3. Mis amigos y yo pedimos una sopa payés. Quizás mis amigos y yo pidamos sopa payés.
4. El restaurante sirve comida catalana. Quizás el restaurante sirva comida catalana.
5. Tus padres están en Barcelona. Quizás tus padres estén en Barcelona.
6. El conserje es catalán. Quizás el conserje sea catalán.
7. Antonio y Regina pasean por la Plaza de Cataluña. Quizás Antonio y Regina paseen por la Plaza de Cataluña.
8. (Nosotros) aprendemos a bailar la sardana. Quizás nosotros aprendamos a bailar la sardana.

C20 Actividad • ¡A escribir tarjetas postales! Answers will vary.

Imagine that you are visiting a city and you are writing postcards to your friends. Use the answers to the following questions as a guide.

¿Cómo es el lugar? ¿En qué hotel estás? ¿Qué has hecho? ¿Cómo es la gente?
¿Cómo es la comida? ¿Qué otros planes tienes?

C21 Actividad • Repasando lo que he aprendido

Complete the paragraph using the correct forms of either the present indicative or the present subjunctive as needed.

España (ser) _____ un país muy hermoso. Muchas personas (ir) _____ a España   es / van
todos los años. Si tú (pensar) _____ visitar España, te aconsejo que (tener) _____ tu   piensas / tengas
pasaporte listo y que (comprar) _____ los boletos pronto para aprovechar las tarifas   compres
especiales. También es importante que los turistas (hacer) _____ reservaciones en los   hagan
hoteles con tiempo. Si tú y tus amigos (ir) _____ a dar un viaje a España, les   van
recomiendo que (ir) _____ a Barcelona porque (ser) _____ una ciudad muy hermosa.   vayan / es
Al llegar a Barcelona, les sugiero que (visitar) _____ la iglesia de la Sagrada Familia,   visiten
el Barrio Gótico, Montjuich y El Tibidabo. También es importante que ustedes
(dar) _____ un paseo por Las Ramblas porque (ser) _____ muy bonitas. Espero que   den / son
(aprovechar) _____ mis consejos y que les (gustar) _____ mucho Barcelona.   aprovechen / guste

C22 Actividad • ¡A escribir y a hablar!   Answers will vary.

Prepare a description in Spanish of the town or city where you live, taking into account the following suggestions.

    I. Introducción
        A. Mi pueblo (ciudad) se llama . . .
        B. ¿Dónde está?
   II. Desarrollo
        A. ¿Cómo es mi pueblo (ciudad)?
        B. ¿Es grande o pequeño?
        C. ¿Cómo son sus calles?
        D. ¿Cómo es la gente?
        E. ¿Cuáles son los lugares interesantes para visitar?
        F. ¿Qué hacen los jóvenes los fines de semana?
  III. Conclusión
        A. (No) me gusta mi pueblo (ciudad) porque . . .
        B. (No) quiero ir a vivir en otra ciudad porque . . .

1   En la agencia de viajes   Answers will vary.

Write a dialog between a tourist and a travel agent. Base your dialog on the illustration below.

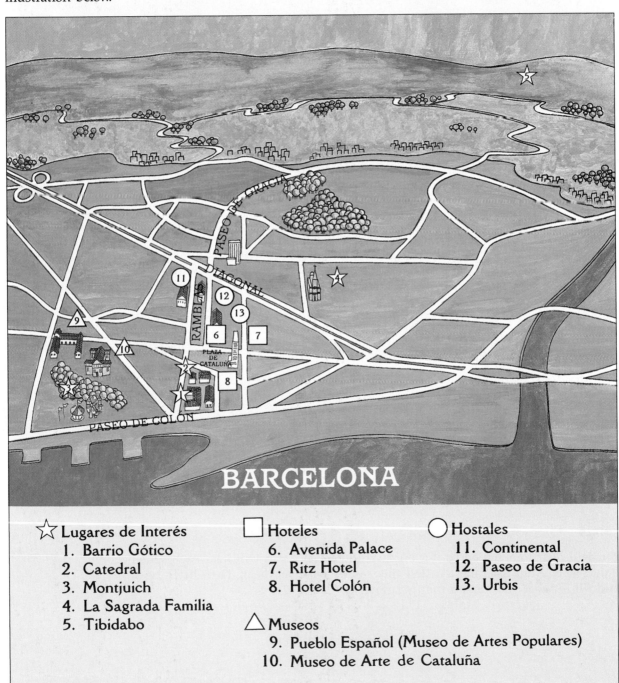

BARCELONA

☆ Lugares de Interés
 1. Barrio Gótico
 2. Catedral
 3. Montjuich
 4. La Sagrada Familia
 5. Tibidabo

☐ Hoteles
 6. Avenida Palace
 7. Ritz Hotel
 8. Hotel Colón

○ Hostales
 11. Continental
 12. Paseo de Gracia
 13. Urbis

△ Museos
 9. Pueblo Español (Museo de Artes Populares)
 10. Museo de Arte de Cataluña

2   Actividad • Mi familia y yo   Answers will vary.

Write five sentences in Spanish. Express your feelings and emotions toward your relatives by using the expressions in the box.

> me encanta   me alegra   me enoja   me gusta   siento

MODELO   Me molesta que mi hermano no me ayude a hacer la tarea.

3   Actividad • Buscando algo perfecto   Answers will vary.

Work with a partner and discuss what you look for in a hotel, a restaurant, a store, and an airline. Follow the model.

MODELO   Busco un hotel que tenga aire acondicionado.

4   Actividad • El premio   Answers will vary.

Your school is giving an award to the class with the best overall performance throughout the year. Try to encourage your classmates by using eight softened commands. Here is a clue: **Vamos a llegar temprano a clase todos los días.**

5   Actividad • Mis recomendaciones para un viaje   Answers will vary.

Using impersonal expressions, give five important recommendations to a person who plans to take a trip.

MODELO   Es importante que Ud. compre cheques de viajero.

6   Actividad • El lugar donde vivo   Answers will vary.

Using Skills 1 as a model, prepare information in Spanish about the town or city where you live. Draw a simple map, showing places of interest, streets, and hotels. Also include a list of places with a brief description of each one.

7   Dictado   For script, see p. T232.

You will hear four sentences. Listen carefully because you will hear each sentence only twice. After listening the first time, write what you hear. Then listen again and fill in what you missed the first time.

Letters *b* and *v*

The **b** and **v** are pronounced identically in Spanish. At the beginning of a breath group, or after the letters **m** and **n,** the sound is similar to the English *b* in *bat.* Listen carefully and repeat the following words.

> Vicente Beatriz viaje cambio
> vida barrio envío también

In all other positions, the sound of the letters **b** and **v** is weaker. Listen carefully and repeat the following words and sentences.

> Isabel sabroso tuvo Tibidabo
> hablar estuve trabajo había

> Vicente baila muy bien la bamba.
> Beba Veléz bebe jugo de uva.
> El bistec que Isabel comió era sabroso.
> Beto estuvo trabajando y hablando mucho.

Intonation

Generally, the intonation for statements in Spanish starts in a low tone, rises to a higher one, and then goes back to the initial low tone at the end of the sentence. Listen to each of the following sentences, and then repeat.

> Yo siento no poder ir a Barcelona con ustedes.
> Es importante que yo estudie informática.
> Les recomiendo que den un paseo por el Barrio Gótico.
> Quizás algún día puedas visitar Barcelona.

Actividad • Práctica de pronunciación

Listen to each sentence and then repeat.

> Balbino no bebe vino.
> Beatriz cambió el viaje.
> Vicente estuvo en el baile.
> Isabel viene en el invierno.
> Victoria vende veinte vestidos verdes.

¿LO SABES?

Let's review some important points you've learned in this unit.

SECTION A

Answers will vary.

Do you know how to make arrangements in Spanish for a trip?
Role-play a brief dialog, detailing your arrangements with a travel agent.

Do you know how to suggest a good hotel in Spanish?
Write five suggestions in Spanish that you would offer to a friend in order to pick a good hotel.

Are you able to express agreement or lack of preference?
Work with a partner. Make suggestions and have your partner reply with the following expressions. Then switch roles.

No me importa.	Me da igual.	¡Maravilloso!
Me da lo mismo.	Como quieras.	¡Regio!
¡Fantástico!	¡Fabuloso!	De acuerdo.

SECTION B

Answers will vary.

Can you offer suggestions to your friends on how to improve their Spanish?
Write five sentences using the following expressions.

es importante	es preciso	es esencial
es necesario	es indispensable	

Can you recommend places to visit in your hometown?
Prepare notes and give five recommendations to the class, concerning places to visit in your hometown.

SECTION C

Answers will vary.

Do you know how to express your wishes in Spanish?
Form five sentences using **¡Ojalá . . . !** to express your wishes for improvements to your school.

Do you know how to convey doubt or uncertainty in Spanish?
Form three sentences with **tal vez** and three sentences with **quizás.**

Do you remember how to write postcards?
Write a postcard to your best friend about a real or an imaginary visit to Barcelona. Don't forget to tell your friend about what you saw in the city, where you ate, and when or if you plan to return.

VOCABULARIO

SECTION A

el **aire acondicionado** *air conditioning*
¡bárbaro! *awesome!*
el **boleto** *ticket*
céntrico, -a *centrally located*
como quieras *as you wish*
costar (ue) *to cost*
de acuerdo *I agree*
¡de película! *out of this world!*
entusiasmado, -a *enthusiastic*
graduarse *to graduate*
la **habitación** *room*
la **ida y vuelta** *round trip*
lamentar *to be sorry*
me da igual *it's the same to me*
me da lo mismo *its all right with me*
molestar *to bother*
no me importa *I don't care*
las **olimpiadas** *Olympic Games*
la **pandilla** *gang*
el **pasaje** *fare*
privado, -a *private*
el **propietario** *owner*
¿qué hay de nuevo? *what's new?*
¡regio! *great!*

la **reservación** *reservation*
sacar (buenas) notas *to get (good) grades*
sorprender *to surprise*
la **tarifa especial** *special fare*
temer *to fear*
el **vuelo sin escala** *non-stop flight*

SECTION B

el **ascensor** *elevator*
el **botones** *bellboy*
el **buró** *desk*
el **casillero** *shelf with dividers*
catalán *Catalan; Catalonian (m.)*
catalana *Catalonian (f.)*
el **conserje** *concierge*
encargarse (de) *to be in charge*
es dudoso *it is doubtful*
es increíble *it is incredible*
es indispensable *it is indispensable*
es preciso *it is essential*
es probable *it is probable*
el **hotel** *hotel*

pintoresco, -a *picturesque*
la **recepción** *reception desk*
recoger *to pick up*
el **registro** *record book*
las **señas** *personal description*
sonreírse *to smile*
¿vale? *okay?*
el **vestíbulo** *lobby*

SECTION C

al aire libre *outdoors*
apurarse *to hurry up*
bellísimo, -a *very beautiful*
la **catedral** *cathedral*
detenerse *to linger, to stop*
estar de vuelta *to be back*
estrecho, -a *narrow*
la **fuente** *fountain*
la **iglesia** *church*
¡ojalá . . . ! *if only; I hope*
recorrer *to travel*
la **región** *region*
la **réplica** *replica*
sobre todo *above all*
la **sopa payés** *Catalonian dish*
la **zarzuela de mariscos** *seafood platter*

PRÁCTICA DEL VOCABULARIO

1. Make a list of all the travel words in the unit vocabulary.
2. Now make up sentences using those words.

1. el boleto, la habitación, la ida y vuelta, la reservación, la tarifa especial, el vuelo sin escala, el conserje, el registro, estar de vuelta, recorrer, sacar fotos, el botones   2. Answers will vary.

VAMOS A LEER

Antes de leer

1. The selections that you are about to read are descriptions of different regions of Spain. Descriptions are usually written in the third person, singular or plural, and thus the sentences will show third person agreement. Knowing this will facilitate your comprehension of the selections.
2. Descriptions use many adjectives that will serve as clues to help you identify the key topic of the reading.
3. By now you are already familiar with cognates. There are several of them in the reading. How many can you readily identify as you quickly scan the selection?

Preparación para la lectura

Before you begin the reading selection, answer the following questions.

1. ¿Has estado alguna vez en España? ¿Has oído música española?
2. ¿Conoces algo de las aventuras de don Quijote?
3. ¿Puedes adivinar el significado de *acueducto, castillo, inmortalizada* y *torre*?
4. ¿Por qué crees que Castilla se llama así?
5. Mira rápidamente la Lectura y busca cuál es el monumento más viejo de Castilla.
6. Busca después la extensión del acueducto romano de Segovia.
7. ¿Por qué crees que se le llama romano?

1. Answers will vary. 2. Answers will vary. 3. acueducto - *aqueduct;* castillo - *castle;* inmortalizada - *immortalized;* torre - *tower* 4. Porque hay muchos castillos. 5. El monumento más viejo de Castilla es el acueducto romano de Segovia. 6. La extension del acueducto es de 728 metros de largo. 7. Porque lo hicieron los romanos.

Panorama de España

La región catalana es sólo una de las muchas y variadas regiones de España. Si bien es verdad que Cataluña es una de las más ricas en recursos naturales, la industria y las artes, hay en España otras regiones que ofrecen al visitante una gran variedad de culturas y paisajes.

El país vasco

Los vascos tienen su propio idioma, euskera, que todavía hoy no sabemos de dónde viene. El traje típico para el hombre es pantalón y camisa blanca, con una boina° roja y un pañuelo al cuello y otro a la cintura del mismo color. El deporte más popular se llama pelota vasca o jai-alai. El baile local es la vigorosa jota vasca. El país vasco es una de las regiones más industriales de España.

---

boina *beret*

Castilla

Ésta es la región de los molinos de viento y de las aventuras de don Quijote.
Además, es donde está Madrid, la capital del país. Como es característico de
España, pero más visible en Castilla, lo antiguo está al lado de lo moderno, en
armonía. Hay en esta región castillos y ciudades medievales, como por ejemplo, la
increíble ciudad de Ávila, que es un monumento nacional por sus murallas° del
siglo once. El famoso acueducto romano, que está en la ciudad de Segovia, con sus
728 metros de largo, es desde luego, unos cuantos siglos más viejo. Allí también
puedes encontrar el Alcázar°, con sus elegantes torres. Un poco más al sur de
Madrid está una de las ciudades más turísticas de España, Toledo, inmortalizada
por el pintor El Greco.

murallas *walls*   **Alcázar** *Spanish fortress or palace*

Andalucía

Aquí vas a encontrar las ciudades más románticas de España. En Sevilla hay casas blancas con las ventanas llenas de claveles.° Ésta es una ciudad llena de gracia, con bellos parques y monumentos. Córdoba, la antigua capital del califato,° tiene entre sus monumentos la inmensa mezquita.° Granada, la más romántica de todas por el famoso palacio de La Alhambra, te lleva en su fantasía a la época de las *Mil y una noches*. Por toda Andalucía puedes disfrutar de guitarras, castañuelas° y baile flamenco. ¿Has leído los *Cuentos de La Alhambra* de Washington Irving?

claveles *carnations*   **califato** *caliphate*   **mezquita** *mosque*   **castañuelas** *castanets*

Actividad • Preguntas y respuestas For answers, see p. T235.

1. ¿En qué región de España está la capital del país?
2. ¿Por qué es un monumento nacional la ciudad de Ávila?
3. ¿Cuál es la ciudad más turística de España?
4. ¿Quién era El Greco?
5. ¿Qué idioma hablan los catalanes? ¿Y los vascos?
6. ¿En qué región de España hay muchas flores en las ventanas?
7. ¿Qué ciudad turística está cerca de Madrid, al sur?

Actividad • ¿Cuál es la ciudad o región?

Match the landmarks or tourist attractions on the left with the names of regions or cities on the right.

1. ciudad con murallas medievales
2. bailes flamencos
3. capital del califato
4. el palacio de La Alhambra
5. jai alai
6. molinos de viento y castillos
7. la capital del país
8. ciudad inmortalizada por El Greco

Granada
Madrid
Andalucía
Ávila
Córdoba
Toledo
el país vasco
Castilla

1. Ávila
2. Andalucía
3. Córdoba
4. Granada
5. el país vasco
6. Castilla
7. Madrid
8. Toledo

Actividad • ¡A escoger!

Use the information in the reading selection to help you choose the answer that best completes each sentence.

1. La ciudad romántica por excelencia es
   • Córdoba.   • Madrid.   • <u>Granada.</u>
2. Hay muchos castillos y ciudades medievales en
   • la región catalana.   • <u>Castilla.</u>   • el país vasco.
3. El Alcázar de las torres elegantes está en
   • Ávila.   • <u>Segovia.</u>   • Toledo.
4. La ciudad que está al sur de Madrid es
   • Córdoba.   • <u>Toledo.</u>   • Ávila.
5. El palacio de La Alhambra está en
   • Córdoba.   • Sevilla.   • <u>Granada.</u>

Actividad • Charla   Answers will vary.

Get together with a classmate and discuss the Spanish city or region you would like to visit and the places you would like to see.

UNIDAD 12 **La última reunión**

Repaso

TEACHER-PREPARED MATERIALS
   Review 12   Poster board

UNIT RESOURCES
Manual de actividades, Unit 12
Manual de ejercicios, Unit 12
Unit 12 Cassette
Transparency 30
Review Test 3
Final Test
Proficiency Tests 2 and 3

Unit 12 combines functions, grammar, and vocabulary that the students have studied in Units 9–11. This unit provides communicative and writing practice in different situations; some of the activities lend themselves to cooperative learning. If your students require further practice, you will find additional review exercises in Unit 12 of the **Manual de actividades** and **Manual de ejercicios.** On the other hand, if your students know how to use the material in Units 9–11, you may wish to omit parts of Unit 12.

OBJECTIVE   To review communicative functions, grammar, and vocabulary from Units 9–11

CULTURAL BACKGROUND   Many graduating classes at Spanish-American high schools sponsor money-making activities throughout the year to finance celebrations. Some of the money is used to pay for a large, formal dinner and dance, which is normally held at an exclusive club or restaurant. As an alternative, students often plan class trips to a foreign country or sight-seeing trips throughout their own country.

MOTIVATING ACTIVITY   Ask the students to form groups to plan an end-of-the-year party that includes typical food, activities, and Spanish music. Combine the groups' ideas to form a master plan for the class.

1   ## Los preparativos

Play the cassette or read the dialog aloud as the students follow along in their books. You may wish to divide the dialog into sections and pause after each section to ask comprehension questions. For cooperative learning, divide the class into groups of four. Then have each group role-play the dialog for the class.

2   ### Actividad • Preguntas y respuestas

CHALLENGE   Have each student prepare five false statements about the dialog in **Los preparativos.** Collect and correct the statements. Then distribute the papers, making sure each student does not receive his or her own. Ask the students to rewrite the false statements to make them agree with the dialog in **Los preparativos.**

ANSWERS:
1. Los estudiantes están organizando la última reunión del año.
2. Miguel no ha llegado todavía.
3. Es probable que no venga porque iba con sus padres a la agencia de viajes.
4. Estrella piensa pasar sus vacaciones en Ecuador.
5. Rafael va a ayudar a su padre en el garaje.
6. Laura tal vez trabaje en un proyecto para mejorar el ambiente de la ciudad.

3   Actividad • Charla

Instruct each student to work with two other students to create a list of four predictions based on the information in the dialog. Call on volunteers from each group to read the predictions aloud to the class.

4   Actividad • Las decoraciones

Have the students work in pairs to complete the activity. Review the exchanges with the class.

ANSWERS:
1. ¿Hiciste las invitaciones?
   Sí, pero no he pedido las flores.
2. ¿Arreglaste las luces?
   Sí, pero no he traído la música.
3. ¿Trajiste una mesa?
   Sí, pero no he conseguido un mantel.
4. ¿Llamaste al profesor?
   Sí, pero no me ha dicho nada.
5. ¿Anunciaste la rifa?
   Sí, pero no he comprado los premios.
6. ¿Compraste las flores?
   Sí, pero no he hecho los arreglos.

5   Actividad • Los cocineros

For cooperative learning, ask the students to work in groups of three to assign tasks for the party. If you are having the students plan an actual party, have them complete the activity using real names and real tasks.

6   Actividad • ¿Refrescos o agua mineral?

Allow five minutes for the students to complete the sentences with the correct verb forms. Review the answers with the class.

7   Actividad • El director

Present the model to the class. Encourage them to use such words as **pues, vale, hala,** and **entonces.** Review the exchanges with the class in the form of short dialogs.

8   Actividad • El proyecto de Laura

Review the impersonal expressions with the class. Then ask the students to write their sentences at home or in class. Call on the students to read their sentences aloud, as you or a volunteer writes them on the board. Discuss with the class the merit of each suggestion.

9 Actividad • ¡A escribir!

Ask the students to make posters for homework. They should write at least five sentences that convince others not to smoke. You may wish to hang the posters throughout the school or in other classrooms.

10 Actividad • Proyecto para mejorar el ambiente

After the students have completed the questionnaire, select a committee to tally the results. Make a graph or a chart to compare the answers. Use the chart to encourage the students to discuss their attitudes toward environmental protection.

11 Actividad • ¡Qué se diviertan!

Assign the activity for homework or to be completed in class within a specific time limit. You may wish to prepare a transparency of the paragraph to correct the answers in class.

12 Actividad • ¡Hasta el semestre que viene!

Brainstorm with the class to create a list of good wishes. You may wish to provide a poster on which the students may write a parting phrase. Place the poster in an accessible location in the classroom. Have the students express their good wishes by writing them on the poster. Then ask the students to complete the activity according to the model. Students may work in pairs, or you may work with the entire class.

13 Comprensión

You will hear a narration of plans for Carolina's going-away party. The narration consists of three paragraphs, each followed by four statements. After listening to each paragraph, decide if the statements are true **(verdadero)** or false **(falso).** Check the appropriate space on your answer sheet.

Pensamos planear una fiesta de despedida para Carolina porque va a Buenos Aires a pasar el verano como estudiante de intercambio. Vamos a invitar a todos sus amigos y a su familia también, especialmente a sus primos, que son muy divertidos.

1. La fiesta celebra el fin del año.   *falso*
2. Carolina va a la Argentina.   *verdadero*
3. Va a Buenos Aires para estudiar.   *verdadero*
4. No piensan invitar a sus parientes.   *falso*

La fiesta será en casa de Eduardo porque tiene un jardín muy grande. Hemos decidido servir los platos favoritos de Carolina, y por supuesto, hemos comprado un regalo muy bonito para ella. Lo mejor de todo es que es una fiesta sorpresa.

5. Escogieron la casa de Eduardo por su jardín.   *verdadero*
6. No le compraron un regalo a Carolina.   *falso*
7. Piensan servir comida argentina.   *falso*
8. Van a sorprenderla con la fiesta.   *verdadero*

Quique preguntó si habría música y yo contesté que sí. Él ofreció traer el tocadiscos y su colección de música latina. Irene va a tocar la guitarra y todos podrán bailar en el patio. Por fin, Alfonso y Gabi ofrecieron hacer las decoraciones.

  9. Quique pidió música. *falso*
10. Escucharán discos de música latina. *verdadero*
11. Nadie sabe tocar la guitarra. *falso*
12. Las chicas van a preparar las decoraciones. *falso*

Now check your answers. *Read each paragraph and accompanying statements again, and give the correct answers.*

UNIDAD 12

La última reunión

Repaso

1

Los preparativos

Un grupo de estudiantes está organizando la última reunión del año. Quieren que sea muy buena y desean que todos se diviertan mucho. Algunos se ocuparán del programa musical y otros de la comida y de los refrescos. Algunos de ellos van a decorar el salón. Mientras hacen los preparativos, conversan un poco.

LAURA   ¡Caramba! Miguel no ha llegado todavía y hay tanto que hacer.

ESTRELLA   Dudo que venga hoy, Laura. Recuerda que iba con sus padres a la agencia de viajes para preparar el viaje de vacaciones.

PEPE   ¡Huy, cómo pasa el tiempo! Ya se termina el curso.

RAFAEL   ¡Qué maravilla! Tres meses sin clases.

LAURA   Bueno, sí . . . Pero después de todo, hemos aprendido mucho. Y también nos hemos divertido mucho.

ESTRELLA   ¿Qué planes tienen ustedes para el verano . . . y el año que viene?

PEPE   Estrella, para el año que viene no sé. En el verano es posible que vaya a casa de los abuelos en Puerto Rico.

RAFAEL   No creo que vaya a ninguna parte. Papá necesita que yo lo ayude en el garaje.

LAURA   Tal vez trabaje en el proyecto para mejorar el ambiente. Como saben hay mucha contaminación y tenemos que hacer algo.

ESTRELLA   Me alegra que todos tengamos muchos proyectos y que pasemos unas buenas vacaciones. Yo pienso ir de vacaciones a Ecuador. ¡Ojalá que estemos juntos otra vez en la próxima clase de español!

TODOS   ¡De acuerdo!

La última reunión   **407**

Actividad • **Preguntas y respuestas**   For answers, see p. T236–237.

Use the information in **Los preparativos** to answer the following questions.

1. ¿Qué están organizando los estudiantes?
2. ¿Quién no ha llegado todavía?
3. ¿Por qué es probable que no venga?

4. ¿Qué planes tiene Estrella para el verano?
5. ¿Qué va a hacer Rafael durante el verano?
6. ¿En qué proyecto va a trabajar Laura?

3   Actividad • **Charla**   Answers will vary.

Pair up with a classmate and discuss **Los preparativos.** Make at least three predictions on what kind of summer you think Laura, Pepe, and Rafael are going to have. Use **creo que** and **no creo que** and be prepared to support your opinions.

4   Actividad • **Las decoraciones**   For answers, see p. T237.

The organizer of the decorations committee gets together with the group and wants to know what has been done. Work with a partner. Follow the model.

MODELO   preparar los letreros / poner las decoraciones
—¿Preparaste los letreros?
—Sí, pero no he puesto las decoraciones.

1. hacer las invitaciones / pedir las flores
2. arreglar las luces / traer la música
3. traer una mesa / conseguir un mantel

4. llamar al profesor / decirme nada
5. anunciar la rifa / comprar los premios
6. comprar las flores / hacer los arreglos

5   Actividad • **Los cocineros**   Answers will vary. Possible answers are given.

You are in charge of the food committee. You are efficient and like to be in control. What do you say? Follow the model.

MODELO   comprar el queso   — No compres el queso, que lo compre Ana.

1. cortar las papas
2. lavar las frutas
3. poner las servilletas allí
4. empezar la ensalada
5. preparar los bocadillos
6. traer el pan

1. No cortes las papas, que las corte Felipe.
2. No laves las frutas, que las lave Marta.
3. No pongas las servilletas allí, que las ponga Mario.
4. No Empieces la ensalada, que la empiece Ramón.
5. No prepares los bocadillos, que los prepare María.
6. No traigas el pan, que lo traiga Mariana.

6 Actividad • ¿Refrescos o agua mineral?

The director of the beverage committee is very polite to the assistants. Complete the sentences with the appropriate verb form.

1. Te aconsejo que no ____ (traer) el hielo todavía.   traigas
2. Necesito que tú ____ (conseguir) más tazas.   consigas
3. Les recomiendo que ____ (comprar) más jugos.   compren
4. Dudo que nosotros ____ (tener) suficientes refrescos.   tengamos
5. Creo que ____ (haber) limonada.   hay
6. ¿Les molesta que ____ (cerrar) la puerta?   cierre
7. Yo sé que no ____ (tener) agua.   tengo
8. ¡Ojalá que ____ (tener) bastante hielo!   tenga

7 Actividad • El director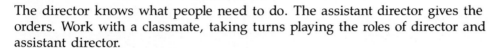

The director knows what people need to do. The assistant director gives the orders. Work with a classmate, taking turns playing the roles of director and assistant director.

> MODELO   bajar al gimnasio
> — Es necesario que bajen al gimnasio.
> — Bajemos ahora.

1. aprender las canciones
2. probar el micrófono
3. abrir las puertas
4. descansar un rato
5. limpiar esa esquina
6. conectar el estéreo

1. Es necesario que aprendan las canciones. Aprendámoslas ahora.
2. Es necesario que prueben el micrófono. Probémoslo ahora.
3. Es necesario que abran las puertas. Abrámoslas ahora.
4. Es necesario que descansen un rato. Descansemos ahora.
5. Es necesario que limpien esa esquina. Limpiémosla ahora.
6. Es necesario que conecten el estéreo. Conectémoslo ahora.

8 Actividad • El proyecto de Laura   Answers will vary.

Make a list of at least five tasks you think Laura must accomplish in order to beautify the city. Use **hay que.**

9 Actividad • ¡A escribir!   Answers will vary.

It is health week and the wrestling coach wants a poster for all to see. He needs five sentences beginning with **NO FUMES** in capital letters, followed by **porque . . .** Write five or six suggestions for him.

10 Actividad • Proyecto para mejorar el ambiente Answers will vary.

The environmental committee also wants to remind everyone about their
responsibilities, so they prepared this questionnaire. Answer it.

1. ¿Has recogido periódicos para salvar los árboles?
2. ¿Has tratado de usar papel en vez de plásticos?
3. ¿Has cortado árboles sin necesidad?
4. ¿Has ayudado a alguien a no fumar?
5. ¿Apagas el aire acondicionado cuando es posible?
6. ¿Caminas para ahorrar gasolina y por ejercicio?
7. ¿Reparas cosas a veces en vez de comprar nuevas?

11 Actividad • ¡Qué se diviertan!

Before the party, the organizers talked and thanked everybody. Complete the
paragraph with the appropriate forms of the verbs in the box.

> ayudar   estar   haber   estar
> trabajar   discutir   pasar   venir

Agradecemos mucho que nos _____ hoy. Nos alegra ver que todos _____ juntos. Me   ayuden / trabajen
sorprende que _____ de acuerdo y no _____ . Esperamos que _____ refrescos para   estén / discutan / haya
todos. Nos gusta que la _____ bien aunque _____ trabajando. Quizás el director de la   pasen / estén
escuela _____ hoy por la tarde.   venga

12 Actividad • ¡Hasta el semestre que viene!   Answers will vary.

Now it's time for good wishes and goodbyes. Make up sentences, using **quizás**
or **ojalá.**

   MODELO   divertirte   ¡Ojalá que te diviertas!

1. vernos durante las vacaciones
2. ver a mis primos en Buenos Aires
3. ir de viaje

4. conseguir un trabajo interesante
5. escribirte una carta
6. pasarla bien

13 Comprensión   For script, see p. T238–239.

You will hear a narration of plans for Carolina's going-away party. The narration
consists of three paragraphs, each followed by four statements. After listening to
each paragraph, decide if the statements are true **(verdadero)** or false **(falso).** Check
the appropriate space on your answer sheet.

	1	2	3	4	5	6	7	8	9	10	11	12
Verdadero		✓	✓		✓			✓		✓		
Falso	✓			✓		✓	✓		✓		✓	✓

FOR REFERENCE

SUMMARY OF FUNCTIONS

The term *functions* can be defined as what you do with language—
what your purpose is in speaking. Here is a list of all the functions
with the expressions you have learned related to these functions.
The number indicates the unit in which the expression is introduced,
followed by the section letter and number in parentheses.

EXCHANGING INFORMATION

Describing what one did
1(A16)   . . . dio dinero . . .
Dimos una vuelta
Dimos un viaje . . .
Dieron un paseo . . .
. . . dio la clase . . .

Reporting past events
1(B1)   Hice un viaje a Colorado.
Pesqué muchas truchas.
Visitamos muchos lugares.

Asking and explaining how something was
1(B16)   ¿Qué tal estuvo (el partido de béisbol)?
¿Cómo fue . . . ?
No sé. Yo no fui, pero Antonio fue.
Fue (un partido) muy bueno.
Estuvo muy bueno.
Fue (un partido) muy malo.
No fue muy bueno.

Comparing age and quality
2(A6)   . . . menor(es) que . . .
. . . mayor(es) que . . .
. . . mejor(es) que . . .
. . . peor(es) que . . .

Identifying what you want
3(B1)   . . . estamos buscando unos jeans . . .
Yo quiero una chaqueta de cuero, talla . . .

Talking about past events
3(C1)   ¿Qué les pasó?
Ramiro fue conmigo a la Nación.
La tienda cerró hoy por inventario.
. . . ahorramos plata en . . .

Asking for directions
3(A22)   Perdone, ¿sabe dónde está . . . ?
Con permiso, ¿sabe dónde queda . . . ?
¿Podría decirme cómo llegar a . . . ?

Giving information (directions)
3(A22)   Sí, con mucho gusto.
Sí, está a la derecha.
Sí, queda a la izquierda.
Sí, queda a . . . cuadras de aquí.
Sí, . . . al lado de . . .
Sí, . . . enfrente de . . .
Sí, . . . detrás de . . .
Sí, . . . cerca de . . .
Sí, . . . lejos de . . .
3(A27)   Sigan derecho.
Doblen a la derecha.
Doblen a la izquierda.
. . . en la esquina.
. . . en la intersección.
. . . en la calle . . .
. . . en la plaza . . .

Asking for and giving information in a store
3(B5)   ¿En qué puedo servirle?
¿Lo están atendiendo?
¿Qué desea?
¿Cuál es su talla?
¿Algo más?
Aquí está el vuelto.

Inquiring about age
5(A19)   ¿Cuántos años tienes?
¿Cuántos años cumples?

Describing events in the past
5(B19)   Había dos fiestas.
Había poco tiempo.
Había muchos discos.

Talking about what one does every day
6(A1)   . . . se levanta temprano.
Ella corre media hora todos los días.

Describing emotions
6(A17)   Se pone furioso(a).
Se pone triste.
Se pone contento(a).
Se pone nervioso(a).

Discussing unplanned events
6(C11) ¿Me prestas tu espejo?
        No puedo. El espejo se rompió.
        Luis, ¿dónde está el reloj que compré?
        Ay, se perdió ayer.
        Antonio, ¿qué pasó?
        Nada, la taza se cayó.

Expressing time (morning, afternoon, or evening)
5(A12) ... por la mañana.
        ... a las diez de la mañana.
        ... a las cuatro de la tarde.
        ... por la noche.
        ... a las nueve de la noche.

Expressing time factors
7(B10) en un par de horas
        en un dos por tres
        a la carrera
        en un abrir y cerrar de ojos
        dentro de un rato
        a menudo

Reporting what others say
9(A4)   Mi hermano me dijo que ...
        Alguien me dijo que ...
        La gente dice que ...
        Dicen que ...

Describing things you have done in the past
10(A1) He estado en Buenos Aires ...
        ... ya todos han desayunado.

Reporting, describing, and narrating
10(A5) He visto ...
        Hemos visitado varios ...
        Me siento muy contento de ...
        Quiero que veas ...
        Hay pocas actividades ...
        Estoy seguro de que ...

EXPRESSING ATTITUDES AND OPINIONS

Comparing and expressing preferences
2(A1)   A Miguel le gusta mucho la música.
        ¿Cuál creen que es mejor?

Making excuses
2(B6)   Lo siento, no puedo ayudarlos.
        ¡Tengo tantas cosas que hacer!
        ¡Estoy tan ocupado(a) ...!
        ¡Estoy tan cansado(a) ...!
        La próxima vez... Hoy no, otro día.

Expressing points of view
2(B1)   Siempre tienes una excusa.
        Tú crees que como eres menor ...

Expressing logical conclusions
7(C5)   por lo tanto
        de hecho

a la corta o a la larga
por consiguiente

Expressing obligation or necessity
10(C6) Hay que + (verb in infinitive) ...

Expressing what is needed or expected
11(B4) Es preciso ...
        Es necesario ...
        Es importante ...

EXPRESSING FEELINGS AND EMOTIONS

Expressing satisfaction and dissatisfaction
1(B10) Me fue bien ...
        La pasamos muy bien ...
        Nos fue de lo mejor ...
        La pasamos de maravilla ...
        No nos fue bien.
        Nos fue muy mal.
        La pasamos muy mal.

Expressing satisfaction or displeasure with emphasis
3(C4)   ¡Uf! ...
        ¡Ay! ...
        ¡Huy! ...
        ¡Bah! ...
        ¡Basta! ...
        ¡Caramba! ...
6(B9)   ¡Cuánto me alegro!

Expressing intention
5(B6)   Iba a ...
        Quería ...
        Pensaba ...

Expressing regret
5(C1)   Ay, ¡qué pena!
        Lo siento, pero no pude ir.

Expressing how you feel about others and about yourself
5(C12) Tere estaba aburrida.
        Víctor era aburrido.
        Luis estaba listo.
        Anita era lista.

Asking and stating how one feels
6(B9)   Me siento bien.
        Me siento mal.
        Me siento mejor.
        Tengo un dolor de ...
        Me duele ...
        Lo siento (mucho).
        ¡Cuida tu salud!
        ¿Qué tienes?
6(B9)   ¿Cómo te sientes?

Expressing displeasure
7(A4)   Estoy harto de (caminar).
        Me estoy volviendo loca.
        Me tiene hasta la punta de los pelos.

Expressing surprise, amazement, sympathy, or pity
6(B9)   ¡Qué lástima!
9(B8)   ¡Qué suerte!
        ¡Qué pena!
        ¡Qué horror!
        ¡Qué barbaridad!

Expressing desire
9(B1)   . . . quería ir a la playa . . .
9(B15) Preferimos alguien con experiencia.

Expressing likes and dislikes
10(B6) ¡Me encanta!
        ¡Cómo me gusta!
        ¡Cómo me divierto!
        ¡No hay nada igual!
        ¡Cómo lo odio!
        ¡Qué asco!

Expressing doubt, disbelief, or denial
10(C1) Dudo que necesites . . .

Expressing emotions
11(A5) ¡Cuánto me alegro de que . . . !
        ¡Estoy muy contento de que . . . !
        Me sorprende mucho que . . . !
        Me molesta que . . .

Expressing uncertainty
11(C13) Quizás algún día puedas . . .

PERSUADING

Making suggestions
2(B1)   . . . poner todas las notas del
        refrigerador en un sombrero y, . . .

Confirming expected courses of action
2(C5)   Me llamas luego, ¿verdad?
        Puedes hablar con ella, ¿no?
        Te llamo esta tarde. ¿Está bien?

Directing others to do something
7(A1)   Comienza otra vez y haz todo de nuevo.
        No . . . hazlo tú.
        . . . saca el manual, léelo bien y aprende
        las instrucciones.
9(C9)   Pídale que me traiga la solicitud.
        Dígale que pase a mi despacho.

Requesting favors, asking for help or giving a warning
7(A4)   Por favor, ayúdame.
        ¿Me puedes dar una mano?

7(C17) ¿Serías tan amable de . . . ?
        ¿Podrías hacerme el favor de . . . ?
        ¿Querrías decirme (darme, prestarme,
            etc.) . . . ?
        ¿Me podrías ayudar (prestar, decir,
            etc.) . . . ?
        ¿Tendrías la bondad de . . . ?
9(A20) ¡Auxilio!
        ¡Socorro!
        ¡Fuego!
        ¡Cuidado!
        ¡Alto!

Giving advice using proverbs
7(B4)   Más vale pájaro en mano que cien
            volando.
        Más vale precaver que tener que
            lamentar.
        Del dicho al hecho hay un gran trecho.
        En boca cerrada no entran moscas.
        Más vale tarde que nunca.

Warning others to refrain from doing something
10(B1) No comas tantos duraznos que te vas a
            enfermar.
Making suggestions
11(B11) Les recomiendo que den un paseo.

SOCIALIZING

Meeting and greeting people
1(C4)   ¡Hola, + name!
        ¿Qué tal?
        ¿Cómo estás?
        Muy bien, + name.
        Te presento a + name.
        Mucho gusto.
        Encantado.

*Sending greetings and saying that someone sends
regards*
1(C7)   Recuerdos a . . .
        Saludos de . . .
        . . . manda recuerdos.
        . . . dio saludos.
        . . . mandan muchos saludos.
        . . . mandan recuerdos.

Writing salutations
1(C15) Querido(a) + name   *(informal)*
        Queridos(as) + name   *(informal)*
        Estimado(a) + name   *(formal)*
        Estimados(as) + name   *(formal)*

Writing salutations for business letters
9(B23) Distinguida señora:
        Estimado señor:
        Muy señores míos:
        Muy señor nuestro:

Writing common introductions for business letters
9(C4)   Acusamos recibo de su carta . . .
          En relación con su carta del 7 del
              presente . . .
          Nos es grato comunicarle(s) . . .
          Por medio de la presente tenemos el
              gusto de comunicarle(s) . . .
          Sentimos comunicarle(s) . . .

Writing complimentary closings
1(C15)   Cariñosamente, *(informal)*
          Un abrazo de, *(informal)*
          Muchos recuerdos/saludos de,
              (informal)
          Todos te mandan saludos, *(informal)*
          Afectuosamente, *(formal)*
          Cordialmente, *(formal)*
          Saludos, *(formal)*
          Atentamente, *(formal)*

Writing complimentary closings for business letters
9(B23)   Muy agradecido(a) por su atención, . . .
          Atentamente, . . .
          Queda de Ud. affmo.(a.) s.s., . . .
          Suyo(a) afectísimo(a), . . .

Extending an invitation
3(A5)   ¿Quieres ir de compras?
          ¡Vamos de compras!
          ¿Tienes ganas de ir de compras?
          ¿Por qué no vamos de compras?
5(A7)   Te llamaba para invitarte . . .
          Quería invitarte . . .
          ¿Quieres ir a la fiesta?
                   . . . a la graduación?
                   . . . al picnic?
                   . . . a la boda?

Accepting invitations
3(A5)   Sí, ¡cómo no!
          Sí, ¡por supuesto!

Refusing invitations
3(A5)   No, gracias. No puedo. Tengo que . . .
          Lo siento, pero no puedo.
          Hoy no. No tengo ganas. Otro día.

Paying compliments
6(C18)   ¡Qué linda estás hoy!
          ¡Qué vestido más elegante!
          ¡Qué bien bailas!
          ¡Qué simpático eres!
          ¡Qué guapo estás!
          ¡Estás a la última moda!
          ¡Qué bien te queda!
          ¡Cuánto me alegro!
          ¡Qué alegría verte!
          ¡Qué bien luces!

Congratulating someone
5(A19)   ¡Muchas felicidades!
          ¡Feliz cumpleaños!
          ¡Felicidades en el día de tu santo!
9(C11)   Te felicito.
          ¡Enhorabuena!
          ¡Felicitaciones!
          ¡Felicidades!

Attracting attention
11(C5)   Un momento . . .
          Un minuto . . .
          Escuchen, por favor.
          ¡Oigan!
          ¡Miren!

EXPRESSING AND FINDING OUT MORAL ATTITUDES

Expressing agreement or lack of preference
11(A11) No me importa.
          Me da igual.
          Me da lo mismo.
          Como quieras.
          De acuerdo.

Expressing approval or satisfaction with emphasis
11(A16) ¡Maravilloso!
          ¡Fantástico!
          ¡Regio!
          ¡Fabuloso!
          ¡Magnífico!
          ¡De película!
          ¡Bárbaro!

GRAMMAR SUMMARY

ARTICLES

DEFINITE ARTICLES

	MASCULINE	FEMININE
SINGULAR	el chico	la chica
PLURAL	los chicos	las chicas

INDEFINITE ARTICLES

	MASCULINE	FEMININE
SINGULAR	un chico	una chica
PLURAL	unos chicos	unas chicas

CONTRACTIONS OF THE DEFINITE ARTICLE

a + el → al

de + el → del

ADJECTIVES

		MASCULINE	FEMININE
Adjectives that end in -o	SING PL	chico alto chicos altos	chica alta chicas altas
Adjectives that end in -e	SING PL	chico inteligente chicos inteligentes	chica inteligente chicas inteligentes
Adjectives that end in a consonant	SING PL	examen difícil exámenes difíciles	clase difícil clases difíciles

DEMONSTRATIVE ADJECTIVES

este			ese		
	MASCULINE	FEMININE		MASCULINE	FEMININE
SINGULAR PLURAL	este chico estos chicos	esta chica estas chicas	SINGULAR PLURAL	ese chico esos chicos	esa chica esas chicas

POSSESSIVE ADJECTIVES

SINGULAR		PLURAL	
MASCULINE	FEMININE	MASCULINE	FEMININE
mi hijo tu hijo su hijo nuestro hijo	mi hija tu hija su hija nuestra hija	mis hijos tus hijos sus hijos nuestros hijos	mis hijas tus hijas sus hijas nuestras hijas

STRESSED POSSESSIVE ADJECTIVES

SINGULAR		PLURAL	
MASCULINE	FEMININE	MASCULINE	FEMININE
mío	mía	míos	mías
tuyo	tuya	tuyos	tuyas
suyo	suya	suyos	suyas
nuestro	nuestra	nuestros	nuestras

PRONOUNS

SUBJECT PRONOUNS	DIRECT OBJECT PRONOUNS	INDIRECT OBJECT PRONOUNS	OBJECTS OF PREPOSITIONS
yo	me	me	mí
tú	te	te	ti
él, ella, Ud.	lo, la	le	él, ella, Ud.
nosotros, -as	nos	nos	nosotros, -as
ellos, ellas, Uds.	los, las	les	ellos, ellas, Uds.

NEGATION:
NEGATIVE EXPRESSIONS

no	nadie
nada	ningún
nunca	ninguno, -a
ni . . . ni	tampoco

AFFIRMATIVES:
AFFIRMATIVE EXPRESSIONS

algo	algún
alguien	siempre
alguno, -a	también
alguno, -as	o . . . o

INTERROGATIVES:
INTERROGATIVE WORDS

¿Cómo?	¿Cuál?	¿Por qué?
¿Cuándo?	¿Dónde?	¿Qué?
¿Cuánto?	¿De dónde?	¿Quién?

COMPARATIVES
COMPARISONS OF UNEQUAL QUANTITIES

más / menos	+	adjective	+	que		más / menos	+	de	+	number (expression of quantity)

COMPARISONS OF EQUALITY

tan	+	adjective or adverb	+	como

SUPERLATIVE CONSTRUCTION

el, la, los, las	+	(noun)	+	más menos	+	adjective	+	de

IRREGULAR FORMS OF COMPARATIVES AND SUPERLATIVES

Adjectives	Regular	Irregular
bueno(a)	**más** bueno(a)	**mejor**
malo(a)	**más** malo(a)	**peor**
grande	**más** grande	
viejo(a)	**más** viejo(a) }	**mayor**
pequeño(a)	**más** pequeño(a) }	
joven	**más** joven }	**menor**

VERB INDEX

REGULAR VERBS

Model **-ar, -er, -ir** verbs

INFINITIVE

trabajar *(to work)*   **comer** *(to eat)*   **vivir** *(to live)*

-NDO FORM

trabajando *(working)*   **comiendo** *(eating)*   **viviendo** *(living)*

PAST PARTICIPLE

trabajado *(worked)*   **comido** *(eaten)*   **vivido** *(lived)*

SIMPLE TENSES

Indicative mood

PRESENT

(I work)		*(I eat)*		*(I live)*	
trabajo	trabajamos	como	comemos	vivo	vivimos
trabajas	trabajáis	comes	coméis	vives	vivís
trabaja	trabajan	come	comen	vive	viven

IMPERFECT

(I used to work)		*(I used to eat)*		*(I used to live)*	
trabajaba	trabajábamos	comía	comíamos	vivía	vivíamos
trabajabas	trabajabais	comías	comíais	vivías	vivíais
trabajaba	trabajaban	comía	comían	vivía	vivían

PRETERIT

(I worked)		*(I ate)*		*(I lived)*	
trabajé	trabajamos	comí	comimos	viví	vivimos
trabajaste	trabajasteis	comiste	comisteis	viviste	vivisteis
trabajó	trabajaron	comió	comieron	vivió	vivieron

FUTURE

(I will work)		*(I will eat)*		*(I will live)*	
trabajaré	trabajaremos	comeré	comeremos	viviré	viviremos
trabajarás	trabajaréis	comerás	comeréis	vivirás	viviréis
trabajará	trabajarán	comerá	comerán	vivirá	vivirán

CONDITIONAL

(I would work)		*(I would eat)*		*(I would live)*	
trabajaría	trabajaríamos	comería	comeríamos	viviría	viviríamos
trabajarías	trabajaríais	comerías	comeríais	vivirías	viviríais
trabajaría	trabajarían	comería	comerían	viviría	vivirían

Subjunctive mood

PRESENT

([that] I [may] work)		*([that] I [may] eat)*		*([that] I [may] live)*	
trabaje	trabaj**emos**	coma	com**amos**	viva	viv**amos**
trabaj**es**	trabaj**éis**	comas	com**áis**	vivas	viv**áis**
trabaje	trabaj**en**	coma	coman	viva	vivan

Imperative mood

(work)	*(eat)*	*(live)*
trabaj**a** (tú)	come (tú)	vive (tú)
trabaj**e** (Ud.)	coma (Ud.)	viva (Ud.)

trabaj**emos** (nosotros)	com**amos** (nosotros)	viv**amos** (nosotros)
trabaj**ad** (vosotros)	com**ed** (vosotros)	vivid (vosotros)
trabaj**en** (Uds.)	com**an** (Uds.)	vivan (Uds.)

COMPOUND TENSES

Indicative mood

PRESENT PERFECT

(I have worked)		*(I have eaten)*		*(I have lived)*	
he trabajado	hemos trabajado	he comido	hemos comido	he vivido	hemos vivido
has trabajado	habéis trabajado	has comido	habéis comido	has vivido	habéis vivido
ha trabajado	han trabajado	ha comido	han comido	ha vivido	han vivido

STEM-CHANGING VERBS

The **-ar** and **-er** stem-changing verbs

Stem-changing verbs have a spelling change in the stem. Verbs ending in **-ar** and **-er** change from **e** to **ie** and **o** to **ue**. These changes occur in all persons except the first and second persons plural of the present indicative, present subjunctive, and imperative.

INFINITIVE	PRESENT INDICATIVE	IMPERATIVE	PRESENT SUBJUNCTIVE
querer *(to want)*	quiero	———	quiera
	quieres	quiere	quieras
	quiere	quiera	quiera
	queremos	queramos	queramos
	queréis	quered	queráis
	quieren	quieran	quieran
cerrar *(to close)*	cierro	———	cierre
	cierras	cierra	cierres
	cierra	cierre	cierre
	cerramos	cerremos	cerremos
	cerráis	cerrad	cerréis
	cierran	cierren	cierren

INFINITIVE	PRESENT INDICATIVE	IMPERATIVE	PRESENT SUBJUNCTIVE
probar *(to try)*	pruebo pruebas prueba	——— prueba pruebe	pruebe pruebes pruebe
	probamos probáis prueban	probemos probad prueben	probemos probéis prueben
volver *(to return)*	vuelvo vuelves vuelve	——— vuelve vuelva	vuelva vuelvas vuelva
	volvemos volvéis vuelven	volvamos volved vuelvan	volvamos volváis vuelvan

Verbs that follow the same pattern:

acordar(se) *(to remember)*
acostar(se) *(to lie down, to go to bed)*
atender *(to attend, to wait on someone)*
comenzar *(to start, to begin)*
costar *(to cost)*
despertar *(to wake up)*
doler *(to hurt, to ache)*

empezar *(to begin, to start)*
encontrar *(to find)*
jugar *(to play)*
llover *(to rain)*
pensar *(to think)*
perder *(to lose)*
poder *(to be able, can)*

recomendar *(to recommend)*
recordar *(to remember)*
resolver *(to solve)*
sentar(se) *(to sit)*
sonar *(to ring)*
soñar *(to dream)*

The -ir stem-changing verbs

There are two types of stem-changing verbs that end in **-ir**: in one type, stressed **e** changes to **ie** in some tenses and to **i** in others, and stressed **o** to **ue** or **u**; in the second type, stressed **e** changes to **i** only in all the irregular tenses.

-ir: e → ie / o → ue or u

Present Indicative: all persons, except the first and second plural, change from **e** to **ie** and **o** to **ue**. *Preterit:* third person, singular and plural, changes from **e** to **i** and **o** to **u**. *Present Subjunctive:* all persons change from **e** to **ie** and **o** to **ue** except the first and second persons plural, which change from **e** to **i** and **o** to **u**. *Imperative:* all persons, except the second person plural, change from **e** to **ie** and **o** to **ue**; first person plural changes from **e** to **i** and **o** to **u**. The **-ndo** form changes from **e** to **i** and **o** to **u**.

INFINITIVE	Indicative		Imperative	Subjunctive
sentir *(to feel)*	PRESENT	PRETERIT		PRESENT
	siento sientes siente	sentí sentiste sintió	——— siente sienta	sienta sientas sienta
-NDO FORM sintiendo	sentimos sentís sienten	sentimos sentisteis sintieron	sintamos sentid sientan	sintamos sintáis sientan

	Indicative		Imperative	Subjunctive
	PRESENT	PRETERIT		PRESENT
dormir *(to sleep)* -NDO FORM durmiendo	duermo duermes duerme dormimos dormís duermen	dormí dormiste durmió dormimos dormisteis durmieron	———— duerme duerma durmamos dormid duerman	duerma duermas duerma durmamos durmáis duerman

-ir: e → i

The verbs in this second category are irregular in the same tenses as those of the first type. The only difference is that they only have one change: e → i in all irregular persons.

INFINITIVE **pedir** *(to ask for, request)* -NDO FORM pidiendo	Indicative		Imperative	Subjunctive
	PRESENT	PRETERIT		PRESENT
	pido pides pide pedimos pedís piden	pedí pediste pidió pedimos pedisteis pidieron	———— pide pida pidamos pedid pidan	pida pidas pida pidamos pidáis pidan

Verbs that follow this pattern:

competir *(to compete)*   seguir *(to follow)*
conseguir *(to get)*   servir *(to serve)*
repetir *(to repeat)*   vestir(se) *(to dress)*

VERBS WITH SPELLING CHANGES

Some verbs have a change in the spelling of the stem in some tenses, in order to maintain the sound of the final consonant. The most common ones are those with the consonants **g** and **c**. Remember that **g** and **c** in front of **e** or **i** have a soft sound, and in front of **a, o,** or **u** have a hard sound. In order to maintain the soft sound in front of **a, o,** or **u,** the letters **g** and **c** change to **j** and **z**, respectively. In order to maintain the hard sound of **g** or **c** in front of **e** and **i, u** is added to the **g (gu)** and the **c** changes to **qu**. The following verbs appear in the text.

1. Verbs ending in **-gar** change from **g** to **gu** before **e** in the first person of the preterit and in all persons of the present subjunctive.

> **entregar**   *to hand in*
> *Preterit:*   entregué, entregaste, entregó, etc.
> *Pres. Subj.:*   entregue, entregues, entregue, entreguemos, entreguéis, entreguen.

Verbs that follow the same pattern: **llegar, jugar.**

2. Verbs ending in **-ger** or **-gir** change from **g** to **j** before **o** and **a** in the first person of the present indicative and in all the persons of the present subjunctive.

> **proteger**   *to protect*
> *Pres. Ind.:*   protejo, proteges, protege, etc.
> *Pres. Subj.:*   proteja, protejas, proteja, protejamos, protejáis, protejan

Another verb that follows the same pattern is **recoger.**

3. Verbs ending in **-guir** change from **gu** to **g** before **o** and **a** in the first person of the present indicative and in all persons of the present subjunctive.

> **conseguir**   *to get*
> *Pres. Ind.:*   consigo, consigues, consigue, etc.
> *Pres. Subj.:*   consiga, consigas, consiga, consigamos, consigáis, consigan

Another verb that follows the same pattern is **seguir.**

4. Verbs ending in **-car** change from **c** to **qu** before **e** in the first person of the preterit and in all persons of the present subjunctive.

> **explicar**   *to explain*
> *Preterit:*   expliqué, explicaste, explicó, etc.
> *Pres. Subj.:*   explique, expliques, explique, expliquemos, expliquéis, expliquen

Verbs that follow the same pattern: **buscar, fabricar, sacar.**

5. Verbs that end in **-cer** or **-cir** and are preceded by a vowel change from **c** to **zc** before **o** and **a** in the first person of the present indicative and in all persons of the present subjunctive.

> **conocer**   *to know, be acquainted with*
> *Pres. Ind.:*   conozco, conoces, conoce, etc.
> *Pres. Subj.:*   conozca, conozcas, conozca, conozcamos, conozcáis, conozcan

Verbs that follow the same pattern: **agradecer, aparecer, desaparecer, obedecer, ofrecer, parecer, traducir.**

6. Verbs ending in **-zar** change from **z** to **c** before **e** in the first person of the preterit and in all persons of the present subjunctive.

> **comenzar**   *to start*
> *Preterit:*   comencé, comenzaste, comenzó, etc.
> *Pres. Subj.:*   comience, comiences, comience, comencemos, comencéis, comiencen

Verbs that follow the same pattern: **almorzar, garantizar, gozar.**

7. Verbs ending in **-eer** change from the unstressed **i** to **y** between vowels in the third person singular and plural of the preterit, in all persons of the imperfect subjunctive, and in the **-ndo** form.

> **creer**   *to believe*
> *Preterit:*   creí, creíste, creyó, creímos, creísteis, creyeron
> *-ndo Form:*   creyendo
> *Past Part.:*   creído

Another verb that follows the same pattern is **leer.**

8. Verbs ending in **-uir** change from the unstressed **i** to **y** between vowels (except **-quir,** which has the silent **u**) in the following tenses and persons.

> **destruir**   *to destroy*
> *Pres. Part.:*   destruyendo
> *Pres. Ind.:*   destruyo, destruyes, destruye, destruimos, destruís, destruyen
> *Preterit:*   destruí, destruiste, destruyó, destruimos, destruisteis, destruyeron
> *Imperative:*   destruye, destruya, destruyamos, destruid, destruyan
> *Pres. Subj.:*   destruya, destruyas, destruya, destruyamos, destruyáis, destruyan

Another verb that follows the same pattern is **construir.**

IRREGULAR VERBS

Only those tenses with irregular forms included in this book will be shown.

> **abrir**   *to open*
> *Past. Part.:*   abierto

> **caer**   *to fall*
> *Pres. Ind.:*   caigo, caes, cae, caemos, caéis, caen
> *Preterit:*   caí, caíste, cayó, caímos, caísteis, cayeron
> *Imperative:*   cae, caiga, caigamos, caed, caigan
> *Pres. Subj.:*   caiga, caigas, caiga, caigamos, caigáis, caigan
> *Past Part.:*   caído

> **dar**   *to give*
> *Pres. Ind.:*   doy, das, da, damos, dais, dan
> *Preterit:*   di, diste, dio, dimos, disteis, dieron
> *Imperative:*   da, dé, demos, dad, den
> *Pres. Subj.:*   dé, des, dé, demos, deis, den

> **decir**   *to say, tell*
> *Pres. Ind.:*   digo, dices, dice, decimos, decís, dicen
> *Preterit:*   dije, dijiste, dijo, dijimos, dijisteis, dijeron
> *Future:*   diré, dirás, dirá, diremos, diréis, dirán
> *Conditional:*   diría, dirías, diría, diríamos, diríais, dirían
> *Imperative:*   di, diga, digamos, decid, digan
> *Pres. Subj.:*   diga, digas, diga, digamos, digáis, digan
> *-ndo Form:*   diciendo
> *Past Part.:*   dicho

> **escribir**   *to write*
> *Past Part.:*   escrito

> **estar**   *to be*
> *Pres. Ind.:*   estoy, estás, está, estamos, estáis, están
> *Preterit:*   estuve, estuviste, estuvo, estuvimos, estuvisteis, estuvieron
> *Imperative:*   está, esté, estemos, estad, estén
> *Pres. Subj.:*   esté, estés, esté, estemos, estéis, estén

haber *to have*
Pres. Ind.: he, has, ha, hemos, habéis, han
Preterit: hube, hubiste, hubo, hubimos, hubisteis, hubieron
Future: habré, habrás, habrá, habremos, habréis, habrán
Conditional: habría, habrías, habría, habríamos, habrías, habrían
Pres. Subj.: haya, hayas, haya, hayamos, hayáis, hayan

hacer *to do, make*
Pres. Ind.: hago, haces, hace, hacemos, hacéis, hacen
Preterit: hice, hiciste, hizo, hicimos, hicisteis, hicieron
Future: haré, harás, hará, haremos, haréis, harán
Conditional: haría, harías, haría, haríamos, haríais, harían
Imperative: haz, haga, hagamos, haced, hagan
Pres. Subj.: haga, hagas, haga, hagamos, hagáis, hagan
Past Part.: hecho

ir *to go*
Pres. Ind.: voy, vas, va, vamos, vais, van
Imp. Ind.: iba, ibas, iba, íbamos, ibais, iban
Preterit: fui, fuiste, fue, fuimos, fuisteis, fueron
Imperative: ve, vaya, vayamos, id, vayan
Pres. Subj.: vaya, vayas, vaya, vayamos, vayáis, vayan

mantener(se) *to maintain, to keep* (See **tener**)

oír *to hear*
Pres. Ind.: oigo, oyes, oye, oímos, oís, oyen
Preterit: oí, oíste, oyó, oímos, oísteis, oyeron
Imperative: oye, oiga, oigamos, oid, oigan
Pres. Subj.: oiga, oigas, oiga, oigamos, oigáis, oigan
-ndo Form: oyendo
Past Part.: oído

poner *to place, put*
Pres. Ind.: pongo, pones, pone, ponemos, ponéis, ponen
Preterit: puse, pusiste, puso, pusimos, pusisteis, pusieron
Future: pondré, pondrás, pondrá, pondremos, pondréis, pondrán
Conditional: pondría, pondrías, pondría, pondríamos, pondríais, pondrían
Imperative: pon, ponga, pongamos, poned, pongan
Pres. Subj.: ponga, pongas, ponga, pongamos, pongáis, pongan
Past Part.: puesto

producir *to produce*
Pres. Ind.: produzco, produces, produce, producimos, producís, producen
Preterit: produje, produjiste, produjo, produjimos, produjisteis, produjeron
Imperative: produce, produzca, produzcamos, producid, produzcan
Pres. Subj.: produzca, produzcas, produzca, produzcamos, produzcáis, produzcan

(All verbs ending in **-ducir** follow this pattern.)

proponer *to propose* (See **poner**)

romper(se) *to break*
Past Part.: roto

saber *to know*

Pres. Ind.:	sé, sabes, sabe, sabemos, sabéis, saben
Preterit:	supe, supiste, supo, supimos, supisteis, supieron
Future:	sabré, sabrás, sabrá, sabremos, sabréis, sabrán
Conditional:	sabría, sabrías, sabría, sabríamos, sabríais, sabrían
Imperative:	sabe, sepa, sepamos, sabed, sepan
Pres. Subj.:	sepa, sepas, sepa, sepamos, sepáis, sepan

salir *to leave, go out*

Pres. Ind.:	salgo, sales, sale, salimos, salís, salen
Future:	saldré, saldrás, saldrá, saldremos, saldréis, saldrán
Conditional:	saldría, saldrías, saldría, saldríamos, saldríais, saldrían
Imperative:	sal, salga, salgamos, salid, salgan
Pres. Subj.:	salga, salgas, salga, salgamos, salgáis, salgan

ser *to be*

Pres. Ind.:	soy, eres, es, somos, sois, son
Imp. Ind.:	era, eras, era, éramos, erais, eran
Preterit:	fui, fuiste, fue, fuimos, fuisteis, fueron
Imperative:	sé, sea, seamos, sed, sean
Pres. Subj.:	sea, seas, sea, seamos, seáis, sean

tener *to have*

Pres. Ind.:	tengo, tienes, tiene, tenemos, tenéis, tiene
Preterit:	tuve, tuviste, tuvo, tuvimos, tuvisteis, tuvieron
Future:	tendré, tendrás, tendrá, tendremos, tendréis, tendrán
Conditional:	tendría, tendrías, tendría, tendríamos, tendrías, tendrían
Imperative:	ten, tenga, tengamos, tened, tengan
Pres. Subj.:	tenga, tengas, tenga, tengamos, tengáis, tengan

traer *to bring*

Pres. Ind.:	traigo, traes, trae, traemos, traéis, traen
Preterit:	traje, trajiste, trajo, trajimos, trajisteis, trajeron
Imperative:	trae, traiga, traigamos, traed, traigan
Pres. Subj.:	traiga, traigas, traiga, traigamos, traigáis, traigan
-ndo Form:	trayendo
Past Part.:	traído

valer *to be worth*

Pres. Ind.:	valgo, vales, vale, valemos, valéis, valen
Future:	valdré, valdrás, valdrá, valdremos, valdréis, valdrán
Conditional:	valdría, valdrías, valdríamos, valdríais, valdrían
Imperative:	vale, valga, valgamos, valed, valgan
Pres. Subj.:	valga, valgas, valga, valgamos, valgáis, valgan

venir *to come*

Pres. Ind.:	vengo, vienes, viene, venimos, venís, vienen
Preterit:	vine, viniste, vino, vinimos, vinisteis, vinieron
Future:	vendré, vendrás, vendrá, vendremos, vendréis, vendrán
Conditional:	vendría, vendrías, vendría, vendríamos, vendríais, vendrían
Imperative:	ven, venga, vengamos, venid, vengan
Pres. Subj.:	venga, vengas, venga, vengamos, vengáis, vengan
-ndo Form:	viniendo

ver   *to see*

Pres. Ind.:	veo, ves, ve, vemos, veis, ven
Imp. Ind.:	veía, veías, veía, veíamos, veíais, veían
Preterit:	vi, viste, vio, vimos, visteis, vieron
Imperative:	ve, vea, veamos, ved, vean
Pres. Subj.:	vea, veas, vea, veamos, veáis, vean
Past Part.:	visto

This vocabulary includes all the words and expressions appearing in the text of **Nosotros, los jóvenes.** Exceptions are names of people and of most countries and places.

Nouns are listed with their definite articles. Nouns referring to persons are given in the masculine and feminine forms. Adjectives are listed in the masculine singular form with the feminine ending shown after each adjective. Verbs are listed in the infinitive form. Verb forms introduced as vocabulary items are listed in the form they appeared in the text.

Active vocabulary and expressions that were introduced in **Nuevos amigos** are followed by a roman numeral **I,** for example: el **árbol,** *tree,* **I.** Active and passive vocabulary introduced in **Nosotros, los jóvenes** are followed by a roman numeral **II** as well as a number that refers to the unit in which the word or expression is introduced, for example, el **caballero,** *gentleman,* **II, 3.**

The following abbreviations are used in this list: *adj.* adjective, *adv.* adverb; *com.* command; *dir.* direct; *f.* feminine; *fam.* familiar; *ind.* indicative; *inf.* infinitive; *m.* masculine; *obj.* object; *pl.* plural; *pol.* polite; *prep.* preposition; *pron.* pronoun; *sing.* singular; *sub.* subjunctive.

A

a at, to, I; **a cambio de** in exchange for, II, 3; **a casa** (to) home, I; **a dieta** on a diet, I; **a final de** by the end of, II, 10; **a la (última) moda** latest style, II, 3; **a la carrera** in a hurry, II, 7; **a la corta o a la larga** sooner or later, II, 7; **a la derecha** on the right, I; **a la fuerza** by force, II, 2; **a la izquierda** on the left, I; **a la una** at one o'clock, I; **a lo dicho, hecho** no sooner said than done, I; **a menudo** often, I; **a partir de** as of, II, 10; **a pie** on foot, I; **a primera hora** as early as possible, I; **¿a qué hora?** at what time?, I; **a veces** sometimes, I; **a ver** let's see, I
abajo below, I
la **abeja** bee, II, 10
abierto, -a open; opened, II, 10
el **abrazo** hug, embrace, II, 1; **un abrazo de...** a hug from..., II, 1
el **abrigo** coat, I
abrir to open; **abrir una cuenta** to open an account, II, 3
aburrido, -a boring, I
aburrirse to get bored, II, 6
acabar to finish, II, 5
acampar to camp out, II, 1
el **accidente** accident, II, 6

acompañar to accompany, II, 10
aconsejar to advise, II, 9
acordar(se) (ue) to remember, II, 6
acostar(se) (ue) to lie down; to go to bed, II, 6
la **actividad** activity, I; **actividad cultural** cultural activity, II, 10
el **acuario** aquarium, II, 2
el **acuerdo** agreement, II, 2
acusar: acusar recibo de to acknowledge receipt of, II, 9
adecuado, -a adequate, II, 6
el **adelanto: el adelanto tecnológico** technological advance, II, 7
adelgazar to become thin; to lose weight, II, 6
adiós goodbye, I
adjuntar to enclose, II, 9
¿adónde? (to) where?, I
la **aduana** customs, I; **aduanero** customs agent, I
el **aeropuerto** airport, I
afectuosamente affectionately, II, 1
afeitar(se) to shave, II, 6
agarrar to grab, II, 9
agencia: la agencia de viajes travel agency, II, 1
agitado, -a excited, II, 2
agradecer (zc) to thank; to be grateful, II, 5
agrícola agricultural, II, 7; **la revolución agrícola** agricultural revolution, II, 7

el **agua** water (*f.*), I; **agua de colonia** cologne, II, 6
el **aguacero** downpour, II, 3
ahí there, I
ahora now, I; **ahora mismo** right now, II, 3
ahorrar to save, I
el **aire: el aire acondicionando** air conditioning, II, 11; **el aire puro** pure air, II, 10
al (a + el) to the, at the (contraction), I; **al aire libre** outdoors, II, 11; **al contrario** on the contrary, I; **al día** up to date, II, 3; **al día siguiente** the following day, II, 5; **al fin** finally, II, 5; **al lado de** beside, I; **al principio** at the beginning, II, 10; **al pueblo** people, II, 6
Alcázar Spanish fortress or palace, II, 11
alegrarse to get happy, II, 6
la **alegría** happiness, I
el **álgebra** algebra, I
algo something, I
el **algodón** cotton, I
alguien someone, II, 6
algún any; some, II, 6
algunos, -as some, I
el **alimento** food, II, 6
allá (over) there, I
allí there, I
el **almacén** store, II, 3

almorzar (ue)   to eat lunch, **II, 3**

el **almuerzo**   lunch, **I**

¿aló?   hello?, **I**

alquilar   to rent, **II, 9**

alrededor de   around, **II, 3**

alto   loudly, **II, 3; alto, -a**   tall, **I**

¡alto!   stop!, **II, 9**

amable   kind, polite, **I; ¿serías tan amable . . . ?**   would you be nice enough to . . . ?, **II, 7**

amarillo, -a   yellow, **I**

el **ambiente**   environment, **II, 10**

la **amiga**   friend (*f.*), **I**

el **amigo**   friend (*m.*), **I**

el **amor**   love, **I**

anaranjado, -a   orange, **I**

ancho, -a   wide, **II, 10**

anfibio   amphibious, **II, 2**

el **anillo**   ring, **II, 3**

el **aniversario**   anniversary, **II, 5**

anoche   last night, **I**

anotar   to write down, **II, 3**

la **antena: la antena parabólica**   satellite dish, **II, 7**

antes   before, **I**

antipático, -a   not nice; unpleasant, **I**

anunciar   to advertise, **II, 5**

el **anuncio: el anuncio clasificado**   classified ad, **II, 9**

añadir   to add, **I**

el **año**   year, **I; el Año Nuevo**   New Year's Day, **II, 5**

apagar   to turn off, **II, 3**

el **aparato: el aparato eléctrico**   appliance, **II, 10**

aparecer (zc)   to appear, **II, 3**

el **apartado: el apartado postal**   post office box, **II, 9**

el **apartamento**   apartment, **I**

el **apio**   celery, **II, 6**

apoyar   to support, **II, 10**

aprender   to learn, **II, 1**

apretar (ie)   to press, **II, 7**

aprovechar   to take advantage of, **II, 3**

apuradísimo, -a   in a big hurry, **I**

apurarse   to hurry up, **II, 11**

aquel, aquella   that, **I**

aquél, aquélla   that one, **I**

aquellos, -as   those, **I**

aquéllos, -as   those ones, **I**

aquí   here, **I; he aquí**   here is; here are, **II, 7**

arar: arar la tierra   to plow the land, **II, 10**

el **árbol**   tree, **I**

los **aretes**   earrings, **II, 3**

arreglado, -a   arranged, **I**

arreglar   to fix, **II, 9**

arriba   up (there), **I**

el **arroz**   rice, **I**

las **artesanías**   arts and crafts, **II, 10**

el **artículo**   article, **II, 3; los artículos de tocador**   toiletries, **II, 6**

el **ascensor**   elevator, **II, 11**

asegúrate   make sure, **II, 9**

así   that way, then, **I; así que**   therefore, **II, 5; así, así**   so-so, **II, 1**

el **asiento**   seat, **I**

la **aspiradora**   vacuum cleaner, **II, 2**

la **aspirina**   aspirin, **II, 6**

atender (ie)   to attend; to wait on someone, **II, 3**

atentamente   sincerely; very truly yours, **II, 3**

atento, -a   attentive, **II, 3**

el **atleta**   athlete (*m.*), **I**

la **atleta**   athlete (*f.*), **I**

el **átomo**   atom, **II, 7**

atractivo, -a   attractive, **II, 9**

el **atún**   tuna, **I**

aumentar   to increase, **II, 10; aumentar de peso**   to gain weight, **II, 6**

aunque   although; even though, **II, 5**

el **auto**   car, automobile, **I**

el **autobús**   bus, **I; autobús escolar**   school bus, **I**

¡auxilio!   help!, **II, 9**

avanzado, -a   advanced, **I**

la **aventura**   adventure, **I**

el **avión**   airplane, **I**

¡ay!: ¡ay, caramba!   for heaven's sake!, **II, 2**

ayer   yesterday, **I**

el **ayudante**   assistant, **II, 9**

ayudar   to help, **I**

el **azúcar**   sugar, **I**

azul   blue, **I**

B

¡bah!   c'mon!, **II, 3**

bailar   to dance, **I**

el **baile**   dance, **I**

bajar   to get off, **I**

bajarse   to step down, **II, 9**

bajo, -a   short, **I**

el **balcón**   balcony, **II, 6**

la **ballena**   whale, **II, 10**

el **balón**   ball (basketball, volleyball, soccer ball), **I**

bañar   to bathe, **II, 2**

bañar(se)   to bathe (oneself), **II, 6**

el **baño**   bathroom, **I**

barato, -a   cheap, **I**

¡bárbaro!   awesome!, **II, 11**

barrer   to sweep, **II, 9**

el **barrio**   neighborhood, **I**

la **base**   foundation (makeup), **II, 6; base de datos**   data base, **II, 7**

basta: ¡basta de . . . !   enough . . . !, **I**

bastante   enough; a lot, **I**

el **bastón** (*pl.* **bastones**)   ski pole, **I**

la **basura**   trash, **II, 2**

la **bata**   robe, **II, 3**

el **bate**   bat, **I**

batir   to beat, **I**

beber   to drink, **I**

belgas   Belgians, **II, 6**

bellísimo, -a   very beautiful, **II, 11**

bello, -a   beautiful, **II, 9**

la **biblioteca**   library, **II, 10**

la **bicicleta**   bicycle, **I**

bien   well; good; fine; very, **I**

bienvenido, -a   welcome, **I**

el **bigote**   moustache, **II, 6**

el **billete**   ticket, **I**

el **bistec**   beefsteak, **I**

el **bizcocho**   cake, **I**

blanco, -a   white, **I**

blandas   soft, **II, 7**

la **blusa**   blouse, **I**

la **boca**   mouth, **II, 6**

el **bocadillo**   snack; sandwich, **I**

la **boda**   wedding, **II, 5; las bodas de plata**   silver wedding anniversary, **I**

la **boina**   beret, **II, 11**

el **boleto**   ticket, **II, 7**

el **bolígrafo**   ballpoint pen, **I**

el **bolsillo**   pocket, **I**

la **bomba: la bomba atómica**   atomic bomb, **II, 7**

bonito, -a   pretty, **I**

bordado, -a   embroidered, **I**

borrar   to erase, **II, 7**

el **bosque**   forest, **II, 1**

la **bota**   ski boot, **I**

la **botella**   bottle, **II, 6**

el **botón**   button, **II, 7**

el **botones**   bellboy, **II, 11**

el **brazo**   arm, **II, 6**

la **broma**   joke, **II, 5**

buen: ¡buen provecho!   enjoy it! (meal), **I**

buenísimo, -a   very good, **I**

bueno, -a: buena suerte   good luck, **II, 9; buenas noches**   good evening; good night, hello, **I; buenas tardes**   good afternoon, **I; bueno**   well, all right, **I; ¿bueno?**   hello?, **I; buenos días**   good morning, **I**

la **bufanda**   scarf, **II, 3**

el **buró**   desk, **II, 11**

el **burro**   donkey, **II, 5**

buscar   to look for, **I**

C

el **caballero**   gentleman, **II, 3**

el **caballo**   horse, **II, 1**

la **cabeza**   head, **II, 6**

cada   each, **I**

caer   to fall; **caer un rayo**   to strike lightning, **II, 3**

la **cafetería**   cafeteria, **I**

la **caja**   cashier's desk, **I; cash register**, **II, 9**

la **cajera**   cashier (*f.*), **II, 9**

el **cajero**   cashier (*m.*), **II, 9**

el **cajón**   drawer, **II, 7**

el **calcetín** (*pl.* **calcetines**)   sock, **I**

la **calculadora**   calculator, **I**

el **calendario**   calendar, **II, 5**

la **calidad**   quality, **I**

calmar(se)   to calm (oneself), **II, 7**

la **caloría** calorie, **II, 6**
los **calzoncillos** men's briefs, **II, 3**
la **cámara** camera, **I**
la **camarera** waitress, **I**
el **camarero** waiter, **I**
  cambiar to cash, **I; cambiar (de)** to change, **I; cambiar impresiones** to exchange views, **II, 1**
  caminar to walk, **I**
el **camino** road, **II, 5**
la **camisa** shirt, **I**
la **camiseta** undershirt, **II, 3**
las **campanitas** little bells, **II, 2**
el **campeón** champion (*m.*), **I**
la **campeona** champion (*f.*), **I**
la **campesina** country dweller (*f.*), **II, 10**
el **campesino** country dweller (*m.*), **II, 10**
el **campo** countryside, **II, 10; el campo de la medicina** medical field, **II, 7**
la **canasta** basketball hoop; basket, **I**
la **cancha: la cancha de tenis** tennis court, **I**
la **canción** song, **I**
el **candidato** candidate (*m.*), **II, 9**
  cansarse to get tired, **II, 6**
  cantar to sing, **I**
la **cantidad** amount, **II, 10**
el **canto** song, **II, 2**
la **cañería** pipe, **II, 9**
la **capital** capital, **II, 10**
la **cara** face, **II, 6**
  cara, -o expensive, **I**
  ¡caramba! heavens!, **II, 3; ¡ay, caramba!** for heaven's sake, **II, 2**
el **carapacho** shell, **II, 10**
  cargar to carry, **II, 9**
el **Caribe** Caribbean, **I**
el **cariño** affection, **II, 1**
  cariñosamente affectionately, **II, 1**
  cariñoso, -a affectionate, **I**
el **carnaval** carnival; Mardi gras, **II, 5**
la **carne** meat, **I; carne sin grasa** lean meat, **II, 6**
  caro, -a expensive, **I**
el **carpintero** carpenter, **II, 9**
la **carrera: a la carrera** in a hurry, **II, 7**
el **carro** cart, **I**
la **carta** letter, **I**
la **cartera** purse; schoolbag, **I**
el **cartero** mail carrier, **II, 9**
la **casa** house, **I;** business firm, **II, 3; casa de cambio** money exchange office, **I**
  casado, -a married, **I**
  casarse to get married, **II, 7**
la **caseta** booth, **II, 9**
el **casete** cassette, **I**
  casi almost, **I**
el **casillero** shelves with dividers, **II, 11**
las **castañuelas** castanets, **II, 11**
  catalán Catalan; Catalonian (*m.*), **II, 11**

  catalana Catalonian (*f.*), **II, 11**
el **catarro** head cold, **II, 6**
la **catedral** cathedral, **II, 11**
la **categoría** category, **I**
la **cebolla** onion, **I**
  celebrar to celebrate, **II, 5**
la **cena** dinner; supper, **I**
  cenar to have dinner, **I**
  céntrico, -a centrally located, **II, 11**
el **centro** downtown, **II, 1; el centro comercial** shopping center, **II, 10; el centro de trabajo** work place, **II, 10**
  cepillar to brush, **II, 2; cepillar(se)** to brush, **II, 6**
el **cepillo** brush, **II, 6**
la **cerámica** ceramics (material), **I**
  cerca (de) near, **I**
el **cerdo** pig, **II, 5**
la **cereza** cherry, **I**
  cerrar (ie) to close, **II, 3**
el **césped** lawn; grass, **II, 7; cortar el césped** to mow the lawn, **II, 7**
el **cielo** sky, **II, 10**
la **ciencia** science, **I; ciencia ficción** science fiction, **I**
la **científica** scientist (*f.*), **II, 7**
el **científico** scientist (*m.*), **II, 7**
el **cine** movies; movie theater, **I**
la **cintura** waist, **II, 6**
el **cinturón** (*pl.* **cinturones**) belt, **I**
la **cita** appointment, **II, 9**
la **ciudad** city, **I**
  claro, -a light (in color), **I**
la **clase** class; classroom; kind, **I**
los **claveles** carnations, **II, 11**
el **cliente** customer (*m.*), **I**
la **cliente** customer (*f.*), **I**
el **coche** car, **I; el coche de topetazos** bumper car, **II, 9**
la **cocina** kitchen; cooking; cuisine, **I**
  cocinar to cook, **I**
la **cocinera** cook (*f.*), **II, 9**
el **cocinero** cook (*m.*), **II, 9**
el **colegio** school, **I**
  colocar to place, **II, 9**
el **color** color, **I**
el **colorete** rouge, blush, **II, 6**
  "comecocos" Pac-man, **II, 7**
el **comedor** dining room, **I**
  comentar to comment, **II, 3**
  comer to eat, **I**
  cómico, -a comic, funny; comical, **I**
la **comida** food; meal; dinner, **I**
  como about; as; like, **I; como de costumbre** as usual, **II, 3; como quieras** as you wish, **II, 11; ¿cómo?** how?, **I; ¿cómo es?** what's he, (she, it) like?, **I; ¿cómo está?** how are you? (*pol. sing.*), **I; ¿cómo estás?** how are you? (*fam. sing.*), **I; ¡cómo lo odio!** how I hate it!, **II, 10; ¡cómo me divierto!** I'm having so much fun!, **II, 10;**

  ¡cómo me gusta! I like it a lot!, **II, 10; ¡cómo no!** of course!, **I; ¿cómo se llama él (ella)?** what's his (her) name?, **I; ¿cómo se llaman?** what are their names?, **I; ¿cómo te llamas tú?** what's your name?, **I**
  cómodo, -a comfortable, **I**
la **compañera: la compañera de clase** classmate (*f.*), **II, 1**
el **compañero: el compañero de clase** classmate, (*m.*), **II, 1**
el **compás** compass, **I**
  competir (i) to compete, **II, 6**
  complacer (zc) to please, **II, 5**
  completo, -a complete, **I**
la **compra** shopping, **I**
  comprar to buy, **I**
la **computadora** computer, **I**
  con with, **I; con cariño** with affection, **II, 1; con mucho gusto** I'd be glad to, **II, 3; con permiso** excuse me, **I; con una semana de anticipación** with a week ahead of time, **I**
  conceder to concede, **II, 9**
el **concierto** concert, **I**
el **conejo** rabbit, **II, 2**
  cogelarlas to freeze them, **II, 6**
  conmigo with me, **I**
  conocer (zc) to know; to meet; to be acquainted with, **I**
el **conserje** concierge, **II, 11**
  conservar to preserve, **II, 7**
  constantemente constantly, **II, 1**
  construir to build; to construct, **II, 3**
  consultar to consult, **II, 9**
la **contaminación** pollution, **II, 7; contaminación ambiental** environmental pollution, **II, 7**
  contaminar to pollute, **II, 10**
  contento, -a happy, **II, 2**
  contestar to answer, **I**
el **continente** continent, **II, 7**
  contribuir contribute, **II, 9**
el **coraje: ¡qué coraje!** what nerve!, **II, 2**
la **corbata** tie, **I**
  cordialmente cordially, **II, 1**
el **coro** choir, **II, 2**
el **correo** post office, **I**
  correr to run; to jog, **I**
el **corrido** a type of Mexican song that tells a story, **II, 10**
  cortar (se) to cut oneself, **I; II, 6; ¡la comunicación se cortó!** we were cut off!, **I**
  cortésmente courteously, **II, 9**
  corto, -a short, **I**
la **cosa** thing, **I; cosas que hacer** things to do, **II, 2**
la **cosecha** harvest; crop, **II, 7**
los **cosméticos** cosmetics, **II, 6**
  costar (ue) to cost, **II, 11**
  crear to create, **II, 10**
  crece grows, **II, 2**

creer to think; to believe, I

la **crema: la crema de afeitar** shaving cream, II, 6

creó created, II, 6

el **crimen** crime, I

el **cuaderno** notebook, I

la **cuadra** city block, II, 3

¿**cuál?** what?; which?, I

cualidad quality, II, 9

cuando when, I; ¿**cuándo?** when?, I

cuánto, -a: ¡cuánta gente! what a lot of people!, I; ¿**cuánto?** how much?, I; ¿**cuánto cuesta?** how much does it cost?, I; ¿**cuánto cuestan?** how much do they cost?, I; ¡**cuánto me alegro!** I am so happy!, II, 6; ¿**cuánto vale?** how much does it cost?, I; ¿**cuántas veces?** how many times?, I; ¿**cuántos, -as?** how many?, I; ¿**cuántos años cumples?** How old are you?, II, 5; ¿**cuántos años tiene?** How old are you (is he/she?), I; ¿**cuántos años tienes?** How old are you?, II, 5; ¿**cuántos cuartos hay?** How many rooms are there?, I

el **cuarto** room, I; quarter; fourth, II, 6; **un cuarto de pollo** a quarter chicken, II, 6

la **cuchara** spoon, I

la **cucharita** teaspoon, I

la **cuchilla** razor blade, II, 6

el **cuchillo** knife, I

el **cuello** neck, II, 6

la **cuenta** bill, check, I

el **cuero** leather, I

el **cuerpo** body, II, 2

cuesta it costs, I; **cuestan** they cost, I

cuidar to take care of, II, 2; ¡**cuida tu salud!** take care of your health!, II, 6; ¡**cuidado!** watch out!, II, 9

la **culpa** blame, II, 3; **la culpa la tuvo . . .** the one to blame was . . . , II, 3; **tener la culpa** to be at fault, II, 3

el **cumpleaños** birthday, I

cumplir: cumplir años to have a birthday, I

la **cuna** cradle, II, 10

curar to cure, II, 7

el **curso** course, II, 1

CH

el **champú** shampoo, II, 6

chao so long, 'bye, I

la **chaqueta** jacket, I

el **cheque: el cheque de viajero** traveler's check, I

la **chica** girl, I

el **chico** boy, I

el **chile: chile con carne** dish of beans, ground beef, and chilies, I

el **chocolate** chocolate, I

la **churrería** churro store, II, 9

el **churro** doughnut-like pastry, II, 9

D

dar to give, II, 1; **dar una clase** to teach a class, II, 1; **dar un concierto** to give a concert, II, 1; **dar dinero** to give money, II, 1; **dar recuerdos (a, para)** to give regards (to), II, 1; **dar recuerdos de** to give regards from, II, 1; **dar un paseo** to take a trip, II, 1; **dar una mano** to lend a hand, II, 7; **dar una película** to show a movie, I; **dar una vuelta** to go for a walk, I; ¿**me podrías dar . . . ?** could you give me . . . ?, II, 7; **darse cuenta de que** to realize that, II, 9

de from; of; made of, I; **de acuerdo** all right, I; I agree, II, 11; ¿**de dónde?** from where?, I; **de él** his, I; **de ella** her, I; **de ellas** their, (f.), I; **de ellos** their, (m.), I; **de hecho** as a matter of fact, II, 7; **de la mañana** in the morning, A.M., I; **de la noche** at night, P.M., I; ¡**de lo mejor!** wonderfully!, II, 1; **de maravilla** marvelous; great, II, 1; **de nada** you're welcome, I; **de novela** from a novel, II, 1; **de nuevo** again, I; ¡**de película!** out of this world!, II, 11; **de plástico** (made of) plastic, I; ¿**de qué es?** what's it made of?, I; **de usted** your (sing.), I; **de ustedes** your (pl.), I; **de vez en cuando** once in a while, II, 7; **de visita** visiting, II, 2

debajo (de) under, I

deber should, I

débil weak, I

¿**debo . . . ?** should I . . . ?, I

decidir to decide, I

décimo, -a tenth, II, 5

decir (i) to say, I; **dice que . . .** he (she) says that . . . , I; ¡**diga!** hello?, I; ¿**me podrías decir . . . ?** could you tell me . . . ?, II, 7

dedo: el dedo de la mano finger, II, 6; **el dedo del pie** toe, II, 6

dejar to leave (behind); to allow; let, I; **le dejo la cartera en . . .** I'll let the purse go for . . . , I

del (de + el) of the, from the (contraction), I

delante (de) in front (of), I

delgado, -a thin, I

delicioso, -a delicious, I

demasiado too (much), I

demostrar: demostró demonstrated, II, 6

dentro (de) in, within (a period of time), I; II, 5; **dentro de un rato** in a while, II, 7

la **dependienta** salesclerk (f.), II, 3

el **dependiente** salesclerk (m.), II, 3

los **deportes** sports, I

desaparecer (zc) to disappear, II, 5

el **desastre** disaster, II, 7

de **desayuno** breakfast, I

descansar to rest, II, 3

descendiente descendant, II, 10

desde from, I

desear to like; to want; to wish, I

el **desfile** parade, II, 5

el **desodorante** deodorant, II, 6

el **despacho** office, II, 9

la **despedida** complimentary closing, II, 1

despedir(se) to say goodbye, II, 6

el **desperdicio** waste, II, 10; **el desperdicio radioactivo** radioactive waste, II, 10

el **despertador** alarm clock, II, 6

despertar(se) (ie) to wake up, II, 6

después then, I; **después de** after, I

destruir to destroy, II, 3

detenerse to linger, to stop, II, 11

detenido, -a suspended; detained, I

detrás (de) behind, I

el **día** day, I; **Día de la Hispanidad** Columbus Day, II, 5; **Día de la Independencia** Independence Day, II, 5; **Día de la Raza** Columbus Day, II, 5; **Día de las Madres** Mother's Day, II, 5; **Día de los Enamorados** Valentine's Day, II, 5; **Día de los Inocentes** Fool's Day, II, 5; **Día de los Padres** Father's Day, II, 5; **Día de Reyes** Epiphany (Day of the Three Wise Men), II, 5; **Día del Trabajo** Labor Day, II, 5; **los días de la semana** days of the week, I

diabólico diabolic, II, 6

el **diario** diary, I

el **dibujo** drawing, I; **dibujo animado** animated cartoon, I

el **diccionario** dictionary, I

dicho said; expressed, II, 10

los **dientes** teeth, II, 6

la **dieta: la dieta balanceada** balanced diet, II, 6

difícil difficult, I

la **dificultad** difficulty, II, 7

el **dinero** money, I

la **diosa** goddess, II, 1

los **dioses** gods, II, 10

el **disco** record, I

la **discoteca** disco, I

discutir to discuss, II, 5

disponible available, II, 9

el **disquete** disk, II, 7

distinguido, -a: distinguida señora dear madam, II, 9
distinto, -a different, II, 1
divertido, -a fun, I
divertirse (ie) to have fun, II, 6
dividir to divide, II, 2
la **división** division, II, 2
doblar to turn, II, 3; **doblar a la derecha** to turn right, II, 3; **doblar a la izquierda** to turn left, II, 3
el **doble** double, I
doler (ue) to hurt; to ache, II, 6
el **dolor; dolor de garganta** sore throat, II, 6; **dolor de estómago** stomachache, II, 6
doña title of respect for mature women, II, 1
dorarse to brown, I
dormir (ue) to sleep, II, 6
dormir(se) (ue) to fall asleep, II, 6
dos two, I; **dos veces** twice, I; **los dos** the two (m.); **las dos** (f.), I
dudoso: es dudoso it is doubtful, II, 11
dulce sweet, II, 6
duradero, -a lasting, II, 7
durante during, II, 1
durar to last, II, 5
el **durazno** peach, II, 10
duro, -a hard, II, 7

E

echar: echar al agua to throw in the water, II, 9
el **edificio** building, II, 10
la **educación: la educación física** physical education, I
egoísta selfish, I
él he; him, I; **de él** his, I
el **the** (m.), I; **el (de)** the one (made of), I
el **elefante** elephant, II, 10
elegante elegant, I
ella she; her, I; **de ella** hers, I
ellas they (f. pl.), I
ellos they (m. pl.), I
el **embotellamiento** traffic jam, II, 10
emigrar to emigrate, II, 10
empezar (ie) to start, I
la **empleada** employee, (f.), I
el **empleado** employee, (m.), I
en in; at; by; on, I; **en busca de** in search of, II, 10; **en calma** calm, II, 9; **en cuanto a** in regard to, II, 9; **en fin** really; actually; after all, II, 1; **en forma** in shape, II, 6; **en persona** in person, I; **¿en qué puedo servirle?** how may I help you?, I; **en relación con** regarding, II, 9; **en todo momento** every time, I; **en un abrir y cerrar de ojos** in a second; in a flash, II, 7; **en un dos por tres** in a jiffy, II, 7; **en un par de horas** in a couple of hours, II, 7; **en venta** for sale, I; **en voz alta** out loud, II, 5; **en voz baja** in a low voice, I
enamorado, -a in love, II, 5
enamorarse to fall in love, II, 6
encantado, -a pleased to meet you, II, 1
encantar to delight, I
encargarse (de) to be in charge (of), II, 11
la **enchilada** rolled tortilla filled with meat or cheese, I
encontrar (ue) to find, I; **encontraron** they met, II, 5
la **energía** energy, II, 6; **energía nuclear** nuclear energy, II, 7
enfadarse to get angry, II, 6
enfermar(se) to become ill, II, 6
la **enfermedad** disease, II, 6
enfermo, -a sick, II, 1
¡enhorabuena! congratulations!, II, 9
el **enjuague** hair rinse, II, 6; **enjuague para la boca** mouthwash, II, 6
enojarse to get angry, II, 6
enrollar to roll up, II, 9
la **ensalada** salad, I
el **ensayo** rehearsal, II, 2
enseñar to show; to teach, II, 3
entender: has entendido have understood, II, 9
entonces then, I
la **entrada** entrance; admission ticket, I
entrar to enter, I
entre between, I
entregar to deliver, II, 9
la **entrevista** interview, I
entrevistar to interview, I
entusiasmado, -a enthusiastic, II, 11
la **envidia** envy, I; **¡qué envidia!** what envy (I feel)!, I
la **Epifanía** Epiphany, II, 5
el **equipaje** baggage, I
el **equipo** equipment, II, 9
equivaler to be equivalent, II, 10
la **erosión** erosion, II, 10
es: es dudoso it is doubtful, II, 11; **es increíble** it is incredible, II, 11; **es indispensable** it is indispensable, II, 11; **es la una** it's one o'clock, I; **es un placer** it's a pleasure, I; **es probable** it is probable, II, 11; **es verdad** it's true, I
escalar to climb (a mountain), II, 1
Escocia Scotland, II, 6
escribir to write, I
escrito written, II, 10
el **escritorio** desk, II, 7
escuchar to listen (to), I
el **escudo** coat of arms, II, 3

la **escuela** school, I; **la escuela secundaria** secondary school, I
ese, -a that, I
ése, -a that one, I
el **esmalte: el esmalte de uñas** nail polish, II, 6
ésos, -as those ones, I
esos, -as those, I
espacial: el transbordador espacial space shuttle, II, 7; **la misión espacial** space mission, II, 7
el **espacio** space, II, 10
la **espalda** back (of the body), II, 6
España Spain, I
el **español** Spanish language, I
especial special, I
la **especialidad** specialty, I
la **especie** species, II, 10
el **espejo** mirror, II, 6
esperar to wait (for), I; to hope, II, 9
las **espinacas** spinach, II, 6
la **esposa** wife, I
el **esposo** husband, I
esquiar to ski; skiing, I
la **esquina** corner (street), I
los **esquís** skis, I
esta: esta noche tonight, I; **esta tarde** this afternoon, I
está: está ocupado it's busy, I
estaba(n): estaba dando was giving, II, 5; **estaban descansando** were resting, II, 5
la **estación** season, I
estacionar to park, II, 9
los **Estados Unidos (EE.UU.)** United States (U.S.), I
la **estancia** cattle ranch, II, 10
el **estanque** pond, I
el **estante** shelf, II, 9
estar to be, I; **estar a punto de** to be about to, I; **estar aburrido, -a** to be bored, II, 5; **estar al día** to be up to date, II, 3; **estar casado, -a** to be married, I; **estar de acuerdo** to be in agreement, II, 2; **estar de compras** to be shopping, I; **estar de vuelta** to be back, II, 11; **estar enojado, -a** to be angry, II, 10; **estar harto de . . .** to be sick and tired of . . . , II, 7; **estar listo, -a** to be ready, II, 5; **estar muerto, -a** to be dead (tired), II, 3; **estar tan cansado, -a** to be so tired, II, 2; **estar tan ocupado, -a** to be so busy, II, 2
estás: estás en tu casa make yourself at home, I
este, -a this, I
éste, -a this one, I
estimado, -a dear; esteemed, II, 1; **estimado señor** dear sir, II, 9
el **estómago** stomach, II, 6
estos, -as these, I

éstos, -as these ones, **I**
estrecho, -a narrow, **II, 11**
la **estrella: la estrella de cine** movie star, **II, 6**
el **estudiante** student (*m.*), **I; el estudiante universitario** college student, **II, 10**
la **estudiante** student (*f.*), **I**
estudiar to study, **I**
estupendo, -a great, **I**
eurpopeo, -a European, **II, 10**
evitar to avoid, **II, 10**
el **examen** exam, **I**
la **excursión** excursion; pleasure trip, **I**
la **excusa** excuse, **II, 2**
el **éxito** success, **II, 9**
la **expansión** expansion, **II, 10**
extenso, -a extensive, **II, 10**
extrañar to miss (someone or something), **II, 1**
extraño strange, **II, 5**

F

la **fábrica** factory, **II, 10**
fabricar to manufacture; to construct, **II, 7**
fácil easy, **I; fácilmente** easily, **II, 1**
la **falda** skirt, **I**
falta: la falta de lack of, **II, 10**
la **familia** family, **I**
el **fanfarrón** braggart, **I**
fantástico, -a fantastic, **I**
fascinar to fascinate, **II, 10**
favorito, -a favorite, **I**
la **fecha** date, **II, 5**
¡felicitaciones! congratulations!, **II, 9; ¡felicidades en el día de tu santo!** congratulations on your saint's day!, **II, 5**
feliz: ¡feliz cumpleaños! happy birthday!, **II, 5**
el **fémur: el fémur humano** thigh bone, **II, 10**
feo, -a ugly, **I**
la **feria** fair, **I**
la **ferretería** hardware store, **II, 9**
el **fertilizante** fertilizer, **II, 10**
los **fideos** noodles, **II, 6**
la **fiebre** fever, **II, 6**
la **fiesta** party, **I**
la **fila** line, **I**
el **fin: Fin de Año** New Year's Eve, **II, 5; el fin de semana** weekend, **I**
finalmente finally, **I**
el **flan** baked custard, **I**
la **flauta: flauta dulce** recorder, **II, 10; las flautas de bambú** bamboo flutes, **II, 10**
el **folleto** brochure, **I**
la **foto** photo, **I; la fotografía** photograph, **I**
el **francés** French language, **I**
frecuentemente frequently, **II, 1**
freír to fry, **I**

la **frente** forehead, **II, 6**
frente: frente a across from, **I**
la **fresa** strawberry, **I**
fresco, -a fresh, **II, 6**
los **frijoles** beans, **I**
la **fruta** fruit, **I**
la **frutería** fruit store, **I**
el **fuego** fire, **II, 9**
la **fuente** source, **II, 7; fountain, II, 11**
fuera (de) outside, **II, 6**
fuerte heavy, **I; strong, II, 5**
fumar to smoke, **II, 6**
funcionar to work; to operate, **II, 7**
furioso, -a furious, **II, 5**
el **fútbol** soccer, **I**

G

la **gallina** hen, **II, 10**
el **gallinero** henhouse, **II, 10**
el **gallo** rooster, **II, 10**
el **ganado** cattle, **II, 10**
ganar to win, **I; to earn (money), II, 1**
la **ganga** bargain, **I**
el **garaje** garage, **I**
garantizar to guarantee, **II, 3**
la **garganta** throat, **II, 6**
la **gaseosa** soda, **I**
la **gasolina** gasoline, **II, 10**
gastar to spend; to use up, **II, 1**
gemelo, -a twin, **II, 2**
la **generación** generation, **II, 10**
generalmente generally, **I**
generoso, -a generous, **I**
el **genio** genius, **I**
la **gente** people, **I**
la **geografía** geography, **I**
la **geometría** geometry, **I**
el **gigante** giant, **II, 7**
la **gimnasia** gymnastics, **I**
el **gimnasio** gym, **II, 6**
la **goma** eraser, **I**
gordo, -a fat, **I**
gozar (de) to enjoy, **II, 7**
grabar to record (on tape), **II, 3**
gracias thank you, **I; mil gracias** thank you very much, **II, 1; muchas gracias** thanks a lot, **I**
gracioso, -a funny, **II, 2**
la **graduación** graduation, **II, 5**
graduarse to graduate, **II, 11**
grande large, **I**
la **granja** farm, **II, 10**
la **grasa** fat, **II, 6**
la **gripe** flu, **II, 6**
el **grupo** group, **I**
el **guante** glove; mitt, **I**
guapo, -a handsome, **I**
la **guerra** war, **II, 7**
la **guía** guidebook, **I; guía de turistas** tour guide, **II, 1**
la **guitarra** guitar, **I**
gustar to like; to be pleasing to, **I; me gusta** I like, **I; le gusta** you like, he (she) likes, **I; te gusta** you like, **I; les gusta(n)** you (they) like, **I; nos gusta(n)** we like, **I**

gusto: ¡qué gusto (verte)! what a pleasure (to see you!), **II, 1**

H

había there was; there were, **II, 5; había que** it was necessary to, **II, 5**
la **habitación** room, **II, 11**
el **habitante** resident, **II, 10**
hablar to speak, talk, **I**
hace: hace (mucho) calor it's (very) hot, **I; hace (mucho) frío** it's (very) cold, **I; hace (mucho) sol** it's (very) sunny, **I; hace (mucho) viento** it's (very) windy, **I; hace (muy) buen tiempo** it's (very) nice, **I; hace (muy) mal tiempo** the weather is (very) bad, **I; hace fresco** it's cool, **I; hace una hora** an hour ago, **I**
hacer to do; to make, **I; hacer cuentas** to do calculations, **I; hacer la maleta** to pack a suitcase, **I**
hacía: hacía frío it was cold, **II, 5**
la **hamburguesa** hamburger, **I**
la **harina** flour, **II, 6**
hasta as far as, **I; hasta la punta de los pelos** fed up, **II, 7; hasta luego** see you later, **I; hasta mañana** see you tomorrow, **I**
hay there is; there are, **I; hay que** one must; you must, **II, 10**
hecho made; done, **II, 10; hecho, -a a mano** handmade, **I**
el **helado** ice cream, **I**
la **hembra** female, **II, 2**
el **hemisferio** hemisphere, **II, 10**
la **herencia** heritage, **II, 10**
el **hielo** ice, **I**
la **hierba** grass, **II, 10**
la **hija** daughter, **I**
el **hijo** son, **I**
los **hijos** children; sons and daughters, **I**
hilar: hilan la lana spin wool, **II, 10**
la **historia** history; story, **I**
la **hoja** leaf, **II, 2**
hola hello, **I**
el **hombre** man, **I**
el **hombro** shoulder, **II, 6**
la **hora** time; hour, **I**
el **horario** schedule, **I**
la **hormiga** ant, **II, 2**
el **hotel** hotel, **II, 11**
hoy today, **I; hoy mismo** today, **II, 3**
el **huerto** fruit and vegetable garden, **II, 10**
el **hueso** bone, **II, 10**
el **huevo** egg, **I**
humano, -a: el ser humano human being, **II, 7**

húmedo, -a moist, **II, 2**
humilde humble, **II, 6**
¡huy! wow!, **II, 3**

I

iba: iba a ir (I) was going to go, **II, 5**
la **ida: la ida y vuelta** round trip, **II, 11**
el **idioma** language, **II, 7**
la **iglesia** church, **II, 11**
igual (que) the same (as), **I**
igualmente likewise, **I**
imaginario, -a imaginary, **I**
imaginarse to imagine, **II, 9**
el **impermeable** raincoat, **II, 3**
importante important, **I**
el **impresor** printer, **II, 7**
impuro, -a not pure, **II, 10**
incómodas uncomfortable, **II, 7**
increíble: es increíble it is incredible, **II, 11**
indispensable essential, **II, 10**
la **industria** industry, **II, 7**
industrial: la revolución industrial industrial revolution, **II, 10**
la **información** information, **I**
informar to inform, **II, 9**
la **informática** data processing, **II, 7**
la **ingeniería: la ingeniería espacial** aerospace engineering, **II, 7**
Inglaterra England, **II, 6**
el **inglés** English (language), **I**
inmediatamente immediately, **II, 7**
inmigrante immigrant, **II, 10**
el **insecticida** insecticide, **II, 10**
insistir (en) to insist, **II, 9**
interesante interesting, **I**; **interesantísimo, -a** very interesting, **II, 1**
el **intérprete** interpreter, **II, 9**
inventar to invent, **II, 5**
el **inventario** inventory, **II, 3**
el **invierno** winter, **I**
la **invitación** invitation, **I**
ir to go, **I**; **ir de compras** to go shopping, **II, 3**; **ir de excursión** to go on a trip or excursion, **II, 2**; **voy a** I am going to (to indicate intention), **I**
invitar to invite, **II, 5**
las **islas** islands, **II, 6**

J

el **jabón** soap, **II, 6**
la **jalea** jelly, **I**
el **jamón** ham, **I**
el **jarabe: el jarabe tapatío** Mexican hat dance, **II, 10**
el **jardín** garden, **I**
la **jaula** cage, **II, 2**
los **jeans** jeans, **I**
la **jefa** boss (f.), **II, 9**

el **jefe** boss (m.), **II, 9**
los **jóvenes** young people, **I**
el **juego** game, **I**; **los juegos olímpicos** Olympic Games, **I**
jugar (ue) to play, **I**
el **jugo** juice, **I**
juntos, -as together, **II, 5**
la **juventud** youth, **I**

K

el **kilo** kilogram (2.2 pounds), **I**

L

la you (pol. sing.), her, it, **I**; **la** the (f. sing.), **I**
los **labios** lips, **II, 6**
la **labor** labor; work, **II, 7**; **las labores domésticas** household chores, **II, 7**
el **lado** side, **I**
el **lago** lake, **II, 1**
lamentar to regret, **II, 7**
la **lana** wool, **I**
el **lápiz** (pl. **lápices**) pencil, **I**; **lápiz labial** lipstick, **II, 6**; **lápiz para los ojos** eyeliner, **II, 6**
largo, -a long, **I**
las the (f. pl.); you (pl.); them, **I**
lavar(se) to wash (oneself); **lavarse la cabeza** to wash one's hair, **II, 6**
la **lección** lesson, **II, 10**
la **leche** milk, **I**; **leche descremada** skim milk, **II, 6**
la **lechuga** lettuce, **I**
leer to read, **I**
lejano, -a distant, **II, 7**
lejos (de) far (from), **I**
el **lema** slogan, **II, 3**
lentamente slowly, **II, 1**
la **lente de contacto** contact lens, **II, 6**
les you (pl.); them, **I**
levantarse to get up, **II, 6**
la **ley** law, **II, 10**
la **libra** pound, **II, 6**
librar(se) to free (oneself), **II, 7**
la **librería** bookstore, **II, 10**
la **libreta** notebook, **II, 7**
el **libro** book, **I**
ligada linked, **II, 3**
ligero, -a light (meal), **I**
la **lima: la lima de uñas** nail file, **II, 6**
el **limón** lemon, **I**
la **limonada** lemonade, **II, 6**
limpiar to clean, **II, 2**
limpio, -a clean, **II, 9, 10**
lindo, -a pretty, **I**
el **lío** complication, **I**
listo, -a ready, **I**
lo you (pol. sing.), him, it, **I**; **lo menos posible** as little as possible, **II, 2**; **lo mismo (que)** the same (as), **I**; **lo que** what; that, **I**; **lo siento** I'm sorry, **I**

la **loción** lotion, **II, 6**
loco, -a crazy, **I**; **volverse loco, -a** to go crazy, **II, 7**
la **locura** madness, **II, 3**
el **loro** parrot, **II, 2**
los the; you (pl.); them, **I**; **los demás** the rest, **I**
la **lucha: la lucha libre** wrestling; wrestling match, **II, 6**
luego then; later, **II, 1**
el **lugar** place, **I**

LL

la **llamada** phone call, **II, 5**
llamar to call, **I**
la **llave** key, **II, 7**
el **llavero** key ring, **II, 3**
la **llegada** arrival, **I**
llegar to arrive, **I**; **llegar a un acuerdo** to come to an agreement, **II, 5**
llenar to fill (out), **II, 9**
lleno, -a full, **II, 1**
llevar to take, **I**; to take (with you), **II, 3**; **llevas** (you) have, **II, 1**; **llevo . . . aquí** I have been here for . . . , **II, 10**
llorar to cry, **I**
llover (ue) to rain, **II, 3**; **llueve** it's raining, **I**
la **lluvia: la lluvia ácida** acid rain, **II, 10**

M

los **macarrones** macaroni, **II, 6**
macho male, **II, 2**
la **madrastra** stepmother, **I**
la **madre** mother, **I**
magnífico, -a excellent; very good, **I**
el **maíz** corn, **II, 10**
mal bad, **I**
la **maleta** suitcase, **I**
la **mamá** mom, **I**
mandar to command; to send, **I, II, 9**
la **mano** hand, **I**
mantenerse to keep in shape, **II, 6**
la **mantequilla** butter, **I**
el **manual** manual, **II, 7**
la **manzana** apple, **I**
mañana tomorrow, **I**; **la mañana** morning, **I**; **por la mañana** in the morning, **I**
la **manera** way; manner, **II, 6**
el **mapa** map, **I**
el **maquillaje** makeup, **II, 6**
maquillar(se) to apply makeup, **II, 6**
la **máquina** machine, **II, 7**; **la maquinilla de afeitar** razor, **II, 6**

maravilloso, -a marvelous, II, 10
el **marcador** felt-tip marker, I
marcar to mark, I
marearse to get dizzy, II, 9
mariscos: zarzuela de mariscos seafood platter, II, 11
marrón brown, I
más more; else; other; most, I; **más . . . que** more . . . than, I; **más barato** cheaper, II, 3; **más caro** more expensive, II, 3; **más de . . .** more than . . . , I; **más dulce** sweeter, II, 1; **más grande que** bigger than, I; **más o menos** more or less; so so, II, 9; **más tarde** later, I
el **mástil** mast, II, 9
las **materias** subjects, I
maya Mayan, II, 1
la **mayonesa** mayonnaise, I
mayor bigger; older, II, 9; el **mayor** biggest; oldest, II, 9; **mayor que** older than, II, 2
mayoría: la mayoría de the majority of, II, 6
el **maíz** corn, II, 6
me me; **me da igual** it's the same to me, II, 11; **me da lo mismo** it's all right with me, II, 11; **me di cuenta** I realized, II, 5; **¡me encanta!** I love it!, II, 10; **me fue bien** things went well for me, II, 1; **me fue mal** things went badly for me, II, 1; **me llamo . . .** my name is . . . , I; **¿me podrías dar (decir, prestar) . . . ?** could you give me (tell me, lend me) . . . ?, II, 7
el **mecánico** mechanic, II, 9
la **medalla: la medalla de oro** gold medal, I
la **medicina** medicine, II, 7; **el campo de la medicina** medicine field, II, 7
el **médico** doctor, II, 6
medio, -a one half, II, 6; **el medio ambiente** environment, II, 7
el **mediodía** noon, I
mejor better; best, I; **lo mejor** the best (thing), I; **el mejor** best, II, 9; **mejor . . .** it would be better to . . . , I; **mejor que . . .** better than . . . , II, 2
mejorar to improve, II, 6
el **melocotón** peach, I
el **melón** melon, I
menor smaller; younger, II, 9; **el menor** smallest; youngest, II, 9; **menor que** younger than, II, 2
menos less, I; **menos de . . .** less than . . . , I; **lo menos posible** as little as possible, II, 2
el **menú** menu (at a restaurant), I; menu (computer), II, 7
la **mercancía** merchandise, II, 3
la **merienda** snack; light meal in the afternoon, I

la **mermelada** marmalade, I
el **mes** month, I; **los meses del año** months of the year, I
la **mesa** table; **a la mesa** to the table, I
el **metro** subway, I
mexicanoamericano, -a Mexican American, II, 1
México Mexico, I
mezquita mosque, II, 11
mi my, I
mí me, I
el **miembro: los miembros de la familia** family members, I
mientras while, II, 1
miles thousands, II, 6
la **milla** mile, II, 7
el **minuto** minute, I
mío, -a mine, II, 2
mirar to look at; watch, I; **¡mira! look!**, I
mis my (pl.), I
la **misión: la misión espacial** space mission, II, 7
mismo, -a same, I
la **moda** fashion; style, II, 3; **a la (última) moda** in the latest style, II, 3
la **moderación** moderation, II, 6
el **mole** spicy chocolate sauce, I
molestar to bother, II, 11
molían used to grind, II, 6
la **moneda** coin; currency, II, 3
el **monedero** change purse, II, 3
la **montaña** mountain, II, 1; **la montaña rusa** roller coaster, II, 9
montar to ride, I; **montar (a caballo)** to ride (on horseback), II, 1
morder to bite, II, 2
moreno, -a dark (hair, complexion), I
la **mosca** fly, II, 10
el **mosquito** mosquito, II, 10
la **mostaza** mustard, I
el **mostrador** counter, II, 3
mostrar(ue) to show, II, 9
el **motivo** reason, II, 2
la **moto** motorcycle, I
la **muchacha** girl, II, 2
el **muchacho** boy, II, 2
muchísimo very much, II, 3
mucho a lot, I; **mucho gusto** nice to meet you, I; **muchos recuerdos** many regards, II, 1; **muchos, -as** many; a lot, I; **¡muchas felicidades!** congratulations!, II, 5
mudar(se) to move, II, 10
muerto, -a: estar muerto to be dead (tired), II, 3
la **multivitamina** multivitamin, II, 6
la **muñeca** wrist, II, 6
las **murallas** walls, II, 11
murió she (he) died, I
el **muro** outside wall, II, 9

muy very, I; **muy mal** awful; terrible, I; **muy señor nuestro** dear sir, II, 9; **muy señores míos** gentlemen, II, 9

N

nace is born, II, 2
el **nacimiento** birth, II, 5
la **nación** nation, II, 7
nacional national, II, 10
nadar to swim, I
la **naranja** orange, I
la **nariz** nose, II, 6
la **natación** swimming, I
la **naturaleza** nature, II, 2
la **Navidad** Christmas, II, 5
la **necesidad** need, II, 10
necesitar to need, I
negocios business, II, 3
negro, -a black, I
ni . . . ni neither . . . nor, I
el **nido** nest, II, 2
nieva it's snowing, I
ninguno, -a none, II, 6
no no; not, I; **no contestan** there's no answer, I; **no crecía** did not grow, II, 7; **no hay más remedio** it can't be helped, I; **¡no hay nada igual!** there's nothing like it!, II, 10; **¡no importa!** it doesn't matter!, I; **no me gusta nada** I don't like it at all, I; **no me importa** I don't care, II, 11; **¡no me digas!** you don't say!, II, 9; **no tengo tiempo para nada** I don't have time for anything, II, 1; **¿no?** right?, I
la **noche** night, I; **la Noche Buena** Christmas Eve, II, 5
norteamericano, -a American, I
nos us, I; **nos es grato informarle** we are pleased to inform you, II, 9
nosotras we (f.); us (f.), I
nosotros we (m. or m. and f.); us (m. or m. and f.), I
noveno, -a ninth, II, 5
la **novia** girlfriend, II, 2
el **novio** boyfriend, II, 2
la **nube** cloud, II, 10
nuclear: la energía nuclear nuclear energy, II, 7; **la planta nuclear** nuclear plant, II, 7; **el reactor nuclear** nuclear reactor, II, 7
nuestro, -a, -os, -as our, I
nuevo, -a new, I
el **número** number, I; **número equivocado** wrong number, I
nunca never, I; **nunca más** never again, II, 3

O

o or, I; **o . . . o** either . . . or, II, 6
obedecer (zc) to obey, II, 5

la **obligación** obligation; duty, II, 5
la **ocasión** occasion, II, 2
octavo, -a eighth, II, 5
ocupado, -a busy, II, 7
odiar: odio I hate, I
odioso, -a hateful; odious, II, 3
la **oferta** offer, I
la **oficina** office, I
oír to hear, II, 6
¡ojalá! if only; I hope, II, 11
el **ojo** eye, II, 6
las **olimpiadas** Olympic Games, II, 11
olvidarse to forget, II, 6
la **operación** operation; surgery, II, 7
operar to operate, II, 9
la **oreja** ear, II, 3
organizado, -a organized, I
oscuro, -a dark, I
el **otoño** fall; autumn, I
otro, -a other; another, I; **otro día** another day, II, 3
la **oveja** sheep, II, 10
¡oye! hey!, I; listen!, II, 5

P

la **paciencia** patience, I
el **padrastro** stepfather, I
el **padre** father, I; **padres** parents; fathers, I
pagar to pay, I
el **país: país extranjero** foreign country, II, 7
el **pájaro** bird, II, 2
las **palomitas: las palomitas de maíz** popcorn, II, 6
el **pan** bread, I
la **panadería** bakery, II, 10
la **pandilla** gang, II, 11
la **pantalla** screen, II, 7
los **pantalones** pants, I
la **pantera** panther, II, 10
el **pañuelo** handkerchief, I
la **papa** potato; **papas deshidratadas** instant (dehydrated) potatoes, II, 6; **papas fritas** french fries, I
papá dad, I
el **par** pair, II, 3
para for; to; in order to, I; **¿para qué?** for what?, I
parabólica: la antena parabólica satellite dish, II, 7
la **parada** stop, I
el **paraguas** umbrella, II, 3
parar to stop, I
parecer to seem, I
la **pareja** couple, II, 5
el **parque** park, I
el **partido** game, match, I
pasa come in, I; **pasa de moda** is no longer fashionable or popular, II, 10
pasado, -a last; past, I; **la semana pasada** last week, I
el **pasaje** fare, II, 11

el **pasaporte** passport, I
pasar to spend (time); to come in, I; **pasar la aspiradora** to vacuum, II, 2; **la paso muy bien** I'm having a good time, II, 2, II, 5; **pasarla bien** to have a good time, II, 1; **pasarla mal** to have a bad time, II, 1
el **pasatiempo** pastime, I
la **Pascua: la Pascua Florida** Easter; Passover, II, 5
pasear to go for a walk, I
el **paseo** sightseeing trip, I
el **pasillo** hall, I
la **pasión** passion, II, 10
la **pasta: la pasta de dientes** toothpaste, II, 6
el **pastel** pie, I
la **pastelería** pastry; pastry shop, I
la **patata** potato (Spain), I
patinar to skate, I; **patinar en hielo** to ice skate, I
el **patio** inner courtyard, I
el **pato** duck, II, 10
el **pavo** turkey, II, 10
el **pedido** order, I
pedir: pedir la palabra to ask permission to speak, II, 2
peinar(se) to comb one's hair; II, 6
el **peine** comb, II, 6
la **película** film; movie, I; **película de terror** horror movie, I; **película del oeste** Western, I; **película musical** musical, I; **película policial** detective movie, I
el **peligro** danger, II, 7; **peligroso, -a** dangerous, II, 7
pelirrojo, -a redheaded, I
el **pelo** hair, II, 6
la **pelota** ball (baseball, tennis ball), I
los **pendientes** earrings, II, 3
pensar (ie) to think; plan, I
peor worse, II, 2; **peor que** worse than, II, 2; **el peor** worst, II, 9
pequeño, -a small, little, I
la **pera** pear, I
perder (ie) to lose, II, 6; **se perdió** it got lost, II, 6
perdón excuse me; I; **perdone** excuse me (pol.), II, 3
perfecto, -a perfect, II, 6
el **perfume** perfume, II, 6
el **periódico** newspaper, I
perjudicado, -a harmed, II, 7
permiso excuse me; permission, I
pero but, I
pesar(se) to weigh (oneself), II, 6
el **pescado** fish, I
pescar to fish, II, 1; **pescar un resfriado** to catch a cold, II, 9
la **peseta** monetary unit of Spain, I
el **peso** monetary unit of Mexico, Bolivia, Chile, Colombia, I
el **petróleo** oil, II, 10

el **pez** (pl. **peces**) fish, II, 2
el **pie** foot, II, 6
la **pierna** leg, II, 6
la **pimienta** pepper, I
pintar(se) to apply makeup, II, 6
pintoresco, -a picturesque, II, 11
la **pintura** painting, I
la **piña** pineapple, I
la **pirámide** pyramid, II, 1
la **piscina** pool, I
el **piso** floor, I
el **placer** pleasure, I
el **plan** plan, I
planear to plan, I
la **planta: la planta nuclear** nuclear plant, II, 7
la **plata** silver, I; silver; (coll.) money, II, 3
el **plátano** banana; plantain, I
el **platillo** saucer; small plate, I
el **plato** dish; plate, I; **plato del día** specialty of the day, I; **plato hondo** soup dish, I; **plato llano** dinner dish, I
la **playa** beach, I
la **playera** tee shirt, II, 3
la **plaza** square, II, 10
la **plomería** plumbing, II, 9
el **plomero** plumber, II, 9
la **pluma** fountain pen, I
poco, -a a little, I
el **poder** power, II, 3
poder (ue) to be able; can, I; **¿podrías hacerme el favor de . . . ?** would you do me a favor and . . . ?, II, 7
el **pollo** chicken, I
el **polo** polo, II, 10
el **polvo** powder, II, 6
poner to put, I; **poner la mesa** to set the table, I; **poner(se) en contacto** to get in touch (with), II, 7
ponerse to put on; to wear (something), II, 6; **ponerse furioso, -a** to get furious, II, 6; **ponerse triste** to get sad, II, 6; **ponerse contento, -a** to become happy, II, 9; **puesto** put; placed, II, 10
popular popular, II, 9
por for; through, I; **por consiguiente** consequently; thus, II, 7; **por correo** by mail, I; **por favor** please, I; **por fin** finally; at last, I; **por la noche** at night, I; **por lo tanto** as a result; therefore, II, 7; **por medio de la presente** hereby, II, 9; **¿por qué no . . . ?** why don't we . . . ?, I; **¿por qué?** why?, I; **por semana** per week, I; **por separado** separately, II, 5; **¡por supuesto!** of course!, I; **por tanto** therefore, II, 5; **por último** finally, II, 9
la **porción** portion, II, 6

porque because, **I**

porteño, -a person from Buenos Aires, **II, 10**

posible possible, **II, 2**

la **postal** postcard, **I**

el **postre** dessert, **I; de postre** for dessert, **I**

practicar to practice; play, **I**

el **prado** meadow, **II, 10**

precaver to take precautions, **II, 7**

el **precio** price, **I**

la **preciosura** thing of beauty, **I**

la **precipitación: la precipitación radioactiva** radioactive fallout, **II, 7**

preciso: es preciso it is essential, **II, 11**

preferido, -a favorite, **I**

preferir (ie) to prefer, **II, 6**

la **pregunta** question, **I**

preguntar to ask, **I**

el **premio** prize, **I**

preocupado, -a worried, **II, 6**

preocupar(se) to worry, **II, 6**

preparar to prepare, **I**

prepararse to get ready, **II, 6**

el **preparativo** preparation, **II, 5**

presentar to introduce; to present, **II, 1**

prestar to lend, **II, 2; ¿me podrías prestar . . . ?** could you lend me . . . ?, **II, 7**

la **primavera** spring, **I**

primero first, **I**

principal main, **I**

el **principiante** beginner (*m.*), **I**

la **principiante** beginner (*f.*), **I**

privado, -a private, **II, 11**

probable: es probable it is probable, **II, 11**

el **probador** fitting room, **II, 3**

probar to try, **I**

probarse (ue) to try on, **II, 3**

el **problema** problem, **I**

producir (zc) to produce, **II, 7**

el **profesor** teacher (*m.*), **I**

la **profesora** teacher (*f.*), **I**

el **programa** program, **I**

la **programación** programming, **II, 1; computer programming, II, 7**

progresar to progress; to advance, **II, 7**

el **progreso** progress, **II, 7**

prohibido, -a off limits, **I**

prohibir to forbid, **II, 9**

prometer to promise, **I**

pronto soon, **I**

el **propietario** owner, **II, 11**

la **propina** tip, **I**

proponer to propose, **II, 2**

proteger to protect, **II, 10**

el **provecho: ¡buen provecho!** enjoy it! (meal), **I**

el **proverbio** proverb, **II, 7**

próximo, -a next, **I; la próxima vez . . .** next time . . . , **II, 2**

la **prueba** test, **II, 7**

el **pueblo** village, **II, 5**

el **puente** bridge, **II, 10**

la **puerta** door; gate, **I**

pues well, **II, 1**

el **puesto** put; placed, **II, 10**

el **puesto** position; job, **II, 9**

el **pulpo** octopus; amusement park ride, **II, 9**

puntual punctual, **II, 9**

Q

que that, **I; qué** what?, **I; ¡qué asco!** how disgusting!, **II, 10; ¡qué barbaridad!** how terrible!, **II, 9; ¡qué bien luces!** you look great!, **II, 6; ¡qué confusión!** what a mixup!, **I; ¡qué coraje!** what nerve!, **II, 2; ¡qué cuarto tan bonito!** what a pretty room!, **I; ¡qué quapo!** how handsome!, **I; ¡qué gusto (verte)!** what a pleasure (to see you)!, **II, 1; ¡qué gusto de verlo!** what a pleasure to see you! (*pol.*), **II, 3; ¿qué hay de nuevo?** what's new?, **II, 11; ¿qué hora es?** what time is it?, **I; ¡qué horror!** how horrible!, **II, 9; ¡qué lástima!** what a shame!, **I; ¿qué más necesitas?** what else do you need?, **I; ¿qué más?** what else?, **I; ¡qué pena!** what a pity, **I; ¡qué suerte!** what luck!, **I; ¡qué suerte!** how lucky!, **II, 9; ¿qué tal?** how are things?, **I; ¿qué tiempo hace?** how's the weather?, **I; ¿qué tienes?** what's wrong with you?, **II, 6**

quedar to be (located), **II, 3; to be left over, II, 5; quedar bien** it looks nice on, **I; quedarse** to stay; to remain, **II, 6**

la **queja** complaint, **I**

querer (ie) to want, **I; to love, II, 5; ¿querrías decirme (darme, prestarme) . . . ?** would you tell me (give me, lend me) . . . ?, **II, 7**

querido, -a dear, **I**

el **queso** cheese, **I**

¿quién? who?, **I**

la **química** chemistry, **I**

quinto, -a fifth, **I**

quitar: quitar la mesa to clear the table, **II, 2**

quitarse to take off, **II, 6**

quizás maybe; perhaps, **II, 6**

R

la **ración** portion, **II, 6**

la **radiación** radiation, **II, 7**

radioactivo, -a radioactive, **II, 7; la precipitacion radioactiva** radioactive fallout, **II, 7; los residuos radioactivos** radioactive waste, **II, 7**

la **rana** frog, **II, 2**

rápido quickly, fast, **I; rápidamente** rapidly, **II, 1**

la **raqueta** racquet, **I**

el **rascacielos** skyscraper, **II, 1**

el **ratón** mouse, **II, 2**

el **rayo** lightning bolt, **II, 3; el rayo láser** laser beam, **II, 7**

la **razón** reason, **II, 9; razonable** reasonable, **II, 9**

el **reactor: el reactor nuclear** nuclear reactor, **II, 7**

la **rebaja** discount, **I**

rebajado, -a reduced (in price), **I**

rebajar to reduce (price), **II, 3**

la **recepción** reception desk, **II, 11**

el **recepcionista** receptionist (*m.*), **II, 11**

la **recepcionista** receptionist (*f.*), **II, 9**

recibir to receive, **I**

el **recibo** receipt, **I**

la **reclamación** claim, **I**

el **reclamo** claim, **I**

recoger to pick up, **II, 11**

la **recomendación** recommendation, **II, 9**

recomendar (ie) to recommend, **II, 6**

recordar (ue) to remember, **II, 5**

recorrer to travel, **II, 11**

el **recreo** recess, **I**

los **recuerdos** regards, **II, 1; dar recuerdos** to send regards, **II, 1; mandar recuerdos** to send regards, **II, 1**

la **red** net, **I**

el **refresco** soda, **I**

el **refrigerador** refrigerator, **II, 2**

regalar to give (away), **II, 3**

el **regalo** present, **I**

regatear to bargain, **I**

el **régimen** diet plan, **II, 6**

¡regio! great!, **II, 11**

la **región** region, **II, 11; región andina** Andean region, **II, 10**

el **registro** record book, **II, 11**

la **regla** ruler, **I**

regresar to return, **I**

el **regreso** return, **II, 1**

regular so-so, **I**

el **reino** kingdom, **II, 6**

reír(se) to laugh, **II, 6**

el **reloj** watch, clock, **II, 2**

remar to row, **I**

el **remitente** sender, **II, 9**

el **renacuajo** tadpole, **II, 2**

la **reparación** repairs, **II, 2**

repetir (i) to repeat, **II, 2**

la **réplica** replica, **II, 11**

la **reservación** reservation, **II, 11**

reservar to reserve, **I; reservar los pasajes** reserve the seats, (tickets), **II, 11**

el **residuo: los residuos radioactivos** radioactive waste, **II, 7**

resistente resistant, **II, 7**

resolver (ue) to solve, **II, 10**

respirar to breathe, **II, 10**

la **responsabilidad** responsibility, **II, 10**

el **responsable** the person in charge, II, 9

las **respuestas** answers, II, 9

el **restaurante** restaurant, I

la **reunión** meeting, II, 2

reunirse to get together, II, 5

la **revista** magazine, I

revivir: reviven relive, II, 10

la **revolución: la revolución agrícola** agricultural revolution, II, 7; **la revolución industrial** industrial revolution, II, 10

rico, -a tasty, delicious (food), I

la **rifa** raffle, II, 9

el **rifle** rifle, II, 9

el **río** river, II, 3

la **riqueza** riches, wealth, II, 10

riquísimo, -a delicious, II, 5

la **rodilla** knee, II, 6

rojo red, I

romper(se) to break, II, 6

la **ropa** clothes, I

rosa pink, I

roto, -a broken, II, 6; **roto** broken, II, 10

rubio, -a fair, blond(e), I

la **rueda: la rueda giratoria** Ferris wheel, II, 9

el **ruido** noise, I

las **ruinas** ruins (archeological), II, 1

la **ruta** route, I

S

saber to know (a fact), I

saber (+ inf.) to know how (+ inf.), I

sabroso, -a tasty, delicious, I

sacar to take, II, 2; to take out, II, 9; **sacar buenas notas** to get good grades, II, 1; **sacar fotos** to take pictures, II, 5; **sacarse la rifa** to win the raffle, II, 9

el **saco** jacket, I

la **sal** salt, I

la **sala** living room, I; **la sala de espera** waiting area, I; **la sala de estar** family room, I

salir to go out, I; **salir bien** to turn out well, II, 2; **salir en defensa de** to go out in the defense of, II, 6

la **salsa** sauce, I

la **salud** health, II, 6

salvar to save, II, 10

las **sandalias** sandals, II, 3

la **sandía** watermelon, I

sano, -a healthy, II, 6

el **santo** saint's day, II, 5

la **sartén** frying pan, I

satisfecho, -a satisfied, II, 9

se: se dirige is steered, II, 7; **se hizo** became, II, 6; **se llama...** his (her) name is..., I; **se ponían de acuerdo** came to an agreement, II, 5; **se reía** (he) was laughing, II, 5

sea: sea como sea whatever it may be; anyway, II, 10

la **secadora** hair dryer, II, 6

la **seca** dry season, II, 2

secar to dry, II, 2

sección: la sección de equipaje baggage claim, I; **la sección de quejas y reclamos** customer service department, I

la **seda** silk, I

seguir (i) to follow; to continue, II, 2; **seguir derecho** to go straight ahead, II, 3

según according to, II, 1

segundo, -a second, I

seguro, -a sure, I

el **sello** stamp, I

la **semana** week, I; **la semana que viene** next week, II, 2; **Semana Santa** Holy Week, II, 5

el **sembrar** sow, II, 10

la **semilla** seed, II, 10

sencillamente simply, I

sentarse (ie) to sit, II, 9

sentirse (ie) to feel, II, 6; **sentir(se) bien** to feel good, II, 6; **sentir(se) mal** to feel bad, II, 6; **sentimos comunicarle** we regret to inform you, II, 9

las **señas** personal description, II, 11

el **señor** man, I; (abbreviation **Sr.**) Mr., sir, I

la **señora** woman, I; (abbreviation **Sra.**), Mrs., ma'am, I

la **señorita** Miss (abbreviation **Srta.**), I

séptimo, -a seventh, II, 5

ser to be, I; **ser aburrido, -a** to be boring, II, 5; **ser listo, -a** to be smart, II, 5; **¿serías tan amable de...?** would you be nice enough to...?, II, 7

la **serpiente** snake, II, 2

la **servilleta** napkin, I

servir (i) to serve, I

sexto, -a sixth, II, 5

sí yes, I

si if, I; **¿si vamos...?** what if we go...?, I

siempre always, I

el **siglo** century, II, 10

significado meaning, II, 1

el **silencio** silence, II, 2; **¡silencio!** be quiet!, II, 5

simpático, -a nice, I

sin without, I; **sin parar** without stopping, I; **sin falta** without fail, II, 2

sobre about, I; **sobre todo** above all, II, 11

el **sobre** envelope, II, 9

¡socorro! help!, II, 9

solicitar to apply, II, 9

la **solicitud: la solicitud de empleo** job application, II, 9

solo, -a alone, II, 1

el **sombrero** hat, I

son: son las diez it's ten o'clock, I

sonar (ue) to ring, II, 5

sonreír(se) to smile, II, 11; **sonríe** smile, II, 9

soñar (ue) to dream, II, 7; **soñaste con** dreamed of, II, 7

la **sopa** soup, I; **sopa payés** Catalonian dish, II, 11

sorprender to surprise, II, 11

su your; his; her; its (*sing.*), I

subir to go up, I

subirse to get on, II, 9

submarino, -a underwater, II, 7

sucesos events, II, 10

sucio, -a dirty, II, 10

sucursales branches, II, 9

el **sueldo** salary, II, 9

suena sounds, II, 1

el **sueño** dream, I

la **suerte** luck, II, 6

el **suéter** sweater, I

sugerir (ie) to suggest, II, 9

el **suministro** supply, II, 7

el **supermercado** supermarket, II, 10

el **surtido** stock, II, 3

sus hers; his; yours; theirs, I

suyo, -a yours, II, 2; **suyo afectísimo** sincerely yours, II, 9

T

la **tabla: la tabla hawaiana** surfboard, II, 7; **la tabla vela** windsurfing, II, 9

el **talco** dusting powder; talcum powder, II, 6

tal vez perhaps, II, 11

la **talla** size, I

también also; too, I

tampoco neither, II, 6

tan so, I; **tan...como** as...as, II, 2

el **tango** tango, II, 10

tanto, -a so (that) much, I

tanto, -a como as much as, I

tantos, -as so (those) many, I

tantos, -as como as many as, I

la **taquilla** ticket booth, II, 9

tarde late, I; **más tarde** later, I

la **tarde** afternoon, I; **por la tarde** in the afternoon, I

la **tarea** homework, I

la **tarifa: la tarifa especial** special fare, II, 11

la **tarjeta: la tarjeta de crédito** credit card, I

la **tarta** tart, pastry, I

te you, I; **te acuerdas** you remember, II, 9; **te hace falta** you need to, II, 9

el **té** tea, I

el **teatro** theater, I

teclear to type, II, 7

la **tecnología** technology, II, 7

el **tejido: los tejidos a mano** hand-woven fabrics, II, 10

el **teléfono** telephone, I; **por teléfono** on the telephone, I

temer to fear, II, 11

temprano early, I

tender (ie): tender la ropa to hang clothes, II, 9

el **tenedor** fork, I

tener to have, I; **tener (mucha) hambre** to be (very) hungry, I; **tener (mucha) sed** to be (very) thirsty, I; **tener . . . años** to be . . . years old, I; **tener dolor de . . .** to have an ache or pain . . . , II, 6; **tener ganas de** to feel like, I; **tener la culpa** to be at fault, II, 3; **tener miedo** to be afraid, II, 5; **tener noticias de** to hear from (about), II, 1; **tener paciencia** to be patient, II, 7; **tener prisa** to be in a hurry, II, 5; **tener que** to have to, I; **tener tantas cosas que hacer** to have so much to do, II, 2; **tener razón** to be right, II, 9; **¿tendrías la bondad de?** would you be so kind as to?, II, 7; **tenemos el gusto de comunicarle** we are pleased to inform you, II, 9

el **tenis** tennis, I

la **terminación** ending, II, 1

terminar to finish, I

la **terraza** terrace, II, 9

el **tesoro** treasure, II, 6

ti you, I

el **tiempo** time, I; **tiempo libre** free time, I; **no tengo tiempo para nada** I don't have time for anything, II, 1

la **tienda** store, I

tiene it has, I

la **Tierra** Earth, II, 10

la **tijera** scissors, II, 6

el **timbre** doorbell, II, 3

la **tintorería** dry cleaning store, II, 10

el **tiovivo** merry-go-round, II, 9

típico, -a typical, I

tirar: tirar al blanco to shoot at a target, II, 9; **el tiro al blanco** shooting gallery, II, 9

el **tobillo** ankle, II, 6

tocar to play (a musical instrument), I

todavía still, I

todo everything, I; **todo el tiempo** all the time, I; **todo, -a, -os, -as** all; every, I; **todos los días** every day, I

tomar to take, I; **tomar** to have (eat or drink), I; **tomar el sol** to sunbathe, II, 1; **tomar fotografías** to take photographs, I; **tomar las cosas con calma** to take things calmly, II, 9

el **tomate** tomato, I

tonto, -a dumb, I

la **tormenta** storm, II, 3

el **toro** bull, II, 10

la **toronja** grapefruit, II, 6

la **torta** cake, II, 5; **torta de cumpleaños** birthday cake, II, 5

la **tortilla** omelette, I

la **tortuga** turtle, II, 2

trabajar to work, I

el **trabajo** job, II, 1

traducir (zc) to translate, II, 5

traer to bring, II, 5

el **traje** suit, I; **traje de baño** bathing suit, I

el **transbordador: el transbordador espacial** space shuttle, II, 7

el **tránsito** traffic, II, 3

el **transplante: el transplante de órgano** organ transplant, II, 7

el **trigo** wheat, II, 6

el **trofeo** trophy, I

tropical tropical, II, 10

el **trozo** piece, I

la **trucha** trout, II, 1

tú you (*fam.*), I

tu your, I

el **turismo** tourism, I

turístico, -a touristic, I

tus your (*pl.*), I

el **tuyo** yours, II, 1

tuyo, -a your, II, 2

U

Ud. (abbreviation of **usted**) you, I

¡uf! ugh!, II, 3

el **último, -a: a la (última) moda** in the latest style, II, 3; **el último piso** top floor, II, 3

un, una a, an, I; **un abrazo de . . .** a hug from . . . , II, 1; **un momento** just a moment, I; **una vez** once, I

único, -a only, II, 5

la **universidad** university, II, 7

unos, unas some, I

la **uña** nail, II, 6

usar to use, I

usted you (*pol.*), I

ustedes (abbreviation **Uds.**) you (*pl.*), I

útil useful, II, 9

la **uva** grape, I

V

la **vaca** cow, II, 10

la **vacación** vacation, I

vacío, -a empty, II, 6

¿vale? okay?, II, 11

valen they cost, I

¡vamos! let's go!, I

van they go, I

varias several; **varias veces** several times, II, 1

el **vaso** glass, I

el **vendedor** salesman, I

la **vendedora** saleswoman, I

vender to sell, I

venenosa poisonous, II, 6

venir to come, I

la **venta** sale; **en venta** on sale, I; **venta-liquidación** clearance sale, II, 3

la **ventana** window, II, 3

la **ventanilla** ticket window, I

ver to see, I

el **verano** summer, I

la **verbena** fair; carnival, II, 9

la **verdad** truth, II, 3; **de verdad** in truth; really, II, 3; **¿verdad?** really?; right?, I

verde green, I

la **verdura** green vegetable, I

el **vestíbulo** lobby, II, 11

el **vestido** dress, I

vestir (i) to dress, II, 6; **vestirse** to get dressed, II, 6

la **vez** (*pl.* **veces**) time, I

viajar to travel, II, 7

el **viaje** trip, I

la **vida** life, II, 2

venir: vino a ser came to be, II, 3

la **visita** visit; visitor, I

visto seen, II, 10

la **vitrina** display window, II, 3

vivir to live, I

el **volibol** volleyball, I

volver (ue) to return, I

volverse: volverse loco, -a to go crazy, II, 7

vosotros, -as you (*fam. pl.*), I

el **vuelo** flight, I; **vuelo sin escala** non-stop flight, II, 11

vuelta: estar de vuelta to be back, II, 11; **ida y vuelta** round trip, II, 11

el **vuelto** change (money), II, 3

vuestro, -a, -os, -as your (*fam. pl.*), I

Y

y and, I

ya already, I; **ya está todo** everything's finished, I; **¡ya sé!** I know it!, I; **ya viene** he (she) is coming, I

yo I, I; **yo no** not me, I; **yo no sé** I don't know, I

el **yogur** yogurt, II, 6

Z

la **zanahoria** carrot, II, 6

el **zapato** shoe, I; **zapatos de tenis** tennis shoes, I

los **zarcillos** earrings, II, 3

la **zarzuela: la zarzuela de mariscos** seafood platter, II, 11

ENGLISH-SPANISH VOCABULARY

This vocabulary includes all the active and passive words in the text of **Nosotros, los jóvenes.** Active words are those listed in the vocabulary at the end of each unit. Passive words are those glossed at bottom of the readings. Spanish nouns are listed with the definite article. Spanish expressions are listed under the English words that the student would be most likely to look up.

Active vocabulary and expressions that were introduced in **Nuevos amigos** are followed by a roman numeral **I**, for example: **tree,** el árbol, **I.** Active and passive vocabulary introduced in **Nosotros, los jóvenes** are followed by a roman numeral **II** as well as a number that indicates the unit in which the word is presented, for example **gentleman**: el caballero, **II, 3.**

The following abbreviations are used in this list: *adj.* adjective; *adv.* adverb; *com.* command; *dir.* direct; *f.* feminine; *fam.* familiar; *ind.* indicative; *inf.* infinitive; *m.* masculine; *obj.* object; *pl.* plural; *pol.* polite; *prep.* preposition; *pron.* pronoun; *sing.* singular; *sub.* subjunctive.

A

a un, una, **I; a hug from** . . . un abrazo de . . . , **II, 1; a little** poco, -a, **I; a lot** bastante; mucho, -a, **I; a week ahead of time** con una semana de anticipación, **I**
about como; sobre, **I**
above: above all sobre todo, **II, 11**
accident el accidente, **II, 6**
to **accompany** acompañar, **II, 10**
according (to) según, **II, 1**
to **ache** doler, **II, 6**
across (from) frente a, **I**
activity la actividad, **I**
ad: classified ad el anuncio clasificado, **II, 9**
to **add** añadir, **I**
adequate adecuado, -a, **II, 6**
admission: admission ticket la entrada, **I**
to **advance** avanzar; progresar, **II, 7**
advanced avanzado, -a, **I**
adventure la aventura, **I**
to **advertise** anunciar, **II, 5**
to **advise** aconsejar, **II, 9**
aerospace: aerospace engineering la ingeniería espacial, **II, 7**
affection el cariño, **II, 1**
affectionate cariñoso, -a, **I**
affectionately afectuosamente; cariñosamente, **II, 1**
after después de, **I**
afternoon la tarde, **I; in the afternoon** por la tarde, **I**
again de nuevo, **I**
agree: I agree de acuerdo, **II, 11**

agreement el acuerdo, **II, 2**
agricultural agricultural, **II, 7; agricultural revolution** la revolución agrícola, **II, 7**
air: air conditioning el aire acondicionado, **II, 11; pure air** el aire puro, **II 10**
airplane el avión, **I**
airport el aeropuerto, **I**
alarm: alarm clock el despertador, **II, 6**
algebra el álgebra, **I**
all todo, -a, -os, -as, **I; all right** de acuerdo; bueno, **I; all the time** todo el tiempo, **I; it's all right with me** me da lo mismo, **II, 11**
to **allow** dejar, **I**
almost casi, **I**
alone solo, -a, **II, 1**
already ya, **I**
also también, **I**
although aunque, **II, 5**
always siempre, **I**
American norteamericano, -a, **I**
amount la cantidad, **II, 10**
amphibious anfibios, **II, 2**
an un, una, **I; an hour ago** hace una hora, **I**
and y, **I**
Andean: Andean region región andina, **II, 10**
animated: animated cartoon el dibujo animado, **I**
ankle el tobillo, **II, 6**
anniversary el aniversario, **II, 5**
to **answer** contestar, **I**

answers las respuestas, **II, 9**
ant hormiga, **II, 2**
any algún, **II, 6**
anyway sea como sea, **II, 10**
apartment el apartamento, **I**
to **appear** aparecer, **II, 3**
apple la manzana, **I**
appliance el aparato eléctrico, **II, 10**
application: job application la solicitud de empleo, **II, 9**
to **apply** solicitar, **II, 9: to apply makeup** maquillar(se); pintar(se), **II, 6**
appointment la cita, **II, 9**
aquarium el acuario, **II, 2**
area: waiting area la sala de espera, **I**
arm el brazo, **II, 6**
around alrededor de, **II, 3**
arranged arreglado, -a, **I**
arrival la llegada, **I**
to **arrive** llegar, **I**
art: arts and crafts artesanías, **II, 10**
article el artículo, **II, 3**
as como, **I; as a matter of fact** de hecho, **II, 7; as a result** por lo tanto, **II, 7; as early as possible** a primera hora, **I; as far as** hasta, **I; as little as possible** lo menos posible, **II, 2; as much . . . as,** tanto, -a . . . como, **II, 2; as many. . . as** tantos, -as . . . como, **II, 2; as of** a partir de, **II, 10; as usual** como de costumbre, **II, 3; as you wish** como quieras, **II, 11**

camera la cámara, I
to **camp out** acampar, II, 1
candidate el candidato (*m.*), II, 9
capital la capital, II, 10
car el coche; auto, I; **bumper car** el coche de topetazos, II, 9
card: credit card la tarjeta de crédito, I
care: I don't care no me importa, II, 11
Caribbean el Caribe, I
carnations claveles, II, 11
carnival el carnaval, II, 5
carpenter el carpintero, II, 9
carrot la zanahoria, II, 6
to **carry** cargar, II, 9
cart el carro, I
to **cash** cambiar, I
cash: cash register la caja, II, 9
cashier la cajera (*f.*); el cajero (*m.*); II, 9
cassette el casete, I
castanets castañuelas, II, 11
Catalan; Catalonian catalán, II, 11; **Catalonian dish** la sopa payés, II, 11
to **catch: to catch a cold** pescar un resfriado, II, 9
category la categoría, I
cathedral la catedral, II, 11
cattle el ganado, II, 10; **cattle ranch** la estancia, II, 10
to **celebrate** celebrar, II, 5
celery el apio, II, 6
centrally (located) céntrico, -a, II, 11
century el siglo, II, 10
ceramics (material) la cerámica, I
champion la campeona (*f.*); el campeón, (*m.*), I
change (money) el vuelto, II, 3; **change purse** el monedero, II, 3
to **change** cambiar (de), I
cheap barato, -a, I; **cheaper** más barato, II, 3
check: traveler's check el cheque de viajero, I
cheese el queso, I
chemistry la química, I
cherry la cereza, I
chicken el pollo, I
children los hijos, I
chocolate el chocolate, I
choir el coro, II, 2
chores (household) labores domésticas, II, 7
Christmas la Navidad, II, 5; **Christmas Eve** la Noche Buena, II, 5
church la iglesia, II, 11
churro: churro store la churrería, II, 9
city la ciudad, I; **city block** la cuadra, II, 3
claim la reclamación; el reclamo, I
class la clase, I

classified: classified ad el anuncio clasificado, II, 9
classmate el compañero de clase (*m.*); la compañera de clase (*f.*), II, 1
classroom la clase, I
clean limpio, -a, II, 9, 10
to **clean** limpiar, II, 2
cleaning: dry cleaning store la tintorería, II, 10
to **clear: clear the table** quitar la mesa, II, 2
clearance: clearance sale la venta-liquidación, II, 3
to **climb** escalar, II, 1
clock: alarm clock el despertador, II, 6
to **close** cerrar (ie), II, 3; **complimentary closing** la despedida, II, 1
clothes la ropa, I
cloud la nube, II, 10
coat el abrigo, I; **coat of arms** el escudo, II, 3
coffee el café, I
coffeeshop el café, I
coins monedas, II, 3
cold: it was cold hacía frío, II, 5; **it's (very) cold out** hace mucho frío, I; **head cold** el catarro, II, 6
college: college student el estudiante universitario, II, 10
cologne el agua de colonia, II, 6
color el color, I
Columbus Day el Día de la Hispanidad; el Día de la Raza, II, 5
comb el peine, II, 6
to **comb (one's hair)** peinar(se), II, 6
to **come** venir, I; **he (she) is coming** él (ella) viene, I: **to come to an agreement** llegar a un acuerdo, II, 5; **come in** pasa, I
comfortable cómodo, -a, I
comic(al) cómico, -a, I
to **command** mandar, II, 9
to **comment** comentar, II, 3
compass el compás, I
to **compete** competir, II, 6
complaint la queja, I
complete completo, -a, I
complication el lío, I
complimentary: complimentary closing la despedida, II, 1
computer la computadora, I; **computer programming** la programación, II, 7
to **concede** conceder, II, 9
concert el concierto, I
concierge el conserje, II, 11
congratulations! ¡muchas felicidades!, II, 5; ¡felicitaciones!; ¡enhorabuena!, II, 9; **congratulations on your saint's day!** ¡felicidades en el día de tu santo!, II, 5
consequently por consiguiente, II, 7

constantly constatemente, II, 1
to **construct** construir, II, 3
contact: contact lens la lente de contacto, II, 6
continent el continente, II, 7
to **continue** seguir, II, 2
contribute contribuir, II, 9
to **cook** cocinar, I
cook la cocinera (*f.*); el cocinero (*m.*), II, 9
cooking la cocina, I
cool: it's cool out hace fresco, I
cordially cordialmente, II, 1; atentamente, II, 9
corn el maíz, II, 10
corner (street) la esquina, I
to **cost** costar (ue), II, 11; **it costs** cuesta, I; **they cost** cuestan; valen, I
cotton el algodón, I
could: could you give me (tell me, lend me) . . . ? ¿me podrías dar (decir, prestar) . . . ?, II, 7; **could you tell me (give me, lend me) . . . ?** ¿querrías decirme (darme, prestarme) . . . ?, II, 7
counter el mostrador, II, 3
country el campo, II, 10; **country dweller** el campesino (*m.*), la campesina (*f.*), II, 10
couple la pareja, II, 5
course el curso, II, 1
courteously cortésmente, II, 9
cow la vaca, II, 10
cradle la cuna, II, 10
crazy loco, -a, I; **to go crazy** volverse loco, -a, II, 7
cream: shaving cream la crema de afeitar, II, 6
to **create** crear, II, 10
created creó, II, 6
credit: credit card la tarjeta de crédito, I
crime el crimen, I
crop la cosecha, II, 7
to **cry** llorar, I
cuisine la cocina, I
cultural: cultural activity la actividad cultural, II, 10
cup la taza, I
to **cure** curar, II, 7
custard: baked custard el flan, I
customer el cliente (*m.*), la cliente (*f.*), I; **customer service department** la sección de quejas y reclamos, I
customs la aduana, I; **customs agent** el aduanero, I
to **cut** cortar, I; **to cut (oneself)** cortarse, II, 6; **cut off: we were cut off!** ¡la comunicación se cortó!, I

D

dad papá, I
to **dance** bailar, I

dance el baile, I; **Mexican hat dance** el jarabe tapatío, II, 10
danger el peligro, II, 7
dangerous peligroso, -a, II, 7
dark oscuro, -a, I; **dark (hair, complexion)** moreno, -a, I
data: data base la base de datos, II, 7; **data processing** la informática, II, 7
date la fecha, II, 5
daughter la hija, I
day el día, I; **another day** otro día, II, 3; **the following day** al día siguiente, I, 5; **days of the week** (see p. 68) los días de la semana, I; **saint's day** el santo, II, 5
dear querido, -a, I; **dear madam** distinguida señora, II, 9; **dear sir** estimado/distinguido señor, II, 9
to **decide** decidir, I
delicious delicioso, -a, I; riquísimo, -a, II, 5
to **delight** encantar, I
to **deliver** entregar, II, 9
demonstrated demostró, II, 6
deodorant el desodorante, II, 6
descendant descendiente, II, 10
desk el escritorio, II, 7; el buró, II, 11; **cashier's desk** la caja, I; **reception desk** la recepción, II, 11
dessert el postre, I; **for dessert** de postre, I
to **destroy** destruir, II, 3
detective: detective movie la película policial, I
diabolic diabólico, II, 6
diary el diario, I
dictionary el diccionario, I
die: (he died) murió, I
diet: balanced diet la dieta balanceada, II, 6
different distinto, -a, II, 1
difficult difícil, I
difficulty la dificultad, II, 7
dining: dining room el comedor, I
dinner la cena, I
dirty sucio, -a, II, 10
to **disappear** desaparecer (zc), II, 5, 7
disaster el desastre, II, 7
disco la discoteca, I
discount la rebaja, I
to **discuss** discutir, II, 5
disease enfermedad, II, 6
dish el plato, I; **dinner dish** el plato llano, I; **Catalonian dish** sopa payés, II, 11; **dish of beans, ground beef, and chilies** el chile con carne, I
disk el disquete, II, 7
display window la vitrina, II, 3
distant lejano, -a, II, 7
to **divide** dividir, II, 2
division la división, II, 2
to **do** hacer, I; **to do calculations** hacer cuentas, I

doctor el médico, II, 6
done hecho, II, 10
donkey el burro, II, 10
door la puerta, I
doorbell el timbre, II, 3
double el doble, I
doubt: it is doubtful es dudoso, II, 11
downpour el aguacero, II, 3
downtown el centro, II, 1
drawer el cajón, II, 7
drawing el dibujo, I
dream el sueño, I; **dreamed of** soñaste con, II, 7
to **dream** soñar (ue), II, 7
dress el vestido, I
to **dress** vestir (i), II, 6
to **drink** beber, I
dry: dry cleaning store la tintorería, II, 10
to **dry** secar, II, 2; **dry season** la seca, II, 2
duck el pato, II, 10
dumb tonto, -a, I
during durante, II, 1
dusting: dusting powder el talco, II, 6

E

each cada, I
ear la oreja, II, 6
early temprano, I
to **earn (money)** ganar, II, 1
earrings los aretes; los zarcillos, II, 3
Earth la Tierra, II, 10
easily fácilmente, II, 1
Easter la Pascua Florida, II, 5
easy fácil, I
to **eat** comer, I; **to eat lunch** almorzar (ue), II, 3
egg el huevo, I
eighth octavo, -a, II, 5
either... or o... o, II, 6
elegant elegante, I
elephant el elefante, II, 10
elevator el ascensor, II, 11
embroidered bordado, -a, I
to **emigrate** emigrar, II, 10
employee la empleada (f.); el empleado (m.), I
empty vacío, -a, II, 6
to **enclose** adjuntar, II, 9
ending la terminación, II, 1
energy la energía, II, 6
engineering: aerospace engineering la ingeniería espacial, II, 7
England Inglaterra, II, 6
English (language) el inglés, I
to **enjoy** gozar (de), II, 7; **enjoy it! (meal)** ¡buen provecho!, I
enough...! ¡basta de...!, I
to **enter** entrar, I
enthusiastic entusiasmado, -a, II, 11

entrance la entrada, I
envelope el sobre, II, 9
environment el ambiente, II, 10; **environmental pollution** la contaminación ambiental, II, 7
envy la envidia, I
Epiphany la Epifanía; el Día de Reyes, II, 5
equipment el equipo, II, 9
to **erase** borrar, II, 7
eraser la goma, I
erosion la erosión, II, 10
essential indispensable, II, 10; **it is essential** es preciso, II, 11
esteemed estimado, -a, II, 1
European europeo, -a, II, 10
events sucesos, II, 10
every todo, -a, -os, -as, I; **every day** todos los días, I; **every time** en todo momento, I
everything todo, I; **everything's finished** ya está todo, I
exam el examen, I
excellent magnífico, -a, I
to **exchange: exchange views** cambiar impresiones, II, 1
excited agitado, -a, II, 2
excursion la excursión, I
excuse la excusa, II, 2; **excuse me** con permiso; perdón; permiso, I; perdone, II, 3
exit salida, II, 9
expansion la expansión, II, 10
expensive caro, -a, I
expressed dicho, II, 10
extensive extenso, -a, II, 10
eye el ojo, II, 6
eyeliner el lápiz para los ojos, II, 6

F

face la cara, II, 6
factory la fábrica, II, 10
fair la feria, I; la verbena, II, 9; rubio, -a, I
fall el otoño, I
to **fall** caer, II, 3; **to fall asleep** dormirse (ue), II, 6; **to fall in love** enamorarse, II, 6
family la familia, I; **family members** (see p. 171) los miembros de la familia, I; **family room** la sala de estar, I
fantastic fantástico, -a, I
far (from) lejos (de), I
fare el pasaje, II, 11
to **fascinate** fascinar, II, 10
fashion la moda, II, 3; **is no longer fashionable or popular** pasa de moda, II, 10
fat gordo, -a, I; **fat** grasa, II, 6
father el padre, I; **Father's Day** el Día de los Padres, II, 5
favor: would you do me a favor and...? ¿podrías hacerme el favor de...?, II, 7
favorite favorito, -a; preferido, -a, I

fault: to be at fault tener la culpa, II, 3

to fear temer, II, 11

to feel (ie) sentirse, II, 6; **to feel bad** sentir(se) mal, II, 6; **to feel good** sentir(se) bien, II, 6; **to feel like** tener ganas de, I

felt-tip: felt-tip marker el marcador, I

female hembra, II, 2

ferris: Ferris wheel la rueda giratoria, II, 9

fertilizer el fertilizante, II, 10

fever la fiebre, II, 6

fifth quinto, -a, I

to fill (out) llenar, II, 9

finally finalmente; por fin, I; al fin, II, 5; por último, II, 9

to find encontrar (ue), I

fine bien, I

finger el dedo de la mano, II, 6

to finish terminar, I; acabar, II, 5

fire fuego, II, 9

first primero, I

fish el pescado, I; el pez (*pl.* peces), II, 2

to fish pescar, II, 1

fitting: fitting room el probador, II, 3

to fix arreglar, II, 9

flight el vuelo, I

floor el piso, I

flour harina, II, 6

flu la gripe, II, 6

flute: bamboo flutes las flautas de bambú, II, 10

fly la mosca, II, 10

to follow seguir, II, 2

food la comida, I; el alimento, II, 6

fool: Fool's Day el Día de los Inocentes, II, 5

foot el pie, II, 6

for para; por, I; **for heaven's sake!** ¡ay, caramba!, II, 2; **for sale** en venta, I; **for what?** ¿para qué?, I

to forbid prohibir, II, 9

forehead la frente, II, 6

foreign: foreign country el país extranjero, II, 7

forest el bosque, II, 1

to forget olvidarse, II, 6

fork el tenedor, I

foundation (makeup) la base, II, 6

fountain la fuente, II, 11

to free (oneself) librar(se), II, 7

free: free time el tiempo libre, I

to freeze (them) congelarlas, II, 6

French (language) el francés, I; **french fries** las papas fritas, I

frequently frecuentemente, II, 1

fresh fresco, -a, II, 6

friend el amigo (*m.*); la amiga (*f.*), I

frog la rana, II, 2

from de; desde, I; **from a novel** de una novela, II, 1; **from where?** ¿de dónde?, I

fruit la fruta, I; **fruit and vegetable garden** el huerto, II, 10; **fruit store** la frutería, I

to fry freír, I

frying: frying pan la sartén, I

full lleno, -a, II, 1

fun divertido, -a, I; **I am having so much fun!** ¡cómo me divierto!, II, 10

funny gracioso, -a, II, 2

furious furioso, -a, II, 5

G

to gain: gain weight aumentar de peso, II, 6

game el juego, I; **Olympic Games** los Juegos olímpicos, I

gang la pandilla, II, 11

garage el garaje, I

garden el jardín, I

gasoline la gasolina, II, 10

gate la puerta, I

generally generalmente, I

generation la generación, II, 10

generous generoso, -a, I

genius el genio, I

gentleman el caballero, II, 3

gentlemen muy señores míos, II, 9

geography la geografía, I

geometry la geometría, I

to get: to get angry enojarse; enfadarse (ue), II, 6; **to get bored** aburrirse, II, 6; **to get dizzy** marearse, II, 9; **to get dressed** vestirse (i), II, 6; **to get furious** ponerse furioso, -a, II, 6; **to get good grades** sacar buenas notas, II, 1; **to get happy** ponerse contento, -a; alegrarse, II, 9; **to get in touch (with)** poner(se) en contacto, II, 7; **to get married** casarse, II, 7; **to get off** bajar, I; **to get on** subirse, II, 9; **to get ready** preparar(se), II, 6; **to get sad** ponerse triste, II, 6; **to get tired** cansarse, II, 6; **to get together** reunirse, II, 5; **to get up** levantarse, II, 6; **to get wet** mojarse, II, 9

giant gigante, II, 7

girl la chica, I; la muchacha, II, 2

girlfriend la novia, II, 2

to give dar, II, 1; **to give a concert** dar un concierto, II, 1; **to give money** dar dinero, II, 1; **to give away** regalar, II, 3; **to give regards (to)** dar recuerdos (a, para), II, 1; **to give regards from** dar recuerdos de, II, 1; **could you give me . . . ?** ¿me podrías dar . . . ?, II, 7; **was giving** estaba dando, II, 5

glad: I'd be glad to con mucho gusto, II, 3

glass el vaso, I

glove el guante, I

go: they go van, I

to go ir, I; **I am going to (to indicate intention)** voy a, I; **to go crazy** volverse loco, -a, II, 7; **to go for a walk** dar una vuelta; pasear, I; **to go to bed** acostar(se) (ue), II, 6; **to go on a trip or excursion** ir de excursión, II, 2; **to go out** salir, I; **to go out in the defense of** salir en defensa de, II, 6; **to go shopping** ir de compras, II, 3; **to go straight ahead** seguir derecho, II, 3; **to go up** subir, I; **(I) was going to go** iba a ir, II, 5

goddess la diosa, II, 1

gods los dioses, II, 10

gold: gold medal la medalla de oro, I

good bien, I; **good afternoon** buenas tardes, I; **good evening, good night, hello** buenas noches, I; **good luck** buena suerte, II, 9; **good morning** buenos días, I

goodbye adiós, I

to grab agarrar, II, 9

to graduate graduarse, II, 11

graduation la graduación, II, 5

grape la uva, I

grapefruit la toronja, II, 6

grass la hierba, II, 10

great estupendo, -a; ¡regio!, I

green verde, I

group el grupo, I

grow: did not grow no crecía, II, 7; **grows** crece, II, 2

to guarantee garantizar, II, 3

guidebook la guía, I

guitar la guitarra, I

gym el gimnasio, II, 6

gymnastics la gimnasia, I

H

hair el pelo, II, 6; **hair dryer** la secadora, II, 6; **hair rinse** el enjuague, II, 6

hall el pasillo, I

ham el jamón, I

hamburger la hamburguesa, I

hand la mano, I; **hand-woven fabrics** los tejidos a mano, II, 10; **handmade** hecho, -a a mano, I

handkerchief el pañuelo, I

handsome guapo, -a, I

to hang: to hang clothes tender la ropa, II, 9

happiness la alegría, I

happy contento, -a, II, 2; **I am so happy!** ¡cuánto me alegro, II, 6; **Happy Birthday!** ¡Feliz cumpleaños!, II, 5; **to become**

happy   ponerse contento, -a, II, 9

hard   duras, II, 7

hardware: hardware store   la ferretería, II, 9

harmed   perjudicado, -a, II, 7

harvest   la cosecha, II, 7

hat   el sombrero, I

hate: hateful   odioso, -a, II, 3; **I hate**   odio, I

have: you have understood   has entendido, II, 9

to **have**   tener, I; **to have (to eat or drink)**   tomar, I; **to have a bad time**   pasarla mal, II, 1; **to have a birthday**   cumplir años, I; **to have a good time**   pasarla bien; pasar un buen rato, II, 5; **to have an ache or pain . . .**   tener dolor de . . . , II, 6; **to have dinner**   cenar, I; **to have fun**   divertirse, II, 6; **to have so much to do**   tener tantas cosas que hacer, II, 2; **to have to**   tener que, I; **it has**   tiene, I

he   él, I

head   la cabeza, II, 6; **head cold**   el catarro, II, 6

health   salud, II, 6

healthy   sano, -a, II, 6

to **hear**   oír, II, 6

to **hear from (about)**   tener noticias de, II, 1

heavens!   ¡caramba!, II, 3; **for heaven's sake**   ¡ay, caramba!, II, 2

heavy   fuerte, I

hello   hola, I; **hello?**   !aló!; ¿bueno?; ¡diga!; ¡hola!, I

to **help**   ayudar, I; **it can't be helped**   no hay más remedio, I; **help!**   ¡auxilio!; ¡socorro!, II, 10

hemisphere   el hemisferio, II, 10

hen   la gallina, II, 10

henhouse   el gallinero, II, 10

her   de ella, I; la (pol. sing.); su; I

here   aquí, I; **here is; here are**   he aquí, II, 7

hereby   por medio de la presente, II, 9

heritage   herencia, II, 10

hers   suyo (-a, -os, -as), II, 2

hey!   ¡oye!, I

him   lo, I

his   de él; su, I

history   la historia, I

holy: Holy Week   la Semana Santa, II, 5

home (to)   a casa, I

homework   la tarea, I

hope: I hope   ¡ojalá!, II, 11

to **hope**   esperar, II, 9

horse   el caballo, II, 1

hot: it's (very) hot out   hace (mucho) calor, I

hotel   el hotel, II, 11

hour   la hora, I

house   la casa, I

how: ¿cómo?, I; **how annoying!**   ¡qué coraje!, II, 2; **how are things?**   ¿qué tal?, I; **how are you?** *(fam. sing.)*   ¿cómo estás?, I; **how are you?** *(pol. sing.)*   ¿cómo está?, I; **how handsome!**   ¡qué guapo!, I; **how horrible!**   ¡qué horror!, II, 9; **how I hate it!**   ¡cómo lo odio!, II, 10; **how lucky!**   ¡qué suerte!, II, 9; **how many rooms are there?**   ¿cuántos cuartos hay?, I; **how many times?**   ¿cuántas veces?, I; **how many?**   ¿cuántos, -as?, I; **how may I help you?**   ¿en qué puedo servirle?, I; **how much do they cost?**   ¿cuánto cuestan?; ¿cuánto cuesta?; ¿cuánto vale?, I; **how much?**   ¿cuanto?, I; **how old are you (is he/she?)**   ¿cuántos años tiene?, I; ¿cuántos años cumples?, II, 5; **how revolting!**   ¡qué asco!, II, 10; **how terrible!**   ¡qué barbaridad!, II, 9; **how's the weather?**   ¿qué tiempo hace?, I

hug   el abrazo, II, 1; **a hug from . . .**   un abrazo de . . . , II, 1

human: human being   el ser humano, II, 7

humble   humilde, II, 6

to **hurry (up)**   apurarse, I, 11; **in a hurry**   a la carrera, II, 7

to **hurt**   doler, II, 6

husband   el esposo, I

I

I   you, I

ice   el hielo, I; **ice cream**   el helado, I

to **ice skate**   patinar en hielo, I

if   si, I; **if only**   ¡ojalá!, II, 11

imaginary   imaginario, I

to **imagine**   imaginario, -a, I

immigrant   el inmigrante, II, 9

important   importante, I

in   en; dentro (de), I; **in a hurry**   a la carrera, II, 7; **in order to**   para, I; **in a big hurry**   apuradísimo, -a, I; **in a couple of hours**   en un par de horas, II, 7; **in a hurry; in a flash**   en un abrir y cerrar de ojos, II, 7; **in a jiffy**   en un dos por tres, II, 7; **in a low voice**   en voz baja, I; **in a while**   dentro de un rato, II, 7; **in exchange for**   a cambio de, II, 3; **in front (of)**   delante (de), I; **in love**   enamorado, -a, II, 5; **in person**   en persona, I; **in regard to**   en cuanto a, II, 9; **in search of**   en busca de, II, 10; **in shape**   en forma, II, 6; **in the morning,** A.M.   de la mañana,

to **increase**   aumentar, II, 10

incredible (it is)   es increíble, II, 11

independence: Independence Day   el Día de la Independencia, II, 5

indispensable (it is)   es indispensable, II, 11

industry   la industria, II, 7

industrial: industrial revolution   la revolución industrial, II, 10

to **inform**   informar, II, 9; **we are pleased to inform you**   nos es grato informarle, II, 9

information   la información, I; **inner: inner courtyard**   el patio, I; **insecticide**   el insecticida, II, 10

to **insist**   insistir (en), II, 9

instant: instant (dehydrated) potatoes   papas deshidratadas, II, 6

interesting   interesante, I; **very interesting**   interesantísimo, -a, II, 1

interpreter   el intérprete, II, 9

interview   la entrevista, I

to **interview**   entrevistar, I

to **introduce**   presentar, II, 1

to **invent**   inventar, II, 5

inventory   el inventario, II, 3

invitation   la invitación, I

to **invite**   invitar, II, 5

irresponsible   irresponsable, II, 11

islands   islas, II, 6

it   lo (*pol. sing.*), I

its   su, I

J

jacket   la chaqueta; el saco, I

jeans   los jeans, I

jelly   la jalea, I

job   el trabajo, II, 1; **job application**   la solicitud de empleo, II, 9

to **jog**   correr; trotar, I

joke   la broma, II, 5

juice   el jugo, I

K

to **keep: to keep in shape**   mantener(se), II, 6

key   la llave, II, 7; **key ring**   el llavero, II, 3

kilogram   el kilo, I

kind   amable; la clase, I

kingdom   reino, II, 6

kitchen   la cocina, I

knee   la rodilla, II, 6

knife   el cuchillo, I

to **know**   saber, I; **I know it!**   ¡ya sé!, I; **to know (a fact)**   saber, I; **to know how (+ inf)**   saber (+ inf), I; **to know, meet, be acquainted with**   conocer, I

L

labor   la labor, II, 7; **Labor Day**   el Día del Trabajo, II, 5

lack: lack of la falta de, II, 10
lake el lago, II, 1
language el idioma, II, 7
large grande, I
laser: laser beam el rayo láser, II, 7
to **last** durar, II, 5
last pasado, -a, I
lasting duradero, II, 7
late tarde, I; **later** más tarde, I
to **laugh** reír(se), II, 6; **he (she) was laughing** se reía, II, 5
law la ley, II, 10
lawn el césped, II, 7; **mow the lawn** cortar el césped, II, 7
leaf hoja, II, 2
lean: lean meat carne sin grasa, II, 6
to **learn** aprender, II, 1
leather el cuero, I
to **leave (behind)** dejar, I
leaves hojas, II, 6
leg la pierna, II, 6
lemon el limón, I
lemonade la limonada, II, 6
to **lend** prestar, II, 2; **to lend a hand** dar una mano, II, 7; **could you lend me . . . ?** ¿me podrías prestar, II, 7
less menos, I; **less than . . .** menos de . . . , I
lens: contact lens la lente de contacto, II, 6
lesson la lección, II, 10
to **let** dejar, I; **I let the purse go for. . .** le dejo la cartera en . . . , I; **let's go!** ¡vamos!, I; **let's see** a ver, I
letter la carta, I
lettuce la lechuga, I
library la biblioteca, II, 10
to **lie down** acostar(se) (ue), II, 6,
life vida, II, 2
light (in color) claro, -a, I
light (meal) ligero, -a, I
lightning: lightning bolt el rayo, II, 3
like como, I
to **like** gustar, I; **you (they) like** les gusta(n), I; **we like** nos gusta(n), I; **I like** me gusta, I; **I don't like it at all** no me gusta nada, I; **you like, he (she) likes** le gusta, I; **I like it a lot!** ¡cómo me gusta!, II, 10; **you like** te gusta, I
likewise igualmente, I
line la fila, I
to **linger** detenerse, II, 11
linked ligado, -a, II, 3
lips los labios, II, 6
lipstick el lápiz labial, II, 6
to **listen (to)** escuchar, I; **listen!** ¡oye!, II, 5
little pequeño, -a, I; **little bells** las campanitas, II, 2
to **live** vivir, I
livestock el ganado,, II, 10
living: living room la sala, I

lobby el vestíbulo, II, 11
to **look (at)** mirar, I; **to look (for)** buscar, I; **look!** ¡mira!, I
to **lose** perder (ie), II, 6; **to lose weight** adelgazar, II, 6; **it got lost** se perdió, II, 6
lotion la loción, II, 6
loudly alto, II, 3
love el amor, I; **I love it!** ¡me encanta!, II, 10
loved quería, II, 5
luck la suerte, II, 6
lunch el almuerzo, I

M

ma'am señora, I
macaroni los macarrones, II, 6
machine la máquina, II, 7
made hecho, II, 10; **made of** hecho de, I
madness la locura, II, 3
magazine la revista, I
mail: mail carrier el cartero, II, 9
main principal, I
to **maintain** mantener(se), II, 6
majority: the majority of la mayoría de, II, 6
to **make** hacer, I; **make sure** asegúrate, II, 9; **make yourself at home** estás en tu casa, I
makeup el maquillaje, II, 6; **to apply makeup** maquillar(se), II, 6
male macho, II, 2
man el hombre; señor, I
manual el manual, II, 7
to **manufacture** fabricar, II, 7
many muchos, -as, I; **many regards** muchos recuerdos, II, 1
map el mapa, I
to **mark** marcar, I
marker: felt-tip marker el marcador, I
marmalade la mermelada, I
married casado, -a, I; **to get married** casarse, II, 7
marvelous de maravilla, II, 1; maravilloso, -a, II, 10
mast el mástil, II, 9
match el partido, I
matter: it doesn't matter! ¡no importa!, I
Mayan maya, II, 1
maybe quizás, II, 6; tal vez, II, 11
mayonnaise la mayonesa, I
me mí, I
meadow el prado, II, 10
meaning significado, II, 1
meat la carne, I
mechanic el mecánico, II, 9
medal: gold medal la medalla de oro, I
medical: medical field el campo de la medicina, II, 7
meet: they met encontraron, II, 5
meeting la reunión, II, 2
melon el melón, I

member: family members los miembros de la familia, I
menu el menú, I; **menu (computer)** el menú, II, 7
merchandise la mercancía, II, 3
merry-go-round el tiovivo, II, 9
Mexican American mexicanoamericano, -a, II, 1
Mexico México, I
mile la milla, II, 7
milk la leche, I; **skim milk** la leche descremada, II, 6
mine mío, -a, II, 2
minute el minuto, I
Miss la señorita (abbreviation Srta.), I
to **miss (someone or something)** extrañar, II, 1
mitt el guante, I
moderation moderación, II, 6
moist húmedo, II, 2
mom la mamá, I
moment: just a moment un momento, I
money el dinero; I; **money exchange office** la casa de cambio, I; **monetary unit of Mexico, Bolivia, Chile, Colombia** el peso, I; **monetary unit of Spain** la peseta, I
month el mes, I; **months of the year** (see p. 111) los meses del año, I
more más, I; **more . . . than** más . . . que, I; **more expensive** más caro, II, 3; **more or less; so-so** más o menos, II, 9; **more than . . .** más de . . . , I
morning la mañana, I; **in the morning** por la mañana, I
mosque mezquita, II, 11
mosquito el mosquito, II, 10
most más, I; **the most** el más, la más, II, 9
mother la madre, I; **Mother's Day** el Día de las Madres, II, 5
motorcycle la moto, I
mountain la montaña, II, 1
mouse el ratón, II, 7
moustache el bigote, II, 6
mouth la boca, II, 6
mouthwash el enjuague para la boca, II, 6
to **move** mudar(se), II, 10
movie: movies; movie theater el cine, I; **detective movie** película policial, I; **horror movie** la película de terror, I; **movie star** la estrella de cine; II, 6
Mr. (sir) el señor (abbreviation Sr.), I
Mrs. (ma'am) la señora (abbreviation Sra.), I
multivitamin la multivitamina, II, 6
musical la película musical, I
mustard la mostaza, I
my mi; mis (*pl.*), I

N

nail la uña, **II, 6; nail file** la lima de uñas, **II, 6; nail polish** el esmalte de uñas, **II, 6**
name: my name is . . . me llamo . . . , **I; his (her) name is . . .** se llama . . . , **I**
napkin la servilleta, **I**
narrow estrecho, -a, **II, 11**
nation la nación, **II, 7**
national nacional, **II, 10**
nature naturaleza, **II, 2**
near cerca (de), **I**
necessary: it was necessary to había que, **II, 5**
neck el cuello, **II, 6**
need la necesidad, **II, 10**
to **need** necesitar, **I**
neighborhood el barrio, **I**
neither tampoco, **II, 6**
neither ni, **I**
nerve: what nerve! ¡qué coraje!, **II, 2**
nest nido, **II, 2**
net la red, **I**
never nunca, **I; never again** nunca más, **II, 3**
new nuevo, -a, **I; New Year's Day** el Año Nuevo, **II, 5; New Year's Eve** el Fin de Año, **II, 5**
newspaper el periódico, **I**
next próximo, -a, **I; next time . . .** la próxima vez . . . , **II, 2, next week** la semana que viene, **II, 2**
nice simpático, -a, **I; it's (very) nice out** hace (muy) buen tiempo, **I; nice to meet you** mucho gusto, **I; to look nice on** quedar bien, **I; would you be nice enough to . . . ?** ¿serías tan amable . . . ?, **II, 7**
night la noche, **I; last night** anoche, **I**
ninth noveno, -a, **II, 5**
no no, **I; no sooner said than done** a lo dicho, hecho, **I**
noise el ruido, **I**
non-stop: non-stop flight el vuelo sin escala, **II, 11**
none ninguno, -a, **II, 6**
noodles los fideos, **II, 6**
noon el mediodía, **I**
nor ni, **I**
nose la nariz, **II, 6**
not no, **I; not me** yo no, **I; not pure** impuro, -a, **II, 10**
notebook el cuaderno, **I;** la libreta, **II, 7**
now ahora, **I**
nuclear: nuclear energy la energía nuclear, **II, 7; nuclear plant** la planta nuclear, **II, 7; nuclear reactor** el reactor nuclear, **II, 7**
number el número, **I; numbers** (see p. 66 and p. 79) los números, **I; numbers from 100**
to 1000 (see p. 310) los números del 100 al 1000, **I**

O

to **obey** obedecer (zc), **II, 5**
obligation la obligación, **II, 2**
occasion la ocasión, **II, 2**
octopus (amusement park ride) el pulpo, **II, 9**
of de, **I; of course** cómo no, **I; of course!** ¡cómo no!, **II, 3; of course!** ¡por supuesto!, **I; of the** del (de + el), **I**
off: off limits prohibido, -a, **I**
offer la oferta, **I**
office el despacho, **II, 9**
office la oficina, **I; post office** el correo, **I; post office box** el apartado postal, **II, 9**
often a menudo, **I**
oil el petróleo, **II, 10**
okay? ¿vale?, **II, 11**
older (than) mayor (que), **II, 2**
oldest el mayor, **II, 9**
olympic: Olympic Games los juegos olímpicos, **I; Olympic Games** las olimpiadas, **II, 11**
omelette la tortilla, **I**
on en, **I; on a diet** a dieta, **I; on foot** a pie, **I; on the contrary** al contrario, **I; on the left** a la izquierda, **I; on the right** a la derecha, **I**
once una vez, **I; once in a while** de vez en cuando, **II, 7**
one uno, -a, (de) **I; one half** medio, -a, **II, 6; the one (made of)** el (de), **I; the one to blame was . . .** la culpa la tuvo . . . , **II, 3**
onion la cebolla, **I**
only único, -a, **II, 5; if only** ¡ojalá!, **II, 11**
to **open: open an account** abrir una cuenta, **II, 3; open** abierto, **II, 10**
to **operate** operar, **II, 9**
operation la operación, **II, 7**
or o, **I**
orange la naranja, **I; (color)** anaranjado, -a, **I**
order el pedido, **I**
organ: organ transplant el transplante de órgano, **II, 7**
organized organizado, -a, **I**
other más; otro, -a, **I**
our nuestro, -a, -os, -as, **I**
out: out loud en voz alta, **II, 5; out of this world!** ¡de película!, **II, 11**
outdoors al aire libre, **II, 11**
outside fuera (de), **II, 6; outside wall** el muro, **II, 9**
owner el propietario, **II, 11**

P

Pac-man "comecocos", **II, 7**
to **pack: to pack a suitcase** hacer la maleta, **I**
painting la pintura, **I**
pair el par, **II, 3**
panther la pantera, **II, 10**
pants los pantalones, **I**
parade el disfile, **II, 5**
parents los padres, **I**
park el parque, **I**
to **park** estacionar, **II, 9**
parrot el loro, **II, 2**
party la fiesta, **I**
passion la pasión, **II, 10**
Passover la Pascua Florida, **II, 5**
passport el pasaporte, **I**
past pasado, -a, **I**
pastime el pasatiempo, **I**
pastry la pastelería, la tarta, **I; pastry shop** la pastelería, **I**
patience la paciencia, **I**
to **pay** pagar, **I**
peach el melocotón, **I;** el durazno, **II, 10**
pear la pera, **I**
pen la pluma, **I; ballpoint pen** el bolígrafo, **I**
pencil el lápiz (*pl.* lápices), **I**
people al pueblo, **II, 6;** la gente, **I**
pepper la pimienta, **I**
per: per week por semana, **I**
perfect perfecto, **II, 6**
perfume el perfume, **II, 6**
perhaps quizás, **II, 6;** tal vez, **II, 11**
permission el permiso, **I**
person: person in charge el responsable, **II, 9; person from Buenos Aires** porteño, -a, **II, 10**
personal: personal description las señas, **II, 11**
peseta (monetary unit of Spain) la peseta, **I**
peso (monetary unit of Mexico, Bolivia, Chile, Colombia) el peso, **I**
phone: phone call la llamada, **II, 5**
photograph la fotografía, **I**
physical: physical education la educación física, **I**
to **pick up** recoger, **II, 11**
picturesque pintoresco, -a, **II, 11**
pie el pastel, **I**
piece el trozo, **I**
pig el cerdo, **II, 5**
pineapple la piña, **I**
pink rosa, **I**
pipe la cañería, **II, 9**
place el lugar, **I**
to **place** colocar, **II, 9**
placed puesto, **II, 10**
plan el plan; régimen, **I**
to **plan** planear, **I**
plantain el plátano, **I**
plastic: (made of) plastic de plástico, **II**
plate el plato, **I**
to **play** jugar (ue), **I; to play (a musical instrument)** tocar, **I**
please por favor, **I**

to please complacer, (zc), II, 5
pleased: we are pleased to inform you nos es grato comunicarle; tenemos el gusto de comunicarle, II, 9; **pleased (to meet you)** encantado, -a, II, 1
pleasure el placer, I; **it's a pleasure . . .** es un placer . . . , I; **what a pleasure (to see you)!** ¡qué gusto (verte)!, II, 1
to plow: to plow the land arar la tierra, II, 10
plumber el plomero, II, 9
plumbing la plomería, II, 9
pocket el bolsillo, I
poisonous venenosa, II, 6
polite amable, II, 9
to pollute contaminar, II, 10
pollution la contaminación, II, 7
polo el polo, II, 10
pond el estanque, I
pool la piscina, I
popcorn las palomitas de maíz, II, 6
popular popular, II, 9
portion la porción; ración, II, 6
position (job) el puesto, II, 9
possible posible, II, 2
post office el correo, I; **post office box** el apartado postal, II, 9
postcard la postal, I
potato la patata (Spain); la papa; I; **instant (dehydrated) potatoes** las papas deshidratadas, II, 6
pound la libra, II, 6
powder el polvo, II, 6; **dusting powder; talcum powder** el talco, II, 6
power poder, II, 3
to practice practicar, I
to prefer (ie) preferir, II, 6
preparations los preparativos, II, 5
to prepare preparar, I
present el regalo, I
to preserve conservar, II, 7
to press apretar, II, 7
pretty bonito, -a; lindo, -a, I
price el precio, I
printer el impresor, II, 7
private privado, -a, II, 11
prize el premio, I
probable: it is probable es probable, II, 11
problem el problema, I
to produce producir, II, 7
program el programa, I
programming la programación, II, 1
progress progreso, II, 7
to progress progresar, II, 7
to promise prometer, I
to propose proponer, II, 2
to protect proteger, II, 10
proverb el proverbio, II, 7
punctual puntual, II, 9
pure: pure air el aire puro, II, 9

purse la cartera, I
put puesto, II, 10
to put poner, I; **to put on** ponerse, II, 6
pyramid la pirámide, II, 1

Q

quality cualidad, II, 9; la calidad, I
question la pregunta, I
quickly rápido, I

R

rabbit el conejo, II, 2
racquet la raqueta, I
radiation la radiación, II, 7
radioactive radioactivo, -a, II, 7; **radioactive fallout** la precipitación radioactiva, II, 7; **radioactive waste** el desperdicio radioactivo, II, 7
raffle la rifa, II, 9
to rain llover (ue), II, 3; **it's raining** llueve, I; **acid rain** la lluvia ácida, II, 10
raincoat el impermeable, II, 3
rapidly rápidamente, II, 1
rather bastante, I
razor la maquinilla de afeitar, II, 6; **razor blade** la cuchilla, II, 6
to read leer, I
ready listo, -a, I
realize: I realized me di cuenta, II, 5; **to realize that** darse cuenta de que, 9
really en fin, II, 1; **really?** ¿verdad?, I
reason el motivo; razón, II, 2
reasonable razonable, II, 9
receipt el recibo, I
to receive recibir, I
receptionist el recepcionista (m.), II, 11, la recepcionista (f.), II, 9
recess el recreo, I
receipt: to acknowledge receipt of acusar recibo de, II, 6
to recommend recomendar (ie), II, 6
recommendation la recomendación, II, 9
record el disco, I; **record book** el registro, II, 11
to record (on tape) grabar, II, 3
recorder flauta dulce, II, 10
red rojo, I
redheaded pelirrojo, -a, I
to reduce (price) rebajar, II, 3
reduced (in price) rebajado, -a, I
refrigerator el refrigerador, II, 2
regarding en relación con, II, 9
regards los recuerdos, II, 1; **to send regards** mandar recuerdos, I
region la región, II, 11
regret: we regret to inform you sentimos comunicarle, II, 9

rehearsal el ensayo, II, 2
relive reviven, II, 10
to remember acordarse (ue), II, 11
to rent alquilar, II, 9
repairs la reparación, II, 2
to repeat repetir (i), II, 2
replica la réplica, II, 11
reservation la reservación, II, 11
to reserve reservar, I; **reserve the seats** reservar los pasajes, II, 11
resident el habitante, II, 10
resistant resistente, II, 7
responsibility la responsabilidad, II, 10
rest: the rest los demás, I; **to rest** descansar, II, 3; **were resting** estaban descansando, II, 5
restaurant el restaurante, I
return el regreso, II, 1
to return regresar; volver (ue), I
revolution: agricultural revolution la revolución agrícola, II, 7; **industrial revolution** la revolución industrial, II, 10
rice el arroz, I
riches la riqueza, II, 10
ride el juego, II, 9
to ride montar, I; **to ride (on horseback)** montar (a caballo), II, 1
rifle el rifle, II, 9
right: all right bueno, I; **right now** ahora mismo, II, 3; **right?** ¿no?; ¿verdad?, I
ring el anillo, II, 3
to ring sonar (ue), II, 5
river río, II, 5
road camino, II, 5
robe la bata, II, 3
to roll up enrollar, II, 9
roller: roller coaster la montaña rusa, II, 9
room el cuarto, I; la habitación, II, 11; **dining room** el comedor, I; **family room** la sala de estar, I; **fitting room** el probador, II, 3; **living room** la sala, I
rooster el gallo, II, 10
rouge el colorete, II, 6
route la ruta, I
to row remar, I
ruins (archaeological) las ruinas arqueológicas, II, 1
ruler la regla, I
to run correr, I

S

said dicho, II, 10
saint: saint's day el santo, II, 5
salad la ensalada, I
salary el sueldo, II, 9
salesclerk el dependiente (m.), la dependienta (f.), II, 3
salesperson el vendedor (m.), la vendedora (f.), I
salt la sal, I

same   mismo, -a, **I**; **it's the same to me**   me da igual, **II, 11**; **the same as**   lo mismo que, igual que, **I**

sandals   las sandalias, **II, 3**

sandwich   el bocadillo; sandwich, **I**

satellite: satellite dish   antena parabólica, **II, 7**

satisfied   satisfecho, -a, **II, 9**

sauce   la salsa, **I**

saucer   el platillo, **I**

to **save**   ahorrar, **I**; salvar, **II, 10**

to **say**   decir, **I**; **he (she) says (that) . . .**   dice que . . . , **I**; **to say goodbye**   despedir(se), **II, 6**; **you don't say!**   ¡no me digas!, **II, 9**

scarf   la bufanda, **II, 3**

schedule   el horario, **I**

school   el colegio; la escuela, **I**; **school bus**   el autobús escolar, **I**

schoolbag   la cartera, **I**

science   la ciencia, **I**; **science fiction**   la ciencia-ficción, **I**

scientist   la científica (*f.*); el científico (*m.*), **II, 7**

scissors   la tijera, **II, 6**

Scotland   Escocia, **II, 6**

screen   la pantalla, **II, 7**

seafood: seafood platter   la zarzuela de mariscos, **II, 11**

season   la estación, **I**; **dry season**   la seca, **II, 2**

seat   el asiento, **I**

second   segundo, -a, **I**; **in a second**   en un abrir y cerrar de ojos, **II, 7**

secondary: secondary school   la escuela secundaria, **I**

to **see**   ver, **I**; **see you later**   hasta luego, **I**; **see you tomorrow**   hasta mañana, **I**

seed   la semilla, **II, 10**

to **seem**   parecer, **I**

seen   visto, **II, 10**

selfish   egoísta, **I**

to **sell**   vender, **I**

to **send**   mandar, **I**

sender   el remitente, **II, 9**

separately   por separado, **II, 5**

to **serve**   servir, **I**

to **set: to set the table**   poner la mesa, **I**

seventh   séptimo, -a, **II, 5**

several: several times   varias veces, **II, 1**

severity: severity of the weather   las inclemencias del tiempo, **II, 7**

shampoo   el champú, **II, 6**

to **shave**   afeitar (se), **II, 6**

shaving: shaving cream   la crema de afeitar, **II, 6**

she   ella, **I**

sheep   la oveja, **II, 10**

shelf   el estante, **II, 9**

shell   carapacho, **II, 10**

shirt   la camisa, **I**; **tee shirt**   la playera, **II, 3**

shoe   el zapato; **I**; **tennis shoes**   los zapatos de tennis, **I**

to **shoot: to shoot at a target**   tirar al blanco, **II, 9**

shooting: shooting gallery   el tiro al blanco, **II, 9**

shopping   la compra, **I**; **shopping center**   el centro comercial, **II, 10**

short   bajo, -a; corto, -a, **I**

should   deber, **I**; **should I . . . ?**   ¿debo . . . ?, **I**

shoulder   el hombro, **II, 6**

to **show**   enseñar; mostrar (ue), **II, 3**; **to show a movie**   dar una película, **I**

sick   enfermo, -a, **II, 1**

side   el lado, **I**

sightseeing: sightseeing trip   el paseo, **I**

silence   el silencio, **II, 2**

silk   la seda, **I**

silver   la plata, **I**; **silver wedding anniversary**   las bodas de plata; **I**; **silver**   la plata; (*coll.*) money, **II, 3**

simply   sencillamente, **I**

sincerely: sincerely yours   suyo afectísimo, **II, 9**; **sincerely, very, truly yours**   atentamente, **II, 1**

to **sing**   cantar, **I**

to **sit**   sentarse (ie), **II, 9**

sixth   sexto, -a, **II, 5**

size   la talla, **I**

to **skate**   patinar, **I**; **to ice skate**   patinar en hielo, **I**

to **ski**   esquiar, **I**

skiing   esquiar, **I**

ski: ski boot   la bota, **I**; **ski pole**   el bastón (*pl.* bastones), **I**; **skis**   los esquís, **I**

skim: skim milk   la leche descremada, **II, 6**

skirt   la falda, **I**

sky   el cielo, **II, 10**

skyscraper   el rascacielos, **II, 1**

to **sleep**   dormir (ue), **II, 6**

slogan   el lema, **II, 3**

slowly   lentamente, **II, 1**

small   pequeño, -a, **I**

smaller   menor, **II, 9**

smallest   el menor, **II, 9**

smile   sonríe, **II, 9**

to **smile**   sonreír(se), **II, 11**

to **smoke**   fumar, **II, 10**

snack   la merienda; el bocadillo, **I**

snake   la serpiente, **II, 2**

snow: it's snowing   nieva, **I**

so   tan, **I**; **so (as, that) much**   tanta, **I**; **so long, 'bye**   chao, **I**; **so-so**   así, así, **II, 1**; regular, **I**

soap   el jabón, **II, 6**

soccer   el fútbol, **I**

sock   el calcetín (*pl.* calcetines), **I**

soda   la gaseosa; el refresco, **I**

soft   blandas, **II, 7**

to **solve**   resolver (ue), **II, 10**

some   algunos, -as; unos, unas, **I**; **algún, II, 6**

someone   alguien, **II, 6**

something   algo, **I**

sometimes   a veces, **I**

son   el hijo, **I**

song   canto, **II, 2**; la canción, **I**

soon   pronto, **I**

sorry: I am sorry   lo siento, **I**; **sooner or later**   a la corta o a la larga, **II, 7**

sounds   suena, **II, 1**

soup   la sopa, **I**; **soup dish**   el plato hondo, **I**

source   la fuente, **II, 7**

space   el espacio, **II, 10**; **space mission**   la misión espacial, **II, 7**; **space shuttle**   el transbordador espacial, **II, 7**

Spain   España, **I**

Spanish (language)   el español, **I**; **Spanish fortress or palace**   Alcázar, **II, 11**

to **speak**   hablar, **I**

special   especial, **I**; **special fare**   la tarifa especial, **II, 11**

specialty   la especialidad, **I**; **specialty of the day**   el plato del día, **I**

species   la especie, **II, 10**

to **spend**   gastar, **II, 1**; **to spend (time)**   pasar, **I**

to **spin: spin wool**   hilan la lana, **II, 10**

spinach   las espinacas, **II, 6**

spoon   la cuchara, **I**

sports   los deportes, **I**

spring   la primavera, **I**

square   la plaza, **II, 10**

stamp   el sello, **I**

to **start**   empezar (ie), **I**

to **stay**   quedarse, **II, 6**

steer: is steered   se dirige, **II, 7**

to **step: to step down**   bajarse, **II, 9**

stepfather   el padrastro, **I**

stepmother   la madrastra, **I**

still   todavía, **I**

stock   el surtido, **II, 3**

stomach   el estómago, **II, 6**; **stomach ache**   dolor de estómago, **II, 6**

stop   la parada, **I**; **stop!**   ¡alto!, **II, 9**

to **stop**   parar, **I**

store   el almacén, **II, 3**; la tienda, **I**

storm   la tormenta, **II, 3**

story   la historia, **I**

strange   extraño, **II, 5**

strawberry   la fresa, **I**

to **strike (lightning)**   caer un rayo, **II, 3**

strong   fuerte, **II, 5**

student   la estudiante (*f.*), **I**; el estudiante (*m.*), **I**; **college student**   estudiante universitario, **II, 10**

to **study**   estudiar, **I**

style   la moda, **II, 3**; **in the latest style**   a la (última) moda, **II, 3**

subjects (see p. 67)   las materias, I
subway   el metro, I
success   el éxito, II, 9
sugar   el azúcar, I
to **suggest**   sugerir (ie), II, 9
suit   el traje, I; **bathing suit**   el traje de baño, II
suitcase   la maleta, I
summer   el verano, I
sun: it's (very) sunny   hace mucho sol, I
to **sunbathe**   tomar el sol, II, 1
supermarket   el supermercado, II, 10
supper   la cena, I
supply   el suministro, II, 7
to **support**   apoyar, II, 10
sure   seguro, -a, I
surfboard   la tabla hawaiana, II, 7
to **surprise**   sorprender, II, 11
suspended   detenido, -a, I
sweater   el suéter, I
to **sweep**   barrier, II, 9
sweet   dulce, II, 6; **sweeter**   más dulce, II, 1
to **swim**   nadar, I
swimming   la natación, I

T

table   la mesa, I; **to the table**   a la mesa, I
tadpole   renacuajo, II, 2
to **take**   llevar; tomar, I; **to take (with you)**   llevar, II, 3; **to take advantage of**   aprovechar, II, 3; **to take care of**   cuidar, II, 2; **to take off**   quitarse, II, 6; **to take out**   sacar, II, 9; **to take photographs**   tomar fotografías, I; **to take pictures**   sacar fotos, II, 5; **to take precautions**   precaver, II, 7; **to take a trip**   dar un viaje, II, 1; **to take things easy**   tomar las cosas con calma, II, 9; **to take a walk**   dar un paseo, II, 1; **to take a trip**   dar un viaje, II, 1; **take care of your health!**   ¡cuida tu salud!, II, 6
talcum: talcum powder   el talco, II, 6
to **talk**   hablar, I
tall   alto, -a, I
tango   el tango, II, 10
tart   la tarta, I
tasty (food)   sabroso, -a; rico, -a, I
tea   el té, I
to **teach: to teach a class**   dar una clase, II, 1
teacher   la profesora (f.); el profesor (m.), I
teaspoon   la cucharita, I
technological: technological advance   el adelanto tecnológico, II, 7
technology   la tecnología, II, 7
teeth   los dientes, II, 6
telephone   el teléfono, I; **on the telephone**   por teléfono, I

tell: could you tell me . . . ?   ¿me podrías decir . . . ?, II, 7
tennis   el tenis, I; **tennis court**   la cancha de tenis, I; **tennis shoes**   los zapatos de tenis, I
tenth   décimo, -a, II, 5
terrace   la terraza, II, 9
terrible   muy mal, I
test   la prueba, II, 7
thank: thank you   gracias, I; **thank you very much**   mil gracias, II, 1; muchas gracias, I
to **thank**   agradecer (zc), II, 5
that   aquel, aquella; ese, -a, I; que, I; **that one**   aquél, aquélla; ése, -a, I; **that way, then**   así, I
the   el (m. sing.), la (f. sing.), los (m. pl.), las (f. pl.), I; **the one (made of)**   el (de), I; **the one to blame was . . .**   la culpa la tuvo . . . , II, 3; **to the, at the (contraction)**   al (a + el), I
theater   el teatro, I
their   de ellas (f. pl.), de ellos (m. pl.), I
them   las; les; los; (pl.), I
then   así; después; entonces, I; luego, II, 1
there   ahí; allí, I; **there is, there are**   hay, I; **there was, there were**   había, II, 5; **there's no answer**   no contestan, I; **(over) there**   allá, I; **there's nothing like it!**   ¡no hay nada igual!, II, 10
therefore   así que; por lo tanto, II, 5
these   estos, -as; éstos, -as, I
they   ellas (f. pl.), ellos (m. pl.), I
thigh: thigh bone   el fémur humano, II, 10
thin   delgado, -a, I
thing   la cosa, I; **thing of beauty**   la preciosura, I; **things to do**   cosas que hacer, II, 2; **things went badly for me**   me fue mal, II, 1; **things went well for me**   me fue bien, II, 1
to **think**   creer, I; pensar (ie), II, 5
this   este, -a, I; **this afternoon**   esta tarde, I; **this one**   éste, -a, I
those   aquellos, -as; esos, -as, I; **those ones**   aquéllos, -as; ésos, -as, I
thousands   miles, II, 6
throat   la garganta, II, 6; **sore throat**   dolor de garganta, II, 6
through   por, I
to **throw: to throw in the water**   echar al agua, II, 9
thus   por consiguiente, II, 7
ticket   el billete, I; el boleto, II, 11; **ticket booth**   la taquilla, II, 9; **ticket window**   la ventanilla, I
tie   la corbata, I
time   el tiempo; la vez (pl. veces), I; **I don't have time for anything**

no tengo tiempo para nada, II, 1; **time**   la hora, I; **I'm having a good time**   la paso muy bien, II, 2
tip   la propina, I
to   a; para, I
today   hoy, I; hoy mismo, II, 3
toe   el dedo del pie, II, 6
together   juntos, -as, II, 5
toiletries   los artículos de tocador, II, 6
tomato   el tomate, I
tomorrow   mañana, I
tonight   esta noche, I
too (much)   demasiado, -a, I
toothpaste   la pasta de dientes, II, 6
top: top floor   el último piso, II, 3
tour: tour guide   el guía de turistas, II, 1
tourism   el turismo, I
touristic   turístico, -a, I
traffic   el tránsito, II, 3; **traffic jam**   el embotellamiento, II, 10
to **translate**   traducir (zc), II, 5
transplant: organ transplant   el transplante de órgano, II, 7
trash   la basura, II, 2
to **travel**   viajar; recorrer, II, 11; **travel agency**   la agencia de viajes, II, 1; **traveler's check**   el cheque de viajero, I
treasure   tesoro, II, 6
tree   el árbol, I
trip   el viaje, I; **round trip**   la ida y vuelta, II, 11; **sightseeing trip**   el paseo, I
trophy   el trofeo, I
tropical   tropical, II, 10
trout   la trucha, II, 1
truth   la verdad, II, 3; **it's true**   es verdad, I; **really**   de verdad, II, 3
to **try**   probar, I; **to try on**   probarse, II, 3
tuna   el atún, I
turkey   el pavo, II, 10
to **turn**   doblar, II, 3; **to turn left**   doblar a la izquierda, II, 3; **to turn off**   apagar, II, 3; **to turn out well**   salir bien, II, 2; **to turn right**   doblar a la derecha, II, 3
turtle   la tortuga, II, 2
twice   dos veces, I
twin   el gemelo, II, 2
two: the two   los dos; las dos, I
to **type**   teclear, II, 7
typical   típico, -a, I

U

ugh!   ¡uf!, II, 3
ugly   feo, -a, I
umbrella   el paraguas, II, 3
uncomfortable   incómodas, II, 7
under   debajo (de), I
undershirt   la camiseta, II, 3

INDEX

The numbers and letters after each entry refer to the unit and section where the entry first appears.

UNIT 10, 330, HBJ Photo/Peter Menzel; 331(all), HBJ Photo/Peter Menzel; 333, HBJ Photo/Peter Menzel; 336, HBJ Photo/Peter Menzel; 339 HBJ Photo/Mark Antman; 341(background), K. Kummels/Shostal; 341(tl), K. Schulz/H.Armstrong Roberts; 341(tr), Victor Englebert/Black Star; 341(c, br), Pedro Luis Roata; 346(both), HBJ Photo/Peter Menzel; 348, Georg Gersten/Photo Researchers; 349(tl), Joe Viesti; 349(tr), Wesley Bocxe/Photo Researchers; 350(tl, background), Dr. E. R. Deggingen; 350(br), George Holton/Photo Researchers; 362, H. Armstrong Roberts; 363(cl), Jack Karson/D. Donne Bryant Stock Photo; 363(tr), Wendy Watriss/Woodfin Camp & Assoc.; 363(all), HBJ Photo; 364(all), Peter Menzel

UNIT 11, 366, HBJ Photo; 367(all), HBJ Photo; 368(both), HBJ Photo; 369(both), HBJ Photo; 370(both), HBJ Photo; 382(t), Renate Hiller; 382(b), HBJ Photo; 383(both), HBJ Photo; 384(both), HBJ Photo; 386(both), Renate Hiller; 387(all), Renate Hiller; 388(tl, tr, br), HBJ Photo; 388(bl), Renate Hiller; 394(both), HBJ Photo; 402(t), D. Corson/H. Armstrong Roberts; 402(b), Craig Aurnes/Woodfin Camp & Assoc.; 404(all), HBJ Photo

UNIT 12, 406, HBJ Photo/Peter Menzel; 407(all), HBJ Photo/Mark Antman; 408(both), HBJ Photo/Mark Antman

ART CREDITS Agustín Fernández: 17, 18, 20, 21, 23, 24, 28, 30, 31, 32, 33, 34, 36, 39, 41, 56, 58, 63, 64, 66, 67, 70, 78, 92, 97, 101, 103, 104, 108, 109, 111, 119, 121, 122, 148, 149, 150, 151, 159, 163, 166, 170, 175, 180, 186, 187, 188, 192, 194, 197, 198, 201, 204, 212, 214, 216, 217, 220, 236, 238, 245, 251, 252, 256, 257, 258, 259, 263, 268, 269, 270, 271, 275, 276, 293, 305, 309, 337, 343, 345, 352, 353, 356, 357, 373, 374, and 397

Don Crews: 14, 52, 60, and 115

Intergraphics, Stephanie Pershing: 26

C 0
D 1
E 2
F 3
G 4
H 5
I 6
J 7
K 8